FULL
SPECTRUM

CoreStates Spectrum

THE
COMPLETE
HISTORY
OF THE
PHILADELPHIA
FLYERS
HOCKEY CLUB

FULL SPECTRUM

JAY GREENBERG

DAN DIAMOND AND
ASSOCIATES

TORONTO

U.S. trade distribution:
ISBN 1-57243-158-X (cloth)
ISBN 1-57243-212-8 (paper)
Triumph Books, 644 South Clark Street, Chicago, Illinois 60605
312/939-3330; FAX 312/663-3557

Canadian trade distribution:
ISBN 0-920445-48-9
North 49 Books, 193 Bartley Drive, Toronto, Ontario M4A 1E6
416/750-7777; FAX 416/750-2049

Production Editor: Richard Hennessey
Copy Editor: Lloyd Davis
Production and Editorial Staff: Eden Alcantera, Tony Jansen,
        Janet Miller, John Miller, Linda Watson, Tom Watson
Contributing Editors: Ralph Dinger, James Duplacey, Mona Greenberg, Stu Hackel

Film Production: Stafford Graphics, Toronto
Printed and bound in Canada by Metropole Litho, Montreal and Drummondville.

 97 98 99 00 01   2   3   4   5

                    Produced by Dan Diamond and Associates, Toronto

FULL SPECTRUM

CONTENTS

To Mona,
who for six years was willing to sacrifice a life with her husband,
but never her principles on redundancy.
As a result, this book is almost as tight as our marriage.

Chapter 1

♦♦♦

"Soccer Will Never Go in Philadelphia"

A ny hockey player who ever trudged back to the Spectrum's visiting locker room after being bloodied, beaten or bedazzled by the Flyers has had only one person to blame for his pain.

It has all been Juggy Gayles's fault.

Gayles took Ed Snider to his first hockey game.

The year was, well ... the Flyers' majority owner isn't exactly sure. But sometime in the early sixties, Snider, a young phonograph record salesman from Washington, D.C., was in New York having what he presumed to be a predinner cocktail at Al & Dick's Bar with Gayles, a buddy who was a sales manager for Carlton Records. As it turned out, Juggy wasn't hungry, which is not to say he didn't have good taste. He announced that rather than dinner, he was taking Snider to a hockey game at Madison Square Garden.

"What's a hockey game?" asked Snider.

"You can't not like it," said Juggy. "It's a great sport."

Snider, the son of a self-made grocery store chain owner, knew Redskins football, and as a kid had enjoyed Senators baseball and Washington Capitols professional basketball. But he had never seen anything like Gump Worsley, the porky little guy bouncing around in the New York Ranger goal that night. "Maybe it was the fact that he didn't look like an athlete or that he wasn't wearing a mask, I'm not sure," says Snider. "But I know I was fascinated with Worsley. I thought, 'This is the greatest spectator sport I've ever seen.'"

Unfortunately, hockey was the greatest spectator sport you couldn't see in Washington, which is where Snider returned to peddle his wares. He and his partner, Gerald Lillienfield, went national,

Three members of the braintrust: GM Bud Poile, left, president Bill Putnam, center, and coach Keith Allen.

overextended themselves, and soon decided to sell their record company. "I wasn't enjoying it anymore," Snider said. In the meantime, he had met an ambitious young builder named Jerry Wolman, whose attorney, Earl Foreman, had married Snider's sister, Phyllis.

Wolman, Foreman and Snider purchased the Philadelphia Eagles football team in 1964, and Snider, a 7 per cent shareholder, moved to Philadelphia to become the team's treasurer. While visiting Boston one weekend, Snider went to watch basketball's dream matchup—Wilt Chamberlain and the Philadelphia 76ers versus Bill Russell and the Celtics. When Snider came out of the Boston Garden that Sunday afternoon, he saw a long line at a ticket window. "What are those people doing?" he asked his companion.

"Waiting for Bruins tickets. That's the hockey team."

"Are they in the playoffs or something?"

"Oh, no, they're in last place. They put 1,000 tickets on sale on game day. Those are the only tickets you can get."

"People line up for tickets for a last-place team?"

"Oh, sure."

"The game in New York and that Boston ticket line left an indelible impression," Snider says. In 1965, however, he was the chief operating officer of the Eagles, talking business with Bill Putnam, the executive at Morgan Guaranty Trust Company in New York who had helped arrange for the loan that enabled Wolman and Foreman to buy the football team, when Snider learned something that would change his life.

Putnam told Snider that he would soon be leaving his bank job to move to the West Coast to work for Jack Kent Cooke, a minority owner of the Washington Redskins who was applying for a National Hockey League franchise in southern California.

"What do you mean you're applying for a National Hockey League franchise?" Snider asked. "Is one available?"

"Not just one," Putnam said. "Six."

The NHL, a moneymaking but static six-team fiefdom since 1942, was being forced to open its eyes to progress. Within the last decade, baseball and basketball had established franchises on the West Coast, the American Football League had been founded, and national television rights fees for professional sports had swollen. Owners of profitable teams in the Western Hockey League were dropping hints that they might declare the WHL a major league and compete for talent and television money.

In addition, Jim Norris, owner of the NHL's westernmost franchise, the Chicago Blackhawks, owned a large, decrepit arena in St. Louis that he wanted to palm off on an expansion franchise. Gradually, NHL president Clarence Campbell, who for years had answered expansion speculation with warnings of the dangers of diluting a successful product, had begun to speak about television and the future.

The NHL owners had originally envisioned adding two teams at a time, starting with Los Angeles and San Francisco, but after hiring a media consultant and receiving expressions of interest from several cities, they began to see a windfall in a mass expansion. "It was really the same plan that Branch Rickey (the legendary executive) had wanted (but did not achieve) for baseball in the late fifties," recalls Putnam. "Create a bunch of teams at once so they can at least be instantly competitive among themselves."

On March 11, 1965, when NHL owners met at the Plaza Hotel in New York and announced that they hoped to give birth to a second six-team division, Putnam was in attendance shaking hands and taking notes.

Born in Twin Falls, Idaho, Putnam had spent his high school years in Fort Worth, Texas, where he was a star quarterback and a prized recruit by the University of Texas. Injuries prematurely ended his football days, but Putnam earned his degree, entered a training course at Morgan, and worked his way up from the mail room to a vice presidency. He had seen some minor-league hockey games in Fort Worth that whetted his appetite for the sport when he got to New York, where, as both a Ranger regular and a banker specializing in financing sports franchises, Putnam had heard rumblings about the NHL's expansion.

He had first met Cooke when the Canadian-born multimillionaire had approached Putnam's bank about financing a bid to buy out Redskins majority owner George Preston Marshall. Although that effort was unsuccessful, Putnam later negotiated Cooke's purchase of the National Basketball Association's Los Angeles Lakers from Robert Short. Cooke took a liking to the young banker and hired him even before the sale of the basketball team was finalized. "I decided sports was more fun than banking," Putnam recalls. His next project was to handle Cooke's NHL bid.

On June 25, 1965, at another meeting in New York, the NHL detailed its expansion plans and announced it was taking applications. The next day, the report made only one Philadelphia paper, a six-paragraph story buried in the *Daily News*.

As he spoke to Putnam, Snider could not remember seeing it. But he did recall the Boston ticket line, the Gumper and a conversation he had with Ike Richman, part owner of the 76ers, six months earlier.

After becoming the Eagles' chief operating officer, Snider had been involved in the planning of Philadelphia's new multipurpose stadium which, pend-

Snider went to Wolman and told him they should build an arena and apply for a hockey franchise. Wolman, who owned Yellow Cab of Philadelphia and Connie Mack Stadium, was financing the building of the John Hancock Center in Chicago, and had extensive plans for redeveloping Camden, thought it was a great idea. The two men pledged a partnership. "With his reputation as a developer and entrepreneur, and my ideas, we went forward," Snider said. "It became my project."

The short-lived Philadelphia Quakers won only four of their 44 games before folding in 1931.

ing the next gust of ever-changing political winds, was scheduled to rise at the south end of Broad Street. Snider was so identified with the stadium project—his influence had helped kill another suggested site over the Pennsylvania Railroad tracks at 30th and Market Streets—that Richman had come to Snider to ask if Wolman had any interest in building an arena.

Snider had told Richman, who wanted to move the 76ers out of Convention Hall, that the Eagles were only interested in a lease at a city-owned stadium, not in building their own facility.

Now, with Putnam telling Snider that major-league hockey teams were for sale, the wheels between his ears were turning. A hockey team would need an arena, which would probably require another regular tenant, like a basketball team.

On a whim, Snider asked Putnam if he thought Philadelphia had a chance to get one of the NHL teams. Putnam said the guy with the answers was Bill Jennings, president of the New York Rangers and chairman of the NHL's expansion committee.

Snider phoned Jennings, introduced himself, and set up a meeting in New York. During their visit, Jennings outlined what had already gone down. Applications were expected from groups in Pittsburgh, Minnesota, Los Angeles, San Francisco-Oakland, Buffalo, Vancouver and Baltimore. The fee to apply was $10,000; the required minimum seating capacity for any home arena was 12,500. The league had no specific timetable, but hoped to grant six franchises on or before June 30, 1968.

The applicants would have to pitch their plans and provide evidence of their financial wherewithal—$2 million for the franchise fee, another $1 million for operating expenses—at an as-yet unscheduled meeting. Los Angeles, with its new arena, and St. Louis, with the Arena burning a hole in the pockets of Norris, the Chicago owner, already satisfied the building size requirements and had been publicly declared front-runners by Campbell.

"What do you think Philadelphia's chances would be?" Snider asked Jennings. Jennings said he was aware of the size of the market (fourth largest in the country), but expressed concern about the city's checkered history with the sport. All the other applicants were from cities that liked hockey. Philadelphia, from all appearances, did not.

The Jersey Devils of the Eastern Hockey League were the surviving descendents of seven failed Philadelphia minor-league teams over thirty-eight seasons. The Devils, playing at the Cherry Hill Arena in Haddonfield, were existing on an average of about 2,000 fans and what seemed like two hundred fights per game.

A Philadelphia NHL franchise had been brought to the city from Pittsburgh in 1930 by Benny Leonard, the former light-heavyweight champion, but had lasted only one year. "It's the coming sport in Philadelphia," Leonard had declared after renaming his Pirates the "Quakers." But when the team won only 4 of its 44 games and was outdrawn by the minor-league Philadelphia Arrows of the Canadian-American Hockey League, the Quakers folded, forcing Leonard, $80,000 poorer, to return to the ring.

Philadelphia remained a minor-league hockey town, but not a particularly good one. As the Arrows, Falcons, Rockets and Ramblers struggled through various incarnations in the American and Eastern Hockey Leagues, the only constants in Philadelphia hockey were Herb Gardiner, who coached every team that represented the city from 1929 to 1947, and complaints about the ramshackle Philadelphia Arena at 46th and Market Streets, the city's hockey home through 1964.

Snider pitched Jennings that Philadelphia was too strong a sports town to turn its back on a major-league team playing in the modern 15,000-seat building that Wolman was pledging to build. Snider agreed to submit the $10,000 franchise application fee on the condition that the Philadelphia bid remain a secret.

"We didn't want competition," Snider says. "There must have been ten groups that had expressed interest in the Eagles when Wolman bought them, driving up the price. I knew Cooke (who planned to build an arena in Inglewood, California) already had competition for the L.A. franchise. Dan Reeves (the Rams owner) had applied for one to play in the Los Angeles Sports Arena. Nobody else in Philadelphia seemed to be aware that the NHL was even expanding. That's the way I wanted to keep it."

Snider went to Paul D'Ortona, the Philadelphia City Council president who had worked with the Eagles on the stadium project, and presented his idea. The city had already purchased the land for the South Philadelphia stadium; Snider said he wanted to put an arena in the parking lot planned between the new facility and JFK Stadium. Wolman's group would lease the land and parking lots from the city, but the building would be privately constructed and owned.

"You have to understand, I was talking to a guy who had been involved with a stadium project that had been delayed ten years in haggling over the use of city funds," Snider said. "It had become a huge political football. And I'm talking about putting down an arena at no cost to the city, that would generate all kinds of revenues to help pay off the (stadium) debt. Well, D'Ortona flipped out. He thought it was wonderful and took me to see Mayor (James) Tate.

"Tate said he loved it, and called in his finance director and instructed him to work up a plan whereby the total cost of the land and prime interest would be divided by the term of the lease. That was the principle by which they determined how much it would cost to lease the land. Tate then turned to the city solicitor and said, 'I want you to do everything humanly possible to cut through all the garbage so that they can get this thing done.' I asked the mayor to follow up with a call and letter to both Campbell and Jennings and tell them what he had done. He did that while I was sitting there."

Snider then had to prepare the franchise bid. "At this point," he recalls, "I'm in over my head because I'm still, remember, running the Eagles. So when I happened to talk to Putnam and he told me that the job with Cooke was not working out the way he thought it would, I told him I had the perfect opportunity for him."

Putnam, who had found working for the demanding Cooke both educational and impossible, was offered by Snider the job of president of Philadelphia's team-to-be. Putnam firmed up his deal with all the partners—Snider, Wolman and Snider's brother-in-law, Jerry Schiff—during a meeting at the 1965 NFL Pro Bowl in Los Angeles. It was decided that Putnam would own 25 percent of the team and Schiff, Wolman and Snider each 22 percent. Several friends of Wolman and Snider came in as small investors to account for the remaining 9 percent.

Wolman's job was to secure financing for the team and construction of the new arena. Snider's responsibility was to keep the project moving through city channels. Putnam's task was to follow up on Snider's application and obtain the franchise.

A five-page brochure for presentation to the NHL owners was prepared by Hal Freeman, the Eagles' director of special events and publications. On the cover was a picture of a hockey player in a red and grey uniform, with a yellow Liberty Bell in a circle on the front of the jersey. Entitled "The NHL in Philadelphia," it blamed the city's past hockey failures on the poor facilities. The brochure emphasized the area's 5.5-million population and the base of established spectator support for the other major-league teams—the Eagles, 76ers and Phillies.

"Philadelphia has residents representing a wide variety of national origins," the brochure read, "in-

cluding many from Canada and Scandinavia, countries where hockey is so popular." The pamphlet closed outlining Wolman's credentials as a developer and Philadelphia's role as a major economic center. "I remain," it was signed, "William R. Putnam, President of Philadelphia Professional Hockey Club."

Amidst speculation that the six-team expansion might be cut to two or even postponed a year in the hopes of driving up the franchise price, NHL owners convened three days of meetings on February 7, 1966, at New York's St. Regis Hotel to interview applicants and make decisions. The governors first heard presentations from Baltimore, considered the front-runner for the additional Northeast Corridor franchise the NHL was expected to award, San Francisco, Buffalo, Los Angeles, Pittsburgh and Oakland. The next day, groups from Minneapolis-St. Paul, Cleveland, Louisville, plus additional applicants from Pittsburgh and Los Angeles were interviewed along with Wolman and Putnam. The owners promised a decision the following morning.

Asked about Philadelphia's chances as he left the meeting, David Molson, president of the Montreal Canadiens, said, "You have to be impressed by anyone who offers to build a new rink." Putnam, however, does not remember any enthusiasm from the owners as he and Wolman made their pitch. "I remember Norris pounding his fist on the table and saying, 'Philadelphia is a lousy sports town,'" Putnam said. "But they did seem impressed with the arena proposal. I was hopeful, but I wouldn't say I was optimistic."

Putnam and Wolman's presence at the New York meeting finally blew the cover off the Philadelphia group's application. The *Evening Bulletin* broke the news at the top-of-the-sports-page: "Local TV Market Could Influence NHL." An enthusiastic column by the *Bulletin*'s Hugh Brown was headlined, "Who Says We Don't Like Ice?"

Snider had remained in Philadelphia so that if the Philadelphia group secured a franchise, he could be at City Hall to immediately announce plans for the new 15,000-seat arena. Putnam, meanwhile, spent the fateful morning of Wednesday, February 9, pacing the floor in his suite at the Plaza Hotel. He had just told his wife, Josie, "in about ten minutes that phone will ring and I'll be out of business again," when the call came. It was Jennings.

"You're in," he said.

So were Cooke's Los Angeles group, Minnesota, Oakland and Pittsburgh. St. Louis was accepted too, although nobody from there had actually applied for a franchise. Norris still was trying to find someone to buy the team and his arena. In announcing the six winners, Campbell said St. Louis had "geographical feasibility" and set a deadline of April 5 to find ownership in that city. The team was soon purchased by Sidney Salomon Jr.

Philadelphia was the only winner without a high minor-league franchise. Obviously, the size of the market and Wolman's reputation had made the difference. Baltimore, with a well-supported American Hockey League team, lost out because the permanent stage at one end of its Civic Center left room for only

The ownership group from left, Joe Scott, Ed Snider and Fitz Dixon discuss plans with VP Lou Scheinfeld.

12,700 hockey seats.

"I'd warned [Baltimore applicant Zanvyl Krieger] to do something about that stage," Jennings told the *Baltimore Sun.* "This league has already outgrown rinks that size." Baltimore, jilted along with Vancouver and Buffalo, was named the alternate city should any of the awarded applicants prove unable to pay the $2-million franchise fee by June, 1967.

Tate, with Snider at his side, announced the plans for the new "ice stadium"—as the *Bulletin* put it—later that afternoon at City Hall. "Philadelphia is for-

Philadelphia Mayor James Tate breaks ground for the Spectrum.

tunate to have a man like Jerry Wolman," the mayor said.

At first, things moved smoothly. A citizens' committee argued that the land for the proposed arena was not being used in the best interest of the public and threatened a lawsuit, but it was never filed. Wolman selected Freeman, who had prepared the brochure that helped land the franchise, as president and manager of the new arena. Lou Scheinfeld, a *Daily News* city hall reporter who had won Snider's heart with his relentless positivism in his coverage of the ongoing story to develop the baseball/football stadium, was hired as an arena vice president in charge of public relations and creativity.

Putnam established offices for the team on the ground floor of the Life of Pennsylvania Building at 15th and Locust Streets. One of the first knocks at the door was from remnants of the EHL's Rambler Rooters who, represented by president John Wagner and vice president Lou Damia, pledged allegiance as the yet-unnamed team's fan club. "I couldn't believe it when they showed up," said Scheinfeld, "because apathy was too weak a word to describe the way people were looking at us."

To generate publicity, Putnam had to make news. On April 4, 1966, he used a speaking engagement at the Vesper Club to announce that the Chicago firm of Skidmore, Owings and Merrill had been hired as architects for the new arena. Ground would be broken by July. Putnam also reported that a contest was being planned to name the team and that the colors of orange, black and white had already been selected.

"The hot colors are always more attractive from a marketing standpoint," recalls Putnam. "Montreal and Detroit were already in red, and orange was as close as we could be to that. Of course, the fact that I graduated from the University of Texas, where the colors are orange and white, might have had something to do with the choice."

It was after Putnam had made his selection that he realized the NHL logo was also orange and black. He offered to switch to only orange and white, but Campbell did not object to the use of black.

Even before the awarding of the franchise, Putnam had asked hockey people for ideas on general managerial candidates. Jennings and Emile Francis, the Rangers' general manager, pointed Putnam toward Jack Adams, who had managed the Detroit Red Wings for thirty-five years. Adams recommended Bud Poile, the 42-year-old GM of the San Francisco Seals of the Western Hockey League. Poile had worked in the Red Wing organization for fourteen years, primarily as general manager of Detroit's top farm club in Edmonton.

Poile had told Putnam that Mel Swig, the Seals' owner, was an applicant for the NHL's Bay Area expansion franchise. "But as it became apparent that we weren't going to get it," recalls Poile, "my calls to and from Putnam became more frequent." After the franchise went to Oakland and a group headed by

New York investment banker Barend Van Gerbig, Poile accepted Putnam's offer to come to Philadelphia.

On May 31, one day before Mayor Tate and Wolman, with ceremonial flourishes of hockey gloves and sticks, broke ground on the new arena at Broad and Pattison Streets, Poile was introduced at the Philadelphia Hockey Club's new center city office as vice president in charge of personnel. "I didn't think he was going to be available," Putnam told

reporters. "I feel fortunate."

Poile was asked at the press conference about his choice for coach. "He won't be a big name," he said. "I'm looking for a man with an extensive minor-league background. We need someone familiar with all the kids playing in the minors. The kind of coach we want is somebody like Keith Allen, the coach (and GM) of Seattle (Totems of the WHL). I've already talked with him, as well as with two other men. We should have an announcement on that next week."

Poile doesn't remember who the other two guys were, if they ever existed at all. "I knew I wanted Keith," he recalls. "In fact, I had recommended him to the guys in Seattle when he went there. He was knowledgeable and an even-keel kind of guy, which is what I thought a new team would need. I figured

my personality would get us in enough trouble for the both of us."

For Allen, the timing of the offer was perfect. Caught between factions of a large and argumentative Seattle ownership group, he had already decided it was time to leave and was in San Diego, secretly interviewing for the GM job of the WHL Gulls, when Poile called his home. Allen had left instructions with his wife, Joyce, not to disclose his whereabouts, but Poile got her to divulge Allen's phone number in California. Allen had all but decided to accept the job there, maybe even as early as the next day, when he returned to the hotel and saw the message from Poile.

"I didn't know anything about Philadelphia," Allen recalls. "But I knew Bud, and I knew it was the NHL. I didn't really want to coach anymore and that's one of the reasons why I had been interested in the San Diego job. But Bud told me he wanted me behind the bench for a few years, then I could move into the front office. It just seemed like the right opportunity."

Allen, who had played his only 33 NHL games with the Red Wings from 1953 to 1955 and was later a member of Poile's teams at Edmonton of the Western League, was introduced six days after Poile. "Our original thinking was that we wouldn't need a coach until next season," Putnam said in making the announcement, "but quite frankly, when a guy like Keith Allen becomes available, you'd better take him. He'll be a tremendous asset to us because of his scouting ability."

In reality, scouting was the one thing the 43-year-old Allen, who had served as Seattle's coach, GM, publicist and advertising salesman, had not done.

"I don't profess to have any magic formula," said the unpretentious Allen to a small gathering of the Philadelphia media. "There's a lot of work ahead."

Lots of names were suggested for the team, but "Flyers" felt right from the start.

On July 12, Putnam announced a contest to give the team a name.

Naturally, there had been no shortage of ideas. "Quakers" and "Ramblers" were two traditional suggestions, but Snider saw that the Philadelphia Quakers, that sorry NHL entry of 1930-31, remained in the league record book with a half-share of the mark for the fewest victories in a season. He and Putnam wanted a fresh identification. They also feared the name Ramblers could conjure old images of the seedy minor-league team and the Arena. People had to be made to understand that this was a new, *major-league*, team playing in a modern, comfortable building.

In early correspondence, Putnam had proposed the names Lancers, Raiders, Royals, Knights and Sabres as possibilities. Liberty Bells also held some intrigue, but there was already a harness track in Philadelphia by that name and besides, "Liberty Bells" would not connote action or strength, only history. Huskies, Blizzards, IceCaps, Bashers, Bruisers and Keystones all were suggested.

But Putnam and Snider don't remember anything grabbing them until one night on the New Jersey Turnpike when Snider and his wife, his sister Phyllis and her husband Earl Foreman, and the Putnams stopped at a Howard Johnson's, ordered from the list of twenty-eight flavors, and kicked around a similar number of names.

On their way home after seeing a Broadway show, they were looking for a stopper of a name for their hockey team. "I was thinking of people skating and sliding around the ice," Phyllis recalls, "and 'Flyers' just popped into my head. Everybody thought it was great."

The "Philadelphia Flyers" had alliterative pizzazz, conveyed motion and excitement, and was short enough to fit into newspaper headlines. Snider told Phyllis, "That's the name, but you can't win the contest." Flyers, it would be.

The ballots, distributed by Acme Markets, had only a space for write-in suggestions and it was clearly noted that management would select the name it deemed most appropriate. All entries bearing the winning name would be eligible for a grand-prize drawing. First prize would be a twenty-one-inch color television set, plus two season tickets for the first year. Second and third prizes would be two season tickets. Another hundred entries would receive two tickets for one home game.

The contest ran for ten days in July. More than 11,000 entries were submitted, including Ice-picks, Acmes, Philly-Billies, Greenbacks, Scars and Stripes and Croaking Crickets. Liberty Bells and Quakers got the most votes, but Flyers, of course, got the only votes that really counted.

On August 3, the team announced its new name

at an outdoor luncheon press conference at the arena construction site. The excavation noise, coupled with the Broad Street traffic, made it impossible at times for Putnam to be heard. After explaining reasons for the rejected names, a compact car pulled up next to the platform. Three models dressed in orange and black climbed out. "You will notice that the girls are wearing the team's new colors," said Putnam.

"It is comforting to know that the team's colors are orange sweatshirts and black mesh stockings,"

said. "Somebody said to me the two nights you definitely don't want are Thursday and Sunday. They said Philly was a very traditional town. Sunday was church day and Thursday was the maid's day off. So I made the decision that we would try to capture Thursdays and Sunday because there wasn't anything else to do on those days."

The team's logo and uniform design were commissioned to Mel Richman Inc., a Philadelphia advertising and graphics design firm. Tom Paul was the sales

Minority owner Joe Scott, third from left, instructs the club's young sales force on the art of selling tickets.

wrote Stan Hochman, the *Daily News* columnist. "Let's hope the players can fight."

Hochman stopped short of predicting a reunited Germany and the development of the VCR, but was clearly on a prophetic roll, even if he couldn't hear Putnam's announcement over the truck noise on Broad Street. "The name of the team is the [chugamugg-kapoww-beep-beep]," Hochman quoted the team president as saying.

Alec Stockard, a 9-year-old boy from Narberth, one of the untold number of entrants who had submitted the name "Flyers," won the television in a drawing conducted on the spot by Putnam. Hochman noted, however, that Stockard had spelled it "Fliers." None of the team founders recall why the second dictionary spelling of the word—with a "y" instead of an "i"—was chosen.

When the NHL requested schedule dates, Snider pondered which evenings of the week should become hockey nights in Philadelphia. "All these different nights were taken with basketball and things," he

manager. "We wanted to come up with something with motion," said Paul. "We wanted it to refer to Philadelphia and to the sport of hockey."

In early correspondence, Putnam suggested something like a winged skate, but artist Sam Ciccone, who drew the logo, doesn't remember any specific instructions. Ciccone drew four wings on a stylized *P* to make it fly and an orange dot inside the *P* to represent a hockey puck. The logo was simple, clever and reflective of both the nickname of the team and the city it represented.

Ciccone did other designs, but when the choices were spread out on Snider's sofa for his, Scheinfeld's and Putnam's consideration, the winged *P* was the clear choice. If there was a close second, nobody involved remembers it.

The Flyers' first uniforms were also Ciccone creations. "Bill Becker (an account executive at Mel Richman Inc.) went out and bought a plain sweatshirt and some white, black and orange felt," recalls Ciccone, now retired and living in West Chester. "He put it on and I started sticking things on it."

A stripe across the shoulder and down each arm gradually widened into a swirl that, at the bottom, encompassed the entire sleeve. "It was supposed to look like wings," Ciccone said. "Like the logo, the concept behind the uniform was speed and motion."

"If those shoulders made the players look a little bigger, well, as an expansion team, we thought we'd take any edge we could get," recalls Putnam.

Ciccone also created Freddy Flyer, a character in a Quaker hat holding a hockey stick that the club

them I represented the Philadelphia Flyers," Scheinfeld remembers. "They'd say, 'Who'd you say you were with? Breyers?' I'd have to explain that I wasn't selling ice cream. Then they'd say, 'We don't think Philadelphia is going to be interested in soccer.'"

Putnam went on the prayer breakfast and civic luncheon circuit, while Snider buttonholed his friends and associates for season tickets. Meanwhile, Poile, Allen and Marcel Pelletier, a well-traveled, 38-year-old ex-goalie who had been hired in a scouting and

The Spectrum under construction.

would use in its advertising during the first year.

Freddy figured to get a workout. The team received approximately six hundred inquiries for season tickets, almost entirely from Rambler and Devil diehards. These people were offered seats before the public sale. The first five hundred season subscribers became charter members of the Flyers Club.

A ticket push began on November 29 with Philadelphia's "Mr. Hockey," Herb Gardiner (the NHL Hall of Fame player who had coached Philadelphia's minor-league teams for eighteen years), on hand at the Flyers' center city offices to fill out the first application. "I think we sold a few that day," Putnam remembers, "but there wasn't exactly a line down the block."

The Flyers' phones failed to ring with offers of corporate involvement. "I'd call companies and tell

promotional capacity, hit the road to look for players.

"I think we reached a consensus almost from the start that we were going to think young," Poile recalls. "We didn't just want to have a team that could be competitive with the new clubs, but one that in a few years could compete with the old ones."

Putnam told the newspapers it would take six years to build a Stanley Cup team, but there was good reason to believe that it would require longer. The best players would not be available to the new franchises in the amateur draft for at least their first two seasons.

The system of junior-club sponsorship—where teams could lock up prospects at age 14 or 15—was being phased out as part of the expansion plan. But almost four hundred 20-year-old players, including all the best ones, were untouchable in the first amateur draft in which the Flyers could participate. It would be 1969 before there would be completely open selection (Montreal's privilege of selecting the two best Quebec-born 20-year-olds would expire after that draft). This made Poile, Allen and Pelletier all the more determined to look for young players that the established clubs might be giving up on too quickly.

"We'd go on the road, usually alone, for as many as two weeks at a time," recalls Pelletier. "Then we'd

come back to the office and have mock drafts. Each of us would pick for two teams and we tried to see how we thought the draft would go.

"I'd played in St. Paul (of the Central League), so I had a real good idea of the players in that league. Bud and Keith had been in the Western League, so they knew that, too. We also scouted the American League heavily. The National League we did less. We knew what was there."

In the meantime, the big hole at Broad and Pattison Streets was beginning to fill with concrete. In a city where a baseball and football stadium had been the subject of a decade of fighting and procrastination, tangible evidence that the new $12-million arena was actually being built—and was a month ahead of schedule—was mind-boggling. With only nineteen months between conception and planned

September 1967 occupancy, there was no time to consider a multitude of schemes. As the architects were drawing, Philadelphia-based McCloskey and Co. was building.

"The architects said they didn't even want to look at any other buildings because they didn't want to be influenced," Scheinfeld said. "But that was silly. We did go look at a few—the plans for the new Madison Square Garden, the new Oakland Colsieum Arena, the San Diego Sports Arena that was still under construction, and the Civic Center Coliseum in Portland."

A two-tier design, with the entrances at mid-level, had become fairly standard during this building boom of new arenas. So were capacities of 15,000 seats for hockey and 16,500 for basketball. The tiers were tapered sharply to provide the best possible sight lines. "The guideline the architects used was that if you were sitting in the last row, you could see the goalies," says Freeman, now director of special events at Garden State Park. "There were no blind spots. I thought about things like press access to the locker rooms, and placement of bathrooms and concession stands. I'm not an artistic guy. I was thinking in terms of function and comfort."

The creativity was left to Scheinfeld, who struggled with finding an appropriate, yet innovative, name. Scheinfeld says Freeman pushed for the Keystone Arena. "A boring, crummy name," Scheinfeld said. "I didn't want 'arena' even in there."

Freeman says he, too, was against using the 'A' word. He wanted to call the building the Keystone. "And it was just a suggestion," Freeman said. But Scheinfeld wanted something unique, so he sought the opinion of Bill Becker, the Mel Richman Inc. executive who had been involved with the uniform and logo designs. In the spring of 1967, Becker and

Scheinfeld went to the arena site, put on helmets and boots, walked through the uncompleted shell and brainstormed names. Scheinfeld says he doesn't remember who said "Spectrum" first. Becker insists that he did.

"I was graphically oriented," Becker recalls, "so I'm thinking in terms of how any name could be applied that way. I'm thinking about how this building will host a number of different events. I thought of color and this being a stadium or auditorium and 'Spectrum' popped into my head and out my mouth.

"I remember Lou saying, 'Doesn't that sound a little pharmaceutical?' I told Lou no, that it suggested blocks of colors which would be great for a billboard and a logo."

"As we walked around," Scheinfeld recalls, "we started throwing out names. 'Special ... spectacular ... splendiferous ...' and then I don't know who said 'Spectrum.' I went to the dictionary to look up what it meant and it said something like 'a series of colorful images created when light comes through a prism.' I thought, 'What could be more perfect?'

"For the presentation to Snider and Wolman, we worked out this thing that the *SP* would stand for sports, the *E* for entertainment, *C* for concerts and circuses, *T* for theatrics, *R* for recreation and relaxation and *UM* for auditorium, stadium, etc."

Scheinfeld built his case against the use of Keystone by going to the phone book and reporting back to Wolman and Snider that there were at least fifty businesses in the Delaware Valley by that name. He made special mention of the Keystone Exterminators and Keystone Pickleworks. "I was really heavy-handed when it came to the presentation before we voted," Scheinfeld says. "We showed all these beautiful Spectrum graphics against an as-bland-as-possible Keystone logo."

If Freeman was upset—and he insists today that he wasn't—he certainly sounded enthusiastic about the name of the new arena when it was announced on May 2. "Spectrum is a series of images which form a display of colors," Freeman said. "We have the only Spectrum in the whole world. It sounds like spectacle and spectacular."

"It sounds like they've reached too far in groping for something unique," wrote Hochman. "There are no Orangutan dry cleaners in the phone book either, and orangutans are big and bold and colorful."

Hochman's wasn't the only dissenting opinion. "People were coming up to me and saying, 'It sounds like a doctor's instrument,'" Snider remembers. "The word 'spectrum' at that time was practically out of the vocabulary. People just couldn't believe that name. I was really shook."

The Spectrum was planned to have a four-color arrangement of seats, a series of concentric swirls conceived by Becker. But the blue, apple green, magenta and orange had to be scrapped when the fabric manufacturer couldn't provide the multitude of tones to the seating company in time for August installation.

The change to all dark red seats wasn't the only alteration in plans as construction continued. Wolman had become overextended on other business ventures and his creditors were starting to call. The wolf was at the Spectrum door, before it even *had* doors.

That spring, Wolman had been contacted by two investors (Putnam has notes identifying their last names as McConnell and Wetenhall) who were interested in buying the hockey franchise. Wolman saw the possibility of fresh capital and asked Putnam to meet with the two men. "They made it clear that they wanted 100 percent of the team," Putnam recalls. "They didn't want to be our partners."

Wolman called a meeting of Snider, Putnam and Schiff and announced he had an offer that would enable the four of them to split $1 million for a franchise for which they had not yet paid. "Wolman said these guys wanted to move the franchise," Snider recalls, "but when I asked where, he said it was 'confidential.' I asked, 'What about the building?' Wolman said he thought the building would be successful anyway, but that the hockey team couldn't help it.

"Schiff said, 'I agree with Jerry, let's sell and take the million.' But Putnam said, 'I've moved here, and we've put a lot of sweat and blood into getting this thing off the ground. I think it's going to succeed. I don't want to sell.'

"I don't think I said anything," Snider recalls. "The whole thing was preposterous anyway. The league had granted us only a conditional franchise for Philadelphia. I didn't think we had any right to sell it.

"Wolman said, 'It has to be unanimous. If you don't want to sell, then that's okay.' That was the beginning of the end for Wolman and me. But I didn't know it at the time.

"We walked out of the room together, and he told me, 'Ed, you've been very excited about getting this team. I think you ought to see if you can put something together to take over. I really don't want to be involved in the hockey team anymore, just the arena.'

"But he said he would still come up with the $1

million (of the $2-million franchise fee due in June) he had promised, and that I could pay him back within a short period of time (once the team was refinanced). So I started working on a deal with Wolman to exchange my 40 percent of the Spectrum for his 22 percent of the Flyers. I bought out Jerry Schiff, too.

"I had become the majority owner of the Flyers before we had to pay for the franchise, and he had become the sole owner of the Spectrum. I had never wanted to own more than 22 percent of the team. I didn't think I could afford it."

Truth was, Snider couldn't. But he started to sign his life away. He remortgaged his home. He borrowed $25,000 from one bank, $50,000 from another.

"Earl Foreman (Snider's brother-in-law and Wolman's ownership partner with the Eagles) negotiated the deal with Wolman for me," recalls Snider. "Afterwards, I remember going out to celebrate and my hand was shaking as I held my drink. If we failed, I was belly-up in every way known to man. But I still thought that if we had a successful product, we'd work it out some way."

Putnam retained his 25 percent interest and the title of team president while Snider, who remained the salaried vice president and treasurer of the Eagles, searched for an investor to come in for the remaining shares of the Flyers. "Wolman and I worked together on the Spectrum like we were still partners even though we weren't anymore," Snider said. "I worked day and night to get it open, selfishly, of course, for the Flyers, but unselfishly, too, for him."

While Snider and Freeman hustled the building along, Putnam was constructing the hockey organization. The Flyers were beaten out by the Los Angeles Kings in an attempt to buy Eddie Shore's Springfield (Massachusetts) Indians of the American Hockey League, so Putnam purchased the AHL Quebec Aces from Gerald Martineau, a Quebec businessman, for $350,000. The sale, announced on May 8, gave the Flyers their first sixteen players. "We'll be well protected by veterans now and we can go for the best available young talent," Allen said.

What the coach did not know was that the Flyers needed to scout for another bank. Because of Wolman's financial problems, they almost didn't make it to the drafting table.

"About the beginning of May, five weeks before the $2 million for the franchise was due, I started to ask Wolman for the $1 million he had promised," Putnam recalls. "Our other million was coming on a loan from Fidelity Bank. When I started to get

put off, I began to have my suspicions. With all the other indications that Jerry was in trouble, it wasn't really hard to figure it out.

"To my recollection, it was seven to ten days before the money was due (on June 5) that Jerry told me he didn't have it."

Putnam and Snider began scrambling. Putnam went to Kaiser Broadcasting, the owners of Channel 48, and undersold three years of the team's broadcast rights for $350,000. Snider borrowed $150,000 independently. Still $500,000 short, he then went to Bill Fishman, the president and founder of ARA Services, which had already put up a $2-million advance for the food service rights at the Spectrum.

Snider hoped the company's vested interest in the project would lead it to volunteer additional money to save the arena's prime tenant. Fishman was agreeable, but to raise the $500,000, he would have to borrow from a bank willing to take his personal ARA stock as collateral.

A desperate Putnam called Jennings and offered New York the Flyers' first two choices in the expansion draft for the $500,000. Putnam says Jennings told him he would try to find funds somewhere in the Madison Square Garden structure.

It was Saturday, June 3, 1967. The money was due in Montreal at 2 P.M. Monday. If Putnam and Snider didn't have it, and had no prospects to get it, the league would face a huge dilemma: whether or not to allow the Flyers to participate in Tuesday's expansion draft.

"I still remember that Saturday morning sitting at breakfast with my wife in our place in the Greenhill Apartments (on City Line Avenue)," said Putnam. "She asked, 'What are you going to do?' I said I had no idea. I would just go down to the office and start making some calls.

"I called Fishman. He said he was working on the loan at Provident Bank and had been promised an answer on Sunday. I didn't wait. I called [Provident executive] Roger Hillas at home. I got him off his lawn mower. He came to the phone and said he would do it."

Provident issued the $500,000 loan check on Monday morning. Fishman signed it over to the Philadelphia Hockey Club.

"Bill Fishman is responsible for my owning the Flyers," Snider recalls. "I've always said that. If it hadn't been for Bill Fishman, I'm history."

Since Putnam had left the previous day for Montreal and the draft, it was up to Snider to make the transfer at Fidelity, which would issue the $2-million credit to be wired to Montreal by the 2 P.M. deadline.

Snider was at the bank when the lights went out.

At 10:23 A.M. a power failure blacked out a 15,000-square-mile area extending north and south from New Jersey to Maryland and east and west from Harrisburg to the Jersey shore. Philadelphia came to an absolute stop. People were trapped in elevators, subways and streetcars, and traffic jams snarled intersections suddenly without functioning stoplights. Phones were out and the banks couldn't do business. Snider had no way to get the money to Montreal.

"Putnam was up there in his hotel room dying,"

Bernie Parent, center, with Bud Poile, left, and Bill Putnam.

Snider recalls. "He can't get in touch with me or anybody. I don't really know what would have happened, but I was thinking that after all we'd been through, they were going to give the franchise to somebody else."

"Somehow I found out, maybe through Jennings, that there was this blackout affecting the East Coast," Putnam recalls. "As I remember, [the league] was aware of the reason for the delay, but they were waiting impatiently."

Power wasn't restored in center city until noon. Snider was able to wire the money through New York to the Royal Bank of Canada, where Scheinfeld and Putnam were waiting. They drew the check and ran back to the league meetings at the Queen Elizabeth Hotel.

"I still remember jumping over the divider on [Dorchester] Street in front of the hotel," recalls Scheinfeld, "and running upstairs to the room where they were waiting for us. We were so excited. It was like, 'Yeah, we're here, we did it, we're in the league.' And I still remember Clarence Campbell sitting there with his dour look on his face saying, 'Do you have the check?' He didn't say 'welcome' or 'happy to have you' or 'congratulations' or anything."

"He didn't even say thank you," Putnam recalls.

Each of the six new clubs had been directed to make out its check to one of the six established franchises. The Flyers' check was payable to the Toronto Maple Leafs. Campbell turned it over to Leafs president Stafford Smythe.

"The way this thing has gone," Putnam remembers Smythe saying, "this will probably bounce."

For their $2 million, the Flyers got to pick eighteen players and two goaltenders in the draft that began at 10 A.M. the next day. After much internal debate and many delays, the league had come up with an expansion formula that was relatively generous.

Each team could protect its best eleven players and one goalie. Anyone who had not completed two full seasons as a professional was draft-exempt. Once a team lost a player (theoretically its twelfth-best), it could then freeze a thirteenth, leaving No. 14 available for claim. The established club could then make one more freeze before all its remaining players became available. Once a team lost a goalie, it could then protect a second one.

Each of the six new clubs drew letters—A through F—which determined their selection place in the two separate drafts of goalies and skaters. The Flyers drew B, which meant they would have the second pick in the two-round goalie draft and fifth choice in the eighteen-round draft of forwards and defensemen.

Los Angeles opened the goaltending selections by taking Terry Sawchuk, who had just lifted Toronto to the Stanley Cup. This left plenty of established veterans available to the Flyers, including future Hall of Famer Glenn Hall, Montreal's Charlie Hodge and Boston's Ed Johnston and Don Simmons. So Poile sent a murmur through the hotel ballroom when he selected 22-year-old Bernard Parent from the Boston Bruins.

Parent, a Montreal native who had recorded a 3.69 goals-against average in 39 games with a last-place Bruins team during his rookie 1965-66 season, had struggled as a sophomore and completed the season in Oklahoma City with a 2.70 goals against average and 4 shutouts in 14 games.

"He was supposed to be immature," recalls

Flyers were unimpressed with the picked-over selection of veterans. They decided to go with the Bruins' other goalie at Oklahoma City, Doug Favell. Two days younger than Parent, Favell was considered the lesser prospect because of his flopping style.

With the fifth-overall choice in the draft of forwards and defensemen, the Flyers selected Ed Van Impe, a 27-year-old Chicago blueliner who, after five seasons at Buffalo of the American League, had just been a distant runner-up to Bobby Orr for rookie of the year. Orr's good friend and rookie teammate in Boston, Joe Watson, a 23-year-old defenseman, was the Flyers' second-round pick.

Ed Van Impe defends with his stick.

Pelletier. "And he probably was. But when I saw him play at Oklahoma City, I thought he looked like the perfect goalie."

As the draft proceeded, three clubs, according to Poile, approached the Flyers about trading Parent. "One of them (Chicago) made a cash offer that staggered the imagination," Poile told the *Inquirer*'s Jack Chevalier.

Having chosen one young goalie, the Flyers hoped to select a veteran next. But Hall went to St. Louis on the third pick, Hodge to Oakland on the fourth and Boston, after losing Parent, protected Johnston. When the eleventh choice came up, the

Chicago and Boston, who had hoped to slip Van Impe and Watson through, both immediately tried to make deals to re-obtain them. "Good offers," Poile said, "but I turned them down." True to their promise, the Flyers were refusing the aging players the established clubs were trying to unload.

The Flyers' third choice was Brit Selby, a 22-year-old Toronto center who only one season earlier had been the NHL's rookie of the year. "He had broken his leg and they had given up on him, but we thought he was still a good prospect," Pelletier recalls.

The Flyers next chose 29-year-old Chicago center Lou Angotti ("We thought he'd be a character guy and good two-way player," recalls Pelletier), then 28-year-old Montreal right wing Leon Rochefort.

Five defensemen were taken with Philadelphia's first nine picks. John Miszuk, 26, was a Chicago farmhand who had played for Poile in Edmonton. Dick Cherry, 30, was from the Boston organization and Jean Gauthier, 30, had kicked around the Montreal chain.

The Flyers felt the best of the forwards they took after Selby was left wing Don Blackburn, a Toronto farmhand. They also chose center Garry Peters (from Montreal's system) and center Jimmy Johnson (from New York's) before selecting Gary Dornhoefer, a 24-year-old, skin-and-bones right wing who had flunked three different trials with the Bruins. Veteran forwards Forbes Kennedy (from Boston's organization), Pat Hannigan (Chicago), Dwight Carruthers (Detroit), Bob Courcy (Montreal), Keith Wright (Boston) and defenseman Terry Ball (New York) rounded out the twenty Flyer selections.

Though Parent lived in Montreal, he did not attend the draft. He heard the news of his selection on the radio at a golf driving range. Parent felt rejected, but was not nearly as upset as Watson.

"I'd beaten out Dallas Smith and Gary Doak for a regular job," Watson recalls. "The Bruins had an up-and-coming team. Orr called and was really upset. Harry Sinden (the Bruin coach) called and told me, 'We didn't think we would lose you.'"

If Watson felt sick with betrayal, misery knew no greater company than Van Impe's when he heard the news on the radio in his hometown of Saskatoon. "The Blackhawks didn't call, they just didn't do those things in those days," Van Impe remembers. "I was very unhappy. After five years, I'd finally made that team. We had just finished first for the first time in the team's history (Chicago had been upset by Cup winner Toronto in the first round), and now I'm going to Philadelphia to start all over again. Chicago had just (in May) made the (Phil) Esposito trade (to Boston) and had gotten Gilles Marotte. That made me expendable."

Cherry was so overjoyed to become a Flyer that he informed Poile he was retiring to teach school. As low as some Flyer draftees were feeling, the media and hockey people were high on the team's selections.

Joe Watson, at 23, was the Flyers' second-round pick.

The consensus was that Philadelphia had done the best and that Boston had suffered the greatest losses.

Campbell, previously a skeptic about expansion, bragged competitive balance wasn't far away. "I estimate that the two divisions (new teams in the West Division, old clubs in the East) will have achieved parity by 1970," the league president said.

Everything appeared to be on schedule. But the Flyers were again in need of refinancing. Fishman had decided not to exercise the option of applying his $500,000 loan into shares of the team and needed to be repaid. Snider and Putnam were already in as far as they could go. Although there were pledges from many small investors, a percentage of Flyers stock remained unsold.

Thus the phone call to Joe Scott. Snider, who had gotten to know Scott when his beer distributorship, Scott and Grauer, ran promotions with the Eagles, had inquired almost a year earlier whether Scott would be interested in buying a share of the hockey team.

Scott, who had served on the board of many Delaware Valley charities and had sponsored practically every amateur athletic endeavor in the tri-state area, was also one of the few known regulars at Rambler games. In fact, before the club moved to Haddonfield in 1964, Scott almost bought a significant share of the team. "Then, I came to my senses," he recalls.

Those senses remained as sharp as ever after Scott sold the beer business in 1966. At age 59, the only thing getting old was retirement.

"My wife, Pat, had just had another child and I turned into a big pain in the butt around the house,"

Scott recalls. So when Pat answered the telephone one morning and Snider told her about his plan, she thought her prayers had been answered.

"Joe," she said, "Ed Snider has a proposal for you. You are going to say 'yes.'"

Actually, Scott didn't agree right away. But he did attend the Spectrum groundbreaking and the party that followed at Bookbinders, where Snider again applied the squeeze. Months earlier, Scott had turned Snider down because he had been asked to join a group of as many as twelve or thirteen own-

ers.

"With twelve or thirteen investors, you don't want me," Scott had said. "I'd be the oldest guy and the worst pain in the ass in the group. I'd want my way."

But now, Snider was proposing an ownership group of three—himself, Putnam and Scott. "Then," recalls Scott, "I got serious. I told Ed that my wife didn't just want me to invest. She wanted me to work."

"Great, you can have a job," said Snider.

The Flyers needed a Philadelphian known to every banker in town. Although Snider was a name in the city because of his Eagles involvement, in business circles he was still the recently transplanted Washingtonian. Putnam, the ex-banker from New York, was even more of an outsider. Snider

felt confident there was a bank president somewhere in Philadelphia who could not turn Scott down.

This belief was retained all the way through their sixth rejection.

"The guy from Industrial Valley Bank fell asleep while Putnam and I were talking to him," Scott remembers.

The seventh bank they approached was Girard. Putnam, Snider and Scott don't remember what their eighth option was, but it might have involved masks and revolvers.

Girard had been placed down the list for a good reason. "It was by reputation the most conservative of all the Philadelphia banks," Scott recalls. "It was the old Quaker bank that wouldn't take a gamble on anything."

As it turned out, Girard president Steve Gardner wasn't a typical, hockey-hating Philadelphian, but a puck-charmed Bostonian and Harvard graduate. The bank also had a vice president, Bill Baer, who, although a Philadelphia native, had also been exposed to the sport at Harvard. "It was a high-risk loan, no question," Baer remembers. "Not the kind we usually made. It was a tough sell to the board, but we did it. We charged them the prime rate plus one-and-a-half, fair, we thought, for the degree of risk. Ed and Bill pledged their socks and underwear and we made the loan."

Girard extended the Flyers $1.5 million which, coupled with the $375,000 from Kaiser for the broadcast rights and the money Scott put into the franchise, assured that a team would be on the ice in the fall.

Scott tried to sell more of the team's stock. "But not one of the five richest guys in town was interested," he said. "They told me, 'You're tossing your money out the window.' Myself, I didn't have any doubts because I thought with national television we'd be riding clear within two to three years."

On August 26, two weeks before training camp was scheduled to open in Quebec City, Wolman's trading of his Flyers shares for Snider's Spectrum shares and the refinancing of the hockey team were made public. Snider now owned 60 percent of the Flyers, Putnam 25 percent, and Scott 15 percent. "Jerry Wolman is rearranging his holdings," Snider told the

Ed Snider, left, with Doug Favell.

newspapers. "He intends to stabilize his finances and stop the rumors that are floating around the city. He just thought it was in his best interest to sell his per cent of the hockey team. His main concern is football."

Snider, still the Eagles' chief operating officer, believed his first job would remain football, too, once the hockey team got off the ground. He took the position of chairman of the board of the Flyers. Putnam remained the president and day-to-day head of operations. "We're giving Bill Putnam a long-term contract as president, signing a long-term lease with the Spectrum and we're here to stay," Snider announced. "If I didn't think hockey would become popular in Philadelphia, I wouldn't have made the deal."

The Flyers pushed nothing but confidence in their newspaper ads. "Landslide Season Ticket Sale Crushes Hockey Fan," they warned their customers-to-be in early September. But at that point, the landslide consisted of only 1,200 season tickets, many of which were attributable to Scott. "He was a bulldog,"

recalls Scheinfeld.

Not only did Scott set up a platoon of college kids that worked off commission selling tickets by phone, he personally walked into the office of every corporate type who had ever heard of him and his Ballantine beer. "I was the jolly fellow well met," said Scott. "They knew me, they gave me a break."

Two weeks before their first training camp, the Flyers had more obligations than assets. All they posssesed, really, was a bunch of hand-me-down players, a trickle of season-ticket deposits, and the faith of Snider, Putnam and Scott. They faced every crisis with the underlying belief that if they could get their team onto the ice, the NHL in Philadelphia could not fail.

"I didn't need a market survey to tell me that the fourth-largest city in the United States needed a modern arena, and that people would come to watch an exciting, major-league sport," said Snider. "I was young and full of energy. I never doubted we could make this work."

Chapter 2

◆◆◆

The Regular Guys

Although most of the hockey players checking into Quebec City's Orleans Motel on September 10, 1967, for the Flyers' first training camp were not excessively talented, they were extremely grateful. "If you weren't picked in an expansion draft with six new teams starting, you knew you were going to be buried in the minors for a long time," said right wing Gary Dornhoefer.

Only the few who had gained precious NHL jobs with the six established clubs were less than thrilled. Defensemen Joe Watson and Ed Van Impe wanted compensation for the disruption in their lives. Expected to fill leadership roles with the Flyers, they decided to test their indispensability with a dual contract holdout.

Watson contacted Alan Eagleson, the young attorney who had represented Bobby Orr and founded the NHL Players Association in 1966, then met with Van Impe and talked him into a strike. This left Bud Poile, the Flyers' GM, grumbling about having to deal with agents, insisting no one on the team would earn more than $20,000 a year, and refusing to negotiate with either Watson or Van Impe until they showed up at camp.

By the time they did, Lou Angotti, the only Philadelphia forward to have played the full previous season in the NHL, was already out with a broken thumb suffered in an opening-day scrimmage fight with Paul Cates, one of the minor-league players the Flyers acquired in their purchase of the American Hockey League Quebec Aces.

Thus, the first Flyer camp was hardly off to a flying start. Watson and Van Impe sat on the bench but did not play as Philadelphia was embarrassed 6-1, in its premier exhibition game by Quebec at Le Colisee. "The bright side," said Poile, "is that our own farm club beat us."

Jimmy Johnson scored for the Flyers, but Bernie Parent allowed four goals before being replaced by Gilles Banville, another Quebec acquisition. "The biggest reason we look so bad is me," Parent said. "It's bad how I play today."

The young goalie slept one night on his humility. The next day, Parent, who had been announced in August as the Flyers' first official player under contract, revealed he had not actually signed Poile's $20,000 offer, and was now thinking about leaving camp. "I been talking to other players and I think I am worth more than those guys," Parent said.

The Flyers managed only a 2-2 tie in a second attempt against Quebec

Favell heads to practice at the Flyers' first training camp, Quebec, 1967.

The first Flyers, from left: Rochefort, Kennedy, coach Allen, Peters.

and needed a late goal by Leon Rochefort to edge another AHL team, Springfield, 5-4 for their first exhibition win. Parent decided to sign after all, but Van Impe and Watson refused to budge and were suspended. The Flyers lost to the Los Angeles Kings, 3-1, in their first preseason game against a new NHL club, then were bombed by the Pittsburgh Penguins, 7-3.

"The team looks bad," Eagleson told the media on behalf of Watson and Van Impe, and Poile obviously agreed. On September 30, Van Impe signed a two-year contract totalling $45,000 plus team performance bonuses. Three days later, Watson accepted a two-year deal worth $38,500.

Doug Favell surprised management with the best performance of any goalie in camp and beat out Banville for the backup spot at the start of the NHL season. Four Quebec players—Ed Hoekstra, Bill Sutherland, Wayne Hicks and John Hanna—were included on the Flyers' roster announced October 6, five days before their opening game in Oakland:

Goaltenders:	Parent and Favell
Defensemen:	Van Impe, Watson, Jean Gauthier, John Miszuk, Jim Morrison and Hanna
Centers:	Angotti, Hoekstra, Forbes Kennedy and Garry Peters
Left wings:	Brit Selby, Don Blackburn and Sutherland
Right wings:	Rochefort, Dornhoefer, Hicks and Pat Hannigan

Allen predicted for the media that the Flyers would end the season in the top three of the new West (expansion) Division. The team finished its exhibition schedule with a win in Providence over the AHL Providence Reds, then flew to Philadelphia to let the players spend a day looking for housing.

Watson's first impression of the city as the team bused in from the airport was the piles of crushed cars in the auto graveyard off the Penrose Avenue Bridge. "When I asked the bus driver about it," Watson remembers, "he said there were people still in them." Was this the place, Watson wondered, where hockey careers came to die?

The Flyers, anxious to do things right, advanced each player $1,000 for an apartment deposit. Most of them put their money down on places in South Jersey, then headed back to the airport and the flight to California for the first game. Management had issued orange sport coats for the players to wear on the road. "I remember telling Watson not to wear his at the front entrance of the hotel," Kennedy said. "Someone would ask us to go get their car."

Van Impe, who already had reservations about the orange and black uniforms, was mortified by the traveling jackets. "Going through airports," he said, "we looked like a herd of pumpkins."

The Philadelphia newspapers ran features introducing the players and the rules of hockey. "It's important to keep your eye on the puck," said one story authored by coach Keith Allen.

"A professional hockey player can skate forty-four feet in one second," read a Flyer advertisement. But

Flyers get set to leave
on their first road trip
in October, 1967. From
left John Hanna, Jean
Gauthier, coach Allen,
Wayne Hicks, Jim
Morrison, Brit Selby.

since no one warming up at the Oakland Coliseum Arena on October 11, 1967, fit that description, it begged the question of just how professional the presentation would be.

At 11 P.M. Philadelphia time, Allen sent Gauthier, Miszuk, Angotti, Selby and Hicks to the center-ice circle. As 6,686 pioneers settled into their seats, referee Art Skov signaled checks of the red lights behind Parent and Seals goalie Charlie Hodge. Then, like an obstetrician cutting an umbilical cord, Skov dropped the puck. The Philadelphia Flyers had begun competition in the National Hockey League.

The expansion era had actually started three hours earlier in Pittsburgh with the mighty Montreal Canadiens having an astonishingly difficult time subduing the new Penguins, 2-1. The game in Oakland, however, between two expansion clubs, had neither a real plot nor live exposure to the Delaware Valley. Channel 48 had not included West Coast telecasts in its 25- game package and the Flyers were still without a radio contract.

Kent Douglas gave Oakland a 1-0 lead 3:23 into the contest. "How are we doing?" Ed Snider, the naive new hockey owner, asked *Bulletin* writer John Brogan between the first and second periods. Not well, it turned out. Sutherland scored the first-ever Flyer goal at 10:07 of the second period to tie the game, but Billy Harris and Bill Hicke responded within two minutes to give the Seals a 3-1 lead.

"It was like ninety degrees outside," Watson remembers, "and Keith put Eddie and I together on defense even though we had almost no training camp." The pair was on for three goals against as Oakland won 5-1, completely "outclassing the Flyers" in the view of *Daily News* writer Ed Conrad.

Let the record show that Angotti, named the team's captain that day, took the initial penalty in Flyer history—for interference—after only 22 seconds. Dornhoefer was the first Flyer to be officially wounded in a league game, suffering a deep bruise to the left instep when hit by a puck in the opening period. The Flyers did little forechecking of the Seals or foreshadowing of later events: there was not one fight in the game.

Allen attributed the loss to a shortage of preparation time. Poile blamed Eagleson for the way Van Impe and Watson played. Two nights later in Long Beach, where the Los Angeles Kings were holed up pending midseason completion of owner Jack Kent Cooke's Fabulous Forum in Inglewood, the Flyers jumped to their first-ever lead when Sutherland's weak shot hopped over goalie Wayne Rutledge's stick before a minute had been played. But Philadelphia lost the

Allen behind the
Flyers' bench during
team's first game at
the Montreal Forum.

game 4-2 as L.A. racked up a 38-15 shot advantage. "Favell was exceptional," said Allen, "but we can't mount any offense."

With three days off before a game in St. Louis, the Flyers flew home and were greeted at the airport by thirty-five fans. The next day, the team was officially welcomed at City Hall. Mayor James Tate sent his regrets and a deputy to do the honors. Then, following a reception at Wanamakers, the Flyers were put into open convertibles for a parade to the Spectrum.

dashers or pucks. With renewed determination, the Flyers faced off two nights later in yet another apathetic setting, St. Louis. As Channel 48 presented the team to the Delaware Valley for first time, Putnam and Blues owner Sid Salomon III glanced at the 5,234 in attendance, then at each other, and wondered why they had become owners of hockey clubs.

The Blues scored on a two-man advantage to jump ahead, 1-0, but Favell hung tough. With 35 seconds remaining in the second period, Angotti put the tying goal up over goalie Glenn Hall's shoulder and off

With Gary Dornhoefer (12) down, Jimmy Johnson battles Los Angeles during the Flyers' second regular-season game.

Watson did not expect wildly cheering fans to line the sidewalks of South Philadelphia, but he hardly anticipated overt hostility. "About halfway down to the Spectrum, I swear to gosh there was this guy there giving us the finger," Watson remembers. "He yelled, 'You'll be in Baltimore by December.' I'll bet there were twenty people, tops, all the way down Broad Street, who actually stood there to watch. All the rest were people on lunch hour wondering who the hell we were."

The public had an open invitation to the Flyers' first-ever practice in their new home that afternoon, but largely declined. When the team came onto the ice, there were about ten spectators in the building. The workout was hampered by the absence of boards, the installation of which had been delayed by a manufacturers' strike. "We started shooting at the workers, getting a big kick out of watching them scramble," Watson recalls.

Concerned about the team's level of conditioning, Allen directed a marathon skate that did not need

the crossbar. Hoekstra put the Flyers in front 2-1 with 7:40 remaining in the game and Favell, despite a 35-21 Flyer shot disadvantage, made the lead stand up.

In the next day's newspaper standings, to the right of "Philadelphia" and beneath the "W," was an historic "1." "The first of many," Poile proclaimed.

"I knew we couldn't be as bad as we looked in our first two games," a relieved Allen said.

As the Flyers chartered back to Philadelphia for the next night's home opener against Pittsburgh, the Spectrum still showed many signs of construction. Wall paint was on hold until $30,000 for the job could be spared, and the overhanging scoreboard was empty of its lower portion designed for messages and cartoons. Both an $800,000 television studio and a $23,000 electronic turnstile system that would have displayed a running attendance total had been scrapped because of a lack of funds.

"[Jerry] Wolman's troubles were affecting an already skeptical situation through that whole summer," recalls Lou Scheinfeld, the Spectrum's vice president. "Snider, by his sheer brilliance and will-power, got it done."

The hockey boards, while forcing cancellation of the Spectrum's first two events—exhibition games featuring the Flyers against Pittsburgh, and the New York Rangers versus the Canadiens—had finally been delivered. Snider had had someone bribe a union guy to open the doors at the construction company so trucks could come in and make their escape with the goods. "Honest to God, that's how we did it," recalls Snider. "or we wouldn't have had

boards for the first game.

"Down the stretch, we'd have a meeting seven days a week at six o'clock at night. We'd go over what was done and what still had to get done. Sometimes those meetings lasted until four o'clock in the morning."

It had been a rush all the way, but the toilets were flushing and the concession stands operating when the Spectrum opened its doors on Saturday, September 30, for the first performance of a two-night Quaker City Jazz Festival. "We hope the public will indulge us for a while until we're settled," said Spectrum manager Hal Freeman.

Patrons encountered huge traffic tie-ups going into the parking lots, delaying the show fifty-five minutes. As organist Jimmy Smith began the program, the Spectrum was only half filled. The jazz remained more mellow than the music lovers when they realized all the restrooms were located in the basement, eighty-five feet below the top row of seats.

The last of the six main acts, which included headliners Ramsey Lewis, Hugh Masekela and comedian Flip Wilson, did not finish until after 3 A.M..

The second night of the festival drew a full house of 17,500 persons, to that point the largest indoor audience in Philadelphia history.

A twelve-day run of Holiday on Ice was the next Spectrum booking. The first sports event, on Tuesday, October 17, was a fight card featuring Joe Frazier versus Tony Doyle. The following morning, as the 76ers prepared for that evening's opener against the Los Angeles Lakers (the Sixers would win, 103-87), the building's official dedication took place under a canopy by the main entrance.

No one hailed the Spectrum as an architectural wonder. *Bulletin* columnist Sandy Grady called it "The Fish Can on the Delaware Flats," and some found it incongruous that a building named for a series of colors would have such a bland exterior of brown (if native Pennsylvanian) brick.

Although the concept of a multihued seating scheme died when the manufacturer could only provide red on short notice, Snider's wife did her part to enliven the building's aesthetic appeal. Usherettes were outfitted in burnt-orange blazers and hot pink miniskirts; ushers wore blue suits.

Thankfully, most of the patrons cared more about function than beauty. While ground for Veterans Stadium remained unbroken, a modern arena with excellent sight lines had been built and opened within fifteen months. "It's the happiest thing to happen to Philadelphia sports in years," wrote Grady. "And without a nickel of the taxpayers' money."

Few of the dollars saved, however, were being spent on hockey. The Flyers sold only 2,100 season tickets and had an advance sale of just 6,000 for their home debut. "We need 8,500 a game to keep from losing money," Bill Putnam said when announcing the team had signed a thirty-year lease. "But even if we don't do that well, we'll be back. We're convinced that, in the long run, we'll draw as well as the older clubs."

That long run appeared to be up a ninety-degree grade when 7,812 attended the Flyers' premier game in Philadelphia on October 19. "Somebody told me this was a gate town," Putnam, who had hoped for 12,000, said disappointedly. High ticket prices, scaled from $2.00 to $5.50, were blamed for the empty seats, but NHL president Clarence Campbell, who dropped the first puck, insisted the league had to "charge luxury prices for a luxury product."

This, however, was not haute hockey. Public ad-

Bill Sutherland tips home a goal against the Blues' Glenn Hall.

dress announcer Gene Hart explained icing and offsides well and often. Favell and Pittsburgh goalie Les Binkley each fielded only 14 shots through two scoreless periods. "I think it was the worst hockey game ever played," Putnam recalls. Nothing worthy of a cheer occured until 2:59 of the third period, when Hoekstra knocked down a Penguin clearing attempt, Rochefort shot through a screen, and Sutherland shoved the rebound and first-ever Spectrum goal past Binkley.

The Flyers slinked away with a 1-0 victory, thanks to the furtive efforts of Sutherland and four of his teammates. Earlier in the evening, a door guard had refused to let them enter the building. "Nobody gets in without a ticket," he had told the players. Not even Putnam, dressed in his orange jacket could convince the employee to allow the players to pass. An unprotected door on the main level finally enabled them to sneak inside.

After the game, Putnam and Snider were hosting a reception in the unfinished Blueline Club. For Snider, the party ended abruptly when he was shown the headline from an early edition of the next day's *Inquirer*: "Snider Fired by Wolman in Struggle over the Eagles."

"Bullbleep, I was fired," Snider seethed.

Despite trading his Spectrum shares for Wolman's Flyer stock during the summer, Snider had retained his position as vice president of the football club. "He's in Washington trying to save his empire," recalls Snider. "I'm building the Spectrum for him. I thought we were still friends."

But that relationship was blown apart both by Wolman's financial problems and a disagreement over Eagles coach Joe Kuharich.

Snider had grown increasingly contemptuous of the methods and personality of Kuharich who, like himself, had been given a fifteen-year contract by Wolman. "I noticed that Kuharich's attitude toward me was changing," recalls Snider. "I'm supposed to still be running the Eagles, but he wasn't listening to anything I said. He was nasty to me in front of everybody at meetings. So that put the antenna up and I called a meeting (on the day of the Flyers' home opener) to bring things to a head.

"Wolman told me he could do a better job with Kuharich than I was doing. I said, 'OK, I'd like an orderly transition and a [contract] buyout (of his 7 percent interest in the football team).' Actually, I wanted to be involved with the hockey team, and I looked at it like a new chapter of my life was beginning in perfect time.

"That night, Wolman released to the press that I was fired. Egotistically, I was destroyed."

The following day, at a bizarre and bitter press conference, Kuharich maintained Snider had been spending so much time on the Spectrum and the Flyers that his Eagle responsibilities were being neglected. In Snider's presence, Kuharich gloated, "I think we should have parties like this more often."

"Maybe yours will be next," Snider shot back.

Wolman says today that Kuharich was not the cause of Snider's firing but refuses to elaborate.

Wolman's supporters have maintained that Snider took unfair advantage of his mentor's financial problems to gain control of the Flyers.

Wolman says that he had the promise of a $43-million loan from Kuwaiti interests if he could acquire more collateral. During a summertime meeting in Hershey, Wolman had asked Snider to sign back his share of the Flyers to help secure the credit.

According to Wolman, Snider verbally consented, then, after driving home, changed his mind. "It wasn't the fact that he said no," Wolman says. "It's that he agreed and reneged after I had done all the work. It blew the whole deal apart."

Snider says he never agreed to sell his share of the Flyers back to Wolman or put them up as collateral for any loan Wolman was seeking.

"I said no because after Wolman had not come up with the money he pledged for the franchise fee, we (he and Flyer partners Putnam and Joe Scott) had gotten our own loan for which we were responsible," recalls Snider. "We had borrowed $500,000

(in June) from Bill Fishman at ARA which we had to pay back in ninety days. So we had to go to Girard Bank to borrow [$1.5 million] that we needed to repay Fishman and operate the team. After going through all that, there was no way I ever would have agreed to give the team back to Wolman."

Snider still does not believe that Wolman even had a pledge for a loan that was dependent upon the value of the hockey team.

"At that point the Flyers were not an asset worthy of an additional loan." he says. "They were already encumbered in and of themselves up to their value.

"The idea that someone was offering to make this big loan to Wolman only if the hockey team was part of the collateral is preposterous. Nobody thought the Flyers were worth anything. We had to beg at bank after bank for money.

"Here's Wolman, who owned all these wonderful things (the Spectrum, Connie Mack Stadium, Yellow Cab of Philadelphia and other properties), needing this new hockey team, for which failure was predicted, to save himself? Wolman's story has grown more and more plausible in people's eyes because the Flyers have grown in value. At that time, though, they had none.

"Over the years, Wolman has managed to confuse every element of what happened and people have believed him. He has told people that his money bought the Flyers. The truth is he put no money of his own into the team. The money to finance the Spectrum and the Flyers was all borrowed from various sources.

"I showed Fred Byrod (the *Inquirer* sports editor at the time) the documents that proved Wolman's money didn't buy the team. (The story ran on November 3, 1967.)

"Wolman never gave me any money. His gift to me was his wherewithal and reputation. I went to him as my mentor and the owner of the Eagles and asked for his support in building the Spectrum and getting an NHL franchise and, to his credit, he agreed. If I had knocked on doors myself at that stage of my ca-

NHL president Clarence Campbell conducts a ceremonial face-off before the first game in the Spectrum. Taking the draw are Pittsburgh captain Ab McDonald and Flyer captain Lou Angotti.

reer, I think people would have told me to get lost. I've never denied Wolman's importance, but monetarily, I never owed him a damn thing.

"He told people he picked me up out of the gutter (when Snider's phonograph record business became overextended in the early sixties). My partner (Gerald Lillienfield) and I sold the record company because we would have needed a lot more capital to go national and I wasn't enjoying it anymore.

"Wolman told people that he bought me my house. The truth is, he once tried to pay off my mortgage. When Putnam, who was my (Morgan Guaranty Trust Co.) banker at the time, told me what had happened, I had him send the money back."

Wolman, now a builder in Washington, denies the account by Snider and Putnam that in May, 1967, he wanted to sell the franchise to investors who planned to move it to another city. "I was buying in those days, not selling," Wolman recalls.

Putnam and other principals involved in the founding of the Flyers verify Snider's account that Wolman ran out of money prior to the June deadline for payment of the NHL's $2-million expansion fee, a shortfall that necessitated the scramble by Snider to refinance. Wolman, however, scoffs at the story, insisting that his trading of Flyer shares for Snider's Spectrum shares took place after the team had begun playing. In fact, it was announced on August 26.

Wolman came to feel betrayed that, after giving Snider his Eagle, Spectrum and Flyer opportunities, his partner refused to come to the rescue. Snider, however, would have risked losing the hockey team into receivership by signing it back over to Wolman. (In 1969, Wolman relinquished the Eagles and Spectrum as part of his bankruptcy settlement.)

As Wolman drowned in red ink, Snider, Putnam and Scott paddled furiously to keep the Flyers, on

the hook for a $1.5-million loan, afloat. "I'm sure it was a struggle to pay some bills," recalls Poile, "but [the hockey operation] never felt it. It was nothing but first class all the way."

Snider, the majority owner, felt it best that Putnam, who had more hockey background, remain as president. "I thought the image he was portraying was what we needed," recalls Snider. "My role stayed mostly behind the scenes where Joe Scott and I were working to keep the club solvent. Bill knew how to spend money. There were a few times I had to tell him no."

Attendance figures at the start of the season continued to be discouraging. The Flyers drew 5,783 for their second home game, a 5-2 victory over the Oakland Seals. The Red Wings sent Gordie Howe in a day early for a promotional press conference that helped draw 10,859 for the Flyers' first matchup against an established team. (Detroit's Ted Hampson scored after only 35 seconds and the Flyers lost 3-1.) But crowds of only 4,708 (for Oakland) and 4,203 (for the Minnesota North Stars) showed up at the next two home games.

On the season's second weekend, Poile tried to inject some color and character into the Flyers' personality by signing defenseman Larry (The Rock) Zeidel. It appeared at first that expansion had come too late for Zeidel, a 39-year-old defenseman for the AHL Cleveland Barons who had last performed in the NHL fourteen seasons earlier. Undiscouraged, Zeidel had sent the six new teams a professionally prepared brochure with pictures of himself in both uniform and business suit. "In case someone wanted me as a coach or manager, I had to look dignifed," he recalls.

"I can help your organization in the front office with my experience in ticket sales and public relations, as well as on the ice," the brochure began. Poile and Allen, both of whom had coached the hard-nosed

Sutherland scored the winning goal in the home-opener.

and multi-scarred Zeidel in the Western Hockey League, decided to fulfill his dream.

Declaring himself as the kind of guy who "will take four punches to land one," Zeidel pasted a picture of the Stanley Cup in his locker. "All I have to do is see this carpeting in the locker room, and I'm motivated," he said. "We never had carpeting in the minors."

But his former teams did have fans, something the Flyers lacked as they played a tedious, defen-

Detroit match.

On nights when regular play-by-play man Stu Nahan was describing road games on Channel 48, Gene Hart would be on radio. The hockey broadcast would be delayed when there was a basketball conflict, but Scheinfeld was happy for any exposure on the station synonymous with Philadelphia sports.

"The big thing to me," Scheinfeld remembers, "was that billboard WCAU had on the Expressway with the Sixers', Eagles' and Phillies' logos. I would drive

Joe Watson, left, and Andre Lacroix bang one in against Detroit.

sive style of hockey in the more-than-half-empty Spectrum.

"There's no such thing as a major-league hockey game before a small, reserved audience," wrote columnist Frank Dolson in the *Inquirer*. The Flyers' profile was so low that the morning paper would not send a reporter to cover the road games. "They said we had to prove ourselves first," Scheinfeld explained.

The team could command no radio rights fees, so it bought time on WCAU-AM for $35,000. One week after the home opener, the Flyers announced they would broadcast the third period of 61 of the 69 remaining games, starting with the October 28

by and see us up there, too, and feel like we had it made."

Scott wrote schools, offering free tickets to deserving students. "We thought that adults already knew what they liked, but kids might try something new,'" recalls Scott. "So I brainwashed thousands of them.

"At first I had to make a lot of calls to get even one school to go along with me. But then it started to pick up. If I saw a school had won a championship in something, I'd offer them tickets figuring they'd be appreciative of the opportunity to treat the kids. It was up to the principal or headmaster to decide how many tickets we'd give them—within reason, of course—but the idea was that if the adults came along, they'd have to buy a ticket. That was the way to expose the game to the parents.

"We sat them in the upper deck, sometimes with the school band, so that they wouldn't disturb what customers we had. There was lots of room at the Spectrum for bands in those days."

There was also plenty of room on the Flyers' bandwagon when the team went to Montreal on November 4 for their first road game against an established team.

"If playing the best brings out the best in you, our best is good enough to beat Montreal," Rochefort, the ex-Montreal farmhand, told the *Bulletin's* Brogan as the team flew to the hockey Mecca. It seemed obvious Rochefort was talking through his hat until one landed at his feet following his third goal the next night. Rochefort's stunning performance and 33 saves by Parent, who was starting the first time since the opening-night disaster in Oakland, propelled the Flyers to an astonishing 4-1 victory.

The next evening, before 9,188 at the Spectrum, the Canadiens got a goal by Yvan Cournoyer with 6:09 left to pull out a 1-1 tie. Getting three out of four points in one weekend against Montreal was a significant step towards credibility. And when the Flyers also won their first game in Boston the following week, they were suddenly looking brash and ambitious. "Coming back here and beating these guys is the greatest thing that's ever happened to me," said Watson, who scored 1:12 into the game to lead the Flyers to their 4-2 victory against his former teammates.

Four days later, the Flyers beat New York 3-2 for their first home success over one of the original six teams. The crowd of 11,276 gave the upstarts a standing ovation as they left the ice. The next week, when Blackburn's goal put away a 4-2 victory over Detroit and set off another celebration, the *Bulletin's* Sandy Grady declared "at 9:16 last night, Philly was ... a hockey town."

On November 26, fans chanted "We're Number One" as the Flyers beat Los Angeles, 7-2, to take over the West Division lead. "People are starting to come

up to me on the street and talk hockey," Allen said. "A few months ago, nobody even recognized me."

Reality set in, however, when the Flyers lost their next eight games against established teams. But they opened the Fabulous Forum, the new home of the L.A. Kings, with Favell's 2-0 shutout, and continued to grind out points when playing clubs in their division.

One rival, the Blues, was fast becoming an archenemy. After Van Impe high-sticked St. Louis's Gordon Kannegiesser at the end of a 3-2 Philadelphia victory and Noel Picard retaliated by punching Zeidel in the face, Flyer fans were witness to their first-ever bench-clearing altercation. The next meeting between the two clubs in St. Louis brought another brawl and a Philadelphia win.

The Flyers followed up early-season victories in Montreal and Boston with success in their first visit to another hockey shrine. "Do you believe this?" asked Favell after stoning Toronto 2-1 at Maple Leaf Gardens. Obviously, Philadelphia was becoming convinced. At the start of February, the Flyers drew their first two home sellouts for back-to-back games against Chicago and Toronto. Scalpers, reported to be getting $10 for $3.25 seats, had no unhappy customers as the Flyers won both games.

"I honestly thought it would take two or three years to build to this," said Snider.

He did not know how fleeting satisfaction could be. The Flyers hit the road. And the wind hit the roof.

On Saturday, February 17, 1968, 11,000 ticketholders were settling into their seats for a matinee performace of the Ice Capades when they suddenly heard a sound many thought was a low-flying airplane. The next thing they knew, portions of the roof above sections 39, 40, 1 and 2 were coming down.

A few patrons screamed, but the Ice Capades band calmly improvised "Off We Go Into the Wild Blue Yonder" and helped prevent panic. Most of the debris—almost entirely tar paper from the roof covering—was whipped away by winds gusting to 48 m.p.h. The performance was cancelled and only minor injuries were reported by three people in the

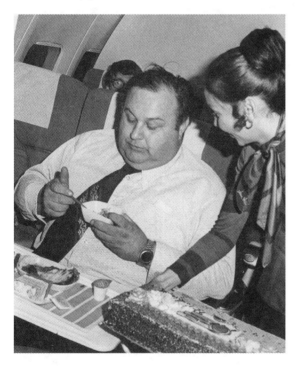

parking lot.

The damaged area was 100 feet long and 50 feet wide. There was no actual hole one could stick a hand through, but light was visible because perforations in the sheetmetal had been exposed by the missing tar paper.

Three other weekend performances of the ice show were cancelled and on Monday, the *Inquirer* called for the facility to be closed pending a complete investigation. Mayor Tate, expressing concerns that the roof might not withstand a snowstorm, said he also favored locking the doors. But after meeting with Spectrum officials and construction representatives from builder McCloskey and Co., city managing director Fred T. Corleto promised that his staff would continue to double-check the safety of the structure after it reopened.

Corleto revealed that the Spectrum had never

received a final certificate of completion from the city, but he called the damage "freakish" and declared the building safe. A fifteen-man crew repaired the roof on Monday, and on Tuesday night an NBA doubleheader was played.

Certainly the hastily repaired ceiling was under no additional stress from tornados in the Flyer offensive end. As the team struggled to score, Poile dug into Quebec for an entire line—Andre Lacroix, Jean-Guy Gendron and Rosaire Paiement—that was dominating the AHL. In his first game with Philadelphia, the 5-8, 170-pound Lacroix saved a tie in Pittsburgh with a third-period goal. Back at the Spectrum, the 22-year-old center assisted on all of Rochefort's three scores (he had both the first road and home hat tricks in team history) in a 7-3 rout of Minnesota.

But the French Line's spark quickly flickered out and the Flyers were booed off the Spectrum ice for the first time when they lost 3-1 to Los Angeles. With a 1-5-1 record in their last seven games, the Flyers suspected they were in trouble. Turns out, they didn't know the definition of the word.

Engineers who surveyed the Spectrum roof damage had theorized that open doors on windy days created a tunneling effect and made the roof prone to blistering. Workers were, in fact, repairing one of those bubbles at 9:45 A.M. on Friday, March 1, when gusts tore off three layers of roofing paper and decking. This time, the Spectrum had three different holes above Sections 2 and 3—20 by 40 feet, 2 by 4 feet and 6 by 8 feet.

At midday, with television news cameras rolling, Mayor Tate, police commissioner Frank Rizzo, Spectrum superintendent Wayne Lalor, and builder and roofing company representatives climbed a ladder to inspect the damage. The mayor came down and immediately declared the Spectrum closed indefinitely.

The Flyers, who had reported to the building that morning for a practice, ate lunch and got on their bus for a game the next afternoon in New York. With the first of seven remaining home contests scheduled to be Sunday's CBS Game of the Week, Philadelphia's match against Oakland was officially moved to Madison Square Garden by the league. After losing to the Rangers 4-0 on Saturday, the Flyers spent another night at the New York Sheraton, dressed in the same clothes, returned to the Garden and played again, this time as the home team against the Seals.

Two thousand of the 12,493 persons holding tick-

Right from the start, announcer Gene Hart could pack away the vittles.

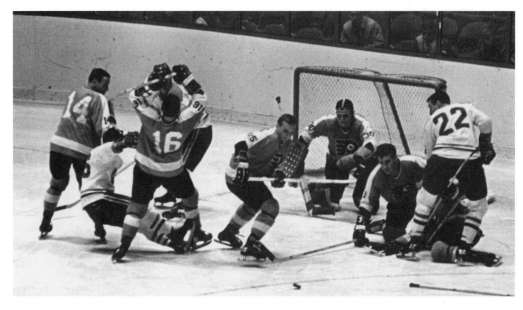

"Playing the best brings out the best in you." Flyers versus Montreal Canadiens.

ets for the game at the Spectrum exchanged them for seats in New York, but their cheers were increasingly drowned out. The Rangers had allowed anyone with a ticket from the Saturday game to attend on Sunday for free, and the majority of fans, inspired by the presence of former Rangers Larry Cahan and Larry Popein in Seals uniforms, cheered for Oakland. The Flyers got a first-period goal from Blackburn, held on for a 1-1 tie that kept their divisional lead at three points, and took the bus home.

Well, at least it used to be home. The next day, Corleto said the Spectrum would not reopen for at least a week, until repairs were made and the still-missing certificate of occupancy issued. A team of inspectors began to check for fire and electrical code violations. When finished, contractors would then have to submit a reroofing plan, subject to city approval, before repairs could begin. Obviously, this was going to take time.

"It is unbelievable that the building was in use for almost five months without the necessary permit," District Attorney Arlen Specter said. He suggested prosecutions might be in order and asked several employees of the city's department of licenses and inspections to take a lie detector test. The DA then accused Wolman and Freeman of failure to cooperate with his office.

Corleto tried to control the damage over the missing certificate. "It was just a case of the [Spectrum operators] trying to get opened for [that September] weekend," he insisted. "I am told the structure is perfectly safe."

Tate nevertheless rejected a plan for a temporary

fix and said any blueprint for permanent repairs would be subject to the binding arbitration of scientists at the Franklin Institute. The *Inquirer*, run by staunch Republican Walter Annenberg, could not pass up the opportunity to embarrass McCloskey, the Spectrum builder and a long-standing Democratic rival. The newspaper continued to vent concern over the public's safety, and the building remained closed.

The 76ers were severely inconvenienced by having to switch games back to their former home at Convention Hall. But the Flyers, with the decrepit

Rough going with the St. Louis Blues. Ed Van Impe throws the check, goalie Parent watches.

4,000-seat Cherry Hill Arena being the only other building in the area with an ice plant, were on the street. Caught between rock-headed bureaucrats and hardened politicians, "Snider's hair turned white," Scheinfeld recalls.

Their next home game, against Boston, was scheduled for Thursday, the night after a Wednesday evening visit to Toronto. Harold Ballard, the Leafs owner, called Putnam and suggested the Flyers stay over and play their Boston match at Maple

Flyers moved Sunday's game against Minnesota to Quebec City while they pondered what to do with the rest of their schedule.

The divisional lead, possibly even a playoff spot (they led fifth-place Pittsburgh by only nine points), was slipping away. And so was the self-esteem of the homeless team.

At least that was Zeidel's view as he dressed for the Boston game at Maple Leaf Gardens. "I look at the mood, I see the team is down," he recalls. "I fig-

Fans protest political delays in repairing damage to the Spectrum roof.

Leaf Gardens. "Harold said we had a lot of Ontario-born players and that Boston was Toronto's most hated rival, so he thought we could get a crowd," Putnam remembers. "He offered us the building for 50 percent of the gate. What a guy. Then he kept our program money and sent us a bill for the ambulance service."

The Flyers trooped off to Toronto with big suitcases and stiff upper lips. They had no idea where the next stop would be. "We can't think of this as a catastrophe," said Blackburn, "because if we do, it *will* be a catastrophe. Maybe this will be the best thing that ever happened to us. We've been having all kinds of trouble at home; maybe the change will do us some good."

Toronto ripped the Flyers 7-2 on Wednesday night. Even that didn't seem bleak when compared to the latest news from Philadelphia. After conferring with scientists at the Franklin Institute, the city ordered an entirely new roof for the Spectrum, which would take two to five weeks to install. The

ure, I'm going to turn it up to high.

"I didn't need an excuse. I'd had a thing going with (the Bruins') Eddie Shack for a long time. The last time we were in Boston (January 20), the two of us had [an incident] where we bumped during the warm-ups. I figured it was time to balance the books. So I go into the game like a kamikaze."

Shack and Zeidel collided and traded insults in the opening minute. At 9:33 of the first period, they again came together along the boards and Zeidel snapped. He swung his stick and opened a three-stitch cut on Shack's head.

Enraged, the Bruin began flailing away, in the words of the *Inquirer's* Chevalier, "like a butcher attacking raw beef." Shack swung seven times at Zeidel, who held his stick horizontally in front of his face to protect himself and escaped with only a three-stitch cut on his scalp.

Wire-service pictures of the two hockey players taking swings at each other, with close-ups of blood running down their faces, chilled two nations. Even longtime hockey people were aghast. "It was one of the worst stick fights I've ever seen," said NHL officials supervisor Frank Udvari.

After the game, Zeidel said the incident had been prompted in part by anti-Semitic remarks made by the Bruins. "I don't mind being called a dirty Jew," he said. "I can take that. But they went further. My grandparents and a lot of relatives were wiped out by that Nazi stuff during the war."

With Zeidel banished from the remainder of the game and Gauthier in bed with the flu, the Flyers were down to a three-man defense of Van Impe, Watson and Miszuk. They tried to rally in the third period, but a goal from the sideboards by Hannigan still left them one score short in a 2-1 defeat. The team was now 1-8-2 in its last eleven starts.

Still, their stronger third period seemed to galvanize them. "I think we're beginning to get our spirit back," said Van Impe. "The bench really came alive after we scored. They may have put us out of the Spectrum, but that's not going to bother us. We're still going to win this thing and we're going to win it for the fans of Philadelphia."

"I was probably saying what I wanted to say, not what I really believed," Van Impe says today. "It just seemed endless to us. We wondered if the team would get into financial trouble."

The Flyers' insurance would cover some of their losses, but revenue from more than 11,000 tickets already sold for each remaining home game might have to be refunded. Bill Baer, the vice president at Girard Bank, called Snider.

"How are you going to handle this?" Baer asked.
"I don't know," Snider replied.
"Suppose we handle it. How much do you need?"
"A million?" said Snider.
"It will be in your account tomorrow morning," said Baer.
"They were good bankers," recalls Snider. "They

NHL president Clarence Campbell presents the Campbell Bowl to Ed Van Impe, GM Bud Poile and coach Keith Allen after the Flyers won the NHL's West Division in their first season.

saw our situation had been getting healthier and they wanted to protect their investment. Still, I'm forever grateful. Without people like that, I never would have made it."

The politicians, failing to move the Spectrum ten yards, continued to punt it back and forth while the NHL pressured the Flyers for playoff dates that could not be provided. "This is a travesty," Snider told the newspapers. "I agree the safety factor is tremendously important, but everyone should be working twenty-four hours a day to get this solved. This is supposed to be a major-league city, you know."

Putnam, using what little leverage he had, suggested publicly that the team might be forced to permanently leave Philadelphia. He entertained Flyer adoption offers from arena managers in Winnipeg, Ottawa, Vancouver and Chicago, but settled on Quebec City, the site of their training camp and minor-league team.

The Quebecers were thrilled. More than 1,000 fans watched the Flyers practice after they arrived from Toronto. Despite a heavy snowstorm, a standing-room-only crowd of 10,971 watched the Flyers beat Minnesota 2-0 on third-period goals by Watson and Kennedy.

The losing streak was over, but the stick fight controversy raged on. Clarence Campbell suspended Zeidel for four games and Shack for three. Poile raged about the unfairness of the verdict, arguing that if Zeidel had swung first, Shack had swung harder and more often. Two Toronto fans informed the NHL president by telegram that they had heard the Bruins utter anti-Semitic remarks.

Zeidel, however, wanted to put it all behind him. "I made my reputation as The Rock," Zeidel, a Philadelphia stockbroker, says today, "and the image of me as the poor little Jewish kid they beat up on rubbed me the wrong way."

Snider announced the Flyers were dropping the issue and gradually the stain on the game dissolved. So did the stains on their clothes when they stopped

the city of dragging its feet on repairs. When the city rejected reroofing plans submitted by Spectrum officials because the covering wasn't thick enough, approximately three hundred members of the Flyers fan club marched on City Hall.

"It's depressing," Allen told the *Inquirer's* Sandy Padwe. "Some of the players are already sending their wives and kids back to Canada. I keep telling them 'Soon, soon,' but I don't know when this is going to end. How many times can I tell my players that a first-place team wins on the road?"

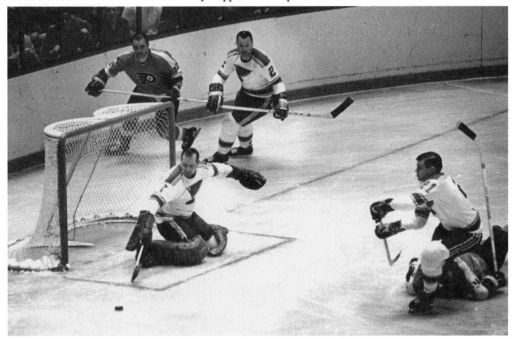

Glenn Hall kicks aside a shot as Doug Harvey (2) guards Forbes Kennedy in Game 7 of the Flyers' 1968 playoff series vs. St. Louis.

overnight to do laundry in Philadelphia. The next day in Minnesota, the Flyers cleaned up on the North Stars, 4-2, before traveling all night to Quebec, where Parent backstopped his exhausted teammates to a scoreless tie.

Despite having played seven straight games—and fourteen of the last seventeen—on the road, the Flyers still held first place and were fast gaining martyrdom back home. "Only Philadelphia would reward two winners (the Sixers were defending NBA champions) by throwing them out of the house," Grady wrote in the *Bulletin*. "Philadelphia's $12-million toy is busted and there are no grownups to fix it. Instead, there are 50-year-old children throwing temper tantrums, blaming each other for breaking it and claiming that it was a lousy toy anyway."

While scientists pondered which roof fasteners would work best, Specter, who had been defeated by Tate in the last mayoral election, was accusing

The Flyers kept listening, though. They broke a tie against the Leafs in Quebec City on a tip-in goal by Lacroix, and Parent survived a two-man disadvantage in the final minute before his teammates twice hit the empty net to wrap up a 7-4 victory. "It was our biggest win ever," said Allen. The team celebrated its success and the latest news: Corleto had approved a resubmitted roof proposal and work had begun.

The resurgent Flyers smoked the Seals 5-1 in Oakland, to clinch a playoff spot with five games remaining. "Our bench was so hopped, I had to yell for them to sit down," said Allen. "I couldn't see half the game."

But they were beginning to see the way home. The city announced that the Spectrum would reopen the following week provided the fasteners could withstand tests at a laboratory in Northbrook, Illinois. Arnold Stark, a Wolman crony, personally transported the screws. "I felt like a Jewish Paul Revere," Stark said. The fasteners proved themselves against 100 m.p.h. forces. "The guys there say the walls will come down before the roof comes off," reported Stark.

Somehow, that didn't immediately set city officials' minds at ease.

But on March 28, twenty-seven days after the ordeal began, Corleto emerged from a six-hour meeting to announce that the fasteners could be applied on the already laid roof following the building's re-opening. A temporary occupancy permit was issued.

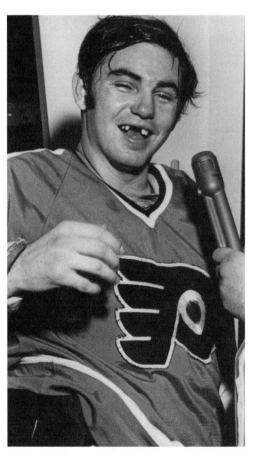

Game 4 goalie Doug Favell. With a 5-2 victory, the Blues pulled away to a 3-1 series lead.

Although they Flyers were committed to playing their final "home" game in Quebec City, the Spectrum began selling playoff tickets only eighty-five minutes after the all-clear was sounded. Fans expressed their joy by getting in line and their faith by not wearing helmets.

The Flyers, who had awakened late after another all-night flight back to Quebec City, responded to the good news by shutting out the Blues, 2-0. Favell was as outstanding as the prospect of finally going home. "I've been feeling seedy for a month," Angotti said. "Every day we wake up and we're on the go. Anything that could ever happen would rank second to this."

The Flyers needed only one point in their final weekend set with the Penguins to clinch the first-ever West Division championship. But they didn't get it on their initial try. Pittsburgh goalie Binkley stopped Rochefort's excellent chance at the tying goal in the final minute, the Penguins hit the empty net, and the Flyers lost 2-0 in their Quebec farewell. As they flew to Pittsburgh after the game, they knew that if the last-place Seals did not get at least a tie against the second-place Kings that night, Philadelphia would still be required to win or tie the season finale.

Poile herded the Flyers into a meeting at Pittsburgh's Carlton House Hotel. "He just about put a gun to our heads and told us to win," said one player. "Then he sent us to bed."

Snider waited for the Seals-Kings updates in the hotel lounge. Poile went to his room with a nosebleed. Allen, too, was in his quarters when he heard Watson's horse laugh from the floor below. "I know only one guy who sounds like that," the coach had said, suspecting something good must have happened in Oakland.

Indeed, Wally Boyer had scored in the third period to pull the Seals into a 2-2 tie. The Flyers were fifteen minutes away from a championship. Snider telephoned the Oakland press box and had someone countdown the scoreless final 40 seconds that gave the Flyers the division title.

With only a .500 record, they were the beneficiaries of a collapse by second-place Los Angeles in the final week. But for all the Flyers had been through, they deserved a celebration. And they were going to have one.

Allen rushed to tell Poile what had happened, Snider hugged Putnam, and the players poured into the tenth floor hallway. Hannigan and Kennedy, just returning after a curfew-breaking fast-food run, got the news as they exited the elevator. Kennedy threw his bag of hamburgers against the wall.

Favell wandered out of his room. "Do we have to win right now?" he asked. "I just took three sleeping pills, and 'The Slime People' is the late movie." Joe Kadlec, the team's road secretary, knew an after-hours place in the East Liberty section of the city, so off into the night the Flyers went.

At the bar, Snider toasted "the greatest team in the world." Then he spilled wine on Selby, who took over the pouring. The party ended sometime before the Flyers lost their season finale 5-1 that night, and long after they ceased to care about finishing with a winning record.

A group of fans waiting at the Philadelphia airport held up a sign—Welcome Home Champs—when the Flyers arrived home at 12:05 A.M. But the celebration was short lived. The Flyers still would have to win two best-of-seven playoff series to prove themselves as the undisputed best of a West Division in which only six points separated the first and fifth-place clubs.

Philadelphia's first-round opponent, third-place St. Louis, had beaten the Flyers only once in ten meetings. But since November, when Scotty Bowman had replaced Lynn Patrick as coach, the Blues had looked like the strongest of the expansion teams. Poile was not worried, however. "I wouldn't be surprised if we won in four straight," he said.

When the Blues triumphed in Game 1, 1-0, on a third-period goal by Jimmy Roberts, Poile explained he had meant that even if the Flyers lost the opener, they could still win four straight. The slightly-disappointing Spectrum crowd of 10,649 and St. Louis's 33-14 shot advantage threw a cold bucket of water on the team's homecoming, and not just in the figurative sense. A reporter relayed the news to Putnam that there was still a leak above row 15 in section 8. Having heard enough about the roof, Putnam blew his. "I don't give a damn," the team president exploded. "People sit out in the snow to watch the Eagles."

The Flyers refused to be dismayed. "We'll get 'em, I know we'll get 'em," Kennedy said. They did, too, in Game 2, breaking a 3-3 tie on Rochefort's early third-period goal and hanging on to win, 4-3.

Although Game 3 in St. Louis was postponed two days because of the assassination of Dr. Martin Luther King Jr., the Blues' concentration hardly seemed broken. Again they dominated play, but the Flyers shook off the loss of Dornhoefer (with a broken leg) to twice erase one-goal deficits. Watson's goal, which deflected off the Blues' Gary Sabourin, tied the score 2-2 with 6:06 remaining in the game.

St. Louis outshot the Flyers 13-4 in the first overtime, but the Flyers had the best chance and lost it when Rochefort was clearly hooked after breaking away. Referee Skov ignored the infraction, par for the course during sudden-death in those days, and the Flyers paid. At 4:10 of the second overtime, all three forwards were caught behind the net, leaving Larry Keenan unguarded at the post. Parent had no chance as Keenan scored on the Blues' 57th shot of the game, giving them a 3-2 victory and a 2-1

series edge.

The Flyers, with Favell in goal, jumped ahead early in Game 4 on a goal by Lacroix. But the Blues twice scored shorthanded and pulled away to a 5-2 victory and a 3-1 series lead. "They're flexing their muscles at us," said Allen. "What we have to do is show them some muscle back."

Although Watson had engaged Blues tough guy Bob Plager, the best Philadelphia punches of the night were thrown after the game by Parent, who twice connected on Flyer trainer Dick Bielous as the goalie was being restrained from going after a taunting fan.

The next day, the Flyers returned to the Spectrum and what they thought would be a tirade from their general manager. Instead, Poile calmly asked each player to speak his mind about what was going wrong. "I could have passed," Zeidel recalls, "but I said, 'It looks like we're being intimidated, but I don't think we are. I think we're worried about penalties.'

"So Forbsie (Kennedy) jumps up and says, 'Bleep the penalties. We'll kill them.'"

And that was exactly what the Flyers did in Game 5. Rosie Paiement, just recalled from Quebec City, scored a hat trick and the Flyers went to the net all night. In the third period, Flyer Claude Laforge took a punch in the jaw from Picard, and Kennedy retaliated on Plager. Picard then suckered Van Impe and the Flyers poured off the bench en route to a 6-1 victory.

Bowman told reporters after the game that Laforge had been sticking the Blues the whole series and had only gotten what was coming to him. Poile, listening to the Blues' coach from the the fringe of the press conference, yelled, "Tell the truth!" and called Bowman a quitter.

The Flyer GM then hired two off-duty Philadelphia policemen to act as his bodyguards for Game 6 in St. Louis. He also threatened to resign after Clarence Campbell, who had been at Game 5, fined the Flyers more heavily than he did the Blues. Campbell ignored Poile and his resignation, of course, went untendered.

But with Laforge, his mouth a mess, joining Dornhoefer on the injured list, the depleted Flyers came out for Game 6 with less fire than their GM was breathing. They fell behind 1-0 on a late first-period goal by Jerry Melnyk and managed only three shots in the second period. Parent held them in the game as Allen benched Lacroix and went more to Angotti, who gave the Flyers some spark. But as time ran down, they still had not pushed a puck past Hall.

With a little more than a minute to play, Allen

pulled Parent and put Lacroix on as a sixth attacker. Dickie Moore's 90-foot attempt at the empty net went barely wide and the Flyers were still alive. While the fans counted down the seconds, Hoekstra avoided two forecheckers and got the puck ahead to Rochefort, who shot from the top of the circle. Hall made the save, but Sutherland got to the rebound first and fed Van Impe at the point.

The defenseman lobbed the puck towards Hoesktra, who deflected it towards Lacroix. Hall, who had played Van Impe's pass like a shot, was fooled and helpless on the ice as the puck settled on Lacroix's stick. The goal was wide open and so was every mouth in the St. Louis Arena when the little center flipped in the tying goal fifteen seconds before the Flyers' season would have expired.

Parent stoned Red Berenson off a two-on-one in sudden death and the the two teams went to an additional overtime for the second time in the series. At 11:18, Blackburn's innocent backhand lob from the blueline tipped off the glove of defenseman Ray Fortin past a startled Hall.

Blackburn's disbelief was interrupted by Zeidel, who jumped on the winning goal-scorer's back, then draped himself over Parent. "Money can't buy a thrill like this," said Zeidel in the afterglow of the Flyers' incredible 2-1 victory. Thanks to their goalie's 63 saves, they were going home for Game 7.

"I figured that we had 'em," Zeidel recalls. "We all did. But Scotty had a secret weapon."

The St. Louis coach recalled Doug Harvey, the future Hall of Fame defenseman who had spent the season in Kansas City as a 43-year-old player coach for the Blues' top farm club. When the fired-up Flyers, inspired by a sold-out Spectrum, charged into the St. Louis end in the first period, Harvey slowed the pace of the game and took control.

The Blues' Frank St. Marseille beat Parent from twenty-five feet out to give St. Louis a 1-0 lead. The Flyers then tied the contest when Sutherland tipped in a Kennedy drive on a power play. But midway through the second period, a shot by Keenan went off the post and slid lengthwise across the crease behind Parent. Zeidel, trying to clear the puck, accidentally tipped it over the line. Referee Vern Buffey overruled the goal judge, who had not turned on the light.

Harvey blocked shots and moved the puck out of trouble until Red Berenson, from a face-off just outside the Flyers' blueline, hit the empty net from 115 feet to assure the Blues' 3-1 victory. "It was the hardest-fought series ever played," Bowman would tell reporters. "It was the hardest-fought series that ever will be played."

"I guess we just ran out of miracles," Blackburn said.

The Flyers received a standing ovation as they left the ice. They had lost the series but had gained a presence that would help sustain them through some tough years ahead. "No question," recalls Brogan, "the roof thing turned out to be a plus. People felt sorry for the team and fell in love with it."

The original Flyers won less than half of their games, but captured whole hearts. They were sustained by Allen's unflappable demeanor, the patience of Putnam, and the energy and deep convictions of Snider, who never thought an NHL team in Philadelphia could fail.

"I just had the belief that if you're a regular guy and know what regular guys like, you can't be wrong," Snider recalls.

The 1967-68 Flyers were largely a collection of aging pros and career fringe players, thrilled with the opportunity to play in the NHL. "I always thought I was too old," recalls Sutherland. "I never thought I would get this chance. That's the way most of us were. We had no stars, nothing really."

Only regular guys.

Chapter 3

♦♦♦

The First Coming

As they headed into Year Two, the Flyers desperately needed to transfuse young blood into an offense that had averaged only 2.3 goals per game in 1967-68. Unfortunately, the league was still a year away from conducting an amateur draft in which all the best 20-year-olds would be available to teams in the reverse order of the previous season's final standings.

Established clubs had retained their rights to junior players sponsored prior to expansion. Philadelphia's top selections in 1967 (center Serge Bernier) and 1968 (Lew Morrison) came from lists of the few unattached athletes. Because the established teams continued to have a monopoly on the stars and best prospects, the relative success of the veteran-laden Blues, who had lost four close games to Montreal in the 1968 Stanley Cup finals, exerted pressure on the other new franchises to trade future draft choices for instant respectability.

Even the Flyers, who had consciously opted for young players in the expansion draft, took the bait. In the summer of 1968, GM Bud Poile revealed that the "future considerations" in the deal that brought right wing Rosaire Paiement to the Flyers from Boston the previous October, was Philadelphia's first-round pick in the 1970 draft.

Paiement, who spent most of the Flyers' first year in Quebec, was moved up to the big club for the 1968-69 season, along with left wing Jean-Guy Gendron and right wing Simon Nolet, two players acquired with the purchase of the AHL franchise, and center Jimmy Johnson, an expansion draft pick.

The Flyers reasoned that 42-year-old defenseman Allan Stanley, obtained from Toronto in the intraleague draft, had more left than 40-year-old Larry Zeidel. So The Rock, largely the spirit of the Flyers' first team, was let go, as was winger Bill Sutherland, in the intraleague draft.

Defenseman Dick Cherry, who had spent a year teaching school after being selected by the Flyers in the expansion draft, reported for camp. But captain Lou Angotti, never happy to be a Flyer, was

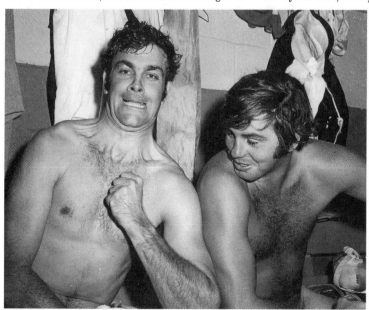

traded to Pittsburgh in a three-way deal that moved Ab McDonald from the Penguins to St. Louis and brought Blues center left wing Jerry Melnyk to Philadelphia.

After the 34-year-old Melnyk suffered chest pains during a skating drill, doctors determined that he had had a mild heart attack and advised him to retire. Poile told Melnyk he could earn his $16,500 salary working as a scout out of his home in Edmonton. "He said he'd pay me that over two years instead of one," Melnyk recalls. "I almost had another heart attack, but what could I do?"

Melnyk went to western Canada to look for future Flyers. The present ones would need some help. With a changed cast and a diminished esprit de corps, the team struggled from the start of the season. On November 3, Johnson's 75-foot goal beat Montreal, 3-2, before 12,431 at the Spectrum and fleetingly recaptured the excitement of Year One. But five days later, the reality of how far St. Louis had moved beyond its expansion brethren was hammered into 9,164 Spectrum patrons when Red Berenson scored an NHL record tying six goals in an 8-0 pasting of the Flyers.

Berenson had the first five scores of the game, with four in the second period coming on only four shots (of his total of ten). After tying the league mark with 5:56 remaining in the contest, Berenson earned both an ovation from the fans and a vicious chop on the legs from Ed Van Impe, who had been on the ice with Joe Watson for all six goals.

"Just say he was great and I was lousy," said Doug Favell. The goalie bounced back for a shutout victory in Pittsburgh, but the punchless Flyers soon lapsed into an 11-game winless streak.

Dick Sarrazin was called up from Quebec to replace the disappointing Nolet. Team president Bill Putnam complained about complacency. "All over the division, kids who fought so hard to prove themselves last year no longer are giving that extra effort," Putnam said.

As the losses mounted, Poile boiled. Seated in the Spectrum press box during a December 8 game with St. Louis, he overheard the analysis of Blues' broadcaster Gus Kyle and didn't wait for a commercial to voice displeasure. "Why don't you tell the truth?" Poile yelled to the nation on 50,000-watt KMOX radio. "You better get your eyes fixed!"

After the Blues complained to the league, Poile accused them of going for "cheap publicity."

Following his stand for broadcast integrity, the cantankerous Flyer general manager blamed nagging women for his team's lack of achievement. "Players shouldn't be babysitting or taking their wives or girlfriends on shopping trips during the season," he said. "These girls like the nice clothes that hockey buys and they like to go to Florida after the season. They have to sacrifice if they want that. They should let the players concentrate on hockey during the winter."

The GM may have fired up women's rights activists, but not his team. On January 30, the Flyers were beaten 12-0 by Chicago at the Spectrum. After six of the goals, coach Keith Allen decided the slumping Favell had suffered enough and called down to the end of the bench for Parent. "He had his head down, pretending he didn't hear me," Allen remembers. "I called a second time and he still ignored me. Finally I had to go down and grab him and tell him to get in the goddamn goal NOW!"

Favell was just as reluctant to heed a postgame summons to Poile's office, where the goalie was told he and Quebec netminder Dunc Wilson were changing places. "Dougie knows he's lost it," said Poile. "He'll be back." But after giving up 19 goals in 13 AHL periods, Favell was hardly reenergized when he returned two weeks later.

Not only were the Flyers having trouble getting up for games, they were having difficulty getting *to* them. After a 6-5 loss in Boston on February 8, a snowstorm forced the team to take the train to New York City for their match the following night. When a frozen switch required an unscheduled stop in Pelham, New York, Allen borrowed Gary Dornhoefer's boots and deboarded to call the Rangers and inform them of the travel difficulties. When the train began to move before Allen returned, the players assumed their coach had been left behind in the raging blizzard. A few minutes later, however, Allen reappeared with snow on his head, frost on his cheeks and exasperation on his face. "Another half-hour out there and I'd have been dead," he said. "I was just lucky I saw the train start moving. The conductor kept the door open, so I climbed aboard as it was pulling out."

For a pregame meal, some players found a passenger willing to share a birthday cake. The train, which took more than eight and a half hours to go from Boston's South Station to New York's Penn Station, arrived at seven o'clock, an hour before the scheduled start of game, which finally began at 9:15 P.M. To end their perfect day, the Flyers blew a 3-0 lead in the final ten minutes and were tied with 42 seconds remaining when the Rangers' Bob Nevin scored through a maze. "I never saw it," said Parent, near tears.

Fortunately, the Penguins and North Stars were also struggling, so Philadelphia never fell more than one point out of a playoff spot. With the 76ers in decline and the Eagles and Phillies showing no signs of improvement, the Flyers always received their fair share of media coverage. Attendance continued to grow, up 1,500 per game from the 9,625 average in Year One. "[The fans] are still very much behind

us despite everything," Ed Snider said. "We've proven Philadelphia doesn't only support a winner."

The Blues, however, were playing before enthusiastic, standing room only audiences, so Snider asked Larry Ferrari, the Spectrum organist, to go to St. Louis to hear Norm Kramer, master of the Blues' keyboard, work the crowd. Ferrari, a disc jockey at WFIL, said he couldn't travel because of work commitments and was fired.

Nerves were rubbed raw on the ice, too. The Flyers were hanging onto a 3-2 lead with 2:45 to go in a February 16 game at the Spectrum against Oakland when Forbes Kennedy took high-sticking and spearing penalties. Before play resumed, Kennedy left the penalty box and skated to the Seals' bench, where he threw punches and a glove at coach Fred Glover to earn both a misconduct and game misconduct. "Those two penalties were very stupid," said Allen after the Flyers held on to win.

Kennedy was used sparingly in a loss at St. Louis three nights later. As the team flew to Montreal after the game, he made nasty remarks while playing cards with other players. "Sarcastic things that were

intended for my ears, I'm sure," Allen recalls. "But he hadn't made it a confrontation yet, so I didn't do anything."

While waiting for the team bus at nearly 5 A.M., Kennedy asked his coach if ice would be available that day. Allen told him no, but Kennedy insisted he wanted to skate. "You can't," Allen said, but Kennedy kept badgering until Allen told him to shut up.

"Don't tell me to shut up," said Kennedy. "I'm not a kid. There's a lot of other guys on this team who do a lot of yapping. Nobody tells them to shut up."

"They don't yap as loud or as much as you," Allen said.

"Then get rid of me."

"Is that a threat?"

"You're the coach, get rid of me."

When the Flyers arrived at the hotel, Allen announced that Kennedy was suspended. "There have been other incidents involving not only Kennedy, but most of our other players as well," said Poile. "But this is something I just can't overlook."

Kennedy refused a demotion to Quebec and went home to Charlottetown, Prince Edward Island, to await a trade.

Although Allen was supported by team members in anonymous quotes, there was no improved response on the ice. A 9-1 loss in Detroit on February 23 dropped the Flyers' record to 13-33-15. "None of the Philadelphia players wants [the puck]," said NHL president Clarence Campbell, who watched the game from the press box.

Putnam, pressured by Snider, ordered Poile to do something. Desperate for a scorer, the GM tried acquiring Toronto's Mike Walton, who was feuding with Toronto boss Punch Imlach. After Walton scored a late third-period goal that gave his team a 1-1 Spectrum tie with the Flyers, Poile completed a lesser deal with the Leafs, reacquiring Bill Sutherland in addition to center Gerry Meehan and right wing Mike Byers for Kennedy and the stone-handed Brit Selby. "We made some mistakes," said Poile about the off-season planning, "and losing Sutherland was the biggest."

The trade seemed to awaken the Flyers. On March 2, Dornhoefer's first score in almost four months climaxed a three-goal rally and pulled Philadelphia into a 4-4 tie at Oakland. One week later at the Spectrum, a three-goal third period brought another victory over the Seals. The *Inquirer's* Jack Chevalier wrote that

Coach Keith Allen looks on as the losses mount.

the win, before 13,885, produced "the kind of unrestrained roars you hear in the established cities."

The remodeled French Line—Andre Lacroix, Gendron and Sarrazin—keyed a 7-1-2 run and the Flyers wrapped up a playoff spot on March 23 with a 4-3 triumph over the Blues at a sold-out Spectrum. It was Philadelphia's only success in eight tries against the West Division champions, who finished 27 points ahead of the third-place Flyers (20-35-21).

Poile thought his team would avenge the previous year's seven-game playoff loss to St. Louis. "The Flyers are equal in talent," he said. "We have momentum and we're due to beat the Blues."

His confidence lasted fifty seconds into Game 1, when McDonald gave St. Louis a 1-0 lead. Johnson limped off with a back strain after being body-checked by Al Arbour, and Bob Plager discouraged Lacroix by smashing the little center into the boards. The Blues won easily, 5-2.

In Game 2, Van Impe, who had sat out the opener with a broken finger, knocked down McDonald, but was cross-checked from behind by Noel Picard. Reluctant to fight because of his hand injury, the Flyer defenseman backed up, waving his stick, before he was tripped by goalie Jacques Plante, robbed of his weapon, and left flat on his back amidst hostile Blues. The Flyers came off the bench, but it was mostly to hold on. "[Picard] thinks he can run us out of the playoffs," said Van Impe after the Blues' 5-0 victory.

Picard thought correctly. The games in Philadel-

phia were more tame, but just as one-sided. Plante's 3-0 shutout before a sellout crowd gave St. Louis a stranglehold on the series. The next day, Easter Sunday, only 10,995 fans were in attendance as the Blues completed the Flyers' humiliation, 4-1. A meaningless late goal by Johnson was waved off, giving fans an excuse to pelt the ice with garbage—an ugly end to a season of regression.

"I made up my mind after that series that we had to get big, tough players," Snider recalls. He did not

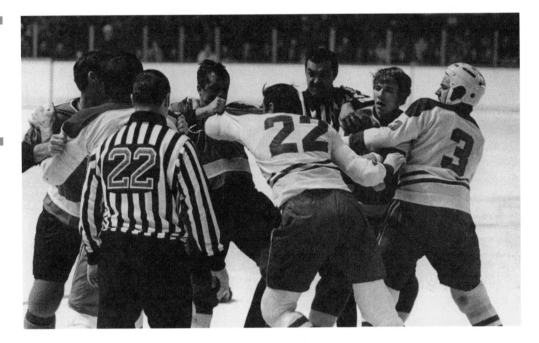

Nolet mixes it up with and John Ferguson (22) of the Canadiens.

publicly announce the new approach, but the Flyers soon traded Don Blackburn and Leon Rochefort to the Rangers for the more aggressive Reggie Fleming. "I'm no Lady Byng man," the 33-year-old Fleming said when introduced to the Philadelphia media. "I'd really like to get that Barclay (Plager) in a room alone." The Flyers also traded the slow and docile John Miszuk to Minnesota for a more muscular defenseman, Wayne Hillman.

While Snider wanted intimidators on the ice, he was more uncomfortable than ever having one as a general manager. "Bud would call guys into his office, threaten them, scare them half to death and send them back to Quebec on the slightest whim," Snider says. "I didn't like the way he operated.

"I had been involved in football, which I found way ahead of hockey thinking at that time. Whenever I would ask a question of Putnam and Poile, they'd say, 'Look, this isn't football, it's hockey.' I accepted it for awhile, but other things bothered me, too.

"I didn't like that we'd shipped out a lot of people that were an integral part of a (regular-season) championship team to make room for some kids from Quebec. I always thought the younger guys should push the older ones out of a job, not have one made for them. I also didn't like the trade of a No. 1 pick (for Paiement) at a time when we figured to be picking high.

"A group of players came to me with their un-

happiness about the way things were being run. I did let Bill and Bud know that I expected things to change. Mostly, I talked to Bill, who disagreed with me. He was a very strong backer of Bud Poile and that made it difficult to get my point across.

"In the meantime, Joe (Scott) was getting mad because Putnam and Poile were treating him like bleep. Here's a guy who came to our rescue and they were acting like he was a bother."

Scott, indeed, was burning. "Putnam wanted to run the whole show," Scott recalls. "He had this grandiose style about him; he didn't want to be interfered with. When Eddie started asking questions, Putnam resented it.

"Now Putnam tries to say that Eddie wasn't involved much the first few years, but that's bullbleep. Putnam must have been blind if he didn't see Eddie. One time we had a ticket foul-up and Eddie and I worked all night with the [office] to get it straightened out. I didn't see Putnam in there sorting tickets. He was going to league meetings and entertain-

ing and couldn't be bothered with us little elves."

Snider, however, was able to maintain a good working relationship with Putnam. "He gave us what I wanted—a first-class image for the team," recalls Snider. "He was cool and collected, he worked hard and did a lot of good things.

"We debated about Poile, but never argued. I was, however, becoming more and more impressed with Keith, the way he thought, his ability to take a cool, detached evaluation of things. I thought if we made him assistant general manager, Keith would have more input, and that it might resolve my differences with Bud."

Since Allen had been recruited to Philadelphia with the promise of a front-office position, and Quebec coach Vic Stasiuk had led the Aces to the AHL finals, the timing was perfect for both men to be promoted. On May 19, the Flyers made Stasiuk the new man behind the bench and named Allen assistant general manager.

"Let's put the cards on the table," said Poile at the press conference. "I'm still running the Philadelphia Flyers."

The media, however, failing to read the clue that Allen's contract had been extended by a year and Poile's had not, criticized the team for making Allen the scapegoat for its miserable playoff showing.

The Flyers continued to make better decisions than the newspapers covering them. Three weeks later, at the NHL meetings, two tremendous twists of fate drew only casual mention.

Poile, who had claimed Wayne Hillman's brother, Larry, from Montreal in the intraleague draft, exposed the injury-ridden Dornhoefer, who had scored just 8 goals in 60 games. "I put [Dornhoefer and defenseman Larry Hale] out there like sitting ducks," Poile told the media. "After we lose one, we'll protect (Dick) Cherry and that will end our worrying."

Dornhoefer went unclaimed.

The next day, so did a 19-year-old, 137-point scorer through round one of the league's first universal amateur draft.

Snider had been sitting near scout Jerry Melnyk at the far end of the table when the Flyers used the

Dick Sarrazin, Reggie Fleming and Andre Lacroix lace 'em up.

sixth selection overall to take center Bob Currier from the Cornwall (Ontario) Royals. "I saw Jerry grimace," Snider said. "I asked him, 'What's wrong?' He said there was a kid who could step right onto our team that we didn't take. I asked, 'Who?' He said, 'Bobby Clarke from Flin Flon.'

"So I asked Keith why we took this Currier, and he said Bud and (chief scout) Alex Davidson liked him. I asked if he'd heard anything about this kid

Reggie Fleming celebrates a goal against the L.A. Kings.

Clarke, and Keith said he'd heard Clarke was a good player, but he was a diabetic.

"When I went back to Jerry, he said, 'The kid is fine. I guarantee he's a good player.' So I pushed Keith to go around and ask about him. When he still wasn't taken as the second round started, Keith asked Bud about taking Clarke next, but Bud said they had already picked a center in Currier. I was still gun-shy about ordering anybody to do anything, but I told Keith, 'You have to persuade him.' And Keith did."

"I didn't see any games in the East," recalls Melnyk, who had scouted for only one season, "so I didn't know this Currier. But our second pick comes up and still nobody's taken Clarke and holy bleep, I can't believe it. I'm saying, 'We have to take him,'

and they're all saying, 'No, he has diabetes.' I'm saying, 'I don't care what he has. I played pro for fourteen years and this kid is already a better player than I ever was.'

"Poile wasn't going to listen to me. It was Keith who said, 'Wait a minute, maybe we'd better listen to Jerry.' And I remember Ed Snider agreed."

The Flyers took Clarke in the second round, with the seventeenth pick overall. Within the hour, Detroit GM Jimmy Skinner, who had selected goalie Jim Rutherford in the first round and had hoped to get another crack at Clarke with the twenty-second pick, offered Poile two players for the center. The Flyers declined.

The Red Wings were one of ten teams, including the Flyers, who had passed on Clarke at least once. Boston took three other players (Dan Tannahill, Frank Spring and Ivan Boldirev) instead of Clarke. Both Minnesota (picking Dick Redmond and Dennis O'Brien) and the Rangers (choosing Andre Dupont and Pierre Jarry) ignored Clarke twice.

"The only reason everybody passed on him was that they were scared about the diabetes," recalls Allen. "I know Alex was high on Currier. We had decided that we had to make size a priority and though Currier was no bruiser, he was bigger than Clarke. I know Jerry was very insistent, and I remember him talking to Eddie, but I honestly don't recall talking Bud into it."

Melnyk, Snider and Allen have no memory of who the Flyers' No. 2 pick would have been had they not drafted Clarke, but the owner has a vivid recollection of how sour that day left him towards Poile. "I had a lot to do with the Eagles' drafts," says Snider, "not as an eye for talent, but in how we processed and evaluated our information. I wanted to put the Flyers into computerized scouting and to be head and shoulders above everybody else.

"So I see Bud draft this guy Currier, who obviously (from Melnyk's reaction) wasn't a consensus pick. Bud just made the decision based on whoever he had talked to."

Poile, now retired and living in Vancouver, denies this. "Whoever we picked was the consensus of the scouts," he recalls. "If they say they talked me into [taking Clarke], I won't argue. It was a long time ago and it's hard to remember. The scouts always get the credit for the good picks and the general manager [gets credit] for the bad ones. It was an organizational decision that we wanted a big strong center man, so we took Currier.

"I do remember a friend from another club, and I won't mention his name, tipping me off that they weren't going to take Clarke because of the diabetes. He didn't agree with their decision and thought maybe it would be a smart thing for us to draft him."

"Look, the bottom line is we did draft Bobby Clarke. A lot of teams passed."

In Putnam's version, Clarke's selection was a calculated gamble. "Clarke had been tested at the Mayo Clinic and we had discussed him beforehand with our team doctor (Stanley Spoont)," Putnam remembers. "Because of the way hockey people thought at the time, we believed we could get him in the second round."

After taking Clarke, the Flyers again made size a priority, drafting defenseman Willy Brossart and goalie Michel Belhumeur. Philadelphia then used its fifth and sixth choices on Sorel, Quebec, left wing Dave Schultz and Regina, Saskatchewan, right wing Don Saleski, two players who had little to recommend them besides their aggressiveness.

June 12, 1969 turned out to be the most pivotal day in Flyer history, but there was no foreshadowing its potential impact. The *Inquirer's* report of the annual hockey meetings did not mention the amateur draft. In the *Bulletin*, John Brogan put draft notes at the end of his story about Parent signing a new contract:

"The Flyers drafted seven players in the amateur draft, only one under six feet. Chief scout Alex Davidson said the club was lucky enough to nab its top two choices—Bob Currier and Bob Clarke. Currier was picked first. However Clarke, a 5-10, 176 pounder ... might be the best of the lot. Detroit offered two professional players right off the bat for Clarke, but the Flyers rejected the offer ... Some hockey people believe [he] will be able to skate right in and play with the Flyers next season—without any seasoning at Quebec."

Clarke, on vacation from his job in the mines on draft day, was driving with his girlfriend Sandy to visit a teammate near Brandon, Manitoba. When they arrived, the center called home and was told that Flyer scout Roy Frost had phoned to say Clarke was drafted by Philadelphia.

Clarke did not care who had chosen him or in what round. "I just wanted to play," he remembers. "I guess when you know you're better than some of the guys who were drafted ahead of you, it creates some apprehension, but I don't really remember being anxious about where I would go. It seems strange, but the draft didn't get the hype it does now, so we didn't think about it much."

Three months later, the Flyers gathered for training camp in Quebec City and Melnyk got his first look at Currier. "He could skate like the wind, but he had no hands and was dumb like a stone," recalls the scout.

Clarke, however, showed up exactly as Melnyk had advertised him. "From shift one of day one of camp, he was our best player," says Allen.

The rookie wore a brush cut, thick black glasses and a pleasant smile that masked his two fears—public speaking and being perceived as handicapped. Clarke neither mentioned his diabetes nor took any precautions with it until he passed out during one of the first morning workouts. "This kid faints," recalls Watson, "and we don't know what the hell is going on."

"Lew Morrison and I were rooming together and overslept," Clarke remem-

After Keith Allen, center, moved up to assistant general manager following the Flyers' second season, GM Bud Poile, right, inked Vic Stasiuk as coach.

bers, "and I didn't want to take a chance of being late, so I skipped breakfast." Trainer Frank Lewis convinced Clarke of the need to eat a good meal at the start of the day and took charge of monitoring his blood sugar. Lewis provided a Coke before games, juice between periods, and carried pure glucose in the training kit for emergencies.

Clarke would talk about his condition only after extracting promises from writers that they not belabor the medical facts. He feared any drop-off in

Bobby Clarke, right, with linemate Lew Morrison.

his play would be attributed to a lack of stamina caused by low blood sugar. It never became an issue because Clarke never faltered.

"He sure does a lot of things well," said Fleming after Clarke assisted on two goals in his first exhibition game. "I especially like the way he forechecks. You don't see that in kids who just turn pro."

Stasiuk was playing Clarke on a regular shift with Fleming and Morrison, a former Flin Flon teammate, even before the Flyers moved to Hershey, Pennsylvania, for the third week of camp. "I'd like a chance myself to play left wing with Bobby Clarke," the new coach said.

Through the exhibitions, Clarke scored the most points on the team and said the fewest words. He spoke up, however, when Poile offered him a standard contract with different rates of NHL and AHL

pay. "I argued more about the Quebec salary than the NHL one," Clarke recalls. "That's where I thought I was going. Bud tried to intimidate me, but I was stubborn."

Clarke signed on the trunk of Allen's car in a Hershey motel parking lot for a $5,000 bonus and a $14,000 Flyer salary. If he played in the minors, the center would earn $10,000. Clarke had made $7,500 the previous year working in the mines.

After failing to score against the Aces at the Spectrum in the Flyers' final exhibition game, Clarke was still worrying aloud about being sent down. But by that time, he was the least of Poile's concerns. "The thing that really disturbs me," said the GM, "is that Clarke and Morrison have been our best players so far and they've never appeared in an NHL game. It doesn't say much for our veterans."

On that optimistic note, the Flyers flew to Minnesota to begin Year Three. "I remember how scared to death I was walking over to the rink from the hotel," recalls Clarke. Two minutes into the game, with Philadelphia already trailing 1-0, Clarke took his first shift and had the puck stolen by Bill Goldsworthy. Goldsworthy promptly fed Claude Larose for another goal and the Flyers went on to a dismal 4-0 loss.

"They looked like the same old Flyers to me," said defenseman Miszuk, whom Poile had traded to the North Stars over the summer. "They can't score and I think those kids (Clarke and Morrison) were kind of overwhelmed."

Undeterred, the Flyers sent Meehan and Byers to Quebec while Stasiuk kept Clarke on a regular shift through ties with Pittsburgh and Montreal. In his fourth game, at Toronto, Clarke fed Morrison through the crease for his first NHL assist. The two kids teamed to kill penalties like veterans, Clarke was named one of the three stars, and the Flyers, on a Lacroix hat trick, recorded their first victory of the season, 4-3.

It took seven games for Clarke to score his first goal. The Rangers, who had once trailed 2-0, held a 3-2 lead with four minutes remaining at the Spectrum when Clarke dug the puck out in the Flyer end, avoided a Ranger forechecker, worked a give-and-go with Sutherland, and entered the New York zone two-on-one with Morrison. When defenseman Arnie

Brown played for a pass, Clarke put his head down and fired past goalie Ed Giacomin's short side before crashing into the boards.

The rookie climbed to his feet and leaped so high that after the 3-3 tie, he was asked about being on the high school track team. "No," Clarke said, flashing one of his earliest recorded gap-toothed grins. "I wasn't around high school long enough to go out for anything. I quit in the tenth grade to go play junior hockey."

Clarke scored 9 points in his first 20 games and the Flyers tied nine of those matches. Lacroix, ever the team's scoring hope, and the cavalier Favell drifted into Stasiuk's doghouse. The coach juggled lines constantly and railed about a shortage of effort after practically every loss. Stasiuk couldn't stop talking about his former Detroit teammate and idol, Gordie Howe, and his players resented it.

"Vic was really good to me," recalls Clarke. "He kept playing me and I thought all coaches acted like he did. But he really got on the nerves of the veterans. One day Reggie Fleming told Vic he'd 'kick the bleep out of [him] and goddamn No. 9 (Howe) too.'"

Not all of the coach-player tensions remained private. "I've never seen guys jerked around so much," Fleming told the *Daily News'* Ed Conrad. Stasiuk had the soda machine taken out of the locker room and complained about the players' eating habits. "Soda and pizza and hot dogs are for hot dogs, not hockey players," said the coach.

By December 11, the Flyers were tired of Stasiuk's old song. Flyer vice president Lou Scheinfeld felt the same way about "The Star Spangled Banner." He stunned a crowd of 10,059 gathered for the contest with Toronto by ordering the playing of Kate Smith's "God Bless America."

"It was a troubled time, with (Vietnam) antiwar protests and dwindling patriotism," recalls Scheinfeld. "And it bothered me that more and more people at Flyers games were ignoring the anthem. Some laughed, talked, ate or even consciously refused to stand.

"I thought I'd do something to shake things up. I listened to tapes and records of various patriotic songs, tested them over the PA system in an empty Spectrum and decided on Kate. I thought it would wake the fans up and make them miss the anthem.

"When Snider heard it, he shot me a murderous look, cursed me out and said, 'Are you out of your mind?' I had told him what I was thinking about, but had never informed him that I was going to actually do it. At the end of the period, some fans

walking past Snider's box were angry; others liked it."

The three goals the Flyers had scored within 3:42 of the first period to take a 4-3 lead may have helped change a few tunes. After the 6-3 victory, the owner received congratulations for both the win and musical change of pace. "I still think you're crazy," Snider told Scheinfeld after the game, but by then the boss was smiling.

In their game stories, writers devoted space to Lacroix's hat trick and Clarke's first NHL fight (with Mike Walton) without mention of Kate. The following day, however, the *Inquirer's* Chevalier speculated that the Flyers, having won one in a row with Miss Smith, might keep her in the lineup. "I haven't decided for sure," Scheinfeld told the newspaper. "It depends on how I feel just before game time."

Two nights later, Scheinfeld coyly played "The Star Spangled Banner" before a Boston game, and the Flyers lost, 5-3. The next home match against Pittsburgh looked easier, so Scheinfeld cued Kate again, and the Flyers shut out the Penguins, 4-0.

It was only Philadelphia's sixth victory of the season but, as Chevalier noted, Kate remained unbeaten. She won another before suffering her first defeat, 6-4, to the Penguins, but when she bounced back to shut out the hated Blues, 2-0, on January 25, the fascination with the good luck charm took hold.

"Joe Kadlec (the Flyers press relations director and traveling secretary) and I had the routine down," recalls Scheinfeld, now principal at Myriad Associates, an event marketing and managing firm in Philadelphia. "Joe would have both Kate and the anthem cued and then, sometimes on impulse, I'd make a decision and he would call the control booth. I remember once I was in Mexico when I got the impulse just before game time. I had trouble getting an operator and got through with about thirty seconds to go, but Joe was ready and it played. I tried to save it for when we absolutely had to win."

As the gimmick gained notoriety, Snider received a telephone death threat from a patriot in Buffalo. The Flyer owner ignored it. Life wasn't worth living without Kate, anyway. And besides, Snider had more confidence in her than in his general manager.

An incident on December 17 turned out to be the final straw. After tying the Rangers 2-2 at Madison Square Garden, the Flyers were traveling home on their chartered bus when Poile, unhappy that Flyers' television producer Harlan Singer had arranged for Snider to be interviewed between periods, went into a tirade.

The following afternoon, Poile, Allen and Putnam went to Liberty Bell Park, where it had been designated Flyers Day. Poile won $35 on a horse named Bold Moment and, after returning home, received a call from Snider.

The owner asked if what he had heard about the bus ride home was true. "[Poile] said it was a bunch of BS and so forth," recalls Snider, "but I told him I was going to check with some of my sources and that I would call him back. I spoke to enough people to be

Bobby Clarke smiles after scoring his first NHL goal in 1969-70, his rookie season.

convinced it was accurate, then called Putnam and told him I was going to fire Poile."

Putnam, pointing out how close it was to Christmas, tried to get Snider to change his mind, but the majority owner would not relent. Snider called Allen, who was at home writing Christmas cards with his wife, Joyce, told the assistant general manager what was about to happen, and asked to meet with him at the Spectrum.

"I was shocked," Keith remembers. "I didn't know Bud was in trouble with Eddie. Bud and I always had a good relationship. Bud could be blustery, and I know he got carried away on occasion, but he was never that way with me. I wasn't afraid to tell him when I thought he was wrong and I felt bad for him.

"Anyway, I asked Eddie if I could meet him someplace a little closer [to my home]. So, we had a cocktail at the (City Line Avenue) Marriott. He offered me the job right there. I felt so loyal to Bud, who had brought me here, that I said I wanted to think about it."

Snider told Allen he would name him acting general manager while he was making up his mind, then called Poile back at around 11 P.M. to tell him he was finished.

"Bud will get his Christmas bonus and his contract (with a year and a half remaining) will be honored," Snider said the following day. The media made the holiday timing of the firing as large an issue as Poile's job performance, which Snider termed "sporadic."

"I've never talked about [my firing] publicly and I don't think I should," says Poile today. He did, however, make his bitterness apparent to the *Inquirer's* Frank Dolson on the day after his termination. "[Snider] doesn't like some of my friends. I don't like some of his," Poile said. "I don't like bell-bottoms and big flashy rings. He does. Look, I'm upset. I'm sick today because I don't like to get fired. And anyway, I don't look good in bell-bottoms. To be successful, one man has to make the decisions. Not five men."

Poile went to Allen's house that day and told his friend to take the job. After flying with the team to St. Louis, Allen accepted. "Getting away helped clear my head," he recalls. "If I didn't take it, I knew that somebody else, who might bring in his own people, would. Then I'd be out of a job." Allen was officially named two days later, prior to a 4-0 Spectrum victory over Pittsburgh.

Stasiuk stayed on as coach. But Putnam, his handpicked GM gone, realized the Flyers were no longer his team to run. Within a few months, he secretly began offering for sale his 25 percent share of ownership. "Eddie and I didn't fight," recalls Putnam. "But it just wasn't fun for me anymore."

The Flyers continued to grind out monotonous ties and Chevalier began referring to them as the "Flying Tyers." On February 13, they were an odd 13-21-19, but were in second place, three points ahead of Pittsburgh. Three consecutive deadlocks the first week of March gave the Flyers twenty-three, matching a mark set by the 1962-63 Canadiens.

Five games later, against the Rangers at the Spec-

Vic Stasiuk, the Flyers'
second coach,
watches action from
behind the bench.

trum, the Flyers broke the record. New York's Orland Kurtenbach scored 2:45 into the third period and fate's hand, manifested in several good stops down the stretch by Parent and Giacomin, saved a 2-2 tie that was celebrated by fans tossing neckties from the upper level.

The Flyers and Rangers finished their season series a weird 0-0-6, but Ranger general manager Emile Francis was hardly fit to be, uh, you know. "I've never heard of such a thing," he said, "but it takes a lot of perseverance, patience, goaltending and defense to tie 24 games. I'll tell you, those ties have put Philadelphia in the playoffs."

Or so it seemed. With eight games to play, the Flyers were one point back of second-place Pittsburgh, seven ahead of fourth-place Minnesota and eight ahead of fifth-place Oakland. Many Flyers were banged up—Watson, Dornhoefer, Wayne Hillman and Favell (who had partially severed a tendon in his foot when he backed into a skate in the locker room) were out of commission—but Parent was on top of his game. Philadelphia was shutout in Montreal on March 21, but rebounded the next night to beat the Seals 3-2 at the Spectrum. When the team headed to the West Coast, one vic-

tory in the final six games figured to be enough to clinch a playoff spot.

The Flyers had a 2-1 lead with 3:40 remaining in the third period against Oakland, but Fleming fumbled away the puck and Don O'Donoghue tied the score. Joe Hardy recorded the Seals' winning goal with 12 seconds left in the game. Stasiuk blamed his players' giveaways on their use of curved sticks.

Two nights later in Los Angeles, Real Lemieux's goal with only one second left in the second period turned out to be the winner in a 3-2 Kings victory. "We must be kissed by the devil," said Stasiuk.

Back at the Spectrum, the Flyers gave up their third goal in three games during the final seconds of a period—this time on a Van Impe cough-up to Dean Prentice—and the Penguins won, 2-1.

In their next contest, a rematch in Pittsburgh, Clarke faced a wide-open net with the Flyers down a goal late in the game, but slid the puck against the post. The Penguins scored into the empty Flyers net and won, 4-2. "It's gotten to be a mental thing now," said Stasiuk. "Everybody's tightened up."

With two games left, both at home, the Flyers had to beat either St. Louis or Minnesota to make the playoffs. They played desperately and well against the Blues, but were stoned 1-0 by Ernie Wakely's 34 saves. Jimmy Roberts' winning goal came on a shorthanded breakaway after Paiement and Lacroix each thought the other would pick up a loose puck at center. "This is unbelievable," said Clarke. "We go out there and play our hearts out and wind up with nothing."

It was down to a single Saturday afternoon game at the Spectrum against the North Stars, a team that earlier in the season had recorded one win in a 34-game stretch. The victor would be in the playoffs, the loser would be out. A tie could still qualify the Flyers, if Oakland lost Saturday night in Los Angeles.

The Flyers' fifteenth straight sellout crowd watched a timid, scoreless two periods. Early in the third, Parent stoned Goldsworthy on the North Stars' best chance of the game. Minnesota goalie Gump Worsley robbed Johnson, then Larry Hillman's shot from the blue line tipped off Worsley's glove, rolled down his back and dribbled inches wide.

With less than twelve minutes to play, referee Bill Friday whistled a North Star hand pass that resulted in a face-off outside the Flyer blueline. Tommy Williams beat Johnson and the puck came back to Minnesota rookie Barry Gibbs. From the red line, he lobbed the puck into the air, where it floated towards the goal like a watch dangling from a hypnotist's hand.

Parent didn't move until the last instant, when he twitched slightly to his right. The puck dropped into the net and clanged against the metal base support like a bell tolling for the season.

Worsley stopped good power-play chances by Gendron and Terry Ball and, in the final minute, smothered a shot by Lacroix. As the buzzer sounded, there were tears in Allen's eyes. "It just seems so un-

real," he said. "I never could have believed this was possible."

The Flyers had lost consecutive 1-0 games to end their season. Parent had allowed only 18 goals in his last 10 contests. But one from the red line had denied his team a playoff spot.

"I lost the puck at the blue line," he said. "Someone stepped in front of me. I moved to my left and didn't see it until it was next to me. I lost it, it happens sometimes. You just lose it."

The smoke rising from the cigarette of the ashen-faced Snider was symbolic of the season. "We never lost six in a row before," he said. Five of those losses were by one goal. The Flyers had scored 12 times in their last 10 games, only one of which they won.

Stasiuk told his players he was sorry and disappeared. Hours later, he was found sitting by himself in the deserted stands.

"Maybe I played too conservatively," he said. "Instead of raising hell, I took an everything-will-be-alright attitude. If we'd gotten beaten, 10-0, maybe I could have tongue-lashed somebody and relieved the tension, but that never happened. It never entered my head that we wouldn't make the playoffs. We were always close, always respectable."

The Flyers kept their commitment to attend a fan club party that night. Parent received a standing ovation when he entered the room. "It's a wonder I didn't get shot, for crissakes," he says today.

The papers compared the collapse to that of the 1964 Phillies, but were generally sympathetic. As disappointingly as the Flyers' season had ended, interest in them continued to grow. Average attendance had climbed to almost 13,000 per game and hockey began to sprout roots as a participatory sport. The Coliseum Club, the first in a series of rinks to be

Keith Allen and Ed Snider are all smiles after Allen inked a contract as the team's second general manager.

built in the Delaware Valley, opened in Voorhees, New Jersey, with Lacroix directing the area's initial summer hockey camp.

Putnam, meanwhile, had found a buyer for his 25 percent share of the Flyers—Widener fortune heir F. Eugene Dixon—and in June received $2.3 million for what three years earlier had been a $500,000 investment.

Poile landed on his feet as GM of the new Vancouver Canucks, who were entering the NHL along

zling" in an unbylined *Bulletin* story, but when the 1970-71 season opened with him immediately injecting grit and steadiness into the Flyers' defense, the only mystery was why he had remained buried in the minors for three years following the original NHL expansion.

Kelly, a human pinball, was an instant hit with the fans and became Clarke's left wing. Goal scoring was not a Kelly strength, however, which left Allen bemoaning how Clarke, who had scored 46 points in

Bernie Parent goes down to make a save as the Hillman brothers, Larry, left, and Wayne, try to head off more trouble.

with the Buffalo Sabres. During the expansion draft, the Flyers lost Meehan and Fleming to Buffalo, and the Canucks took Wilson and Paiement, the disappointing right wing acquired by Poile three years earlier for a 1970 first-round amateur pick. A frustrated Allen watched Boston, drafting fourth overall, use that choice for Rick MacLeish, a Peterborough center about whom Flyer scouts had raved.

All players with obvious scoring potential were gone by the time Philadelphia selected in the second round, so Allen focused on size, drafting Bill Clement, a sturdy 6-1, 190-pound center who had been used mostly in a defensive role with the Ottawa 67s. With their third-round choice, the Flyers took Bob Kelly, a rambunctious, barrel-chested left wing from Oshawa.

In his first trades as general manager, Allen moved minor leaguers, sending Byers to Los Angeles for defenseman Brent Hughes, then two days later dealing Darryl Edestrand and Larry McKillop to Hershey for Barry Ashbee, a 31-year-old defenseman.

Ashbee's acquisition was termed "small and puz-

his rookie year, did not have finishers to hasten his journey to stardom.

Dornhoefer, the team's leading sniper in 1969-70 with 26, remained oft-injured, and Gendron was the only other Flyer forward with 20-goal capability. Speedy Bill Lesuk, claimed from Boston in the intraleague draft (the Bruins responded by claiming Cherry), had minor-league hands, and Bernier, the 1967 amateur pick promoted from Quebec, had appealing size but a minor-league heart.

Thus, the Flyers' fourth season progressed at a familiar win one, lose two, tie one pace. On December 9, the team won its first game in St. Louis in three years, but there was no sign that the Blues, still the class of the expansion clubs, had slipped. In fact, with Chicago's movement into the Flyers' West Division to balance the addition of Buffalo and Vancouver to the East, the likelihood of Philadelphia challenging for first place seemed more remote than ever.

Stasiuk kept complaining about his team's work ethic and Lacroix's inconsistency, but the Flyers were doing the best they could. There would be no upward movement until they acquired a scorer.

"Because of expansion, there aren't many players around, and getting a star in a trade is almost impossible," said Allen as he approached his first anniversary as GM. "We need big, strong wingers who can score, and a defenseman who can move the puck."

When asked if he would trade a goalie, Allen said, "In the right kind of deal, I would give one up."

As a winless streak reached 11 games on January 5, 1971, Snider was approached by reporters who questioned whether a trade would prevent the team from missing the playoffs for a second consecutive

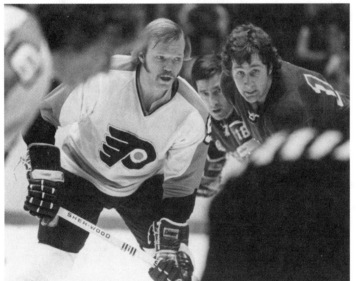

Bob Kelly, the rambunctious left wing from Oshawa.

season. The owner exploded about the expansion mindset that valued such a short-term, modest reward. "What the hell good is making the playoffs if you get wiped out (like St. Louis in the previous final) by Boston in four straight?" said Snider. "There are expansion teams doing pretty well with older players but, in ... two or three years when those players retire, they'll be back where we are today. And we'll be way ahead of them.

"It must get discouraging for our fans, but I hope they understand what we're trying to do."

Allen fished for interest in both Flyer goalies and, to his disappointment but not surprise, found a stronger market for Parent than for the hot-and-cold Favell. If Parent had to go, the GM was determined to get more than just a veteran scorer who could push the Flyers ahead of the other expansion teams. For a top, 26-year-old goalie, Allen wanted multiple pieces around which the franchise could grow.

On January 31, after Philadelphia rallied for three third-period goals to beat Detroit 3-1 and move one point ahead of Minnesota into third place, Parent was summoned to Allen's office. The goalie had

been puzzled by Stasiuk's decision to use Favell for a second consecutive game, but was not prepared for the words that came out of Allen's mouth.

"Bernie, we've traded you to Toronto."

Parent started to cry. Allen bit his lip.

The emotions were much simpler than the three-way deal the Flyers had struck. Parent and a second-round 1971 draft choice were going to the Leafs for center Mike Walton, goalie Bruce Gamble and a first-round 1971 pick. Philadelphia was then sending Walton to Boston for center-winger Rick MacLeish and right wing Danny Schock.

"In spite of having two fine goalies, we have been struggling for four years," Allen explained to the media after Parent had left the office. "I think we've reached the stage where we have to break through.

"We could have gone ahead and kept trying to build this team by adding a player here and a player there, or we could make this deal and try to strike it rich, and live or die with kids. Most expansion teams have traded away their No. 1 picks. We've got two (in the 1971 draft). And in MacLeish, we're getting a helluva prospect."

The reporters were skeptical, questioning why Walton, the established scorer in the deal, was being relayed to Boston for a player who had scored only 28 points in 46 games with the Bruins' Oklahoma City farm club.

"[MacLeish] will get 15 goals the rest of the season," boasted scout Les Moore, in Philadelphia for midseason meetings. "He's got a good wrist shot and slap shot. Nine out of ten times he goes into the corner, he'll bring the puck out."

Allen, who had seen MacLeish play only once, accepted the judgment of his scouts, just as the owner, philosophically in tune with his GM, let Allen do what he thought best. Still, Snider felt he had sold off part of the team's birthright in trading Parent, the first-ever and most popular Flyer, and had trouble consoling himself or reassuring the crushed goalie before he drove away. "I'll never forget looking back over my shoulder at the Spectrum," Parent recalls, "knowing it was *el gonzo*."

Watson also was crying in the locker room. "I've

been traded, too," he said. "I'm going to Boston."

"I don't know where Joe got that idea," Allen said. "He hasn't been traded."

Watson wasn't any more confused than Favell, who felt his body for bullet holes. "I can't believe they traded Bernie and not me," he told reporters. "Vic doesn't like my style, and I've had to work like hell to convince him I could play. He really liked Bernie. Keith really put me on the spot with this trade."

Favell wasn't the only guy in the hot seat. Calls to the Flyers' switchboard were almost totally negative and, when MacLeish made his debut four nights later against Chicago, the Spectrum was filled with signs: " I s Keith Allen really Joe Kuharich in disguise?" "Judas, Benedict Arnold and Keith Allen."

MacLeish eased the tension with a rousing body check of Keith Magnuson 30 seconds into the game, helping to jump start the Flyers toward their second victory ever over the Blackhawks, 6-2. "I guess I have to do the job to make the deal look good," said the new Flyer. "I thought I did okay, but I should have had a couple of goals."

MacLeish scored only twice in the 26 remaining games of the regular season. Fortunately, Favell began to play well, at least until he fell backwards during a March 16 practice and struck his head on the ice. "Why's that guy there and not Bernie?" Favell asked, pointing to the other goal as he was helped off the ice.

That guy was Gamble, the 33-year-old throw-in on the deal, who did an excellent Parent imitation by keeping the Flyers comfortably ahead of stumbling fifth-place Pittsburgh. Favell looked sharp in his return, a 3-1 loss at Chicago on March 27, but Gamble was in goal the next night at the Spectrum when the Flyers wrapped up a playoff spot with three games to spare. Kelly had thrashed the Penguins' Sheldon Kannegiesser in a first-period fight and had set up both of Clarke's goals in the 3-1 victory.

"I've never felt this way before, just so relaxed and happy," said Clarke, his skates still tied long after most of his teammates had showered. "I just want to keep the feeling a little longer."

The euphoria figured to be short-lived if the Flyers maintained third place and drew a match against the Blackhawks, the division leaders by twenty points. Dropping down a spot to secure a series with runner-up St. Louis was obviously a more prudent idea. Thus, when the fourth-place North Stars came to the Spectrum for the next-to-last game of the season, Clarence Campbell was in the building paying close attention. "I'm going to satisfy myself that both teams play as well as they are capable of playing," the NHL president said. "I proposed the 1-4, 2-3 plan last year, but it was turned down. I think everybody now realizes we made a mistake."

The Flyers played it straight and hard, beating the North Stars, 3-2. Predictably, they were not rewarded for their integrity.

In Game 1 of the playoffs, the Blackhawks scored three power-play goals, two by Bobby Hull, to win, 5-2. "I'm not trying to place the entire blame on Dougie, but he was only fair to middlin'," said Stasiuk of his goalie.

Several Flyers, however, were less reluctant to finger their coach after Chicago rolled up a 5-0 lead and won Game 2, 6-2. Stasiuk had flip-flopped right and left wings on several lines trying to get better defensive matchups, and the players, simmering all season, finally had had enough.

"There's only one way to beat Chicago," said Lacroix, "and that's to play offensive hockey. If they score six goals, you have to score seven." Nolet, ripped by Stasiuk for letting Hull get away on two goals, said, "Bleep [Stasiuk]. I took a run at [Hull] and he got the puck away off one leg while he was falling. Nobody can stop a guy like that."

In Game 3 at the Spectrum, the Flyers received goals from MacLeish and Nolet to carry a 2-1 lead into the third period. But Lesuk twice took penalties trying to stop Hull and the superstar scored on both

Barry Ashbee learned to play with pain. He often wore this collar.

power plays to give Chicago a 3-2 victory.

The Blackhawks' clear superiority and the seeming unfairness of the penalties struck a nerve with the fans, who threw trash at Hull as he left the ice. "We need a boomer like Hull," said Stasiuk, pacing the corridor after the game. "But what we need even more is an expansion referee. [Established refs] bend over backwards to give the old teams all the breaks."

The next afternoon, Jim Pappin scored the first of his three goals only 21 seconds into the game. The 6-2 victory and four-game sweep ended with a barrage of Easter eggs—some hard-boiled, some not—flying down from the upper deck. "Losing to a team like Chicago is not so disappointing," said Clarke, held pointless in his first playoff series by Stan Mikita. "But going out in four straight is sickening, just sickening."

"I thought something good would happen because we didn't lay down and finish fourth," Stasiuk said. The coach then spoke of his team's youth and predicted a brighter future, assuming he would be part of it. But on May 27, Stasiuk was summoned to Allen's office and fired.

"I know I shocked the hell out of him when I called him in," recalls Allen. "But I was never really a Stasiuk guy. I had inherited Vic from Bud's regime. I'd gotten a lot of feedback from the players and they really didn't like him. He was awfully stubborn. Gordie Howe was his ideal player and nobody else measured up."

Allen pulled no punches in explaining Stasiuk's demise to the media. "There was almost unanimous undercurrent," the GM told Bill Fleischman of the *Daily News*. "We'd be sitting on a firecracker. There's no way Vic could change his rapport with this team.

I told him he's an idealist. Some guys don't want to be as good as Bobby Orr or Phil Esposito. Vic could never buy that."

Stasiuk conceded his inflexibility. "My stubbornness in not accepting a so-so effort got me in trouble," said the Flyers' second coach, 45-68-41 in two seasons. "I've been told I have to change with the times ... but I have to be shown my ways are wrong before I believe it."

After the press conference, Allen kept a checkup appointment with Dr. Stanley Spoont, the Flyers' physician. "When I told him that I had just fired Vic," Allen recalls, "he said, 'You're a cool customer; your blood pressure is normal.'"

But had Allen been attached to a polygraph when reporters inquired about likely coaching candidates, the needle would have left the paper. "I have no idea," the GM lied.

Several months before, during an off-the-record chat over beers with *Bulletin* writer Brogan, Allen had said if he ever replaced Stasiuk, he would try to hire Fred Shero, the 45-year-old coach of the Rangers' Central League farm team in Omaha. The day after Stasiuk was fired, Brogan wrote the job was Shero's if he wanted it.

"I didn't know Freddie well, but I had followed his career and he had won everywhere," Allen recalls. "The only thing that made me wonder was why Emile Francis had given other guys a chance (to coach the Rangers) and never given one to Freddie. But his record was so good and I'd never heard anyone say a bad word about him."

Allen called Francis and received permission to talk to Shero. When the prospective coach came to Philadelphia on June 1, five days after Stasiuk's firing, the Flyers' interest in him was an open secret. Three writers and two photographers barged into Allen's office during the interview. "This is liable to be embarrassing," said the GM. But his recruit affably posed and answered questions. When the two men were again alone, Shero quickly agreed to a three-year contract.

Parent and Flyers' officials Marcel Pelletier, left, and Joe Kadlec, right, appear stunned after learning of the goalie's trade to Toronto.

The next day, during the formal announcement in the Blueline Club, Shero was asked why he had spent thirteen years in the minors before receiving an NHL offer. "There was talk, that was unfounded, my discipline wasn't strong enough," said the new coach. "I've never believed in socializing with management. Because of that, I've never made many contacts there. Maybe that's why I was never asked before."

Regarding how he handled players, Shero said: "You've got to be ready to defend the players from

criticism. In fact, once the season starts, I think I'll do more for my players than I'll even do for my family ... I've hardly ever fined a player. Nowadays, you fine a player and he laughs at you. You sit him on the bench though, and it's embarrassing ... I tell my guys, I don't want you to do what I say unless I can prove that I'm right."

Asked what would happen if he couldn't prove himself correct to a player, the coach replied, "He'll do it anyway because I'm the boss."

Shero likened hockey to pool—"It's not what you make, it's what you leave"—and said that the Flyers, forced since birth by limited firepower to play a conservative style, would now attack in five-man units. He predicted that before the season ended every player on the team would have played every position except goal.

The following day, the *Inquirer's* Dolson called Snider the "Charlie Finley of the Atlantic Seaboard" for changing coaches and sarcastically referred to Shero's naiveté for joining "this big, happy, hockey club."

Indeed, any good cheer enjoyed by the new guy behind the bench would depend largely upon upgrading the quality of the players in front of him. The 1971 draft figured to be critical. With the eighth

overall pick, Philadelphia selected center Larry Wright of the Regina Pats; with the ninth-overall choice (from the Parent trade), the Flyers took right wing Pierre Plante of the Drummondville Rangers. "[Wright] had a problem with his stamina last year," said head scout Alex Davidson, "but when he builds that up, he'll be as good as anybody."

Due to sagging attendance in Quebec, the Flyers moved their American Hockey League team to Richmond, Virginia. Training camp, however, was held in Ottawa, Ontario where barbers rejoiced over an edict from the new coach. "All I said was that I don't want hair in their eyes," said Shero. "Before Johnson could take a faceoff, he had to brush the hair [away]. If [a player] has a lot of hair around his face, it's going to take too much time to put in the stitches. In hockey we demand that a man get back in action as soon as possible.

"Another thing is we'll be rushing to catch planes and won't have time to wait for players to dry their hair. They'd catch colds if they rushed outside. And we can't afford to pay for nineteen hair dryers."

"I already have a hair dryer," said Schock.

On the whole, the team submitted to clippers without complaint. The Flyers noticed that, unlike Stasiuk, this coach had something to teach. Shero patiently explained his drills, then had players repeat them until they were done correctly. "He's installing a system," said Favell. "We didn't have a system last year."

Shero wanted his players to be more organized. But who would better organize Shero? After the first exhibition game, writers unsuccessfully searched the arena in Flint, Michigan, for fifteen minutes until the Flyers' coach finally materialized, explaining that he had gone for a walk to sort out his thoughts and had locked himself out of the building. "I had to climb a fence and go around to a door that was open," he said.

Watson, sour at being used in only one playoff game, had reported to camp out of shape. He spent a few days vomiting over the boards and announced his retirement before pep talks from buddy Orr (in Boston) and Van Impe changed Watson's mind. He was less stubborn than Davidson, who clung to his belief

Fans express their displeasure at the Parent trade.

in Currier, the draft choice taken ahead of Clarke. "(Phil) Esposito didn't come into his own until he was 27," argued the scout. But Currier, benched for twenty consecutive games the previous season by Quebec coach Eddie Bush, was again farmed out.

The Flyers opened the 1971-72 season in Pittsburgh, where Plante made a strong first impression by elbowing goalie Binkley in the head, enabling Clarke to score into an empty net. When Bryan Watson retaliated against Clarke, the Flyers cleared the bench but went down to a 3-2 loss in Shero's debut. They then blew two leads in Oakland before Dornhoefer's goal with 51 seconds remaining produced the coach's first victory, 5-4. Shero celebrated by complaining that Gendron had almost been caught up ice before the winning goal.

Lacroix, the Flyers' first false messiah, did not impresss his new coach any more than the old one,

General manager Keith Allen poses with Flyers' new coach Fred Shero.

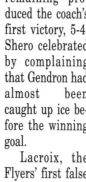

and was traded to Chicago for Rick Foley, a 6-4 defenseman who had run up 306 penalty minutes and averaged more than a point per game in 1970-71 at Portland (WHL).

Foley made a good first impression in a 1-0 victory in Los Angeles, but the Kings avenged their loss with a 7-0 blasting of the Flyers in Shero's home opener. "I thought we played extremely well in the first two periods," the contrary coach said.

The Flyers won only two games in a stretch of fourteen. Clarke, who had reported to camp sick and underweight with a tooth problem he had let slide over the summer, was off to a poor start. Bernier was a total bust and Foley was putting on pounds. MacLeish showed few signs of life and, along with Plante and Wright, was sent to Richmond.

"Don't worry, MacLeish is going to be great," Allen would tell Snider while trying to reassure himself. The GM gave firm instructions on developing MacLeish to Bush, the Richmond coach. "Drive him," said Allen.

Clement came up from Richmond and Watson gradually conditioned himself into Shero's good graces, but Nolet and Dornhoefer were the only Flyers scoring. Inexplicably, the team was unbeaten in three games against Montreal, but Shero was not impressed. "I just wish we would beat somebody else," he sighed.

Stasiuk, hired as coach of the renamed California Seals two weeks into the season, came to Philadelphia on December 5 and couldn't resist a dig at the sixth-place Flyers. "I see where they've been having trouble scoring, but that's nothing new," he said. "Maybe it wasn't the coach's fault after all."

The Flyers avoided further embarrassment by beating Stasiuk's team 3-0 but continued to slide while Shero dropped hints that passing, shooting and checking were not the only fundamentals his team needed to learn. After Foley, finishing a fight with Brad Park by making obscene gestures and spitting at Ranger coach-GM Emile Francis, was high-sticked by Glen Sather in a 5-0 loss to New York at the Spectrum, Shero took his team to Madison Square Garden the following week and made a statement.

The coach quickly changed to a line with three of his biggest players—Kelly, Bernier and Foley (suddenly an experimental left wing)—right after the opening faceoff. No fights materialized, but during a second-period altercation between Ashbee and Pete Stemkowski, Foley sought out Sather and threw several punches in the fiesty Ranger's face. "I wanted the rough stuff," Shero said after the 6-2 loss. "I just wanted to let them know they weren't going to get away with anything."

While the Flyers' coach extracted his pound of flesh, his team's home had been bled dry. Jerry Wolman, who had secured construction financing before becoming hopelessly overextended, had surrendered his rights to the Spectrum in September

1969, reducing his obligations in the pending bankruptcy settlement. A U.S. district court had placed the facility under the trusteeship of David Webb, senior vice president of Industrial Valley Bank, and attorney Harvey Schmidt.

Despite good attendance, the building's debt had reached $10 million by 1971. Convinced the Spectrum needed more aggressive management, Snider and his brother-in-law, Earl Foreman—an original partner of Wolman's who still held Spectrum stock—proposed a reorganization plan under which they would take ownership and pay off the creditors.

Judge A. Leon Higgenbotham, taking time to criticize Wolman for making withdrawals of more than $2 million from the Spectrum and Eagles to save his other enterprises, had approved the Snider-Foreman plan on September 1, 1971. With financ-

ing secured from First Pennsylvania Bank, Snider and Foreman took control on January 1, 1972, and, in time, all creditors were paid.

With the Flyers playing to only scattered empty seats, Snider had plans drawn up to add a third level to the Spectrum for the 1972-73 season. Despite little tangible evidence that the team was close to turning the corner, the fans remained content.

Well, at least most of the time. On January 6, with Philadelphia leading St. Louis 2-0 at the end of the second period, Blues coach Al Arbour walked across the ice to complain to referee John Ashley about the way the puck had been dropped for a faceoff that led to a Johnson goal. When Arbour, hit with a two-minute penalty for unsportsmanlike conduct, started to follow Ashley down the runway leading to the officials' dressing room, a spectator doused the coach with beer.

The Blues charged into the tunnel, while Bob Plager went into the stands after the fan. Policemen rushed in and the St. Louis coach suffered a ten-stitch gash in his head, apparently caused by a billy club. Several Blues—center Garry Unger being the most noticeable—swung their sticks wildly at onlookers and police reinforcements arrived in two busloads to restore order.

St Louis defenseman John Arbour needed forty stitches to close a scalp cut. Several spectators had been hit, but none required hospitalization. Al Arbour, whose shirt was torn in the melee, coached the third period wearing his sportsjacket and undershirt. The aroused Blues scored three goals, including one from the blueline by Phil Roberto, and stunned the Flyers and Favell, 3-2.

After Plager flashed the "V-for-victory" sign to the fans, Al and John Arbour, Floyd Thomson and Roberto were all taken to the police station at 24th and Wolf Streets to be charged with disorderly conduct, and

Coach Fred Shero barking out a line change.

assault and battery of policemen. "The worst case of police brutality I've ever seen or heard about," said Blues' owner Sidney Salomon Jr.

Snider said he was "sick." But not about the brawl. "This was a very important game and our guys blew it," he said. Shero, meanwhile, lamented that some players were never going to change, so Allen began changing players.

By the end of January, the GM had a deal on the table that would send Bernier, Lesuk, Johnson and defenseman Larry Brown to Los Angeles for center Eddie Joyal, left wing Ross Lonsberry, right wing Bill (Cowboy) Flett and defenseman Jean Potvin. "I did all the talking to (Kings owner Jack Kent) Cooke," recalls Snider. "Keith told me what to say." After Allen watched the Flyers lose 4-2 in Boston on January 27, he told Snider to say "yes."

"I got so goddamn mad at Bernier in that game," Allen recalls. "He could have been a great player. I remember some great practice battles he had with Clarke.

"Johnson and Lesuk gave us everything they had, but they were fourth-line players. Lonsberry and Flett were wingers we thought could score. Cooke wanted us to take Bob Berry, but we held out for Lonsberry."

The Flyers were almost immediately vindicated. Lonsberry scored in a 4-0 Spectrum victory over Pittsburgh that sparked a small turnaround. When the Blues came back to town on February 6 to face both the Flyers and justice (their cases were then continued until June), Philadelphia rallied for goals in the final three minutes by Nolet and Dornhoefer to pull out a tie.

The team was unbeaten in four games since the big trade. By no coincidence, Foley, who tipped the scales at 223, had sat out all four contests. When thyroid tests suggested no medical reason for the bloating, the defenseman was suspended.

Gamble, the throw-in on the thirteen-month-old Parent deal, also carried a few too many pounds for Shero's liking. But with Favell faltering, Gamble was called upon more often. As the Flyers began a six-game trip in Vancouver on February 8, the shy, chain-smoking, 33-year-old seemed on his way to becoming the No. 1 goalie.

Early in the first period during a Canuck siege, Gamble dropped to his knees, then slumped over. Ashbee blocked a shot and referee Ron Wicks whistled the play dead. By the time Warren Elliott, the Flyers' assistant trainer, reached the goalie, he was back on his pads and yanking off his mask. Gamble

asked what had hit him, but all Elliott had seen was Ashbee blocking the shot.

Gamble shrugged and not only continued, but played sensationally. On two goals by Clarke and one by Kelly, the Flyers were leading 3-0 with six minutes to play when the goalie summoned Ashbee to the crease. Gamble said he felt so ill that he doubted he could finish the game.

He did though. Gamble lost his shutout with 1:58 remaining and his lunch in the dressing room following the 3-1 victory, but he was hale enough to do a radio interview and speak to the writers. He told them he had not felt well all day and as a result had eaten little. But he was puzzled about what had happened in the first period and why, for the first time in his life, he had thrown up after a game.

Clarke thought the Flyers had gotten away with a sick performance, thanks to the heroic efforts of their under-the-weather goalie. "If anybody here prays, they should say [thanks] for Bruce tonight," said Clarke.

By the time the Flyers' bus reached the airport, prayer had become appropriate. "Bruce had the color of a dead man," recalls Favell. Elliott tried to make the goalie comfortable on the flight to Oakland, but the trainer told Allen he was worried about something more serious than the flu or dehydration.

The next morning, Gamble was taken to Merritt Hospital, where Dr. Joseph Clift determined the goalie had suffered a heart attack. As his wife, Virginia, flew to his bedside, Gamble's condition stabilized. His career, however, was probably over.

The Flyers recalled Bobby Taylor, a 27-year-old college marketing major who was enduring the minors as a way to pay for his education. In his first start, Taylor was on his way to a shutout and Philadelphia to its initial win at Chicago Stadium until a three-goal burst within 2:11 early in the third period brought the Blackhawks back to a 3-3 tie.

With five weeks left in Year Five, the Flyers were in their same old position, scuffling for one of the final two West Division playoff spots, when a former teammate made headlines. On February 27, Toronto's Bernie Parent became the first big name to sign with a new league—the World Hockey Association. Parent committed to a five-year, $750,000 contract with the Miami Screaming Eagles.

"Clarence Campbell had been adamant (at an NHL meeting) that either the WHA wouldn't be able to start or that they wouldn't last a month," Snider recalls. "I got up and said, 'It doesn't matter, they will start. They'll move franchises and flip and flop, but they will survive.' I was in football; I saw it with the American Football League."

While Blackhawks owner Bill Wirtz scoffed at the idea of losing Hull, who was being courted by the Winnipeg Jets, Snider quaked at the thought of the Flyers without Clarke. The team that had drafted his center's WHA rights, the Alberta Oilers, made an offer through agent, Howard Casper, so Snider immediately moved to get the emerging star under long term contract. "I'd made a determination that I didn't want to go through this year after year," recalls Snider.

On March 18, during a seven-hour session at the Spectrum, Snider, Allen and Casper negotiated a five-year, $500,000 deal.

Clarke's previous salary had been $25,000. "Let's just say I won't have to worry about eating for a while," he smiled when the contract was announced on March 21. "I like Philadelphia. The NHL is really the only place to play."

The signing was unprecedented in length for an NHL player and Snider said it was "the biggest step forward the Flyers ever made." Indeed, Clarke's commitment was the foundation for the owner's building plans. "Bobby said he wanted to win the Stanley Cup, not hold management up for all the money in the world," recalls Snider. "The fact that he was satisfied helped make the other players satisfied.

"Campbell said I was destroying the salary structure of the league. I got calls from other owners who said I was out of my mind. Many of those same people later lost their clothes."

Favell, who had been kept on a hanger in Shero's closet, was dusted off for the season's stretch drive and the Flyers, keyed by the surging Clarke, entered the final two weeks grinding out points in critical games. They shut out California 3-0, beat Van-

couver 4-1, and earned a 2-2 tie in Minnesota. Two nights later, the reinstated Foley broke the spell of Buffalo goalie Dave Dryden with a third-period score that sparked a three-goal rally and a thrilling 3-1 Spectrum victory.

The 3-0-1 spurt had put the 26-37-13 Flyers two points behind third-place St. Louis and two ahead of fifth-place Pittsburgh. With two games remaining—at home against the Penguins, and at Buffalo—the Flyers needed only two points to make the playoffs.

Scheinfeld cued Kate Smith, a mind-boggling 21-2-1 over three losing Flyer seasons, and Clarke scored two goals to help build a 4-2 lead over the Penguins. In the third period, a right circle drive by Pittsburgh's Bob Leiter went in off Favell's skate, but Philadelphia still led, 4-3, into the final minute when Penguin coach Red Kelly pulled goalie Rutherford and called his team to the bench. Clarke, who had just finished his shift, had time to catch his breath, but Shero sent out the fresher Clement to take the draw.

Syl Apps whacked the puck out of Clement's feet and Greg Polis deflected Eddie Shack's point drive past Favell with 46 seconds remaining, giving the Penguins a 4-4 tie and life going home for their final game with St. Louis the following night. As the Flyers flew to Buffalo to play the 15-43-19 Sabres, Shero's team could finish third with a win and a Pittsburgh victory. But the Flyers still needed a point to guarantee fourth place.

Nine seconds before the end of the first period, Clarke, lying on his stomach, swept a Hughes' setup past goalie Roger Crozier to give the Flyers a 1-0 lead. Foley made it 2-0 with a blast from the left circle midway through the second period.

The cushion lasted only 1:44, until Hughes twice lost the puck and Gil Perreault cut the lead in half.

Goaltender Bruce Gamble, who beat the Vancouver Canucks after suffering a heart attack early in the game.

As Pittsburgh ran up a big score on St. Louis, Van Impe took a penalty and Rene Robert's goal at 8:47 of the third period tied the game.

The Flyers could no longer worry about third place. They had to think defensively to insure the playoff spot. "The Sabres weren't all over us in that third period," recalls Clement. "We felt pretty confident."

On radio, Gene Hart began a countdown: "Three minutes and the Flyers are in the playoffs ... one minute and the Flyers are in the playoffs ... 30 seconds and the Flyers are in the playoffs."

When Favell glanced at the clock with :13 left, his teammates were making their last change of the game. Gerry Meehan, the former Flyer, started behind the Buffalo goal and fed the puck to Byers, another former Flyer, fifteen feet in front of the Philadelphia bench. "The puck went right by me," recalls Clarke, who was coming on for Clement. Clarke turned and tripped Byers, but the return pass to Meehan was already away.

As Meehan accepted the puck and skated diagonally through center ice, Flett made the mistake of picking up Jim Lorentz cutting through the middle, leaving Morrison, the left wing, unsuccessfully chasing all the way across the ice to catch Meehan. Buffalo's Tracy Pratt was waiting on Meehan's left as he hit the blue line, so Van Impe, respecting the possibility of a pass, decided to back in.

"I was surprised when nobody challenged me at the blue line," recalls Meehan.

Ten feet in front of Van Impe and forty-five feet from the goal, Meehan half-wristed, half-slapped his shot. Favell had not come out to cut down the angle. The goalie kicked with his left leg and lunged with his glove as the puck came across his body. He fell backwards on his rear end as the puck hit the net.

Clarke, reaching the blue line when the light went on, looked back over his head at the clock. It read :04. He tossed his face upwards, then sank to his knees in the corner. Favell remained on his haunches until teammates summoned him to the bench for the perfunctory face off.

After Meehan missed the empty net at the buzzer, those Flyers who still couldn't believe their season was over sat dazed in the locker room. "It was like getting shot," Clement remembers. "It was that stun-

ning, that abrupt. It wasn't really happening, like we stepped into a time warp. I couldn't put it in any perspective at all, just couldn't handle it."

Those Flyers who accepted the reality did not control their emotions. "I cried, knowing I'd let the team down," recalls Favell. "Eddie didn't screen me. I didn't choke. I just missed it. And it was awfully hard living with it."

Clarke, his complexion the color of chalk, met the media in an adjoining locker room. "I feel dead inside," he said. "I'll bet if you look back since hockey's started, there's never been anything like that happen. I'll bet you'll never see it again in fifty years."

When Shero was asked for his feelings, he paused for almost 30 seconds. "The same way I did when my mother and father died," he said.

Dornhoefer felt as badly for the coach as he did for himself. "The first thing I thought about was how good Freddie had been to us and we lost for him," he told reporters. "Then I thought, why didn't someone jump off the bench and tackle Meehan? The penalty would have been worth it."

The loss was the only one the Flyers suffered in their last six games. Nevertheless, for the second time in three seasons, they had blown a playoff spot on a long, bad goal in the final contest.

They numbed themselves against the pain into the wee hours at Sinatra's, their Buffalo hangout. Few players had slept when they staggered onto the airport bus the next morning for the trip home. Snider walked around repeating to the team what he had said to Shero after the game: nobody would lose his job over one disastrous goal.

"It was unbelievable what had happened," Snider says today, "but once I got used to it, I realized we had made great strides. I was still totally and completely confident."

"All the right things were said," Clarke recalls. "If they weren't, it could have been devastating. Some teams blow a season and don't bounce back for three or four years."

The next day Allen called the loss more crushing than the one in 1970. "It's the worst thing that has happened to me in hockey," he said. But the GM insisted he was not going to tear his team apart. Soon enough, there would be other people trying to do that for him.

Chapter 4

◆◆◆

The Breeding
of the Bullies

The installation of a third level of Spectrum seats for the 1972-73 season would allow an additional 1,980 fans to see the Flyers. Hockey was becoming so popular in Philadelphia that the new World Hockey Association felt the town could support two hockey teams.

Jim Cooper, an Atlantic City attorney, bank chairman and Flyer season-ticket holder, and Bernie Brown, a Vineland, New Jersey, trucking tycoon, had acquired the stillborn Miami franchise and the rights to its players for $3 million. On June 3, the club named itself the Blazers, announced its colors as orange and yellow, and introduced its first player—Bernie Parent.

The former Flyer, who had left the Maple Leafs to sign with Miami, had his five-year, $750,000 contract renegotiated to be personally guaranteed by Cooper and Brown against the team or league folding. Parent was also promised a new car every season to drive around the city he had been heartbroken to leave eighteen months earlier. "I didn't enjoy Toronto too much," Parent told the media.

The Blazers named Johnny McKenzie, the longtime right wing of the Stanley Cup champion Boston Bruins, as player-coach, and lured Andre Lacroix, the former Flyer center whose production had never approached his popularity, from the Chicago Blackhawks.

When the Blazers inquired about available dates at the Spectrum, they were given a choice of forty-two for a 39-game schedule. "We were offered Christmas Eve, New Year's Eve and New Year's Day, Monday nights opposite the NFL game, Super Bowl Sunday and only one date in February," said Cooper.

The City of Philadelphia came to the rescue by advancing Cooper and Brown $359,000 to install an ice rink, refurbish locker rooms and set up offices at Convention Hall. Mayor Frank Rizzo talked about building a 20,000-seat arena for the WHA team so that the facility could also be used for both the Democratic and Republican National Conventions during the 1976 U.S. Bicentennial celebrations.

As the Blazers made big headlines, the Flyers' off-season news seemed mundane. With the seventh overall pick in the amateur draft, they selected Kitchener center Bill Barber. After taking Edmonton defenseman Tom Bladon in the second round, their third choice was Calgary defenseman Jimmy Watson, Joe's younger brother.

The Flyers also announced the hiring of one of the NHL's first assistant coaches, longtime Hershey center Mike Nykoluk. "Eddie (Snider) came from football, where they had assistant coaches, and thought Freddie could use some help," recalls Allen. "Mike had never been fast enough to play in the NHL, but he was a smart player and I had a lot of respect for him."

The National Hockey League continued to grow. Two new franchises—the Atlanta Flames, headed by Bill Putnam, and the New York Islanders—were introduced in June 1972. Atlanta plucked Lew Morrison from the Flyers in the expansion draft while Rich-

Mike Nykoluk was the first full-time assistant coach in the NHL.

Coach Fred Shero's blackboard philosophy.

mond defenseman Jim Mair was taken by the Islanders. The Flyers had no plans for either player, but when the WHA New York Raiders announced the signing of right wing Bill Flett and defenseman Brent Hughes, Snider counterattacked.

Flyer legal counsel Gil Stein warned Howard Casper (who represented Flett and the majority of the Flyers) that the team would try to prove in court that the agent had received a bounty to deliver players to the WHA. "Casper called Snider and threatened him," remembers Stein, but when the Raiders missed a $50,000 advance payment to Flett, Casper had legal grounds to bring him back to Philadelphia for an even larger contract.

When Flett's return was announced on June 27, the former rodeo rider had grown a beard which he denied was a necessary disguise after jumping two teams within a month. "I knew what I was doing when I signed with New York," the Cowboy insisted, "and I know what I'm doing now."

The WHA had thrown back a minnow to hook a much bigger fish. On the day Flett rejoined the Flyers, Bobby Hull signed a ten-year, $1.75-million contract with the Winnipeg Jets.

On August 3, the Blazers also signed a big name—Derek Sanderson, the play-

boy blowhard center of the Bruins–to an astonishing ten-year, $2.65 million contract, the largest in professional sports history. At a press conference in Philadelphia's Bellevue-Stratford Hotel, Cooper pointed to two five-foot-high pictures of Sanderson near the podium. "Wallet-sized," the Blazer owner joked. He then announced Sanderson's deal as "a declaration of independence for all hockey players."

Sanderson signed his contract before two thousand screaming teeny-boppers and curiosity seekers in JFK Plaza, where he was asked whether the city seemed too staid for his taste. "Boston was quiet, too, until I got there," he said. After predicting he would have a 45-goal season (he had achieved 25 with Boston), Sanderson announced that the Blazers would draw better than the Flyers. "When the

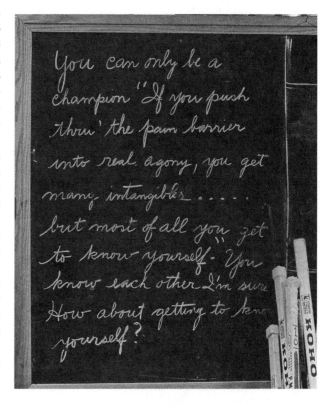

Bruins would play the Flyers, you had to feel, who are they?" he said.

Cooper told the media that Sanderson's contract would result in the Blazers' absorbing a small deficit, even if they sold out the 9,200-seat Convention Hall for the season. The owner recounted that when his majority partner, Brown, who was not a sports fan, had asked why one man was worth so much money, Cooper had replied that Hull, Bobby Orr and Sanderson were the three most recognizable names in hockey.

The Flyers were incredulous. "[Sanderson] is colorful and a good hockey player," Allen said, "but he's no superstar. I wouldn't trade Bobby Clarke for him.

"We're just to the stage where we sell out almost every game and they're cashing in on all our work. I think Philadelphia fans are knowledgeable enough to know [the Blazers] have three or four National Leaguers and the rest are who-he's."

The Flyers, however, also had their share of no-names and were coming off a 26-38-14 season. "I was very nervous," Snider recalls. "The WHA teams

could just switch [their rights to specific players] and sign anybody they wanted.

"The flip side was that we had the substantial league with the drawing power of the visiting clubs. And Convention Hall as a hockey arena didn't exactly send shivers up my spine. Still, it certainly could have been a turning point for us if they succeeded."

Cooper challenged the Flyers to a game for charity. "Loser leaves town," he smirked. Clarke, meanwhile, went off to defend the bragging rights to larger turf. He was selected to play in the eight-game series between NHL players and the supposedly amateur Soviet national team that had been dominating world competition.

Team Canada, undertrained and overconfident, jumped to a quick 2-0 lead during Game 1 on September 2 in Montreal, but was left gasping as the Soviets won, 7-3. Canada, its heroes victorious in only one of the first four contests, was suffering a nervous breakdown until Clarke helped turn the tide by putting Soviet star Valeri Kharlamov out of the series with a vicious slash to the leg.

Canada rallied to win the last three games in Moscow, climaxing a three-goal third period in Game 8 on Paul Henderson's goal with 34 seconds remaining. Clarke, not only his team's meanest player but one of its best, came home a national hero and an NHL superstar in full bloom.

As the Flyers began training camp in Ottawa without him, snakebites from the devastating goal in Buffalo seemed to have healed. Although they had received publicity beatings all summer from

Gloves and sticks litter the ice in this heavyweight battle between the Flyers and Flames.

Dave Schultz, the baddest of the big, bad Broad Street bullies.

the Blazers, Snider's team suffered negligible player losses to the WHA compared with their NHL divisional rivals. Center Eddie Joyal, who had scored only 7 points in 26 games after being acquired in the multiplayer Los Angeles trade, went to the Alberta Oilers, and 38-year-old Jean-Guy Gendron signed with the Quebec Nordiques. Snider, meanwhile, talked Hughes back from the Raiders, who were happy to be relieved of the financial burden.

Allen made headlines by telling reporters that the

Bill Barber, right, with Moose Dupont, scored his first Flyer goal in his fourth game and never looked back.

and American Hockey League records in compiling consecutive seasons of 259 and 348 penalty minutes, figured to make the team, as did Don Saleski, a 6-2, 200-pound right wing.

"I really like our muscle up front," said Shero, who was also pleased with the most recent draft picks. Bladon was a sensation during training camp; Barber looked skilled and poised. "(Rick) MacLeish or (Larry) Wright weren't ready last year, but this kid Barber might be," said the coach. "He's a smart player."

Nevertheless, the Flyers wanted to take another look at Wright, so they farmed Barber to Richmond along with the unseasoned Jimmy Watson and the rotund Foley. Shero wasn't sure Schultz was prepared for the NHL, but as the team flew to St. Louis for their season opener, the rookie seemed ready for the Blues. Asked if he was aware of the bad blood that flowed between the two teams since their births, Schultz licked his lips. "Yeah, I've heard there's been some trouble," he said.

Schultz was barely used,

Flyers could beat out the Hull-less Blackhawks for the West Division championship. Snider wasn't making predictions, but believed his team was close to a breakthrough. "If we don't have a club fighting for first or second place in two years, if our young players don't come through by then, the fans can say we don't know what we're doing," said the owner.

Defenseman Barry Ashbee, who had to be talked out of a sudden request to be traded, did not share management's enthusiasm. Bitter about contract negotiations and curfew-breaking teammates, Ashbee had an especially low threshold for Rick Foley, who reported to camp weighing 243 pounds, twenty-eight over his assigned weight. "I've talked and talked and talked to the guy," said coach Fred Shero. "The more I talk, the more weight he seems to put on."

Shero wanted a bigger, not rounder, team. And Allen had provided one. "You know," said Joe Watson, as he leaned over the boards to Bill Fleischman of the *Daily News*, "I think I'm the smallest guy here now."

Left wing Dave Schultz, who had smashed faces

however, as Philadelphia survived a two-man disadvantage in the final minute to hang onto a 4-4 tie. Five nights later, the Flyers' largest Spectrum crowd—14,929—watched Vancouver get blasted, 7-3, in the home opener.

That same night, the Blazers debuted against the New England Whalers at Boston Garden, where the homecoming Sanderson excited a capacity crowd by scoring on a breakaway early in the 4-3 Philadelphia loss. The following evening, there were spotlights, a band, and traffic tie-ups outside Convention Hall as the WHA team warmed up for its first home game.

The date was Friday, October 13, 1972, but Brown apparently was not a superstitious man. "See, you didn't think we could do it," the co-owner crowed to the *Bulletin's* John Brogan. But as the crowd filed in while the Blazers and Whalers warmed up, players felt the ice crack, then buckle under their feet.

The Zamboni, which was still being assembled as the teams took the ice, finally made its appearance twenty minutes after the scheduled starting time, but gouged up huge chunks of the surface. Every piece referee Bill Friday touched came away from the floor. When Cooper stood in front of the penalty box and began a postponement announcement to approximately 5,000 fans, he was assaulted with souvenir first-night Blazer pucks. Sanderson was summoned from the locker room to apologize and plead for another chance. As always, he knew just the right thing to say.

"This is a first," Sanderson said into the microphone. "Philadelphia has suffered a first here."

More pucks came down. "Please come back, we need your support after they get this bloody ice fixed." Sanderson then added, "I hope you can get out of the building. The parking situation isn't that great."

Flyer minority owner Joe Scott–in attendance only because of his deep love of hockey, of course–ran to call Snider, then went to see Cooper at ice level. In what was either a magnanimous gesture or a spectacular grandstand play, Scott offered the Blazers the use of the Spectrum the next afternoon.

"We're competitive in all ways, but in a situa-

tion like this ..." Snider said to calling reporters.

"Thank you, Lord," Snider said to himself.

Cooper politely declined the offer, then ripped into the city for being unable to do a decent ice installation in five days. The facility was not usable until the Blazers' third scheduled home game, which they lost while on the way to an 0-7 start. Sanderson soon suffered a herniated back disc and Parent a broken toe, leaving the WHA team hemorrhaging.

Meanwhile, the Flyers' transfusion was proving to be successful. Barber, a center when sent to Richmond, scored 9 goals in 11 games as a left wing and was recalled on October 28. He recorded his first Flyer goal in his fourth game, a 5-3 victory over Buffalo, and looked completely at home in the NHL. MacLeish replaced the slow-starting Bill Clement on a line with Ross Lonsberry and Gary Dornhoefer and scored two goals in a 5-2 win at Toronto.

Shero decided Ed Van Impe, the Flyers' sole captain since 1968, should share those responsibilities with Clarke, Dornhoefer and Joe Watson. The coach also told Bobby Taylor that he had been elevated to No. 1 goalie over the inconsistent Doug Favell. Taylor warmed to the challenge until he kicked out a Greg Polis shot in Pittsburgh and felt like his leg had caught fire. The hard luck netminder was helped off with a severe hamstring pull, and the cold Favell was bombed with four quick scores. The Flyers, despite Barber's second and third goals, lost 5-2.

The team bounced back the next night, however, when MacLeish's first NHL hat trick helped produce a rousing 5-3 victory over Chicago. "If anybody would have told me MacLeish would be carrying the team now," said Shero, "I'd have asked how much he'd been drinking." Schultz, although used sparingly, raised eyes and a welt on Keith Magnuson's head with a barrage of punches, while Saleski kicked out the Chicago tough guy's skates. "I

Coach Shero was convinced that Moose Dupont was a key missing ingredient for the Flyers.

never heard of Schultz before," the battered Magnuson said afterwards.

Clarke was on pace for 100 points and Flett, his right wing, had a chance at 40 goals. MacLeish scored 13 times in his first 19 games, and Barber artfully manned the left point of a power play that was among the league's best.

"Were those the Philadelphia Flyers?" asked Montreal coach Scotty Bowman after the Canadiens outlasted Philadelphia 6-5 at the Forum. "What happened to that 1-0, 2-1 team I used to know?"

On the road, the Flyers remained the same kittens they had always been. Their away record was 1-10-3. "I guarantee we will win our share [of away games]," Shero said. He fiddled with his goaltending—Michel Belhumeur got some starts while Taylor's hamstring was taking six weeks to heal—and juggled his lines. After Philadelphia fell behind Boston 4-1 on December 9 at the Spectrum, the coach used Schultz on a regular shift and made an interesting discovery. "They were letting him go where he wanted around the net," Shero told reporters after a Flyer comeback fell short in a 4-3 loss. "Maybe I'll use him more and try to intimidate [teams] early."

Allen realized the Flyers needed some muscle on the backline to complement their increasingly rambunctious forwards. Snider telephoned Sid Salomon III, the Blues' itchy-handed president, and inquired about Andre (Moose) Dupont, a 23-year-old defenseman whom Shero had coached in the Ranger organization.

As always, St. Louis was anxious to deal. Since Barclay Plager was hospitalized with stomach and bladder problems, the Blues wanted a defenseman who could move the puck and asked about Hughes. They also desired a young forward, a commodity the Flyers suddenly had in surplus. Wright and Pierre Plante, the disappointing first-rounders playing in Richmond, had become expendable.

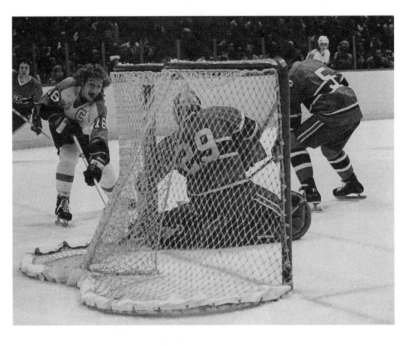

On December 14, Salomon agreed to send Dupont and a third-round pick to the Flyers for Hughes and Plante, but insisted Hughes be in the Blues' lineup for that night's game at the Spectrum. Snider argued unsuccessfully. "I said, 'Sid, that's unconscionable,' but he was worried about somebody getting hurt and insisted." So at 4:45 P.M., Allen told Hughes he would be dressing in the visiting locker room.

Playing on an ankle injured during the previous evening's 7-2 loss at Minnesota, Hughes was minus-3 as Philadelphia jumped ahead, 3-0. Fans who had rarely been kind to the defenseman delighted in his misery. After the Flyers blew the lead, then recovered on Clement's late goal to win 5-3, Hughes was bitter. "Allen didn't even have the common courtesy to tell me who I was traded for," he said.

Dupont, however, was delighted. "I'm happy to play for Freddie again," he said. Shero, who had come to appreciate Dupont's fearlessness two seasons earlier in Omaha, was convinced the Flyers had found a missing ingredient. "The Blues panicked," Shero said. "[Dupont] is a good team man. And he'll adjust quickly because he knows my systems."

Instead, the aloof, sensitive, and mistake-prone Dupont struggled. He and Ashbee were on for four goals against as the Flyers went down to Boston, 5-3, at the Spectrum. The team's road record fell to 2-12-3 when Favell was bombed 6-1 at St. Louis, but in Vancouver on December 29, Philadelphia was ahead in the third period when Bob Kelly and the

Clarke's inspired play, here against Montreal, earned him the full-time captain's "C."

Canucks' Jim Hargreaves grappled.

As the linesmen took too long to separate the combatants, Saleski and Barry Wilcox got into a secondary scuffle along the boards. Saleski put a stranglehold on Wilcox. "He was turning purple and I thought his eyes were going to pop," said the Flyers' right wing.

As Wilcox struggled, an outraged fan reached over the boards. Dr. J.J. Lederman, a dentist by trade, attempted to extract Saleski's hair without anesthesia. "I thought he was going to pull me right off the ice," said Saleski.

Taylor left the bench to grab the doctor, who was then punched several times by Ashbee. Van Impe, Dupont and Flett jumped into the stands swinging sticks as spectators scurried away or ducked under seats. Lederman was bruised and cut, a little girl was grazed by a stick, and police officer Donald Brown, who tried to pull Taylor away from the melee, was knocked down. Flett rescued Taylor, but the Canucks used their power plays to pull out a 4-4 tie.

Canuck fans gathered by the visitors' locker room after the game, booing and calling the Flyers "animals," but the players were becoming impossible to insult. Although Philadelphia lost to Los Angeles 5-3 the following night, Schultz beat up the Kings' Terry Harper.

Three nights later in Atlanta, Barber rocked Larry Romanchych over the boards on the first shift, Saleski menaced Jacques Richard (the NHL's top draft pick) and Dupont took three roughing minors as the Flyers jumped to a lead. While accumulating 43 penalty minutes to Atlanta's 17, Philadelphia confidently and belligerently checked the game away. The 3-1 victory, only the Flyers' third on the road, was punctuated by Dornhoefer giving referee Wally Harris the choke sign at the end of the game. The *Bulletin's* Jack Chevalier had a clear sense of the transfor-

mation that was taking place:

"The image of the fightin' Flyers is spreading gradually around the NHL and people are dreaming up wild nicknames. They're the Mean Machine, the Bullies of Broad Street and Freddy's Philistines. Living up to their reputation, the Flyers learned last night that winning on the road can be easy and profitable fun. They swaggered into the Omni, ordered the Atlanta Flames up against the wall and fleeced them for a 3-1 win."

Chevalier had used "Blue Line Bandidos" instead of "Bullies of Broad Street" when he filed his story, but on the red-eye flight home after the game, he had second thoughts and called in a change. Pete Cafone wrote the headline: "Broad Street Bullies Muscle Atlanta."

It had a ring to it. Midway through Year Six, the Flyers had a personality.

"I used to have a club in the minors they called 'The Magnificent Malcontents' and we won the championship easy," Shero said. "Eighteen choirboys never won the Stanley Cup and they never will."

Philadelphia lost at Buffalo, 2-0, to a team unbeaten in its first 21 home games but, as the Flyers announced a contract extension for Allen, the GM proclaimed their road woes were near an end. "We need that one big win and I think we're about to break through," he said.

Two nights later in Chicago, Cliff Koroll's goal gave the Blackhawks a 2-1 lead early in the third period that seemed typically backbreaking. But Clarke

The Flyers were becoming the terror of the league. Bob Kelly steamrolls another goaltender.

scored on a tip-in, Dornhoefer broke the tie in the final five minutes and, behind Belhumeur's 33 saves, the Flyers recorded their first-ever victory at Chicago Stadium, 3-2. "It only means a lot," Shero said, "if the players think it means a lot."

It meant a lot. The Flyers went 6-3-1 in their next ten away games while continuing to dominate in Philadelphia. Clarke became the full-time captain on January 17, the day before a smashing 6-1 Spectrum win over Minnesota. Schultz cruised for trou-

Gary Dornhoefer battles for the puck in front of Montreal goalie Ken Dryden.

ble almost every night. "It's too bad these home games aren't exciting anymore," he lamented. "Nobody wants to fight back."

A few did verbally. "They are pretty brave in their own building," said the Penguins' Al McDonough after the Flyers won the first game of a home-and-home at the Spectrum. Two nights later in Pittsburgh, Ashbee punched referee Bryan Lewis to protest a call, the Flyers took 80 minutes in penalties, and players were on their way into the stands when Shero called them back. "We kicked the bleep out of them and their fans, too," sneered Schultz after the 5-3 vic-

tory.

"I like to think we're winning on finesse," said Shero, "but it's good to soften them up first."

Clarke's stick was doing much of the advance work. "It's brutal what he gets away with," complained Bowman after the Canadiens beat the Flyers 6-3 in Montreal. But for the first time, the old guard had to respect the team from Philadelphia.

When mighty Chicago scored a bad-angle goal on Taylor with eight minutes remaining in a February 3 game at the Spectrum, the Blackhawks were happy to play for a 2-2 tie. "That's all they could get," Dupont said, "and they knew it."

With Philadelphia down 2-1 and shorthanded in the third period in Boston, Dupont goaded Orr into a penalty that nullified the power play. Clarke scored to give the Flyers a 2-2 tie, their only point earned against the Bruins at the Garden since their first-ever game there.

An 8-game winning streak ended when Schultz tipped a puck into his own net in Los Angeles, but the Flyers knew they were no flukes, so they refused to be deterred by one.

The team was neither humbled by Ashbee's 8-game suspension for hitting the referee, nor remorseful during a ten-minute visit to the Vancouver police station on February 9 to hear various assault and creating-a-disturbance charges laid against Flett, Van Impe, Lonsberry, Saleski, Watson and Ashbee. The cases from the December 29 riot were continued until June, but Vancouver fans who wanted the judge to throw the book at the Flyers were expected to toss anything but accolades from their seats at the Pacific Colsieum that night. "I really don't think anything will happen," said Shero, "but sometimes situations like these get the adrenaline up for the visitors."

Comments made through the media served the same purpose. The Flyers were seething over Vancouver tough guy Bobby Schmautz's words to a radio interviewer following a 5-4 Canuck loss at the Spectrum eight days earlier. "My wife hits harder than Dave Schultz," Schmautz had said.

For opening his mouth, Schmautz had eleven stitches sewn into his face after it was perforated by Dupont's stick two minutes into the game. Eggs splattered onto the ice as the Philadelphia defenseman went to serve a five-minute penalty. By the time he got out of the box, Clarke and MacLeish had scored shorthanded goals.

After eight minutes, the Flyers led, 4-0. Schultz beat up Schmautz (delivering a few shots for his wife, too) and Saleski, who twice fought Vancouver's Richard Lemieux, was ejected for going after the diminutive Canuck center a third time. "I think I'm crazy," said Saleski, after the Flyers recorded a 10-5 victory, the most smashing road triumph to that point in their history. "I thought it would be a quiet game."

As Dupont described the afterglow of success, it was clear that calm Flyer games had been canceled due to lack of interest. "That was a lot of fun," Gene Hart recalls Dupont saying afterwards. "We don't go to jail, we beat up their chicken forwards, we score ten goals and we win. And now the Moose drinks beer."

The only Flyer failing to have the time of his life was Favell, who had not played for 15 games. "Do you feel like you're being boycotted?" Favell was asked by the *Inquirer's* Chuck Newman.

"Am I a grape?" Favell said. "What do I look like, a head of lettuce?"

The goalie replaced Taylor when he was bombed 7-2 in Chicago, and began to climb back into Shero's good graces.

On February 17, the Flyers swaggered into Montreal, where Schultz punched Guy Lafleur, wrestled Henri Richard, then later ran at Serge Savard. Schultz lost the fight with Savard, but picked another with Pierre Bouchard as the Flyers jumped to 3-0 and 6-4 leads. The Canadiens rallied and tied, but Clarke stole the puck from Bob Murdoch behind the net, fought his way to the front and, facing away

from goalie Ken Dryden, scored the game-winner on a low backhander. Clarke's first NHL hat-trick, coming in a hockey mecca, announced him as a serious MVP candidate. When Shero was asked about the exhilarating 7-6 triumph, he shrugged. "They played one goal dumber than we did," he said.

The league was becoming wise to the Flyers' act. Clarence Campbell threatened Snider and Allen with disciplinary action if they failed to control their players. The NHL president said he had no problem with the penalties, only the team's histrionics before reporting to the penalty box. It was clear to him that the Flyers' behavior was hardly spontaneous. "Obviously," he said, "nobody on the Philadelphia club is trying to stop it."

Management's resolve had been only to build a big team. "Freddie took it from there," recalls Allen. As their reputation and advantage grew, the Flyers offered no apologies for their conduct. "You can see teams coming in here are a little worried," said defenseman Wayne Hillman. "They're hearing that we're a bunch of animals. Some guys don't want any part of that."

St. Louis tough guy Steve Durbano was one of the few to take his chances. He responded to Flyer trainer Jimmy McKenzie's taunting by reaching over the boards and jamming his stick into McKenzie's mouth. Kelly jumped off the bench and pounded Durbano as the Blues, the organization that had terrorized the Flyers in their early days, watched.

"We had been victims for a long time," recalls Clarke. "Teams felt it was their right to hammer us. We enjoyed returning the favor."

The Flyers were having almost as much fun as their fans. A group in Section E, calling itself Schultz's Army, was led by Phil Stein, who wore an old German military helmet that was painted orange and black and later sported blinking lights.

As Favell rendered the red bulb behind him useless in a 7-0 rout at Oakland, Shero finally was getting caught up in the excitement. "With Dougie playing the way he did and all the other things going for

Phil Stein, the general of Schultz's Army.

Rick MacLeish sweeps the puck away from Atlanta defenseman Pat Quinn.

us, we are on our way," proclaimed the coach.

Meanwhile the Blazers, who had seemed to be a threat at the beginning of the season, were on their way out of town. Phil Watson, who took over as coach, refused to play Sanderson even after his back had healed, and a contract settlement was reached so that the star could return to the Bruins.

Parent's broken toe had mended and he was performing yeoman's duty in goal as the WHA team worked its way back towards the .500 mark. But the Blazers, despite a midseason cut in ticket prices, were only averaging 4,325 fans per game. Owner Bernie Brown had bought out his free-spending partner, Cooper, in midseason, but had little stomach for running the franchise and no clue what to do with it. When Brown went to Snider for general advice and to ask again about Spectrum dates, the Flyer owner recommended that the Blazers leave town. "Well, he asked me and I told him," recalls Snider. "There were plenty of other marketplaces."

On March 4, MacLeish amassed four goals in a 10-0 romp over Toronto to reach No. 42, and on March 22, Lonsberry's hat trick in a 9-0 Spectrum rout of Vancouver clinched a playoff spot and the Flyers' first-ever winning season.

As they drove for home-ice advantage in the first round, Allen traded spare defenseman Jean Potvin to the New York Islanders for center Terry Crisp, a playoff-tested checker and face-off man. The Islanders, expected to make defenseman Denis Potvin their first pick in the upcoming draft, wanted his brother as an inducement to keep the prospect from signing with the WHA.

Clarke, with two goals in a 4-2 victory over At-

lanta on March 29, became the first player on an expansion team to reach 100 points. In the season's next-to-last game, MacLeish scored Nos. 48 and 49 during an eight-goal second period that gave the Flyers a 10-2 victory over the Islanders and the second playoff position behind Chicago and ahead of Minnesota.

The following night in Pittsburgh, MacLeish dug the puck from beneath defenseman Dave Burrows and flipped it past netminder Cam Newton to become the eighth man in NHL history to score 50 goals. It was also MacLeish's 100th point. "To have two centers with 100 points is just unreal," marveled Snider, who renegotiated both MacLeish and Clarke's contracts and offered them cars as bonuses. Clarke asked for a dune buggy instead.

Any Philadelphian would have gladly chauffeured either player. The Flyers, who had broken the NHL season mark for penalties by 385 minutes, were a smash. One fan arrived at the ticket booth at 10 P.M., twelve hours before the remaining 1,500 playoff seats went on sale, and was the eleventh person in line. By daybreak, 10,000 were waiting.

Flett, with 43 goals, and Barber and Dornhoefer, each with 30, gave the Flyers' deep firepower for their best-of-seven series against Minnesota, a team that had taken defending champion Montreal to six games the previous spring.

Tom Bladon moves the puck as Ted Harris watches.

day left the Flyers facing a short night and a 3-1 deficit in games unless they immediately bounced back. After Clarke, scoring his first playoff goal, gave the Flyers an energizing lead, their younger legs began pumping. Favell's glove glowed, snatching superior chances by Lou Nanne and Dean Prentice, and Philadelphia evened the series with a 3-0 victory.

"You're damn right I'm proud," said Allen. "I don't think Favell has ever played better. Clarke and Lonsberry were very strong and Ashbee was just great."

The North Stars, with six players 35 or older, had a clear edge in experience, and it showed in Game 1. Dennis Hextall broke a scoreless tie midway through the second period and Minnesota dominated the nervous Flyers before a Spectrum crowd that turned from roaring to subdued to terrified when Clarke took an accidental stick in the eye during the third period and lay face-down on the ice, his legs thrashing wildly.

The Flyer star's vision had returned by the time Minnesota goalie Cesare Maniago completed his 3-0 shutout. At Lankenau Hospital, doctors removed two fragments of Clarke's hard contact lens, gave him ointment and sent him home.

The next night, the captain was back in the lineup and the Flyers were recharged. MacLeish threw a body check on the first shift, Saleski's rebound of Simon Nolet's shot 5:48 into the first period put Philadelphia ahead, and Ashbee had three assists in a solid 4-1 victory that was the Flyers' first in ten playoff matches.

Hextall again gave Minnesota a 1-0 lead in Game 3 at Bloomington, and Maniago, back in goal after being rested in Game 2, was flawless once more. The North Stars broke the game open with a four-goal third period before Schultz tried to break apart Hextall's skull with a head butt. The Hammer had picked fights in the final minute of all three games, but Philadelphia was nailed with a 5-0 shutout.

An afternoon CBS telecast the next

"So far, this is the greatest thing that's ever happened to me," said Favell. "I've always been considered a terrible playoff goaltender."

The North Stars had a day to rest, and no reason to quit as Game 5 began at the Spectrum. MacLeish sent 16,600 fans—many of whom beat the combined Flyers-Phillies traffic by riding the four-day-old extension of the Broad Street subway—into ecstasy by scoring twice to turn a 1-0 deficit into a 2-1 lead. But Bill Goldsworthy's goal at 13:00 of the third period sent the Flyers into overtime.

The two teams flew at each other furiously for more than eight minutes until Dornhoefer took a pass from Ashbee and headed into the Minnesota zone. The North Stars seemingly were in good defensive position, but Goldsworthy missed a poke check just as Dornhoefer took a step inside Barry Gibbs. The defenseman got a piece of the puck, but Dornhoefer

still pushed it ahead, then switched to his backhand.

Tom Reid then grabbed at the Flyer winger as he lifted his shot. The puck flew waist-high to the far side across Maniago's body as he dropped to his knees. Dornhoefer, tumbling over the goalie, had his stick up in celebration as he flew through the air, and the Spectrum was bedlam with leaping, joyous fans even before the hero hit the ice. At 8:35 of overtime, the Flyers had won, 3-2.

"I was near the end of the shift and I was so tired. I didn't want to go out there again," said Dornhoefer.

Boston's Bobby Orr presents Bobby Clarke with the Hart Trophy for the 1972-73 season.

"One mistake and the game's over, you have to force the issue. You could try that play one hundred times and it wouldn't work."

The Flyers returned to Minnesota a victory away from advancing to the semifinals. Goldsworthy's goal put Minnesota ahead, but Crisp deflected in a Bladon point drive, Favell made a big stop on Prentice, and Lonsberry flicked a wrist shot past Maniago at 16:42 of the second period to put Philadelphia up 2-1. Just 1:19 later, Schultz bounced off Ted Harris and went to the net to put in a Flett rebound. Ahead 3-1, the Flyers were in control.

Favell, playing with a bad back, was forced to lean on the goal after making saves, but the Flyers checked the tired North Stars into mostly long-distance shots. Lonsberry, praised by Shero as the best player in the series, hit the empty net with 12 seconds remaining, putting a bow on the 4-1 triumph.

"Dougie was the man," said Van Impe in a locker room that was more glowing than ecstatic. The workmanlike clincher of the franchise's first series victory had seemed anticlimactic following the drama of Game 5, but the Flyers had to quickly refocus on Montreal, where the semifinals would begin two nights later.

Although Barber was playing with a bad shoulder and Ashbee's knee would need surgery during the summer, the Flyers were feeling no pain as they traveled to Montreal for a nothing-to-lose series against a club that had lost only 10 games in the regular season.

The second of two long-distance goals by Guy Lapointe gave the Canadiens a 3-2 lead in the third period of Game 1, but Nolet dug a Barber rebound from Dryden's pads and Dornhoefer redirected a MacLeish drive to put the Flyers back ahead. Montreal tied the game 4-4 on a goal by Jacques Lemaire and looked poised to make short work of the overtime. But Frank Mahovlich lost the puck in a puddle left by the Zamboni and MacLeish swept in to startle Dryden and the hockey world with an unassisted 15-footer at 2:56. The Flyers were 5-4 winners.

When Dupont and Dornhoefer scored in the first nine minutes of Game 2, the Montreal fans almost fainted. Even after the Canadiens fought back to tie, a goal by Flett gave the Flyers a 3-2 lead that they carried well into the third period. But Dryden held firm and Yvan Cournoyer picked Bob Murdoch's rebound out of Favell's skates to tie the game. At 6:35 of overtime, Larry Robinson banked the puck around Dornhoefer, stepped ahead, and beat Favell with a 50-foot dipper to even the series.

Bowman, who had read too much about Shero and his bold, young Flyers in the papers, awarded three goat horns: to Dornhoefer, for his mistake on the game winner; to Shero, for having Schultz out against Cournoyer on the tying goal and to Favell, for fanning in overtime. But the Philadelphia team was hardly intimidated. "I had some doubts [coming into the series]," said Lonsberry. "But we're working harder than they are. We may have played better tonight than we did [in Game 1]."

Flyer fans, who had not seen their heroes since sending them off to Minnesota with a 3-2 lead, stood and cheered for six minutes as the team took the Spectrum ice for Game 3. "You could not talk over it," recalls Dornhoefer. "I will never forget it."

The troops were fired up. Unfortunately, so was the throat of MacLeish, who became a late scratch due to tonsilitis.

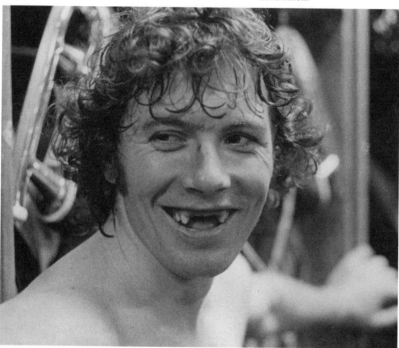

The Flyers pounded shots at Dryden, who kept the game scoreless until Rejean Houle launched a catchable 25-foot backhander that got under Favell's glove. Richard finished off a two-on-one pass from Mahovlich, while Crisp's rebound was the only shot to beat Dryden. "Montreal wasn't better tonight," grumbled Dupont after the 2-1 loss, "Dryden was better, that's all."

The Flyers cranked up Kate Smith (now 29-2-1) for Game 4 and Clarke put the team ahead. But Dryden stopped six shots during a two-man disadvantage and the Canadiens scored three times in the second period to go on to a 4-1 win. Checking tighter with each game, they had the series in a 3-1 vise.

For Game 5 in Montreal, the Flyers recalled Jimmy Watson from Richmond to replace the injured Hillman. Surviving five shorthanded situations in the first period, Philadelphia went ahead 3-2 when

Dryden flubbed a Flett shot early in the third. The advantage lasted only fourteen seconds as Frank Mahovlich beat Favell with another long goal and Richard, who battled Clarke valiantly throughout the series, jammed in a Savard feed. Yvan Cournoyer finished off Montreal's 5-3 series clincher.

Snider called referee Dave Newell "a donkey," but Flyer frustrations were short-lived. Before Barber took his uniform off, he said he couldn't wait until next year. "They know we've got something going," said Allen.

Shero, who during the playoffs had conveniently mentioned to the media that he'd received a WHA offer, was given a contract extension through three more seasons.

Ticket demand became so great that half-season plans were discontinued. Fans gladly paid for all 39 games and the privilege of watching the NHL's most valuable player. Clarke, although outscored by 26 points by Phil Esposito, was voted the winner of the Hart Trophy. "It's hard for me to believe he's won it," Shero said, "because it always seems to go to the big clubs."

The Flyers, however, had become one of those big clubs. Still, Allen felt his team lacked the consistent goaltender it needed for a chance at the Stanley Cup. "It wasn't any particular goal or goals in the Montreal series," he recalls. "It was just the realization that Dougie was the kind of goalie who could win you a series in four straight or lose you one in four straight." The best alternative had become a man Allen once traded away.

On the advice of his agent Howard Casper, Bernie Parent had quit the Blazers one game into their first-round series against Cleveland because of the withdrawal of a $600,000 bank deposit that guaranteed his contract.

"[Parent] deserves equal parts pity and scorn," wrote Stan Hochman in the *Daily News* as the Blaz-

Upside: with Clarke leading, the Flyers were ready to advance to the NHL's elite tier.

ers lost in four straight. But to the Flyers, public sentiment was a secondary consideration. Parent, having shared the net with Jacques Plante for a season and a half in Toronto, had perfected his style under the tutelage of a master. Now that his WHA contract had been breached, the Flyers only had to work a trade with the Leafs, who held the goalie's NHL rights, to bring him back.

Even before May 11, when the Blazers were sold and moved to Vancouver, Casper had informed Toronto that Parent did not want to return. "Casper told (Leafs VP) King Clancy that there wasn't a snowball's chance of him coming back," recalls Jim Gregory, then Toronto's general manager. "I argued we should force the issue, but (Leafs owner) Harold Ballard (who was serving a year's prison sentence for misappropriation of Maple Leaf Gardens stock) listened to Clancy."

On May 15, just before the amateur draft in Montreal, the Flyers announced that they had acquired Parent's rights from Toronto. Philadelphia gave up the tenth pick overall in exchange for the twentieth (they took defenseman Larry Goodenough), and also promised the Leafs a choice of future considerations. Toronto could take draft choices or Favell, who was immediately guessed by the media to be headed for the Ontario city.

Parent, 28, had expressed enough bitterness towards the Flyers during his year in the WHA to burn the Walt Whitman Bridge. "When someone even mentions the Spectrum, I get an upset stomach," he had said. But the Flyers, who had never wanted to trade the goalie, were anxious to forgive him. "Bernie is one of the classiest guys I ever met," said Snider. "I'm sure he must have been put in a bad situation [when he left the Blazers]."

On June 22, Parent was signed to a new multi-year contract for close to the $750,000 over five years he had signed for with the Blazers. "Everyone knows I want to be in Philadelphia," he said. "This is the first time I'll be playing for a team with a great chance at the Stanley Cup. I saw some Flyers' playoff games at the Spectrum and got goose bumps."

Meanwhile, the skin of Favell, a hero of those playoffs, was crawling as he awaited Toronto's decision. Gregory kept up the intrigue by acquiring two other veteran goalies—Eddie Johnston and ex-Flyer Dunc Wilson—but on July 27, after a push from Allen, the Leafs accepted Favell.

"I tried to convince [Gregory] to go the [draft choice] route," said Allen, "but they had decided they needed help right now."

Favell was finally out of limbo, but more let down than relieved. "I never really thought it was true until Keith told me this morning," he said at a press conference. "The greatest disappointment is that I'm going to a team that's still struggling and the Flyers are past struggling now.

"You can't knock them for trying to improve the team. I realize the difference between Bernie and me is consistency, but I feel people jumped on me a little too quickly when I had a few bad games."

During an interview with CBS's Tom Brookshier, Favell suddenly asked to be excused. "I guess it finally hit me," he said, crying as he walked the same corridor where Parent had left a trail of farewell tears two and a half years earlier.

It was no easier for Allen to send away the likable Favell than it had been to say goodbye to Parent. After the press conference, the GM left orders that he was not to be disturbed and headed for the Jersey shore. From the balcony of his motel in Wildwood Crest, he looked up and saw an airplane with a trailing sign: "Bring Back Favell."

As popular as Parent had once been, the Flyers had just traded the goalie who brought them their first winning season for a player who jumped a contract in the middle of a playoff.

Reporters called Parent for his reaction. "Gee, this will be a little pressure on me, won't it?"

Chapter 5

♦♦♦

The Cup Years

When the Flyers reached the end of the handshake line after being eliminated by Montreal from the 1973 playoffs, they wanted to go back to center ice and immediately drop the puck for the next season. "I went to Canada that summer and told everybody that I thought we were going to win the Stanley Cup the next year," Don Saleski recalls. "Our whole club thought we had a chance."

Fred Shero mailed letters to team members informing them that training camp, moved from Ottawa to the University of Pennsylvania's Class of '23 Rink, would be for learning, not conditioning. To prepare, some players shortened their vacations by two weeks and began skating at the (Voorhees, New Jersey) Coliseum.

"We entered last year hoping we could do it," wrote Bobby Clarke in his first weekly column in the *Bulletin*. "Now, we know we can. We've got more experience and depth, and Bernie Parent is as good as any goaltender around."

When the reacquired Parent was bombed for seven goals in twenty-two minutes by the Rangers during the exhibition opener at the Spectrum, Clarke looked like another know-nothing sportswriter. Shero pulled Parent, who was serenaded with boos, mostly from Doug Favell loyalists. "I had trouble concentrating," Parent said after the 10-3 loss. "Maybe I was a little tight."

Four nights later, in the more sanguine setting of Windsor, Ontario, Parent stopped 29 Red Wing shots in two shutout periods. He finished the exhibition season strongly, as did rookie defenseman Jimmy Watson, who seized the lineup spot created by Wayne

Coach Fred Shero describes a new drill.

Hillman's departure to the WHA Cleveland Crusaders.

Bill Clement worked hard to win back the ice time he had lost following Terry Crisp's acquisition in March. But both centers faced competition from Orest Kindrachuk, a 23-year-old free agent who had missed his draft year to attend college and was then signed at the urging of scout Jerry Melnyk. Asked early in the 1973 camp what he liked about Kindrachuk, who had scored 86 points at Richmond in 1972-73, Shero

Orest Kindrachuk was a strong cornerman, the perfect anchor for Schultz and Saleski on the third line.

said, "Everything."

Though only 5-10, 175, Kindrachuk was a strong cornerman, puckhandler and checker, the perfect anchor for Dave Schultz and Saleski on the third line. Kindrachuk's set-up skills, however, still were dwarfed by the NHL schedule maker's, who sent Favell's Maple Leafs to Philadelphia for the Year Seven opener. This drama promised to be so compelling, the appropriate musical accompaniment was needed.

Previous efforts by Flyers' vice president Lou Scheinfeld and Spectrum promotions chief Jay Seidman to have Kate Smith appear live had been rebuffed by her agent, Raymond Katz. "Miss Smith has sung for presidents, emperors and queens," Katz huffed. "She does not sing at sporting events."

Neither Seidman nor Katz was aware, however, that an 88-year-old uncle of Smith's, Fred Ditmars, lived in West Philadelphia and had been sending her newspaper clips chronicling the "God Bless America"

phenomenon. The singer told her agent that she wanted to go to the Spectrum, and he telephoned Seidman to discuss appearance fees.

"Make an offer that doesn't insult us," Katz said. So Seidman promptly offended Katz with an offer of $1,000. "Miss Smith's normal fee is $25,000," said her agent, who finally agreed upon $5,000.

"I went into [Ed] Snider's office to tell him what we were up to," recalls Scheinfeld. "We talked about some other stuff first, then he said, 'You know, I've been thinking. Why don't we try to get Kate Smith here?' I said, 'Oh Ed, I don't know, that could cost us a lot of money.'

"So I pretended like I was checking on it, and then went back to Snider a few days later and told him, 'We got her.' He said, 'Great, how much?' I said, '$10,000,' and he said, 'Boy, that's a lot of money, but I guess it's worth it. Go do it.' Then I told him it was already done for $5,000. He called me a son of a bitch. And I'd just saved him five thousand bucks.

"We sent a limo to pick her up in New York and sneaked her in." Nevertheless, rumors of Kate's appearance swept through the Spectrum on game day and hardly lessened Favell's anxiety. "When I heard she was here, I knew we were in trouble," he would say later.

By the time the red carpet was rolled onto the ice, Miss Smith's presence was an open secret, but no element of surprise was needed to produce a thunderous ovation. "The cheers went right through me," she said. "I've played before larger crowds, but I've never had a bigger ovation. It was fantastic and I'm sorry that is such a mediocre word."

Before game time, Favell had joked to Channel 10's Hugh Gannon that Crisp was the ex-mate he feared the least, but the checking center with the popgun shot got the goal that broke the scoreless tie. The Flyers then killed a five-minute spearing penalty called on Ed Van Impe, Barber scored an insurance goal, and Parent ran Kate's record to 29-3-1 with a 2-0 victory.

"Bernie is the greatest goalie I ever coached," Shero declared after one game.

The season's second match did not sway his opinion. Bill Flett fleeced Denis Potvin, the NHL's top draft choice, and fed Clarke for a shorthanded goal that started the Flyers to a 6-0 victory over the New York Islanders at the Nassau Coliseum. It was the second of 4 shutouts Parent recorded in his first 10 games as the Flyers jumped to a 6-point lead over the Chicago Blackhawks.

Although Barry Ashbee was suffering from a pinched neck nerve that sent stabbing pain through his left shoulder and numbed his hand, the 34-year-old defenseman was playing the best hockey of his career. "The pain he goes through every game is like somebody shooting bolts of electricity through you," said Dr. John Wolf, the Flyers' orthopedist. "If Barry took two weeks off, he'd probably be okay, but he won't do it."

Jimmy Watson, whose first NHL goal beat the Islanders 2-1 on December 1, added mobility to the backline. Kindrachuk became another excellent penalty killer on a team that went to the box often and without fear. Through seventeen contests, the Flyers were 7-0 in games in which they had scored shorthanded.

"I stand here, watch us take penalties and score goals," said an amazed Parent. Clarke, Flett and Rick MacLeish were behind their offensive paces of the previous season, but Philadelphia had a more efficient team. Thanks to Shero's well-practiced system, Parent was tested with only three to five good chances a night and was rarely beaten on more than two.

"I thought the Parent trade was just another deal when we made it," recalls Clement. "Then I saw what a difference he made. He was so much more consistent than Dougie. Every game you knew exactly what you were going to get."

As the Flyers grew more confident, they also became more belligerent. Schultz would spend the afternoon visualizing a fight with the opposition's toughest player, then go straight for him at the first opportunity. An increasingly rambunctious Clarke would also wield his stick without fear of retaliation. But on December 2, during the second period of a Spectrum game against California, he paid.

Seals' rookie defenseman Barry Cummins had absorbed a stick in the face from Clarke and snapped. Cummins took a full two-handed swing at No. 16's head, driving Clarke to his knees with a twenty-stitch

Singer Kate Smith belts out *God Bless America* in a live performance at the Spectrum.

Goalie Bernie Parent in his second time around with the Flyers.

cut and bringing the Flyers off the bench. Flett arrived first, throwing his gloves at the rookie's head before the Flyers began pounding. When the linesmen pulled Cummins away from the mob, he had blood pouring down his face.

"That bleepin' stupid fool," said Flett. "You never hit a guy over the head with a two-hander. It doesn't take much to kill a person."

Clarke, who returned to take a few shifts in the third period, received a phone call and an apology from Cummins after the Flyers' 5-1 victory. "[Clarke] cut me below the eye (for three stitches) and I was mad," the defenseman told the media. "It was an impulse action that I regretted a second after it happened. You always do when you hurt somebody."

Cummins was fined $300 by the league and suspended for three games. "I guess that's fair," said Allen sarcastically.

The meaner the Flyers played, the more they were penalized, and the stronger their convictions became that they were unjustly targeted by referees and NHL officials. Yet, they took delight in living up to their image.

"As much as we were loved at home, we were hated everywhere

Bill Barber battles Bobby Orr for the puck as goalie Gilles Gilbert looks on.

we went," says Clement. "So we began to feel like it was us against the world. We thought, 'If that's what the fans expect, then we'll give it to them.'"

The Broad Street Bullies drew both severe criticism for their tactics and begrudging recognition for their skills and work ethic. "In Canada, where they understood the game, we were largely complimented," Snider recalls. "It's in the retelling that we have gotten worse and worse.

"As much as the Bullies stuff was played up, we were also looked at as colorful, a Gashouse Gang on skates. That's part of the legend, too."

In many ways, the team reflected the personality of its majority owner. "I'd sit in the stands at playoff games and get in fights," Snider recalls. "They finally had to get me a private box at Madison Square Garden because I got into something almost every time I was there.

"I was always getting Keith (Allen) in trouble, too. One time in Minnesota some guy challenged me and I said, 'C'mon, let's go outside.' So we go through the tunnel and I'm looking at this guy. He has tattoos and big muscles on each arm and let me tell you, I'm nervous. I'm getting ready to square off and in comes Keith grabbing me and the guy and saying, 'Cut this out!' He saved me."

Snider and his GM almost perfectly complemented each other. The owner probed, pushed and sometimes lost his temper, but his trust in Allen's judgment was so complete that disagreements were rare.

"I don't think there has ever been a greater judge of talent than Keith," recalls Snider. "I just asked questions so that we were absolutely sure all the

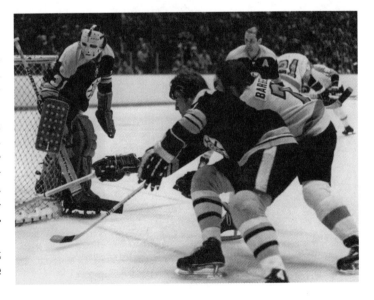

bases were covered before we made a move. He needed a push from me sometimes. And I needed him to force me to take a dispassionate view."

Publicly, Allen was always "putting irons in the fire," "cogitating," "exploring the parameters" of his next deal, or lying that he had "nothing going in the way of trades at this time." But "Keith The Thief"—so nicknamed by *Daily News* writer Bill Fleischman—knew exactly what the Flyers needed and was usually trying to steal it.

Allen's relationship with Shero was only as warm as the coach's personality would allow it to be. While waiting thirteen seasons for an NHL job, Shero had developed a generic distrust of management that sometimes made him a difficult employee. "He'd take some kind of a shot at us in the papers," said Allen, "and then when I'd get him in the office and ask him what he meant, he'd say he was misquoted or his words were taken out of context."

Nonconfrontational by nature, Shero never argued against any move the front office wanted to make. His sporadic jabs were often calculated to convince team members that the coach was on their side. "I found out a long time ago that [the players] are the only thing that wins for you," Shero said. "Maybe that's why it took me so long to

Reggie Leach blossomed in the Shero system.

make the majors. I catered to no one but them."

The appreciation was mutual. Almost to a man, the Flyers liked their coach to a greater degree than they comprehended him. "We understand the fact that everything he does is aimed to helping us win," Clarke said, "but we just don't understand some of the things he does."

For example, the Flyers were sometimes put through nonsensical drills until somebody, usually Clarke, would challenge their worth. "Now we're getting somewhere," Shero would say. "I wanted to see who was thinking."

Shero searched libraries for inspirational quotations and dropped them in players' lockers. He philosophized about life, discussed the game in theoretical terms, and rattled on endlessly about his respect for Anatoli Tarasov, the Russian coaching master. Yet Shero succeeded with a pragmatic system that was the virtual antithesis of that used by the Soviets.

He drilled Philadelphia's big, strong, essentially plodding, team on skating in straight lines, dumping the puck, and not taking unnecessary chances. Although the coach sometimes used unusual props like tennis balls and folding chairs at practices and almost always left time at the end of workouts for fun, he adhered to the fundamental philosophy of repeti-

This goal by Dornhoefer assured the Flyers of their first berth in the Stanley Cup finals.

tion.

Essentially shy, Shero sat by himself in coffee shops and bars, and often would not acknowledge the players when they passed on streets and in hotel corridors. They nicknamed him "The Fog" because he would materialize in rooms or hallways and then, just as quickly, disappear.

"Sometimes I don't think he knows Wednesday from Thursday," said Montreal coach Scotty Bowman, "and sometimes I think he's a genius who's got us all fooled."

Shero embellished the Fog persona because it gave him an excuse to avoid confrontations, questions and people. Yet an essential part of the loner's coaching philosophy was to bond his team together. Shero would gather the Flyers in his hotel room at midevening for beers. The real purpose of these meetings was to disrupt the players' barhopping and keep consumption at modest levels, but the sessions were far less resented than any strict curfews.

The Flyers felt Shero treated them like adults. He never embarrassed them before their peers and would sometimes go to ridiculous lengths to publicly defend them. Once when Tom Bladon, under heavy Blackhawk forechecking, backed up, stumbled and put the puck into his own goal, the coach insisted the defenseman had been wise not to risk a pass.

Shero told his players and the media outrageous stories about events from his minor-league past, but kept the Flyers looking forward by assigning a monthly quota of points. Before the team could think about the Cup, they set their sights on becoming the first expansion franchise to beat an established club (Chicago) for the (West) division title.

On December 12, Philadelphia bounced back from a two-goal deficit to tie 2-2 at Chicago Stadium. Ten days later, relentless Flyer bodying and three third-period goals sent the Blackhawks to a 4-2 Spectrum defeat. "Schwartz and Saleski don't belong in the league," groused Chicago coach Billy Reay. But Dave

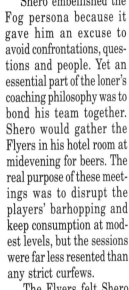

Defenseman Barry Ashbee after his accident.

"Schwartz" and his teammates never surrendered first place throughout the winter, and after Philadelphia won eight straight games in March, the club led the division by seven points.

When Clarke scored the hat trick in a 3-3 Atlanta tie on March 28, the Flyers were in position to wrap up the West championship at the Spectrum against Boston, a team they had not beaten in 27 games (0-23-4). Flett stole the puck from Bobby Orr and snapped a 2-2 tie 22 seconds into the second period, then circled the net 50 seconds later to set up a score by Clarke. Schultz engaged the Bruins' Terry O'Reilly in a bloody fight, Ross Lonsberry added a third-period insurance goal, and black and orange balloons fell from the rafters at the completion of the 5-3 victory.

"This is the best team I've ever seen in hockey for discipline and desire," Shero said softly. "I don't think I'll ever see one better."

Even though the Flyers were vying with the Blackhawks for the Vezina Trophy, which was then awarded to the team with the fewest goals against, Shero rested Parent, Clarke and Van Impe in Pittsburgh on the next-to-last night of the season. Bobby Taylor was bombed 6-1 in the contest. "It's a horsebleep award," said Shero. "The big thing is getting the club ready for the playoffs."

The coach sat out Simon Nolet for the regular-season finale the next night at the Spectrum, even though the right wing, a part-time player most of the year because of his size and defensive deficiencies, needed only one goal to reach 20. "I've taken a lot of bleep this winter without saying a word," said Nolet. "But I never expected this tonight."

Parent tuned up for the playoffs with a 6-2 victory over Minnesota and the Flyers still earned a half-share of the Vezina when Chicago's Tony Esposito allowed four goals to Detroit (the last by Marcel Dionne with 1:06 remaining). But Shero was more concerned that his team, only the sixth in NHL history to win 50 games in a season, be in a checking groove for its

opening-round series with Atlanta, the fourth-place finisher in the West.

Nolet was dressed for Game 1, but another right wing led the charge into the Flames' zone. Gary Dornhoefer, who had missed two 9-game stretches during the regular season with knee and wrist injuries, opened the scoring shorthanded with 4 seconds remaining in the first period. Two goals by Kindrachuk paced the Flyers' 4-1 victory.

MacLeish's hat trick gained Philadelphia a 5-1 win over the Flames in Game 2, but Atlanta GM Cliff Fletcher guaranteed his team would be bolder at the Omni.

Indeed, with Philadelphia leading Game 3, 2-1, Clarke received a retaliatory shove from Curt Bennett. Schultz then challenged the Atlanta bench and was answered by Butch Deadmarsh, who eventually emerged from beneath Schultz with a bloody nose. "Did he hit his face on the ice?" someone later

asked Schultz. The Hammer held up his fist. "He hit his face on this," Schultz said.

Sixteen seconds after play resumed, the officials failed to wave off a goal by MacLeish that had never entered the net. Atlanta goalie Daniel Bouchard flew into a rage, swinging his stick at linesman Neil Armstrong and punching referee Dave Newell. Newell, who always worked nervously in Flyer games, did not eject Bouchard. "If a [referee] gets hit and doesn't know it, he's got to be stupid," said Clarke after Philadelphia took a 3-0 series lead with the 4-1 victory.

Bouchard, however, didn't swing nearly as hard as the person who attacked Shero during one of his nocturnal wanderings the following night. When the coach was awakened at 11 A.M. the morning of Game 4 by a call from assistant coach Mike Nykoluk, Shero wondered why he was still in bed, then went to the mirror and found out. His face was bruised and cut, his right thumb was broken and he had a six-stitch gash on his left arm.

Shero said he had no idea how he was injured. "I remember the word 'animal' upset me," he said. "If I had a fight in a bar, it wouldn't be the first time." A police report revealed there had been a disturbance at 2:08 A.M. outside the hotel, but there were no arrests or details.

"From now on, when I'm going for a walk, I'm taking Schultz," said Shero. Allen put the coach on a 6 P.M. flight home and placed Nykoluk behind the bench. The Flames, desperate to avoid a sweep, opened up a 3-0 lead on Ray Comeau's goal at 16:19 of the second period, but Schultz quickly seized the moment and head-butted Bryan Hextall into submission. Andre Dupont scored on Atlanta's Phil Myre before the intermission and goals by Dornhoefer and Bladon tied the game before the third period was seven minutes old. At 5:40 of overtime, Schultz finished off a two-on-one pass from Clarke to score the series-clinching goal, then slid headfirst into the boards, where the hero of the 4-3 victory was

conked by a thrown air horn.

Schultz's mind cleared in time for him to ponder the Flyers' opponents in the semifinals. "I hope we play New York because they have a reputation of choking," he said. When the Rangers upset the Canadiens in six games and posted Schultz's quote in their locker room for inspiration, the Hammer was concerned that he had hurt his team's cause. "I never brag that I can beat the bleep out of somebody, he said. "But if I did, I [could] back it up myself. What I said could hurt the whole team." His contriteness was short-lived, however. "I'm just waiting for one of [the Rangers] to say something to me about that quote," said Schultz, shaking his right fist. "I'll have an answer for 'em."

With only two days to prepare for the rested Flyers, the Rangers put up no arguments in Game 1 at the Spectrum. Dornhoefer parked himself at the edge of wandering goalie Ed Giacomin's crease, once knocking the stick out of his hands before Lonsberry scored. Parent, supported by a pair of MacLeish goals and one by Bill Barber, shut out New York, 4-0.

In Game 2, the Rangers cut a Flyer lead to 2-1 in the third period, but Lonsberry stole the puck from point man Pete Stemkowski and soloed for a shorthanded goal. Brad Park quickly halved the deficit, but MacLeish scored off Jim Neilson's skate and the Flyers pulled away to a 5-2 victory and a 2-0 series lead.

"The Rangers are the best team in the league," warned Shero before the next match at Madison Square Garden. But overzealousness, not overconfidence, was the Flyers' problem in Game 3. They jumped to 2-0 and 3-1 leads, but were shorthanded constantly and eventually ran out of gas. Park's goal early in the third period, one of three Ranger power-play scores, proved to be New York's game-winner in the 5-3 victory.

The Flyers had lost not only the game, but Bob Kelly– to torn knee ligaments suffered in a hip check by Ron Harris, one of the few clean hits of the contest. "Intimidation, my butt," said Francis after Schultz had cruised for trouble in the final minutes and was ejected by referee Bryan Lewis. "The best way to stop that bull is to score on the power play."

Although warned by NHL president Clarence Campbell to cool it in Game 4, the Flyers were called for 17 penalty minutes in the first period. Joe Watson's goal had given Philadelphia a 1-0 lead, but Bobby Rousseau grazed the crossbar to tie the game late in the second period and the less-penalized Rangers were again fresher down the stretch. Only Par-

ent, who had 37 saves, kept the Flyers alive into overtime.

At 1:27 of the extra period, Ranger defenseman Dale Rolfe fired from the point. Ashbee had pushed to get around Stemkowski to face Rolfe's shot, but the puck rose too quickly for the Flyer defenseman to get his glove up for protection. "It looked like it hit him in the eyelid and pushed the eyeball down," said Rolfe later.

Ashbee dropped his stick and covered his face with both hands as blood dripped onto the ice. "It was like a softball was stuck in my eye, and then there was just a big red ball of fire," he said later. A woman fainted at the sight as the defenseman was carried off on a stretcher.

The ambulance had not pulled out of the Garden garage when Rod Gilbert, jostling with Joe Watson, deflected a Steve Vickers setup through Parent's legs at 4:20 of overtime, giving the Rangers a 2-1 victory and a 2-2 tie in the series.

At St. Clair Hospital, Dr. Frances Stovolla immediately ruled Ashbee out for the playoffs. A few days later, the Flyer was transferred to Philadelphia's Wills Eye Hospital, where both eyes remained patched while doctors waited for the blood to drain so that the extent of retinal damage could be determined.

Although Clement had injured his knee ligaments during a practice and was also scratched for Game 5, the Flyers refused to let their weakened manpower situation affect their approach. During the first period, Philadelphia twice faced two-man disadvantages, one of which enabled Stemkowski to score for a 1-0 Rangers' lead.

For the third consecutive game Parent was brilliant, buying time for his teammates to get moving. Bladon, dressed because of Ashbee's absence, gambled to get to the net and shoved in a Lonsberry rebound. MacLeish then broke the tie with Dornhoefer in Giacomin's lap. "I can't spend all my time slashing at guys like Dornhoefer," said a frustrated Giacomin later. "If I do that, the puck gets by me. I need some help. You don't see our forwards screening their goalie."

Nolet, playing in place of Kelly, whipped in a 35-footer during the second period and MacLeish put the game away into the empty net. The Flyers, 4-1 winners, had been saved by their bench and goalie.

Although Philadelphia had recorded only one victory at Madison Square Garden in their history, the Flyers returned to New York for Game 6 hoping they had weakened the Rangers' resolve. But with the score tied 1-1 and Giacomin sprawled, Clarke flipped a rebound over the glass to revitalize New York. Spare defenseman Ron Harris fooled Parent with a wrist shot from the boards 4:10 into the third period and the Rangers pulled away to win, 4-1.

The Flyers were going home for Game 7 of a series in which the visiting team had yet to win a game, but Shero feared he held no advantage. "The players are so frightened at taking a penalty, they don't play their normal game," he said.

Schultz, however, suffered no pangs of caution.

ers played as though frightened to make a mistake. Vickers eluded Dornhoefer to complete a pretty play from Tkaczuk and Fairbairn at 8:49, and the lead was cut to 3-2.

A contrite and determined Dornhoefer was at Giacomin's doorstep to restore the two-goal advantage only 12 seconds later, but the Rangers were not finished. Stemkowski, who had battled Clarke hard throughout the series, flipped in a rebound of a Rod Seiling shot to make the score 4-3 with 5:26 remaining.

Rick MacLeish scores what proves to be the Cup-winning goal in a 1-0 victory over Boston, May 9, 1974.

When Kindrachuk, trying to jab a puck away from Giacomin, was pushed by Rolfe in the first period, Schultz went after the defenseman and poured left hands to his face. "That took something out of New York," said Shero later. "They didn't do as much hitting after that."

The Rangers did, however, score first when Bill Fairbairn finished a three-way passing play from Park and Walt Tkaczuk. Less than a minute later, MacLeish tied the score on a goalmouth pass from Clarke on a power play. Throughout the second period, the Flyers drove to the net like possessed men. Rebound goals by Kindrachuk and Dornhoefer presented Philadelphia with a 3-1 lead, and a 37-19 shot advantage going into the last twenty minutes gave the illusion of total control.

But with a berth in the finals so close, the Fly-

As 17,077 fans fidgeted, Shero's best defensive hands smartly forechecked and stoutly blocked all routes through center ice. The Rangers were forced offside twice and managed only two long-distance shots over the next three minutes. As Giacomin was being pulled, New York's last hope died when a sixth skater jumped the boards too early. Linesman John D'Amico called too many men on the ice and the Rangers didn't get the puck out of their end until less than 10 seconds remained. Clarke controlled at center, and skated back into his end as the final seconds ran out to a cathartic roar.

The Flyers succeeded in becoming the first expansion team to beat one of the old guard in a playoff series, but took deep breaths, rather than deep gulps, to celebrate. Philadelphia had won by the closest of margins on sheer determination.

Scoreboard says it all
as fans help players
celebrate first Cup on
Spectrum ice.

Scoreboard says it all as fans help players celebrate first Cup on Spectrum ice.

"Every time you think you're about to gain some ground on them, they kick everything out from under you," said Giacomin with deep respect. "They won because they were all over us all the time."

Park, however, was bitter. "After the fifth game, I was so fed up with the bleep they were pulling, I wanted to give it right back," he told the media. "But I decided that if I had to maim somebody to win the Stanley Cup, then it wasn't worth it. I look around this locker room and I'm prouder to lose with these guys than I would be winning with another club."

When Lonsberry read Park's comment, he understood why the Rangers had lost in the semifinal round for four straight springs. "That statement just epitomized their whole team," Lonsberry recalls.

Dornhoefer, whose two Game 7 goals from Giacomin's lap had summarized the Flyers' effort, feared it would take a toll. "We're an awfully tired hockey club," he said. "I worry about our legs. But whatever we've got left, we'll give Boston all of it."

The Bruins, who had eliminated Chicago in a Game 6 that was played five days earlier than Philadelphia's Game 7, figured to be fresher. They were also very confident. The Flyers, opening on the road, had not won at Boston Garden since their first visit

in 1967.

The aura surrounding the Bruins, who had won Cups in 1970 and 1972, obscured the fact that Philadelphia had collected only one point less than Boston during the regular season. Having minimized the damage done by the Rangers' top line of Jean Ratelle, Rod Gilbert and Vic Hadfield in postseason play, the Flyers were not overly intimidated by the challenge of checking Phil Esposito, Ken Hodge and Wayne Cashman, the highest-scoring line in hockey. "I really believed we had already beaten the best team," recalls Clarke.

But the Flyers had yet to face the best player— Bobby Orr. Philadelphia had nothing remotely comparable to the defenseman whose offensive abilities had revolutionized the position, but Shero applied smart tactics and clever psychology in his plan to counter the superstar. Rather than respect No. 4, Shero told his players to work him, even to the point of dumping the puck in his direction. The more tired Orr became, the more human he would seem.

After Wayne Cashman opened the Game 1 scoring with Barber in the penalty box, and just 56 seconds later Greg Sheppard made it 2-0, it was the Flyers who appeared weary. But following Boston's initial burst, the Bruins' legs died from the week's lay-off and the Flyers summoned emotion for another series. Kindrachuk poked in a second-period rebound and Clarke, jamming ferociously for a loose puck, tied the game at 5:32 of the third period.

In the final minute, Clarke led a three-man rush into the Boston end. Flett took the captain's pass, faked goalie Gilles Gilbert and cut in front to a wide-open net, but slid the puck against the post. Orr smothered the rebound and soon after the ensuing face-off, the Bruins carried back into the Flyer zone. Cashman held Dupont so Hodge could feed back to Orr, whose shot went though a crowd and Parent's legs with 22 seconds remaining.

It seemed like the underdogs had given their best effort and had still fallen short, yet instead of being demoralized by the 3-2 loss, the Flyers felt energized. "We were still living in the New York series in the first period," Parent said. "But when we went back to our system in the second period you saw what happened. We'll beat those SOBs the next game."

"We'd outplayed them and we knew it," recalls Clarke. "We were in better shape than the Bruins."

Orr warned his teammates they could lose the series unless they picked up the tempo. In Game 2, Boston did, jumping to another 2-0 first-period lead on goals by Cashman and Esposito. Clarke redirected a Flett shot from the blue line early in the second to make the score 2-1, but Gilbert was Parent's equal as the teams played through a tense third period. With one minute to go, the Flyers were still a goal short.

As Parent came to the bench, Lonsberry spun away from Esposito, dumped the puck into the Boston zone, then hurried Orr as he rimmed the puck to Hodge. Clarke jammed the Bruin winger and the puck slid down the boards to MacLeish, who heard Dupont yelling as he moved up to the hashmarks. MacLeish threw the puck out blindly but perfectly and the Flyer defenseman slapped it waist high before Gilbert could set himself. Dupont was into his Moose Shuffle even before the light went on. The only sound in Boston Garden came from the joyous Flyer bench. With 52 seconds remaining, the game was tied.

In overtime, Gilbert made close-in saves on MacLeish, Nolet and Crisp. John Bucyk, sent in by Sheppard after the puck had reversed direction off the body of referee Art Skov, roared in alone and went to his backhand. Parent stood up to make a pad save.

Shero had been using his top players to go for the quick kill, but as the eleventh minute began and the adrenalin lagged, he sent out Schultz. The Hammer hustled into the Boston end, hurried Carol Vadnais, and worked with Clarke to seal the Bruin outlet up the boards. When Clarke forced O'Reilly to pass down the boards towards Vadnais, Schultz intercepted and fed Flett, who was calling for the puck at the hashmarks.

Flett took the pass on his backhand and had no time to turn and shoot. But Clarke had beaten Andre Savard off the side boards and was crossing in front of the goal. Flett slipped the puck to Clarke, who flicked a backhander. Gilbert sprawled to make the save, but the rebound came back to the Flyer captain who, on his forehand, took an instant to square himself. Then, he lifted the puck off the arm of the diving O'Reilly and high into the net.

At 12:01 of overtime, Clarke was in the air, as was the entire Delaware Valley. The Flyers' first win at Boston Garden in 19 games and six and a half years could not have been more dramatic or buoying. "I don't see how anybody could have doubts about us now," Clarke said in the locker room. "We know we can beat them."

In Game 3, Bucyk's rebound goal gave the Bruins an early lead, but the Spectrum was wired and the Flyers supercharged. Bladon tied the score on a power play, Crisp tallied off Gilbert's glove, and Kindrachuk poked in a puck that Orr was trying to freeze against the post. The Flyers' foot soldiers forged a dominating 4-1 victory that caused Boston coach Bep Guidolin to indict his officers—Esposito and Hodge were benched during the third period.

"We got maybe six guys putting out," said Guidolin. Orr, weary from incessant bumping, said Philadelphia looked hungrier than the Bruins, and Shero, gleefully joining the Boston-bashing chorus, continually criticized their supposed star mentality. The Flyer coach was building the case that hard work could conquer anything, even the loss of Dornhoefer, who suffered a shoulder separation during the third period of Game 3.

"We could really be in trouble," said Shero, who was already missing Kelly and Ashbee. Clement, out since midway through the New York series in Game 4, however, volunteered to play.

The coach went to the blackboard to remind his team that the sacrifices they were making were taking them closer to the ultimate prize. "Win together now and we will walk together forever," he wrote.

The Flyers took the ice intent on putting a stran-

glehold on their own immortality. MacLeish's tip-in of Bladon's point drive and Schultz's wrister off a two-on-one gave Philadelphia a quick 2-0 lead before the Bruins, finally appearing to realize what they were up against, fought back. Esposito scored on a power play and Savard slipped MacLeish and beat Parent through a screen to tie the game before the end of the first period.

Boston continued to carry the play, but the Flyers, keyed by Van Impe's flawless defense, kept the game tied. As the third period progressed, Philadelphia started to come on.

With six minutes remaining, Barber, playing right wing in Dornhoefer's absence, dumped the puck towards the left corner. Lonsberry got his stick against Orr's as the defenseman tried to clear and the puck died against the boards. Barber moved in and heeded the voices who had urged him to shoot his way out of what had become a 9-game goalless streak. He lifted the puck across Gilbert's body, over his glove and just under the crossbar. "The best wrist shot I've ever seen," said Orr later. "Maybe the best ever."

It was so stunning, the Spectrum took a second to explode. "I felt a shiver from my neck through my toes," said Barber. The roar had barely subsided when Clarke crossed the blueline, stopped at the far cir-

cle, and laid a pass on the backhand of the trailing Dupont. The defenseman stickhandled past the feebly waving Esposito and drove a forehander past Gilbert's stick side. The Flyers led by two goals with only 3:20 remaining.

Orr's last rush was steered wide by Van Impe as the clock ran out on a 4-2 victory that put Philadelphia one game away from winning the Stanley Cup. "I can't imagine," said Schultz. "I just can't imagine."

Neither could the Bruins, who from the start of Game 5 played like they would not die at home. Twenty-four seconds after the opening faceoff, Vadnais defiantly put his stick into the chest of the forechecking Schultz. With Dupont and O'Reilly off, Orr used the extra skating room to go the length of the ice to set up Sheppard's rebound goal.

Clement converted Flett's second period shot to tie the game, but Orr put Boston ahead on a 50-footer off Parent's glove. When Hodge made the score 3-1, the Flyers lost control. Their 24 penalties and the combined total of 43 for both teams set playoff records.

"They'll never beat us here in the seventh game and that's true in big black letters," said Guidolin after the Bruins' smashing 5-1 victory. The Flyers, looking outclassed for the first time in the series, didn't argue the point. Almost to a man, they believed they had to win Game 6 Sunday afternoon at the Spectrum or kiss the Cup goodbye.

Shero calmly listed his team's coverage mistakes and scoffed at the Bruins' apparent superiority. "When [they're] ahead by three or four goals, they all look like Orr," he shrugged. But his braggadocio disappeared at the thought of getting this close and losing. "It would be terrible," he said. "Not for me—I'm used to dying—but for the young players."

Since Kate Smith was booked for a taping of *The Mike Douglas Show* in Philadelphia on Monday, there was little suspense as to where she would be on Sunday. "What could be better than being linked with something so wholesome as good, clean sport?" Miss Smith told the *Bulletin's* Joe Adcock.

Obviously, she had not seen the venomous Game 5. But even if she had, on May 19, 1974, the Flyers looked like angels to her and the 17,077 fans who possessed the most coveted ticket ever to a Philadelphia sporting event.

The organ, pushed onto the ice prior to Smith's introduction, drew a standing ovation. The roar of the crowd drowned out Kate's final "home sweet home," but the Flyers already knew where they were and believed it was going to make the difference. When the puck dropped, they were ready to play the game of their lives.

Philadelphia received the first two penalties, but Parent remained composed. When MacLeish, crossing in front of the goal in a four-on-three situation, tipped Dupont's drive past Gilbert's pad at 14:48 of the first period, the Flyers had the precious lead and the resolve to make it stand.

They killed six Boston power plays. Clarke and MacLeish dominated Esposito and Sheppard on key face-offs. Nolet, never a checker, dedicated himself to that task as Dornhoefer's replacement, and Lonsberry was one of the best players on the ice. Dupont settled down after some early giveaways and, as the contest moved along and the margin for error shrunk, Van Impe and Jimmy Watson were faultless.

Orr played for fourteen and a half minutes of the second period under constant bumping by Flyer forecheckers. Defensively, he blocked shots and made up two and three stride deficits to foil Flyer rushes. But on the power play, Orr showed signs of arm weariness, often missing the net.

Parent, positioning himself in front of the traffic at the top of the crease, devoured whatever the

Bruins served. In the third period, Bobby Schmautz stole the puck from Lonsberry behind the goal and Vadnais worked a give-and-go with Sheppard to gain a step on Joe Watson. Parent, at full extension, brilliantly gloved Vadnais's 25-footer.

With less than three minutes remaining, Cashman turned at his own blue line and whipped a cross-ice pass to a breaking Hodge, who took the puck on the blueline and completed his follow-through 10 feet above the top of the circle. The shot, six inches off the ice and close to the inside of the far post, could hardly have been better placed. "Tie game," Crisp thought to himself, but Parent, with perfect balance and timing, kicked the puck away.

Barber chased down the rebound and fed Crisp, who ran a pick at center and sent Clarke on what would have been a breakaway had not Orr made up for a 30-foot head start and grabbed the Philadelphia captain by the arm. Referee Art Skov called a holding infraction that put a raging Orr into the penalty box.

With only 22 seconds left in the game, Orr emerged from the box and mindlessly shot the puck down the ice as the Spectrum went insane. Parent hugged the post as the puck slid by the net and Joe Watson skated back to touch up. He wanted to let the clock expire but, fearing a delay-of-game penalty and a last faceoff in the Flyer end, put his stick on the puck with 2 seconds remaining.

By that time, streamers were already coming down and Flyers were jumping off the bench. Crisp took the souvenir puck from the linesman, and the Bruins, who would have had to go the length of the ice in an impossibly short time, did not argue for the missing seconds. At 5:01 P.M., the Flyers, 1-0 winners, were the Stanley Cup champions.

Fans leaped over the boards and filled the ice surface. The players completed their handshake line, but the Flyers, presented the Cup by Clarence Campbell amidst the bedlam, were able to take only a few feet of their triumphant skate.

At the buzzer, Shero had walked directly from the bench through the tunnel to his office. He took off his glasses, sat down behind his desk, and drank a beer. The coach shook slightly as he answered questions and joined the locker room reverie only long enough to pose for a few pictures.

Ashbee, wearing dark glasses, stood against the wall of the locker room watching the celebration. "You might never see another bunch like this," he told the *Daily News's* Fleischman. "I don't cry much, but I was in tears the last minute and a half. I've never

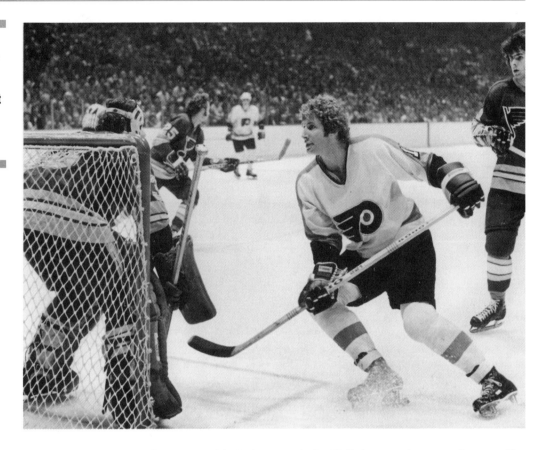

been so proud of a bunch of guys in my life. We've
had so many setbacks."

Orr, looking for Joe Watson, his old roommate,
sneaked into a room where some Flyers celebrated.
Watson offered him champagne. "No, I don't deserve
it," Orr said.

Guidolin complained bitterly about the Orr penalty, criticized the selection of Parent over Clarke
for the Conn Smythe Trophy, and called Kate's appearance a "bleeping circus." But Orr offered the best
analysis.

"We went in spurts," he said. "When you go to the
finals, you don't play in spurts. Call it momentum or
desire, whatever it was, they had more of it than we
had."

The Flyers stayed in the locker room with wives,
parents and girlfriends for more than two hours.
Asked about his party plans, Clarke said, "I'll just
follow Bernie. I'll walk across the water with Bernie."

The team tried to adjourn to Rexy's, its regular
hangout in Mount Ephraim, New Jersey, but the
place was too mobbed to accomodate the guests of
honor. At Compton's in Haddon Township, the players were given a private room away from the Delaware Valley's public party.

At City Hall, there was dancing in the street. Five
naked men on a flatbed truck tossed their underwear
into a crowd at the intersection of Broad and
Dickinson. Occupants of cars stopped at red lights
were being kissed by pedestrians. On streets and in
taverns, drunken renditions of "God Bless America"
were performed endlessly. About 10,000 persons
jammed the area of Frankford and Cottman Avenues,
where police assistance was needed when vandals
overturned a bus and smashed windows.

Parent woke up the next morning wondering if it
had all been a dream, so he looked to the *Inquirer* on
his doorstep for confirmation. "Miracle Flyers Take
the Cup And City Goes Wild With Joy," read the headline. "I guess we did it," Parent said.

A few hours later, players met with Shero at the
Spectrum to convey their thanks. Then they rode in
open convertibles for a parade to a reviewing stand
at Independence Park.

The police, who had expected a crowd of several
hundred thousand, were staggered by a throng of two
million. The Flyers were overwhelmed—and sometimes frightened—as fans reached into their cars to
offer drinks, touch them and tear at their clothes.

The vehicle carrying Clarke and Van Impe became

so inundated in South Philadelphia that neither player made it to the ceremony. "People were pulling at him, pushing him, throwing things at him," said Sandy Clarke, Bobby's wife. "He got hit on his sore leg with a can of beer and somebody grabbed his hand and almost yanked him out of the car."

As Crisp's automobile passed Broad and Porter Streets, he saw a police horse kick a 6-year-old boy, Frankie Hudson of South Philadelphia, in the face. The youngster, who needed extensive plastic surgery, suffered the only serious injuries during a day of mass euphoria.

"Bernie, Bernie, Impeach Nixon," read one sign along the route. A young man pulled down his pants to reveal "Flyers No. 1" on his bare backside. A State Store on Chestnut Street sold more than 1,000 bottles to parade spectators before employees stopped counting.

It took three hours for the motorcade to reach the historical area, where Shero spoke. "You've got the greatest team in hockey here," he said, "and you're going to win the Cup again next year."

Kindrachuk, who had ridden in the car with the bubbly, acknowledged his introduction, flashed a triumphant peace sign, and swooned backwards into his teammates arms. "Sheer exhaustion," he recalls. "I hate champagne."

Two days later, Parent, *Sport* magazine's MVP of the playoffs, was presented with a car. He gave the keys to Shero. "I have enough happiness the last three days to last a lifetime," the coach said before going to Moscow for a clinic run by his idol, Tarasov.

The Flyers left for a summer of hometown adulation, but five days after the clinching, Allen was already planning the defense of the Cup. For two years, he had been pursuing Seals' right wing Reggie Leach, Clarke's junior linemate in Flin Flon. Flett's decreasing goal production—from 43 to 17, then to zero in the playoffs—and his increasing alcohol consumption gave the GM reason to make a major change on a championship team.

The Seals, being run by the league and appointed caretaker Munson Campbell while they awaited new ownership, accepted Allen's offer of the Flyers' 1976

No. 1 draft choice (fifteenth overall) and Richmond players Larry Wright and Don McCulloch in exchange for Leach. But Clarence Campbell called Allen and threatened to void a deal the NHL president felt was exploiting the orphaned franchise. Campbell accepted Allen's substitution of a better prospect, right wing Al MacAdam, for McCulloch, enabling the trade to be closed.

"[Leach] has never played with a good team or a good center man as a pro," Allen told the media. "He

has a chance to be a star."

Three days later, Flett was traded to the Maple Leafs for two lukewarm Toronto prospects, defenseman Dave Fortier and left wing Randy Osburn. Fortier was quickly lost to the Islanders in the intraleague draft.

A scar in the central portion of Ashbee's right retina took away almost all of his depth perception, so upon the recommendation of Dr. William Tasman, the defenseman retired. "These things happen and you just have to accept them," Ashbee said at a June 4 press conference. "The one good thing I've found out from this is that this old world isn't such a bad place after all. I can't begin to count the number of letters I've had from people offering to give me one of their eyes.

"I'm just happy that I was able to get my name on the Stanley Cup once. I look at it this way. I'm only 35. I've got a long time to live."

Although best known for his fighting, Schultz also recorded two hat-tricks.

Ashbee considered Snider's offer of a job in the organization to have been made out of pity, but later in the summer relented and agreed to a one-year trial as an assistant coach.

Allen found another silver lining in the premature loss of Ashbee. The Flyers had one less player to protect from the expansion draft stocking new franchises in Washington and Kansas City. To keep Joe Watson, the GM struck agreements with the Capitals to take Richmond goalie Michel Belhumeur

Wayne Stephenson answers questions after filling in for an injured Bernie Parent.

who returned from Moscow and told *Maclean's* magazine that he had gone to the famed Gorki Monastery to pray he would not have to leave Philadelphia for a $100,000-a-year offer from the WHA's Minnesota Fighting Saints. "Mr. Snider answered those prayers," said Shero after getting a raise from $28,000 to $75,000 per season.

Snider bought patches in the shape of the Stanley Cup to put on the uniforms of the defending champions, but the players found them ostentatious and declined. "I thought it would start a new tradition," shrugged the owner. It was Snider's only setback of the summer. He became sole owner of the Spectrum by buying out the 50 percent share of his brother-in-law, Earl Foreman. Snider also sold a package of Flyer home games to a test cable system in South Philadelphia. Five thousand subscribers could receive 25 games for $100.

The 1974-75 season opened with Frankie Hudson, the boy kicked by the horse at the Stanley Cup parade, dropping the first puck. The Kings took some of the fun out of the banner-raising ceremony by winning 5-3, and three nights later Nolet tried to play spoiler, too. The ex-Flyer drew a standing ovation at the Spectrum when he bamboozled Clarke on a shorthanded goal. The Flyers barely squeaked by Kansas City, 3-2.

On October 25, Philadelphia trailed 4-0 at Oakland

and with the Scouts to select Nolet.

Allen then made two deals with St. Louis, filling Ashbee's playing slot by purchasing 38-year-old Ted Harris and improving the backup goaltending situation by trading a No. 2 pick in the 1975 draft and the rights to WHA defector Randy Andreachuk, for 29-year-old Wayne Stephenson.

"I'm surprised," said Bobby Taylor, who had played in only 8 games the previous season, "and I'm a little shook up."

Snider's pocketbook was also rattled by Shero,

when Kindrachuk, penalized two additional minutes for a fight with Mike Christie, climbed over the time-keeper's table to wrestle with the Seals' rookie defenseman. Kelly led a charge off the bench and the Flyers virtually sealed Christie away from his teammates' help. While being held by Kindrachuk, Christie was punched in the face by Kelly, then Saleski, before dropping his arms. "Go ahead, you bastards, go ahead and hit me," said the bleeding defenseman. Saleski and Kelly accepted the offer.

Christie needed eleven stitches. The Flyers, in the

opinion of many, needed to be locked up. "It's pretty bad when you have to send three guys against one," said Christie after the Seals' 4-1 victory. The combined total of 237 penalty minutes for both teams was a new NHL single-game high, while the Flyers hit a new low in behavior.

"It's the one thing I look back on with regret," Saleski says today. "I wound up playing with Christie (in 1979-80 at Colorado) and he was a nice guy. He had a big scar under his eye from where I

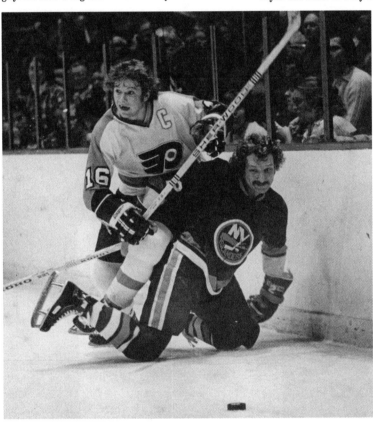

hit him. Who ever thought a punch I threw could do that much damage? It's hard for me to see myself having done those things."

Yet at the time, the Flyers were hardly contrite. They blamed referee Bryan Lewis for lighting Kindrachuk's fuse, rationalized their behavior as frustration from being blown out of the game, and even faulted the Seals for not coming to Christie's aid. When Saleski and Kelly were suspended for six games each (Kindrachuk was only fined $300), Clarke ripped Clarence Campbell. "I think it's time he got out of there and they gave it to somebody who could do a decent job," said the Flyer captain.

Allen made Clarke call and apologize. "[Campbell] was very good about it," recalls Clarke.

Reprehensible as it was, the incident seemed to wake up the struggling Flyers, who immediately began a 10-game unbeaten streak with a 3-2 victory in Vancouver. Soon, they were the runaway leaders of the newly formed Lester Patrick Division, where they had been placed with the Rangers, Islanders and Flames.

Leach, who scored only 4 goals in his first 19 games, began jumping into holes and recorded his first Flyer hat trick to bury Detroit, 6-2, on November 27. Soon Philadelphia reeled off another unbeaten streak of 12 games. Parent had seven shutouts in the first 37 contests and made the cover of *Time* magazine. By February 8, Schultz broke his one-season penalty record, a fete that brought another round of media apoplexy and criticism from a coaching staff trying to get him under better control.

As the Hammer began to watch his step, MacLeish fell asleep. The Flyers, playing 19 road games in a 28-contest stretch, let a 3-7-3 February skid shrink their 14-point lead to four.

But Leach kicked off a February 27 homestand by scoring a goal and two assists in a 3-1 victory over Vancouver, and Philadelphia began another tear. On March 23, a 2-1 win over Montreal broke the Canadiens' 23-game road unbeaten streak and helped the Flyers make up what had been a 9-point deficit in the race for the league's best record.

With a weekend sweep of Chicago on March 29 and 30, Philadelphia moved into the driver's seat. So did Ashbee when his teammates gave him a new camper on a night held in his honor on April 3. Victories over the Islanders and Atlanta on the final weekend climaxed a 16-1-2 finish that gave the Flyers 113 points and 51 victories, one more in each category than the preceeding season. Parent finished with 44 wins and 12 shutouts. Leach scored 45 goals, Clarke was plus-79 and Philadelphia earned home-ice ad-

Clarke runs over Gerry Hart of the Islanders.

vantage throughout the playoffs.

Under an expanded 12-team playoff format, the division champions awaited the winners of best-of-three preliminary rounds. The Flyers drew the 78-point Maple Leafs who had stunned the 105-point Kings, then opened Game 1 at the Spectrum as though they meant to stay in business through another series. Toronto scored twice during a five-minute Dupont match penalty (for head-butting) to take a 3-2 lead into the third period. But Dornhoefer

their charter flight home to the tune of Schultz's debut single, "Penalty Box," scheduled to hit the airwaves of WIBG and WFIL, Philadelphia's AM-radio Top 40 giants, within the week. "Love is like an ice-hockey game," sang the Hammer, "...you get me checking and holding and hooking and then you blow the whistle on me."

Fortunately, the Flyers had a full week to stop laughing before beginning their series with an Islanders' team that had to be taken seriously. After stun-

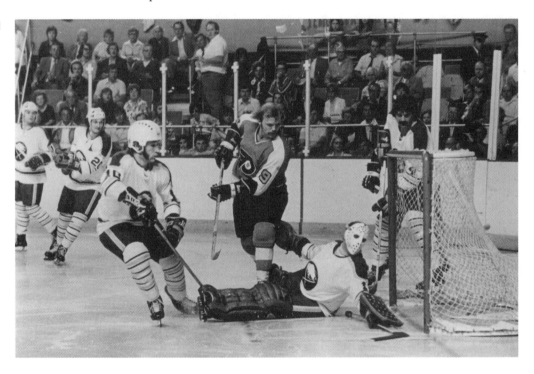

Bob Kelly scores 1975's Stanley Cup-winning goal in Buffalo.

intercepted a clear by Swedish defensive whiz Borje Salming and fed Barber, who ignited a three-goal barrage on goalie Gord McRae within 2:37. MacLeish completed a hat trick into the empty net, giving the Flyers a 5-3 victory.

In Game 2, Kelly banged in the corners twice to set up goals by Crisp, Clarke shut down rising star center Darryl Sittler, and Parent recorded a 3-0 shutout. When the series moved to Maple Leaf Gardens, Parent again blanked the Leafs, 2-0. "I can't believe how good Bernie's become," said Favell, Toronto's backup goalie.

The Leafs put up a determined last stand and Ron Ellis's rebound goal with 6:37 remaining tied Game 4, 3-3. But in overtime, Schultz intercepted a pass, carried into the Leaf end and dropped the puck to Dupont, whose 20-foot wrister went through McRae to wrap up the series. The Flyers boogied on

ning the Rangers in the preliminary round, the third-year franchise from Long Island became the second club in NHL history to rally from a 3-0 series deficit when it eliminated Pittsburgh.

The Flyers, who had played only four games in three weeks, fussed about being rusty until a Dornhoefer warmup shot caught Parent in an unprotected area above the knee before Game 1. Then, the players had real reason to worry.

"I thought, 'Get up, Bernie! Get up!'" said Stephenson, who had played in just 12 games all season. Xrays at the hospital proved negative, unlike the Flyers' response to the crisis. They protected Stephenson grandly in a 4-0 shutout.

In Game 2, the Flyers were ahead 4-1 and seemingly on their way to another routine win when they suddenly hit the wall from the long layoff. After J.P. Parise made it 4-2, Denis Potvin ripped the second of two Islander goals in 14 seconds between Stephenson's legs to tie the game. But the goalie came back to rob rookie right wing Bob Nystrom in overtime, just before Clarke went to the net for a Lonsberry rebound and kicked in the winner at 2:56.

The Islanders screamed the goal should not have counted. But more importantly, they had reason to believe they were not overmatched. "This should be a long struggle now," predicted Potvin.

The two teams held each other scoreless in Game 3 at the Nassau Coliseum until the first shift of the third period, when Leach cut outside on defenseman Dave Lewis. Rookie goalie Chico Resch challenged to the bottom of the circle, so Leach looped a backhander over the glove of Resch that dropped into the goal like an iron shot onto a green. Parent had to make only 14 saves in a 1-0 shutout.

For the second consecutive series, the Islanders found themselves down 3-0. "They've got you right where they want you now," someone joked to Shero. He refused to laugh, especially when New York used two power-play goals to jump ahead 3-0 in Game 4. Not until Schultz beat up Gary Howatt was the tide turned. Dornhoefer fed Lonsberry to get the comeback started in the third period, then MacLeish scored on a wrist shot and on a breakaway to tie the game.

It seemed like the Flyers had regained control. And with one more second, it would have been over. Leach, taking a passout by Barber, fought off Lorne Henning's check and fired between Resch's legs at the buzzer, but the green light signifying the end of the period had flashed briefly before the red one went on. After talking to the timekeeper, referee Newell disallowed the goal. The Flyers barely argued. They believed in their inevitability until Jude Drouin's backhander 1:53 into overtime returned the series to Philadelphia.

The strange turn of events seemed to knock some confidence out of the Flyers. They came out tentatively in Game 5 and Parise's shot deflected in off the post to give New York a 1-0 lead. Philadelphia took 13 shots before the Islanders had one in the second period and appeared to be taking control before Parent muffed a catchable Billy Harris drive. Drouin then undressed Bladon to make it 3-0 and leave the Flyers deflated.

As usual, Schultz attempted to leave a bare-knuckled calling card for the next meeting, but was thrashed by Islander rookie Clark Gillies. "We're starting to find our way out of the woods," said Resch hopefully after New York's shocking 5-1 victory, the

Flyers first home playoff loss in two years.

Larry Goodenough, recalled from Richmond late in the season, replaced the struggling Bladon in Game 6 at Uniondale and Lonsberry tipped in a shot by Joe Watson after only 1:42. Potvin, however, tied the score while Clarke was in the penalty box. Early in the third period, Goodenough attempted to clear after Parent had made superior saves on Ralph Stewart and Gerry Hart, but put the puck right back on Hart's stick. He fired over Parent's glove and the Islanders held on for a 2-1 victory. The Flyers, who had been a split second away from winning the series in four straight, were now going to Game 7.

"We know this shouldn't be happening," said Crisp, "but it's like a bad nightmare where you run and run and get nowhere."

Potvin's voice seemed to come from the grave. "Some external force seems to be driving us," he said. "If I were the Flyers, I'd be damn worried."

Indeed, the Flyer power play—2-for-23 in the series—wasn't exactly confidence-inspiring, but Shero put on his poker face. "A little pressure, a little stress is good for an athlete," he insisted. "The only people not under stress are dead."

The Flyers retreated to a hotel in Valley Forge, enjoyed dinner and a few beers, and searched their souls. "If you don't play hard, we can't win," Clarke scolded the laconic MacLeish. Shero, on the suggestions of Nykoluk and Crisp, decided to turn loose a second forechecker. And an emergency call went out to you-know-who. Kate Smith had been secretly booked for Game 1 of the finals, but the Flyers' moon was in imminent danger of going over the mountain. Seidman reached Philadelphia's lucky charm in West Palm Beach.

The teams were circling the ice before the faceoff when the lights went out and a roar went up. Through the darkness, the fans could see the carpet being unrolled and the organ being pushed into Resch's crease. The Spectrum was bedlam, but the Islanders were nonplussed.

As the accompanist vamped and Kate blew kisses to the crowd, Eddie Westfall handed the singer a flower bouquet that a friend of Hart's had sent with good luck wishes during the day. As the crowd booed, the Islanders lined up one by one to tell Miss Smith "God Bless You." She graciously accepted both the flowers and their handshakes. "Those Islanders tried to shake me up," she said later, "but both my feet were on the ground."

She belted out the Flyer hymnal before 17,077 revivalists and keepers of the faith, who drowned out her last few bars while tears streamed down Joe Watson's face. The building was still vibrating when Jimmy Watson forced Westfall to turn over the puck at center on the first shift of the game. The fans thundered at the sight of Dornhoefer suddenly one-on-one against Bert Marshall, then inhaled as the Flyer winger went into his backswing 40 feet away from the goal. When the puck, whizzing by Resch on the short side, exploded into the back of the net, the earth shook.

over her wires."

Islander coach Al Arbour, conceded graciously, however. "The teams that should be in the finals are there," he said, although the Flyers, relieved to see Montreal eliminated by Buffalo in six games, secretly disagreed about the Sabres' worthiness.

Buffalo had risen to power in only its fifth NHL season behind the offensive might of the dazzling French Connection line—Gilbert Perreault, Rick Martin and Rene Robert. The Sabres also had a solid

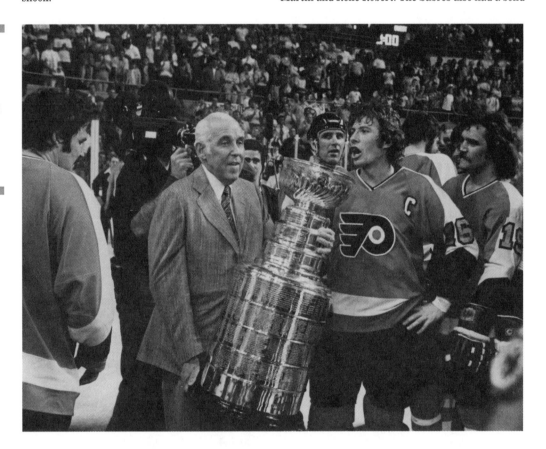

Clarence Campbell presents the Stanley Cup to the Flyers for a second time on May 27, 1975.

After only 19 seconds, the Flyers led. MacLeish made it 2-0 at 2:27 by redirecting Barber's power-play point drive, then countered Drouin's five-on-three goal by beating Resch with a rising wrister before nine minutes had been played. Philadelphia had a working 3-1 lead and the Islanders, who managed just 15 shots in the game, had no chance. When MacLeish completed his hat trick into the empty net, sign man Dave Leonardi held up "Midnight" behind the New York goal.

A bitter Resch sounded as ugly as the stepsisters. "It wasn't fair," he said. "They stuck that organ right in my crease. She must have been out there fifteen minutes. I lost concentration. I should have skated

second unit composed of Don Luce, Craig Ramsay and Danny Gare. But the defense, while big and aggressive, was not very smart, and Buffalo's veteran goalies, Gerry Desjardins and Roger Crozier, were nowhere near Parent's class. The Sabres had managed just one point in their last nine meetings with the Flyers and since birth were 0-11-2 at the Spectrum.

Philadelphia had won most of those games similarly to the way it took Game 1. The Flyers had to kill seven manpower disadvantages in the first forty minutes, but when the contest remained scoreless into the third period, they were confident they would still break through. Sure enough, Desjardins leaned the wrong way as a Van Impe shot came off the end boards, and Barber swept in the carom. Lonsberry and Clarke sandwiched goals around Martin's power-play tally and the Flyers went on to a 4-1 victory.

Again in Game 2, the Sabres fired wildly and the Flyers bided their time. Clarke dug the puck out of a five-man scrum in the right circle and fed Leach for a 1-0 second-period lead. Jim Lorentz got away from Saleski to feed defenseman Jerry Korab's tying goal early in the third period, but on the next Flyer power play, Barber drew Korab out of position and slipped the puck along the left side of the net to Clarke. Desjardins didn't square to the shooter and Clarke hit the long side at 6:43. The Sabres did not manage a shot the rest of the game and the Flyers, 2-1 winners, took a 2-0 lead to Buffalo.

When Dornhoefer converted a Barber-forced giveaway after only 39 seconds, and Saleski scored less than three minutes later, the Flyers appeared to be in command of Game 3 and the series. But as the late-spring temperatures and an un-airconditioned Memorial Auditorium combined to cause the ice to gradually become enshrouded by fog, Philadelphia's chances of making short work of the series evaporated.

The chamber of horrors where the Flyers had been tortured out of a playoff spot in 1972 was transformed into a Transylvanian castle. A bat flitting above the players' heads was chopped out of the air by Lorentz. It was a game neither the Audubon Society nor the goaltenders enjoyed. Twelve times, play

was stopped so the teams could skate around the ice to dissipate the fog.

Coach Floyd Smith replaced the shaky Desjardins with Crozier and the Sabres began to fight back. Midway through the third period, defenseman Bill Hajt lifted in a rebound to tie the game, 4-4.

As fatigue set in, fewer players chose to participate in the fog-chasing drills. The overtime lasted 18:29 largely because of the energy drain. Barber had come off, probably too early, when Perreault dumped

Parent and Clarke skate a victory lap around Buffalo's Memorial Aud.

the puck toward the corner from center ice. Robert, almost on the goal line, one-timed the carom towards the net. Parent looked set but the puck whizzed past his skates to end the game.

The Fog, of course, was not annoyed by the fog. "In 1948, in Houston," said Shero, "it was so bad we were on our hands and knees looking for the puck. We couldn't find it, so they called the game."

The Sabres hired local skaters to gather the condensation in bedsheets during Game 4, in which the Flyers twice grabbed one-goal leads. But the Sabres drew even both times on power plays and took a 3-2 lead when Lorentz jammed in a goalmouth feed late in the second period. After Lonsberry hit the post with 3:01 to go, Gare scored into the empty net and Buffalo, 4-2 winners, tied the series.

The Flyers had given the French Connection, usu-ally well contained by the MacLeish-Lonsberry-Dornhoefer unit, too much room to skate. And Clarke was disgusted with the effort. Before the locker room was opened to the media, the captain lectured his teammates, some of whom he knew had imbibed too much the night before, that they were stupidly throw-ing away an opportunity. "I sensed a few players were trying to get by without making a full commitment," Clarke recalls.

More than 2.3 million people turned out for the second Stanley Cup parade, shown here rounding City Hall below the statue of William Penn.

Before Game 5 at the Spectrum, Marcel Pelletier, the Flyers' player personnel director, pointed out to Nykoluk that the team was helping Desjardins by too much passing. The advice was taken to heart. Schultz, who had barely been used by Shero in the series, chased a corner dump-in three minutes into the game, turned and fired a goal off Desjardins' shoulder. Dornhoefer then cranked up from an equally terrible angle in the opposite corner and placed a goal on Desjardins's short side. Nineteen seconds later, Kelly whizzed past Rick Dudley and Larry Carriere and beat the beleaguered goalie from the slot. The Flyers led 3-0 before hardly working up a sweat.

They protected the lead sloppily, but the Sabres packed it in before Schultz scored his second goal on a breakaway feed from Goodenough. The Flyers, 5-1 winners, were one victory away from another Cup, but their coach was unhappy with their poor concentration. Shero did not speak to the media and ordered a change of hotels in Buffalo to get away from fans and reporters.

Desjardins wanted no part of Game 6. "I'm getting to the point where I hate hockey," he said. The Flyers helped Crozier by being shorthanded five times during the scoreless first two periods, when Parent somehow kicked out power-play drives by Korab and Jocelyn Guevremont, making difficult saves look routine. "Any other goalie, I say he was lucky," said Guevremont. "But Parent makes impossible saves with one eye closed."

Shero, worried that his key penalty killers were out of gas, was urged by Nykoluk at intermission to use Kelly, who had enjoyed two strong shifts early in the second period. The rambunctious winger started the third in Barber's place.

Clarke won the face-off and Leach dumped the puck down the right side. Kelly busted diagonally across the ice and got a standoff with Korab until Clarke arrived. The captain shouldered the 215-pound defenseman, spinning him off long enough for Kelly to pop free. He picked the puck off the base of the back of the net, took a big swing out front to keep Crozier from pokechecking, and beat the goalie along the ice just inside the far post. Eleven seconds into the period, the Flyers led, 1-0.

Dornhoefer and MacLeish both made bids for an insurance goal, but Crozier held the Sabres in the game. The Flyers, meanwhile, obsessively protected Parent. Saleski hooked Dudley as he carried to the slot, and Van Impe blocked a dangerous backhander by Martin.

Philadelphia carefully dumped the puck out on almost every possession down the stretch, but Buffalo continued to turn up scoring chances. Parent calmly sticked aside a Jim Schoenfeld drive labeled for the far corner, then somehow saw and trapped a Guevremont shot that came out of Joe Watson's legs. Ramsay, set up by a Guevremont pinch on Barber, was all alone thirty feet in front of the goal, but lifted a backhander into Parent's midsection.

With three minutes remaining, Kindrachuk took advantage of Korab's slow backswing and blocked his point shot. Brian Spencer chased Kindrachuk for the puck in the neutral zone, and Korab stupidly did, too, leaving Clement alone in the center of the rink.

"I heard somebody yell," said Kindrachuk. "I had no idea who it was." He laid a soft pass into Clement's path before being buried by Korab. Clement went in one-on-one against Crozier, who spread out expecting the Flyer center to deke and go wide. Instead, Clement held the puck all the way to the hashmarks and scored between the goalie's legs.

From beneath Korab, Kindrachuk saw stars. But he also heard the blessed silence of the air rushing out of the Sabres and the "Aud". Leading 2-0 with only 2:47 left, all the Flyers had to do was play it safe and smart through several more face-offs.

"Congratulations," said Luce to Clarke before they took the last draw in the Philadelphia end with 2 seconds remaining.

"Thank you," said Clarke. He pulled the puck back, dutifully screened Luce, and counted to two. Then the captain leaped, turned, and danced on the toes of his skates toward Parent. The Flyers were champions, again.

As they mobbed Parent, Shero let his players enjoy their own moment. The coach refused Nykoluk's invitation to join the celebration and walked to the locker room. "I'm happier this year than I was last year," said Shero. "We proved it wasn't a fluke. Last year there was no pressure, we got into the finals against Boston and before they woke up, it was over. In these playoffs, we were expected to win."

The Buffalo fans, who had spent the final minute chanting "Thank You, Sabres," applauded when Parent, who had clinched the Cup with a shutout for the second straight year, repeated as Conn Smythe Trophy winner. They also clapped as Parent and Clarke accepted the Cup from Clarence Campbell and led their teammates in the circle around the ice that they had been denied by the Spectrum mob a year earlier.

The Flyers made only one turn, then went to the locker room to splash champagne and drink mostly beer. Van Impe, wanting to make sure he remembered everything, abstained. There had been no thrill comparable to winning the first Cup and no satisfaction like repeating. "We didn't goon it up the whole playoffs," said Lonsberry. "We just played hockey."

Dornhoefer and Kelly, both injured for the clincher the previous May, glowed. "You have to be there in the end to feel like you made a contribution," Kelly said. He then told a guy sitting on the bench in front of his clothes to get the hell out of his seat. Pennsylvania Governor Milton Shapp apologized and moved on to congratulate someone else.

As Ted Harris walked to the team bus, a boy wearing a Sabres shirt asked, "Are you happy, Mr. Harris?" "Yes," said the 38-year-old defenseman, "because that was the last hockey game I'll ever play."

In Philadelphia, horns blared and crowds formed at intersections along Broad Street. Cars were stopped by celebrating fans in the Northeast neighborhoods. Streakers ran, beer cans popped, and marijuana burned. Hospital emergency rooms filled with patients who had suffered twisted ankles jumping off cars, or who were cut from broken beer bottles. Sixty-five persons were treated.

The Flyers partied on their 50-minute jet ride home. Then, after Clarke and Parent insisted Shero carry the Cup down the plane's steps, the team joined their families at the Spectrum Blueline Club at 2:30 A.M. to continue their celebration. They left at 4:30 and were at the parade starting site—18th and Locust Streets—at 11:00 A.M.

Having learned hard lessons in crowd control the previous spring, city officials placed the players on flatbed trucks rather than in open convertibles for the procession down Broad Street to a rally at JFK Stadium. When nervous policemen asked Shero to stop leaning over to shake hands, he frowned.

"I believe this day belongs to the people of the city just as much as it belongs to us," the coach said. "They supported us all year and what are they asking in return? Just a handshake or a chance to touch one of us. I don't think they should be denied that."

Despite thirty six hospital-treated injuries—seven to policemen—the parade went much more smoothly than in 1974. The only delay came when Parent asked off his truck, knocked at the door of a random house in the 1500 block of South Broad Street, and was invited in to use the bathroom.

One hundred thousand fans were in the stadium when the Flyers entered at 12:45 P.M. The crowd, parade route and stadium combined, was estimated at 2.3 million– 300,000 more than the previous May.

The trucks made two turns around the stadium track and came to a stop at a platform set up on the field. There, Shero announced to his wife, Mariette, and the world that he loved her. The coach of the two-time champions said he felt that way towards Philadelphia, too. "This city is beautiful," said Shero. "It doesn't realize just how beautiful yet, but maybe it's learning."

Chapter 6

Dethroned and Defogged

Bill Clement had already been traded when he scored the goal that put away the second Stanley Cup. During the finals, Flyer GM Keith Allen had shaken hands with Washington GM Milt Schmidt on an exchange of Clement, defenseman Don McLean (Philadelphia'a second-round choice in 1974) and the Flyers' first-round pick (eighteenth) to the Capitals for the first-overall selection.

The deal was not announced until the morning of the June draft. Clement, who read rumors involving him and Dave Schultz on the day of Game 6, was hardly surprised. "I remember on the ride home after we won, talking to Davey," recalls Clement. "He told me he had been thinking so much about getting traded, he couldn't get his head into the game."

Because the NHL had allowed each of its clubs to select one underage player in 1974, the 1975 draft did not yield a blue-chip prospect. Nevertheless, Allen and his scouts felt Victoria center Mel

Reggie Leach awaits a pass: "It's so easy. All I have to do is get in the slot and wait for Clarkie to get me the puck."

Bridgman, who scored 157 points in his final junior season, would be the perfect Flyer. Although slower than Clement, the rookie was a more physical player and four years younger.

Bridgman reported to camp fighting homesickness but, with a formidable center-ice corps of Bobby Clarke, Rick MacLeish, Orest Kindrachuk and Terry Crisp, no immediate pressure was put on the recruit.

Preseason was uneventful until seven days before the opener when Bernie Parent came to prac-

Viner, then the Flyers' team physician. "But (Dr.) Fred Simeon (chief of neurosurgery at Pennsylvania Hospital) agreed it should be done."

On October 14, Dr. Simeon performed a cervical laminectomy and Wolf estimated recovery time at three to four weeks. "Doctors don't stop pucks," said Fred Shero, skeptical of the optimistic timetable. The coach then expressed confidence in Stephenson. Sort of. "Unless we get somebody better, we'll go with him," Shero said. "He's never had to play that much be-

Moscow's Central Red Army team leaves the ice en route to the locker room at the Spectrum.

tice complaining of pain in his neck and elbow, a more severe version of a problem he had felt during the Islander series. Trainer Frank Lewis massaged Parent, but as he moved during drills, pain shot down his arm. The goalie went home and tried muscle relaxants prescribed by Dr. John Wolf, the team orthopedist. They didn't work. Neither did a few days of traction at Abington (Memorial) Hospital.

The Flyers' 3-0 start behind Wayne Stephenson did not make the reading of Parent's milogram—a herniated cervical disc—less painful. "Subjecting a high-priced goalie to the trauma of cervical surgery was not an easy decision to make," recalls Dr. Edward

fore. Now his stamina is going to be tested."

"I'm nervous, sure," said the 30-year-old Stephenson. "But I'm ready to go until they don't need me or I drop." Bobby Taylor, who had barely played in two years, went to Springfield to sharpen his skills in case of an emergency, leaving Jerome (Moses) Mrazek, a bearded eighth-round draft choice from the University of Minnesota-Duluth, as the backup.

Mrazek could play guitar, but no one was certain he could tend goal. Fortunately, Stephenson remained healthy while Mrazek kept the Flyers entertained. "A few songs I've written aren't bad," he said. "But they're not that good, either."

The Flyers sang to a 9-1-2 start that included a

2-2 comeback tie in Montreal and an 8-1 Spectrum smashing of Boston. Ed Van Impe needed hernia surgery and missed a month, but Jack McIlhargey, a free-agent signee armed with a windmilling right fist and a healthy knowledge of his own limitations, provided what Allen euphemistically referred to as "that certain element."

When a joust between Gary Dornhoefer and the Penguins' Steve Durbano on November 9 escalated into a scrum, McIlhargey tore 110 feet from the

after his Canadiens were buried by a 49-27 shot disadvantage in a 3-1 Spectrum loss on November 16. "You would expect our team to be as hungry."

Reggie Leach scored his 20th goal during the club's 31st game, a 4-2 victory at Chicago on December 17, while linemates Clarke and Bill Barber were also headed for record seasons. "It's so easy," said Leach. "All I have to do is get in the slot and wait for Clarkie to get me the puck."

Even though Parent experienced arm pain when

NHL president Clarence Campbell talks to the press after the Russian walkout.

bench and dove at Pittsburgh's Harvey Bennett, the top man in a pileup. Bennett ducked and McIlhargey hit the boards headfirst. He was unhurt, unlike Shero's feelings when Penguin trainer Ken Carson insisted he heard the Flyer coach order McIlhargey off the bench. "If he wants to take a lie detector test, he'll take one and I'll take one," said Shero.

It was the truth, the whole truth and nothing but the truth that playing at the Spectrum terrified most visiting teams. As Philadelphia played 18 of its first 28 games at home, most of the shots Stephenson faced were mailed from safe places where opponents would not get hurt. "The Flyers controlled the boards," said coach Scotty Bowman

he tried practicing on November 27 and went back into traction, the Flyers, 22-4-8 at Christmas, looked too good for the rest of the NHL. Intriguingly, a greater challenge was on the way. On Sunday, January 11, the Flyers were to be the last of four NHL teams scheduled to play the Central Red Army, perennial Soviet champions and main supplier of members to the U.S.S.R. national team.

Since Team Canada's skin-of-its-teeth 4-3-1 victory in the 1972 Summit confrontation, the only other series between the Soviet and North American professionals had resulted in a 4-1-3 defeat of a WHA All Star team. The coming tour would either revalidate the NHL's might or measure its decline.

The Red Army opened with a 7-3 victory over the Rangers. "If we play this badly through the series," said NHL president Clarence Campbell, "then it's obvious we shouldn't be playing with them at all." On New Year's Eve, the Canadiens outshot the Soviets 38-13 in a scintillating 3-3 tie, but failed to burst the Army's growing aura of invincibility.

The Bruins, resurgent after trading Phil Esposito and Carol Vadnais to the Rangers for Jean Ratelle and Brad Park, figured to be able to make the small Boston Garden surface work to their advantage, but the fast and free-flowing visitors adapted quickly and won, 5-2. Meanwhile, the No. 2 Soviet team—the Wings—had lost only one of its four contests, a wild 12-6 shootout in Buffalo, and finished with a 2-1 victory over the Islanders.

The Flyers were cynical at the irony of how they, the black sheep of the NHL, were to defend the league's honor, but the responsibility was accepted solemnly. After Philadelphia's final tune-up, a sloppy 6-4 Spectrum victory over Los Angeles, Shero was asked if his players had been looking ahead to the Soviets. "I don't think they were," he said, "but I know I was. You know how long I've waited for this game?"

Shero, the hockey theorist, saw the contest as the ultimate test of conflicting philosophies. The children of a three-decade-long cold war took it from there, turning a sporting event into a clash between gritty, free-enterprising North Americans and highly efficient Russian robots.

Clarke, whose vicious slash had put Soviet star Valeri Kharlamov out of the 1972 series, was asked to reflect on his lingering status as villain in the U.S.S.R. "It wasn't premeditated," said the Flyer captain. "He had speared me and it wasn't a clean series from the start.

"I don't care. I hate the sons of bitches, anyway."

On that note of international goodwill, the weekend's festivities began. The Soviets, just off the plane from Boston, showed up half an hour late for a Spectrum luncheon. "They're always pulling this stuff," Clarke grumbled.

Shero raved about the Stolichnaya vodka that had been placed on the bar and welcomed the guests to the "cradle of liberty." Then, the Tsentalnaya Sovietskaya Krasnaya Armia, perennial champions of the Soviet Union, broke bread with the Broadnaya Streetivska Bullieas, defending champions of the National Hockey League. It wasn't exactly candle-light and soft music. "I watched them," recalls Ross Lonsberry, "and they kept sneaking glances over at Schultz."

Shero assured his players that their system was tailor-made to counter the Soviets. The key was for the third Flyer forward to stay at the attacking blue line, cutting off the Army's long passes up-the-middle. When the Soviets would weave to regroup around center ice, Philadelphia wingers and defensemen were told to drop back and wait at the blue line. Shero was certain the opposition would become disoriented if unable to pass or skate the puck into the offensive zone.

Since the Soviet idea of defense was a poke check and a trapping pass to a cherry-picking forward, the Flyers figured gaining possession would not be a problem and keeping the puck would be the key. The Red Army was not expected to challenge much along the boards, leaving Philadelphia plenty of time to make good, safe plays. Shero believed his team could negate the Soviets' speed advantage by shooting judiciously and avoiding errant, diagonal passes.

The Army went to see *Jaws* at a movie theatre on Saturday night; on Sunday afternoon, they swam nervously in the Spectrum shark tank. Jewish and human rights' groups picketed outside the building while ushers inside removed anti-Soviet signs. Kate Smith's recording never sounded more patriotic as Philadelphia hoped to prove just how blessed America really was. The Flyers felt like the fate of the free world was resting on their backs.

"It was the biggest game in Flyers history," said Shero years afterwards. "We had to win or else."

The Army retreated into their own zone off the opening face-off and made eight passes before starting up ice. Clarke waited at the Soviet blue line, while the rest of the Flyers dropped back. When Alexander Maltsev finally took a 50-foot shot, Leach deflected it into the corner.

After Van Impe went to the penalty box at 9:10 of the first period for tripping Vladimir Lutchenko, Philadelphia started hitting. "It wasn't planned," said Tom Bladon later. "We were just wound up because of the pressure on us. I think it was more emotional than anything."

Andre Dupont laid a clean shoulder check into Boris Mikhailov, the Soviet captain, and Barber nailed both Valeri Vasilyev and Kharlamov. Thus, three jarring hits had been absorbed by the Army before Van Impe, exiting the penalty box, came cross-ice to elbow Kharlamov in the face as he took a pass at the blue line. The Soviet star lay on his knees, head in his gloves, while coach Konstantin Loktev waved disgustedly at NHL referee Lloyd Gilmour.

Kharlamov was helped to the bench, but Loktev

dallied putting his players on the ice. Gilmour skated toward the Army and held up two fingers, assessing a delay-of-game penalty. When the interpreter explained this to Loktev, the coach immediately waved his team into the locker room. "Their one intention," said Loktev later, "was to damage our players."

The Flyers took a few shots to keep Stephenson warm and then went to their own room. They had been warned that walkouts were a trick the Soviets used to intimidate officials. "But who knew what they were thinking?" said Barber. "I really thought they might be leaving."

Campbell, Snider and Alan Eagleson, the players' association director who had arranged the competition, went to talk to the Army. "This is no way to end a series of this kind," Campbell told Vyacheslav Koloskov, the head of the Soviet hockey federation. Koloskov agreed and convinced Loktev to bring his team back to the ice. The visitors tried negotiating their way out of the two-minute delay penalty, but Campbell was firm that it stood.

Later, the NHL president denied he had reminded Koloskov that the Soviets had not yet been paid. "Never," Campbell insisted, "did I mention the money angle. Somebody on the periphery mentioned it, that's all."

"Then I was the guy on the periphery," recalls Snider. "I told them they weren't going to get paid unless they finished the game."

Following a seventeen-minute delay, the contest resumed at 11:21 of the first period. The Flyers won the face-off and Leach hounded defenseman Vladimir Lokotko into throwing a panicked pass to the point. Barber fired the puck towards the net and Leach tipped it past goalie Vladislav Tretiak. Seventeen seconds after the Soviets returned, Philadelphia had taken an electrifying 1-0 lead.

With less than three minutes in the period, Lonsberry's pass from the left boards sprang MacLeish. Vasilyev had an angle to cut off the Flyer center until Dornhoefer ran blatant interference at the blue line. Gilmour didn't make the call and MacLeish beat Tretiak with a rising wrist shot to the glove side.

Early in the second period, Don Saleski got wide of the Army defense in a shorthanded situation and the Soviets failed to look for Joe Watson cutting up the slot. He put in a backhander to make the score 3-0 before the Army recorded its third shot on goal.

"They were scared," said Bladon, "plain and simple. Almost from the beginning, they were holding their sticks in close to their bodies like they were looking for somebody."

As Vladimir Popov was being buried on a massive check by Bridgman, Viktor Kutyergin, the one feisty Soviet, jumped into the slot to fire a 35-footer past Stephenson. But the Army was no more back in the game than it had been while sitting in the locker room. Larry Goodenough, on a feed from Clarke in the third period, scored a window-dressing goal in the 4-1 demolition of the great machine.

Loktev said the hosts, who had outshot his team 49-13, played "like animals." The Flyer owner thought they played like champions. "That was the greatest coaching job I've ever seen," said Snider, interrupting the press conference to shake Shero's hand.

"I had a lot of help," said the Flyer coach. Usually reserved in victory, he was ready to take on anybody. "We are the world champions, and 99 percent of the NHL didn't think we could do it."

Shero exaggerated the level of skepticism, but not the satisfaction. His team celebrated for itself, not for the league, but anyone wanting to join the party was welcome. "I've never been so happy," said Jimmy Watson. "This compares with winning the Stanley Cup."

The emotional energy the Flyers expended soon took its toll. So did a heel bruise Clarke suffered in a 2-0 loss at Chicago, which forced him out of the 1976 All-Star Game at the Spectrum and two other contests during an 0-3-2 trip.

When the Flyers returned home on February 5, Parent, who had tried to melt away his fears on a Jamaican beach, again attempted to practice, found the pain at a tolerable level and decided to fight through it. "When the doctors said I couldn't hurt myself, that's all I wanted to hear," Parent said.

With Clarke back in the lineup that night, the Flyers were blowing away both their black clouds and the Canucks when a clean body check by defenseman Harold Snepsts sent MacLeish to the ice holding his left knee. The next day, Dr. Wolf repaired the center's torn ligaments. The most optimisitic forecast was that he could be back for the Stanley Cup finals.

"[MacLeish] means so much," lamented Clarke, but the team still managed to pick up its pace. With a 2-1 victory over the Canadiens on February 15 at the Spectrum, the Flyers stayed within striking distance of league-leading Montreal. Parent accompanied his teammates to the West Coast the next day, and as the trip closed in Washington, the rusted star returned to the nets, giving up five goals on only 19 shots. "I wonder if I would be ready to face a team like Montreal," said the goalie after the Flyers rallied for a 5-5 tie that stretched an unbeaten streak to 11 games. "It's just not there right now."

Parent looked better in a 2-2 tie at St. Louis, then received practically no work during two routs of Kansas City. The way Philadelphia was scoring, the goaltender was the least essential player. Bridgman was performing well in MacLeish's spot between Dornhoefer and Lonsberry and, with 13 contests remaining, the Leach-Clarke-Barber line was within

Holmgren remembers. But while thinking about returning to the University of Minnesota to play baseball, he was contacted by Allen, invited to Philadelphia, and signed to a contract for the following season.

"I'll see you at training camp," said the GM.

"Isn't there anywhere I can play the rest of this year?" asked Holmgren, who was then sent to Richmond.

Van Impe, meanwhile, was suddenly showing his 35 years and was benched by Shero for 6 of 7 games before the March 9 trading deadline. Just before noon on that day, Allen traded the veteran defenseman and Bobby Taylor to Pittsburgh for 26-year-old goaltender Gary Inness.

Feisty Orest Kindrachuk mixes it up.

"This was hard," said Allen. "[Van Impe] was an original and he'd been our captain. We're the champs and so is he. But McIlhargey must play in order to develop."

Allen was nervous about how little time Parent had to get in shape for the playoffs,

23 goals of the NHL record (140) set by Boston's Esposito, Ken Hodge and Wayne Cashman in 1970-71.

Kindrachuk passed the 20-goal mark with a hat trick that helped sink Detroit 6-1, but neared his own pain threshold with a three-month-long backache. Shero, himself a longtime spinal sufferer, took the center to see a faith healer, who gave both men plastic containers filled with stones and copper wire.

"I'm cured," the coach said.

"Anything to get through the season," said Kindrachuk.

The WHA Minnesota Fighting Saints were not as fortunate, leaving right wing Paul Holmgren, Philadelphia's fifth-round pick in the 1975 draft, out of work. Holmgren, a 6-3, 215-pounder from St. Paul who had signed with his hometown team before being selected by the Flyers, assumed he did not figure into the plans of the loaded Stanley Cup champions. "They had never called after they drafted me,"

but the GM's primary motive in obtaining another goalie had been to convert a declining asset—Van Impe—into a commodity. "I thought Inness had a chance to be a decent backup," Allen recalls. Parent's recovery would mean the Flyers could then trade either Stephenson or Inness.

Van Impe, bitter and despondent, said he would not report to the Penguins, but a contract renegotiation soon changed his mind. Shero proved less flexible about Inness, who flopped too often in practice for the coach's liking. In order to keep Stephenson warm and sharpen Parent in the remaining games, finding starts for Inness could not be part of the agenda.

Montreal, with Ken Dryden back in top form after sitting out an entire season over a contract dispute, was proving to be uncatchable, but the high-scoring Flyers kept on pace to record their best-ever regular season.

Leach became the thirteenth player in history to

reach 50 goals when Philadelphia clobbered Atlanta 6-1 on March 14 and ran its unbeaten streak to 21 games. Two contests later, Barber's 100th point was part of a three-goal burst within 1:23 in the second period that enabled the Flyers to beat Vancouver, 3-2, and tie the NHL record of 23 games without a loss. That mark, set by the 1940-41 Bruins, had lasted 35 years, but most of the Flyers didn't think it was worth 35 cents.

Clarke, who refused to acknowledge that he was

and 4 assists, was called up on March 25 for a contest against the Rangers. The hulking 20-year-old winger promptly deposited Esposito on the seat of his pants. "There's the Stanley Cup," Shero said to himself.

But the following evening in Boston, Holmgren reported for a team meeting with a suddenly-swollen right eye. Barry Ashbee and Clarke took the rookie to the Massachusetts Eye and Ear Infirmary, where doctors found a puncture wound that had apparently been caused by a skate blade when Holmgren had

The LCB Line, Barber, left, Clarke, center, and Leach scored 141 goals in 1976.

in a race for the Art Ross Trophy with Montreal's Guy Lafleur, felt that to liken winning streaks that occurred three decades apart was as silly as keeping track of goals and assists. "How do you compare something that happpened in 1941 to something that happens now?" he asked.

Shero, also openly contemptuous of the streak's significance, played Parent in the next game at Detroit. He gave up two terrible goals and the Flyers lost 4-2. "Do you think if I wanted to win I would have used Bernie?" said the coach. Their impressive and annoying streak finally over, Philadelphia wrapped up the Patrick Division title the next night by beating Toronto 4-2 at the Spectrum.

Dornhoefer had developed viral pneumonia, so Holmgren, who in 6 games at Richmond had 4 goals

been at the bottom of an AHL brawl several days earlier.

An emergency operation was performed to arrest a fluid leak that endangered Holmgren's sight. But a severe reaction to the anesthetic caused convulsions and the Flyer almost died on the operating table. Ashbee stayed with him through a frightening and sleepless night before reporting to Boston Garden for a 4-4 afternoon tie.

Five days later, Leach became the second player in NHL history to achieve 60 goals in a season with a pair during an 11-2 Spectrum rout of Washington. Shero, who had always sneered at statistics, shamelessly gave the LCB line extra shifts, allowing Barber, who scored three goals, to reach 49 and Clarke, who had five assists, to climb within two points of

Lafleur.

Barber then scored his 50th, and Leach his 61st, in a 5-2 Spectrum victory over Buffalo during the next-to-last game of the season. "Sure I wanted to do it," Barber admitted. "I'll probably never do it again." His goal was also the record-breaking 141st for the line.

The Flyers were closing the regular season with a bellyful of grand statistics, but Shero was getting a nervous stomach watching Parent. Before a meaningless finale at Madison Square Garden, he ordered Philadelphia forwards to let the Rangers shoot so that Parent could get work. The Rangers gunned it up more than Clarke, who went scoreless and finished six points behind Lafleur. Although New York only won, 2-0, Parent looked slow getting back to his feet and had trouble with his balance.

"Right now Bernie is not at his best," said Shero while he waited for Toronto to eliminate Pittsburgh and earn a series with the Flyers for the second consecutive spring. Ashbee and Mike Nykoluk convinced Shero to start Parent anyway. "If [Bernie's] ready, we'll find out," said Ashbee. "If not, we'll go with Stephenson."

Dornhoefer returned for Game 1. So, seemingly, did the old Parent, who moved well in a 23-save, 4-1 victory. After losing their 18th straight match to Philadelphia, the Leafs resorted to mysticism. Coach Red Kelly placed pyramids under his team's bench for Game 2, following the ancient Egyptian belief that they transmitted energy, but the Toronto players became mummified and lost, 3-1.

To have any chance, the Leafs knew they had to play tougher, so three minutes into Game 3 at Maple Leaf Gardens, Kurt Walker speared Schultz. The dynamite was lit and the Flyers proved willing to blow themselves up, playing only sixteen of the first forty minutes with five skaters. Even after goals 13 seconds apart by Dornhoefer and Jimmy Watson cut Toronto's lead from 4-1 to 4-3 midway through the second period, Saleski almost immediately took another penalty.

When a fan tossed a chunk of ice at the winger in the penalty box and Saleski angrily turned around, an overreacting policeman grabbed the Flyer's stick and initiated a brief tug-of-war. Joe Watson, perceiving his teammate as about to become defenseless in a hostile circumstance, swung his stick from the ice over the glass, striking Constable Art Malloy on the shoulder. Saleski quickly pushed the weapon back to Watson.

During the third period, Bridgman punched out star defenseman Borje Salming, but with sixteen power-play opportunities and 52 shots, the Leafs won, 5-4.

Afterwards, the Flyers learned they had bigger problems than just Toronto's sudden belligerence. William McMurtry, a Toronto attorney whose government commission on hockey violence had cited the NHL for setting a bad example, told newsmen that Saleski, Joe Watson and Bridgman had committed indictable offenses.

"What for?" said an incredulous Watson. "I didn't hit anybody. I never made any contact."

"Why don't they just handcuff [Watson] and take him away right now?" said an angry Snider. "The official (referee Dave Newell) was the whole game. They got McMurtry, they got Newell, they got everybody."

The next day, Bill McMurtry's brother, Roy, the Ontario attorney general who was already pursuing charges against Detroit's Dan Maloney for an on-ice beating of Toronto's Brian Glennie, announced he was laying charges against Saleski and Watson for the penalty box incident and against Bridgman for beating up Salming. "If the leagues would police themselves," the attorney general said during an afternoon press conference at his home, "none of this would be necessary."

That night, the three Flyers surrendered at Toronto's 52nd police division and were released on their own recognizance.

"Maybe Joe ought to plead insanity," said Parent, but Watson wasn't laughing. "It was just pure frustration," he said. "I never tried to hurt anybody or anything in my whole life."

"They call you animals and you do something back," said Saleski. "You can only take so much. The policemen should have been looking up in the stands."

Toronto fans seated around the Philadelphia bench told reporters that Nykoluk had shouted, "Get that bleeping Swede" about Salming. "Maybe I did say it," the assistant coach confessed., "but it's ridiculous. Guys are always saying, 'Get that guy or this guy.'"

"We always used to say, 'Get (Maurice) Richard,'" said Shero. "We'd get him and he'd still score a thousand goals."

Salming was embarrassed at being the focal point of controversy. "They want to take me out of the game," he said, "but there are some guys on other teams who do the same thing."

In Game 4, the brilliant defenseman was unintimidated as he held off Flyer forecheckers, blocked shots, continually rushed up ice, and scored a second-period goal. Parent, meanwhile, muffed a soft 40-footer by George Ferguson and, despite two goals by Toronto's Public Enemy No.1—Bridgman—the Flyers lost 4-3 and returned to the Spectrum with the series tied 2-2.

Philadelphia District Attorney Emmett Fitzpatrick, a diehard hockey fan, accused McMurtry of committing a "perversion of office." Even Clarence Campbell, who had a background in law and a record for repeatedly rapping misbehaving Flyers on the knuckles, suggested that this time the Philadelphia players were victims. "They are playing with much more restraint than they did a few years ago," he said. "Before the game was a couple minutes old, Walker went out of his way to cross-check Schultz, so Toronto's intentions were quite obvious."

A jury of the Flyers' peers produced 17,077 jeers for the Leafs as they appeared for Game 5. Less than six minutes after the booing of "O Canada", Barber scored, and within 1:33 of the second period, three Philadelphia goals broke the game wide open. Saleski completed a hat trick in the 7-1 rout.

"I want to jam [a victory] down the throats of those fans," said Barber as the Flyers returned to Toronto leading 3-2. But the Leafs again summoned courage before their home crowd and another game degenerated. While Schultz was en route to the locker room after receiving fighting and misconduct penalties, he was elbowed by a 65-year-old man named George Crawford. Although the Hammer was restrained by police from retaliating, his teammates clustered at the scene and Bob Kelly threw a glove into the stands that struck usherette Jan Brown in the face.

In the third period, Schultz returned to the game long enough to be ejected for fighting with Dave (Tiger) Williams, then saluted the taunting crowd by holding his nose on the way to the locker room. "Because it stinks," the Hammer explained.

Unquestionably, the Leafs were taking advantage of the Flyers' dilemma. "I felt like I was being strangled out there," said Schultz. "The referee on one side and McMurtry on the other."

Both Williams and Scott Garland tried to pick fights with Bridgman who, fearing further legal difficulties, just held on while Darryl Sittler scored five goals in Toronto's 8-5 victory that forced a Game 7. "We didn't play like Stanley Cup champions," said Clarke. "We were undisciplined, unorganized."

Both Kelly and the fan who hit Schultz were charged with assault the following day, but before

their court battle the Flyers would face a one-game trial-by-ordeal. Clarke was hiding stretched ligaments in his left knee and Parent, who had given up four bad goals in Game 6, was unraveling.

He was beaten by Jack Valiquette before Game 7 was two minutes old. Dupont, who had given the puck away, atoned with a tying goal nine minutes later, but Schultz, checked by Garland, accidentally spun his stick into Ferguson's mouth and earned a major penalty. Forty-seven seconds later, Bob Neely put Toronto ahead, 2-1.

The Flyers had fifteen long minutes between periods to consider their predicament. "God, if we don't come back, that's it," Parent thought. They also had 3:09 to kill on Schultz's major. Lonsberry was working at it when his skates locked with those of Toronto defenseman Claire Alexander. After they tumbled, only Lonsberry got up. Alexander was taken to the locker room and the Leafs' defense was down to skin, bones and Salming.

"We had been bringing the puck up the center the whole series and Claire was part of that," Sittler said later. "Without him, we started throwing it around the boards." When Schultz's penalty was finally over, Philadelphia started pinching in and the puck began coming loose. Saleski drove in a rebound, Bridgman scored twice and Lonsberry completed a four-goal burst within 3:16 to put the Leafs away.

Kindrachuk offered the only gloat after the 7-3 victory. "The pyramids have withered," said the Flyer. "Red Kelly had better go back to King Tut and find something else."

Overall, the team felt more relief than joy. "As a whole, we were disappointed with our play and didn't feel it should have gone seven," said Crisp.

One consolation was that Boston, the Flyers' semifinal opponent, had also played seven games in eliminating Los Angeles. The Bruins, with Bobby Orr sidelined for the season following the fifth knee operation of his career, had become a grinding team that in Game 1 outworked Philadelphia. Goals 1:48 apart in the third period against an unsteady Parent broke open a 2-2 tie, giving coach Don Cherry's team a 4-2 victory.

Before the second contest, Shero was spared a painful decision. "I'm tired," said Parent, asking to be taken out. "I'm not in playoff shape. I don't want to cost the team a game. Let's make the move before it happens."

Stephenson, who had not played in a month, walked his teammates along a tightrope in Game 2. The Flyers jumped in front when Saleski beat goalie

Gerry Cheevers from 70 feet, but after John Bucyk's third-period shot from the slot slipped past a screened Stephenson, Philadelphia was forced into a nervous overtime. Only one mistake away from going to Boston in a deep hole, the Flyers picked up momentum, controlled the extra session, and won when Leach beat Cheevers to the post for a broken-down Jimmy Watson shot that had come off the end boards.

In Game 3, the Bruins were about to take a 2-1 lead into the second period break when Barber beat goalie Gilles Gilbert off a two-on-one. After Bridgman's bloop rebound of a Goodenough drive early in the third gave Philadelphia a 3-2 advantage, Stephenson stopped Bobby Schmautz on a breakaway and the Bruins deflated. The Flyers went on to a 5-2 victory.

Early in the second period of Game 4, Leach scored in his 8th straight playoff match to erase another 2-1 Boston lead. When Jean Ratelle had to leave the game with back spasms, joining Schmautz and Wayne Cashman on the sidelines, the visitors wore the undermanned Bruins down. Kindrachuk, off a backhand pass from Schultz, put Philadelphia ahead and Joe Watson, with Dornhoefer lying on Cheevers, got the puck over a goalmouth pileup with 2:01 remaining to ensure the 4-2 victory.

The Flyers still needed one more win to reach the finals, but Leach was already celebrating. After failing to report for the morning skate on the day of Game 5, teammates found him passed out in the basement of his Cherry Hill, New Jersey, home. When a shower and coffee didn't achieve a complete revival, the right wing had a few more beers.

Clarke talked Shero into letting Leach play and the Rifle scored five goals as Philadelphia put away Boston, 6-3. Backhanders beat Gilbert on the short side, the long side, and in the top of the net. Forehanders were driven to the overwhelmed goalie's stick side and between his legs. Three of the scores came after Leach had crossed over to left wing. All five came when he was in no condition to play.

Leach had 15 playoff goals and the NHL a dream matchup for its finals. "People have been waiting for this for three years," said left wing Steve Shutt after Montreal defeated the Islanders in five games. "It's a natural, our speed against their strength."

The Canadiens, eliminated by the Rangers and Sabres the two previous springs, had retooled with the Bullies in mind. Second-year forwards Doug Risebrough and Mario Tremblay added feistiness, and rookie center Doug Jarvis had been acquired from Toronto as a face-off antidote to Clarke. Mon-

treal also lined up three of the five best defensemen in the league—Guy Lapointe, Serge Savard and Larry Robinson—and, with Parent's confidence gone, Ken Dryden provided a clear edge in goal.

The Flyers' strength advantage at center had dissipated significantly because of MacLeish's unavailability, Kindrachuk's back problems and Clarke's knee. Nevertheless, Shero's team had earned an aura of invulnerability by not losing an essential game in three years. On intangible factors, Philadelphia was still favored in many minds.

"At the start of the season I wondered if, after winning two Stanley Cups, they would be as hungry as they once were," said Dryden before the finals began. "I know this sounds impossible, but to me they look hungrier."

The Canadiens, under intense hometown pressure to rescue the Holy Grail from the heathens, started nervously. Leach's record 16th playoff goal gave Philadelphia a 1-0 lead after only 21 seconds. Lonsberry then converted a Bridgman pass to make it 2-0. But Montreal's speed soon caused the Flyers to break down. McIlhargey and Jim Watson were trapped at center on a Jimmy Roberts' goal and Joe Watson was caught when Robinson tied the game off a two-on-one.

Stephenson, far busier than Dryden, kept the score tied until Goodenough's power-play goal 5:17 into the third period put Philadelphia ahead. But Jacques Lemaire scored on a backhand swipe off a loose puck in the slot and Bladon was caught gambling when Lapointe gave the Canadiens a 4-3 lead with only 1:22 remaining.

Leach, hounded by left wing Bob Gainey on practically every shift, sneaked behind Lapointe in the final minute, but had to reach for the pass and hurried his shot wide. In losing Game 1, 4-3, the Flyers had blown two leads, but their mistakes were mostly caused by Montreal's speed.

"We were picking them up late tonight, but we'll adjust," said Lonsberry. "We always come up with something."

Philadelphia was more disciplined in Game 2, only to be sobered by the Canadiens' awesome strength. Dornhoefer was nailed by a Robinson check so hard that play had to be stopped to repair the boards. "Lean on them! Lean on them!" Dryden shouted to his teammates every time the Flyers would get the puck. Scotty Bowman had reminded his deep club that its opponent could be worn down.

Clarke, Barber and Leach were held to one shot apiece by the checking unit of Jarvis, Gainey and

Roberts. Jarvis dominated Clarke 14-4 on face-offs. Lemaire fleeced Goodenough for a shorthanded score late in the second period and Guy Lafleur stole the puck from Bladon early in the third to build a 2-0 lead.

Late in the game, Schultz beat Dryden from a bad angle, but that was the only type of opportunity that Philadelphia could manage against the impregnable Lapointe, Robinson and Savard. "They're so big you can't go through them, and so strong you

ways managed to have a fresh defensive center—Jarvis, Risebrough or Lemaire—on the ice. "All I can do is give [Clarke] shorter shifts," Shero said later. "But when I do that, I'm putting out a player who isn't as good. I don't have as many good swing men as [Bowman] does. I can't be as flexible."

At 9:16 of the third period, Pierre Bouchard took a pass out of the corner from Wilson and beat Stephenson with a 40-footer through Rick Chartraw's screen. The Flyers did not muster a good chance the

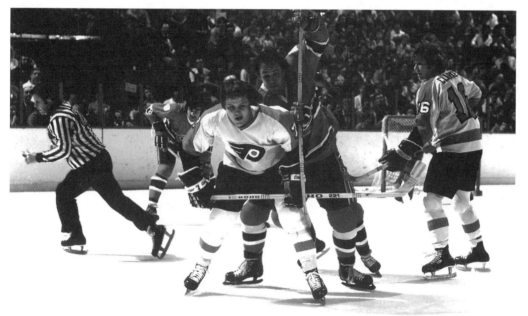

Barber battles the Canadiens.

can't get around them," said Lonsberry after the Canadiens' 2-1 victory gave Montreal a 2-0 series lead.

Still, as formidable as their opponents looked, the Flyers had lost both games by only one goal. They hoped home ice and last change would get them back in the series. Even after Stephenson missed Shutt's 70-foot fluttering sinker, Philadelphia fought back. Clarke finally got his hands free long enough to feed Leach for the tying goal, then the smoking Rifle scored again off a giveaway by Bill Nyrop to put the Flyers ahead, 2-1.

Although Shutt put in his own rebound, Stephenson stopped second-period breakaways by Murray Wilson and Yvan Cournoyer to keep the game tied. But Philadelphia was spending less time in the Montreal zone as the game progressed. Attempting to get Clarke away from Jarvis, Shero at one point played his captain with Lonsberry and Dornhoefer, but Bowman, changing on the fly, al-

rest of the way and lost 3-2 to Superteam. For the first time in three years, Philadelphia could not will itself to victory. "We played our best, too," said Barber with pained eyes. "But there wasn't much we could do. That's what makes it so hard to accept."

The defending champions had two days off to dread the thought of being swept. "I'd be embarrassed," said Crisp. "We're too good for that."

Schultz, increasingly torn by the fear of bad penalties, examined himself publicly. "When Chartraw hit a few of our guys, I should have just walked up and drove him," said the Hammer. "I don't know why I didn't. Ever since the Toronto series, we can't help but be affected by all the publicity we got. If I take an extra penalty, it probably would hurt us."

As the Grim Reaper knocked at the Spectrum door, the Flyers were not abandoned by their fans. "Win or Lose, You've Given Philly a Lot to be Proud Of," read one sign rimming the balcony before Game 4. The crowd, certain their team would not go down without

Montreal coach Scotty Bowman shakes hands with Reggie Leach, the leading goalscorer in the playoffs.

Kate and a fight, roared as Miss Smith, appearing live for the fourth time, belted out "God Bless America". Sure enough, after only 41 seconds, Leach stuck a 45-foot dart past Dryden's feet.

Shutt and Bouchard replied for Montreal on power plays, but the hobbled and heroic Clarke set up a Barber deflection that tied the game 2-2 by the end of the first period. Philadelphia then applied its best sustained offensive pressure of the series and grabbed a 3-2 lead on Dupont's power-play goal. When Lemaire took a penalty, the Flyers had the opportunity to add insurance, but 33 seconds into the power play, Dornhoefer was called for hooking Jarvis. "I didn't touch him," the veteran argued. When Lemaire returned, Cournoyer scored with Dornhoefer still in the box and only 11 seconds left in the second period.

Stephenson kept his deflated team alive through much of the third period. "Their injuries were catching up with them," said Pete Mahovlich. "They were really dragging. I was sure we'd get the break eventually."

It came after Dornhoefer swiped at a loose puck

in the crease and hit the crossbar. On the next shift, Lafleur, free in front of Stephenson, tapped in the go-ahead goal with 5:42 remaining. Less than one minute later, Mahovlich, fed by Lafleur, backhanded an insurance goal and the Spectrum fell silent.

The Flyers, 5-3 losers in the only game of the series not decided by one goal, went down with dignity and to respectful applause. The Canadiens received an ovation as captain Cournoyer took a lap around the rink with a Cup that had been harder to earn than the sweep suggested. "Somewhere down the line people will see that we won in four straight games and think that it was easy," said Dryden, as his mates popped their corks. "But they will not be more wrong. If you'll notice, we're drinking our champagne sitting down."

Leach, who finished with 19 playoff goals in 16 games, became only the third player from a losing team to win the Conn Smythe Trophy. It wasn't much consolation. Neither was any credit Philadelphia received for getting to the finals minus MacLeish, and with Clarke, Kindrachuk, Dornhoefer and Parent all at far less than 100 percent.

"We'll be back after that Cup again next year," said Joe Watson bravely. Then his voice dropped. "But damn it, so probably will the Canadiens."

In June, Clarke won his third Hart Trophy by a landslide vote of the writers. He also was elected president of the NHL Players Association, which recommended the elimination of fighting. Instead, the owners opted for a new rule calling for a major penalty and misconduct to a player deliberately starting a fight.

Clarke was asked whether the legislation would damage Schultz's career. "Not at all," said the Flyer captain. "It gives him a chance to play hockey."

Fans in the Delaware Valley would also have increased opportunity to watch the sport. For two years, South Philadelphia bars that had been serviced by an experimental cable company were packed during home games. With suburban areas due for wiring, the market was soon to explode.

Home Box Office, the dominant channel in the fledgling industry, had offered $200,000 for a package of Flyer contests, but Snider had a better idea. Spectacor, the new parent company of the burgeoning Spectrum operation, would create its own sports and movie station targeted for a local audience.

On July 15, president Lou Scheinfeld announced the creation of Philadelphia Regional In-Home Sports and Movies. PRISM would show Flyers, Phillies and 76ers home games not available on over-the-air television, plus motion pictures that had just completed their theatrical runs.

The cost for the service, initially available only in Upper Darby (one of the few Delaware Valley communities cable-ready) would be $9 to 10 a month. Hugh Gannon, the sports director of PRISM, and former goalie Bobby Taylor would announce the Flyer telecasts.

In August, Clarke, Barber, Leach and Jimmy Watson went to defend Canada's honor in the first Canada Cup, a six-nation tournament organized by Eagleson. Clarke suffered a sprained ankle in Team

Canada's opening-game rout of Finland and limped through the rest of the competition. He still fared better than Watson, who spent much of the tournament in Montreal General Hospital after sustaining a fractured cheekbone, cuts and a concussion when hit with a shot by Team USA's Gary Sargent.

Leach started poorly, lost confidence and was a virtual nonfactor. Barber, the only Flyer to distinguish himself, got the lead goal in an emotional 3-1 win over the Soviets at Maple Leaf Gardens and the tying score in Canada's series-winning overtime victory against

Czechoslovakia at the Montreal Forum.

Because of their Canada Cup involvement, Watson and Clarke were excused from training camp at the Class of '23 Rink. Stephenson, meanwhile, claimed to have been promised a contract renegotiation by

Despite losing to Montreal, Leach won the Conn Smythe Trophy as the most valuable player in the 1976 playoffs.

Allen and refused to report. While the GM said he had agreed only to look over certain clauses pertaining to bonuses, the goalie's agent, Mark Stewart, insisted he would deal only with Snider or Allen and declined to work with Flyer counsel and troubleshooter Gil Stein. Stephenson, being fined $250 per day, flew to Florida to play golf and "look into business opportunities."

Allen, optimistic that Parent would make a full comeback with the benefit of a complete training camp, was content to let Stephenson stew. The GM had something else on his agenda. Believing that the deciding factor in Montreal's triumph had not been speed, but its newfound ability to match the Flyer muscle, Allen hoped to recycle Schultz.

"I thought Davey reached a point where he [believed] he was a better player than he really was and didn't want to go out and fight like he had been," recalls Allen. "After O'Reilly [beat] him up in the playoffs, I think fighting had become distasteful."

With McIlhargey and Bridgman expected to take larger roles and Holmgren given medical clearance to resume his career, the GM thought his club still capable of defending itself. Allen had once promised Kings owner Jack Kent Cooke that if Schultz was ever up for trade, Hollywood's hockey team would be given first chance to bid.

"I thought Davey had a showbiz flair and that something might happen for him out there," recalls Allen, who never shopped the left wing anywhere else. "In spite of everything people might believe, every once in a while I did try to help the players."

On September 29, after completing negotiations with Los Angeles for two draft choices—one in the second round, one in the fourth—the Hammer was called to Allen's office and hit with a roundhouse right. He was no longer a Flyer.

Actually, the punch had been telegraphed by rumors for more than a year, so Schultz was somewhat braced for it. "He thanked me and I thanked him," the Hammer told reporters later in the day. "He doesn't have to justify to me what he's doing. I told a writer yesterday that I wanted to play hockey. The Flyers didn't seem to want me to. What are you going to do? I've had four good years here, I really couldn't ask for more. The people in Philly have been great and the press has done everything for me."

Allen diplomatically told reporters a half-truth: the move was made so that Bridgman could play regularly. But while Schultz's assets were probably replaceable, his impact had been unique. "What Schultz had was in here," said Shero, pointing to his heart. "He was a major part of our success. He's a winner and I won't forget him."

Neither would the fans. "We want Schultz," they chanted while the Canadiens lit up a shaky-looking Parent, 8-2, in an exhibition game the night after the deal. "I feel good," said the goalie. "Sometimes."

During the final weekend of preseason, Allen agreed to Stephenson's request for a one-on-one meeting. Following their talk, the goalie practiced with the team. According to management, his contract was not being renegotiated and the $4,250 in fines levied against him would stand.

On Monday, the Flyers learned that Parent had suffered a broken toe the previous night during the final exhibition game in Buffalo and would be out for four weeks. The next day, Stephenson insisted on a new contract. Believing that Parent's injury was being used as leverage, Allen again suspended Stephenson, only this time with a smile. Parent had been fitted with a pad that Dr. Joe Torg, the team's new orthopedic consultant, believed would enable him to play. "It's a miracle," said Parent. "It's a bleeping miracle."

When the Islanders came to the Spectrum to open the Flyers' tenth season, No. 1 was in goal. Also in the lineup were Jimmy Watson, after playing in only one exhibition game; Clarke, who had played in none; and Kindrachuk, who had missed the final week of camp with damaged rib cartilage. Not unsurprisingly, New York made Philadelphia look dead on its feet in a 3-0 shutout. Shero's team fought back from a 3-1 deficit in Atlanta, but lost when Rey Comeau's centering pass went in off Dupont's skate. Thus, the Flyers were 0-2 when Schultz's Kings came to town.

The Hammer dressed in purple and gold was a disorienting sight. So was the push he gave Bridgman after Kelly and L.A.'s Don Kozak shoved at each other 35 seconds into the first period. The crowd, which offered Schultz a huge pregame ovation, had giggled when he shoved Bridgman, but when the ex-Flyer cross-checked MacLeish, the boos began.

"My game plan was to play," Schultz said later. "But I was wired up, no doubt. For the last three or four nights, I couldn't sleep."

After he was knocked down by Dornhoefer, the Hammer slashed Dupont, then stood on the bench taunting the Flyers. When the Kings' Dave Hutchison– dumped by Bridgman– retaliated with a high stick, Dupont led a charge off the Philadelphia bench. Schultz sought out Holmgren and baited the rookie into taking off his visor and fighting. "I had a feeling I'd be the guy he would go after," said

Holmgren. "I was the one he hadn't played with."

Dupont had to be restrained from going after his former teammate who, along with six other players, was ejected from the game. "I know nobody's supposed to hit the Flyers in their own building," Schultz sneered after Lonsberry's goal held up for a 1-0 Philadelphia victory. "About four guys grabbed Hutchison. That's the way the Flyers have always done things, even when I was here. Like (in 1974) when three guys jumped (Oakland's) Mike Christie. I never wanted to be part of that."

Schultz did not tiptoe through his homecoming, and emotional ties were cut without sadness or anger. "It had to be tough for him to start hitting our guys late," said Lonsberry sarcastically. "He went out and did the same thing with them that he did with us."

Ironically, the Hammer had become the first player to test the Hammerless Flyers. "There's a lot of teams that are going to try us," said Clarke. The full effect of Schultz's departure remained to be seen, but the team struggled during the early weeks of the 1976-77 season. Parent's toe was healing, but his confidence was not, as the Canadiens swept Philadelphia with ease, 7-1, at the Spectrum.

Two nights later in Toronto, Shero pulled Parent for Inness with the Leafs ahead 4-0. Holmgren's first two NHL goals climaxed a five-goal rally within sixteen minutes before Inness, attempting to put his glove on a slow, slithering puck, knocked it over the line to create a 5-5 tie.

As the Flyers' patience was being tried, Saleski, Joe Watson, Kelly and Bridgman went to court for a preliminary hearing on the charges laid the previous spring.

The doctor who had examined Jan Brown, the usherette hit by Bob Kelly's glove, testified that the only treatment she required was reassurance. Constable Arthur Malloy said he was not aware that he had been struck by Joe Watson's stick until he discovered a bruise while bathing the next day, and Salming, battered by Bridgman, stated under cross-examination that fighting was part of the game. The only case the Crown had against Saleski was that he had tried to conceal Watson's stick by passing it back over the glass. Nevertheless, Judge James Crossland ruled prosecutor Robert McGee could pursue all four cases at a later date.

The North Stars, guilty of ignoring a hometown prospect—Holmgren—were prosecuted when the St. Paul kid scored a goal to complement Clarke's six-point night in a 9-1 rout of Minnesota that high-lighted a 6-0-1 Flyer run. But when Philadelphia went winless on a trip to Detroit, Buffalo, Chicago and Cleveland (where the California Seals had moved over the summer), Allen sounded the alarm publicly.

"In the past, if we lost a game, it was never because we were outhustled," said the GM. "I can't say that's the case this year. We're just not the desperate, driving, hockey club that we were."

The Flyers did not win a road game until November 26—a 4-2 victory over the Colorado Rockies– the transplanted Kansas City Scouts. Philadelphia beat the division-leading Islanders 5-3 at the Spectrum and swept the Bruins in a home-and-home series, but despite a 15-7-6 record and appearances that the surgically repaired MacLeish was almost as good as new, the team's play was still vaguely suspect. Shero benched Leach for a game. "He'll play when he checks," said the coach, and although Barber's effort was not in question, he was in a horrific slump. "Nothing I do is right– nothing," the left wing said.

Suddenly nervous about not having enough muscle, Allen picked up 6-foot-4-inch winger Harvey Bennett from Washington. Stephenson, his cash reserves dwindling, returned on December 7. "There are some things I would like to do with my family," he said. "And if I wasn't going to continue playing hockey, I might have to wait until I was 55 or 60."

There were nights when Parent looked that old, but the goalie played 24 straight games anyway. He fleetingly flashed his brilliance in a 38-shot, 2-0 shutout in St. Louis. "It was a pleasure to watch him," said Clarke. "And that's what we did all night, too." Still, the Flyers kept winning, even after losing Jimmy Watson for two weeks with retinal damage caused by an accidental clip from the stick of Blues' Jerry Butler.

In Stephenson's first start, Philadelphia struggled past Colorado, 4-3, at the Spectrum to go into the top spot ahead of the inconsistent Islanders. A 7-2 victory in Cleveland on January 1 extended the Flyers' unbeaten streak to 20 games and took the team into Montreal for a true test. They failed, surrendering a club-record 55 shots in the 6-4 loss. "This doesn't help our confidence any," said a glum Bladon.

Two days later, Watson was cleared to return, but with a visor and the knowledge that his vision would probably never be the same. "I've been told it might get better, but not to count on it," he said. "My other eye should take care of my depth perception, but [the left eye] is blurry."

Even the incredible sight of McIlhargey scoring a breakaway goal in a 4-4 tie at Madison Square Garden did not shock Watson back to 20/20 focus. "The puck found a hole I didn't think was there," said the Wolfman.

A crater could have developed in Philadelphia's lineup after Barber suffered a partial ligament tear in his right knee from a collision with Ranger Pat Hickey. "The doctor who examined me in New York said I had a big problem," recalls Barber. But Dr. Torg recommended against surgery and the winger was in the lineup after missing only one game.

Bob Dailey wasn't sorry to be leaving Vancouver after clashing with Canuck coach Phil Maloney.

Holmgren, meanwhile, had a scare that sent him to Wills Eye Hospital. Taunted by St. Louis players about his visor, the rookie threw a punch at Bob Gassoff, who then reached under Holmgren's shield in an attempt to pull it off before trading blows. The Flyer thought the Blues' tough guy was attempting a gouging and, after both players were given game misconducts, walked down the Spectrum corridor looking for another fight before being discouraged by an attendant.

Philadelphia went on to a 7-1 victory over St. Louis and Holmgren's eye checked out fine, but the Flyers were humiliated in an 8-3 road loss to the Islanders. "It was just a total embarrassment," said Joe Watson.

Thus did the Canadiens come to the Spectrum for the first do-or-die January 20 game in NHL history. "If we don't beat them now, I don't know when we will," said a grim Clarke. But the Stanley Cup champions took Philadelphia apart, 6-2. "This is three [straight blowouts by Montreal] now," said Dornhoefer. "It doesn't leave a very good taste in your mouth."

Convinced the gap between the Canadiens and Flyers was becoming a canyon, Allen traded between periods of the Montreal game for two of the longest arms in the business. McIlhargey and Goodenough were dealt to Vancouver for 6-5, 220-pound defenseman Bob Dailey.

While Goodenough was a decent offensive defenseman and McIlhargey's muscle, enthusiasm and dedication were assets, Dailey, the ninth player taken in the 1973 draft, was strong and mobile, with a bazooka shot. "He can be another Larry Robinson if he wants to be," said Ashbee.

Dailey had a restaurant in Vancouver, but was sinking in the Canucks' lethargy and had no qualms about leaving. "I felt like a guy getting paroled," he recalls. "I loved the city, but didn't see eye to eye with (coach-GM Phil) Maloney, and the travel beat the hell out of everybody who played there.

"I knew I was probably going to be traded. Eagleson (his agent) had told me to take some extra suits on one of the last few road trips. I thought I was going to the Bruins. I had no idea it would be the Flyers."

Dailey had always been referred to as "The Giant" by Shero and "Moose" by his Canuck teammates. But Dupont declared, "There's only one Moose around here." When the new Flyer joined the team in Atlanta with a coat draped over his shoulders like a cape, Dupont, a *Sesame Street* enthusiast, quickly christened his new teammate "The Count."

"Because you can count on him," said Dupont. Indeed, Philadelphia was about to go down in Dailey's debut before his blast from the point set up a last-minute goal by Leach to seal a 4-4 tie at the Omni. "Can that guy shoot?" asked Shero, rolling his eyes at his own rhetorical question.

As the Flyers continued their five game trip, spouses and girlfriends stayed busy at home preparing for the first Flyers Wives Fight for Lives Carnival.

Sylvan Tobin, a season ticket holder and Snider's friend, had referred the owner to Dr. Isadore Brodsky (Tobin's brother-in-law), who was looking to form a board for Hahnemann Hospital's fledgling cancer institute. Snider accepted a position and brainstormed with other members for revenue-generating ideas. "We had enough dinners," recalls Snider. "I told them I'd go back to my (Spectrum) people and try to come up with some fundraising ideas where we could use the Spectrum. I gave it to Ed Golden (the hockey team's public relations director) and he came up with the carnival."

The Flyers' wives, mostly Canadian citizens prohibited by immigration laws from holding jobs, had often involved themselves in charitable endeavors. "But they were always small, like fashion shows," recalls Mary Ann Saleski. "And the expenses were always so high, we never made much money. We had wondered if there was anything else we could do."

Fran Tobin, Sylvan's wife, and her sister, Estelle Brodsky, solicited advice from carnival people in the Delaware Valley. "We still had the idea of doing different things for different charities each year," Saleski's wife explained. "For all anyone knew, the first carnival would be the last."

The concept proved too good to abandon. About 6,500 tickets, priced at $6 apiece, were sold in advance for the February 1, 1977, event and walk-ups brought attendance to approximately 8,000. Clarke's 1972 Team Canada jersey was auctioned for $1,055. Long lines formed to takes shots for $1 apiece at Parent, Inness and Stephenson, none of whom made a save the entire night. Leach and Dornhoefer volunteered for the dunk tank. Ashbee and his wife Donna spent much of the evening on their hands and knees retrieving coins tossed at saucers.

The carnival raised $85,167.35, which enabled the institute to purchase an electron microscope, critical in researching blood disease-causing retroviruses. "This is a good cause," Parent told Bill Fleischman of the *Daily News*. "We're all made of flesh. This damn disease can happen to any of us."

Dailey's acquisition triggered a 6-0-3 run, but the Flyers were tripped up 2-1 at Nassau Coliseum on February 12, leaving them 1-6-1 against the Canadiens and Islanders. Injuries suffered by

Holmgren (shoulder) and Bennett (collarbone) forced the team to dip into their farm club at Springfield, Massachusetts, where the Flyers had switched their affiliation from Richmond at the beginning of the season.

Al Hill, a free agent whose play during a preseason tryout had earned him an AHL contract, was proceeding towards career anonymity with a modest 10 goals and 22 assists. He had arrived home following a Sunday-night game in Rochester at 4:30 A.M. only to be summoned at 11 o'clock to Philadelphia for a game that night against St. Louis. The 21-year-old left wing arrived at the Spectrum at 5:30 P.M., and at 7:35 was on the ice for the first shift.

His initial NHL shot, a 40-footer, was driven between goalie Yves Belanger's pads. Hill then deflected in a MacLeish shot, circled the goal to feed Leach, and set up two other scores to complete a five-point night. "I didn't even know we had the guy," said Shero following the 6-4 victory.

Hill was as flabbergasted as his coach. "I was shaking before the game," he said, "and I'm still shaking. I was very lucky."

It took several days for the league to confirm that Hill had recorded the greatest statistical first night of any individual in NHL history. By that time, however, the rookie had gone scoreless in his next 3 games and had been returned to Springfield.

Holmgren saw the eye doctor while waiting for his shoulder to heal and learned that his right-side vision, reduced to 20/300 by the skate cut eleven months earlier, had improved to 20/30. All the better to see the bodies he was leaving splattered. "He must have 50 minutes in penalties just because he hits so hard," said Shero. "Is it my fault he hits so hard? It's his father's fault, not mine."

On February 17, the resurgent MacLeish scored his 35th goal in a 7-1 rout of the Rangers, while Allen again slipped into his office between periods to trade. This time the GM acquired two defensemen—Rick Lapointe, the fifth player taken in the 1975 draft, and Mike Korney—from the Red Wings in exchange for defenseman Terry Murray and minor-leaguers Steve Coates, Bob Ritchie and Dave Kelly.

Murray, who had been signed as a free-agent after being let go by California, played capably and had become the Flyers' sixth defenseman. But Ritchie, a third-round pick in 1975, was the only NHL prospect of the three farmhands. Allen didn't expect the 21-year-old Lapointe, who had lost his confidence in the chaotic Detroit organization, to make an instant impact the way Dailey had, but believed he had all-star potential.

Lapointe was thrilled. "Who wouldn't be happy to get traded to Philadelphia?" he said. In his debut two nights later at Montreal, he proved to be the only thing new. The Canadiens completed a four-game sweep of the season series with a 5-2 victory.

"It sure is psychological," said Parent about the Flyers' inability to contend with Montreal. When Philadelphia routinely handled its Sabre cousins, 4-2, one night later at the Spectrum, Dupont said,

The Islanders, two points behind with 3 games remaining, took their last stab at the division title on March 29 at the Spectrum. "We're more confident against the Flyers than against any other team," boasted Clark Gillies, but Philadelphia came up with a big-game performance that was as masterful as any since its rise to power. MacLeish dominated and Holmgren came from behind the net to score the winning third-period goal in a redeeming 3-1 victory.

One night later, the Flyers clinched their fourth

The valiant Barry Ashbee in action.

"We're so tight against [the Canadiens], we ought to pretend we're playing Buffalo."

Clarke, Leach and Barber were statistically behind the previous season's pace, but MacLeish reached 40 goals in a 4-1 victory at Detroit on March 5 and the Flyers maintained a 7-point Patrick Division lead. When Toronto won at the Spectrum, 4-2, on March 7, it was the first home game Philadelphia had lost to a team other than the Islanders, Boston or Montreal in two seasons.

Parent, who missed two weeks with a knee sprain, returned to help the Flyers rally from a 3-1 third-period deficit to a 5-3 victory in Los Angeles. Three nights later at Vancouver, Clarke fed Leach with only 18 seconds remaining to pull out a 4-4 tie. The galvanizing trip closed with a startling 6-2 blowout of the Bruins in Boston. "Put Montreal in our division," said a proud Shero. "Then we'll see how tough they are. They were under no pressure all year."

consecutive division title with a 3-3 tie in Cleveland. "I'm happy for the players; they had to work like hell for this," said Shero.

Indeed, after suffering so much self-doubt early in the season, holding off the rising Islanders had become a huge point of pride. The players celebrated like they had won for the first time. While Dornhoefer machine-gunned the Richfield Coliseum locker room with champagne, Joe Watson sat in the corner quietly with Parent. "You're good now, Bernie," said Watson. "You're good. Two years ago, it was unbelievable what you were doing, the saves you were making. Now, you're good."

"Just watch me during the playoffs," said Parent.

On the next-to-last day of the season, MacLeish reached 49 goals with a pair in a 4-1 victory over the Rangers. But the next afternoon, he was stopped five times by Atlanta goalie Phil Myre and fell short of No. 50. "I'm not disappointed," MacLeish lied. "I'm young. I've got lots of time."

Montreal's 132 points dwarfed Philadelphia's 112, but the Flyers still had the second-highest total in the league and were expected to reach the finals. First stop would entail another series with Toronto, where legal matters remained unresolved. "You're afraid to play your game there," said Shero. "It's getting to be a joke."

Certainly, the Leafs' coach had a sense of humor. Having failed to level Philadelphia with the power of pyramids the previous spring, Red Kelly announced his team would achieve victory through the power of ions. "I haven't read up on them," smiled Darryl Sittler. Yet some inexplicable force seemed to be at work during Game 1 at the Spectrum when Toronto jumped to a 3-0 lead in the first ten minutes and held on for a 3-2 victory.

Afterwards, Crisp, Dailey and Lonsberry were reminding themselves that one loss was not calamitous when Ashbee joined them in the players' lounge. He showed some bruises on his arms and hands to Crisp.

"I read a medical book," Ashbee said. "Bruises like this could be the first sign of leukemia."

"Get out," said Crisp. "You must have fallen down a flight of stairs or something."

Ashbee went to the training room where Dr. Viner was making postgame consultations. Viner did a visual examination and his heart sank.

"Normal bruises caused by a blow don't have an infiltrative feel to them," he recalls. "These did. I told Barry to come to my office the next morning and we'd do tests. But I told my wife on the drive home that Barry had acute leukemia."

The next day, the blood count and bone marrow samples confirmed Viner's fears. The doctor called Ashbee at his Delaware County home that night to say he was coming out to see him. "He had to know the significance of it," recalls Viner. "My wife and I got there at about 10 o'clock. I told Barry and Donna in the living room. Barry didn't cry. He never cried."

Barry and Donna called Heather, 15, and Danny, 12, from their bedrooms and told them the horrifying news. The family stood in the living room with their arms around each other.

Viner didn't sugarcoat a grim prognosis. Ashbee had the most virulent form of the disease. Chemotherapy could achieve a remission, but it would not last long unless it was followed up by a bone-marrow transplant, which was still a controversial and little-used procedure.

"They were doing [transplants] on an experimental basis at Hahnemann," recalls Viner. "And Barry had siblings (a brother and sister) who might have given us an opportunity to find a match. It was really the only hope.

"We told the media there was a fifty-fifty chance of achieving remission, which statistically was true. But we didn't explain that the remission, without the transplant, still only gave Barry a twelve to eighteen month life expectancy.

"I was totally honest with Barry, though. I don't take away hope from patients, but when they ask I give honest answers. He understood everything and said whatever chance we had, he would go for it."

The next morning, the day of Game 2, Ashbee called Clarke with the thunderbolt. The assistant coach said he would be at the Spectrum before practice to tell the team.

"I used to ride in with Clarkie to practices," recalls Lonsberry. "He called that morning and said he was going in himself and would meet me there. He didn't say why. When I walked in, he was pacing."

After all the players had arrived and Ashbee still had not, Clarke ordered the door to the locker room closed. "I thought he wanted to tell us how bad we were playing," Holmgren recalls. "Then he told us about Barry. It was like getting hit with a brick."

Nykoluk, who'd spent three seasons with Ashbee in Hershey, had seen him defy despair with so many injury problems that this news was impossible to digest. "Nobody's stronger than Barry," Nykoluk said. But he also remembered a practice three weeks earlier. "One of our defensemen got hurt and Barry filled in," said Nykoluk. "He skated up the ice and back just once and got all red. So red it was unbelievable."

Ashbee arrived during the skate. Afterwards, he spoke to the team. "The last thing I want is sympathy," he said. "I'll beat it. I'll win." He went to check into Hahnemann, where his chemotherapy would begin the next day.

That night, the Flyers were thinking about life and death, not hockey. After a pregame press conference by Dr. Viner, the Leafs clicked on two first-period power plays, jumped to their second 3-0 lead in two games and dumped the puck the rest of the contest. Barber scored six minutes into the second period to give his team a brief spark, but Sittler stole the puck from Clarke and beat a shaky Parent to wrap up a convincing 4-1 Toronto victory.

Sittler had been told of Ashbee's illness by linesman John D'Amico and had asked Clarke about it on the ice. Clarke nodded in confirmation, but the Toronto captain didn't share the information with his mates until after the game. If Tiger Williams was aware of Philadelphia's emotional baggage, his glee at the Leafs' two victories was still unrestrained. "Don't count the Flyers out," he said. "But they are out. We know their system now. I don't see how they can come back."

Ashbee called a press conference in his hospital room the next day. A small group of invited newsmen crowded in, shook his hand and then awkwardly waited for someone to ask the first question. When no one did, Ashbee, seated on the edge of his bed in a bathrobe, began. "The reason I'm having this [conference] is I don't want everybody in town to think I'm lying up here dying. Heck, I'm lucky. The doctors are optimistic. They think they caught it in time.

"At first I was in shock. My family took it pretty tough. They were in tears for awhile. But they know they can help me by being strong. I told them three weeks (the hospital stay required for a cycle of chemotherapy) is no different than any other long road trip. They say that chemotherapy treatments make you nauseous. I'm not worried about that. I've had hangovers that made me feel that way.

"I don't want this to be written up as a 'Win One for the Gipper' story. The players know I'm sick and I'm going to get better, that's all. They have their battle to win in Toronto and I have mine right here. I want to be ready for the parade when we win the Stanley Cup."

The Flyers practiced at the Spectrum that morning before their flight to Toronto. The mood was improved. As unimportant as the game had seemed after receiving the news of Ashbee's plight, their helplessness was triggering a need for something they could control, like a stronger effort to pull out the series. "We'll get back on our game and it'll be different," said Barber. "Toronto is playing the same guys a lot. It will take its toll."

At least the team's judicial burden lightened the following day. Trials for Saleski, Watson, Bridgman and Kelly had been set for June, but with Philadelphia in town for another series, George Finlayson, the Toronto lawyer handling the Flyers' defense, pushed for a plea bargain. Charges against Saleski and Bridgman were dropped in favor of guilty pleas from Watson and Kelly, whose actions had involved spectators.

"Dan Maloney (the Red Wing arrested for an on-ice fight with the Leafs' Glennie) had been found not guilty, so the Crown knew it didn't have a case against Bridgman," recalls Gil Stein, then the Flyers' in-house legal counsel. "And the charges against Saleski

for trying to conceal Watson's stick (which had struck a police officer on the shoulder) were ludicrous.

"Technically, they could prove recklessness by Watson and Kelly (for throwing the glove that hit the usherette)."

Crown attorney Robert McGee pushed for heavy fines and a probation period extending through the Toronto-Philadelphia series. As evidence of the Flyers' incorrigibility, he read a Lonsberry quote from the previous day's *Toronto Star*. "We'll do what we have to do [to win] even if it means the entire team must be bailed out of jail for the games," Lonsberry had said.

Judge Hugh Locke doused the prosecutor with a dose of perspective. "I don't know that something a hockey player says under questioning during a moment of enthusiasm has any bearing on this," said the magistrate. "[This] was not an important crime."

Watson was sentenced to a $750 fine or thirty days in jail; Kelly had the choice of a $200 fine or a five-day term. They paid and left. "We were told this would be best for everyone," said Watson.

Thus the Flyers were no longer a menace to society when they reported to Maple Leaf Gardens that night. But at the start of Game 3, they continued to endanger their own playoff lives. Stephenson, who had finished Game 2 for Parent, gave up a soft goal to Sittler at only 3:23. Ian Turnbull made it 2-0 on a power play.

Desperate for a break, Philadelphia caught one when Toronto goalie Mike Palmateer opened his legs and allowed Lonsberry to score from a bad angle three minutes into the second period. When Stephenson stopped Sittler on a shorthanded two-on-one, the Flyers broke up ice. Dailey's shot from deep along the boards went in off Kindrachuk's leg to tie the game.

Palmateer toughened, however, and with only 4:09 to play in regulation, Errol Thompson, from 20 feet up the slot, pounced on a deflected centering pass and backhanded a floater through four players. "You could read the label on it," said Joe Watson, but Stephenson, rising to his feet, couldn't reach the puck as it fluttered past his shoulder. The Gardens exploded; the Leafs were about to put a 3-0 stranglehold on the series.

Philadelphia fiercely refused to accept that fate and pounded the puck into the Toronto end. The nervous Leafs began to fumble and bumble under heavy pressure. Palmateer made saves on Clarke, Lonsberry and Dupont before covering the post on Leach with 44 seconds remaining.

On the face-off, Sittler beat Clarke and the puck

came to Salming at the goal line. He spun to his forehand and tried to clear, but MacLeish, standing inside the top of the circle, coolly knocked the puck down with his right glove. As Dailey moved to blot out the sun in front of Palmateer, MacLeish took two strides toward the boards and launched a low wrist shot, scoring just inside the far post to tie the game with 38 seconds left in regulation time.

The air escaping from the crowd poured into the Flyers' lungs. "I have never seen the bench so keyed up," said Shero. "There was no way we could lose now." At 2:55 of overtime, MacLeish, on a feed from Dailey, beat Palmateer with another wrister to give Philadelphia a 4-3 victory.

"Sudden Life," read the placard of sign man, Dave Leonardi.

The Flyers, nevertheless, fell right back into a hole during Game 4. With the Leafs leading 2-1 in the second period, Dornhoefer cracked Palmateeer with his stick during a struggle in front of the net, causing the goalie to retaliate on the back of the winger's head. Dupont, believing Mike Pelyk had done the dirt, went after the Toronto defenseman. Upon leaving the penalty box to go after a taunting Tiger Williams, The Moose was given a game misconduct by referee Bruce Hood.

Leach tied the score during a four-on-four, but when Holmgren was given a penalty for unnecessarily tripping Turnbull, Lanny McDonald cashed the power play. He scored again early in the third period to lengthen Toronto's lead to 4-2. When Hood next called Dornhoefer for tripping Palmateer, McDonald made it 5-2 and the Flyers lost control. Both Dornhoefer and Lonsberry unloaded on Hood and were thrown out of the game. With 7:16 remaining, Philadelphia was down by three goals, short by three players, and faced with killing Lonsberry's unsportsmanlike conduct penalty.

Even when Bridgman put in Dailey's rebound 9 seconds before Lonsberry's penalty expired, the team hardly looked like it was going to mount a comeback. But as the Flyers took a faceoff in the Toronto end with two minutes remaining, Clarke pushed the puck ahead of Sittler and Holmgren fed Bladon, whose rising shot from the point ricocheted off a Salming-Clarke struggle in front and accelerated into the top of the net with 1:49 on the clock.

"All of a sudden," said Bladon, "it was right there for us." Trailing 5-4, Philadelphia dumped the puck in. Leach got a standoff with Mike Pelyk, and Dailey, under pressure, hurriedly shot from the point. Palmateer flopped needlessly after the

unthreatening drive and the rebound bounced out to Clarke, who flicked it high into the net with 1:33 to play.

The Flyers—eighteen Houdinis who had been freed from a locked, submerged trunk—raced gleefully off the bench. They had tied a game that they had given up on.

Toronto survived the shock. Palmateer made a big save on Barber's riser early in overtime and the Leafs began to skate. Stephenson got his blocker up to stop Turnbull's screecher and Joe Watson slid in front of a George Ferguson shot off a two-on-one. He retrieved and tried to center again, but MacLeish picked off the puck and headmanned to Leach, two-on-one with Kelly.

Pelyk backed up to respect the possibility of the pass, but the Rifle was shooting all the way. His 45-footer dropped under Palmateer's glove at 19:10 of overtime. "The greatest comeback I have ever seen," said Nykoluk, and nobody argued otherwise. Philadelphia had pulled out a mind-boggling 6-5 victory to tie the series.

A huge ovation warmed the Flyers when they skated out for Game 5 at the Spectrum. This time, they were ready from the start. Leach scored in the first period and the millions of ions coach Kelly was deploying were unable to preserve the ten players he was using to death. From his knees, Leach tallied again with five minutes remaining to wrap up a solid 2-0 victory.

The Leafs' owner ripped his team. "How can I be proud of them," Harold Ballard asked, "especially blowing those games the way we did in Toronto?" But his players, down 3-2 in a series they had once controlled, refused to fall easily. When Stephenson misplayed a McDonald shot five minutes into the final period of Game 6, the Leafs took a one-goal lead for the third time in the contest.

Pelyk, however, tripped Bridgman, enabling MacLeish to tie the score. With three minutes remaining, Dailey, Philadelphia's best player in the series, raced to the line to keep the puck in. His slapshot was blocked by Turnbull, but Jimmy Watson lifted the carom as he was belted to the ice by Sittler. The puck flew past goalie Wayne Thomas and the Flyers checked away their clinching 4-3 victory.

A bitter Williams was restrained from starting a brawl at the buzzer, while his teammates accepted that the proud Bullies had fought their way off the mat. "I believe we did our best," said Sittler. "It just wasn't good enough."

Philadelphia had every reason to expect semifinal opponent Boston, which had run out of healthy bodies during the previous year's five-game playoff loss to the Flyers, to be tougher this time. But as Game 1 began at the Spectrum, Shero's team was not emotionally geared for another series and fell behind 3-0. Although none of the goals had been Stephenson's fault, the coach gambled that a change to Parent, who had not played since Game 2 with Toronto, might awaken the team.

It worked. Clarke ignited a charge with a lucky

Rick MacLeish was a natural talent who played his best hockey when pushed.

carom off goaltender Gerry Cheevers's stick and Dailey took a feed from MacLeish to cut the lead to 3-2 with 3:25 remaining in the game. The Spectrum crowd begged for a third incredible comeback and, sure enough, the Flyers tied the score. With Parent pulled, Clarke knocked down Brad Park's clearing attempt, fed Leach, then went to the net to jam in MacLeish's rebound with only 29 seconds left on the clock.

Parent had barely touched the puck during the period, so Shero considered reinserting Stephenson

for the overtime. "I was thinking about it," the coach said later. "I felt it wouldn't have been right."

He turned out to be wrong. Early in sudden death, Jimmy Watson angled off Rick Middleton, who put a routine 35-foot shot on Parent. The goalie made the stop but allowed the rebound to drop behind him. He reached back with his stick and fanned. Trying again, Parent knocked the puck over the line to give Boston a 4-3 victory.

It was the Flyers' first-ever overtime loss at the Spectrum, but they were making such a habit of bouncing back that it hardly seemed crippling. Philadelphia took a 3-1 lead late into the second period of Game 2 and appeared to be in control. But Wayne Cashman got away from a struggling Lapointe and fed Gregg Sheppard to bring the Bruins within one. Peter McNab then slipped Bladon and fed Mike Milbury for a stuffer that tied the game. Quickly, Dornhoefer netted a corner feed from MacLeish to put the Flyers ahead, but 23 seconds later, Jean Ratelle's breakaway evened the score.

Twenty minutes of overtime could not produce a winner, so the teams entered a second sudden-death period. Cheevers, a scientist at cutting angles, showed Philadelphia nothing but his roly-poly body, and Stephenson made a heartstopping save on what had appeared to be a certain game-winner by Park. Finally, Don Marcotte retrieved Gary Doak's point shot, circled out from behind the net and laid the puck between Joe Watson's legs to Terry O'Reilly at the post. O'Reilly jammed in the winning goal at 10:07 of the second overtime.

The Flyers did not kid themselves about their chances of coming back from a 2-0 deficit for the second consecutive series. "We're not playing Toronto anymore," said Lonsberry. "The Bruins match us line for line."

Dailey gave Philadelphia a 1-0 lead in Game 3 at Boston Garden, but the Flyers could not carry the play. After McNab scored, only Stephenson kept the match tied into the third period. With seven minutes gone, Lapointe pinched down the boards, Kelly didn't support, and Milbury blooped a two-on-one feed over the sprawling goalie. Cheevers stopped the only good chance down the stretch, a Dupont backhander off a scramble, and Philadelphia, losing 2-1 on a paltry 15 shots, was one game away from being swept.

"Hell, maybe we can be loose now," said Barber. Instead, the Flyers panicked, running all over the ice as the Bruins thoroughly dominated Game 4. Clarke, hobbled since the last match with a charley horse, was outplayed by Ratelle, and the absence of Dornhoefer, whose knee locked before the opening faceoff, left Philadelphia with practically no forechecking.

Stephenson fumbled a Ratelle rebound back to the Boston center, who broke a scoreless tie in the second period. Marcotte made it 2-0 with six minutes remaining in the game. It ended 3-0; the Flyers exited in humiliation.

"When we beat them for the Stanley Cup, they had all the good players and we worked like hell," said Joe Watson. Now, we have all the good players and they worked like hell."

Breaks had decided the first three games, but the more diligent Bruins deserved every bounce they received. Most of their players, including ex-Rangers Park and Ratelle, had suffered playoff losses to Philadelphia in 1974 and 1976. "After they beat us last year, I swore I'd square the books," said Cheevers.

Cherry told the *Daily News*'s Fleischman that he had copied the Flyers' system and had used it against them. But the major difference in the series was the four-man Boston defense that had proved more reliable than Philadelphia's supposedly improved six-man unit.

Perhaps that was because Ashbee wasn't around for guidance. Throughout the Toronto series, while enduring the hell of chemotherapy, the assistant coach had watched his team on television and had called the locker room with advice and encouragement. "I was supposed to report to Barry every day," recalls Joe Watson. "He'd critique us and I'd relay it.

"When we were in Boston, I started to hear a change in him. Barry couldn't remember conversations we'd had and that made it difficult. When you asked him how he felt, he didn't want to talk about it."

Ashbee was slipping away. Two rounds of chemotherapy had failed to achieve a remission. When the players returned to Philadelphia, they were shocked to see how much his condition had deteriorated.

"I don't think I ever felt more busted up and impotent in my life," said Dr. Brodsky. Ashbee's kidneys became infected and his body, overloaded with white blood cells, was incapable of fighting back. Chills alternated with fevers. "I saw him every day,"

said Saleski, Barry's Delaware County neighbor. "And to see a strong-willed guy like that wasting away was so hard."

Ashbee did not complain about the pain. Never, to anyone, did he curse or question his fate.

Donna spent her strong moments with Barry. She took her weaker ones in the corridors and waiting room. When Clarke went to Hahnemann on Wednesday, May 11, he was told he would probably be seeing his friend for the last time.

Ashbee was sleeping when Clarke walked into the room, but suddenly he awoke and said he wanted some ideas for the defense written down. Before verbalizing them, he drifted off. Clarke was told Ashbee would soon be given a shot and would not likely regain consciousness.

"Jimmy and I got there just as Clarkie and Crispie were coming out," said Joe Watson. "Barry didn't know we were in the room at first and then all of a sudden he told Jimmy and me to stop fighting. We weren't fighting, we were just talking. That was the last thing he said to us. Sometimes I wish I hadn't seen him like that."

Before he went to sleep for the last time, Barry told Donna that he was tired. "But in the morning," he said, "I'll have this thing licked."

She was with him when he died at 8:50 A.M. the next day.

Saleski told Heather and Danny their father was gone before the announcement was released to a stunned public. It had been only thirty days since Ashbee was diagnosed.

On Monday, May 16, the Flyers chartered a plane to attend the funeral in Toronto. More than five hundred persons filled St. Andrew's Presbyterian Church in suburban Weston, Ontario, and heard Clarke eulogize the bravest man he had ever known.

"It took an incurable blood disorder to quell a spirit that the loss of sight in one eye, a spinal fusion, torn ligaments in his knee and a pinched nerve in his neck could not dampen," said Clarke. "Barry never gave in to the luxury of exhaustion or pain. He always played the hand the way it was dealt.

"Barry was well liked and highly respected for his unselfish attitude of always being willing to give and expecting nothing in return. His blunt, hard-nosed exterior was often a cover-up for a warm, gentle and considerate human being. A man can be counted if he thinks he is doing right and Barry stood to be counted.

"He may be gone from us physically, but he will never be forgotten because he left a little bit of himself with all of us.

"Barry, you were a heckuva guy. Barry, we thank you."

Clarke's knees quivered as he looked at the closed casket before walking back to his first-row pew.

The Reverend J. Donald Joyce tried to bring sense to the 37-year-old's passing. "Death does not have the final say," he said. "I can't believe that white blood cells growing blindly in a body are ultimately stronger than a human being. Neither life nor death can separate us when we're loved. If you really be-

the fathers I've met, I've never met one so warm, so loving, as Barry Ashbee."

While the service was being held graveside, more than 800 persons attended a memorial observance at the Spectrum. Mourners were given cards with Ashbee's picture. "We will walk together forever" was written on the back.

"I hope the Lord has prepared the greatest for him," said Father John Casey, the Flyer chaplain. "A place where there's nothing but the greatest

Bernie Parent, right, with his mentor Jacques Plante.

lieve the things Bobby Clarke said, then we only hope that someone here will be determined to take Barry Ashbee's place. To say to himself: 'For me to be as he was to me.'"

The song the organist played as the procession filed from the church was in tribute to Barry's musical taste: "Take Me Home, Country Roads." Many who thought they would be strong learned otherwise when Ashbee was laid to rest at Glendale Memorial Gardens Cemetery. As roses were snipped one at a time and taken from a bouquet on the casket, Heather buried her head in the arms of Donna, and Danny leaned on Saleski. "Those children are so strong, but they idolized their father," said Saleski later. "Of all

defensemen ... [a place where] the ice is always smooth. And if they have a Stanley Cup there, I hope he wins it every year."

Ashbee's death was not the only lesson the team received in May 1977 about the fragility of life. MacLeish attended the funeral wearing a body cast, the result of a compression fracture of a neck vertebrae suffered in a van accident on May 4.

MacLeish and Dailey had been traveling to a dinner after a golf tournament when their vehicle hydroplaned on the curve of a rain-slickened Burlington County highway. The van flipped three times before resting on its roof. "We were only doing about 45," recalls MacLeish. "It was just one of those things on a rainy highway."

MacLeish, the driver, wound up underneath Dailey, but both men crawled out of the vehicle before help arrived. "We asked each other if we were all right," MacLeish recalls, "and I sat down on the guardrail. When I tried to get up, I couldn't."

The center, kept in traction at Pennsylvania Hospital for several days, was expected to fully recover by training camp.

His good fortune was a ray of light in a terrible month for the Flyers who, in three seasons, had gone from Cup winners to finalists to semifinalists. "I don't think this is a team on the decline," said Allen. "But Bobby Clarke made the point that when you lose four straight, there's something wrong somewhere. It seems to me we've got more talent than we've ever had, but maybe we lack some of the grinders."

The GM, hoping to upgrade Philadelphia's speed, selected two excellent skaters—defenseman Kevin McCarthy of the Winnipeg Monarchs and University of Minnesota right wing Tom Gorence—with his club's first two draft picks. The coaching situation was also a priority, with the late Ashbee's position not the only one needing to be addressed. The front office had become upset with the work habits of Nykoluk.

"Mike always gave the appearance of liking the (horse) racing more than hockey," Allen recalls. "He'd be in (press relations director) Joe Kadlec's office smoking a cigar and reading the *Racing Form*, and we started to wonder if his focus was right."

When Nykoluk, who had a year left on his contract, was given the nebulous title "coordinator of player development," his reaction confirmed a lack of ambition. "I enjoyed what I was doing even more than being a head coach," he said. "I don't know if I'm going to take the job."

He did, however– requiring Allen to fill both Flyer assistant spots, as well as the position of head coach for the Flyers' new AHL franchise in Portland, Maine, sixty miles from Snider's vacation home.

Allen asked Jack Parker, the Boston University coach, and Pat Ginnell, the coach-GM of the Victoria (British Columbia) Cougars, if they had any interest in the Maine job. Neither wanted to relocate for a minor-league post. However, a call from Morris Snider, longtime general manager of the Port Huron Flags of the International Hockey League, turned up a prospect. Bob McCammon, 36, coach of the financially troubled Port Huron team, had heard about the plans for Maine and asked his GM to contact the Flyers.

Allen heard good things about McCammon from Ken Ullyot, the coach-GM of the Fort Wayne Komets of the IHL, and after getting to know the aspirant at the June meetings in Montreal, hired him. McCammon's eleven years—eight as a player—at Port Huron figured to help him relate to the veteran minor-leaguers the Flyers would use to stock their Maine team. He could also be groomed to eventually take over for Shero.

Ashbee's successor also had head coaching potential. "I'd heard a lot of good things about Pat Quinn as a person," recalls Allen. Quinn, a 34-year-old Atlanta defenseman who was being phased out of his playing career after he suffered a broken leg in a fall off his daughter's skateboard during the summer of 1976, had spoken casually to Snider and Clarke during a swimming-pool break at the players' association meetings in Bermuda.

"They asked about my interests," recalls Quinn. "I probably wouldn't even remember it if I hadn't gotten a call from Keith." The defenseman planned to play at least another year but, learning Flames' GM Cliff Fletcher had given Allen permission to approach him, saw the writing on the wall. Quinn felt dumped, but was convinced by Clarke that the Flyers were presenting a bridge to a new career.

Nykoluk's position was offered to Terry Crisp, the 34-year-old center who had spent more time in the broadcast booth during the 1976-77 season than in uniform. With the firing of Don Earle after five and a half seasons, a full-time opening at the microphone had also become available, but Crisp decided to try coaching. Bobby Taylor moved from PRISM to become Gene Hart's color analyst.

Dornhoefer mended from another operation on his knee and asked for a two-year contract. The Flyers gave him a raise but only a one-year deal. "I have to look at it from their standpoint," Dornhoefer, 34, said. "I'm not a young guy anymore."

Neither was Clarence Campbell who, at age 71, was replaced as NHL president by John A. Ziegler Jr., the chairman of the NHL's board of governors and the alternate governor of the Detroit Red Wings.

Snider pushed hard for a merger with the WHA, which was down to eight teams and no longer able to attract big-name players. After months of negotiations, the NHL consented to accept franchise applications from WHA clubs once a new player-owner bargaining agreement was signed. The war appeared over. "I've never worked so hard in my life for something," said Snider triumphantly.

But the plan died as L.A. owner Jack Kent Cooke rallied opposition, and the WHA continued operation for another year. This gave goalie Inness, who obviously did not fit into Shero's plans, the opportunity to land with the Indianapolis Racers.

Allen exchanged his disappointing 1976 first-round pick, defenseman Mark Suzor, to Colorado for its first 1975 choice, left wing Barry Dean. Jacques Plante, Parent's mentor during his Toronto years, was brought to camp to pump up the goalie's sag-

Wayne Cashman had grabbed at Holmgren's face and the Flyer, convinced he was the victim of another gouging attempt, snapped. Both players were ejected from the game but continued to threaten each other in the Spectrum hallway. As Holmgren charged Cashman, the Bruin reached into his locker room and grabbed a stick for self-defense. Holmgren, in tears, began kicking at his antagonist as both teams poured into the corridor. "All these guys slipping and sliding on the concrete, nobody could stand up," said Jimmy

Bladon, after his record-breaking eight-point night vs. Cleveland at the Spectrum.

ging confidence.

The Flyers held unsupervised precamp workouts at the Coliseum and talked about rekindling their old spirit. "In a way, the thrill of winning disappeared," Clarke told the *Bulletin's* Ray Didinger. "A few years ago, it was a big deal every time we won a game. That excitement wasn't there last year."

Shero's enthusiasm hardly seemed dimmed, however. When McCarthy had an impressive camp, the coach almost instantly proclaimed the No. 1 draft choice "the greatest passer in the history of the NHL." The team spoke publicly of a renewed vow to defend each other and Holmgren kept that promise when he went to Jimmy Watson's aid during an exhibition match with Boston.

Watson. "It was kind of funny when you think about it."

A second brawl broke out less than four minutes after play resumed. Sixteen game misconducts were called, leaving eight Boston players and nine Flyers to skate themselves into exhaustion over the final 31:54 of the contest.

A gate was installed between the two locker rooms, and Holmgren and Watson (the first man off the bench) were suspended for the Flyers' regular-season opener, a 5-1 victory over Chicago. So was Kelly, who had led another charge off the bench during an exhibition game at Madison Square Garden.

Saleski, in danger of losing his third-line spot to Holmgren, saved himself with a hot start, scoring 6 goals as Philadelphia won its first 4 games. Parent, meanwhile, had to be financially rescued by Snider after learning his taxes had not been paid by former agent Howard Casper. The goalie received pledges of patience, too, when he struggled while Stephenson was out with a knee hyperextension.

"Bernie's going to have his ups and downs but I think we're overreacting," said Allen.

When Stephenson returned, he alternated starts and declared himself happier than he had ever been as a Flyer. "Not playing put me in a bad mood," he said after shutting out Detroit, 3-0. "To put it bluntly, I had some growing up to do."

So did Leach, who, nagged by Shero to check, took up residence in the coach's doghouse. MacLeish was not playing much better, but received more sympathetic treatment. "I think he needs a pat on the back more than anything else," said Shero.

McCarthy's performance forced Lapointe onto left wing or into street clothes and Barber was enjoying a fine comeback season. Still, Philadelphia was playing more inconsistently than its 9-3-3 record indicated. On November 17, the team rallied from a 3-0 third-period deficit to take a 4-3 lead on the Islanders, only to be tied by Bryan Trottier with 10 seconds remaining.

Allen signed the franchise's first European player—defenseman Rudy Tajcnar (pronounced TIGHTS-ner), a former Czechoslovakian national team member who had defected following an altercation with police in Switzerland. Louis Katona, a Toronto resident and Czech expatriate who brought Tajcnar to the GM's attention, told of more talent in their homeland.

The Flyers advanced Katona $20,000 to arrange for the defection of brothers Peter, Anton and Marian Stastny, stars of the Czech national team. Katona was sent to Europe with five-year contracts worth $1.25 million for Peter and Marian and $850,000 for Anton. Katona would earn $300,000 upon delivery of the three players.

The agent never produced the brothers and, despite repeated Flyer threats of legal action, failed to return the $20,000. But Tajcnar, who was sent to Maine for conditioning purposes, looked like a find. He spoke virtually no English, yet Shero insisted the language barrier would not present a coaching problem. "The players don't listen to you anyway," he said.

In his seventh Philadelphia season, Shero seemed sharper than ever, thanks to the sobriety strongly recommended by his doctors and Snider.

After his 500th game, a 4-2 Spectrum victory over Chicago on December 10, the coach reflected upon his longevity with one team. "Any job I've ever taken," he said, "I expected to be there forever."

The following night, against Cleveland at the Spectrum, Bladon took his own try at immortality. He opened the scoring by ripping in a carom of a blocked Bridgman shot, then started plays that led to goals by Saleski and Bridgman 25 seconds apart. When the defenseman scored twice more on slap shots to complete a hat trick before the end of the second period, Clarke retrieved the puck. Bladon said he did not want it.

"What, you think you're going to get more?" Clarke laughed.

As a matter-of-fact, Bladon did. He tallied his fourth goal early in the third period and assisted on a MacLeish score to amass seven points and a share of Bobby Orr's four-year-old NHL record for points in one game by a defenseman. "It was like I was on autopilot," Bladon recalls. "Everything was going so well."

With 6:13 remaining, Barber redirected a Bladon point shot to break the mark. After Philadelphia's 11-1 victory, the inconsistent, often booed player who had become trade bait with the acquisitions of Dailey, Lapointe and McCarthy, seemed as dazed as he was thrilled. "This is really a freak thing," he said.

The club tried to prove there was nothing fluky about an 11-game unbeaten streak when they put it on the line against Montreal. But the flu-ridden Canadiens made Shutt's first-period rebound goal stand up until they hit the empty net in a 2-0 victory. Snider, feeling a late penalty call on Holmgren had been pivotal, berated referee Bob Myers in his dressing room while the Flyers tried to take heart with its best performance against the defending champions in two seasons. But on December 23 at Boston Garden, the Bruins exposed Philadelphia as a team unwilling to pay the physical price in a 6-1 thrashing.

"Except for Dupont," said Clarke, "nobody threw a check all night." The Moose, already badly beaten around the face by Boston's pit bull, Stan Jonathan, stepped in to rescue the glaring Saleski from imminent death at the hand of Bruins tough guy John Wensink.

"I think we have as much muscle as we ever did," said Allen. "But we aren't using it. Somebody's got to set the tone. Holmgren has played his role fine, but there are times he needs a little help."

The GM rejected the theory that Schultz's trade had been a mistake. Still, fans and Snider wanted the Hammer—whom the Kings had dealt to Pittsburgh the previous month—in Philadelphia. Instead, Allen reached into Maine for left wing Dave Hoyda, who had punched his way to 112 penalty minutes in less than half an AHL season, plus defenseman Frank Bathe, a former Detroit farmhand who had followed McCammon from Port Huron to Portland.

Allen hoped to trade a defenseman and wanted to find out if the bearded Bathe represented depth. Shero, however, resented that he was not told Bathe was coming up and barely played him. After only one

Bobby Clarke was determined not to lose.

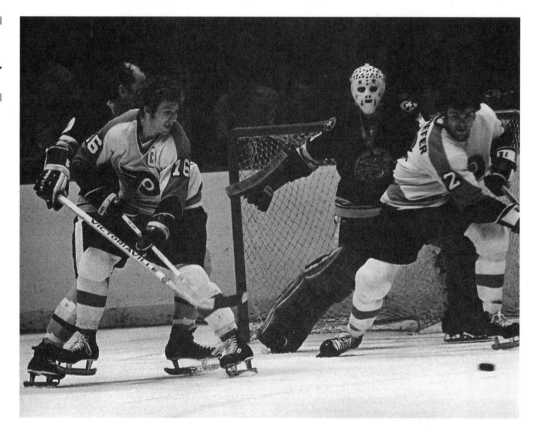

disfavor—Kelly with Shero and Dailey with the fans. Joe Watson, a victim of the youth movement, was no longer dressing for every game. Philadelphia got its biggest point in two years when Holmgren's goal just before the buzzer pulled out a 3-3 tie in Montreal. "This is like a cloud off our team," said Clarke. But two nights later it stormed again as the Flyers blew a lead and lost 5-4 in Chicago.

With neither goalie thriving in a rotation, Shero started to go with Parent, but the Islanders smashed

game, he was returned to Maine, where Tajcnar was laying an egg. The same Czech who had appeared so robust during his tryout wanted no part of any contact. "A pussycat," Allen complained.

Following a 3-2 loss to the woeful Blues on New Year's Eve in St. Louis, Flyer fans were hardly purring. A burger chain offered freebies with the presentation of home-game ticket stubs on the day following victories. "We want the Cup, not hamburgers," read a sign over Section P.

On January 5, during a 4-4 tie with Los Angeles, Dornhoefer suffered torn left knee ligaments that appeared to kill his final season. Kelly and Dailey, both going for points instead of hits, fell into

Philadelphia 6-1 at the Nassau Coliseum and took over the divisional lead after the Flyers blew a 4-2 third-period edge into a 6-4 loss at Colorado.

"My patience is wearing thin," said Shero, "and so are the soles of my shoes."

Allen recalled three Mariners—Al Hill, Blake Dunlop (acquired from Minnesota for Bennett) and Drew Callander—but Shero still played and defended his vets. "I know the effort is there," he said. "What else can I do? You want to jump in the river with me?"

Indeed, there were doubts whether the players were as willing to follow their coach as they had once been. "There was a deterioration of our ability to listen to Freddie," recalls Lonsberry. "In the transition to become more of a Montreal-style team, more free-flow rather than a static system, we started taking short cuts."

"As I think back on it, [Shero] was trying to get us to play the game differently," recalls Clarke. "But it was too ingrained in us. Old habits were hard to break.

"I thought players became individually more selfish, too. That's what destroys most teams. People start going their own ways and doing their own things. When we first came together, somebody who got a good deal on a new car would tell everybody. Later, they would just tell their closest friends and little cliques broke out. Guys would go out and wouldn't tell others where they were going."

The Flyers' heartiest fans were still bonding, even if the team was not. On February 6 when 14 inches of snow fell, 5,148 diehards made it to the game. Management opened the doors, offering free admission to anyone wanting sanctuary, free hot chocolate and a choice of the best seats to view a 2-0 victory over St. Louis.

Dornhoefer's knee healed earlier than expected, but Clarke suffered a broken thumb in a stick-swinging duel with Vancouver's Pit Martin and was lost for 9 games. The Islanders then added injury to insult when Potvin's check put McCarthy out of commission with torn knee ligaments during New York's 4-1 Spectrum victory on February 19. "We're in front and they have to feel we're better than them now," said defenseman Hart as the Islanders opened up a 6-point lead.

When Stephenson developed bursitis in his groin and Parent failed to part the waters, Allen pitched Pittsburgh for goalie Denis Herron. The GM couldn't close the deal, so the Flyers called up Rick St. Croix, a 1975 fourth-round draft choice, for trial by fire on a 6-game trip. Hoyda confronted Boston's Wensink and MacLeish scored in the final minute for a 4-4 tie, but at Montreal, Philadelphia closed its 2-3-1 excursion with a 7-1 defeat.

"They are on their way down," gloated Canadiens' defenseman Serge Savard. "They have problems in the nets, they don't have the same drive from their forwards that they used to have, and their defense isn't too strong. Bobby Clarke can't lift that club all by himself.

"Everyone knows what their system is—just control the wingers at center ice, the wings keep coming back and they try to scare everybody. They scared a lot of people. I'm glad they're in trouble

because hockey was becoming a farce."

Trying to recapture their lost swagger, the Flyers watched films of the Cup years before a March 11 Spectrum game with Boston. Thanks to a shaky performance by Bruin rookie goalie Jim Pettie, Philadelphia recorded a 6-2 victory, only its second of the season against one of the top five teams, and seemed to regain some confidence. As the chance to win a fifth consecutive division title became more remote and the trading deadline passed, players relaxed and focused on preparing for the playoffs.

St. Croix, no panacea, returned to Maine and Shero went back to Stephenson and Parent. When Danny Gare scored with 7:25 remaining to give Buffalo a 2-2 tie at the Spectrum, the Flyers logged their 14th game in which a win or tie had escaped them on a third-period goal. But on March 21, they defeated the Islanders 4-2 after MacLeish's penalty shot beat Billy Smith.

The exasperating center who had suffered a miserable season was coming alive. But in Los Angeles on April 1, he left his feet to knock down a pass and almost made the supreme sacrifice. MacLeish's neck was cut by Marcel Dionne's skate. Almost every towel on the bench was used to get the Flyer to the locker room, and eighty stitches were needed to close two gashes. "I didn't realize I was in trouble," he said, unperturbed as always, "until I took a drag of a cigarette and the smoke came out my neck."

While MacLeish's cuts were being closed, Barber, one constant in a season of ups and downs, went for the Kings' jugular by scoring two shorthanded goals on the same shift and Philadelphia won, 4-2.

Nevertheless, a well-played 3-3 tie at Nassau Coliseum failed to gain the Flyers any ground and, as they awaited an evening game in Atlanta on the next-to-last day of the season, the Isles clinched the Patrick Division championship with a 7-2 afternoon victory over the Rangers. Philadelphia assured itself of home-ice advantage through at least two rounds by tying the Flames 1-1, then came home to close the regular season by celebrating Gary Dornhoefer Night.

Organist Allan Pallar played "Nobody Does it Better" as the original Flyer accepted three standing ovations and a trip to Florida. Dornhoefer stood at center ice with tears streaming down his cheeks. "I think I cried a cupful," he said after scoring the only goal in a 3-1 loss to Minnesota. "That's right, a Stanley Cupful."

Philadelphia, 45-20-15, earned a matchup with the bottom qualifier, 19-40-21 Colorado, in the best-of-three first round. But the Rockies' Doug Favell was the kind of hot-and-cold goalie that could make a short series terrifying.

Sure enough, in Game 1 at the Spectrum, the ex-Flyer was at his flopping, diving, death-defying best. Despite 17 third-period shots, Philadelphia was unable to break a 2-2 tie. "I could just see a puck jumping over somebody's stick and some guy getting a breakaway and beating us," said Kindrachuk. Overtime, however, was virtually painless. Bridgman's wraparound beat Favell between his legs after only 23 seconds.

In Game 2 at McNichols Arena, Dennis Owchar's goal through a screen evened Leach's earlier score, but defenseman Barry Beck, the Rockies' rookie-of-the-year candidate, was limping with a knee injury suffered in Game 1, and the Flyers resolutely ground their opponent down.

Saleski put in a rebound by Bridgman, the best player in the series, to give Philadelphia a third-period lead, then Kelly beat Beck to score the clincher. The Flyers, 3-1 winners, were safely into the second round. "Now," smiled Kindrachuk, "you can say that [finishing] first in the division didn't mean anything."

Buffalo, meanwhile, had defeated the Rangers in three games and arrived at the Spectrum confident that its days of inservitude to Philadelphia were over. "We *own* this bleeping team now," an exuberant Jerry Korab had said after the Sabres went 3-0-1 against the Flyers during the season.

But the start of the series looked like 1975 all over again. Parent was strong; MacLeish scored two goals and Philadelphia forechecked the Sabres at will in the 4-1 victory. "It's no fun when things are going tough," said Parent, "but it makes it more fun when things get better."

In Game 2, second-period goals by Dupont and MacLeish broke open a 1-1 tie and the Flyers triumphed again, 3-2.

Sabre star Gilbert Perreault, who had performed his usual disappearing act at the Spectrum, snapped a 1-1 tie with a deflection early in the third period and Buffalo won Game 3, 4-1, at the Memorial Auditorium. But the following night, Kelly scored off a steal from Jim Schoenfeld, Lonsberry tallied on a setup by Bridgman, and MacLeish poked the puck past Korab to score on a breakaway, giving Philadelphia a 3-0 lead after only 14:13. Craig Ramsay sneaked behind Dailey to get one of the goals back, but the Flyers checked strongly the rest of the way. Parent looked like his old self in the 4-2 victory, Philadelphia's first all year on the road against one of the top five NHL teams.

Early in Game 5, Parent stoned Ramsay and Rene Robert just before Clarke put in a Dailey rebound on the power play. Holmgren gave away a goal to Terry Martin midway through the second period, but MacLeish stole the puck from Schoenfeld and fed Holmgren for a redemptive score only 14 seconds later. MacLeish then set up Lonsberry, Saleski overpowered goalie Don Edwards with a wrist shot and the fans chanted "Bernie! Bernie!" down the stretch of the 4-2 victory that gave Philadelphia its five-game triumph.

"The truth is they just checked us to death," said Ramsay.

The Flyers beamed with satisfaction. "People looked at us and said we were finished," glowed Jimmy Watson. "You don't know how much that hurt."

Every doubt the team experienced during the season seemed washed away. While Snider predicted a Philadelphia upset of Montreal, Shero announced he wanted another crack at (third-seeded) Boston. The coach got his wish when Toronto shocked the Islanders in a Game 7 overtime.

Both the Flyers and the Bruins, who had mowed down Chicago in four straight, were off for a week between series, so Game 1 at Boston Garden started creakily. Clarke set up Leach, then put in a Barber rebound to erase 1-0 and 2-1 Bruin leads. Philadelphia had two great chances down the stretch to go ahead, but Bridgman hit a post and MacLeish fumbled the puck in front of an open net. In the second minute of sudden death, Clarke was tied up on a faceoff by Jean Ratelle, who chased down a rebound and put a shot off McCarthy's skate. The puck bounced to Rick Middleton, unguarded at the opposite post, and the Boston winger lifted it off Parent's arm high into the goal.

The Bruins' 3-2 victory was their third in the last three overtimes against the Flyers and left Philadelphia feeling unlucky, but not overmatched. Boston's four-man defense, including journeymen Rick Smith and Dennis O'Brien, looked even thinner than it had the previous spring. Nevertheless, it was the Bruins who exploited Philadelphia's backline in Game 2.

Bobby Schmautz scored off a Bladon giveaway, then Middleton got outside Lapointe and caught the far corner of the net behind Parent. Wayne Cashman held off Dupont and batted a Gregg Sheppard feed out of the air to make it 3-0 and Middleton poked the puck from Clarke to Ratelle, who raced past Bladon for Boston's fourth goal. In the second period, Schmautz made it 5-1 after Don Marcotte lost his balance and took Parent's legs out from under him.

The Flyers came back, however. Barber scored off a feed from MacLeish, who then went around O'Brien to cut the lead to 5-3. Dailey steamed outside Brad Park for another goal and Clarke tied the game less than two minutes into the third period.

Unfortunately, all that hard work and momentum quickly went for nought when Mike Milbury's dive at the blueline stopped a Philadelphia clearing attempt and Middleton redirected a pass over Parent. The light went on, even though television replays showed the puck hitting the crossbar and never entering the net. The Flyers, unaware, did not argue. Nor did they score again. With 3:21 remaining, Sheppard converted a Park rebound and the Bruins, 7-5 victors, had a 2-0 lead in the series.

"I hope the Flyers think that God is against them," said Park. "They gave us two pretty good games here."

Shero benched McCarthy in Game 3 at the Spectrum, but instead of dressing Joe Watson, who had been sitting out the entire playoffs, the coach went with five defensemen. Philadelphia played more steadily and received goals from Dupont, Kindrachuk and Barber to win, 3-1. After six consecutive playoff losses to Boston—in every game the teams had been no more than a goal apart at one point of the third period—the Flyers had finally broken through.

But the Bruins took control early in Game 4. Ratelle hit a breaking Schmautz, who raced outside Jimmy Watson and caught the far corner of the net behind Parent. Marcotte converted a backhand feed across the goalmouth from Milbury, and Cashman scored on a setup from Park after Parent had lost his stick in a collision.

Philadelphia, down by three goals, began an uphill climb. Jimmy Watson converted some strong cornerwork by Holmgren and, with 13:26 remain-

ing in the game, Kindrachuk redirected a power-play feed from Dailey between Gerry Cheevers's legs to make the score 3-2 and bring the fans to a full roar.

"I honestly felt intimidated," said Boston coach Don Cherry, but his team did not and flawlessly protected its lead.

The Flyers, hoping to hit a man for a breakaway, repeatedly failed to connect on long passes and were called for icing. For almost nine minutes, they did not get a shot on goal. In a final, desperate rush, Kindrachuk's tip was deflected by Cheevers's glove and Park cleared a Barber rebound from Holmgren before it could be pushed over the line. Schmautz hit the empty net to clinch a 4-2 Boston victory, leaving Philadelphia one game from elimination. "How could we let them get ahead of us 3-0?" asked a tortured Jimmy Watson.

Clarke and Dupont were lost early in Game 5 at the Garden. Clarke, hit on the hip by Terry O'Reilly, skated one more aborted shift and spent the rest of the game on the bench while Dupont had to go to the hospital for a precautionary checkup after taking a punch in the eye from Jonathan. Kindrachuk scored two goals 11 seconds apart late in the second period to give the Flyers a 3-2 lead, but within four minutes they had reverted to their series-long tendencies and were caught up ice.

Peter McNab passed the puck over Lapointe's stick to Schmautz, who went around Parent to tie the game. Marcotte put the Bruins ahead when he converted McNab's rebound 6:18 into the third period and Schmautz tipped the puck away from Bridgman to McNab, who completed a five-point night by scoring between Parent's legs. Ratelle hit the empty net to finalize the 6-3 victory. Boston had followed up its previous season's sweep of the Flyers, by winning in five.

"When they beat us a few years ago they were a different team," said O'Reilly. "There was always

The unthinkable happened, Shero quit the Flyers: "The organization needs a change, whether they realize it or not."

somebody coming at you, taking you out, getting to the puck first. They would get up quick, now they get up slower. We wanted to win more."

Flyer veterans did not disagree. "Did you see O'Reilly and Middleton diving to make plays?" asked Joe Watson, who had dressed for Game 5 but had barely participated. "Do you think the Bruins would have beaten us in the second game if Milbury wouldn't have dived to keep [the puck] in on the winning goal? I don't see that around here anymore.

The Flyers had not played wisely, either. "We had a plan that could have won the series and never followed it," said Crisp. "We knew we had to hit Cheevers, but how many times did anyone do it? Can you count three?"

Despite that strategy, Dornhoefer, the master crease crasher, had been used little by Shero. But the retiring winger was reflective, not bitter, as he took off his uniform for the last time. "I realized, 'Hey, this is it, big boy, you're finally finished with hockey.' Right now, I'm kinda numb."

Snider spoke calmly in the locker room. "What we've done is slip behind Boston while we were chasing Montreal," said the owner. "We've lost some proven winners and one of the problems is that the kids we have are not ready to take on the attitude that the Van Impes, the Ashbees and the Schultzes had. When you get down to the short strokes, you've got to have some guys ready to go through a wall to win.

"We'll make some changes, but we never do anything just to be doing something."

Throughout the season, Allen had been trying to decide whether Shero had lost his effectiveness, but leaned towards keeping him. "I'm sort of a believer that you have to change coaches every once in a while, and I did wonder if [the players] were still getting Freddie's message," the GM recalled. "But [Shero] had a year left on his contract and there was a strong feeling to make a move after it ran out."

The coach, however, forced the issue. On Thursday, May 18, seven days after Philadelphia's elimination, he dropped off an envelope at the Flyers' of-

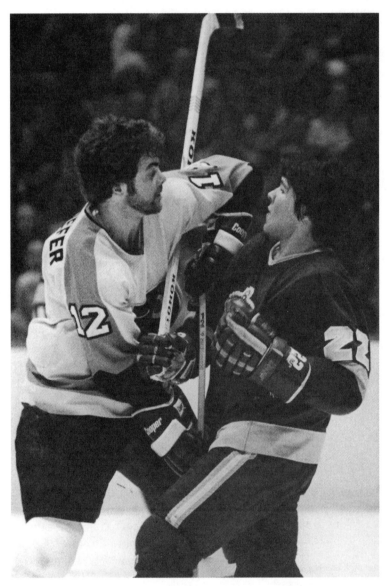

Dornhoefer's final season was 1977-78.

Sure, we played Buffalo a good series, but that's because Buffalo wasn't a physical team. When we came up against [Boston], some guys didn't work as hard because they knew the Bruins would fight back."

fice. Allen opened it to find a letter of resignation.

Although there were vague rumors during the playoffs about the Rangers wanting Shero, Allen was taken aback. So was Snider, who at first took the letter at face value. Two days later, the owner told the coach he was overreacting to the disappointing Boston series.

On that same day, however, Shero and his agent, Mark Stewart, met with Sonny Werblin, the new Madison Square Garden president, at Baltimore's Pimlico racetrack, where the Preakness was being run. Snider was unaware of the rendezvous, although he knew Stewart had become the coach's representative. Distrustful of the agent since his role in Stephenson's walkout, the owner suspected Stewart of trying to manipulate Shero's release.

Allen and Snider had no proof of tampering to take to the league, but thought there could be an opportunity to get compensation for the final year of Shero's contract. Snider had scouting administrator John Brogan write a letter to the coach stating his resignation had not been accepted. The Flyers then wired their mouths shut and waited.

"I issued instructions that no one was to say anything whatsoever concerning the issue to anyone," recalls Snider. "I made it very strong, with the implied threat that anyone saying a word would be fired on the spot."

The report that Shero had quit was broken by the *Daily News's* Stan Hochman on Monday, May 22, two days after Freddie went to the races with the Rangers. The Flyers' only reaction was a brief prepared statement: they had not accepted the coach's resignation.

With the news out, Shero appeared at a press conference arranged by Stewart. "I feel my effectiveness to motivate the players has been exhausted," Shero said. "The organization needs a change, whether they realize it or not. Most of the players have been with me too long and I've been with them too long.

"The idea [of resigning] never hit me until a couple of days after the Boston series. Man for man, I honestly believe we're better than the Bruins. So it must be me. I didn't do the job. I really believe I don't want to coach anymore. Coaching anywhere else would be a demotion."

At some time over the next nine days, Snider received a call from Werblin. "He told Eddie he had read in the paper about our coach," recalls Gil Stein, then the Flyers' legal counsel, "and asked if Snider would have any objections if he talked to Shero about

working for the Rangers. Snider told him, 'Yes, I object. He's under contract.'

"Rather than deal with Werblin, Snider called (Ranger president) Bill Jennings, told him about the phone call he had gotten, and solicited Jennings to serve as a middleman to work something out. Snider told Jennings what he wanted—a No. 1 draft choice and, as I recall, $100,000. The reason for the money was that it would pay for signing the draft choice. I believe Eddie settled for $50,000."

The Ranger president knew his team would never be able to sign Shero without the Flyers taking a tampering charge to the league. "Jennings had been put in a very embarrassing situation," said Snider. "But he was very knowledgeable and wanted to get it worked out. I was being pushed by some of our guys to hang tough (for more money), but I was just so happy to get the No. 1 pick, I didn't want anything to break that up."

Allen and Snider met with Shero for eighty-five minutes on May 31 at the Stadium Hilton. They walked out, shook hands and parted.

Shero left for New York the following afternoon. A few hours later, the Rangers called a press conference for noon the next day, but did not say what it would be about. While the Flyers were announcing that they had acquired the Rangers' first pick (eighth overall) in the upcoming draft for allowing Shero out of his contract, Ranger GM John Ferguson confirmed his dismissal.

Keith Allen was amazed that Shero, who had never shown any interest in administration and often admitted to a sparse knowledge of players on other teams, was now going to be the Rangers' coach *and* general manager. "One time I was talking to him about George Maguire (the Los Angeles GM)," Allen recalls, "and Freddie didn't know who he was. He thought I was talking about Al McGuire, the (Marquette University) basketball coach."

Shero may not have known how to be a GM, but he knew he wanted to be the boss. He said so at least five times at the elaborate luncheon press conference at Madison Square Garden that formalized his hiring. "After twenty years," he said, "I'm tired of people criticizing me, grading me. Here, I have full control. I have no one to answer to, except myself."

The new Ranger boss was taking Nykoluk from his token Flyer job and bringing him to New York as assistant coach. Shero admitted to some annoyance that Nykoluk had been demoted in Philadelphia. "I wasn't happy about it," he said. "They didn't discuss it with me, but I really don't want to talk about it."

Shero spoke like a man who had seen his Flyer years as a way station on his return to New York, where he had spent his brief NHL playing career and coached thirteen years in the system. "I remember twenty-four years ago when I was a young defenseman sent down subject to immediate recall (which never came)," he said. "Ever since that day, [I'd get up and look] at a paper to see how the Rangers did. My heart has always been here."

The Flyers' brass, meanwhile, was telling its side of the story at the Spectrum. Snider was asked if he accepted Shero's rationale that he could no longer motivate the team. "I not only accept it," the owner said, "I agree with it."

Allen admitted to some annoyance with Shero's intractability, but denied ever ordering him to play anybody. Except for St. Croix, the coach had barely used any of the prospects the Flyers had called up at midseason. "I was disappointed," said Allen, "but that's an indication that Freddie made the final decision on who was going to play."

Clarke was openly disillusioned that Shero had left in a fog of lies. "He said he had enough of coaching and he obviously wasn't telling the truth," said the Flyers' captain. "It's fairly obvious he had an idea of where he was going all along. He probably knew during the playoffs. You wonder how much he could concentrate on what we were doing.

"He really has no training to be a general manager. I think they're taking a chance. How do they know he's capable?"

The obvious candidates to replace Shero were McCammon, who coached Maine to the AHL Calder Cup championship, Crisp and Quinn. Allen conceded that the two incumbent assistants lacked bench experience. "It's not a plus," said the GM, "but I think that can be overcome very quickly."

Allen added that he might also interview individuals from outside the organization but didn't expect to make a decision before July. "The thing with Freddie has put us way behind," said Allen, "and there are other things to do first. I'm working on the draft."

Chapter 7

♦♦♦

The Magical Ride

With Fred Shero gone and the Flyers' Stanley Cup core aging, the 1978 draft provided a perfect opportunity for a new direction. Having already acquired the eighth-overall choice from the Rangers as compensation for Shero, Keith Allen believed he had the depth to trade for yet another high pick.

After three NHL seasons of swinging between center and wing, Mel Bridgman was ready to anchor his own line, so 27-year-old Orest Kindrachuk became attractive bait. On defense, the potential of Rick Lapointe and Kevin McCarthy made the inconsistent Tom Bladon expendable. Ross Lonsberry, Don Saleski and Reggie Leach, all of whom had slipped in 1977-78, were also dangled in front of the seven teams drafting ahead of Philadelphia.

Minnesota, Washington, St. Louis and Vancouver were not interested, so Allen pitched the next three teams—Colorado, Cleveland and Pittsburgh—and targeted two prospects: Kingston defenseman Behn Wilson and center Ken Linseman of the WHA Birmingham Bulls.

Linseman, a 168-pounder with spectacular quickness and a Flyer-like chip on his shoulder, was the priority. Birmingham owner John Bassett Jr. had made a business of signing 18- and 19-year-old players to long-term contracts, then peddling their rights when they became eligible for the NHL at age 20. He met with Ed Snider in Florida and agreed to sell Linseman for $500,000 if he was still available when Philadelphia picked. Allen and Snider suspected that the Canadiens also wanted Linseman and tried acquiring a higher selection to get him.

Meanwhile the Flyers brought Wilson to Montreal for an interview two nights before the draft. Although generally considered the most talented

defenseman available, he had played on three different junior teams, was once suspended for "indifferent play" and had a reputation for believing himself smarter than his coaches.

Allen and Snider took the prospect to dinner, then turned him over to scouting administrator John Brogan. "He grilled Behn and grilled him and grilled him," recalls Allen. "I finally said, 'John, you're embarrassing me.'" Wilson didn't rattle. He would be Philadelphia's choice if the team acquired a second pick or if Linseman fell out of reach.

The next day, the Flyers received a break. Cleveland owner Gordon Gund folded the franchise, bought the North Stars and merged the two rosters. Colorado moved up one place into the Barons' drafting position, but turned down Allen's trade advances. So Philadelphia bore down on Pittsburgh, picking sixth.

While Penguin GM Baz Bastien wanted Kindrachuk, useful players were also available from Montreal. "There must have been sixty-five [combinations discussed with the Flyers]," Bastien said later. One of them put Allen and Snider at each other's throats.

The owner urged Allen to reacquire Dave Schultz from Pittsburgh, but the general manager was convinced the Hammer's best days were behind him. "I remember walking out of the [hotel suite] and saying, 'If you want him that goddamn bad, I'll get him for you'," recalls Allen. "Eddie saw how much I was against it and backed off."

The evening before the draft, Philadelphia traded Bladon, Lonsberry and Kindrachuk to the Penguins for their choice, thus giving the Flyers the sixth and seventh selections. Allen, however, was still worried about the strategy of the Rockies, who held the fifth pick overall. Although Colorado was not going to spend the money for Linseman's release, Philadelphia wanted reassurance that GM Ray Miron would not deal to Montreal. At 4 A.M., Allen gave up a second-rounder (acquired from Los Angeles in the Schultz trade) and a third-round choice in exchange for Colorado's second -round pick in 1979 plus Miron's promise to make his own selection.

Since Linseman did not attend the draft, the Flyers used the first of their consecutive choices to take Wilson. The 6-3, 210-pound redhead was asked if he

**Ken Linseman:
spectacular quickness
and a Flyer-like chip
on his shoulder.**

agreed with reports that rated him the best defenseman available. "I don't want to sound over-confident," he said, "but that's what I believe."

The Bulls' buyout, a signing bonus and a three-year deal cost Snider $860,000, but those who had seen Linseman play were certain he was worth it. "A guy like this doesn't come along very often," said Glen Sonmor, his coach in Birmingham. "You can compare him to Clarke in attitude. His skills aren't as well developed, but he's quicker. A loose puck and he's gone."

Believing it had acquired building blocks at defense and center, Philadelphia next went for a sniper. With their own first-round choice, fourteenth overall, the Flyers selected Danny Lucas, a right wing who had scored 50 goals at Sault Ste. Marie. His linemate was a 17-year-old center who had accumu-

lated 182 points in 64 games. Philadelphia liked the kid, too, but unfortunately Wayne Gretzky, who had just signed with the WHA Indianapolis Racers, was not old enough for the NHL. Lucas, considered the best in his class at age 17, had dropped in most evaluations because he lacked intensity. But the Flyers felt they already had adequate grit.

After the draft, Allen retreated to his Jersey shore summer home to ponder his choice for coach. Assistant coach Terry Crisp was a loyal servant and student of the game but had played with many incumbent Flyers; Allen believed the transition would prove awkward. Pat Quinn had made an excellent impression in his year as an assistant coach but, like Crisp, had never run his own bench. The GM decided to go with experience.

Just before 10 P.M. on July 4, he called Maine Mariners' coach Bob McCammon at his Port Huron, Michigan, home. "I have some good news for you," Allen said. "Are you ready to take over the big machine?"

"So many things had gone through my mind over the last month that either yes or no would have been a relief," said the 37-year-old McCammon when he met the media at Ovations two days later. The Flyers' fourth coach admitted to being nervous about following Shero.

As a sign of organizational solidarity, both Quinn and Crisp attended McCammon's coronation. "No doubt Bob will make some mistakes," said Allen, "but with the help of the two assistant coaches, we'll get over those in a reasonable amount of time."

McCammon, however, would not commit to keeping both men on board. Following a meeting that afternoon, he decided to retain only Crisp. Quinn was not thrilled by Allen's offer of the Maine coaching job, but relented twenty days later. "Not everything is handed to you on a silver platter," he said. "You have to be flexible."

Joe Watson, meanwhile, was agonizing over his future. He wanted more ice time but was offered the option of completing his final contract year as a spare player or being moved to a team that could use his experience. Allen asked the 34-year-old for a list of clubs acceptable to him. Colorado promised a big role with the struggling Rockies, so on August

GM Keith Allen, left, and owner Ed Snider confer with Bob McCammon.

31, for a minimal waiver price, the original Flyer became the fifth member of the Stanley Cup teams to depart that summer.

Allen tried to move Leach, but found no takers. With Linseman and Bridgman penciled in at center, veteran Rick MacLeish was also dangled as bait to acquire depth at left wing behind Bill Barber. Unless Leach, coming off 32- and 24-goal seasons, bounced back or Lucas came through, right wing appeared iffy after Paul Holmgren.

But if seeing the first exhibition game was believing, the transition was going to be ridiculously easy. Philadelphia bombed Shero's Rangers 8-2 at the Spectrum. "I've been embarrassed before," shrugged the New York boss after all of the Flyers' first-round picks had scored, including Wilson on an end-to-end rush early in the game.

"Nice goal," said Brogan to John Wilson, Behn's father, between periods.

"Oh, he does that all the time," said Dad.

Philadelphia fans treated the game as a grudge

match. Signs read: "Rangers: Beware, He Lies" and "Win Today and Renegotiate Forever." But Shero played it for the preseason contest it was, leaving home two dazzling Swedes—Anders Hedberg and Ulf Nilsson—who had been signed as free agents following spectacular careers with the WHA Winnipeg Jets.

Both were dressed five days later at Madison Square Garden, at least until Nilsson's shirt was pulled over his head by Linseman, who also speared the Ranger, thus demonstrating how old Flyer tricks could be performed by new faces.

When Philadelphia returned to New York to open its regular season, the players who set the standards for the franchise saved the day. Clarke scored a goal and an assist and Bernie Parent, beaten on three first-period power plays, slammed the door as the team rallied for a 3-3 tie. "Maybe this year will be my last," said the 33-year-old goalie, "and maybe I'll be out there at 75 with a cane."

During their home opener, Philadelphia encouragingly carried the play against the three-time champion Canadiens but lost, 3-2. Fans gave Lonsberry, Bladon and Kindrachuk a polite hand when Pittsburgh came to town and lost to the Flyers 3-1, then cheered when Wilson scored two goals in a 5-0 shutout of Toronto. "How good is he?" asked McCammon rhetorically. "How good was Doug Harvey?"

After Clarke and Barber appealed to McCammon, the benched Leach got a new lease on life and a goal to tie Buffalo, 3-3. But Vancouver's first Spectrum victory in 18 games and back-to-back losses to Atlanta made it obvious the Flyers were still a work in progress.

"I'm scared stiff I'm letting everybody down," said a floundering Linseman before suffering a hairline ankle fracture in Boston. Philadelphia stunned the Bruins 7-3, but lost MacLeish to an accidental stick in the eye and Holmgren to a 3-game suspension for kicking Terry O'Reilly in a fight. Center Blake Dunlop, acquired from Minnesota for Harvey Bennett the previous season, was called up from Maine and scored twice in his debut, a 5-3 victory in Los Angeles. The Flyers then enjoyed a 2-2 tie and a reunion with Joe Watson in Denver.

But two days later in Vancouver, players awoke to learn that Watson's career had ended the previous night in St. Louis when his skate got caught in a rut during a hard check into the boards by Blues' Wayne Babych.

"At first I thought I was just stunned," recalls Watson. "I started to get up and (linesman) John

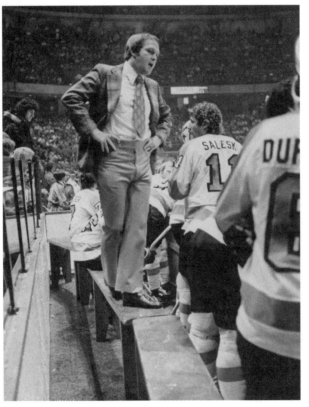

McCammon's first stint behind the bench lasted 49 games in 1978-79.

D'Amico said not to move. I looked down and the knee was here and my left leg over here, at a 45-degree angle. It looked like two legs, not one." His femur broken in thirteen places, Watson faced multiple operations and months in traction. "I never expected to go out this way," he said.

Parent shut out the Canucks 4-0, but fanned on Jim Harrison's shot from the blue line in a 4-3 Spectrum loss to Chicago. The Flyers remained as inconsistent as their goaltending. "I don't know, I still don't trust them," said old adversary Chico Resch, refusing to believe how bad Philadelphia looked in an 8-2 bombing at Nassau Coliseum. But the Flyers had many new parts that were not yet broken in. Lucas was sent to Maine, as was Linseman after his ankle

healed. And Wilson, the lone survivor of the youth movement, was still holding the puck too long and committing alarming giveaways.

Clarke, Leach and Barber kept the Flyers' heads above water. But after Shero's revived Rangers rallied from a 2-0 deficit to a 5-2 Spectrum victory, reports circulated that Bruins' coach Don Cherry would replace McCammon at the end of the season. "I resent the implication that we would be tampering," said Snider. The Flyers took the heat off by blasting Cherry's Bruins 9-3 at the Spectrum.

The following night, Philadelphia shut-out Shero, 4-0, at Madison Square Garden, so critics were temporarily soothed. But Holmgren was not. Playing with an injured knee, the hair-trigger right wing retaliated to Carol Vadnais's spear with a high-stick over the helmet and was suspended for 6 games.

Parent's inconsistency whetted the Flyers' appetite to look at Pete Peeters, an eighth-round pick in 1977 who had backstopped Maine to the AHL championship. "I hope we're not being premature," said Allen, "but we have high hopes for Peeters." Considerably higher, in fact, than the goalie had for himself. The 21-year-old had just returned from a training-camp knee injury and had family coming from Edmonton to Maine for the holidays. After receiving the call-up on December 16, he insisted he wasn't ready for Philadelphia. "McCammon couldn't believe it," recalls Peeters, who lost the argument but beat the Blues 4-1 in his NHL debut at the Spectrum.

Left wing Yves Preston was also brought up and scored two goals and an assist in a 5-2 win over Washington. Although Clarke set up one goal and scored another in the final 2:18 to pull out a 2-2 tie in Detroit, the Flyers suffered a much closer call than almost losing the game. After being hipchecked by Perry Miller, defenseman Bob Dailey landed on the back of his head, swallowed his tongue and went into convulsions. Luckily, Wilson, trained in first aid, got to his teammate and forced open the air passage.

"Once a victim goes into convulsions," said Dr. John Finley, the Red Wings' physician, "there's not much time. They (Wilson and Flyer therapist Matt DiPaolo) worked very fast." Dailey flew home with the club and spent the night at Pennsylvania Hospital.

McCammon was also suffering with his share of headaches. Holmgren's stuffer with 3:22 remaining pulled out a wild 6-5 win over the Rangers that was typical of Philadelphia's skittish play. Yet even with Leach's revival, the team lacked another threat off the wing. On December 29, Allen traded the suddenly little-used and thoroughly perplexed McCarthy, plus right wing Drew Callender, to Vancouver for right wing Dennis Ververgaert.

"Kevin is a very positive kid," said Allen, "but Ververgaert is a guy who should get 30 to 35 goals for us. Everybody is concerned with his attitude, but he's a solid player in every way."

Ververgaert, one of a long series of underachieving high Canuck picks and the subject of Allen's interest for two years, joined the Flyers in St. Louis for a dismal 6-3 loss. "Brutal," said Allen, who called up Tom Gorence, Al Hill and Frank Bathe.

Snider had the patience for a rebuilding season, but none left to play politics against the owners fighting a merger with the WHA. He appointed a politician, Robert Butera, to represent him on the board of governors. The 43-year-old former Republican floor leader of the Pennsylvania House of Representatives and the brother of Dick Butera, Snider's partner in the ownership of radio station WIOQ, became the Flyers' vice president and chief front-

office administrator. "I'll work as closely as I ever have with Keith, and Bob will handle all the other phases of the hockey operation," said Snider.

According to the forgotten Wayne Stephenson, the club was being overoperated. "All the extra players have made the team tight," the goalie told PRISM's Gary Dornhoefer while Parent was beating the first-place Islanders, 3-2. "The best thing that could happen would be for management to take a vacation in Florida."

Stephenson settled for Peeters's all-expenses-paid return trip to Maine, which gave the bitter veteran his first start in a month. He turned back the Caps, but not the other cheek. "I'm beyond the point of having to prove myself," said Stephenson, who revealed after the 5-2 victory that he had already asked to be traded.

While Holmgren, having completed his sentence in NHL purgatory, continued hard time in a leg cast to repair torn knee ligaments, MacLeish failed to pick up the slack. "We have some guys who don't go in the big games," said McCammon after a 5-0 loss in Atlanta on January 16. "If the veterans don't come through, what can we do?"

Indeed, many of the players who had gone to sleep on Shero seemed equally uninspired by McCammon. The team was short of depth and the rookie coach lacked the courage to sit his underachievers. McCammon's excitability behind the bench, a marked contrast to Shero's demeanor, was also a turn-off for some club members. "Not panicky," recalls Barber, "but a few times there was a little loss of composure."

Still, the Flyers were not quitting. They scored in the final minute to pull out ties against Buffalo and at Montreal, then climbed out of a 5-2 third-period hole to tie the Rangers 5-5 in New York. But when they looked sparkless during a 3-1 loss in Minnesota on January 27, and two nights later fell behind the Canadiens 6-1 after two periods at home, Allen had seen enough. He pulled the Maine schedule from his wallet to figure how quickly he would need a replacement for Quinn, whom the GM wanted to bring to Philadelphia.

The few fans who remained until the completion of Montreal's 7-3 victory chanted, "We Want Cherry," but only Allen knew a change was imminent. When he told Snider after the game, the owner was surprised. Although the Flyers had not won in 8 contests, they had tied 5, three times coming from behind in the third period. And while Linseman and Lucas were still in Maine and the goaltending erratic, Philadel-

After only three months McCammon was replaced as Coach by Pat Quinn.

phia, at 22-17-11, had the sixth-best record in the league.

Snider, who had been outspoken about the organization's determination to take a long-range view, worried how the quick hook would be perceived. He asked his GM to sleep on it. "It was probably the only time," recalls Allen, "that Eddie wanted to be patient and I wanted to make the move." Allen agreed to wait until morning but knew his decision would not change.

McCammon, who had just settled into a new office across from the locker room, had no clue his firing was imminent when he unloaded on his veterans after the game. "If the vets play well, the kids look good, it's as simple as that," he said. "We're counting on MacLeish for a line and he's not going. Dupont's not playing his game. And ever since he got injured in Detroit, Dailey hasn't played to his potential. We're playing five defensemen and four (the exception being Jimmy Watson) aren't doing the job. We don't lack talent as much as we do spirit or heart."

Ironically, Quinn had been in town for the game, having met with Allen the previous day. The Mariners' coach learned that the Rockies had expressed an interest in him, but that Allen had denied them permission to talk. Quinn wanted clarification on his future and his contract was extended by a year, but there had been no indication by Allen that McCammon's job was in danger.

After flying back to Portland in the morning, Quinn was surprised when Allen called and offered the promotion. "I told Keith he was making a mistake," Quinn recalls, "and that Bob should be given more of a chance. He told me he was going to make a change whether I took the job or not. I remember wondering whether I wanted to step into that spot, seeing what was happening to Bob. But I said, 'Sure.' I didn't ask why the change was being made."

McCammon and Crisp were called to Allen's office after Flyers' practice at the Class of '23 Rink. "He said the team was disorganized," recalls McCammon. "I was too shocked to press him on what he meant. We didn't talk long."

Both men were given the option of staying in the organization. They walked down the corridor to the coaching office and locked the door behind them.

Two hours later, Allen was slumped on a couch in the directors' lounge, defending his move to the media. "I'm not saying the players are blameless," he said. "A lot of them should be looking in the mirror. But I didn't think the team, not just some players, was playing with any degree of organization.

"I started to think about this a month ago, when it looked to me like we weren't improving. After a while we got better, then we started to drift again."

A few reporters had waited out McCammon when he emerged from his office several hours later. Tears filled his eyes as he spoke.

"We lost our composure in that game last night and that hurt me," he said. "But I didn't expect this; not now. I think the fans had something to do with it, chanting like they did and leaving early.

"The players make more money and have bigger egos than the players in the minors. Maybe I allowed for that too much. I let things go, figuring they'd appreciate and respect it. I guess they're human beings. They'll get away with what they can.

"They were used to Freddie's system. Maybe I should have just kept [my changes] simple. I could have spent more time on it; I was probably a little negligent, maybe foolish. I was too easy. I thought things would work out. I wasn't myself."

Today, McCammon questions whether he was ready to coach an NHL team at that stage of his career. "But I also think replacing a legend was very tough," he said. "I'll say this about the players: some of them had become self-satisfied, but they weren't disrespectful to me. Later, it got in the paper that Dupont had flashed his Stanley Cup rings in my face and said, 'How many of these do *you* have?' but that was really exaggerated.

"What happened was Crisp and Dupont got into a 'f— you' battle in practice. Of course I stood up for my assistant coach and sent Moose off the ice. I went to him afterwards and told him, 'We don't tell you to bleep off, don't you tell us that.' He had calmed down and agreed, and apologized. That was it."

Dupont and most of the veterans were not sorry to see McCammon go. Several, expecting a trade, not a firing, felt reprieved. Jimmy Watson insisted the players were to blame, but inadvertently indicted the sacked coach. "Freddie was a big believer in repetition," said Watson. "Maybe Bob thought we didn't have to practice fundamentals as much."

Closer to the root of the problem were players' suspicions that Allen and Snider pulled the coach's strings, although McCammon insisted when he was fired that every move was his own. "That's what I picked up," recalls Quinn. "Freddie had dropped that bomb about management interference and the players came to believe it. In retrospect, I'm pretty sure it wasn't true, but I would have no credibility with the players unless they perceived me as independent. Keith supported me on that."

Snow delayed Quinn's departure from Portland the next day, so the Flyers' first practice under their new coach began two hours late. He gathered the players at center ice and tried reassurance. "I told them I wasn't going to immediately upset the applecart," Quinn informed reporters. "I see confusion, self-doubt, anxiety. And it can't stop until someone takes control. Bob may have had it, but I don't know if the players believed it."

When McCammon cleaned out his office that day, he left Quinn a message of good luck. The following night, the new coach was reminded he would need it.

Philadelphia played hard against the Islanders but gave up three goals within ten minutes of the third period and lost 4-1 at the Spectrum. "We've been an inconsistent team for a long time," said Clarke. "I don't think it's going to change overnight."

Quinn took the blame for trying to install a new system after practicing it only once, and questioned the club's level of talent. "That's one of the things we have to talk about," said the coach. "[Management's] expectations may not be the same as mine."

With only one game left before the league took a seven-day break for a three-game series matching its All-Stars against the Soviet national team, the Flyers needed a victory to relieve some pressure. Atlanta goalie Rejean Lemelin came through for them, allowing five second-period goals in a 7-4 Spectrum victory that snapped Philadelphia's 9-game winless streak.

After two meetings with Allen, McCammon decided to return to Maine as the Mariners' coach. "I can't just sit around and do nothing," he said. Quinn, wanting to get close to the players and rebuild their confidence, decided to go the rest of the season without the buffer of an assistant. Crisp became a special assignment scout.

During the break, Quinn drilled the Flyers for two hours a day while Clarke and Barber went to Madison Square Garden to take on the Soviets. The NHL won the opener 4-2, but the Soviets rallied in Game 2 from a two-goal deficit to win 5-4, then scarred the NHL's psyche with a humiliating 6-0 defeat in the rubber game. "It hurts," said Clarke. "It was total domination."

But he and Barber came back to a rejuvenated Philadelphia team. Bridgman, playing on a new line with Bob Kelly and Tom Gorence, jammed in a goal with less than five minutes remaining as the Flyers rallied for a 2-2 tie in Toronto. The next night at the Spectrum, they again climbed out of a 2-0 hole

to beat Boston, 5-3.

"We're gaining our confidence back," said Clarke. "Before, it was twenty guys trying to do something but not really knowing what. Obviously [we] didn't have that much respect for McCammon. I don't want to belittle him because he did everything he could to make us a better team, but it wasn't working.

"Pat has everybody's respect. I don't know if it's because of his locker room presence, or the fact that he was here last year and everybody knows him, or that he played in the NHL. It's probably a combination of all those things."

After a strong game in Toronto, things were looking up for Parent, too. But while protecting an early 1-0 lead against the Rangers three days later, he suddenly felt a jolt, then a ferocious stabbing pain in his right eye. Jimmy Watson had pulled rookie Don Maloney's arm, causing the Ranger's stick blade to invade the eyeslit of Parent's mask. The goalie immediately threw it off, clutched his face and skated to the tunnel leading to the Flyers' dressing room.

Dr. David Pollock, the team optometrist, found blood in the eye's interior chamber and sent Parent to Wills Eye Hospital. Pollock was not unduly alarmed. Earlier in the season, MacLeish had suffered an injury that seemed similar and had returned in ten days.

But at Wills, Dr. James Tasman found Parent had suffered two conjunctival tears and admitted him to Pennsylvania Hospital. Both eyes were patched and total bed rest was prescribed for at least seven days. "If all goes well, Bernie could be back in three weeks," said team physician Dr. Edward Viner. "Barring further complications, he should ultimately be all right."

Parent, however, was not nearly as confident as he lay in darkness. "The way the doctor was talking downstairs, the eye is badly damaged," he told the Bulletin's Ray Didinger. "This is what happens to old goalies, I guess. You forget to duck. Something like this hits you when you're 34 years old, it makes you think a little bit."

New York had rallied against Stephenson for a 4-2 victory, but he won three of his next four games as Philadelphia continued its turnaround. Ververgaert, however, had scored only 5 goals in 20 games since his acquisition. So when the Canucks, claiming McCarthy had a preexisting hip condition that forced him out of their lineup after only one game, complained about receiving damaged goods, Allen offered to void the deal. Unwilling to have Ververgaert back, Vancouver GM Jake Milford declined the offer and NHL president John Ziegler found the Flyers innocent of wrongdoing.

Linseman, his ankle healed and his desire burning after 38 games in Maine, was recalled on February 28 to set up three goals in a 4-4 tie at Boston. "On one rush, I started off two steps ahead of Kenny and before I took two more, he was ahead of me," said Dunlop. The Rat, so nicknamed by Clarke ("Because he looks like one," explained the captain), added two more assists in a 6-1 rout at Buffalo.

With Linseman earning a place in the lineup, Saleski, who had become a spare, was traded on March 4 to the Rockies for an exchange of third-round picks in the 1980 draft.

Changes were made in the net, too. Hit on the knee in Boston, Stephenson was questionable for the Buffalo game, so the Flyers summoned Robbie Moore, a 5-foot-5, former University of Michigan goalie who quit dental school for a shot with the Mariners, to back up Rick St. Croix. When Stephenson volunteered to play after all, Quinn decided to give the minor-leaguer a taste of atmosphere by dressing him, not realizing that under NHL rules he was making Moore the one allowable emergency recall and leaving St. Croix in a position where he would have to clear waivers to remain eligibile to play for Philadelphia.

Thus, St. Croix was useless when Stephenson's knee needed further rest. Quinn was forced to use Moore, who stopped 22 easy shots in a 5-0 defeat of Colorado. "The Flyers sent me down for a year to work on my size," he said. "Actually, I figured out that I cover exactly one less square foot than Ken Dryden. As long as I can stand in the middle and touch both posts, I'm okay."

Leach was coming up increasingly big due to Quinn's positive approach. "I think it's fair to say we thought we had lost Reggie," said Allen. "Freddie handled 95 percent of the players right. This was one guy he was wrong about." MacLeish, too, was awakening, and in a reflection of the Flyers' rekindled, uh, spirit, they and the Kings set new NHL game records for penalties (54) and minutes (303) in a 6-3 Philadelphia victory at the Spectrum on March 11.

The Flyers left the fourth-place Flames behind with a 4-1 win in Atlanta and began courting second, despite discouraging reports from Parent. "It looks like there's been a party in a room with a lot of people smoking for five or six hours," he said from his Cherry Hill home.

At least the NHL owners were finally seeing clearly. They announced a plan on March 22 to ad-

mit the four strongest survivors of the six-team WHA—Edmonton, Winnipeg, Quebec and New England—into the NHL the following season for $6 million each. The approval of a balanced schedule (all teams playing each other four times) and a playoff format that would seed teams first through sixteenth for the following (1979-80) season served to render the divisional rankings virtually meaningless just as the Flyers were reasserting their power within the Patrick Division.

Bridgman's goal capped a rally from a 4-0 deficit to a buoying 4-4 tie with New York at Madison Square Garden. "We're better than that team," declared Linseman. The Rangers didn't offer much of a counterargument when they came to the Spectrum on April 1. With second place on the line, Shero started goalie John Davidson, coming off an 18-game absence with back problems, and Holmgren's three points paced the Flyers to a 7-3 victory.

Philadelphia was outclassed by the division champion Islanders 3-1 at the Spectrum and 9-2 at Nassau Coliseum, but wrapped up second place and a sixth-straight 40-win season with a 4-2 Spectrum victory over Atlanta in the regular-season finale. Dunlop, proving to be a fine Allen find, scored his 20th goal and the Flyers, 18-8-4 under Quinn, glowed with their recovery. "A lot of bleep happened around here," said Stephenson, "but we managed to wade through it."

Two nights later, they were back in deeper than ever. In the opener of a best-of-three series against a 63-point Vancouver team, Philadelphia took several early momentum-killing penalties, then surrendered a goal to Thomas Gradin on a three-on-one break. Stephenson flubbed a savable shot by Stan Smyl only nine seconds into the third period and Quinn's team, down two goals, faced a tall problem in a short series.

Clarke got the club on the board, but the Canucks continued to effectively dump the puck until Don Lever converted a carom off Dailey's skate to restore a two-goal lead. Suddenly gagging at the realization of how close it was to the biggest victory in franchise history, Vancouver gave up a breakaway goal by Leach, but netminder Gary Bromley held off the Flyers' desperate final flurry. The 3-2 loss sent both clubs to British Columbia for a contest that could end Philadelphia's season.

Clarke was determined not to let that happen, but as Game 2 began, his teammates looked terror-stricken. With Moore, a goalie of only five games' NHL experience, in the net, the Flyers played 9:23 of the first period shorthanded. Clarke, on the ice for fourteen minutes, checked ferociously to keep Philadelphia in the game until Barber fed Leach to tie the score 2-2 just before the period break.

As the Canucks went to their locker room, coach Harry Neale looked up the hallway and saw Allen following official Bryan Lewis. "Bryan was a stubborn referee, I thought you couldn't get to him," recalls Neale. "But he came out in the second period and called nothing."

Gorence put the Flyers ahead off a Harold Snepts giveaway, but Gradin came right back on a breakaway only 36 seconds later. Quinn cut down to nine forwards (it seemed as if seven of them were Clarke) plus four defensemen, and his team raced across a high wire with no net beneath.

With less than seven minutes remaining, Holmgren buried Bob Manno with a check at the Philadelphia line and Linseman raced away. Snepts had an angle to cut the Rat off, so Linseman pulled up, sending the Vancouver defenseman skidding to the corner. With incredible acceleration, Linseman was back at full stride within fifteen feet. He fought off a hook by Don Kozak and reached out to tip the puck between Bromley's legs.

The rookie turned and sped past the Canuck bench in a triumphant, mocking dance. But three minutes later, Gradin redirected Manno's point drive to tie the score again. "You think maybe fate is taking its hand and it's not meant to be," Quinn later admitted wondering.

With 57 seconds remaining, Clarke was thinking only about winning the most important face-off of the season as he awaited the drop in the Vancouver end. "You see him bearing down and you just know it's coming back to you," said Leach. Clarke won the draw cleanly and backhanded the puck to the Rifle, who blew a shot off Bromley's stick and between his legs. Dailey one-armed Gradin on the last Canuck rush, Barber hit the empty net, and Philadelphia, in one of the greatest clutch performances of Clarke's career, kept its season alive with a hair-raising 6-4 victory.

"Clarkie just never thought we could lose, even with the funny things that were happening," said Linseman, "so we didn't either."

Vancouver figured to have as much chance to win a Game 3 at the Spectrum as the Flyers would allow. "We always talk about not taking stupid penalties," warned Clarke, "and then we go out and do it anyway." But maintaining its discipline, the team jumped to a 2-0 lead on goals by Clarke and Hill. Gradin answered, but Leach, Dunlop and Gorence

scored within the first 10:27 of the second period and the Canucks packed it in. Philadelphia rolled to a 7-2 victory and into the quarterfinals against Shero's Rangers, who had swept Los Angeles.

In Game 1, the Flyers took five penalties and fell behind 2-0, but Moore held them in the contest and they gradually picked up the pace. Kelly hit the net on a first-period power play and Barber tied the score on a backhander with 4:58 remaining in the third. Moore staggered to stop Don Maloney's two-on-one in the final minute, then rejoiced as Linseman's wrist shot 44 seconds into overtime gave Philadelphia a 3-2 victory. "This is all a dream," said the rookie goalie, "and I hope I never wake up."

Unfortunately, the alarm clock rang in Game 2. With the score 1-1 late in the first period, Ron Greschner stole the puck from Clarke and soloed to put the Rangers ahead. Maloney scored off the skate of Norm Barnes – a callup to replace the injured Wilson – and Moore, knocked down when Dailey pushed Phil Esposito during New York's fourth goal, had to be replaced by Stephenson. The only injury Moore suffered was a burst bubble as the Rangers went on to a 7-1 rout.

"That second period was the worst I've ever seen us play in the playoffs," said Allen. The Flyers had survived silly penalties and foolish gambles against the Canucks, but were now up against a team whose defensemen could move the puck. "We're giving them time," said Linseman. "And confidence."

In Game 3 at Madison Square Garden, Philadelphia took a 1-0 lead on a goal by Bridgman. But Maloney tipped a point drive between Stephenson's legs, then stepped outside Gorence to put the puck in off the goalie's pads. Anders Hedberg then soloed off a bad Leach pass to complete a three-goal explosion within 3:24.

Although the Flyers were the more aggressive team, New York, in winning 5-1, continually trapped Philadelphia up ice and controlled the power play. "I can't remember taking a face-off in our end the whole night," said Clarke.

"I want to win this series even more because of the way the Flyers play," said Hedberg, displaying a four-stitch cut on his forehead caused by a Holmgren high stick.

In Game 4, Quinn went back to Moore, who promptly muffed an early Don Murdoch shot to put Philadelphia in a hole. The Flyers stormed the New York end, but Wilson hit the post and John Davidson, glowing hotter with each game, stoned Leach, Linseman and Barber on good chances. Eddie

Johnstone scored from the slot, Phil Esposito put in a rebound, Bobby Sheehan trapped Dupont and scored with a breakaway, and the rout was on. It ended 6-0, the third consecutive lopsided Ranger victory in a series taking place mostly in New York's zone. "It's not like we're playing that badly," said Watson. "I'm shocked."

Before Game 5, Quinn mulled weak options. Moore had been exposed, Peeters had suffered a pulled hamstring in the Mariners' playoff opener and, after being made ineligible, St. Croix had seen no NHL action for the final five weeks of the regular season. So the coach went with Stephenson, who gave up a power-play goal to Greschner and a shorthanded one to Walt Tkaczuk before the first period ended.

Philadelphia skaters thrashed desperately around Davidson, but would either shoot the puck into the flopping goalie or miss the net while leaving the back door open. When Tkaczuk and Steve Vickers cashed giveaways by Leach and Linseman to extend the Ranger lead to 4-0 seven minutes into the third period, Quinn, having nothing to lose, pulled Stephenson. Ron Duguay hit the empty net on a two-on-one, but then the Flyers, their hopes all but gone, finally began to beat Davidson.

Leach scored the team's first goal in 168:59 of playing time, then Dailey and Wilson hit the net to stir the stragglers in a half-emptied Spectrum. But with Stephenson back in goal, Carol Vadnais finished off a three-on-one and New York pulled away to an 8-3 victory. Philadelphia, outscored 28-8 during the five games, had been eliminated short of the semifinals for the first time in seven years.

Shero tried to be gracious, comparing the spirit of his Rangers to both past and present Flyers. But he did not deny the obvious: the smarter club had won. "They had too many guys hitting too much," he said. "We had muscle when I coached the Flyers, but we used it judiciously."

Snider was calm in the locker room. "A lot of this is difficult to understand," he said. "But the Rangers were well disciplined and well coached and they deserved to win. By the same token, I see the future of our hockey club. Despite this holocaust, I think we're going up, not down."

Philadelphia had turned over six new regulars and still won 40 games and one playoff round. But to become an elite team again, the Flyers had to stabilize themselves in goal.

Three of Philadelphia's top eye specialists—doctors Louis Karp, Harold Scheie and William Tasman—concurred that Parent should retire. His lens had been permanently subluxed, or pushed back, resulting in a buildup of pressure in the eye. While medication could control the condition, his ability to focus and his depth perception would never again be normal.

"He can't catch a ball his kids throw to him, let alone stop a puck," said team physician Dr. Viner. "And his eye will forever be more highly vulnerable to future serious injury."

Parent, whose father was very ill in Montreal, was ashen-faced when his retirement was made official at a May 31 press conference. "It's an awful feeling," he said. "Until I got the official word, I still had my hopes."

The Flyers assured Parent a job with the organization for as long as he wanted one. Allen began the task of finding Stephenson employment elsewhere while looking for a younger veteran upgrade to share the net in 1979-80 with Peeters. On June 7, Philadelphia acquired 30-year-old Phil Myre from St. Louis for Dunlop and Lapointe.

Myre had become expendable because the Blues had the rights to a bright WHA goalie, Mike Liut. Dunlop had done a good job, but was behind Clarke, MacLeish, Bridgman and Linseman on the depth chart at center. Lapointe's cause was championed by Quinn—"I felt Rick was on the doorstep," the coach said—but after three inconsistent years, Allen had given up on the once-prized trade acquisition and hoped to find a top defensive prospect in the upcoming draft.

The NHL, having buckled to a right-to-work lawsuit threatened by Art Kaminsky, the agent for 19-year-old prospect Tom McCarthy, had lowered the age of eligibility to 19, thus doubling the size of the 1979 draft pool. The Flyers, selecting fourteenth, felt they could obtain a blue chip prospect.

Keith Brown of the Portland Winter Hawks, a 19-year-old defenseman Allen thought would still be available, went seventh to Chicago. But a sniping left wing, almost as perfect for Philadelphia's needs as a defenseman, remained on the board as picks seven through twelve were used on 19-year-olds. The Flyers thought they had little chance of landing Brian Propp, the 20-year-old from the Brandon Wheat Kings who had scored 94 goals in 1978-79. But only one choice—by the Rangers—remained before Philadelphia's turn.

"Doug Sulliman, left wing from the Kitchener Rangers," came the voice of New York's head scout Danny Summers over the conference call speaker. Allen announced Propp's name next as the Flyers' contingent cheered.

When two good defensive prospects—Brandon's Brad McCrimmon and Kingston's Jay Wells—went fifteenth and sixteenth, Philadelphia took defenseman Blake Wesley from Portland with the twenty-second pick. With 292 penalty minutes, Wesley was a stereotypical Flyer selection, but their next choice came out of the blue and out of Sweden. With the thirty-fifth pick, Philadelphia took Swedish national team goaltender Pelle Lindbergh.

"Jerry [Melnyk] scouted him at the Izvestia Tournament in Moscow and came back raving," Allen told reporters. "We won't get him for another year, he's going to play for Sweden in the Olympics.

To Lindbergh, who had first been told at age 10 that he played like Parent, the call from Melnyk on draft day was flabbergasting. "Bernie was my hero, and the Flyers were the team I dreamed of playing for," Lindbergh later said. "I couldn't believe they wanted me."

Philadelphia selected another Swede, defenseman Thomas Eriksson, in the fifth round, and didn't rest when the draft ended after six rounds. Realizing that only 126 picks were to be made and that some promising players would remain unchosen, Brogan had pitched Snider earlier on aggressively recruiting free agents.

Brogan remembers the Flyers signing more than 30 players to tryout forms before the draft, expecting most of the the forms to be torn up as players were chosen by other clubs. Yet even on draft day, Philadelphia's scouts were in the field trying to talk disappointed undrafted players into determining their own fates now rather than waiting to be picked the following year.

While other teams had the same idea, the Flyers pursued it most ambitiously. By November 1, for bonuses as low as $10,000, Philadelphia had locked up six 19-year-olds who could have been high picks in 1980: two defensemen, Marc-Andre Marchand and Simon Learmouth; two wingers, Bill Barber's younger brother Dan, and Greg Adams; and centers Ron Flockhart and Tim Kerr.

Melnyk had found Flockhart dipsy-doodling to

his heart's content in a British Columbia Tier II league. The Edmonton-based scout had seen Kingston's Kerr on one of his visits east, but wasn't very impressed. "He wasn't aggressive enough," recalls Melnyk. But eastern scout Eric Coville pleaded Kerr's potential to Allen and got the go-ahead to offer him a contract.

"I came to practice one day and a little guy introduced himself as Eric Coville from the Flyers," recalls Kerr. "He wanted to know if we could go out for

The warrior,
Bernie Parent.

dinner. I was about to sign with Detroit. After practice, I was going to go out and look at a car I wanted."

"C'mon, let's go buy it," said Coville.

They looked at the car, then went to eat.

"The money (which included a $60,000 signing bonus) was about the same Detroit had offered," said Kerr, "and my agent told me I probably wouldn't get any more by waiting a year to see who drafted me.

"Jim Morrison, my coach, said the Flyers had a classy organization and I should go with them. I was a pretty confident kid. I knew Clarke and MacLeish were getting older and I thought I'd get a good chance, even if it would be a harder team to make than the

Red Wings."

Joe Watson, meanwhile, went to work for Philadelphia as an advance scout. McCammon won a second consecutive Calder Cup at Maine and agreed to a contract extension through the end of the 1980-81 season. Quinn, who had worked without an assistant through the end of the 1978-79 season, thought the time had come to get help. The *Philadelphia Journal's* Don Wilno broke the news that Clarke had been offered the position as a playing coach.

The captain was torn. Distance had developed between himself and teammates who perceived him as management's confidant, and he worried about how this new authority would affect locker room dynamics.

Holmgren, who had become Clarke's best friend on the team, urged him to accept. "He's been offering what he thinks as long as I've been here," Holmgren said. "What else was he doing but helping to coach? All he wants is what's good for the Flyers."

"Obviously this could backfire and destroy what it's taken me ten years to build," Clarke said when his appointment became official on August 10. "But I think the challenge is worth the risk. If a guy is going to be resentful of me or my position, then he's looking for an excuse."

Stephenson, ignored in the expansion draft (Philadelphia lost only Dave Hoyda, to Winnipeg), was traded to Washington for a third round draft choice. After being bitter for so long in his role as backup, Stephenson was surprisingly gracious towards the Flyers at a Capital Center press conference. "I never really had a future there," he said. "But looking at the overview of it, I had to be very happy with it. The Flyers offered me a home for five years."

Today, the goalie who beat the Russians, saved Philadelphia's 1976 run to the finals, and was uncannily effective coming in cold, holds no grudges. "I guess it's called growing up," said Stephenson, vice-president of a Milwaukee bank. "I didn't fully appreciate what my greatest asset was. They really had to have a lot of confidence in me to stay with me for that long."

Robbie Moore arrived at September's training camp with the false impression that he was the in-

cumbent. "I'll stab somebody in the eyes with knitting needles if I think they're going to take my job," he said. "At least it was my job when I left."

The position actually belonged to Peeters, whom the management projected as goalie of the immediate future. His best friend, St. Croix, had played just as well during the exhibition season, but was sent to Maine.

Propp, averting eye contact at every opportunity, had little to say, but from the beginning of drills

Brian Propp came to the Flyers with a nose for the net.

wasn't shy about finding the net. "You can see how he adapts to changing situations on the ice," said Resch after the rookie scored against the Islanders. "You don't see guys with that kind of ability come along very often."

Hill won a left wing spot behind Propp, removing the need to play MacLeish on wing. Allen had tried to trade the veteran center over the summer for Toronto defenseman Ian Turnbull. "It's pretty hard to get me psyched up," said MacLeish, coming off a 26-goal season and poor playoff. "You could ask Freddie about that."

John Paddock, five years a minor-leaguer, won a designated puncher's spot on right wing behind Leach, Holmgren, Gorence and Ververgaert, whose job was saved when the Flyers could not get the Kings to take him for defenseman Rick Hampton.

With Jimmy Watson and Dupont coming off subpar years, Dailey displeasing the fans and sometimes his coaches, Wilson still overhandling the puck, and Bathe having sixth-man abilities at best, Allen was concerned about the team's defense. He considered Colorado's offer of veteran Dennis Owchar, but passed as Norm Barnes, an eighth-round pick in 1973 who had kicked around the minors for five seasons, outplayed other Flyer blueliners in exhibition games.

Even with a backline that figured to need help from diligently backchecking forwards, the coach installed a system that encouraged defensemen to jump into the play and forwards to exchange lanes. Quinn got no argument from his new assistant. "We've been trying some new things and it's a big boost when they work in a game," said Clarke after Philadelphia pounded defending champion Montreal 8-3 on the way to a 4-2-5 exhibition record.

On opening night of the 1979-80 season, the Flyers honored Parent, the first NHL goalie to have his number retired. "It's not that you're nervous," said No. 1, who was rewarded with a hunting rifle by his old teammates and "Bernie! Bernie!" chants by the fans. "You just remember that it's [the end of] a career."

Parent's eyes misted as he walked up the runway for the last time. The Islanders, however, appeared more choked up after Holmgren, Propp and Hill had scored within 1:41 early in the second period to stake Philadelphia to a 4-0 lead. Myre allowed two third-period goals before Bridgman, named Flyer captain that day, fed Gorence to clinch a 5-2 victory. "I've never seen the Islanders look as confused in their own end," said Allen, "but we forced those mistakes."

Two nights later in Atlanta, Philadelphia forechecked hard again but continually got caught up ice. Myre was embarrassed 9-2 despite his club's 48-25 shot advantage. "You beat the best team in hockey one night," said Quinn, "and [the next game pucks are] going into our net like we don't have a team out there. It causes apprehension. It brings back memories of our playoffs last year."

The Flyers, however, were enjoying their new system too much to worry. At the Spectrum against Toronto the following night, Propp, playing with Leach and Clarke, hit a bull's eye through a six-inch opening on goalie Paul Harrison's far side to boost the team to a 3-0 lead. Lanny McDonald and Darryl Sittler, off giveaways by Watson and Dailey, pulled the Leafs back within one, but Kelly's score with 3:16 remaining made McDonald's late penalty shot goal (called when Quinn tried to sneak an extra skater on the ice in the final seconds) meaningless in Philadelphia's 4-3 victory.

The next day, to build camaraderie, Quinn walked his team from the Spectrum to Roosevelt Park to play a game of soccer. "It was that or football," said the coach, "and we couldn't find a football." Three nights later, the Flyers kicked around the Flames 6-2 at the Spectrum behind two goals by Leach.

With Wilson and Dupont hampered by injuries, Allen recalled defenseman Mike Busniuk from Maine for Philadelphia's final visit to Olympia Stadium. Two goals each by Holmgren and Propp took a wrecking ball to the Red Wings, 7-3.

Returning to the Spectrum, the Flyers jumped to a startling 6-2 lead over Montreal before realizing who they were dominating. The Canadiens scored twice in the second period, then Kelly took a frivolous slash at Rejean Houle to set up Guy Lafleur's power-play goal. With three minutes to play, Dupont charged to center ice to meet Lafleur, became hopelessly trapped, and Houle snapped the puck past Myre to create a 6-6 final.

"We wanted to win badly and we tightened up," said Quinn. But the Flyers' eyes had been opened to another truth: they had skated for sixty exhilarating minutes with the champions.

"We have the speed, we have the movement now," said Barber. "Pat's system is letting us go where we want to go. Sure, it's contributing to some mistakes, but hopefully we'll cut down on them. I have this feeling we're coming on, just like my first year here."

The Flyers continued to forecheck relentlessly, regardless of the score. Dailey and Leach wiped out an early 2-0 Ranger lead, then Propp and Leach fed each other for goals 12 seconds apart in a 5-2 Spectrum victory. Three nights later, Philadelphia scored three third-period goals in six minutes to wipe out a 2-1 Red Wing lead, surrendered two late tallies, then won 5-4 on Leach's last minute score. "I hope our team doesn't expect to do this every time," frowned Quinn.

The Flyers tightened the screws in a 3-1 Spectrum victory over St. Louis and went to Montreal with a 7-

1-1 record and the desire to announce their return to the NHL's elite. "We're getting better," said Clarke, "and I don't think [the Canadiens] are as strong as they were." Montreal's four-year grip on the Stanley Cup seemed to have loosened with the resignation of coach Scotty Bowman–who was replaced by Bernie Geoffrion–and the retirements of Jacques Lemaire and Ken Dryden.

Although Barber's drive sent Canadiens goalie Denis Herron to the hospital with a broken collarbone, Philadelphia lost Dailey to a recurring shoulder problem and trailed 2-1 after two periods. Early in the third, Barnes and Hill popped in rebounds before Mark Napier tied the game, 3-3. But 1:29 later, Barber faked Mario Tremblay and put a low wrist drive past goalie Michel Larocque to restore both the lead and the Flyers' domination.

Leach drove a bullet by Larocque with 1:54 remaining and Philadelphia snapped a 16-game winless streak against the Canadiens, 5-3. "It's been a long time since I've been this happy in Montreal," said Clarke. The Flyers had outshot the Canadiens 19-5 in the third period while playing a defense of Watson, Bathe, Busniuk and Barnes.

"I was concerned about the numbers on defense, not about the people," said Quinn. "These guys were champions in Maine. They must be able to do something right."

Quinn fully expected a letdown the next night against the Sabres in Philadelphia, but Linseman and Holmgren scored to break open a 1-1 second-period tie and the Flyers won again, 3-1. Three nights later, they returned to Quebec's Le Colisee for the first time since their emergency refuge in 1968 and held on to beat the Nordiques, 4-3.

Bringing an 11-game undefeated streak to Long Island figured to challenge the slow-starting Islanders, but Quinn's team dominated 5-2, enjoying it almost as much as winning in Montreal. "[The Islanders] said something in the papers last year, that we aren't the Flyers and just don't have it anymore," MacLeish told Terry Brennan of the *Bulletin*.

The team returned home to Philadelphia and beat an old whipping boy, Vancouver, then a new one, Edmonton. Unbeaten in 14, the Flyers had won 9 in a row–5 short of the NHL record–when they opened a 4-game trip in St. Louis. The rapidly-improving Blues scored twice late in the first and checked tenaciously for two periods before Philadelphia ripped three goals within 7:29 of the third. They were about to congratulate themselves on their comeback victory when Blair Chapman converted a Barnes giveaway with 2:32 remaining for a 3-3 tie.

"You hate to see the [winning] streak end, especially since we were so close," said Quinn. "But when you come back from 2-0 in the third period, you know you accomplished something."

The rallies were becoming routine. In Los Angeles, the Flyers were again down 2-0 halfway through the game before MacLeish and Barber pulled them even; a four-goal burst in the first 11:04 of the third period gave Philadelphia a 6-4 victory.

In Vancouver, Leach scored his 15th goal and Propp his 11th while Linseman provoked his team's first brawl of the season. "He's either crazy or the bravest guy since Audie Murphy," said Canuck coach Harry Neale after the Flyers, playing their best game yet, won 5-2. "And I don't know whether I dislike him more than I admire him."

After jumping to a 2-0 lead the following night in Edmonton, Philadelphia ran out of gas, but Peeters saved a 2-2 tie with a brilliant skate save on B.J. McDonald with 15 seconds remaining.

The Flyers flew the red eye home, caught some Z's, then blew open another game with a machine-gun burst of goals. Leach scored two and Propp one within 5:52 as Philadelphia beat Hartford 6-2 to stretch its unbeaten streak to 18.

Mentions of the NHL record–28 by the 1977-78 Canadiens–began to slip into the newspapers. The Flyers had a long 11 games to go to break the mark, but only three of those contests, including Game No. 29 at Boston on December 22, would be on the road.

Of course, the players thought the streak was just something for media consumption, even after they rallied from a 3-1 first-period deficit to down Minnesota, 6-4. "I don't know if it's mentioned [in the locker room] or not," shrugged Quinn. "There's enough pressure on us without thinking about something like that, but it's hard to ignore."

Dailey still wasn't in the lineup, but the three B's–Barnes, Busniuk and Bathe–were playing astoundingly well. Opponents were slow to catch on to the different ways the Flyers were leaving their zone. And although Peeters and Myre played soundly, the offense was so overwhelming that exceptional goaltending was unnecessary.

Twenty-one games into the season, Clarke had centered Leach to 18 goals and Propp to 12. On the second line, Barber had 25 points, Linseman 23 and Holmgren 17. MacLeish, now a fourth-line center behind Bridgman, had 15 goals. Gorence, Hill, Kelly and even Ververgaert were playing hard and chipping in key points. The power-play percentage was barely in double figures, yet incredibly, the Flyers had been held under four goals in only 4 of the streak's 19 games.

"I thought we'd be better this year," said Allen, "but I don't think anybody expected this. I thought we'd be short one, maybe two, players. Now I don't know. You look around the league [and] there isn't a real strong defensive team anywhere. We might be good enough to win it."

While the Flyers continued to score their way out of any predicament, their defensive concentration inevitably lapsed. "As we went along, they felt they needed me less and less," recalls Quinn. "Our practices were taking on a quality of self-destruction. The night of games was really the only time I was involved. They were in their own bubble and cruising and I could see them headed for a fall."

But even when his players hit the slump Quinn knew was coming, they still couldn't lose. At Toronto they surrendered Dan Maloney's tying goal midway through a third period in which they were outshot 14-5, but Myre held on for a 4-4 result. Against Detroit at the Spectrum the next night, Philadelphia turned a 4-2 lead in the last seven minutes into another 4-4 tie.

A visit from the Bruins helped snap the Flyers back to attention. Goals by Leach and Holmgren 1:08 apart in the second period wiped out a 2-0 Boston lead and Cheevers had to stand up to a 38-14 avalanche of shots to hold Philadelphia to a 2-2 draw. Their third consecutive deadlock pushed the streak to 22, but the Flyers continued to insist they weren't counting.

The Kings came to the Spectrum, put three first-period shots behind Peeters, and the law of averages appeared finally to be asserting itself. Nope. Leach put a rebound behind goalie Ron Grahame, then beat him with a flutterball :20 later and the sharks began to feed. Linseman scored on a breakaway, then fed Ververgaert before Barber and Watson completed a six-goal second period. It ended 9-4. Twenty-three in a row.

"The streak doesn't really have anything to do with it," said Linseman. "We just don't want to lose." Quinn feared otherwise, however. He was afraid the incredible run was becoming a season unto itself and that his team would deflate when it ended.

He even saw signs of boredom. Philadelphia blew 2-0 and 3-1 leads over the Blackhawks into a 4-4 tie when Terry Ruskowski scored with 50 seconds remaining. A few fans—how's this for tough?—booed the Spectrum message-board announcement that the Flyers' 24-game unbeaten streak was the second-longest in NHL history. Everyone but the players seemed to understand that their defensive lapses would eventually catch up to them.

December 13 looked like the day of reckoning when the Nordiques scored twice early in the third to take a 3-1 lead. Quinn thought, "It looks like our number is up." To his players, he said, "Okay, we've got twelve minutes left, let's move our butts." Ververgeart scored, Barber put in a Dailey rebound, Leach ripped in the go-ahead goal with 1:54 remaining, goalie Michel Dion waved feebly at Barber's shot and Hill hit the empty net as the Flyers won 6-4 at a roaring Spectrum. "They can put on the tap when they want to," said a shaken Jacques Demers, the Quebec coach.

So *now* were the Flyers counting? "That's all I hear as soon as I walk out of this [locker room] door," said Jimmy Watson. "And it never comes up in here. Uh, how many is that for us anyway?"

Twenty-five. Into the Spectrum came resurgent Buffalo under new coach and GM Scotty Bowman, trailing Philadelphia by only two points for first place overall. Up went the Sabres, 2-1, on Tony McKegney's goal at 1:31 of the third period. Down they went, 3-2, after Dailey beat goalie Don Edwards to the far corner and MacLeish, set up by a Holmgren hit on Jim Schoenfeld, scored off the stick of John Van Boxmeer. Twenty-six. The Flyers left the ice to a standing ovation.

The next night, at Madison Square Garden, Barber and Steve Vickers traded first-period goals and the teams flew furiously at each other for two periods. But in the third, it was obvious that the numbers were finally making the Flyers think.

They performed cautiously, dumping the puck most of the last twenty minutes, and Myre had to glove Greschner's screamer down the stretch to save a 1-1 tie. For the first time in 27 games, Philadelphia had needed superlative goaltending to keep the streak alive. Finally, the players admitted how much a chance at the record meant to them.

With one game remaining—at the Spectrum against Pittsburgh—to tie the mark, they spoke without fear of being caught looking ahead. "We've been saying it's not affecting us," said Quinn, "but you know that's a crock. This is a once-in-a-lifetime opportunity. You might play 100 years and never get another chance at something like this."

The Flyers wanted Game 28 so much that they played like they were afraid of it. Ron Stackhouse cashed a Propp high-sticking penalty, the Penguins settled into a checking groove, and goalie Greg Millen had a 1-0 shutout after two periods.

The fans stomped and shrieked, wanting their team to make them witnesses to history. On Leach's first shift of the third period, he fired four shots but just missed the corner on three of them while Millen committed robbery on the other. After six minutes, Barber took a pass from Linseman and came in alone, but the goalie stopped the backhand try with his pad. Five minutes later, Hill's deflection of a Barnes drive bounced off the crossbar.

Bobby Clarke tangles with Toronto's all-star defenseman Borje Salming.

On their knees and finally appearing to be out of luck, the Flyers put their hands together and appealed to a higher authority—referee Dave Newell. With 4:39 to go, Penguin defenseman Bob Stewart hooked Hill to the ice. Newell went with the rulebook and against standard operating procedure of the era, awarded a power play in the final minutes of a one-goal game.

And Philadelphia scored. Wilson sneaked behind Greg Sheppard to knock down Ververgaert's pass through the crease and either kicked or sticked the puck over the line with 4:08 remaining. "I stopped it with my skate," recalls Wilson, "and it was sliding towards the line when I rattled my stick against the goalpost as I went to shoot. I got a piece of the puck, but it was an inch either way whether I got my stick on it before it went over the line."

The Penguins, convinced Wilson did not, were furious, but Newell refused to wave off the goal. After Bridgman's backhand flip from the boards hit the post behind Millen and Peeters gloved the last Pittsburgh shot with 2 seconds remaining, balloons fell and "You Were There" coupons fluttered down from

the third level. Penguin Nick Libett gave Newell the choke sign as he left the ice, but it was the Flyers who had breathed laboriously for most of the game. This was the closest call of their record-tying 28 undefeated contests.

"Millen played an exceptional game," said Quinn, "but we helped him. We took shots from bad angles and passed up some better ones. This was a test of how we're going to do in a pressure situation and I'm sure you saw the Phantom out there knocking some of our guys down. There was no one around them."

Nevertheless, his team had persevered for the opportunity to create a new mark two days later in Boston. "We got a piece of the record," said Leach. "To break it isn't that big a deal. Maybe the pressure will be off. Now, it's just the Flyers and the Bruins as usual."

This wasn't as preposterous as it sounded. Quinn believed that the virtual certainty of a physical game at Boston Garden would help his players over any early butterflies. He was more thankful than fearful that they were going for the record in a difficult place to win.

The next day, however, he suspected they wouldn't beat anybody anywhere. "We've had a lot of bad practices," he said at the Boston Sheraton bar, "but today's was the worst."

Yet when referee Gregg Madill dropped the puck at 1:05 the following afternoon, the Flyers were almost eerily focused. They showed none of the nervousness that had almost doomed them the previous two games. MacLeish dominated the second shift and though Hill had to hook down Rick Middleton to save a possible breakaway, Philadelphia killed the penalty without a dangerous Bruin chance.

Five minutes into the period, Clarke pinched along the boards on Boston winger Al Secord, who was attempting to play a hard-around. The Flyer captain lifted Secord's stick, snatched the puck and shot. Clarke's drive went between Kelly's legs as he screened goalie Gilles Gilbert, and hit the far side to give Philadelphia the first score.

Holmgren and Bruin tough guy John Wensink squared off on the next shift for a long, twisting struggle. Both received match penalties for head-butting and the Flyers, who had already scratched Leach due to a sore knee, were without their top two right wings.

Madill penalized Wensink for two extra minutes, however, and Bobby Lalonde took another penalty for slashing Linseman, giving Philadelphia a two-man advantage for 39 seconds. After only 12 seconds, Barber's slap shot rose through a Paddock screen and landed stickside under the crossbar for a 2-0 lead.

Everywhere a Bruin attempted to move the puck, a Flyer was in his way. Terry O'Reilly tried to loosen Philadelphia's resolve with a crushing check on Ververgaert in the first minute of the second period, but Watson picked up the puck and led a rush. He dropped to Linseman, who pulled it just beyond Mike Milbury's reach and sped outside. Gilbert failed to cut down the angle enough to prevent Linseman from wristing the Flyers' third goal just inside the far post.

It wasn't going to be easy, was it? Of course not. Only two minutes later, Dailey accidentally deflected a centering pass by Tom Songin past a startled Myre to get Boston on the board. On the next shift, Myre was caught flat-footed as Milbury's point drive sneaked through traffic and dropped over the line.

Two gift goals within 1:07 pulled the thoroughly outplayed Bruins to within one and supercharged the Garden. After the face-off, Dwight Foster hustled back to break up Linseman's drop to Bridgman, but the Bruin winger hurried his clearing attempt onto Busniuk's stick. The Flyer defenseman relayed to Watson, who fired from the left point. The flopping Gilbert missed the puck completely as Philadelphia needed only :30 to restore its two-goal lead.

The Flyers checked, and checked, and checked. O'Reilly tried to rouse his team with a fierce shift late in the second period, but rookie Ray Bourque missed the one dangerous Boston chance.

The Bruins had only 14 shots as they started the third period. They added 5 when Clarke was sent off for slashing Boston rookie Brad McCrimmon, but Myre dragged his pad to stop Middleton, then stood up to stop both Middleton and Jean Ratelle. Halfway through the period, Busniuk knocked down a McCrimmon wind-around and Kelly wheeled and scored, giving Philadelphia a three-goal lead and removing whatever doubt remained.

Except for one power-play flurry in the third period, the Flyers stuffed the Bruins in a closet. Even before Myre cleared Dick Redmond's shot at the buzzer and pumped an arm into the air in triumph,

Boston fans stood to applaud the culmination of one of the most magnificent feats in NHL history. The Philadelphia Flyers, 5-2 winners, had marched into the record book with a stunningly efficient performance under the severest pressure. "They just never stopped working," said Lalonde. "They're amazing."

There was no presentation on the ice, only a celebration of back-pounding in the locker room. "Like we'd won the Stanley Cup," said Holmgren. Realizing that the streak was not an end unto itself, the Flyers tried to put on their poker faces when reporters were admitted. But they were unable to hide what the streak meant to them.

"There's a tremendous feeling of relief," said Clarke. "Nobody can say we came in the back door. We set the record against one of the top teams and we did it in their building."

No one was more impressed than the Bruins. "My God," said coach Fred Creighton, "it's almost halfway through the season and they only have one loss. It's hard to comprehend." Philadelphia had broken the record on the seventieth day since its last defeat. "You know," Linseman said on the plane ride home, "I've almost forgotten what it feels like to lose."

The following night, the Flyers returned to the Spectrum to play Hartford. The ovation began as soon as fans with views down the tunnel to the locker room saw Peeters leading the team out the door. The entire building was standing as the club stepped onto the ice.

The pregame media release noted the record for longest unbeaten streak in North American pro sports was set by the 1971-72 Los Angeles Lakers, who won 33 games in a row. "Will you guys get off that?" laughed Quinn. Nevertheless, after routinely handling the Whalers 4-2, the players seemed intrigued with how much longer they could go. "If we win just a few more," said Peeters, "I don't think anyone will ever break our record."

They almost lost three nights later in Springfield, Massachusetts, the Whalers' interim home while the Hartford Civic Center was being rebuilt. Gordie Howe, set up by his son Mark, sparked a third-period rally. Philadelphia escaped with a 4-4 tie when Greg Carroll shot over an empty net with four minutes left.

At Winnipeg, the Flyers held off the Jets, 5-3, to run the streak to 32. The next night at Colorado, when they jumped to a 3-0 lead and had to hold on, 3-2, it again looked like they were running out of gas. But after five days off, Philadelphia rolled to a 5-0 lead at Madison Square Garden and stretched the chain to 34 with a 5-3 victory. "We play them again the last day of the season," joked Carol Vadnais. "We'll break their streak then."

Two nights later in Buffalo, the Sabres, still second overall in the NHL, got their third shot at breaking the string. Buffalo led 2-1 late in the second, but Ververgaert tied the game, Barber and Macleish scored third-period goals, and Myre, taking over after the virus-ridden Peeters lost his lunch into his mask, finished up a 4-2 victory. "It ... it ... it's incredible," said Watson, breaking yet another record—the longest pronunciation of the word "it" with one's jaw slack in utter amazement. The Flyers had gone 35 games without losing.

"You look at the travel, the schedule, the balance of the league, it's impossible," said Scotty Bowman. "But it's not impossible. They've done it."

The Flyers flew to Minnesota after the game, where a full house greeted them the following night. "We were like every team waiting to play [them]," recalls Craig Hartsburg, then a North Star defenseman. "We hoped they would keep winning so we could be the ones to end the streak."

Barber opened the scoring, but a screaming Met Center psyched the North Stars to a 3-1 lead. A Holmgren goal, which would have put Philadelphia within one early in the second period, was disallowed as there were too many men on the ice. Hartsburg cashed the power play and the Flyers finally sagged. Minnesota went on to a 7-1 win.

"I remember the feeling I had on the bench when it became obvious that it was over," recalls Bridgman. "It was relief. It was only then that I realized just how much pressure we'd been under."

The 35-game streak, which included 25 wins, lasted eighty-four days. While undoubtedly aided by seven meetings with the four expansion clubs, it was no fluke of the schedule. The Flyers beat every team except Washington. They won at Montreal, Uniondale and Boston Garden. They defeated second-overall Buffalo three times. They rallied from one three-goal deficit and eight two-goal disadvantages, and came from behind in the third period on six occasions.

"It was a magical ride," recalls Quinn. "I pull the picture of that team out and look at it and say, 'How did we do that?' With that team, with that defense, there was no reason to think we could even put a 10-game streak together."

And yet, even after the string was snapped, Philadelphia stayed hot. The team immediately rallied from a 3-1 deficit to beat Winnipeg 5-4 at the Spectrum, and although losing 4-3 in Montreal two nights later, began another streak that went 8-0-3. Clarke

kept it alive at the Capital Center by beating Stephenson with 4 seconds left to pull out a 4-4 tie. And after Philadelphia reeled off five straight road victories, goals by MacLeish and Leach in the final 49 seconds pulled out an incredible 3-3 Spectrum deadlock with Boston.

Two nights after tying the Bruins, the record-setters finally dropped their first home game of the season, 4-1 to Vancouver, but it was 5 more contests before Peeters (22-0-5) suffered his first defeat, 8-6 at Colorado on February 19.

As the Flyers continued their western swing, the hockey world had a new darling—the U.S. Olympic team. Hours after the Americans' miraculous upset of the Soviet Union on the way to the gold medal at Lake Placid, Philadelphia and the Canucks dragged the NHL through the mud with 307 penalty minutes in a 7-3 Flyer victory. Bathe was suspended for leading a charge off the bench, joining Barnes (groin pull) and Wilson (flu) on the sidelines the next night in Los Angeles. Dailey was playing with a bad shoulder and Watson's back was worsening, yet true to its season, Philadelphia rolled over the Kings, 5-1.

The NHL suspended Quinn for 3 games because he had allowed his team to leave the bench in Vancouver, and the Flyers glanced over their shoulders when the Canadiens, playing well since Claude Ruel had replaced Geoffrion as coach, won 5-1 at the Spectrum on March 3.

The Islanders, rallying from a poor start, also left their calling card with a 5-2 Spectrum victory four days later. But Philadelphia was so far ahead of the defending divisional champions that it wrapped up the Patrick Division title with 14 games to spare in a 5-3 victory over Edmonton.

The celebrations continued with Joe Watson Night, a 4-1 success over Colorado. "I want to thank my parents for getting together 37 years ago," said the guest of honor, who received a lifetime pass from the Phillies and a trip to Bermuda from the Flyers.

Snider and Clarke were each presented the Lester Patrick Trophy for service to hockey in the U.S. at a dinner in New York, where they shared the dais with fellow honoree Fred Shero. "We seemed to be getting along," said Shero afterwards. "Today was a happy time."

Clarke hustled to Pittsburgh and the following night set up Leach's 300th career goal in a 4-3 victory. "He's been our best player," said the assistant coach.

The next night, Linseman's two in the third saved a 6-6 tie in Chicago, and Myre from himself. Convinced a wide-angle goal by Ron Sedlbauer had gone through the side of the net, the goalie went berserk, throwing his stick in the air, banging it against the goal judge's glass enclosure and giving up three more goals. "I just couldn't settle down," said Myre. "I told [the judge] he was a crook."

Quinn, meanwhile, was less wild about his team's performance down the stretch. Barnes had played only 3 games since suffering the groin pull in late January and Dailey's shoulder again forced

him from the lineup. Allen had reacquired Jack McIlhargey from Vancouver for cash in early January but, even with the Wolfman back in the house, the wolf seemed to be at the door. Philadelphia blew a 4-0 lead into a 4-4 tie with lowly Colorado at the Spectrum, then was shut out 3-0, by visiting Toronto.

"I'm not going to wring hands around necks," said Quinn, who nevertheless blew up at a practice session after a 7-2 loss in Boston. The winless streak (0-4-3) was stretched to 7 games in a 5-2 defeat at Nassau Coliseum, but the Flyers played their best game in weeks. Two nights later at the Spectrum, McIlhargey bloodied Quebec tough guy Paul Stewart and Philadelphia broke its slump with a 5-2 victory. The team then clinched the overall points title with a 4-2 win over Atlanta.

Leach reached 50 goals in Game 79, scoring into the empty net for a hat trick in a 4-2 triumph over Washington. "Combined with the other things he did for us this year, it's outstanding, just outstand-

ing," said Quinn.

The Flyers finished the regular season 48-12-20, but were 3-5-5 in their last 13 games. "We were scared bleepless going into the playoffs," recalls Myre.

The new playoff format, seeding teams first through sixteenth regardless of divisions, sent Philadelphia into a first-round best-of-five series against Edmonton. Keyed by Wayne Gretzky's 23 points in their final 11 games, the Oilers went 8-2-1 to beat Washington for the sixteenth spot.

After surrendering early scores to Holmgren and Leach in Game 1, Edmonton goalie Ron Low tightened. Gretzky set up Dave Lumley, then struck on a breakaway. When Don Murdoch finished off a two-on-one, the totally outplayed Oilers took a stunning third-period 3-2 lead.

The Flyers remembered their playoff-opening loss to Vancouver a year earlier, but stayed the course. "That's the calming influence Pat has had on us," said Holmgren. The coach was getting ready to pull Peeters for an extra attacker when Linseman forced a turnover and MacLeish caught Low leaning the wrong way with a 30-foot wrister. Reprieved only 1:19 before the buzzer, Philadelphia won the game eight minutes into overtime when Clarke batted in a puck that had popped over the net and off Low's pads.

Linseman's stomach virus made him a Game 2 scratch, helping the outmanned Oilers stay within a goal until Holmgren finished off a two-on-one midway in the third period. Quinn, playing only four defensemen as the game progressed, received a second consecutive superlative performance from Dailey, who acknowledged he would need shoulder surgery following the playoffs. "It won't be too bad," he said after the Flyers pulled away to a 5-1 victory and a 2-0 series lead. "I'll just hold my beer can with my other hand."

For Game 3 in Edmonton, Linseman gave it a go with a bucket behind the bench—just in case. Quinn almost needed to use it when the Oilers took a 2-0 first-period lead on goals by Gretzky and rookie center Mark Messier. Gradually, however, the deeper team

Goalie Phil Myre talks to the press about the Flyers' 35-game unbeaten streak.

took control. Wilson scored during a delayed penalty and Propp slammed in a Linseman rebound seven minutes into the third period to force overtime.

Myre, making his first start of the series, was outstanding. "I sat in the locker room before the overtime thinking how much fun it was to be in that situation," he recalls. The goalie enjoyed himself so much, he forced a second overtime, then saved the game when Murdoch was sent in alone by Gretzky. Linseman immediately broke up ice, went outside

Flyers celebrate the NHL's longest unbeaten streak.

defenseman Pat Price, cut in and pushed the puck past Low's pad at 3:46. "I had to do it," said the chalky-faced hero of the series-sweeping 3-2 victory. "I don't think I could have played tomorrow."

The Rangers finished off Atlanta in four, setting up a rematch of the previous spring's quarterfinals. Philadelphia refused to acknowledge revenge as a motivator, but Mike Nykoluk caught the Flyers' attention by suggesting their streak had been helped by the Islanders' and Canadiens' slow starts. Shero's right-hand man also questioned the vulnerability of Philadelphia's goaltenders to playoff pressure.

"There are 100 ways we are better than we were last year," said Linseman. "If you think about all these things that could go wrong, you can forget we were first in the league this year, and they were eighth."

The confident Flyers launched 19 shots at John Davidson in the first period of Game 1, but the big goalie was just as tough as in 1979. New York tied

the game 1-1 early in the third period on a goal that bounced in off Ray Markham's skate. But two minutes later, Holmgren got a step outside Barry Beck and fed Wilson, who held off Ron Greschner and tipped the puck past Davidson. Philadelphia, so undisciplined away from the puck the previous spring, held the Rangers to only one good chance the rest of the way and won, 2-1. "It was as good a game as we've played in a long time," said Quinn.

In Game 2, the Flyers were even better. Holmgren finished off a two-on-one feed from Linseman midway in the second period to break open a scoreless tie and 14 seconds later Barber lifted in a rebound. With the Linseman-Propp-Holmgren line outplaying the Ranger top line of Nilsson, Hedberg and Vickers, and Bridgman frustrating Phil Esposito, Philadelphia checked relentlessly to a 4-1 victory and a 2-0 series lead.

Even with last change, Shero couldn't crack the Flyers' domination in Game 3 at Madison Square Garden, although Beck broke Watson's collarbone and bruised Linseman's ribs with devastating checks. But Peeters and the team played flawlessly and took a 3-0 series lead with a 3-0 victory.

Helped by the absences of Watson and Linseman, as well as a revived power play, the Rangers stayed alive with a 4-2 victory in Game 4. But Linseman returned for Game 5 wearing a flak jacket and Philadelphia resumed its relentless pounding in the New York end. Bridgman set up Hill, then Wilson, and Holmgren scored off Dave Maloney's skate. The Flyers wrapped up their vengeance on the 1979 debacle with a 3-1 victory.

Shero noted his team had fallen short in abrasiveness and paid tribute to Philadelphia. So did other Rangers. "We were never really in it," said Dave Maloney. "All the things you teach a kid about hockey when he's young, they beat us in every one of those things. They didn't finish thirty points ahead of us for no reason."

While Minnesota unseated the four-time champion Canadiens in seven, the banged-up Flyers rested. And in Game 1, the rust showed. Philadelphia scored three goals within 1:44 late in the first period to take a 4-3 lead, but Mike Eaves got around Barnes to tie the game. Steve Payne then cashed both a Wilson giveaway and a Holmgren penalty to send the North Stars to a 6-5 victory.

The Flyers' power play, 0-for-20 during the Ranger series, sprang to life in Game 2, going 4-for-4. Philadelphia physically dominated Minnesota throughout Myre's 7-0 shutout.

The North Stars girded themselves for a Game 3 war at a wired Met Center, then began to take unnecessary penalties. Paul Shmyr was called for interference and Barber converted on the power play. Two minutes later, Barber scored again on a pass from Clarke. Bridgman put in a Gorence rebound and then Barber, taking a one-handed pass from Clarke while he held off Shmyr, completed his hat trick before the second period was half over.

Having taken a 4-0 lead, and taken the crowd out of the game, the Flyers let Minnesota and its fans back in. Mike Polich stripped MacLeish and fed Tom Younghans for a shorthanded goal, and Tim Young outraced Wilson to tap in Tom McCarthy's feed. McCarthy then whacked in a rebound during a two-man advantage and Philadelphia, ahead by only one, was suddenly in trouble.

"We're still leading this game," Clarke screamed on the bench. The Flyers were shorthanded three times and escaped numerous close calls around their net during a frantic third period before Barber hooked down Payne, broke for a pass from Dupont and, from the top of the circle, fired between goalie Gilles Meloche's legs.

"It was like the building just dropped on the fans," said Holmgren. "They had raised the roof and Billy just dropped it on them." On the strength of Barber's four goals, Philadelphia took back the home-ice advantage with a gut-wrenching 5-3 victory.

Barber was still on fire in Game 4, banking a shot off goalie Gary Edwards, then scoring again on a feed from Linseman to give the Flyers a 3-1 lead. Polich's shot blooped off Busniuk's stick past Myre to pull the North Stars within one with 6:04 remaining, but Philadelphia survived another hair-raising third period for a 3-2 win and a 3-1 series lead. "I've never seen Phil Myre play any better," said Quinn.

Minnesota had taken its best shot at home. Barber, however, still had one left. At the Spectrum, he backhanded his 9th goal of the round to help gain a 4-2 lead. Bridgman maintained his series-long hounding of the North Stars' rising star, Bobby Smith, and with two more power-play goals, the Flyers closed out the series with a 7-3 rout. Philadelphia was back in the finals for the first time in four seasons.

Still wearing his pads, Myre smoked a cigar at his locker stall. "I never would have thought of this a year ago," he said. "The streak was the greatest thing that ever happened to me in hockey. Now, this."

The Islanders finished off Buffalo in 6 games, matching up two Patrick Division teams in the finals. New York, upset in the semifinals in 1978 and 1979, had gotten over the hump due largely to the trade-deadline acquisition of center Butch Goring, who lifted some of the offensive burden from Bryan Trottier and Mike Bossy. Both clubs were loaded with hard-nosed forwards determined to exploit what appeared to be vulnerable spots on the two defenses. The Islanders had two rookies—Ken Morrow and Dave Langevin—taking regular shifts.

The Flyers led early in Game 1, when Bridgman took advantage of goalie Billy Smith's puck-handling error, but Bossy's power-play goal on the third of three rapid-fire shots tied the game. Clark Gillies set up Denis Potvin for a 2-1 Islander lead, but Clarke redirected a Barber shot on the power play and MacLeish put Philadelphia ahead. The Flyers were 3:42 from victory when, with Hill in the penalty box, Bossy fed Stefan Persson up the slot for the tying goal.

Two minutes into sudden death, Watson grabbed John Tonelli around the shoulders to prevent a scoring chance. It was an obvious penalty at any point except during overtime, when officials usually looked the other way. This time, however, referee Andy Van Hellemond did not. With the extra skater, Bob Nystrom overpowered Busniuk, and Tonelli fed Potvin, who beat Peeters on a 25-footer with one second left in the man advantage. On the first sudden-death power play-goal in NHL history, Game 1 went to the Isles, 4-3.

Fans threw garbage at Van Hellemond as he left the ice, but Philadelphia, outplayed more and more as the game went along, had trashed itself. "There isn't a guy in here who thinks we were just unlucky," said Linseman. "We could have gotten beat a lot worse."

Quinn lectured his team about its lack of aggression. And when Wilson retaliated for Gary Howatt's Game 2 strafing of Peeters by cross-checking the fiesty Islander winger, it was clear the Flyers had taken their coach's message to heart. The Islanders led 1-0 on an early goal by Goring, but Peeters stayed strong and Holmgren tied it on a power play seven minutes into the second period.

Kelly put Philadelphia ahead 1:15 later. Clarke then banged in a rebound of Watson's stuffer and set up Barber to start the romp. Holmgren became the first American-born player to record a playoff hat trick, and the Flyers rolled to an 8-3 victory.

"They're a bunch of chicken bleep bleepers," said Isles' coach Al Arbour. "All they do is wield their sticks."

On that note of sportsmanship, the series moved to Long Island, where Quinn again defied a cardinal coaching rule by switching goalies after a playoff victory and going back to Myre for Game 3. The veteran, badly wanting to play in the finals despite a mild flu, was rocked for goals on all five Islander power-play opportunities. New York built a 6-0 lead, coasting to a 6-2 result. "I may have been a little stubborn in following my pre-series plan," said Quinn. "I wanted to play Pete the first two games and Phil the two here. But in my mind, I'd do it again."

Philadelphia was in even deeper trouble than its 2-1 disadvantage suggested. Holmgren had suffered torn knee cartilage during Game 3 and a hit by Bob Lorimer had reopened Watson's hairline clavicle fracture. Neither Flyer played in Game 4, when the Islanders, appearing to be on their way to another trouncing, twice stripped Busniuk of the puck on first- period goals by Bossy and Goring.

Peeters, however, stopped three breakaways to keep his team breathing in the second period and Paddock, who had scored but three goals all season, cut the lead in half with an astonishing shot over Smith's shoulder. "When things like that happen," said Bossy, "you think you're going to lose."

Hill then beat Smith, only to have his backhander stop right on the line. The goalie covered it, and the electricity generated by Paddock's thunderbolt dissipated. Six minutes into the third period, MacLeish missed a center-ice check on Trottier, who restored New York's 3-1 lead.

Linseman, repeatedly frustrated by Smith, finally converted a backhander, but Bob Bourne blocked a hurried Dailey point drive, broke in two-on-one against Barnes and fed Nystrom, who scored. Gillies's shot from the circle set the final at 5-2, leaving the Flyers one game from elimination.

The healthier team was clearly the better one, and Philadelphia's weaknesses on defense were finally being exposed. Quinn's only answer was to press

the attack. "They are a well-positioned club, but they'll make mistakes and we haven't forced enough," said the Flyer coach.

To do that, Philadelphia needed its biggest, bravest player, so Dr. Joe Torg fitted Holmgren with a brace. Flyer fans stood and cheered for two minutes as their team took the ice. The adrenaline kicked in, but Smith kicked out a great chance by Leach, and Persson fired a power-play goal past Peeters midway through the period.

Philadelphia went sixteen minutes without a shot, but Peeters refused to give up a second goal. And when Clarke one-timed Wilson's feed to tie the game in the second period, the Spectrum surged back to life. MacLeish, who had been terrible on Long Island, beat Smith on his glove side to put the Flyers ahead, 2-1.

Trottier tied the game, but within a minute Busniuk came from behind the net to restore Philadelphia's lead. MacLeish, Propp and the gimpy Holmgren added goals and the Flyers, 6-2 winners, forced a Game 6. If they could somehow win it, they would return to the Spectrum to play for the Cup.

"As far as I'm concerned, said Quinn, "we're going to do it." Privately, he wondered how. "We were really beat up," he recalls. "Holmgren was our most valuable player that year and he was a mess. Dailey was in terrible physical condition and I didn't know how much longer Watson could go."

On Saturday afternoon, May 24, 1980, the fans who filled the Nassau Coliseum were wondering how much more tension they could withstand, especially after Leach scored on a five on three to give Philadelphia a 1-0 lead. It lasted only four minutes, until Potvin batted a Bossy rebound out of the air and past Peeters, prompting a vehement Flyer protest that the Islander's stick was above his shoulder when it contacted the puck. The television replay was inconclusive, but 2:12 later, Philadelphia had clear reason to be outraged.

Gillies skated into the Flyer zone and dropped a pass that came two feet outside the blue line before Goring carried the puck back in. Dupont pointed to the line immediately and Propp, who had been backchecking Duane Sutter, let up. Goring's pass went by both Flyers, enabling Sutter to rifle the puck into the top of the net.

Philadelphia's players looked to Leon Stickle, the official who was perfectly positioned on the line, for confirmation that he had blown the whistle. They were incredulous that he had not. Composing themselves before the end of the first twenty minutes,

Propp got behind Ken Morrow to take a Holmgren pass and tie the game.

Nevertheless, the Islanders took control in the second period. With Wilson off for holding Gillies, Bourne half-fanned on Trottier's setup from behind the net and the puck slithered to Bossy who turned and fired New York's 15th power-play goal of the series through Peeters's feet. Before the period was up, Tonelli got past Clarke along the side boards and fed Nystrom, who had bulled past Leach to the

net, and the Isles led, 4-2.

The Flyers appeared exhausted. Watson, the victim of several jarring checks, couldn't make it to the bench for the third period and the emotion that had forced Game 6 seemed spent.

Still, Dailey beat Smith from the point on the first shift of the third period, and less than five minutes later, MacLeish knocked down an attempted clear by Langevin and fed Dupont, whose slap shot hit MacLeish, then Paddock, and caromed past Smith to tie the score.

Philadelphia pressed the stunned Islanders for the next several shifts. Smith had to make a pad save on Dupont's drive from straight up the slot and Linseman, fed by Wilson from the corner, tipped the puck wide of a half-empty net. "It was Scared City," said Smith. "They were really pounding us in the third period. They were playing a great hockey game."

New York also had several good chances. Tonelli missed the net on a close-in backhander and Peeters fought off the deflection of a Potvin shot. Smith then challenged Barber's drive from the top of the circle with 50 seconds remaining to send the game into overtime.

Linseman, set up by Holmgren, had the best Flyer opportunity in sudden death, but Bob Lorimer blocked the shot and Smith covered. Hill also had a chance, chipping over a sliding Potvin, only to have Smith win a race to the fluttering puck and snatch it out of the air.

With almost seven minutes gone, Persson jammed a clearing attempt back into Philadelphia's end, forcing Dailey to absorb a hard check from Nystrom and Hill to merely dump out of the zone. Lorne Henning picked up the puck, retreated over the red line, then suddenly turned and trapped Hill, Bridgman and MacLeish with a pass to a pivoting Tonelli. Dailey moved laterally to stay with the Islander's winger, failing to pick up Nystrom, who had crisscrossed behind his teammate.

Dailey scrambled when he saw that Nystrom had a clear path to the goal. Tonelli skated into the right circle, slowed slightly, and laid a perfect feed past Dupont to Nystrom, who had a long step on Dailey. As Peeters came across, the New York winger put out his stick and deflected the puck from his backhand over the sliding goalie.

Dailey's head jerked upwards as he saw the puck enter the net. Peeters knew Nystrom had scored, but only remembered the significance when he rolled over to the sight of Nystrom jumping up and down along the endboards. "That's when it hit me," recalls the goalie. "It was sickening."

At 7:11 of overtime, the Islanders had won their first Stanley Cup. And as New York fans were letting out a prolonged roar, steam was rising from Snider's head.

"It was an absolute, total, bleeping disgrace," said the Flyers' owner, pacing the hallway outside the locker room within earshot of the *Bulletin's* Didinger. "Anybody who's impartial knows we took a screwing today. I believe the [officials] who come out of Montreal and Toronto don't want [us] to win. I believe that right down to the pit of my stomach.

Reggie Leach opened the scoring in the deciding game of the 1980 Cup finals.

"It was the bleeping penalty they called on Jimmy Watson in (Game 1's) overtime that put us in this damn hole. The problem with this league is (referee-in-chief) Scotty Morrison. He should be shot."

Allen was calmer, but almost as bitter. "You can say they are human and they make mistakes," said Allen, "but this was the Stanley Cup finals and [the offside goal] wasn't even close. I know people think we cry a lot about the officials, but just look at it. You can see it."

Quinn tried to be gracious, pointing out that the Flyers' inability to stop the Islander power play was the major difference in the series. "I don't want to taint their victory," he said. "They worked too hard for it."

But with further questioning, the defeated coach unloaded too. "It's just not right that [the officials] should have an influence like that in a game," he said. "It's at a state now where [the officiating's] the worst part of our business."

Stickle did not deny his mistake. "I guess I blew it," he said. "Maybe I was too close to the play. Maybe there was tape on the stick and it confused me."

Few Flyers could force themselves out of the training room to talk to the media. "I cried," recalls Peeters. "A lot of guys did." Most believed they would not have lost a seventh game at the Spectrum and many Islanders agreed, admitting their fear of going back to Philadelphia had been a prime motivator in Game 6.

In truth, the Flyers might have been too battered to be the stronger team in a seventh game played anywhere. "We were not in good shape," recalls Clarke, "but we'll always wonder what might have happened."

During the summer, Dr. Torg helped the team pick up its pieces by removing several broken ones from Dailey's shoulder and repairing Watson's collarbone. Ververgaert's contract was not renewed, Paddock was sold to Quebec and, on August 21, Kelly received a call from Allen. "In the middle of the summer, you know it's not social," said the Hound. The Flyer veteran had been traded to Washington for a third-round draft choice.

"I still think the biggest thrill was just making this team in 1970," Kelly told reporters. "I feel lucky I was here for 10 years."

The Flyers, in turn, had been blessed by the energy Kelly provided. "Freddie always said he needed guys who had character, not who were characters," said Clarke. "But Hound was both."

The same was true of Dupont, yet despite his strong performance in the finals, Allen had decided Thomas Eriksson, a fifth-round pick in 1979, was ready for a regular spot on defense. On September 14, the evening before training camp opened in Portland, Dupont, 31, was traded to the Nordiques for a seventh-round pick and cash. "I wanted to wait one more year," he said , "but I had asked Keith if he was going to move me, that it be to Quebec."

Allen, not only granted his lionhearted Moose that wish, but gave him the security of a new, three-year contract before closing the deal.

"I hope we are able to compensate for what we've lost," said Quinn, distancing himself as usual from a personnel decision. "I played against [Dupont] and he, as much as any of them, was what the Flyers were all about."

The NHL notified Snider of a $5,000 fine for his post-playoff outburst. The Flyers' organization sent more kindly greetings—a tape of fans singing "God Bless America" before an exhibition game and a 4-by-6-foot get well card with thousands of signatures—to Kate Smith, ailing in Raleigh, North Carolina.

The team was not in the pink, either, as the 1980-81 season opened. Linseman, trying to get even with the Rangers' Ed Hospodar for a nose-breaking cross-check the previous season, missed his target, crashed the boards, and suffered a broken left tibia. "We are trying to get our guys to play within themselves," said a displeased Quinn.

Kerr's strong camp suggested Philadelphia could withstand the expected loss of Linseman for two months, but its defense was an ongoing worry. Watson underwent electric stimulation treatments for his increasingly troublesome back and missed 14 of the Flyers' first 22 games. Dailey's shoulder recovered slowly from surgery and Eriksson, not ready for prime time, joined fellow countryman Lindbergh at Maine.

Nevertheless, Blake Wesley and Terry Murray, the latter of whom had been repurchased from Detroit, stepped in to make Barnes and McIlhargey expendable to Hartford for a second-round pick. Quinn was once again patching holes from game to game, but the Flyers were at the top of the NHL after exploding with a 13-game unbeaten streak. Shero, meanwhile, was fired after the Rangers won only 4 of their first 20 games.

Barber scored his 300th career goal in a 5-2 win over Detroit on November 15, and MacLeish reached the same milestone on December 15 with a last-minute goal to beat St. Louis, 5-4. New Flyers' assistant coach Bob Boucher, hired away from St.

Mary's University in Halifax, diagrammed a vastly-improved power play that solved Philadelphia's one major failing of the preceding season.

Linseman returned on December 10 at Chicago, taking a foolish penalty that turned a late lead into a 2-2 tie. The Flyers, 19-6-4, were aiming to extend another unbeaten streak to seven and wrap up the back end of a home-and-home sweep of Washington, but the Capitals survived a 21-shot first period, lit up Myre and rolled to an astonishing 6-0

victory, their first ever against Philadelphia.

Twelve nights later in Winnipeg, the Flyers trailed the 2-28-7 Jets after one period, 4-1, and suffered a 4-3 loss, their fourth in five games. "We are probably playing well for the same amount of each game as we did earlier in the season," said Quinn after his team lost 4-2 to the Islanders on January 11. "But we're not getting away with it now. There are probably five or six guys who haven't approached the game the way they did last year."

Bridgman's dissatisfaction with contract talks affected his play, and Linseman's refusal to use his speed to go wide caused Propp and Holmgren to fall well behind their previous season's scoring pace. "We always had lots of emotion last year," said Holmgren after a desultory 4-1 home loss to Quebec. "This year

we haven't."

Watson finally submitted to spinal fusion surgery and was lost for the season, so Philadelphia called up Glen Cochrane, a belligerent third-round 1978 draft pick. The team also summoned left wing Greg Adams to light a fire under the catatonic Hill. Adams scored twice in his NHL debut, a 6-4 loss in Boston.

The Flyer goaltenders had problems, too. St. Croix was ticketed for Maine, but Pittsburgh claimed him on recallable waivers. Locked into keeping the young goalie, Quinn watched him outplay Myre, who was sold to Colorado.

Peeters was masterful in a 5-0 shutout at Pittsburgh, and Philadelphia ground out its most impressive road victory since the season's infancy by beating the reborn Blues, 3-2. But Clarke, who had suffered a cracked rib when slashed by the Bruins' McCrimmon early in the season, was having trouble breathing. The Flyers were manic one game and depressive the next.

Eriksson's recall on February 12 upgraded the skill level on the blue line. But the Swede didn't do as much to boost Philadelphia as Kings owner Dr. Jerry Buss, who announced he would canvass the board of governors to censure the Flyers for gooning it up. When the Los Angeles media rallied to his cause, Philadelphia warmed to the fear and loathing by brutalizing the Kings 3-1 at the Forum. Cochrane fought Dean Hopkins three times in fifteen minutes and was topless when finally pushed off the ice. Later, Larry Murphy was crosschecked by Wilson after the ace L.A. rookie had already stepped through the gate to the Kings' bench.

"I think it scared them," said Holmgren. "Hell, that even scared us."

In the good old days, a 270-penalty-minute game would have galvanized the Flyers. But more trouble followed. Two nights later in Vancouver, Dailey, hobbled by right knee problems since November, was forced from a 6-4 loss to the Canucks with torn cartilage. Dr. Torg declared him out for the season, leaving Wilson, an inconsistent third-year pro, as the team's most experienced defenseman.

When the Oilers scored five goals in the third period to blow the Flyers away 6-2, Allen tried sending a message to his team by recalling Flockhart, one of the free agents signed after the shortened 1979 draft. The juking and jiving rookie set up two of three Barber goals in a 5-3 victory at Winnipeg, but two games later, Gretzky and Edmonton again picked Philadelphia apart, 5-3, at the Spectrum.

At the trading deadline, having gone only 15-14-5

since Christmas, Allen failed in his attempts to acquire Pittsburgh defenseman Ron Stackhouse and to get Colorado's right wing Lanny McDonald for Bridgman.

Fans interrupted their grumbling long enough to give Clarke a standing ovation when he scored his 300th goal on March 12, beating Detroit goalie Larry Lozinski on a backhander set up by Leach. Four games later, while Kerr was collecting his first NHL hat trick, Clarke became the fifteenth player to reach 1,000 points when he fired his own rebound past Boston goalie Marco Baron.

"I'm just happy to get a goal," said Clarke. "I haven't been pulling my share of the load lately." Indeed, it was only his 14th point in 26 games. But loyalists, standing and saluting his second statistical milestone of the month, still placed Clarke beyond reproach for the team's decline.

Management absolved Quinn of blame, too, announcing on March 17 that their St. Patrick had been given a new five-year contract. "It's the kind of stablity we feel any organization needs," said Bob Butera, now the team's president.

The wobbly Flyers perked up with a 6-2 Spectrum pounding of the Calgary (formerly Atlanta) Flames, and played a spirited scoreless tie—their first in ten years—at Madison Square Garden. But a 2-0 shutout loss at home to the Rangers on the final night of the regular season left Philadelphia 41-24-15, and in a worrisome first-round best-of-five matchup against the Nordiques, who had enjoyed a 19-5-5 stretch run.

In Game 1, Peter Stastny, the brilliant Slovakian center whose 109-point rookie season had keyed Quebec's rise, set up two beautiful back-door goals. But Linseman, with the second of three assists for the night, fed Propp twice and the Flyers went on to a 6-4 victory.

Philadelphia, unable to put two good games together the entire second half of the season, held true to form in Game 2, but won again thanks to a stone-cold performance by goalie Daniel Bouchard and a hat trick by Barber. Although Bridgman failed to prevent Stastny and his brother Anton from teaming for two goals, the Flyer captain scored twice himself as Philadelphia outgunned the porous Nordiques 8-5 to take a 2-0 series lead.

Quebec coach Michel Bergeron used the advantage of last change to keep Peter Stastny away from Bridgman in Game 3 at Le Colisee. And when Dailey fell, re-injuring his knee in the second period, Quinn's matchup problems were compounded. Skating

against Linseman, Stastny cleverly kicked a Pierre Lacroix point drive to Michel Goulet, who broke a scoreless tie midway in the third period. Peter, set up by Anton, put away Bouchard's 2-0 shutout with a goal in the final three minutes.

The following night, Bouchard misplayed Murray's routine dump-in off the opening face-off into a goal, and Wilson and Gorence added scores that gave Philadelphia a 3-1 lead after one period. Even without Dailey, the Flyers found the checking groove that had eluded them most of the season and were five minutes away from wrapping up the series.

But rookie center Dale Hunter got outside Murray and put Quebec's first shot of the third period in off St. Croix's arm. Less than two minutes later, Lacroix sprung Hunter, who burst between Murray and Wilson and went in alone. St. Croix made the save, but no Flyer saw Jacques Richard coming up the slot. His rebound went under the sprawled St. Croix's stick to tie the game.

Bouchard made a full extension glove save on Linseman with 14 seconds remaining in regulation and, on the first shift of overtime, Richard wriggled past Wilson down the boards and fed Hunter, who had been left unchecked in the slot by both Linseman and Propp. Murray dropped to block the shot and screened St. Croix, who allowed the winner to go between his legs.

Philadelphia had not played this soundly in months, but had still blown a late two-goal lead into a 4-3 loss. "They weren't even getting a smell," said Quinn. "I don't have an explanation for it."

An answer was needed for Game 5 or else the Flyers would go from finalists to first-round losers in one year. The coach, who had benched Leach for Game 4, continued to play Kerr with Clarke and Propp and hoped the younger, smaller Nordiques would be intimidated by a winner-take-all game at the Spectrum. Quinn also decided to go with the rusty Peeters in goal.

Fortunately, Peeters was a spectator almost from the opening face-off thanks to a desperate Philadelphia effort. Bouchard left the net to clear the puck and fell over Barber, allowing MacLeish, until then a no-show for the series, to give the Flyers a 1-0 lead. Goulet tied the score, beating Dailey, who had returned to the lineup on one leg. But a 19-shot first period established Philadelphia's dominance.

Bridgman fed Hill to boost the Flyers ahead, and early in the third period Holmgren blocked a shot and Linseman soloed to give Philadelphia breathing room. Holmgren then jammed in a Linseman rebound and the Flyers finally put Quebec away, 5-2. "We imposed our will on them," said Quinn proudly. "We didn't let fear conquer us."

Several first-round upsets, highlighted by Edmonton's sweeping demolition of Montreal, gave Philadelphia an unexpected home-ice advantage for the quarterfinals. Their opponents were the Flames who, in their premier season in Calgary, had finally advanced beyond the first-round test they had flunked six straight years in Atlanta.

The Flames began Game 1 by admiring the quarterfinals' view and spent the second half firing blanks into a suddenly red-hot St. Croix. Barber's goal and assist paced the Flyers to a 4-0 breeze.

After playing five games in seven nights against Quebec and facing four in five nights against Calgary, Quinn decided to start the rested Peeters for Game 2. Barber and MacLeish scored power-play goals for a 2-1 lead, but the Flames scored the next four, including one by Ken Houston that trickled over the line following a needless flop by Peeters.

Down 5-2, the Flyers mounted a third-period charge. Wilson cut the lead to 5-3 while Willi Plett served a major for cutting Bridgman on the chin. Calgary goalie Pat Riggin then allowed a 55-footer by Gorence between the pads. But the Flames' defense, anchored by Brad Marsh and Phil Russell, clutched and grabbed its way through Philadelphia's frantic final flurry.

"So far, we've played one period out of six." said Holmgren after Calgary's 5-4 victory evened the series.

Two nights later, the Flyers spent the entire game in the opposition end at the Corral, the Flames' temporary 7,226-seat home, but Riggin stopped 47 shots and Calgary won 2-1 on Plett's rebound goal early in the third period. "You look at the films of that game without the scoreboard and nobody would believe we lost it," said Clarke.

Nevertheless, Philadelphia would be in big trouble if it could not find a way to win Game 4. Dailey had to bow out again, and the Flyers entered the third period down 3-1. But Kerr pinched the boards to set up MacLeish, then kept a rebound alive for Clarke, who tied the game. Only 37 seconds later, however, Flame tough guy Randy Holt, goalless the entire season, used a Plett screen to put Calgary back ahead. Incredibly, Holt scored again, off St. Croix's arm, to make the score 5-3.

Barber beat Riggin on a breakaway during a three-on-three, but in the final minutes Bridgman hit the post and Kerr's feed to Clarke at an open goalmouth hit referee Bob Myers and bounced away. "We work and we work and we work, then we bleep up and we're behind again," said a grim-faced Clarke after the Flames' 5-4 victory sent the Flyers home trailing 3-1 in the series.

Backed against the wall, Philadelphia took command of Game 5 early. Propp scored a hat trick before nine minutes had been played and the Flyers raced to a 5-1 lead and 9-4 victory. They were alive, although exhausted from the two-flight, eight-hour trips between cities. Snider hired a $60,000 charter—costing double the commercial fare—for the run to Calgary and the team tried to make it an investment for a Game 7.

The Flames went for the kill early, but St. Croix kept the game scoreless until Holmgren harassed Paul Reinhart into a giveaway and fed Linseman for the critical first goal. The sore-ribbed Clarke, lathered with painkilling DMSO and wired with desperation, beat Riggin on a breakaway to make it 2-0. St. Croix allowed Guy Chouinard's prayer from the red line to bounce off his shoulder and into the net, but Philadelphia struck back quickly. Two minutes later, Linseman chased down Propp's long lead pass and made the score 3-1.

Clarke was suddenly and miraculously back from his living death. And behind him, the Flyers clung to

Recalled by the Flyers, Ron Flockhart twice set up Bill Barber.

the lead and their season. With 6:11 remaining, Ken Houston reached around Murray for a power-play rebound and made the score 3-2, but St. Croix got his pad out to stop a Chouinard deflection with 10 seconds remaining and Murray blocked Reinhart's drive at the buzzer.

The series was tied, 3-3. "It has to be right up there with the best feelings I've ever had," said Clarke in a joyous locker room. The team flew home the next day confidently.

"They haven't been overpowering us," said a defiant Al MacNeil, the Flames' coach. "We're still going to win it in Philly." Not all of his players believed him. Marsh recalls several of his teammates drank to excess the night before the match.

Game 7 opened with a Philadelphia penalty for too many men on the ice. When Plett cashed in for a 1-0 lead, the Flyers began to fall off a cliff in slow motion.

Wilson, gloving a lob at center ice, put the puck down on his forehand and was called by referee Bruce Hood for delay of game. "How many times did I do that in my career without it being called?" Wilson asks today. "Why then?"

Hood quickly made a tripping call on Bill Clement, despite Barber's obvious dive. But Holmgren held Brad Marsh, then tripped Kent Nilsson, and Hood called his third and fourth minors on Philadelphia in the first eight minutes. Houston took a pass Chouinard threaded between Murray's skates and put Calgary up, 2-0.

Cochrane, having taken down Bobby Gould to prevent a breakaway, was in the penalty box when Kevin Lavallee chipped in a Reinhart feed for a third power-play goal. After Kerr beat Don Lever on a face-off and Barber buried a wrister over Riggin's shoulder, the Flames braced for a Flyer charge that never came. Nilsson sent an exhausted Clarke sprawling with a move at the blue line and fed Bob MacMillan for the tip-in and a 4-1 lead.

Calgary iced the puck continually down the stretch and Philadelphia could not fight past the mauling Russell and Marsh. "I remember the look on Holmgren's face," recalls Clement. "He was absolutely bewildered that this could happen.".

The Spectrum emptied silently in the final minutes of Calgary's shocking 4-1 victory.

Quinn, who had switched goalies after St. Croix's Game 1 shutout and taken Kerr off Clarke's line to give the slumping Leach another chance in Game 7, was not blameless in the defeat. But the team did not need a new coach, only new bodies.

MacLeish was fading and Kerr's great hands demanded a regular shift. "Timmy's rough around the edges and isn't the classic playmaking center," said Allen. "But when we won this season, he was playing regularly. I don't think it was a coincidence." Although the GM believed Watson and Dailey would return and that Eriksson and Cochrane,who saw spot duty during the playoffs, were ready to become regulars, the club still needed a defenseman, plus a scoring winger to make up for Leach's declining production.

Hartford, soured on the promise of its last two first round picks—right wing Ray Allison and defenseman Fred Arthur—was in a trading mood. Allen failed in an effort to swap MacLeish for the Whalers' No. 1 pick (fourth overall) in the upcoming 1981 draft, but after the Capitals traded for center Bobby Carpenter, who Hartford wanted, and Philadelphia used the sixteenth pick to take defenseman Steve Smith, the Whalers and Flyers kept talking.

General manager Larry Pleau offered Allison and Arthur for MacLeish, Wesley and Hill, then changed his mind about Hill in favor of prospects from Maine. Allen insisted that if Philadelphia was going to give up another young player besides Wesley, it would have to receive the Whalers' first choice in 1982. Pleau agreed, if Hartford could have the Flyers' first-rounder in return, and asked for Don Gillen.

Thus, on July 3, 1981, Allen traded MacLeish, Gillen, Wesley and Philadelphia's first-, second- and third-round draft choices in 1982 for Arthur, Allison, and the Whalers' first and third 1982 picks. Since the Flyers had already acquired Hartford's No. 2 pick for Barnes and McIlhargey, the two teams had, in effect, exchanged positions for the first three rounds of the draft.

MacLeish got the news at his Jersey shore home, where he did not enjoy a happy Fourth. "I've been here ten (actually eleven) years and look what they get for me," he bitterly told Tim Panaccio of the *Philadelphia Journal*. "Some draft pick. They aren't even sure who it's going to be. Yeah, I do feel a little offended at that."

Allen took the high ground and sent the Spectrum hero away with praise. "Ricky was always one of my favorites," said the GM. "A low-key guy who came through for us so many times under pressure."

But, the Flyers had recycled a player whose best days were behind him for two more top prospects— Arthur and Allison—and what was probably going to be a blue-chip pick. Philadelphia had reason to believe the Eighties were going to be good years.

Chapter 8

◆◆◆

Long Pants
and Long Faces

The Flyers reported to their 1981 training camp in Portland suffering physical and mental strain. Bill Barber's knee and Paul Holmgren's shoulder had been injured in Canada Cup exhibitions, Jimmy Watson remained stiff and sore from spinal fusion surgery, and a July knee operation and back problems had drained Bob Dailey's enthusiasm. "If I had a definite idea of what I wanted to do when I quit playing, I might not be here now," he admitted.

Reggie Leach, beginning his option year and hardly coming off a season than inspired an extension, was refused a new contract and went home. Waiting for his flight back to Philadelphia, Leach was asked if he had talked to Allen before his decision. "I might as well talk to that ashtray," the bitter right wing said.

He returned four days later with a salary upgraded from $115,000 to $140,000, and the promise of a year's extension if he reached 30 goals or 50 points.

An unhappy Mel Bridgman signed for $148,000, the same amount he had rejected a year earlier. Quinn was determined to remove the captain's C from the disillusioned center. "Last year, [Bridgman] was so preoccupied that he wasn't being treated properly that his whole approach suffered," said the coach. The Flyers named Barber captain the day they opened the season with a 2-2 Spectrum tie against lowly Detroit.

Ilkka Sinisalo, a Finnish free agent winger signed at the urging of scout Eric Coville, became only the second player to score his initial NHL goal on a penalty shot when he beat Pittsburgh goalie Paul Harrison in an 8-2 Spectrum rout of the Penguins.

Quinn was slow to work the Flyers' new European talent into regular shifts and Thomas Eriksson, suspecting ethnic bias, returned to Sweden without confronting the coach with his concerns. But Quinn did find one young defenseman, Fred Arthur, NHL-ready. His play encouraged Allen to demote Busniuk to Maine and let Terry Murray go to Washington in the waiver draft.

> Ilkka Sinisalo became
> only the second player
> to score his first NHL
> goal on a penalty shot.

The Flyers brought long pants, popular in junior hockey, to the NHL for the first time, but their 7-0-1 start only disguised their continuing problems. The first loss, 11-2 in Montreal, was crushing. "This is as devastated as I've ever felt in my coaching career," said Quinn. The coach's confidence, most shaken by his goaltending, wasn't restored by St. Croix's unsteady 6-4 win over Pittsburgh two night later.

When Peeters was bombed 8-4 by Vancouver in the next outing, Quinn shocked the media after the

for him," announced the coach. He blasted McKegney for hitting Dailey while his back was turned instead of reaching for the touch up.

Dailey, however, felt cheap-shoted by a far greater being than McKegney. "My God, what else can happen to me?" he asked while being helped from a cab at the Buffalo Hilton after the game.

The next day at the University of Pennsylvania Hospital, Dr. Joe Torg inserted two long screws and one pin, into Daley's leg. He told Allen not to count

Paul Holmgren's return gave the Flyers new life.

game by announcing Pelle Lindbergh, reluctantly enduring a second AHL season, would be recalled for the game in Buffalo the following night. Asked if the Flyers had not already learned a lesson from keeping three goalies the previous season, Quinn snapped, "Right now I'd like to find one."

He was still searching, and trailing 4-1 late in the second period, when Dailey raced the Sabres' Tony McKegney for an icing, caught his skate in a rut and fell backwards into the boards. When Dailey looked, his left foot was at a nine-iron angle from his ankle. "It's broken," he told McKegney.

By the end of the Flyers' 6-2 loss, Quinn had heard from the emergency room at Buffalo General Hospital that both Dailey's tibia and fibula had suffered complex fractures. "It may very well be over

on the 28-year-old defenseman returning. From his bed, the Count tried to search for a silver lining. "Things could always be worse," he said. "In Buffalo, they had to move me out of the emergency room to make room for some poor guy who had the top of his head shot off."

That gentleman could have been a Flyer goalie. Philadelphia was outscored 71-36, while losing 9 of its next 11 games. "This is the worst I can remember since I came to the team," said Clarke. "It's unbelievable. We're down 3-1, 4-1, after every first period. Every game we do some things right, but screw up something else so badly we're not even in the game."

Behn Wilson's idea of turning the team around was to turn his stick into Ranger rookie Reijo Ruotsalainen's face, an act which brought booing even at the Spectrum. "We're lifeless," said Barber after the Rangers completed a 6-2 bombing of St. Croix. "On the bench, there's no yelling, no spark, and no talk on the ice."

Wilson received a 4-game NHL suspension and Quinn got a public vote of confidence from Ed Snider–sort of. "I'm disappointed with the way the goaltending has been handled," said the owner. "It wasn't the time to prove the value of Lindbergh [who had been returned to Maine]. But I have no reason to feel that Pat Quinn is not an outstanding coach."

There was, however, strong evidence that the defense needed help. Not only was Dailey down, but Frank Bathe, the team's steadiest defenseman during the misleading start, was out with a herniated back disc. When the similarly slumping Flames offered a straight one-for-one swap of Brad Marsh for Mel Bridgman, Allen jumped at the opportunity.

"We weren't dissatisfied with the way Mel was playing," said Allen when the deal was completed on November 11. "Center was one area where we did have some depth, and young Marsh is a real winner. He and Phil Russell took our cornerwork away from us in the playoffs last year.

Bridgman, who had 12 points in 9 games, insisted he was leaving without hard feelings. "My attitude had completely changed," he told reporters. "I'm showing that I really want to play and I'm sad I can't continue to do so [in Philadelphia]."

Holmgren's return pepped up the Flyers for Marsh's debut, a 5-3 Spectrum victory over Hartford. Nevertheless, the Flyers lost four of five, including a 10-4 humiliation at the Capital Center. Holmgren, Linseman and Wilson followed the leader, Clarke, in taking repeated penalties out of frustration, the Flyers had little mobility on defense and the goalies surrendered ridiculous goals. Team psychologist Julie Anthony (a former pro tennis player who was the wife of Flyer president Bob Butera's brother Dick) conducted seminars and counseled individual players, but on the ice Flyers seemed beyond help.

Holmgren, trying to defend Quinn, inadvertently damned him. "He's the best coach in the league," said Holmgren. "If we don't listen to him, it's our own fault. We have the worst practices, guys take advantage of him, bleep around."

At first, Quinn was harshly critical. "You see our team right now, it stinks," he said. As the trauma continued, the coach wisely decided to be more supportive, but he remained sensitive to Allen's criticism that Quinn's read-and-react system was backfiring on a team without the confidence to make cor-

rect, instantaneous decisions.

"A lot of the things that are going wrong are attributable to coaching," said the GM. "It is a time we have to go back to the basics."

"We could line up all our players at the blue line and still not even do that correctly," Quinn argued. "We're not thinking." Eventually, the coach relented both on his system and on Lindsay Carson, a third-round pick in 1979 who had stayed on a regular shift despite scoring one point in 18 games. Quinn gave more time to dipsy-doodling Ron Flockhart and two defensive call-ups — Mark Botell, an eighth-round pick in 1980, and Bob Hoffmeyer, a Blackhawk reject recycled through Maine. Botell was a revelation, Peeters' confidence surged in a 3-1 Thanksgiving night victory in Boston and the Flyers began to roll.

Arthur, a bright spot through the slump, continued to shine and Ray Allison was recalled to team with Flockhart, who quickly became a sensation.

"You guys have written that I don't pass the puck enough," said Flockhart, "and that's probably true." Quinn cringed at the rookie's inability to read defenses and his reluctance to use the other players on the ice, but the points kept coming. "I don't want to take away an obvious asset," said the coach, "but there are guys who score one and give up three and we don't want [Flockhart] to become that way."

Linseman, hardly eligible for checking awards himself, at least stopped pulling up at the blue line, which gave linemates Barber and Kerr more room to operate. A Propp-Holmgren-Clarke line was clicking, too, until Paul Baxter elbowed Holmgren during a December 9 game at Pittsburgh. Holmgren retaliated with a left hand, then became enraged as the Penguin defenseman turtled. When referee Andy van Hellemond gave the Flyer right wing a game misconduct for throwing two more punches against an unwilling opponent, Holmgren hit Van Hellemond in the shoulder.

The referee was not injured. But when NHL vice president Brian O'Neill, citing Holmgren's remorse and few league precedents for abuse of referees, suspended him for only 5 games, the NHL officials threatened to strike. It caused the league to institute a 20-game suspension for any future physical transgressions against officials.

The Flyers, 9-3 since their Thanksgiving turnaround, were top-heavy in centers. Nevertheless, when the Toronto Maple Leafs and their popular star center, Darryl Sittler, neared a divorce, Allen paid close attention.

Toronto GM Punch Imlach had precipitated a feud

with the 31-year-old Sittler by trying to deny his participation in 'Showdown', a one-on-one competition shown on Canadian television. Owner Harold Ballard then broke a promise to renegotiate the team captain's contract and insulted him at a face-to-face meeting.

Sittler declared he would waive a no-trade clause in his contract to get out of Toronto. His first relocation choice was Minnesota, but Barber, a fellow client of agent Alan Eagleson, asked Sittler to consider Philadelphia. Allen offered Gerry McNamara, who had replaced the fired Imlach, his choice of either Lindbergh or St. Croix, but was turned down. "They are in no rush to move the guy," said Allen. "I do have a better idea of what they want and we'll talk again."

The Flames were certainly in a conversant mood when the Flyers hit Calgary after Christmas. They were laying for Linseman, who, in a 6-1 Flyer victory three weeks earlier, had put center Guy Chouinard out of the lineup with a finger in his eye. "I don't mind losing to teams like Minnesota with an honest style," said forward Jim Peplinski. "But I hate the Flyers with a passion."

Linseman responded by dancing away with two goals and two assists in a 7-4 Flyer romp. "I didn't really gouge [Chouinard]," argued the Rat. "I just kind of had my finger near his eye."

Two nights later in Edmonton, the Flyers' vision of Wayne Gretzky was perfect, but he blurred reality. Needing 5 goals in 12 games to become the third player in NHL history to record 50 in the first 50 contests of a season, the Great One decided to get them all against the Flyers and Peeters. Gretzky put the last one into an empty net with 3 seconds remaining.

"This is absolutely crazy," said Clarke, who went to the Oiler room to congratulate Gretzky after Edmonton's 7-5 victory. "He materializes out of nowhere. Every time he gets a chance, he scores."

The Flyers handled a January 14 rematch with Gretzky much better, holding him to one goal in an 8-2 Spectrum victory. Two nights later, they beat the Canadiens 4-2 in Montreal, then returned home the next night to blow out Boston 7-3 behind a a dazzling two-goal, one-assist display of Flocky Hockey.

"What's his name?" asked Bruins' coach Gerry Cheevers. "Lockhart? Flockhart? Christ, he looked like Meadowlark Lemon." The Flyers lost Holmgren for three weeks with a slight knee ligament tear during the game, but at 28-15-1, they led the two-time defending Stanley Cup champion Islanders by one

point.

Two nights later in Quebec, Clarke was forced to limp on a sore foot through 1:35 of a late-game penalty to Linseman for flipping the puck into the stands to protest an offside call. The Flyers held on for a 2-2 tie that was not attended by their GM.

Allen was in Phoenix at a general manager's meeting, making his final pitch for Sittler. The Leafs, excited about a recent scoring spurt by rookie Norman Aubin, wanted draft choices and prospects. Minnesota GM Lou Nanne offered winger Steve Christoff and a second-round pick but McNamara– put off by Nanne's shameless broadcasting of his intentions and reluctant to move Sittler to a Norris Division rival– looked for a better offer.

Allen was unwilling to part with the first-round pick the Flyers had acquired from Hartford, but would move the second-rounder and satisfy McNamara's request for center Rich Costello, the Flyers' second-round 1981 pick. McNamara went to play golf and Allen awaited the Leaf GM's promised call. It came at 11:15 P.M., after Allen had already gotten into bed, but he rose, dressed and went to McNamara's room.

McNamara asked for another player to sweeten the deal, so Allen drew up a fifteen-player list that included Hill, Gorence, Eriksson and prospects Mark Taylor, Daryl Stanley and Len Hachborn. The Leafs could choose one at the end of the season (it would be center Ken Strong, a 1981 third round pick). "At least Nanne didn't get him," said McNamara to Allen as they shook hands.

The next morning, the Flyers got the good news about Sittler a few hours before receiving bad news: A second Xray of Clarke's foot, injured in Uniondale ten days earlier, showed a fracture that would put him out for a month. The injury didn't seem quite so crippling, however, when the closest living facsimile of Clarke stepped off a freedom flight from Toronto at 10:25 P.M. As Sittler and his wife, Wendy, were greeted and taken home by Barber, the new Flyer smiled for the first time in a year. "I think the Flyer management is excellent," Sittler told waiting newsmen. "The best in the NHL."

Snider and Eagleson had already agreed on a deal paying Sittler $110,520 for the balance of the season, then $230,000 for each of the following three years. "The guy scored 96 points last year under terrible conditions," said Snider. "For a player of Sittler's caliber, it's a bargain."

Sittler, who had not played during the final eighteen days of the siege, performed on adrenaline the next night at the Spectrum. He had four first-period shots before fading in a 4-2 loss to Montreal. "I'm just anxious for all the excitement to taper off so I can get into some kind of routine," said Sittler.

He had chosen the Flyers assuming that winning would be part of the routine, but as injuries piled up, that became impossible. Kerr, who had missed 12 games in 1980-81 with a knee problem, landed on it again two nights later in a 5-5 tie in Pittsburgh, joining Clarke, Holmgren, Wilson, Bathe, Gorence and Dailey out of the lineup.

In Los Angeles, Ray Allison's empty-net goal appeared to wrap up a 4-2 victory, but the Kings scored twice to pull out a 4-4 tie. "Our defensive skills are deteriorating rapidly," said Quinn after Gretzky's hat trick beat the Flyers 7-4 in Edmonton on January 31. "We've been backing off, whether it's against Gretzky or Arnie Schwartz, and I don't know why."

Botell's flash died in the pan and Arthur, with little meat on his 6 feet, 5 inches of bones, ran out of gas and enthusiasm. Quinn stayed with a lackadaisical Leach, while rookies Greg Adams and Sinisalo were getting limited ice time.

The return of Holmgren and Kerr for a 6-4 win over Buffalo on February 11 was only a finger in the dike. The long layoff had left Sittler a half-step behind and Marsh had grown so hesitant he looked three steps slow. Cochrane could not accept a clean hit without taking a retaliatory penalty and Linseman again ignored Quinn's pleas to use his speed and take the puck wide.

Holmgren crashed the net in Winnipeg and left the lineup with yet another injury, this one to his back, as the Flyers lost to the Jets, 6-2. "Eddie is out of town," said Allen as he watched the Winnipeg debacle from his home. "I'm dreading it when he calls in to find out the score. We seem to be getting worse. I'm really worried."

Quinn finally benched Leach. "I guess they'd rather go with two- and three-goal scorers," sniffed the Rifle-turned-airgun. Marsh drew great personal satisfaction from a goal that beat the Flames 9-8 in Calgary, but the absurd score was only one more manifestation of the Flyers' alarming defensive play.

Clarke returned on March 2 at the Spectrum against Winnipeg, but Willy Lindstrom scored five goals on Peeters to give the Jets a 7-6 victory. "They just keep blowing in on you, how many can you stop?" said the goalie, who had surrendered 21 goals in his last 3 starts. "If I take all the blame on myself like I did in the past, then I'll go crazy."

The constant offsides and horrendous penalty-killing were already driving Snider nuts. With the Flyers 4-10-5 in their last 19 games, the owner summoned Allen and Quinn to his center city office. "Keith never said a word at the meeting," recalls Quinn. "Ed did all the talking. He basically just laid out a collection of opinions about me that he had gotten from different sources.

"One was from [advance scout] Joe Watson, who didn't feel I was listening to him enough. From that, I got that I wasn't using other people, that I had gotten stubborn and closed-minded. That was combined with some things I had said that were perceived as criticism of personnel decisions to make a case against me. It was like I had become too autonomous and become a danger to the organization. I was told it was my job to coach the players I had been given.

"Ed also said something that apparently came from Darryl Sittler about how my practices weren't hard enough. I don't think Darryl went to anybody to complain about me. He probably just gave an opinion when he was asked. There was a criticism that I had not developed a single defenseman, that I was teaching a system that was too complicated for the personnel we had. All these things were being combined to make a case against me.

"I was terribly upset. I was thinking that I had the team in first place in January, but that we had since lost a lot of key people to injury. We had a mishmash of guys we had to call up from Maine just to get through the season.

"We also had some players—and key players, too—who weren't 'Flyers.' These were the players they were supposedly building the new regime around, too. I got the impression that Ken Linseman had gone above me, that some of these opinions about me had come from him."

Linseman recalls being asked his thoughts by Snider and giving them. "I don't remember exactly what I said, but it seemed to me that Pat didn't know what to do when we were falling apart," Linseman says. "His whole tone completely changed, like he was lost, too.

"I never would have gone behind Pat's back to complain about him. I was just a kid and it's ridiculous to think that I would have any influence. I probably was a coaching problem. I hated to practice and I loved to compete. I was torn by a lot of people trying to tell me different ways I should play and just how aggressive I should be, but I was also young and having fun."

Quinn left the meeting with Snider reeling. "I remember thinking it was like something out of a Shakespearean play, with all these subplots," he recalls. "Still, I didn't get the feeling that my job was in immediate jeopardy. Ed didn't really want an immediate answer to any of these things, he just wanted me to think about them and get back to him within a couple weeks."

The Rangers, on a 19-6-6 tear and virtually guaranteed a first-round meeting with the Flyers—the second- and third-place teams in each division would meet in the first round under the new format—came to the Spectrum on March 4 for the first of four remaining games betwen the two rivals. Lindbergh, looking more like the future and less like trade bait as Peeters and St. Croix struggled, was recalled and given the start.

The rookie was three minutes away from a victory when Andre Dore retrieved a loose puck off a loose stick lying on the ice and scored between Lindbergh's legs. Still, he had shown enough in the 4-4 tie for Allen to offer St. Croix to Boston for defenseman Brad McCrimmon. St. Croix was sent into the nets against Washington in a final showcasing for the very interested Bruins, and suddenly glowed so hot in a 7-1 victory that Allen backed out of the deal.

The Flyers rallied from three goals down for a 5-5 tie March 10 in New York. And with everyone but Dailey now healthy, Snider waited to see if the team would come together down the stretch. Instead, he watched the Flyers lose, 6-3, in Washington and saw Barber used on defense for four games. The owner, disappointed with the progress of the young defensemen, interpreted Quinn's move as an act of desperation. A 5-2 loss at Madison Square Garden on March 17 was the final straw.

Snider, Allen and Butera had gone to dinner at Bookbinders, then watched the game on television as the Flyers were hopelessly befuddled by the circling, puck-possession game that coach Herb Brooks had taught the Rangers. Snider became more convinced than ever that the Flyers would have no chance in the upcoming first-round series unless they made a coaching change.

"I think Eddie is a genius, but this was not his finest hour," recalls Butera. "He had lost confidence in Pat and transmitted it in such a way that Pat lost confidence in himself. Players always sense when a superior is in trouble and they protect themselves.

"Eddie had been working on Keith for about three months. When we watched the game that night, Keith for the first time said, 'Okay, maybe we should make a change.' They decided to sleep on it and called a meeting in the morning in Eddie's office, when

Eddie said, 'I changed my mind. You guys do what you want.' But I don't believe Keith thought for a minute that was the case. He knew what he had to do."

The best available replacement was Bob McCammon, who had earned back Snider and Allen's confidence by continuing to win and develop players at Maine. McCammon had attracted a job offer from Islanders assistant GM Jimmy Devellano, which Allen planned to counter in the off-season by making McCammon assistant GM of the Flyers.

On the evening following the Ranger loss, while the Flyers were preparing to play the Blackhawks at the Spectrum, Allen called McCammon and offered him Quinn's job. The startled McCammon responded as Quinn had three years earlier: Wasn't this being rash? Allen gave the exact same answer. He was making a move. If McCammon didn't take the job, the Flyers would look elsewhere.

Quinn worked the bench against Chicago with no idea of his imminent demise. Sittler's 400th career goal with 22 seconds remaining brought a standing ovation and a 4-4 tie, but no change of mind by Allen.

Quinn was upbeat at practice at the Penn rink the next morning. It wasn't until he got the call to come to the Spectrum that he became concerned. "He said on his way down that he thought this might be it," recalls Clarke. "But I told him 'no way at this point in the season.'"

The coach and his assistant, Bob Boucher, were dismissed by Allen in a five-minute conversation. Clarke, whose coaching role had diminished as teammates grew uneasy with his dual status, lost his title of assistant.

Quinn went to his Newtown Square home, then to his daughter Valeri's swim meet, and begged off comment until a later time. It was Allen and Snider —with McCammon at their side—who had all the explaining to do when they met a generally Quinn-friendly media later in the afternoon.

"The Rangers were toying with us," said Snider. "We were going nowhere with the present situation." He bristled at the suggestion that recurring appearances of McCammon and Quinn through revolving doors reflected organizational instability. "Bob McCammon wasn't fired three years ago," said Snider. "He was reassigned. He stayed in our organization and we brought him back when he was more ready to coach the team.

"I wouldn't be surprised if Pat Quinn someday comes back to haunt us. But to wait until after the playoffs would have been throwing in the towel on this season. And I'll be damned if I'm going to do that."

"I don't care what system we're using," added Allen. "I didn't tell [Quinn] what to do. But if it's not working, either we're not executing it right or we don't have the personnel to do it the way he wanted. Either way it's his fault.

"There was confusion. I saw mistakes that I thought should have been corrected long ago. Up front, we should be better than we were two years ago when we went to the finals. Our defense isn't as bad as it's been made out to be. Players have gone backwards."

McCammon immediately put Lindbergh in goal for a weekend series with Hartford. The Flyers won both games, but that hardly made the returning coach a conquering hero. The "Welcome Back Bob McCammon" posted on the Spectrum message-board during the Sunday night game was met with almost stone silence.

"Were you here the last time I coached in this building?" asked McCammon. "I'd say the [lack of] reaction tonight was favorable. I'm not going to run for mayor. I'm just here to do the job."

It was a job Quinn had valued highly. When he called the beat writers together at Cavanaugh's restaurant in West Philadelphia three days after his firing, he termed the dismissal "the biggest disappointment of my life."

"I was the same guy I was two years ago. I treated players like I wanted to be treated as a player. It was pointed out to me a while ago that maybe everybody isn't Pat Quinn. They may have been right. Maybe I needed to smack a few guys. But should I have to threaten somebody to do a job?

"The threat is something that [should be] in management's hands. If I was at the end of my rope with all my motivational skills, then get the guy out of here or send him down. And if you get to that point, then my threatening didn't work anyway."

Quinn said he planned to maintain his Delaware County residence and that he might explore his long-standing curiosity with law school.

McCammon, brought back to prosecute some Flyer repeat offenders, was given his first test case after only five days on the job. Several players were tardy for practice. Cochrane, five minutes late on the ice, was told to stay in the locker room and fined a day's pay. Peeters and Linseman were also docked when they missed afternoon appointments for one-on-one meetings with McCammon.

Leach, twenty minutes late for drills and hav-

ing already cleared waivers at the trading deadline, was told to go home for good. "If we don't show we mean business, we're not going anywhere," said McCammon. "I asked him last week to behave and look after himself."

"He told me he's going to go with young guys." said Leach, as he rushed past reporters in the Spectrum parking lot. "Gotta get the kids to school."

After eight years and 306 Flyer goals, Reggie Leach drove away.

McCammon reinstated Peeters as his goalie. "Pelle's going to be an all-star," said the coach. "But if Pete gets himself together, I think we have a chance to go far." Second place was gone, but a solid 3-1 victory over the Rangers on March 28 rekindled some hope that the Flyers could give New York a good series. The Flyers went 4-2-2 under McCammon to complete an 87-point season, their worst in nine years. "I guess we're ready," said Linseman after the Flyers finished up with a 7-1 victory over Toronto. "I just hope we're confident enough."

The voting for the Barry Ashbee Award winner provided the quintessential statement about the Flyers' defense. Bathe, who played in only 28 games, was the deserving winner. McCammon hoped experience up front and some good old Flyer grit could save the season against the smaller but much quicker Rangers.

Sure enough, Philadelphia played soundly in Game 1 at Madison Square Garden. Sittler scored twice and the Flyers, forechecking with only one man, negated the Rangers' speed through the neutral zone. Peeters made a handful of outstanding stops, Clarke and Sittler dominated on face-offs, and the Flyers won routinely 4-1.

When Clarke nailed a top corner behind goalie Ed Mio only 48 seconds into Game 2, the Flyers had an opportunity to seize control of the series. But the Rangers needed only 1:09 to tie the game. Watson, called for taking down Mikko Leinonen, let up as referee Wally Harris' arm rose and Rob McClanahan fed Carol Vadnais for the tying goal.

The Flyers reverted to their season-long form. With Watson whistled again, Mark Pavelich pushed Arthur off the puck, enabling Ron Duguay to put in Barry Beck's rebound. Leinonen fed Don Maloney for an easy tap-in while Kerr was in the penalty box, and Robbie Ftorek scored after Linseman was caught horse-collaring Pavelich at center. Allison cashed a power play to cut the Ranger lead to 4-2, but Dave Silk was unchecked by Gorence and the Rangers, on a playoff-record six assists by Leinonen, pulled away to a 7-3 victory.

"Philadelphia played silly," said Ranger defenseman Barry Beck. McCammon coached curiously, too, using neither Linseman nor Holmgren on regular shifts.

Flockhart, gonged by a Dave Maloney cross-check, stayed overnight at Pennsylvania Hospital and was unavailable for Game 3 at Spectrum. Obviously, the Flyer center's skull wasn't as thick as that of Cochrane, who ignored the lessons of Game 2 and took an early roughing penalty. Clarke, however, turned it into a shorthanded goal. Wilson then scored on the power play and Propp, set up by Kerr off a face-off, made the score 3-0 before eleven minutes had elapsed.

The Spectrum was roaring, but the Rangers calmed themselves and worked their way back into the game. Mike Rogers scored, then Reijo Ruotsalainen bounced a power-play goal off Marsh while Linseman was sitting out for senselessly slashing Silk. In the final minute of the second period, Don Maloney tied the score.

In the locker room, McCammon screamed at Linseman. "He accused me of only thinking about myself, not the team," recalls Linseman. "I don't remember anything anybody ever said to me in hockey hurting so much."

The Rat was benched in the third period when the Flyers had chances, but the Rangers caught the big break. Cam Connor flagrantly yanked down Holmgren along the boards in the Flyer zone and went to the net to put in a Mike Rogers rebound for the game winner with only 1:09 remaining. The Flyers raged at the non-call by referee Bruce Hood and not enough at themselves for the penalties that had helped them blow a 3-0 lead.

The Rangers were now only one game away from winning the series. And they knew they could count on the Flyers' help. In Game 4, Robbie Ftorek cashed two power plays as the Rangers raced to a 3-0 second-period lead. The Flyers, desperately flailing around Mio, sandwiched goals by Holmgren and Clarke around one by Duguay to climb back to 4-2, but were repeatedly trapped up ice. Mark Pavelich put in a rebound, chasing Peeters, and Maloney went through Watson and Bathe to beat St. Croix from a sharp angle and build the Ranger lead to 6-2 and remove all doubt — except in Clarke and Sittler.

Sittler fed a goalmouth pass to Clarke who backhanded the puck between his own legs to make it 6-3, then Sittler put in his own rebound, cutting the lead to two with 6:27 left in regulation. Wilson, true

to Flyer form, took a frivolous roughing penalty against Ftorek, but the possessed Clarke stripped Silk at the side of the net and set up a shorthanded Barber goal. "The greatest game of all the great ones I've ever seen Bobby Clarke play," Snider would say later. With 3:41 remaining, the Flyers had lifted themselves to a one-goal deficit.

But the visitors regained their composure and put up a roadblock at center ice. Duguay hit the empty net with 7 seconds remaining and the Flyers, 7-5 losers, had encountered first-round failure for the first time since 1971.

"In my mind we should have beaten the Rangers," said McCammon, "but we're still three or four players away from being a real contender. We have to make some hard, fast decisions. Some of the players have been here for a while and we haven't won."

The remaining draft pick acquired in the Rick MacLeish trade had turned into the fourth choice overall, leaving Gary Nylund and Gord Kluzak, the two most coveted defensemen in the draft, out of the Flyers' reach. Though defenseman Scott Stevens had risen lately in the rankings off his strong performance in the Memorial Cup and speedy center Ken Yaremchuk was considered the most skilled player still on the board, the Flyers pulled a major surprise by taking Lethbridge center Ron Sutter, the brother of Duane and Brent of the Islanders.

"Yaremchuk could turn out to be spectacular," Allen said later. "But when he doesn't have the puck, he floats. Sutter is a skilled player, too. It's like taking a Clarke over a Perreault." The Flyer GM then walked table-to-table making offers for each of the next six picks, hoping to be able to draft Sutter's twin brother, Rich. There were no takers. Rich Sutter went to Pittsburgh on the tenth selection.

However, the Flyers did not let draft day pass without getting sorely-needed defensive help. In the third round they took Miroslav Dvorak, a 30-year-old Czechoslovakian national team star who was being allowed to finish his career in the West as part of a program to discourage defections and finance the Czech program. "We know [Dvorak] can play and he gives us two or three years to buy some time." said McCammon.

The Flyers weren't going to wait a day longer for Peeters to mature. During the draft, they announced his trade to Boston for McCrimmon, a 23-year-old defenseman with good skills and a mean streak who had floundered after an encouraging rookie season.

McCrimmon blamed only himself for the difficulties that led to his trade, but Peeters went away throwing darts. "You have to remember the Flyers once traded away Bernie Parent," said Peeters. "Sometimes I think they forgot I'm 23 years old. My rookie year, when we went to the finals, we did great with a defense of guys like Norm Barnes and Mike Busniuk. They let them go without getting anything in return."

Allen was tired of patching the defense with re-cycled minor-leaguers, reclamation projects and kids. Dailey was not coming back ("I can't walk with-out pain," he said on August 16. "How am I going to skate?") and the GM needed an anchor for the Fly-ers' new defense. Flockhart's 72 points in 72 games as a rookie had made Linseman the bait.

One of the defensemen on Allen's list, Rob Ramage, was traded at the draft to St. Louis by Colorado—which had moved to become the New Jersey Devils—but two others were anxious for a change of scenery. Montreal's Rod Langway wanted to be traded to a U.S.-based team and Mark Howe was in Hartford's doghouse over so-called lackadai-sical play.

Howe, 27, had lost 17 games and twenty pounds during the 1980-81 season. His buttocks had been pierced by a metal goal spike following a collision with the Islanders' John Tonelli. Nineteen months later, Whaler GM Larry Pleau questioned why Howe had yet to regain full strength, and was determined to purge what he felt was the team's country-club atmosphere.

Snider had asked Whalers president Howard Baldwin, a former Flyer ticket manager, for first crack at Howe should the Whalers ever decide to trade him. Pleau wanted Linseman—to deal him for Edmonton's Risto Siltanen, an offensive defenseman to replace Howe.

McCammon recalls Allen dreaded telling Snider of the opportunity to trade Linseman, who had been dating the owner's daughter, Lindy. McCammon drew the dirty work. He rode the subway to Snid-er's center city offices and informed the owner what it would cost the Flyers to get Howe. "Eddie said 'Whatever you and Keith think is best,'" recalls McCammon.

Pleau also wanted a No. 1 pick. Allen's scouts, feeling the 1983 draft would not be deep, told the boss not to hesitate. But when Pleau insisted the Flyers also throw in left wing prospect Greg Adams, Allen balked. And when Pleau refused to accept a substitute, the Flyer GM prepared to walk away from the deal.

"I asked Keith what Howe's value would be to

us," recalls Snider. "When Keith said Howe would in-stantly be our best defenseman and that we probably couldn't fill our need another way, I asked if Greg Adams really was worth letting the deal pass." Allen relented. But there was one more obstacle.

Howe, who signed a ten-year deal with the Whal-ers when he, his father Gordie, and brother Marty had left the WHA Houston Aeros, had a no-trade clause in his contract. On the morning of August 19, Pleau called Howe in, explained the deal on the ta-ble, and gave him Keith Allen's phone number. Mark walked down the hall to his father's office and dialed.

"All I wanted to hear was that the Flyers really wanted me," Howe recalls. Reassured, he then asked if the Flyers could relieve him of the burden of sell-ing his recently-completed Hartford home. Snider not only agreed to buy the house, but also assumed some of the Whalers' contractural obligations to the defenseman. It was a done deal.

Linseman, immediately moved by the Whalers to Edmonton for Siltanen, was in San Diego and couldn't be reached by Allen before the trade was announced later in the day. Once informed, the Rat laid as low as he felt, refusing to return phone calls from the me-dia. "I wasn't totally surprised, but I was upset," Linseman recalls. "It took a while before I said, 'Don't be an idiot. Look at the team you're going to.'"

Snider's heart was also giving his head an argu-ment. "I feel like I just sold my son to Siberia," said the owner.

Bobby Clarke's heir apparent had been traded even as Clarke was still going strong, but Allen re-fused to express regret over Linseman's stunted growth during four inconsistent seasons. "I don't want to give the impression we were disappointed with Kenny," the GM told reporters. "I think we all felt a sense of frustration that he could do better if he was a little bit more disciplined, but he certainly played well in a lot of important games."

The move freed Sittler to go back to center from left wing and completed a 50-percent turnover of a defense that had hung in tatters for almost four years. "Mark Howe is one of the finest offensive defensemen in the NHL," said Allen. "I think the Whalers expected him to be a leader. He isn't, but with Clarke, Sittler and Holmgren, he won't have to assume that mantle here."

Dailey made his retirement official five days later. "The pain would be beyond the call of duty," said Dr. Torg. "And to continue to play would facilitate degen-erative arthritis in the joint."

From Day One of the 1982-83 training camp in

Portland, Howe kissed the Flyer defense and made it all better, while Dvorak brought skill and enthusiasm to his new world beyond the Iron Curtain. The Czech's eyes widened at the discovery of two cases of beer on a bus bringing the Flyers back from a preseason game in New York. Two hours later, Dvorak disembarked holding a can in one hand and a cigarette in the other. "America great country," he smiled.

Marsh took Dvorak under his wing while McCammon went out of his way to rebuild the confi-

Mark Howe was the club's dominant defenseman.

with Allen the day before the 1982-83 opener, the best defenseman on the Flyers' Cup teams and a torch-bearer of organizational pride for eight seasons retired, agreeing to complete the final year of his contract as a scout.

"It wasn't as much fun playing with pain," said Watson. "I guess that's why I'm relieved."

The Flyers also made cosmetic changes as they opened the 1982-83 season with a 9-5 victory over Quebec. The stripe disappeared from their long pants while the orange shoulders of their jerseys were reddened, broadened, and bordered in black. But the Spectrum crowd of 16,200, the smallest since 1972-73, was an indication that a first-round defeat had not worn well on the fans.

Fred Arthur, whose career doubts drained his enthusiasm in the second half of his rookie year, refused an early-season demotion to Maine and decided to pursue medical studies. "I can't say I feel at home in the sport or particularly enjoy it," he said. "You have to be totally committed. I can't be, because there is something I want to do more."

After founding and building the security firm Spectaguard, 25-year-old Jay Snider, son of the Flyer owner, was looking for a new challenge, too. On October 21, he was named a Flyer vice president, taking on marketing projects while training to eventually run the organization.

The Flyers, getting only average goaltending from St. Croix, did not bolt from the blocks. But the team was obviously improved. "Bob [McCammon] has really harped on discipline," said Marsh after a 3-2 victory in Winnipeg on October 31 brought the record to 8-5. "And now, when we have a face-off in our end, it makes a big difference when he can have a Darryl Sittler pull it back to a Howe or a Dvorak."

Kerr was lost again to torn knee ligaments on November 10 in Buffalo, the night St. Croix's 7-2 loss convinced McCammon that it was time to give Lindbergh a shot at the top job. The following night at the Spectrum, he beat the hated Rangers, 7-3. The little Swede shut out the Kings 4-0 in Los Angeles, stoned the high-powered Oilers 4-2

dence of McCrimmon. There was no longer a regular spot for Watson, who had endured the 1981-82 season as a shell of his former self. When he played the exhibition season in pain that doctors told him was normal for an overly stressed, surgically fused disc, Watson knew it was time to move on. At a meeting in Edmonton and battled to a scoreless deadlock in Pittsburgh, a game in which Barber was lost with a torn medial collateral ligament in his right knee.

Paired with a maturing Cochrane, Howe was outstanding, notching three assists and completely controlling a 7-2 Spectrum rout of Detroit. "He's better than I thought, definitely," said McCammon. When the rapidly improving Capitals, who had scored three in the final 3:43 to stop the Flyers 3-1 at the Spectrum on December 19, wiped out a 3-0 Philadelphia lead seven days later in Landover, Howe's shorthanded goal restarted his team towards a 6-3 victory.

The following night in Detroit, Clarke's hat trick in an 8-4 rout lifted the 20-12-5 Flyers into a first-place tie with the dawdling Islanders. "People have been counting [Clarke] out, saying he's on his last legs," said McCammon, "and here, in an important game, he wins it for us."

The Flyers caught fire. In his first exposure to the Chicago Stadium air horn, Lindbergh almost jumped out of his skin after being beaten by Al Secord, but the Flyers went on to a 3-1 victory that completed a 6-0 post-Christmas western trip. "I've never won 6 games in a row in my life," said Sittler.

An exhibition game with the Soviet national team drew flag-waving zealots and memories of 1976, but a different result. After the Flyers were shut down 5-1, Ed Snider vowed they would only play Russian club teams, never again the all-stars.

The owner's ego wasn't the only one bruised. Barber was told before the Soviet game, his first outing in a month, that he was being replaced as captain by Clarke. "Billy didn't do anything wrong," said McCammon. "I just think there are only a chosen few who can lead."

"It hurts me," said Barber, who had remained captain after Clarke lost his assistant coach title the previous March, "but if that's what they feel is best, I'll back it."

While Barber tried to wash a bad taste from his mouth, Lindbergh woke up the morning after the Soviet loss to discover he could not brush his teeth. His wrist, severely sprained when it had been kicked, was placed in a cast.

The rusted St. Croix wanted out of Philadelphia, so the Flyers turned to Bob Froese, a 1981 free-agent signee who was sizzling in Maine. He debuted with a 7-4 victory in Hartford. Two days later, St. Croix was moved to to Toronto for 30-year-old goalie Michel (Bunny) Larocque, but McCammon stayed with Froese, who picked up exactly where Lindbergh

left off.

A 10-game league winning streak ended in a 4-4 Spectrum tie with Chicago, but Barber's misfortune continued nonstop. Diving to prevent a breakaway, he caught Blackhawk Peter Marsh's skate in the face. It wasn't until after he had scored a goal and two assists in Froese's 4-0 shutout the following night at Madison Square Garden that the left wing learned his jaw had been broken. Howe, who took a blow to the kidneys against the Rangers, discovered blood in his urine after playing two nights later in a 4-1 defeat at Landover and was lost for four games, while Barber decided to play with a wired jaw.

But the Flyers still were feeling no pain. Sittler scored his 1,000th point — a goal that blew off goalie Don Edwards's glove — in a 5-2 Spectrum victory over Calgary on January 20. The Islanders, six points behind the Flyers, took their best shot at Nassau Coliseum, but Sittler's goal and Froese's 31 saves produced a stunning 1-0 Philadelphia victory. "That's the best-goaltended game I've ever seen," Holmgren told Froese on the bus ride home.

He defeated the Rangers 7-1 the following night at the Spectrum and was unbeaten in 11 starts when Lindbergh returned for the final game before the all-star break to shut out the Kings 2-0 at Inglewood. The Flyers were an astounding 18-1-2 in their last 21 outings.

The Flyer veterans welcomed the Swede back with a particularly brutal rookie shaving. "They do it to everybody, so what could I do?" he said forlornly. The goalie covered his butchered scalp with a hat at the all-star dinner at the Nassau Coliseum, but had no place to hide the following night when he surrendered seven goals—four to Gretzky—in 30 minutes. Lindbergh looked shaky in a 5-2 Spectrum win over St. Louis, then gave up five as the Kings ended a 32-game, nine-season, winless streak against Philadelphia, 5-4 at the Spectrum.

McCammon went back to Froese, who finally suffered a setback in his 14th start, 4-2 in Buffalo. His disappointment was not as acute as Kerr's. The luckless winger broke his leg against the Sabres, only his 6th game since returning to the lineup.

Gradually, the Flyers began to slip backwards. After dominating the fourth place Rangers in four consecutive victories, Philadelphia was routed 8-2 at Madison Square Garden on March 14. "Nobody hit their smurfs all night," complained McCammon.

The coach tried Lindbergh again, with so-so results, and publicly flogged Barber, who had lost weight and stamina trying to play with a wired jaw. "The captaincy thing may have hurt him more than he thinks," said McCammon. "He's not playing well defensively, not jumping into holes. To see a guy of his caliber not going, it hurts us."

Barber seethed. "The coach is always right," he said bitterly. "We're not winning and I'm the reason."

Clarke, Sittler and Dvorak were similarly low on fuel, but Clarke didn't want to rest and McCammon didn't press the issue. Howe had not been dominant since the bruised kidney, Marsh went down with a cracked fibula in a 7-4 win over Toronto, and a slump-

8 on the recommendation of Ted Sator, a guest power-skating instructor at the Flyers' September training camp who had coached Poulin in Sweden. Poulin made his NHL debut in his hometown Toronto on the next-to-last night of the season and scored goals on his first two shots, helping the Flyers win, 6-3.

The following night, the Flyers punished the Islanders with 45 shots in a 4-2 Spectrum victory. "I feel a lot better," said McCammon, whose team finished with 106 points. That was twenty-six more than the fourth-place Rangers, but the Flyer coach, hav-

Dave Poulin, who had been named team captain when this photo was taken, scored his first playoff points in 1983.

ing McCrimmon put the go-ahead goal into his own net in a wretched 6-5 loss on March 25 at New Jersey.

One night later, the Flyers' first division title in three seasons was clinched when second-place Washington tied Pittsburgh. But the celebration was subdued and a 4-2 Spectrum loss to the oncoming Rangers was sobering. "If it makes us think about what's happened in the past, that's good," said McCammon bravely. "We can make sure it doesn't happen again."

Lindsay Carson suffered bruised ribs against the Rangers, so the Flyers recalled left wing Dave Poulin. The undrafted former University of Notre Dame player had been signed and sent to Maine on March

ing been repeatedly burned out the back end in the two late-season losses to New York, was fearful of trying to dictate the play. Instead, McCammon decided to try to contain the smaller, swifter Rangers at center ice.

The strategy failed miserably in Game One. Frank Bathe, back for his second game after missing 12 with strained knee ligaments, was beaten to a rebound by Anders Hedberg, who gave the Rangers a 1-0 lead. McCrimmon and Lindbergh took undisciplined penalties and Mark Pavelich and Hedberg, stashed power-play rebounds. Early in the second period, Mikko Leinonen got outside Cochrane and fed Mike Backman, who eluded Clarke to give the Rangers a stunning 4-0 lead.

Flockhart brought the morose Spectrum crowd to life by lifting in a Howe rebound, but Eddie Johnstone, untended by Sittler at the edge of the net, quickly answered. Poulin, the only Flyer appearing to have any jump or confidence, scored after going around Tom Laidlaw, and Barber redirected a Howe point drive, but the game wasn't as close as the 5-3 final suggested.

"I was uptight," said Howe, who was repeatedly bumped as he tried to carry the puck. A frustrated Clarke publicly faulted McCammon's cautious game plan. "We're trying to change what we've been doing best," said the captain. "We've got to forget about how they play and just bleeping play. If you have to stop and think, it freezes you."

McCammon, chastised by Snider after the game for not having his team prepared, tried to stay calm. "We didn't get 106 points by accident," said McCammon. "Thursday night, we'll be a better team."

And the Flyers were, too. They hit every Ranger they could in the first fifteen minutes and Propp scored on a power play. But in the middle period, Behn Wilson made a sloppy clear and George McPhee's backhander beat Lindbergh. Pavelich then squirted away from Marsh and Sinisalo to feed Laidlaw, whose first goal in 102 games gave New York a 2-1 lead.

Sinisalo, on a feed from Poulin behind the net, tied the game 51 seconds into the third period. But Howe, lined up against Pavelich on a simple two-on-two, inexplicably crossed over to take Rob McClanahan, who appeared to be contained by Cochrane. McClanahan slipped the puck past Howe to the suddenly wide-open Pavelich, and he went around Lindbergh for a deposit. Two minutes later, Marsh made a bad pinch and Pavelich sprung Hedberg on a two-on-one, which Reijo Ruotsalainen finished with a bazooka to the top corner.

Kerr, back in the lineup for the first time since February 23, put in Propp's rebound to cut the lead to one and the desperate Flyers were all around Ranger goalie Ed Mio down the stretch. Mike Allison swept a Sittler jam off the goal line and Kerr shot just wide from 35 feet. In the final seconds, Propp forced a giveaway and Howe fired for the top corner. He missed by three inches.

"We keep coming back and coming back and every time we make a mistake it's in our net," said a morose Clarke after the 4-3 loss. McCammon railed about an obviously accidental high stick by Dave Maloney that had sent Flockhart to the hospital with facial injuries. By the next day, however, the coach appeared to be accepting the inevitable.

"You second-guess yourself," he said. "I remember when we had a big lead over the Islanders, and I was thinking about giving Sittler and Clarke two weeks off. And then the Islanders kept winning and we had to be sure we finished first."

The Rangers had used McCammon's "smurfs" quote for motivation and the Madison Square Garden crowd, astonished by the Rangers' two victories at the Spectrum, waved smurf toys and roared for blood as Game 3 began. The Flyers' heads came off quickly. Lindbergh had to stop two breakaways in the first two minutes. McClanahan, who undressed McCrimmon, and Ron Greschner, on the power play, scored 1:23 apart to give the Rangers a 2-0 lead.

Howe looked rattled early on, then fell backwards into the boards when hit by Kent-Erik Andersson and was knocked from the game with a concussion. Clarke got one goal back after Holmgren was knocked into Mio, but Beck restored the two-goal lead three minutes later through a screen.

McClanahan cut inside Dvorak to make it 4-1 early in the third and the rout was on. The enraged Flyers dished out cheap shot after cheap shot and the Rangers gleefully piled on the humiliation as toy smurfs littered the Garden ice. The most crushing playoff disappointment in Flyer history ended in a 9-3 loss. Their 106-point season had been ruined by their archenemies in three straight games.

"If they don't learn from this," gloated Ron Duguay, "they never will. They can go through the season intimidating teams, but when it gets serious, when it's hockey that matters, we've beaten them two years in a row."

Clarke was inconsolable. "It's the worst I've ever felt after a loss," he said. "It was just so total. Nobody played worth a damn."

McCammon sifted through the ashes for a perspective. "We had a great season," he said quietly. "We had some injuries that hurt us. Paul Holmgren had a shoulder that had to be frozen every couple of games. We had guys [Marsh and Bathe] who were coming off broken legs.

"I kidded about the 'smurfs,' but they are great skating hockey players. Of the 15 other teams in the playoffs, we probably drew the worst one for us to play. Edmonton has speed, but not like the Rangers have speed. Brooks did the right thing. He used the regular season as an exhibition and it worked."

A disillusioned Snider said from now on the Flyers would no longer push it to the floor during the regular season. He gave the embattled McCammon a vote of confidence and promoted Jay to team president.

"I had gone to Ed earlier that year," recalls Butera, "and said, 'Don't you want Jay to run this team?' He said, 'Eventually.' Later that year, Ed came to me and said [New Jersey owner] John McMullen had asked for permission to talk to me. I think it solved the problem." The day after Jay Snider's April 14 appointment, the Devils announced Butera as their new president.

On May 24, Allen was waiting for his tardy coach to begin a draft-planning meeting when scouting director John Brogan called the GM from the board room. Allen followed Brogan to his office, where he was surprised to see McCammon. The coach told Allen that he was about to accept an offer to become coach-GM of the Penguins.

McCammon had never signed the contract he and the Flyers had agreed to the previous summer, putting off a few Allen attempts to tend to the matter. But McCammon insisted the first he heard from Pittsburgh was after the playoffs, when he was approached by Penguin president Paul Martha. Meeting with owner Edward DeBartolo Sr. at his corporate headquarters in Youngstown, Ohio, McCammon was offered the job of rebuilding the rundown franchise.

Allen asked McCammon not to make a decision until he had talked to Ed Snider, who was returning that evening from the funeral of the wife of Blackhawk owner Bill Wirtz in Chicago. The next day in Snider's center-city offices, McCammon was shocked to be offered a promotion to become general manager as well as coach of the Flyers.

"I said, 'I can't, Keith hired me.'" recalls McCammon. "But Eddie said this is what he wanted and he would talk to Keith."

Snider, alarmed by his own impatience leading up to the Quinn firing, had become convinced it was time to take another step back from the operation. In light of the sudden possibility of losing McCammon, the owner felt perhaps Allen, 59, should move into a senior advisory capacity as well.

When Ed relayed his idea to Jay, the new team president, nervous about whether Allen would willingly take orders from the boss's kid, was relieved.

"I thought having Keith to advise Bob, like my Dad would advise me, would be the best of both worlds," recalls Jay. "Keith still had a great mind, but I think he was at a point where he didn't want to

go through the wars anymore."

The next day, Snider called Allen to his office. "I thought nothing of it," recalls Allen. "Eddie and I met all the time. But when he told me that Bob was the new general manager—you could have pushed me over with a feather. I couldn't believe what I was hearing.

"McCammon was there. He was sheepish about the whole thing. I remember asking Eddie, 'What becomes of Keith Allen now?' He reassured me I had a job, but I remember riding back down to the Spectrum on the subway being unable to reconcile why Eddie had done this. I just didn't think our situation dictated it.

"I had talked about going only a few more years and maybe that left him thinking my heart wasn't in it anymore, I don't know. But we had never talked about it and I had no warning. I walked in cold turkey to that meeting and he hit me right between the goddamn eyes."

Suddenly kicked upstairs after 14 seasons as general manager, the builder of two Stanley Cup winners, four finalists and seven semifinalists, kept his pain to himself. The next day at the press conference, Ed Snider announced that among Allen's new duties would be to develop a true world series of hockey involving the Stanley Cup champion and European teams. Snider also said he was convinced Allen was doing what he really wanted.

Allen played the good soldier. "This came up a little bit more quickly than anticipated, but I'm ready for it," he maintained. "I've been letting you guys know I've been winding down."

McCammon was sensitive to the perception that he used the Penguin offer to get Allen's job. "I think my dealings with the Penguins were on the up-and-up," he told the media. "If it was a power play, it was as bad as some of the ones I've run on the ice. If the Flyers had said to me, 'Stay another year and we'll make a decision then about the GM job,' I would have done it."

Today, Ed Snider looks back on the events of May 1983 with huge regret. "In hindsight, we should have let McCammon go," he says, "and Keith should have stayed right where he was. But at the time, I didn't feel he was going to pasture. I felt he was still going to be an integral part of the decision-making process."

McCammon told the press there was a need for changes in the scouting department. Within two weeks, heads began to roll. On June 4, director of player personnel Marcel Pelletier, who had grated on Ed Snider and whom the loyal Allen had refused to fire, resigned. "It was accepted with a smile," Pelletier told the media. Scout Eric Coville, whose work habits had deteriorated, was let go four days before the June 10 entry draft, replaced by former Mariner defenseman Dennis Patterson. McCammon promoted Jerry Melnyk to head scout, a position the Flyers had discontinued after Alex Davidson's demotion in 1978 (Davidson left to scout for the Red Wings a year later).

"If you draft by committee, the decisions are made by who shouts loudest at the meeting," said McCammon. "A head scout eliminates that." McCammon also named Sator assistant coach, replacing Joe Watson, who had served that function without the title the previous year. Watson was retained in a part-time public relations capacity.

Jay Snider was taking over an organization that had sold out only 12 of its 40 home games in 1982-83. While the Flyers never had more than 1,000 empty seats on any night, they had played only two home playoff games and operated $1 million in the red.

The new president cut half the deficit by selling the Maine Mariners to Butera's New Jersey Devils for $500,000. Philadelphia signed with Chicago to share a working agreement with the AHL team in Springfield, Massachusetts, and also exchanged blueliners with the Blackhawks. Wilson, who had become a spare defenseman and part-time left wing, was moved for 23-year-old defenseman Doug Crossman and a second round pick. "I think we got a guy who is a potential star," said McCammon, who was coached through the negotiations by Allen.

Wilson was dealt the morning of a draft that, because of the Howe trade, would not yield a Flyer choice until the forty-first selection. McCammon, ditching not only Coville, but also the computerized rankings the Flyers had been using for several years, relied largely on the judgment of the western-based Melnyk and invited Sam McMaster, general manager of Sault Ste. Marie of the Ontario Hockey League and a Flyer bird dog, to sit at the Philadelphia table for opinions on eastern players. "Jay always called it the mass confusion draft," recalls McCammon.

The Flyers' top selection, Toronto Marlboros center Peter Zezel, had a fireplug build and good playmaking skills. Derrick Smith, the third -round choice, enjoyed outstanding speed and good work habits. McMaster insisted that one of his own Sault Ste. Marie players, Rick Tocchet, possessed softer hands and better skating skills than most scouts believed and pushed the Flyers to take the tough right wing in the sixth round. The seventh choice, Swedish center Pelle Eklund, was highly touted by Sator.

After Western Hockey League president Ed Chenowyth turned down McCammon's offer of an assistant GM position, Bruins head scout Gary Darling accepted the administrative job. The Flyers moved their training camp and permanent practice site to the refurbished Coliseum in Voorhees, New Jersey, where a reinvigorated McCammon plotted to make the Flyers younger and quicker up the middle.

Sittler moved to left wing to make room for Ron Sutter, the 1982 first-round pick who had gained ten

Peter Zezel was the Flyers' top draft selection, 41st overall, in 1983.

pounds and confidence in his final junior season. Poulin, the lone bright spot of the playoff debacle, moved from wing to center when Flockhart showed up overconfident and out of shape.

McCammon announced that Clarke, who had clearly become worn down in the playoffs, would not play 80 games during the 1983-84 season. "We may have to hide his skates," the GM-coach said, "but he said he would go along with it if it is set up ahead of time."

Ron Sutter contributed 51 points as a rookie in 1983-84.

promptly pumped in enough exhibition goals that McCammon canceled plans to trade Sittler to Hartford for Blaine Stoughton.

The NHL passed a uniform conformity rule, so the Flyers dressed in short pants for the first time in three seasons when they opened with a 4-1 Spectrum victory over Washington. Barber achieved goal number 400, going to his backhand to beat Michel Dion on a breakaway, in a 7-1 victory over Pittsburgh on October 9.

Poulin scored 7 times in his first 7 games, locking Flockhart out the door to Pittsburgh, which obtained the flamed-out shooting star along with spare center Mark Taylor, farmhand Andy Brickley and a first-round 1984 pick for Rich Sutter and the Penguins' second-round selection in 1984.

The Flyers did not believe there would turn out to be much difference between their low first-rounder and the Penguins' high second-rounder. Nor could referee Ron Fournier distinguish between Rich and his twin Ron in sending the wrong Sutter to the penalty box for Rich's cross-check during his debut against Toronto at the Spectrum. After Grace Sutter, the boys' Mom, cried for joy at their reunion, the pair celebrated by each scoring a goal in an 8-5 victory.

Clarke took advantage of the NHL's new five-

Rick MacLeish, released by Pittsburgh, asked for a tryout and turned back the clock with 5 points in 7 exhibition games. He became a Flyer again on a 40-game contract. Thomas Eriksson returned from Sweden, adding more mobility to the defense, and Kerr, snakebitten by injuries for three years, vowed that his fourth NHL season would be complete and healthy. "I haven't done a damn thing to prove myself in Philadelphia yet," he said. The big right wing

minute overtime to score the Flyers first-ever regular season sudden-death goal, beating Pittsburgh, 6-5. Holmgren passed Andre Dupont as the Flyers' all-time penalty leader. "I hope my mother doesn't find out," said Holmgren. It was no secret, however, that the veteran right wing's shoulder and knee were wearing out. So were the phone lines between McCammon and Minnesota GM Lou Nanne, who badly wanted to bring Holmgren home to the Twin

Cities to inject character into the underachieving North Stars. Nanne offered U.S. Olympic team winger Paul Guay. "I saw [Guay] once and really wasn't impressed," McCammon told the media. "The chances of making a deal with Lou Nanne are slim and none."

When McCammon began giving Froese, who was outplaying Lindbergh, a fair number of starts, the Swede's play deteriorated. After appearing to make some progress in beating Vancouver 5-4 on November 26, Lindbergh allowed two soft goals in Calgary three nights later, was yanked, and completely lost confidence.

So, increasingly, had the fans in the Flyer management. Several hundred seats went unsold for most home games so Jay Snider, who in his year as a marketing vice president had instituted cheering sections to fill the third-level seats, tried a Score-O game between periods. It was booed, as were the Flyers when they blew a three-goal lead into a 5-5 deadlock with Minnesota on November 17. When Philadelphia was tied 3-3 at the buzzer on a goal by Detroit rookie Steve Yzerman on December 18, it was the third time the 18-10-5 Flyers had been scored upon with a goalie pulled.

With seven new faces — six, actually, since two Sutters had the same face — the Flyers lacked cohesion. Cochrane, who had played capably with Howe the previous season, was feeling so listless that the Flyers sent the defenseman for medical tests. "Come to think of it, *I* haven't felt well watching him play, either," said McCammon. By January 8, he had seen enough of MacLeish, who had scored only 3 points in his last 18 contests. Detroit picked up the 34 year-old center for no compensation.

The long season also began catching up to Clarke. When he scored a goal and two assists in a 7-0 Spectrum rout of Toronto on February 5, it gave him only 5 points in his last 14 outings. "I love this game too much to quit," he said. "I love everything about it—the games, the practices, everything.

"I appreciate what McCammon is trying to do; he's working in two kids, [Dave Poulin and Ron Sutter] who are going to be excellent players. With what we've added, I think we're as good as anybody in the division. I want to be part of it while we take another run at it. I'll know when it's time."

Bunny Larocque, who had only played twice in his year with the Flyers, was sold to St. Louis. Barber returned after missing 5 games with recurring knee problems and played his best hockey in two seasons. But the inconsistency of the aging veter-

ans and inexperience of the kids left Flyers both too old and too young at the same time. On consecutive Saturdays in February, they held two-goal second-period leads at Boston and Washington and lost both games. The special teams were poor and the defense inconsistent.

With 32 points in 43 games, Eriksson was a bright spot, so McCammon tried Howe for 10 games on left wing. He scored little and returned to the blue line, where a series of nagging injuries left him playing less efficiently than a year earlier. Bathe had disc surgery and Marsh and McCrimmon played badly enough to be benched.

When Froese beat the Islanders 7-1 at the Spectrum on January 23, it was the Flyers' first victory over a plus-.500 team since October. Yet, because Froese was playing well and Kerr, on a line with Propp and Poulin, was on a 50-goal pace, Philadelphia remained in a four-way race for first place.

Attempts to revive Lindbergh's confidence were a disaster. Leading Vancouver 5-4 midway through the third period on February 12 at the Spectrum, the goalie got his feet tangled as he tried to clear a Darcy Rota dump-in, and the puck rolled across the goal line. With two minutes remaining, Lindbergh again lost his balance as Marsh tied up Tiger Williams in front of the net. The deflected puck, sliding at centipede speed, went between Lindbergh's legs as he fell on his backside.

The fans booed viciously. "I heard them," said Lindbergh after the 6-5 loss. "But I guess they'd heard enough from me, too. Do you know what it's like to feel like an absolute fool in front of 17,000 people?"

McCammon, as usual, knew just the right thing to say. "There's a plane for Sweden at midnight," he answered before adding, "but we're not that cruel." Instead, Lindbergh went to Springfield for 4 games to try to find himself.

The Flyers beat the Rangers for the first time in nine meetings, 3-2, on Kerr's overtime goal at Madison Square Garden on February 19. But two nights later, against Buffalo at the Spectrum, the Flyers played their season in microcosm. After a catatonic first period, they rallied, blew a 4-2 lead, then were all over the Sabres in overtime, only to get caught on an outnumbered break that led to Phil Housley's sudden-death winner.

Holmgren, who had become a fourth line right wing behind Kerr, Rich Sutter and Ilkka Sinisalo, signed a new three-year contract that looked suspiciously like a going-away present. On February 23, an hour before the North Stars played the Flyers at the Spectrum, McCammon met with Nanne and finally traded Holmgren to Minnesota for Guay and a 1985 third-round pick.

Because McCammon did not want the Flyers distracted by feelings for their departing teammate before a game, Nanne agreed to hold the announcement until afterwards. Following the warmup, trainer Dave Settlemyre informed Holmgren he was sitting out, but not why.

"With the North Stars in town, I figured that's it,

Tim Kerr, the perennial 50-goal scorer.

I've been traded," Holmgren said later. "But then I'm sitting there for two periods and nobody says a word to me. I thought if I'd really been traded, they would have told me, and now I'm upset."

After the second period, the impatient Holmgren left to drive to Reading to see his girlfriend, Doreen. Nanne had already informed a Twin Cities television station of the deal, so after the 3-3 tie, McCammon had no choice but to reveal the deal.

"It was a hard trade to make," McCammon said. Even harder for Holmgren to take. He heard the news

on KYW radio. "I almost drove off the road," he said.

"Why couldn't they tell me?" Holmgren said while packing the next day. "I can understand the team had a game to play and they didn't want the distraction, but I wouldn't have wanted to hang around. Nobody would have had to know but me until after the game."

McCammon never reached Holmgren, but apologized publicly. "Paul deserved better than to hear about it on the radio," the GM said.

Clarke, who was home fighting a viral infection the night of the trade, lost his best friend on the team. "I'll miss him more than anybody we've ever traded away," the captain said, but he understood that time was marching on. "They're making changes they probably had to make," Clarke said. "I'm sure when the season is over, we'll sit down and talk. I won't stay on if it means being a fringe player and I'm not going to play anywhere else."

The Flyers recalled Dave Brown, a hulking 1982 seventh-round draft choice, from Springfield to replace Holmgren's fists. Brown scored a goal and an assist in his debut in Hartford, but the Flyers played out of control in a 9-7 loss. They returned home an evening later to find the Spectrum crowd seething like a lynch mob.

"Ditch McCammon," said one sign. "From Keith the Thief to Bob the Robbed," said another. The Flyers, who had made their own displeasure with McCammon the subject of a players-only meeting before the game, came to his rescue with a 5-3 victory over the Islanders. They then opened a road trip by knocking off the Oilers, 5-3, completing back-to-back victories over the previous season's Stanley Cup finalists.

"I think Cagey [McCammon] is doing a better job," volunteered Clarke after the victory in Edmonton. "He was getting excited behind the bench and I think that was contributing to the panic when we were blowing all those leads. I went to Bob about it and he understood."

The following night in Calgary, Clarke, unable to completely shake the virus that had been plaguing him for more than a week, was coughing on the bench as the Flyers were routed, 5-1. At the airport the following morning, McCammon told Clarke he would not play in St. Louis the next night. Clarke argued but McCammon stayed firm. "I'm going to make sure our key guys are rested for the playoffs," the coach said.

"It's better, but I'm still coughing up a lot of stuff," Clarke admitted as he watched the 4-3 loss to the Blues in street clothes. Two days later, after Clarke practiced with the team at the Coliseum, he was surrounded by media members wanting further reaction to his forced rest.

"It's like arguing with your wife, you can't win," Clarke said. "This has been going on for two years and I'm not tired, just tired of talking and hearing about it. But at this point of the season it would be wrong to make a big deal out of it."

The *Inquirer*, however, had no such compunctions. "Discontent in the Flyers' Ranks" read the headline at the top of the sports page. The story, by beat writer Angelo Cataldi, reported Clarke's reaction without acknowledging he had scored only 11 points in his last 26 games. Clarke, McCammon said, would be in the lineup the following evening at Nassau Coliseum. But before the contest, the Flyers announced he would miss the next 5 games to rest in Florida and that Sittler, Barber and Dvorak would take simultaneous 4-game vacations after the captain returned.

"Coming only a day after Clarke had publicly criticized McCammon for overemphasizing his age ... the announcement raised new questions about the strained relationship between the coach and player," Cataldi speculated.

Certainly McCammon had left himself open to the suggestion that Clarke was being banished for speaking out. Reminded he had said Clarke would play against the Islanders, the coach-GM smiled. "That was just to throw you guys off," he said.

Typically offhanded, McCammon had poorly presented a good—even neccessary—idea and turned it into a public relations disaster. It wasn't until several days later that he offered a credible explanation for the timing of the vacations.

"I was thinking about a 6-game rest starting in St. Louis," he said. "Then, I had some second thoughts. But when you think about it, what good

would one game do? I told [Clarke] yesterday afternoon we were going to go ahead with the full thing. He didn't like it, but ... when he really thought about it, I think he was in agreement. Going to Florida, in fact, was his idea.

"The situation is not what the fans think. Do you really think I'm stupid enough to have a public argument with Bobby Clarke?"

McCammon had alienated many of the players with his sarcasm and hip-pocket style of coaching and management. But most of the Flyers felt Clarke, who went south without further comment, was acting childishly.

Barber publicly backed the coaches. "After what happened last year, I want this team to do well in the playoffs," he said after a 4-1 victory over the Kings. "If this is going to help, I'm all for it."

Privately, however, Barber questioned the wisdom of his taking time off. "For the first time in a year, I felt half-decent," he recalls. "I didn't think I needed time. I told [McCammon and Sator] so at Long Island, too, but they said they thought this was best for the team, so I said I wouldn't make a big deal out of it."

While Clarke golfed in the sun, Holmgren left Cochrane cold to score a goal in a 4-3 North Star victory over the Flyers at the Met Center.

Jay Snider vigorously denied the vacation controversy was a prelude to a Clarke-McCammon confrontation over who would run the club after the Flyer captain moved into the front office. "There is a simple fact that Bobby Clarke does not want to rest," Snider told the *Inquirer's* Al Morganti. "But Bobby Clarke does not run the hockey team.

"He will remain with the club as long as he is working, I hope. But in this case he was wrong to carry on when it was not in the best interest of the club." Snider added that the poor handling of the Holmgren trade had underscored the team president's belief that one man should not be both coach and GM.

Clarke was contrite upon rejoining practice on March 13. "I was thinking of myself instead of the team," he said. "The people are on Bob heavily and a lot of it is unfair. I think there was anger put into my words [in Cataldi's story] that wasn't there. I think [McCammon] has done a helluva job."

Clarke's real feelings for McCammon were thinly veiled. So was the Flyer defense when it blew another two-goal lead and was beaten 6-3 at Madison Square Garden in the captain's return. After the game, Barber headed for his four-game break in the Poconos, where he planned to do an exercise program provided by the coaching staff. Included were modified squat thrusts.

"I thought they were probably not a good idea with my knee," Barber recalls. "But you're not playing and you want to come back in the best shape possible. So I did them."

One morning while Barber was working out, he landed on the leg and heard a crack. "I thought I broke my leg," recalls Barber. The next morning in Philadelphia, Dr. John Gregg drew blood and told

ishing anywhere from first to third in the division. "This year everything is falling into place at the right time."

The following night, the Islanders wrapped up the Patrick title with a 3-1 victory at the Capital Center, guaranteeing a Washington-Philadelphia first-round series. The home-ice advantage would be determined in a Game 80 Flyers-Caps match at the Spectrum.

Giveaways by Propp and Kerr staked Washington to a 2-0 lead and the Flyers did not generate a

**Defenseman Howe:
playing through pain.**

Barber he suspected new knee damage. But the strong muscles around Barber's ravaged joint had given him so many reprieves, he wanted to see if rest would bring a positive response.

Kerr scored goals 50 and 51 in a 13-4 rout of the Penguins on March 22. "I don't want this to be a one-time thing," he said. Clarke was rejuvenated by his vacation and, thanks in part to a string of games with the woebegone Devils and Penguins, the Flyers won 8 straight down the stretch.

"Last year we were a scared team going into the playoffs," said Clarke after a 6-2 victory at New Jersey in Game 79 left Philadelphia still capable of fin-

good chance the entire game. Their only goal, by Guay, was a gift from Washington goalie Pat Riggin, who fanned clearing the puck. The Caps took home a 4-1 victory that the Flyers tried to pretend was not portentious. "We had one bad game," said McCammon. "The series starts Wednesday night."

The Flyers, who finished with 98 points, would be going to the Capital Center without Barber, who was scheduled for arthroscopic surgery to determine the extent of his damage. Philadelphia would start the playoffs with eight rookies in the lineup, including three regular centers—Poulin, Sutter and Len Hachborn, a 1981 ninth round pick who had scored

27 points in 28 games since his January recall. Such inexperience up the middle—Clarke had been moved to left wing to give Hachborn a regular shift— figured to put the Flyers at a disadvantage in a series against the best defensive team in the NHL.

Philadelphia jumped to 1-0 and 2-1 leads in Game 1 on goals by Clarke and Sinisalo. But Bryan Erickson came up the slot for a rebound and tied the score before the end of the second period.

Seven minutes into the third, Rod Langway's shot caromed off Gaetan Duchesne during a goalmouth struggle with Froese, giving Washington a 3-2 lead. Clarke had just returned from serving a penalty when Mike Gartner swept in a rebound from his knees. The Caps' checking line of Duchesne, Glen Currie and Bobby Gould held Poulin to one shot and Kerr to none in the 4-2 victory.

Without Barber, Sinisalo (who suffered a back injury in Game 1) and Carson (out since March 22 with back spasms), McCammon was down to three lines for Game 2. He broke up the Kerr unit, putting Clarke with Poulin, reinserting the slumping McCrimmon, and instructed the Flyers to dump the puck. The Flyers generated more chances and Clarke batted a rebound out of the air to give them a 2-1 lead in the second period.

Scott Stevens, however, saved the puck for Alan Haworth, who tied the score between Froese's legs. In the third period, Sittler missed his man coming out of the corner, enabling Craig Laughlin to put Washington ahead, 3-2. After Crossman tried to knock a pop-up away from the front of the net with his hand and inadvertently put the puck off Froese's shoulder and into the net, the Caps pulled away to a 6-2 victory and a 2-0 series lead.

Barber underwent knee surgery at Graduate Hospital on the morning of Game 3. The damage, which included a fracture of the femur where it entered the joint, was more severe than expected. Barber would have to rehabilitate the entire next season. "[The break] was in the worst possible place," said Dr. Gregg. "All I could tell him was that [eventually] he was going to get a good knee out of it. It will be very tough to come back and play. But I think he's going to try."

Lindbergh had won his last three regular-season starts, so McCammon rolled the dice with a goaltending switch for Game 3 at the Spectrum. The Flyers, one game away from a being swept in the first round for a second consecutive year, came out physically. Carson, back in the lineup, fought with Stevens and Ron Sutter punched with Gartner.

The Flyers outshot Washington 12-2 in the first eight minutes but predictably made the first important mistake. Gould got around Dvorak and poked the puck ahead to Glen Currie, who beat Lindbergh low to the glove side.

Late in the period, McCammon sent out Daryl Stanley, normally a defenseman, on wing against Gartner. Before the face-off, Stanley threw down his gloves and pummeled Gartner, while Ron Sutter jumped Darren Veitch. Stanley and both Sutters were given game misconducts (as were Veitch and the Caps' Bobby Carpenter), but Stanley received an extra two minutes as the instigator.

The Caps cashed in. Alan Haworth's drive from the top of the circle bounced off both of Craig Laughlin's legs and into the goal, giving Washington a 2-0 lead.

McCammon coached the game under a telephoned death threat. From the superbox, Jay Snider resisted the urge to carry out the deed himself. "It was the final straw," Snider recalls. "We were in the game and he sent out a goon line."

The Caps scored three in the second, raced to a 5-0 lead and won easily, 5-1. Just as the previous spring, the Flyers had played out of control facing elimination. "They kept taking stupid penalties," said Caps' captain Rod Langway, "and we kept killing them."

The Spectrum echoed throughout the third period with chants of "Bob Must Go." Both Sniders had come to think the customers were right. Jay had already stated he didn't want McCammon to continue as both coach and GM. Now, he wasn't sure he wanted him at all.

"I thought he did some good things," Jay recalls. "But over the season there were some errors in judgment that had backfired tremendously, like his handling of Clarke. It was clear to me his coaching wasn't going to work. I wanted to press the issue.

"I don't think the players had respect for Bob McCammon. I don't think we had a game plan or discipline. I thought we were clearly outplayed two years in a row in the playoffs because we were predictable in our behavior. We may have lost to Washington, but it should have at least been a good series."

Jay handed McCammon a list of five potential coaching candidates that included Mike Keenan, the 33-year-old coach at the University of Toronto. McCammon replied he felt stigmatized by 9 consecutive playoff losses and wanted to stay behind the bench to work with a team he had made younger and more promising.

Snider, scheduled to go to Florida, and

McCammon, headed for Maine, agreed to take a week to reconsider their feelings. But when they met again on April 23 at the Cherry Hill Hyatt, neither had changed his mind. McCammon not only wanted to redeem himself, but also test where he might stand with the Sniders on the day Clarke moved into the front office.

"That was my thought when I got the Pittsburgh offer the year before," recalls McCammon. "Bobby was the chosen son. Where would I be? I stayed then because Eddie is a great salesman."

With McCammon unyielding, Jay had an excuse to make the complete change he was leaning towards anyway. "There was no gray area, no room for compromise," recalls Jay. "I was only firing the coach, but we both realized we weren't on the same wavelength, so how could we go forward with him as GM? Even though I think McCammon did a good job evalu-ating talent, we couldn't escape that there was a fundamental problem."

McCammon, whom the Flyers would pay $150,000 a year for the next three seasons, spoke with Snider one more time on the 24th, when they agreed on how to announce a mutually agreed-upon resignation. The Flyers released it late that evening.

"If I don't believe a coaching change is necessary, then how, as a GM, do I go along with it?" McCammon said the next day. "There was no animosity. It was probably the best thing for both parties. This was the first big disagreement we ever had.

"We didn't go out with the dignity that [the Sniders] felt we should have. But we made a lot of changes, ones that I felt were going to make us stronger next year. The only sad thing is that I think the Flyers have a pretty good young team. And I'm not going to be there to see it develop."

Four of the Flyers' five Hall of Famers: from left, Clarke, Ed Snider, Barber and Parent. Missing is Keith Allen.

Chapter 9

◆◆◆

Close Enough to Cry

To find Bob McCammon's successor as GM, Jay Snider organized a search committee comprising his father and Keith Allen. It had more members than candidates: both men wanted Bobby Clarke.

Jay was unconvinced the fifteen-year veteran was ready to leave the ice, but on May 2, nine days after McCammon's departure, the Flyer president telephoned a team party Brad Marsh was throwing for Miroslav Dvorak and asked Clarke to come to the Cherry Hill Hyatt the following day. "He said it was going to be a long meeting," Clarke recalls. On the way home, Bobby told his wife, Sandy, that the session would probably be about the GM job.

Behind closed doors, Snider sought Clarke's opinions on organizational strengths and shortcomings and, most significantly, whether he was prepared to hang up his skates. "Bob was wrestling with it," recalls Jay. "But by the end of the meeting, I liked the idea."

Clarke went home with a firm offer, no hard deadline for a decision and extremely torn feelings. "I wasn't afraid of the job," he recalls. "I knew I could lean on Keith and (assistant GM) Gary Darling while I learned. The thing I feared was not playing anymore. I liked being part of a group of men working together and all the stuff that goes on around a locker room, and I was afraid to give that up. I still thought I could be a contributing player.

"Mr. (Ed) Snider had told me I'd always have a job in the organization. But if I wanted to keep playing, they obviously weren't going to hire a GM just for one or two years until I was finished."

Clarke felt getting away on an already planned vacation with Kim and Dave Poulin and another couple to the British Virgin Islands would clear his head and aid his decision. But on the morning of departure, he telephoned Jay from Philadelphia International Airport to accept the position. Several hours later, on an island dock, his vacationmates were informed of his new title.

When Clarke returned on May 14, the team quickly called a press conference at the Franklin Plaza Hotel for the following day. The media, which

Flyers president Jay Snider introduces Bobby Clarke as the team's new GM.

had believed Clarke when he said he was unprepared to stop playing, were shocked.

"I was becoming very frustrated with my contribution as a player," the Flyers' fourth GM said from the podium. "I didn't feel I was doing the job I thought I should do. Obviously, I wasn't capable of doing it anymore.

"If they said the job would have been there in a couple of years, I probably would have chosen to keep playing. But this was sort of a relief for me. Brighter minds than mine thought I was capable of doing this, so I jumped at it."

As much as Clarke had to learn, he did not have to start from scratch to find a coach. Jay Snider, Allen and Darling had already laid the groundwork.

Three successful young candidates—Dave King of the Canadian Olympic team, Bill Laforge of the Kamloops Blazers, and the University of Toronto's Mike Keenan—had been informed of Philadelphia's interest by Darling, while Jay assured assistant coach Ted Sator that he would also be considered.

Keenan had been interviewed by Snider before Clarke accepted the GM position. "Boy, did Jay grill that Mike Keenan when he was here," Allen told Clarke.

Jay had also prepared a written philosophical questionnaire for the candidates. "The introspection it took was fabulous," recalls Keenan. "I told myself that even if I didn't get the job, it would still be a worthwhile experience." Having already scheduled a Florida vacation with his wife Rita and 4-year-old daughter Gayla, Keenan worked in the hotel room preparing a nineteen-page response while his family was poolside.

"Personally, I have experienced a contagious phenomenon whereby the more I win, the more I want to win," wrote Keenan. *"Nothing short of this objective is acceptable. Winning is, perhaps, the single most significant solution for every problem your team may encounter. Therefore, the challenge, as I see it, is to teach the team how to win and to expect to win.*

My approach in motivating the athlete is to maintain an imbalance of predicitability by incorporating incentive, fear and attitudinal methods employed in a very dynamic environment. I would emphasize, however, that within this framework of discipline and team organization ... the players must be kept loose, their creativity unstifled and their intrinsic enthusiasm for the game maintained. It is important that the practice year be well-planned. Practices must be creative, interesting and challenging.

Now is the time to define and implement another *formula for success. The old passions of the Flyers must be rekindled. I am ready for the challenge."*

Clarke had a copy of Keenan's dissertation in hand when he flew to Ontario for the Memorial Cup competition hours after his press conference. "He wrote a book," recalls Clarke.

The two men met twice during the tournament. Laforge, whose boisterous team was participating, accepted an offer to coach the Vancouver Canucks, but not before he had been crossed off Philadelphia's list. "We were trying to get away from the Broad Street Bullies image," Clarke recalls. King had also eliminated himself by re-signing with Team Canada, so the field was narrowed to Sator, who had also met with Clarke at the Memorial Cup, and Keenan.

Sator had won four championships in five seasons with two different teams in Sweden. "All his head-coaching experience was in Europe and that worried me a little," recalls Clarke. Keenan, however, had been hugely successful on three levels in North America.

After taking the Peterborough Petes to the 1980 Memorial Cup final, he coached Buffalo's AHL club at Rochester where, in his third season, the Amerks defeated the Flyers' Maine team to win the Calder Cup. Convinced the Sabre organization was already loaded with head-coaching prospects, Keenan moved to his alma mater, the University of Toronto, and in his first season won the Canadian university championship.

"Everybody I talked to said that his style would cause some problems with players, but that he had always won," recounts Clarke. "I thought we needed discipline."

On May 23, the general manager flew to Toronto, away from a prying media that had already reported Keenan's hiring. At the candidate's home, the men agreed on a three-year contract starting at $80,000, with raises of $5,000 per season plus performance bonuses. Keenan knew Sator from their days as instructors at the Huron Hockey School and was comfortable with him as an assistant.

The next morning Clarke, Mike and Rita flew on the Flyers' private plane to Philadelphia. The new coach informed his other suitor, the New Jersey Devils, of his decision, met with Sator and faced the media at the Bellevue-Stratford Hotel.

"He's the kind of guy that just meeting him and reading his resume, you had to be impressed," the GM told reporters. "When I talked to people about him, it kept coming across how competitive he is. The thing I like about him is he wants our team to develop a personality."

Neither Clarke nor his mustachioed, immaculately dressed, 34-year-old coach would publicly state a goal for the following season. "Some form of excellence," Keenan told reporters. "As for a style of play, I won't even visualize it until I know more."

While he studied videos of the 1983-84 team, Bernie Parent became the first Flyer elected to the Hockey Hall of Fame. "It's difficult to imagine. My God," the goaltender said. "It's like winning the

Stanley Cup. It hasn't sunk in yet."

In June, Ed Snider bought back the ownership shares of 76-year-old Joe Scott, who wanted to relinquish them for estate planning purposes. Snider appointed Scott, a lifesaver during the franchise's infancy, to the position of chairman of the board emeritus and took on new limited partners. Fran and Sylvan Tobin, owners of apparel manufacturer Fishman and Tobin, charter season-ticket holders and driving forces behind the staggeringly successful wives' carnival, purchased 5 percent of the team and would later double their stake.

Philadelphia's first pick in the draft had dropped six places to twenty-second overall as a result of the Rich Sutter trade, and was used to take London, Ontario defenseman Greg Smyth. The Flyers next selected right wing Scott Mellanby, headed for the University of Wisconsin, then Kingston defenseman Jeff Chychrun. "My scouts tell me I'm very pleased," laughed Clarke.

The new executive stuffed his can of snuff into a

drawer, put on a tie, rolled up his sleeves and went to work like he had been going to an office all his life. "An amazing transformation," said Allen. "He's surprised us all. I had been doing contract negotiations for McCammon and I thought maybe I'd continue while Bobby eased into them. He took them right out of my hands. He has the fidgits. He wants to deal."

First, however, Clarke signed 25-year-old free-agent defenseman Ed Hospodar away from Hartford to keep the rough edge that was jeopardized by Glen Cochrane's knee reconstruction and the retirement of Frank Bathe following back disc surgery.

Mark Howe, rehabilitating a shoulder that troubled him through the playoffs, passed up a Team USA invitation to the Canada Cup, leaving Sweden's Thomas Eriksson as the lone Philadelphia representative in the tournament, which was won by Canada.

Edward John (E.J.) McGuire, who had been an unpaid assistant and video aide to Keenan at Rochester while coaching at nearby Brockport State, was hired away from the head job at Ontario's University of Waterloo to complete the assistant-coaching staff.

During August, Keenan met with individual team members, telling Pelle Lindbergh, who had impressed him in the AHL, that he would be the No. 1 goalie. "Just by talking to the players, it was fairly obvious there were a lot of strong people on the club," Keenan recalls.

The coach's expectations grew higher than those of the people who hired him. "I remember Clarke telling me that he just wanted to make the playoffs," Keenan recalls. "He wasn't sure we would."

Young players had filled key rolls on the 98-point team Keenan was inheriting, but with Clarke retired and Barber facing a year-long knee rehabilitation, the roster had potentially traumatic holes. The best prospect, Rick Tocchet, came to camp as Paul Holmgren's heir apparent after scoring 44 goals in his final junior season at Sault Ste. Marie. But after Brian Propp and Lindsay Carson, the Flyers had nothing on left

GM Clarke announces the appointment of Mike Keenan.

wing.

Tim Kerr, angered by the team's first contract offer, publicly asked to be traded, but Clarke remained conciliatory and continued talks with agent Frank Milne. On the fourth day of camp, the burgeoning scoring star signed a five-year deal for $250,000 annually. "It was fun," said Clarke of his first major negotiation.

Darryl Sittler, entering the option year of a contract that allowed Philadelphia to match any offers,

enough to make the team. But that hardly seemed like a great accomplishment when Philadelphia, worn down by a brutal exhibition grind of seven games in seven nights, had won only once heading into its final tuneup.

Keenan finally put together his best lineup and Lindbergh punctuated a bench-clearing brawl by skating the length of the ice to bop Ranger goalie Glen Hanlon over the head with a blocker. The Flyers, 8-3 winners, showed signs of coming together.

GM Clarke watches the action from the press box with Keith Allen.

was easy to satisfy. He and Clarke agreed on a one-year, $250,000 deal that would give the team's lone remaining senior leader a $100,000 bonus if the Flyers did not want him back the following season. Sittler was impressed by his meeting with Keenan and proud when told by Clarke to expect to be named captain.

Tocchet came to camp as hard-nosed as advertised. But the most impressive and surprising rookie through the exhibition season was left wing Derrick Smith, picked forty-fourth overall in 1983, who grew up in the same Toronto suburb, Scarborough, as Tocchet and center Peter Zezel. Zezel, chosen three picks ahead of Smith, beat out Todd Bergen, a fifth-round 1982 choice who, along with Paul Guay, was sent to Hershey.

Tough guy Dave Brown, an eager Sator pupil at summer power-skating school, improved his skills

Two nights later, Keenan reinforced the esprit de corps with a dinner at Kaminski's in Cherry Hill. The coach took Sittler aside to tell him to prepare a speech for the following day, when he would be officially named captain during the Chamber of Commerce face-off luncheon at the Bellevue-Stratford.

Sittler was puzzled when introductions ended without him being called to the podium, but he figured the late-running proceedings had been shortened. There was a "C" next to his name on the program, he answered questions from newsmen about his apparently imminent appointment and, on the bus ride back to the Coliseum, accepted congratulations from teammates. But when the players arrived at the training center, Sittler was summoned to Keenan's office, where Clarke was waiting with words that hit like a sledgehammer. "We've traded you to Detroit," the GM said.

According to Clarke, Red Wings GM Jimmy Devellano had called and asked for Sittler a week earlier. Clarke told him that Philadelphia wanted left wings. "As I recall, when Jimmy got back to me, he offered a choice of two out of three guys," says Clarke. On the list were 24-year-old Joe Paterson and 20-year-old Murray Craven, Detroit's 1982 first-round draft choice. Craven had floundered in two trials for the Wings, but both his junior GM at Medicine Hat, Russ Farwell, and Flyer head scout Jerry Melnyk believed the winger had been mishandled.

"If you looked at Craven's junior record, you'd have to believe he was going to play," recalls Clarke. "Paterson was a big strong kid who could fill a desperate hole for us. You have a chance to get two young players for somebody of Darryl's age, you couldn't turn it down."

Talks had heated up the day before the luncheon. Clarke wanted to close the deal the following morning, but couldn't reach Devellano until after the meal had been served. From a telephone outside the ballroom, Clarke made the trade, then told Keenan just before Sittler was scheduled to be introduced.

Prepared to enjoy one of the biggest days of his life, the 34-year-old former Leaf captain's world had crashed and his heart burned. "Clarke got Devellano on the phone while I was there [in Keenan's office]," Sittler recalls, "and I told him to tell Devellano that I wasn't going.

"I didn't mean it as a threat, it was just the way I felt. Jimmy said something about [redoing] my contract, and I said it wasn't the money. I just wasn't in the right frame of mind. Here I was helping to plan the retirement dinner the Flyers were having for Clarke, and he had just traded me on the day I thought I was being named captain."

Keenan, who lived in the same Voorhees, New Jersey development as Sittler, gave him a ride home. His wife was out and the veteran had not brought his keys, so he sat, crying, on the front steps with Keenan until she drove up. "What's wrong?" Wendy asked.

Sittler watched the sports on the evening news. "When Clarke was asked (at the press conference) whether it was true I had been about to be named captain, he said, 'Mike Keenan makes that decision.' Clarke said it like he wasn't in on it at all. I thought, 'Why, you...' I had been a free agent and didn't shop myself around because he had told me I would be captain. I wanted that very much."

In announcing his first major deal, Clarke told the media he had experienced his first heartache as a general manager. "This has nothing to do with Darryl Sittler," he said. "I have the utmost respect for Darryl as a player and a person. We picked up two solid left wings at a position where we were short. And Murray Craven has a chance to be a star."

Sittler skated alone at the Coliseum before deciding a week later to go to Detroit. "I saw Clarke there one of those days," he recalls, "and in a very calm voice, I basically called him a liar."

Today, Clarke says he felt Sittler had waived the right to any special consideration when he was assured at least a $100,000 buyout at the end of the 1984-85 season. "That was a lot of money in those days," recalls Clarke. "I felt it made him fair game [for a trade] like any other player."

The next day, before the 1984-85 season opener against Washington at the Spectrum, Keenan chose Poulin, about to enter his second full NHL season, as Philadelphia's new captain.

While the Sittler deal had stripped the NHL rookie coach of his last proven leader, Keenan hardly batted an eyelash. "I just thought managers should manage and coaches should coach," he recalls. "Maybe I was naive, but I didn't expect to have any input in personnel decisions. Really, the only pressure I felt was developing the team, not winning. Now there was no Clarke, Barber *or* Sittler. So nobody expected anything."

When the houselights dimmed for the Flyer introductions, Propp was the only remaining member of the 1979-80 finals team. Dvorak was the sole player over age 30. Philadelphia was starting the season with three rookies—Zezel, Smith and Tocchet—and seven sophomores, but Lindbergh was razor-sharp and the kids made a good impression. Len Hachborn slipped Scott Stevens's check and fed Kerr for a goal with only 1:39 remaining, enabling the Flyers to gain a satisfying 2-2 tie. "We had a consistent effort throughout the contest," said Keenan. "We might as well start from Day One."

Two nights later in Landover, the Caps jumped on Philadelphia for 18 first-period shots and a 2-0 lead. But Howe scored from a goalmouth scramble, both Zezel and Hachborn beat Rod Langway to set up goals, and the Flyers roared back for a startling 4-2 victory to give them three of a possible four points against the team that humiliated them the previous spring.

Reality set in during the third game, when Philadelphia fell behind 4-0 and lost 5-2 in Montreal. "I had to increase the expectation levels," Keenan recalls. When the team returned home, he turned a scheduled optional practice into full-scale torture. Snapped back to attention, the Flyers smoked the injury-devastated Canucks 13-2 at the Spectrum.

Philadelphia's first look at the Penguins' Mario Lemieux, the most awaited prospect since Wayne Gretzky, turned into a tough 3-1 loss at the Civic Arena when Doug Shedden scored the winner at 19:23 of the third. But the next night at the Spectrum, the Flyers bounced back to beat Pittsburgh,

Clarke the player says goodbye to the fans on Bobby Clarke Night in the Spectrum.

4-2. "Everybody is so enthusiastic," said Kerr, who had 6 goals in the first 5 games. "The expectations, at least from the outside, aren't as great as they've been the last few years, and so far we're having fun."

Keenan, so organized that every player had his own water bottle at practice, was a marked contrast to McCammon. He used words like "intrinsic" and "synergistic," ran high-tempo workouts, burned veterans and rookies alike with his tongue, and pushed the team as it had never been challenged before.

There was no hiding from the new coach. "He is capable of everything," said Poulin, "and he has figured each of us out very quickly." The veterans, tired of April sorrows, bought the demanding new program while the impressionable kids were willing to skate

through brick walls to keep their jobs.

Paterson went to Hershey, but the four other new forwards—Smith, Zezel, Tocchet and Craven—scored in an astonishingly easy 7-2 rout at Minnesota. Zezel, making out-of-this-world centering passes after only 19 years on the planet, helped lift Kerr's play another notch. The right wing scored three goals within 2:27 during a 7-2 defeat of St. Louis at the Spectrum.

Likewise, Keenan had no interest in dissecting Lindbergh's problems of the previous season. After Bob Froese, who started 3 of Philadelphia's first 10 games, lost a 7-4 clunker to Winnipeg on November 1, the coach became determined to play the Swede, a victim of overanalysis in 1983-84, until he tired of more than just advice.

Zezel suffered a broken hand in a practice collision with Propp. "I've never been hurt before," he said. "I think I'll just sit here and cry." But the Flyers shed far more sweat than tears. Kerr scored twice in one game for the fifth time in the young season during Lindbergh's 6-0 home shutout of St. Louis, then added another goal as Philadelphia stopped Stanley Cup champion Edmonton at a roaring Spectrum, 7-5, ending the Oilers' record 15-game unbeaten streak to start a season.

When the Flyers held Bobby Clarke Night on November 15, they were 9-3-2. Both team and GM seemed to be avoiding withdrawal symptoms. "Watching us beat Edmonton Sunday night was as satisfying to me as any game I ever played in," Clarke said at a black tie dinner given in his honor at Philadelphia's Adams Mark Hotel.

Billy Preston's "I'm Never Going to Say Goodbye" was Flyer television producer Mike Finocchiaro's choice of music to accompany the video of Clarke's career that began the Spectrum festivities. A standing ovation lasted more than four minutes. Cliff and Evonne Clarke, Bob's parents, were given a trip around the world by Ed Snider, who also presented Sandy with a 14-karat gold watch. Clarke received a matching timepiece from the organization, a sterling-silver hockey stick from the players, a set of golf clubs from the visiting Hartford Whalers, and the eternal love of the fans.

Ed Snider handed the No. 16 jersey to Clarke's son Wade, who presented it to his father. As Clarke put it on one last time, the cheers and tears swelled. "I got all I could out of this body for fifteen years," he said from center ice. "I'll cherish this evening for-

Text continues following page S-32

HEROES
of the
SPECTRUM

osing is dying only in the allegorical sense. Yet there was something about the way Bobby Clarke played hockey that suggested he was competing for his very life. Was it the diabetes? Problems associated with the condition can kill. Did he want to get it all in before it was too late? Clarke denied it. His eyes were good. His cuts healed quickly. He took insulin every day as routinely as he brushed his teeth. No, if he was a diabetic, he was one of the lucky ones.

Still, he undoubtedly overcompensated for an affliction that became his burden from the time it was diagnosed at age 14. Doctors at the Mayo Clinic certified in writing prior to the 1969 draft that the medical condition of the 168-point Flin Flon center should not preclude a successful professional career. But eleven teams, including the Flyers, passed Clarke over at least once before Philadelphia made him the seventeenth pick overall.

During his early seasons in the NHL, Clarke cringed whenever the question of his health was broached. "I don't want anyone to think anytime I have a bad game, that it's because I'm a diabetic," he said. Gradually the condition vanished as an interview subject because Clarke began dealing with it more openly. He also never played poorly. A mediocre game was a luxury he would not allow himself.

Even before he knew anything about blood sugar, Clarke's resolve was reinforced by his father, who had told his son, "Nobody ever gets something for nothing in this world." Cliff Clarke's world was his home, family and eight honest, grimy hours a day in the northern Manitoba copper mines. "There you either play hockey or work in mines," Bobby said. "And there was no way I wanted to work in those mines.

"Every kid in Flin Flon played hockey. Some played three nights a week, some played four. I played every night. All I ever wanted to do was play hockey and I just played it the way I thought it had to be played."

The most-cited reason why Clarke became one of the greatest players in the history of the NHL was his work ethic. But in truth, hockey never seemed like labor to him, and for fifteen seasons Clarke forged that passion upon his team.

The Flyers rose to the top of the NHL in 1973-74 and 1974-75 and remained a winner until Clarke's 1984 retirement because nothing was

Clarke became one of the greatest players in the history of the NHL

more important to their captain than his next shift. He relentlessly blocked everything else out. Big leads, hopeless deficits, January road games in half-empty arenas, illness, injuries, fatigue and personal problems were mere excuses to Clarke once the puck was dropped. He was an excellent player, but human. It was his will that bordered on the supernatural.

An examination of his body gave no clues as to where his energy came from. As his career progressed, Clarke's devotion to conditioning became nothing short of fanatical, but hour after hour of pumped iron produced little chest definition and modest lumps for biceps.

His unremarkable physique embellished the legend, but it often led to his skills becoming underrated. Clarke was hardly swift and elusive, but would get a superior jump towards the puck and was exceptionally strong on his skates. His uncanny fac-eoff and corner work manifested a supreme understanding of the principles of body leverage. Almost without fail, he would turn a two-step deficit into an advantage, chasing the puck and the defenseman to the corner, sticking his

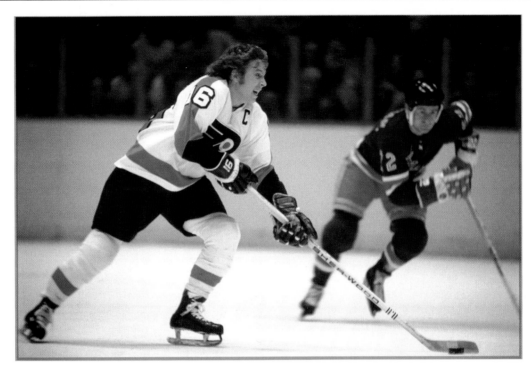

hip and rear end into the opponent, while keeping his own hands free to set up a scoring chance.

Despite an average shot—he hit the net only by perfect positioning or from close-in—Clarke recorded more than 100 points three times. Until Wayne Gretzky came along, nobody passed the puck in a more exacting and creative way or maintained better peripheral vision of the other eleven players on the ice. And there has never been a more tenacious forechecker or smarter defensive forward in the game's history.

Clarke's toothless grin and choirboy looks contradicted his on-ice personality, making him all the more fascinating and beloved. Philadelphia fans, who tortured many of their city's sports Hall of Famers right up until induction, bestowed their greatest compliment on Clarke: never once did they boo him. If they were quick to understand that you can't win them all, it was because they watched No. 16 exhaust himself on nights the Flyers fell short.

The demands he placed on himself prompted admiration from opponents, but his obsession with victory also drew a measure of hatred. Clarke expressed no remorse after putting Valeri Kharlamov out of the epic 1972 Canada-Soviet series with a cold-blooded slash across the ankle and no immediate remorse for spearing Toronto defenseman Rod Seiling, a friend off the

ice, in the face.

The Flyers protected their captain well, but Clarke did not escape retaliation. By the time he retired, his face, scarred by sticks and pucks, had become a road map of his career. One enduring impression came from the 1981 game in which he scored his 1,000th career point. Creased in the forehead by a rising Leach shot, Clarke skated calmly back to the bench, blinking away the blood that poured down his cheeks and onto his jersey.

In 1983, as he lay on the ice at Chicago Stadium clutching his face, Bobby feared he had lost what was left of his career to a skate cut near the eye. Seven stitches, forty minutes and one doctor's go-ahead later, Clarke descended upon Blackhawk defenseman Bob Murray just as he was clearing the Flyers' last chance to tie the game. Murray wound up, dazed, on his back. The puck, fed by Clarke from behind the goal to Miroslav Dvorak, landed in the Blackhawk net with one second remaining.

Of course, Clarke did not always have to bleed to do a good night's work. And he didn't have to give teammates or trainers a dog, a gift certificate, or the flannel shirt off his back every time he or the club won something. It only seemed that way during the Cup years. Too thoughtful to be true when the team was at its peak, Prince

Valiant had to turn politician in later seasons and dodge undercurrents of jealousy. Some Flyers, believing Clarke had a say in personnel decisions, grew to fear him, but those who shared their captain's obsession for winning admired and followed him.

Between the peak years of Bobby Orr and Guy Lafleur, Clarke, the Hart Trophy winner in 1973, 1975 and 1976, was unquestionably the best player in the game. When he retired after the 1983-84 season to become the Flyers' general manager, Clarke was the NHL's fourth all-time leading assist-maker with 852, and its eleventh all-time leading scorer with 1,210 points.

He handled both praise and vilification evenly, was ever gracious and accessible, and served as a thoughtful critic and defender of his sport and team.

On Bobby Clarke Night, November 15, 1984, the fans at the Spectrum stood for more than four minutes cheering the greatest Flyer of them all. The team lavished expensive gifts on him and the people bestowed their love, but the debt for what he had given them remained. To a degree as great as any athlete in the history of sport, Bobby Clarke gave of himself.

Goaltending, the last line of defense, was not a desperate, sweaty act when Bernie Parent played the position: it was an art. His movements were economical and fluid. Parent always seemed to know where the puck had the best chance of hitting him and would patiently wait there for it. He didn't flail at shots but accepted them, cleanly snatching or sticking the puck out of harm's way. Rebounds, the goaltender's quintessential anxiety, were rare when No. 1 was at the top of his game. He reflected a serenity that calmed and inspired his teammates, convincing them that they could beat anybody. For two years, maybe the two greatest any goaltender ever played, the Flyers did exactly that.

In 1973-74, Parent set NHL records for games (73) and games won (47), and compiled 12 shutouts and a goals-against average of 1.89. In the playoffs, he went 12-5 with a 2.02 goals-against average. The next year, Parent had another 12 shutouts and a 2.03 average, followed by a playoff in which he went 10-5 and a 1.89. During the two Cup-winning springs, he recorded a staggering 6 playoff shutouts, including both clinching games.

"He was the best," said Bobby Taylor, then Parent's backup and later the Flyers' radio analyst. "The only one who could come close was Glenn Hall. Bernie played 65 games a year and there would only be a handful of bad performances. The rest were not just good, but great. He was always there, like the sun rising in the east and setting in the west. He never had to move that much. His anticipation was just phenomenal. His feet were the key. He used them better than anybody."

The defensive-minded Flyers protected their goalie well, but rarely ran up big scores, which often left little margin for error. "You get 50 shots against, blow two or three, lose 5-4 but make some spectacular saves and everybody says how great you played," said Taylor. "The 19- or 20-shot shutout or one-goal game is a lot tougher mentally. Think about how often we were shorthanded in those years and the pressure that Bernie was under. He was incredible."

The youngest of seven children of a Montreal cement machine operator, Bernie got his start kicking out rubber balls while wearing galoshes. He then signed with one of the few youth teams not sponsored by the Canadiens, leaving him open to claim by Boston.

"He was the best. The only one close was Glenn Hall."

After winning a Memorial Cup at Niagara Falls in his final junior year, the long-suffering Bruins hurried him into their net. For the first time in six seasons, Boston did not finish last. But in 1966-67, when Parent drank too many beers, stopped too few pucks and heard too many boos, his lack of experience and confidence betrayed him. He was sent to the minors, then left unprotected in the expansion draft.

Parent and Doug Favell, who was also selected from the Bruins' system, instantly became the new Philadelphia team's best and most popular players. Whatever respectability the franchise had was due largely to its kid goalies. Yet when the punchless Flyers grew tired of having to play for a tie, they decided Parent, the more classically styled netminder and marketable commodity, could bring the scorer they desperately needed. Tearfully, Keith Allen traded Parent midway through Philadelphia's fourth season in a three-way deal that sent him to Toronto and brought Rick MacLeish from Boston.

At first, the trade emotionally devastated Parent, but his year and a half with the Maple Leafs allowed him to share a net and thoughts with 41-year-old Jacques Plante, the gray-haired genius of his position. Plante, aloof, frugal and egotistical, had been essentially a loner at his other NHL stops, but took a liking to Parent, was intrigued by his abilities, and set out to refine him.

"He didn't really change my style," Bernie said. "He just taught me how to use my own system." Parent had always stood up well, but didn't challenge or distribute his weight to facilitate movement. Plante recommended that Bernie spring from the right foot to improve his balance, and structured a mental checklist to help him focus more on mechanics and less on fear.

A five-year, $750,000 contract offer—enormous money for a hockey player in 1972—brought Parent to the World Hockey Association Blazers and back to Philadelphia. But the new team that was supposed to steal the town's hockey hearts instead became a cheap substitute for the suddenly emerging Flyers. When the Blazers' paychecks started arriving late, agent Howard Casper advised Parent not to play. When Casper insisted that his client would not return to Toronto, the Leafs, who still held Parent's NHL rights, traded him and a second-round pick to the Flyers for a No. 1 choice and the acrobatic, not-always-dependable Favell.

On opening night of the 1973-74 season, Bernie shut out the Leafs and Favell at the Spectrum. After that, Parent looked back only to see the cars behind his in the parade up Broad Street.

With two championships under his belt, Bernie missed much of the 1975-76 season following neck surgery to repair two discs. Although he never again approached the sustained level of excellence he enjoyed during the Cup years, there were high points in later seasons. Parent was almost as sharp as ever in the 1978 playoffs, when Philadelphia beat Colorado and Buffalo before losing to Boston in the semifinals. And he was still making opponents earn their goals on Saturday afternoon, February 17, 1979, when Jimmy Watson, attempting to move a Ranger from in front of the goal, accidentally put the blade of his stick through the right eyeslit of Parent's mask, ending No. 1's career.

"He can't catch a ball his kids throw to him, let alone stop a puck," said Dr. Edward Viner, the Flyers' physician, when Parent announced his retirement on June 1, 1979.

Suddenly cut from the life he had known, Bernie sank in a vat of booze. Although his biggest save was made by joining Alcoholics Anonymous, it was not the first time he left himself a big rebound. Casper had lost most of the goalie's money from his prime earning seasons. "I understand now that everything in this life that happens to you, even the bad things, is for a purpose," Parent said years later.

Part of what made him so endearing was a willingness to share his anxieties. "Look," Bernie said while combing his grey hair during his unsuccessful struggles to regain his form in the 1976 playoffs, "things are so bad it's turning black again."

The Parent who, sweating out a one-goal lead in the final minutes of the first Cup-clinching victory, called Ed Van Impe over and said, "Some fun, eh?" was the same goalie who told interviewers, "I would not call what I do fun."

In 1984, in his first year of eligibility, Parent became the first Flyer elected to the Hockey Hall of Fame. He later served as Philadelphia's goaltending coach and is currently a vice president of new business development for Rasanaio-Baillet-Talamo, a Cherry Hill, New Jersey marketing firm.

"He always had to bear the burden of how good he was before the neck injury," said Taylor, "and yet he was one of the most together guys I ever came across. Whatever he was going through inside, he was excellent in the locker room before games. He talked about hunting and fishing. He'd laugh, he'd joke, he'd tell stories about his dog Tinker Bell, who always shared a pregame nap with him in his bed."

Tinker Bell slept not only with her master, but *the Master*. There was no confusing the Parent who was vulnerable to life with the one who was impregnable in goal. "Bernie always talked about the pressure," said Allen, "but he seemed immune to it."

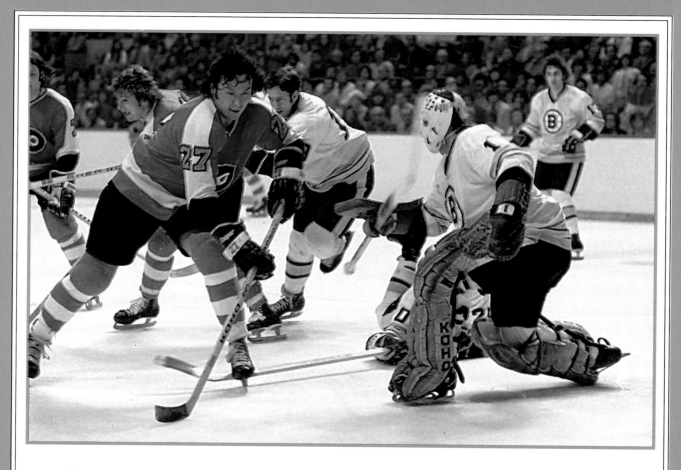

When Reggie Leach had one step on the defenseman and a few inches of net visible behind the goaltender, the puck was as good as in. "He gets his shot off so quickly and with so little body movement," Bernie Parent once said. "He can change in midshot, aiming for a different area entirely, and still pinpoint it."

If only the right wing had managed the same control of his life that he exhibited with a puck, the 306 regular-season goals he scored for the Flyers probably would have represented about half of his career total. As it was, he accomplished much and overcame even more.

Leach's father drifted off to work in the mines before Reggie was born, and his mother, an unmarried young native, soon left Riverton, Manitoba, for a new life in Edmonton. Leach was left with his paternal grandparents, who raised him with twelve of their own children and never discouraged any of the kids from drinking. One of the siblings died in an automobile accident, another froze to death, drunk in a snowbank. Two sisters died young, one of asphyxiation in the front

Leach: "Clarke makes the bombs and I drop them."

seat of a car, the other in a mental hospital.

His grandmother took odd jobs, but money for skates was nonexistent, so Reggie would borrow from older friends and fill the space around his feet with crumpled newspaper. There was no running water, so Leach went to the pump and carried buckets of water to places where he could create a rink, skate and shoot for up to eight hours a day.

Never serious about school, he lived for hockey. "I knew that was all there was for me," Leach said. By age 13, he played on the town's adult team, was spotted by a Red Wings scout and signed to a contract with their junior club in Flin Flon, Manitoba.

Leach struck up a friendship with the team's best player and the town's favorite son, Bobby Clarke, and was fortunate enough to be his right wing for two years. When Clarke went to Philadelphia in the 1969 draft, Leach continued to thrive, scoring 65 goals in 1969-70 and becoming Boston's first pick (third overall) in the 1970 draft.

The Bruins, filling a hole for a successful Stanley Cup run, traded Leach to Oakland in a deal that brought defenseman Carol Vadnais to Boston. In California, Leach floundered like the franchise until, on Clarke's recommendation, he came to Philadelphia in exchange for center Larry Wright, winger Al MacAdam and a No. 1 pick.

Acquired one week after the Flyers' first Cup, the winger contributed 45 goals, plus another eight in the playoffs, toward their second championship. The next year, he scored 61 goals, followed by 19 in sixteen playoff games, and seemed just a trailing pass behind Clarke on the way to the Hall of Fame.

"He makes the bombs and I drop them," Leach said. But Reggie's speed also created offensive opportunities. Of the five goals (on seven shots) that he recorded against Boston to close out a five-game victory in the 1976 semifinals, three were on backhands after he had carried the puck to his off-wing.

To check the Flyers' scoring machine in the finals, Montreal used five players who were later honored in the Hall of Fame for their defensive abilities—goalie Ken Dryden, defensemen Larry Robinson, Guy Lapointe and Serge Savard, and left wing Bob Gainey. Leach still managed four goals during the four tight games that ended Philadelphia's reign and began Montreal's dynasty. His performance throughout that spring was so strong that it earned him the distinction of being only the third player from the losing team in the finals to win the Conn Smythe Trophy.

Unfortunately, Reggie's attention span could be as short as his backswing. He drank too much and at times cared too little. The afternoon of that five-goal playoff game with Boston, teammates alarmed by his failure to show up for the morning skate found Leach passed out drunk in his basement, and had to revive him with coffee, a shower and a few more beers. More than once, Shero—no teetotaler himself—relied on Clarke's judgment to get Reggie ready to play, and looked the other way when he wasn't. The coach, however, did demand that Leach check, and the pouting winger resented the badgering and benchings. By 1978, he slumped to a season average of only 30 goals.

After Bob McCammon replaced Shero, Clarke suggested that Leach's 115-mile-an-hour shot could be refueled with sugar rather than vinegar. McCammon, fired only three-plus months into his first stint, never benefited from the vote of confidence he gave Leach, but successor Pat Quinn continued the stroking and Reggie again had a 50-goal season in 1979-80, when the Flyers ran off a 35-game unbeaten streak and went to the Stanley Cup finals.

Inevitably, Quinn's high opinion of Leach ebbed, as did Reggie's enthusiasm, and the coach's failure to discipline Flyer underachievers eventually prompted his firing. McCammon, brought back with a mandate to get tough, had an instant example at his disposal when Reggie showed up late for practice on the first full day of the coach's second reign. Leach was waived and released.

Reggie scored 15 goals with a bad Detroit team in 1982-83 before finding Alcoholics Anony-

mous and a grass-cutting job that grew into Reggie Leach's Sports Lawn Service in South Jersey. Today, he is sober, successful and is not regretful about his hot-and-cold career.

"I was one of the best at getting into scoring position and I knew I could score from anywhere," he said. "I worked hard on my shot; I would take about 200 after practice. The things they do at NHL skills competitions, I did then. Sometimes I could hit the crossbar ten times in a row from thirty feet out. Shooting was probably the only thing I worked on, though.

"Once I had that big year, they expected me to do it every [season] and that was hard. I know I had as many bad years as good ones, but I still averaged almost 32 goals (in twelve full seasons) and I don't think that's bad. I accomplished everything I wanted in the NHL."

Indeed, a Stanley Cup, a Conn Smythe Trophy, 47 playoff goals, and a place on the 1976 Canada Cup squad was not a poor haul. When the Flyers were feeling as good about Leach as he was about himself, the Rifle was a devastating weapon.

The highest compliment a player can receive in a team game is the one Bill Barber earned: by dedicating his career to blending in, he clearly stood out. For twelve seasons, Barber skated up and down the ice with the reliability of a metronome. He did everything well and with so little fanfare that, even though widely accepted as the best left wing in the game, he was sometimes taken for granted.

"I'm just happy to be here," he would say, usually after insisting team goals came ahead of any of the 420 he scored personally. Ranked seventeenth on the all-time NHL goal-scoring list when he retired, Barber's statistics were far too high for him to warrant anonymity. Yet the "how" to his career still proved more important than the "how many."

"I want to be remembered as being capable of doing my job day in and day out, not just as a goal scorer, but as a good all-around player for every kind of situation," said Barber. His election to the Hockey Hall of Fame in 1990 indicated that the selection committee had perfect recall of the nearly perfect player.

Barber was always where he was supposed to be, doing exactly what the score and clock dictated. On the power play, he performed equally well as triggerman and feeder from the point. On defense, he anticipated so adeptly that he scored 31 career shorthanded goals. Barber combined a grinder's soul with an artist's skills.

His astonishing shot from along the boards detonated over Boston goalie Gilles Gilbert's shoulder in the third period of Game 4 during the 1974 finals, breaking up a tense 2-2 tie and enabling the Flyers to move within one game of their first Cup. "The best wrist shot I've ever seen," Bobby Orr said. Barber also scored four times in a 5-3 victory in Game 3 of the 1980 semifinals against Minnesota. While no Flyer goal was ever a dramatic series-winner, most series would never have been won without him.

So it went for Barber throughout his career. All of Canada remembers the Darryl Sittler shot that defeated Czechoslovakia for the 1976 Canada Cup and forgets that Barber sent the game into overtime.

"Nothing was as important to me as playing on two Stanley Cup winners," Barber says. Second on the priority list was the completion of his career with one team. This distinction, shared by only eight of the twenty-five NHL all-time leading

Barber: The soul of a grinder but the talent of an artist.

scorers at this writing, underlines the fact that Barber was simply too valuable to ever trade.

The strong leg muscles that kept him in the game long after a deteriorating knee should have forced his retirement provided this forward with fine outside speed and a stable base for his underrated corner work. Barber, now head coach of the Flyers' new AHL affiliate, the Philadelphia Phantoms, could shoot equally well off the pass or from full stride.

Barber was happy to be a Flyer long before anyone had good reason to feel that way. With Montreal holding three of the first eight picks in his draft year (1972), the Kitchener center hoped he would be taken seventh by the undistinguished Philadelphia team. "I was afraid I was going to get buried in the Montreal organization," he said.

The Flyers captured two Cups partly because Barber matured quickly. After scoring 9 goals

and 5 assists during a lightning, 11-game crash course at left wing in Richmond, Barber was called up and never looked back, except, of course, for the guy he was supposed to check. The forward scored 30 goals his rookie season and 34 in each of the next two before exploding to 50 in 1975-76.

The LCB Line, consisting of Reggie Leach, Bobby Clarke and Barber, combined for a record-setting 141 goals that year, but never stayed together long enough to again approximate that number. Barber could do so many things well that three coaches—Fred Shero, Bob McCammon and Pat Quinn—used him as a roving cure for whatever, or whoever, ailed the team. He even played a few games on defense for Quinn.

Barber went along with all of it, but never just for the ride. His troublesome right knee, first injured during the 1976-77 season, gradually eroded his effectiveness and probably cost him membership in the 500-goal club.

In August 1985, when this complete player surrendered to the pain and drudgery of an almost year-long rehabilitation, Clarke was asked what it had been like to play with the best left wing of his time.

"Easy," he said.

t broke the Flyers' hearts when Barry Ashbee died, but he was never into flowers. So much of his life could have been set to violin music that his funeral warranted the Hollywood Strings, yet Ashbee would rather have taken a puck in the eye, which he did, than accept your pity.

Tough? You could extinguish cigarette butts on old Ashcan's hardened hide and he wouldn't have flinched. "Look, I don't want this written up as a 'Win One for the Gipper' story," Ashbee said from his hospital bed the day after he was diagnosed with leukemia. "The players know I'm sick and I'm going to get better, that's all."

Thirty days later, he was gone, a reality that was incomprehensible to anyone who had ever known his strength. "He never complained, never batted an eye," said Dr. Isadore Brodsky, who treated Ashbee at Hahnemann Hospital. "All he asked was that we be straight with him."

It was the only way Ashbee knew. His hockey career was full of bad breaks, yet cancer was the only adversity he could not overcome.

Ashbee, whose rights were originally owned by the Bruins, was good enough to be taken by one of the six new teams during the 1967 expansion draft but, because he had missed the entire previous season at Hershey following back surgery, he went unselected.

Three years later, Keith Allen's second trade as Flyers' GM brought the 31-year-old to Philadelphia for Darryl Edestrand and Larry McKillop.

Ashbee was appalled by how many Flyers were content to wallow in their own mediocrity. After learning that players had broken curfew during training camp in 1972, Ashbee had to be talked out of quitting by Allen.

His tolerance of lazy teammates fell considerably short of his pain threshold. In 1972-73, Ashbee played with partially torn knee ligaments. In 1973-74, a chipped neck vertebrae sent searing pain from his shoulder to his hand, but Ashbee taped the arm snug to his body, jammed the stick into his glove and earned a place on the NHL's second All-Star team.

"The strongest guy mentally I've ever seen," Bobby Clarke said. Also, the unluckiest. During the 1974 semifinals, in the overtime of Game 4 at Madison Square Garden, a slap shot by Ranger Dale Rolfe caught Ashbee flush in the right eye, knocking him out of the Flyers' drive to their first Stanley Cup and ending his career. "If he ever asked 'why me?'" recalls Donna, "He

Ashbee: "The strongest guy mentally I've ever seen." (Bobby Clarke)

never said it [out loud]."

Ashbee watched the Flyers win the Cup from behind dark glasses in Ed Snider's suite. "Don't write me up as the great tragic figure," he said. "I'm just happy I was able to get my name on the Stanley Cup. These things happen and you have to accept them."

The injury almost completely ruined the depth perception in his eye, but the assistant coaching job he reluctantly accepted with the Flyers eventually broadened Ashbee's outlook. "He felt it was given out of pity, but he became well into it," recalls Donna.

Allen was thinking of Ashbee as a head-coach-in-training until the April 1977 day when Barry found bruises on his body. Dr. Ed Viner

confirmed the diagnosis the following evening.

The Flyers, reeling from the news, lost to Toronto that night and fell behind 2-0 in the quarterfinals. They fought back to win the series and would have also bet on Ashbee, but two massive doses of chemotherapy failed, along with Barry's kidneys. Not his spirit, though. "I'm tired now, but I'll whip this thing in the morning," he told his wife Donna before going to sleep for the final time.

"He was the bravest man facing death I've ever seen," recalls Allen. Although he could sometimes be gruff and intractable, Ashbee was also the best friend anyone could ever have.

When they laid him to rest in Glendale Memorial Gardens Cemetery outside Toronto at the too-young age of 37, the rough, tough Broad Street Bullies lost their fight to hold back tears.

"The essential thing in life is not to have conquered, but to have fought well," Bobby Clarke eulogized. "Barry never gave into the luxury of exhaustion or pain."

So powerful was his will, so strong was Ashbee's influence on those he touched, that even though he had not played a game in three years, the Flyers' golden era died with him.

Of the 328 goals Rick MacLeish scored for the Flyers, only about 327 looked effortless. His head cocked, the player they called "Cutey" would float from blue line to blue line, with no idea what he'd do when the puck came to him. "My style?" he once said. "Freestyle."

He didn't say much. He didn't sweat much, either. Thanks to hips and arms that swiveled in defiance of the laws of aerodynamics, the center moved around the ice with dispassion at best and indifference at worst. Defensemen knew he would probably cut left to right and goalies understood that the puck would come harder than the slight flick of his wrists suggested, yet the only one who could ever stop MacLeish was himself.

The game came so easily to him that on many nights he forgot to play. Fortunately, the Flyers had no shortage of leaders willing to tie the string around his finger or put their hands around his throat to remind him. Following lectures from Ed Van Impe, Gary Dornhoefer or Bobby Clarke, MacLeish's alarm clock would usually sound in time to save the game.

Although Ricky was never much of a checker, he, Ross Lonsberry and Gary Dornhoefer would often be matched against the opposition's top line by Fred Shero. "I needed somebody to push me," MacLeish says today. "That's why Dorny and Ross were so good for me. They were great to play with. They said, 'Just get open and we'll get you the puck.'"

Nature provided MacLeish with a fluid stride and a river running through the backyard of his family's home in Cannington, Ontario. Each winter, his father would smooth out bumps with a layer of water from the garden hose and Ricky would skate for hours.

After scoring 95 goals in two seasons for coach Roger Neilson's Peterborough Petes, MacLeish was selected fourth overall in the 1970 draft by the Boston Bruins, ironically with a pick Philadelphia had traded three years earlier to obtain Rosaire Paiement. The Flyers realized what they had passed up before Boston understood what it had gained. MacLeish, who had only 13 goals in his first 46 games for the Bruins' farm club at Oklahoma City, became the target of one of the boldest trades in Flyer history.

On February 1, 1971, Keith Allen dealt Bernie Parent to Toronto for center Mike Walton, a No. 1 draft choice and goalie Bruce Gamble, then immediately sent Walton to Boston for MacLeish

A natural talent, MacLeish needed somebody to push him.

and minor leaguer Danny Schock.

For almost a year, Allen heard he should have kept Walton. MacLeish scored only 2 goals in the 26 games following the deal, and managed just one in his first 17 after being recalled from Richmond. But in 1972-73, the season of the Flyers' emergence, MacLeish exploded for 50 goals and 100 points.

He never again reached those statistical standards, but his regular-season totals were hardly the truest measure of value. In the two

Cup drives, MacLeish recorded 13 and 11 playoff goals, and in both years was the NHL's leading playoff point scorer. He got the lone goal in the 1-0 Cup-clinching victory over the Bruins in 1974, a Game 7 hat trick against the Islanders in 1975, and the goal that proved to the game-winner in the Flyers' 4-1 Soviet Red Army victory in 1976. We can only imagine what MacLeish might have done in the 1976 playoffs had he not been out with torn knee ligaments from a February collision. The Flyers lost in the finals to Montreal. Ricky seemed at his best when the Flyers' plight were most dire. In the 1977 quarterfinals vs. Toronto, Philadelphia was down 2-0 in games and 3-2 on the scoreboard when he hit the net with 38 seconds left, and then again in overtime. The Flyers won in six.

In 1980, young Wayne Gretzky and the Edmonton Oilers were about to steal Game 1 when MacLeish forced overtime with 1:19 remaining, and the Flyers went on to a three-game sweep.

MacLeish's failure to respond to Bob McCammon was a major reason the coach was fired halfway through his first season. Pat Quinn successfully appealed to the center's pride, and many of his 31 goals the next year helped maintain Philadelphia's 35-game unbeaten streak. When Tim Kerr showed up the next year, MacLeish was recycled in the deal with Hartford that brought the Flyers the fourth-overall pick they used to select Ron Sutter.

Today, MacLeish is a successful insurance agent in South Jersey. Fitting, considering how often he was the Flyers' insurance policy when they needed him most. As long as they had a minute and a MacLeish, they always had a chance.

Profile / *Ed Van Impe*

He spoke softly and used his stick the way Teddy Roosevelt implied. To suggest that Ed Van Impe played with enormous heart is to say he would rather have cut out yours than let you go around him. Van Impe epitomized the Flyers even before there was much about them to epitomize. Long before the franchise turned the corner, nobody wheeled around Van Impe without getting a stick in the gut as a warning never to do it again. It was a dirty job night after night, holding the opposition to one or two goals so that the early Flyers might have a chance to tie, but the defenseman bloodied his hands willingly, almost gleefully.

He was uncompromising, unflinching unselfish, a smart and tough cookie who the Flyers wisely and luckily pulled from the expansion jar. When Philadelphia drafted Van Impe away from Chicago, he was a 27-year-old Calder Trophy runner-up to Bobby Orr. "There might have been six rookies in the league that year before the expansion," he recalls. "Any similarity between myself and Orr was nonexistent.

"I had played five years in Buffalo (in the AHL) before I finally cracked the lineup in Chicago, but then they traded for Gilles Marotte and I became expendable. At that age, I wasn't sure I wanted to start over again. It turned out getting drafted by the Flyers was the best thing that ever happened to me."

It proved great for the Flyers, too, even if the Spectrum fans needed a few years to be convinced. Van Impe—particularly embarrassed on the November 1968 night that Red Berenson of St. Louis scored six goals at the Spectrum to set an NHL record for a road game—was the subject of boos in his early Flyer seasons.

Even his harshest critics, however, never questioned his toughness. In 1968, a drive by Oakland's Wayne Muloin tore Van Impe's lip for thirty-five stitches, his tongue for another seventeen, and broke seven teeth off at the gums. Van Impe returned to the game in the third period. "It was the popular belief that I couldn't swallow the puck, but I tried," he said. "I felt like I had gone ten rounds with Joe Frazier.

"I got a personal letter from (U.S Senator) Hubert Humphrey, who said he read about it and personally wanted to congratulate me."

Even when Van Impe's mouth was intact, he was never one to flap his jaws. Strong, silent and perfectly suited for Fred Shero's system, the Flyers' second captain was a master of both the

Tough as nails, Van Impe was the mainstay of the defense.

sweep and hip checks, an unerringly effective short passer, and a mainstay of the back-to-back Cup teams. In 1974, after Barry Ashbee's career-ending eye injury in the semifinal series against the Rangers, Shero went with four defensemen. Van Impe, at age 34, was outstanding in the finals against Boston.

Fans were longsince won over, even if opponents remained understandably less warm. The elbow thrown at Valeri Kharlamov that prompted the Soviets to leave the ice during their epic game with the Flyers in 1976 was actually one of the cleaner manuevers of Van Impe's career.

"I couldn't skate that well and my skills weren't polished, so I had to make up for it in other areas," recalls Van Impe, now a successful insurance executive in Delaware County, Pennsylvania. "I had to play that way to be effective.

"Whatever happened, I didn't feel remorse. Whatever I did, or whatever somebody did to me, was all part of the game. Later in my career, there were certain situations I regretted that told me

my career was winding down. You hear cliches about mellowing when you get older and I guess it's true."

Van Impe underwent hernia surgery in October 1975 and struggled to get back into condition. Shero gave his job to rookie Jack McIlhargey and, at the March 1976 trading deadline, one month before the Flyers began their quest for a third straight championship, Keith Allen dealt Van Impe to Pittsburgh for goaltender Gary Inness.

Van Impe was crushed. "I couldn't understand the reasoning," he recalls. "I think I could have helped the way things wound up against Montreal (a four-game Canadiens' sweep)."

Instead of giving Van Impe a new lease on life, the trade sounded the death knell for Van Impe's career. He suffered a shoulder injury at training camp and had to file suit to eventually reach a settlement on his contract. Van Impe was shocked by the adversarial relationship with the Penguins' management and the attitude of his new teammates.

"We weren't winning," he said. "It wasn't what I was used to. A Flyer always gave more than he had, did what he had to do to win, and would do it game in and game out, not just every fourth or fifth time he played."

Ed Van Impe not only fit those criteria, he helped establish them.

The collection of skeletal remains that made up Gary Dornhoefer was good at rattling goalies. This thin-as-a-ghost right wing would climb into the crease and haunt the netkeeper's attic.

"If I was a goalie and had to battle someone like me," Dornhoefer once said, "I would be frustrated as hell. I'd end up being thrown out of the game because I'd blow my cool. They try not to let it bother them, but some guys get so occupied trying to move me out of their way, they forget about the game."

At the same time Dornhoefer was practicing sadism, he was indulging in masochism. There was little to him but elbows and a desire to make the most out of his assets.

When the bag of bones retired after the 1977-78 season, Dornhoefer was a veritable hulk at 190 pounds, although that figure probably included the weight of all the casts ever worn on his body. What the winger did for eleven Flyer seasons was nothing short of heroic.

"I've seen him play some nights when you wonder how he gets out of bed looking the way he does," said Ross Lonsberry, Dornhoefer's longtime linemate.

Dornhoefer, now the Flyers' television color commentator, has had postretirement operations on his back and both knees. He cannot walk a golf course or play racquetball. "Sometimes I think if I had to do it over again, I wouldn't," he said. The Flyers, who took him in their expansion draft, once had even more serious regrets about selecting a player who proved to have so little stamina that he would exhaust himself after one shift or bodycheck. After two seasons, they left him exposed in the 1969 waiver draft.

Nobody claimed him, which turned out to be one of the luckiest breaks in the history of the franchise. "Give me fifteen Gary Dornhoefers on my team and I don't have a care in the world," Fred Shero once said. "He doesn't make excuses."

Instead he made things happen when the Flyers were in need. In Game 5 of Philadelphia's 1973 first-round series with Minnesota, Dornhoefer cut past the North Stars' Tom Reid and tumbled over goalie Cesare Maniago to score the overtime winner. The goal, which inspired the statue outside the south end of the CoreStates Spectrum, set up the Flyers to clinch their first playoff series victory two nights later.

"I had been thinking how much I would love to score that goal," Dornhoefer recalls, "but every player sees himself as a hero."

Dornhoefer had no fear for his body. He only feared losing.

Few, however, actually perform like one every night, as Dornhoefer did for a team destined to burst the buttons on Philadelphia's stuffed shirt. As the Flyers followed up their success over the North Stars with a split of the first two semifinal games with heavily-favored Montreal, Dornhoefer was like a kid in the candy store. "When we hit the ice for Game 3, we had an ovation like I'd never heard before," he recalls. "It had to be eight, nine, ten minutes. You had to holler to talk to the player skating next to you. It's probably still the most memorable moment of my years as a Flyer."

It didn't top a short list, either. In Game 7 of the 1974 semifinals against the Rangers, Steve Vickers got away from Dornhoefer's check in the third period to cut the Flyer lead to a nail-biting 3-2. "I wanted to crawl in a hole," Dornhoefer said, but his heart told him instead to drive to the net. Twelve seconds later, he scored the goal that proved to be the series winner.

Two games into the finals, Dornhoefer suffered a shoulder separation and became an observer as Philadelphia beat Boston for their first Stanley Cup. But the following spring, he had his health and the ultimate satisfaction in helping linemates Lonsberry and Rick MacLeish shut down Buffalo's French Connection line as the Flyers retained the Stanley Cup. "I would have bet every cent we would win that series," Dornhoefer recalls.

Every penny Dornhoefer put up would have been earned in blood and sweat. The tears, he saved for Gary Dornhoefer Night, April 9, 1978, when he went to his retirement a blubbering mess. "They were running down my cheek during the ceremony, he said. "And after the game, I just sobbed." Typical of Dornhoefer that as many bones as he broke, his most painful Flyer experience was saying goodbye.

I t cut through closed locker-room doors, carried clearly over the hiss of spraying showers, pierced the roar of 17,077 fans and occassionally even dented the cement in some of his teammates' heads. One time, the voice of an injured Joe Watson even called an offsides from the press box: actually Watson bellowed so loudly that linesman Neil Armstrong, apparently about to ignore the infraction, blew his whistle.

Joe (Thundermouth) Watson never scored more than 6 goals or recorded more than 30 points in any of his fourteen NHL seasons, but he broke every existing record for decibels.

His style of play was not nearly as loud as his voice. Still, it was never whispered, least of all by Joe, that he was anything but an extremely reliable defenseman. Teammates asked only that Watson keep it down, which he did. The score, that is, not his voice.

It is unclear why a kid who came from a northern British Columbia town with a population of 2,400 had a voice louder than the Canadian Brass. Later, of course, the citizens of Smithers shouted to anybody or anything in earshot—two moose, three elk and a couple of bears—how proud they were of Joe. When his little brother Jimmy joined Watson on two Flyers Stanley Cup teams, the sun stayed up all night through almost the entire summer to celebrate.

The guy who put Smithers on the map was also appreciated in the big city. "If you want to measure a guy in every way," Pat Quinn once said about Watson, "not just what he's done today on the ice, but for everything he's done for a franchise and a city, Joe would come out near the top."

Watson was a throwback, not just to Year One of the Flyers' franchise, but to the youth of every player, when he would skate all day and then talk about it all night. "If you can't enjoy it, you can't do it," Watson said. He adored being in the NHL

"Thundermouth" was the conscience of the locker room.

and respected the privilege of being a Flyer. "A lot of guys mellow and play out the string," said Keith Allen when he sold Watson to the Colorado Rockies in 1978. "Joe's not that kind. It's amazing how he never lost his enthusiasm."

Woe unto any teammate who did. "I guess you've got to know the right thing to say at the right time," Watson once said. "But I hope they all realize it's constructive criticism. It all stays in the locker room and these guys know how I am."

His words had all the subtlety of a bludgeon, and on scoring chances his stick wasn't exactly a precision instrument. When Joe scored in the epic 1976 game against the Soviet Red Army, Fred Shero said the goal set Russian hockey back fifteen years. Watson laughed harder than anyone at Freddie's joke. His good humor was interrupted only by the thought of anyone laughing at the Flyers.

"The word I think of is 'sincere'," said Terry Crisp. "He never embellished the truth. It was just there, good and bad. You never got it from him unless you deserved it, and Joe was there with the right words when you needed it."

In Boston, where Watson broke into the NHL a year ahead of the 1967 expansion, he was a roommate and best buddy of Bobby Orr. With the long-bedraggled Bruins, ready to climb on the revolutionary young defenseman's coattails, Watson's ego was blown to smithereens when he was drafted by the new team in Philadelphia.

He got over it, and became the relentless worker needed by an expansion team wanting to be competitive. Eleven years later, the woebegone Colorado Rockies were looking for that same kind of influence, and Watson was seeking a new challenge.

But one month into the season, Joe was checked from behind by St. Louis's Wayne Babych, fell awkwardly against the end boards, and broke his leg in thirteen places.

Watson spent six weeks wearing a cast up to his chest in a St. Louis hospital and needed six operations. Today, he works in sales for the Flyers, with a left leg two inches shorter than his right.

"The wear and tear is very difficult," Watson says. "Hip replacement is probably down the road. But I'm not complaining. When I turned pro, I wanted to play in the NHL and win a Stanley Cup, and I won two of them.

"Hey, I'm lucky. I know a lot of guys who broke their legs and never got out of Smithers."

Flyers fans never came to the Spectrum for the express purpose of watching Jim Watson play hockey. But once inside, they were happy he was there. For more than nine seasons, Joe Watson's little brother did big, important things. He moved the puck, played the right man, and stayed calm and purposeful amidst the chaos of the defensive zone. The enthusiasm with which the five-time midseason all-star worked made it obvious just how much he cared.

Writers on the Flyer beat were amused to find it virtually impossible to ask the affable Watson any question without getting this answer: "You know, this team has a lot of pride." Those words were true because players like Jimmy Watson looked at their jobs as a trust.

"He gave everything," Paul Holmgren said when Watson retired in 1982, "and everything to him was the team. If there was ever anyone complaining in the locker room, he'd be the first guy to shut them up."

Watson simply liked playing hockey and being a Flyer too much to allow teammates to take the privilege for granted. "I was very proud to be a loyal soldier," he says today. "I had a lot of respect for what that uniform stood for."

Those feelings grew out of brother Joe wearing one for five years before Jimmy. Mary and Joe Watson Sr. produced six sons, all of whom grew up in the small town of Smithers, British Columbia, sharing passions for the outdoors, hockey and the Detroit Tigers. Joe Watson Jr., always the pitcher, burned the palms of his designated catcher, Jimmy, with fastballs, and carved out a career path for him to follow. When Jim struggled during his first junior season with the Calgary Centennials and pondered quitting, Joe had his kid brother come to Philadelphia to see for himself what life was like at the end of the rainbow.

Jimmy stuck it out, but not without further disappointments. Despite being named best defenseman in the Western Canada Hockey League during his final year, Watson was the thirty-ninth player taken in the 1972 NHL draft. He spent a season in Richmond before becoming the final building block of the Flyers' Stanley Cup defense. He quickly became the cornerstone, too. His mobility and intelligence quickly earned him the confidence of coach Fred Shero and brought Watson recognition as one of the most efficient defensemen in the league.

Jim Watson: "I had a lot of respect for what that uniform stood for."

He was playing for Team Canada in the 1976 Canada Cup when his cheekbone was broken by a rising slapshot from Team USA's Gary Sargent. Watson was back with the Flyers for opening night of the season, but during a December game in St. Louis was accidentally hit in the face by the stick of the Blues' Jerry Butler. The blade left a crease in the retina of Watson's right eye, permanently diminishing his vision by ten per cent. The Flyers, who felt Watson would gradually add more offense to his game, instead settled for a strictly defensive defenseman.

While they never had any reason to feel cheated, Watson certainly did. During the second round of the 1980 playoffs, the Rangers' Barry Beck broke Watson's shoulder with a bodycheck, but the defenseman played two more rounds on painkillers and courage before finally surrendering during Game 6 of the finals against the Islanders. Jimmy's surgically repaired shoulder healed by the following season, but back problems continued to plague him. In 1980-81, Watson played only 18 games before undergoing spinal fusion surgery.

The operation was deemed a success, but the patient's hockey career died. Watson participated in 76 games in 1981-82, but was clearly diminished. At training camp the following September, he hurt so much that common sense prevailed. Doctors told him that the recurring stiffness and pain were the usual manifestations of surgically repaired discs and that there was no risk in continuing to play, but they also said he could not expect to do so comfortably. The Flyers had rebuilt their defense that summer around the acquisition of Mark Howe, so on the eve of the 1982-83 regular season, Watson retired, taking a scouting job with the team until his contract expired.

"In a sense, I feel like I could have had more time," he says today. "But I got in ten years, got two rings, two more trips to the finals and was fortunate to play on a good team."

Today, James C. Watson Inc. is a successful contractor in Delaware County, Pennsylvania, where the houses he constructs are as sturdy as their builder's character.

Andre Dupont's knees pumped up near his chest as emphatically as blood flowed through his oversized heart. Fred Shero hated the Moose Shuffle almost as much as he loved the man who performed it. "Why does he have to do that?" the coach would ask, rolling his eyes. Moose Dupont may have celebrated his occasional goals like a hot dog, but his relish for the game was beyond reproach.

That enthusiasm never diminished, even after the chips on the Broad Street Bullies' shoulders were shaved down to sawdust. One night late in December 1978 at Boston Garden, the Flyers were losing 3-0 when Dupont stuck his stick into the gut of Stan Jonathan, perhaps the best fighter of the era. Because Moose's abilities in the fistic arts never matched his ardor, the result was predictable. Dupont needed stitches to close a cut near the eye that was rapidly swelling shut as he returned to the hopelessly lost game. With the Bruins shoving the score and their gloves into Flyer faces during the third period, Dupont pushed Wayne Cashman and, while his teammates stood frozen, had to hold off a challenge from the sinister John Wensink.

"I figured I had to do something to get us going," the Flyer defenseman said afterwards.

The Bruins could have severed the Moose's arms and legs that night, but he still would have stood defiantly asking whether they had already taken their best shot. There were times when Dupont, prone to the spectacular giveaway, played like his head had been lopped off, but Shero never believed even the worst-timed Moose minuses could cancel out his pluses.

"He'll bleeping die for you," the Flyer coach once said. "He'll kill himself. He'll try to beat five guys and then come back and ask you if he did the right thing. He'll drive you crazy because he can't see the forest for the trees sometimes, but he never has to be told to work."

Shero had received an early insight into Dupont's makeup when he coached the eighth-overall choice in the 1969 draft (nine picks ahead of Bobby Clarke) on the Rangers' farm team at Omaha. New York had moved him to the Blues, who were always a few losses away from a panic-stricken purge, and Shero urged GM Keith Allen to find a spot in the Flyers' growing menagerie for a Moose. Most of the muscle being flexed by the emerging Broad Street Bullies was on the for-

Moose gave the Flyers courage, color and heart.

ward lines; Shero wanted a beast of prey to protect the goalie, too.

In December 1972, Dupont showed up with St. Louis for a game at the Spectrum only to be informed that he would instead be playing for the home team. Traded to the Flyers for defenseman Brent Hughes and right wing Pierre Plante, Dupont changed uniforms more quickly than loyalties. Teammates initially found him distant, but soon learned that they never had to place a long-distance call for his help.

The Moose gave the Flyers courage, color, humor and probably the most vital goal of their team's history. Philadelphia had lost Game 1 of the 1974 finals to the heavily favored Bruins, 3-2, and was about to fall short again in Game 2 when Dupont jumped up to the hash marks, took a blind backhand pass from Rick MacLeish, and slapped in the tying goal with 52 seconds remaining. In overtime, Clarke scored to turn the series.

Dupont would valiantly carry the puck to audience calls of "Mooooooooose," but his sense of timing was not always exquisite. When he got caught up ice, it was never because he got caught up in himself, only in his team. All he had he expended on the ice. "As long as they think I'm doing the job, that's all that matters," Dupont, now a Montreal player agent, would insist. Dupont was sensitive to the public image that he was not very bright, but he was an apt student who knew a good teacher when he found one in Shero.

"Everything I know about hockey I learned from Freddie," said Dupont. He also played well for Pat Quinn, and the Moose's final Flyer season proved to be one of his best. Dupont was a mainstay on a defense that produced a 35-game unbeaten streak and took the Flyers to within two victories of the Stanley Cup.

Less than four months later, Allen, anxious to make room for a Swedish prospect named Thomas Eriksson, traded Dupont to his native Quebec for a seventh-round draft choice.

Before the trade was consumated, Allen had given the loyal Flyer a three-year contract. More than a nice gesture, it was an example of the organization taking care of one of its most passionate and loyal servants.

t's hard to believe it lasted only four years. Most *games* Dave Schultz played for Philadelphia seemed to take that long. From the Hammer's first glare to the shove up the tunnel by the linesman, Schultz's ritual was as symbolic of Flyer hockey as Bobby Clarke and Bernie Parent.

Considering the criteria for the team's most significant players of all time—performance, leadership, longevity—the inclusion of Schultz risks the author a misconduct penalty. Or perhaps more fittingly, an overhand right from the Hammer himself. But considering his impact, Schultz belongs ahead of Flyers who played better and longer.

To opponents and their supporters, Schultz was the ultimate hockey thug. But to Philadelphia, he was a liberator from years of losing. Coach Fred Shero always said Schultz gave the team courage on the road. And at home he could do no wrong.

The NHL had had its share of tough guys before Schultz came up in 1972, but no one had ever embellished the act to such a grandiose level. His arms windmilled not only at competitors' faces, but in continuing exasperation with the referees. In other rinks, he dodged airhorns, bottles, right and left hands, and the daggers of do-gooders who thought he was the worst thing that ever happened to the game.

Forever wrestling with the moral dilemma created by his role, Schultz could be as introspective as he was hair-triggered. Always a competent defensive player, The Hammer's unpredictability created a buffer which helped him earn 20 goals in 1973-74. Still, there was never any misunderstanding about his primary role, one he came to resent after the Flyers traded him.

As it turned out, Schultz largely had been play-acting all along, More coward than bully while growing up in rural Saskatchewan, his behavior was more learned than instinctive. "When we went to Flin Flon to play Clarkie's tough team, I was scared as *bleep*," Schultz recalls. "I would hide."

He surprised himself one day in a Junior B game when his right-handed punch staggered a player named Butch Deadmarsh, and as Schultz's body grew, so did his nerve. The Flyers drafted him in the fifth round of the 1969 draft, the first after the team's four-game annihilation by the big, bad Blues.

In his initial game with Roanoke Valley of the Eastern League, he destroyed a player named Denis Romaneski and found the process exhila-

Schultz took the tough guy image to levels never before seen.

rating. Schultz's appetite for blood whetted, he fought his way up the ladder, arriving at the right time—and on the bench of the right coach—to become a phenomenon.

"The fighting gave me notoriety," he recalls. "That part I loved, but [it] never came naturally to me. I would sit there the afternoon of every game thinking about who I was going to fight and visualizing the fight.

"It was nerve-wracking. I was always afraid of that one punch that would knock me out of my career. Fortunately, it never happened. I had some well-publicized losses but I never really got the whipping that would destroy my confidence and value.

"It was different then, the rules were such that you could really help your team if you scared the

right [opponent]. I knew what the Flyers expected and I just totally got caught up in it. I was this kid from Rosetown, Saskatchewan, suddenly a hero in a city of two million, making all this money and being afraid of losing everything. I did what I had to do to keep it going."

Flyers who had not been particularly courageous before Schultz's arrival dropped their gloves and followed him.

Schultz had a quiet playoff in 1976, when Philadelphia surrendered the Cup to Montreal, and the arrivals of Paul Holmgren and Jack McIlhargey made the Hammer expendable to Los Angeles for second- and fourth-round draft choices. He was never the same after that. Subsequently moved to Pittsburgh and finally to Buffalo, Schultz's disillusionment grew. In a book he co-wrote after his retirement in 1980, he said he resented having to fight Bobby Clarke's battles and criticized the pack mentality that had fueled the Flyers' success.

"I don't want to sound hypocritical. As I look back, I can't believe I carried the role as far as I did. Despite all the anxiety, I guess I loved it."

efensemen thought it was unfair for someone with a big body to have such quick hands, so they showed no remorse for what they did in their futile attempts to stop Tim Kerr. Opponents chopped at his legs and clung to his torso while 225 pounds of defiance stood willing to take whatever abuse was necessary for that next goal.

Kerr flipped pucks into nets as easily as coins into the basket at a tollbooth, scoring at a goals-per-game pace that only eight NHL players have bettered. The real price, however, was paid on the surgeon's table. Shoulder and knee problems kept him from achieving totals that could have been among the highest in league history. But he never complained about any of his setbacks, even before they became trivialized by the sudden death of his wife, Kathy, ten days after giving birth.

Kerr kept rising from cross-checks, rehabilitation and suffocating personal loss to continue scoring. "When something happens, I'm angry," he once said. "But I've always been able to channel it. I find positive things and build back up."

He never enjoyed the luxury of skating regularly with a superior playmaking center or without pain. Three knee injuries and a broken leg held him to a combined total of 54 goals in four years until, in 1983-84, he equaled that number in just one season. He then recorded 54 again, and 58 twice. During the Flyers' 1985 drive to the finals, Kerr had 10 goals in 12 games before damage to his knee sidelined him from the playoffs. In 1987, he scored 8 times in 12 contests, most of which were spent in agony with a gradually separating left shoulder that would not allow him to continue past the second round.

After a two-stage operation that summer, a surgical pin came loose and was replaced by another that became infected. Those setbacks took virtually the entire 1987-88 season away from him. Yet the winger rebounded the following year to score 48 times, despite missing 12 games with the still-troubled joint. He gulped aspirin in a regimen that increased his tolerance for anti-inflammatory medication and finally felt robust as he headed into the 1988-89 playoffs. Kerr scored 14 goals in 13 games before his thumb was broken by a slash, rendering him effectively useless during the semifinal series against Montreal.

"Listen, if you're looking for real trouble, you don't have to look too far in this world," he had

Kerr: An awesome goal scorer hampered by serious injuries.

said. A year later, he became a widower with three young daughters. Tim went to the gym two days after the tragedy and returned to the lineup in two weeks. As if not tested enough, he twice more suffered injuries during that season, yet returned both times.

Souls were illuminated watching his repeated, stoic refusal to despair. He passed every trial by running a high-pressure test of the red bulbs mounted behind the nets, achieving seventeen hat tricks during his career and earning the NHL record for most power-play goals in a season (34, in 1985-86).

The enduring image of the classic Kerr score was the sweep of a passout from behind the net. It looked so easy, he rarely bothered to lift his stick in celebration. But this big horse was no one-trick pony. He could beat goalies with wrist shots from thirty-five feet, or step outside a defenseman and pick the far corner with a backhander. He scored while on his knees, his chest, under pile-ups, and uncannily, in first games after long absences.

It was Philadelphia's incredible good luck that Tim fell through the cracks of a six-round 1979

draft, enabling the Flyers to sign the big center from Tecumseh, Ontario who many experts considered too lazy for the NHL. And it was the team's misfortune that he was only available for two games during the 1985 and 1987 finals.

After eleven seasons, the right wing was let go to San Jose in the 1991 expansion draft, then quickly traded to the Rangers. A year-and-a-half later, he was out of the game at the too-young age of 32. Nevertheless, he thanked fate for never giving him more than he could bear and his body for holding up as long as it did.

Today, Kerr is remarried and has five children. An executive with Power Play International, a sports marketing firm, he also runs a nonprofit organization—Tim Kerr Charities—out of his home in Avalon, New Jersey.

"One thing I learned from Kathy's death is that there are no [guarantees]," he said. "There are only privileges. And life is one of them. You have to enjoy it because you can have it taken away from you at any time.

"The rehab was never a big problem because I like a good workout. The games were a lot of fun, so I kept getting up until I couldn't get back up again.

"A lot of people have said to me that they could never have gone through what I have. But people underestimate themselves. When they have to, they handle things."

Of the 363 goals Kerr scored for the Flyers, many came on his own rebounds. It is easy to understand why.

Few players with a skill level as high as Mark Howe's have ever subverted their egos so for the good of their teams. He failed to score more than 480 points in his 594 regular season games only because the Flyers were ahead too often to need more goals.

Those leads were largely due to him. Howe could skate away from pursuers, smother attackers with smart positioning, and pinpoint openings in forechecking mazes. All decisions were based on the clock and the score. And 97 out of 100 were correct.

Those other three situations were fun to watch. Seconds after Howe would miss a pinch down the boards or get trapped up ice, unoccupied segments of the rink would disappear, swallowed by one of Howe's strides. In the four pushes it took an opponent to move thirty feet through the netural zone, Howe would take two steps and pull even.

The best defenseman never to have won the Norris Trophy had neither the muscle of Rod Langway nor the heavy shots and relentless scoring drives of Paul Coffey and Ray Bourque. Howe finished second to each of those players in three different Norris ballotings, proving that while he always picked the right spots to join the rush, his best seasons weren't as well-timed.

The Flyers, who twice fell in the finals to Edmonton's great offensive machine, shared his problem. Still, the defenseman did not see himself as unlucky or unfulfilled. On the contrary. He was one of the three persons in the entire world fortunate enough to be a son of Gordie Howe.

"Maybe my wishes and hopes exceeded my eyesight," said Dad, "but I think I saw all the boys as NHLers almost at birth."

Being as levelheaded as the haircuts of his day, Gordie pressured Murray, Marty and Mark to do only what made them happy. "I guess because he had so much fun playing hockey, he would never make it a chore for any of us," recalled Mark. "He would come to our games and sit and watch, never rant and rave like some of the other fathers. If there were any problems being Gordie Howe's kids, I always thought the advantages far outweighed them."

Brother Marty's real passion was football, although he played hockey professionally in Houston and Hartford. Murray "disgraced" the family and became a doctor, while Mark received an excellent two-for-one deal in DNA spirals—the

Mark Howe, the best defenseman never to have won the Norris.

instincts and grace of his father and the brains of his mother, Colleen.

School was easy for Mark. Homework would get completed in an hour so that hockey could be played until bedtime. In the morning, he would sometimes suggest to Dad that it might be an especially good day to pass by the school and drive to the Olympia. Gordie went along with the scam every once in a while after eliciting an oath that no one tell Mom.

There were financial benefits to being Gordie Howe's kid. Mark would sell the four tickets Dad got for every game, then walk past friendly ushers and sit in the press box. The little hustler grew up to be a bright businessman. And his father could tell early, even before Mark's skills developed, how smart he was on the ice.

The youth hockey program in the Detroit area was not adequate for the training of an aspiring professional, so Colleen took charge of upgrading it. The Junior Red Wings traveled often to compete against Ontario's best clubs, helping Mark, by age 17, earn a place on the silver medal-winning 1972 U.S. Olympic team.

He was awaiting his NHL draft with Toronto's Junior A Marlboros when Bill Dineen, GM of the WHA Houston Aeros (and Howe's coach in his final season with Philadelphia), sounded out Gordie and Colleen about Mark and Marty turning pro early. Dad stunned Dineen by asking if he would be interested in a third Howe. Two years into retirement, Gordie, 43, wanted to play again.

Dineen signed the greatest family act since the Flying Wallendas. Gordie averaged 100 points over three seasons; Mark, scoring 79 points his first season, was named WHA rookie of the year and become regarded as the best young talent outside the NHL.

The Bruins took Mark in the second round of the 1974 draft, but Montreal blocked any Howe reunion in the NHL by selecting Marty one round later. When the Houston team folded following its 1976-77 season, the Howes moved together to the WHA New England Whalers, who in 1979 were accepted into the NHL.

Mark keyed the team to an unexpected playoff berth in its premier season and was on his way to a happy life in Hartford until the Islanders' John Tonelli roared down the slot and hooked up with Howe. Both players went into the net, which came off its moorings, and a sharp piece of metal pierced Mark's buttocks.

Howe remembers his toes being moved by a doctor. "I told him the toes weren't the problem," he recalls. "And he told me he was checking my reflexes. An inch one way and [the metal] could have gone into my spinal cord; an inch the other way, it would have pierced my sphincter muscle and I would have been walking around with a co-lostomy bag. When Dad looked at it and almost got sick, I knew it was serious."

Mark lost thirty-five pounds and, eventually, the will to play for the Whalers. He was weak upon returning to the lineup and coach/GM Larry Pleau thought him a whiner and hypochondriac.

Keith Allen, ill from watching his 87-point Flyer team get knocked out in the first round by the Rangers, bore down on Hartford during the summer of 1982, working a deal for Howe that sent center Ken Linseman and No. 1 and No. 3 picks in 1983 to the Whalers. When Ed Snider agreed to take financial obligation for the resale of Mark's new Hartford home, the player gleefully waived a no-trade clause and joined Philadelphia.

Billed as an offensive defenseman who was difficult to motivate, Howe instead provided half the expected offense, twice the defense and three times the motivation. Whereas the Whalers, desperate for leadership, had seen a moaner and malingerer, the Flyers, short on defensive talent but not players who cared, enjoyed a likable kvetch who made leaving their

zone painless. The more Howe hurt, the more he let you know about it. And the better he seemed to play.

Revitalized, Philadelphia surged to 106 points and a Patrick Division title but was wiped out of the playoffs by the Rangers in three straight first-round games. Howe played nervously and dis-couragingly. The following spring, the Flyers were again eliminated, this time in three straight by Washington. But in 1985, when Philadelphia broke a three-year, nine-game playoff schneid, it was Howe's Game 1 overtime goal that changed the series and his reputation for not coming through in the clutch.

As new coach Mike Keenan raised Mark's conditioning level and his self-esteem, the defenseman's best years began at age 30.

"I had a lot of accomplishments with two pre-vious teams, but there was no way my career would have been complete without my time in Philadelphia," he said. "Other than winning a Cup, the next best thing would be to play 10 years with the Flyers in the eighties."

Back disc problems began to take chunks out of Howe's seasons, but the Flyers remained teth-ered to his lifeline. In Mark's final Flyer year (he signed as a free agent with Detroit in 1992), Phila-delphia was 21-18-3 when he was in the lineup and 11-19-8 when he was not.

The players who have best exemplified the franchise were some combination of brave, ex-plosive or gritty. Howe, the best defenseman the Flyers ever had, added marvelously efficient to this list.

The official notice of Pelle Lindbergh's death in Stockholm newspapers filled the space usually reserved for a biblical passage or inspirational quotation with only one word:

"Why?"

The loss was irreconcilable; the waste of talent impossible to rationalize. Lindbergh was one of the most endearing personalities and brilliant talents ever to perform in an orange and black jersey. The day the best goalie in the NHL died was the worst day in Flyer history.

The compulsion with speed that killed the 26-year-old was a tragic extension of his passion for life. "He was a terrific competitor with an unmatched will to win," Dave Poulin eulogized at a memorial service three days after Lindbergh's red Porsche hit the wall of an elementary school. "Anything he did, he had to be best at, and through his exuberance and personality, he transmitted that to us. He wasn't happy unless there was something on the line."

Lindbergh pushed hard towards his ambition to become the league's first great European goalie. He possessed a grin wider than the Atlantic Ocean and an affability that transcended the status he gained after winning the 1985 Vezina Trophy. Liking the way Pelle stopped the shots had nothing to do with enjoying his company.

The Swede had difficulty saying no to anything besides the puck. After his first start for the Flyers, Lindbergh suffered dehydration, became nauseous and had to leave postgame interviews. When he was forced to excuse himself twice, most of the writers took the hint and moved on. One guy, however, hovered even after the chalk-white goalie returned for the third time. Lindbergh stacked up his pads as pillows, lay down on the locker room floor and, holding his hands over his forehead, continued to answer questions.

Per-Erik Lindbergh was without pretense. His desire to savor everything in life included the people in it and the nuances of a new language that he attacked without embarrassment. Following a slump-ending victory, the goalie was asked if he had the "monkey off his back." Lindbergh looked over his shoulder quizzically. Told it was just an expression for a release of pressure, Pelle used the cliche for a month, declaring an absence

A terrific competitor with an unmatched will to win.

of monkeys after every win.

The third child and first son of Sigge and Anna-Lise Lindbergh was told at age 12 by Curt Lindstrom, the coach of the Hammarby athletic club on the working-class south side of Stockholm, that he had a chance to be the greatest goaltender on earth. Later, Lindstrom, who doubled as the Swedish national team coach, brought a film of the 1975 Stanley Cup final to Hammarby. Watching Bernie Parent, Lindbergh determined that playing for his country would be his means to the NHL, not an end unto itself.

Pelle wore a mask like Parent and was thrilled when anyone mentioned that he resembled his idol. Lindbergh was performing in Sweden's First Division at age 16. By 19, he was a backup for the national team, and at 20, the starter.

Flyer scout Jerry Melnyk spotted the short goalie with lengthy aspirations in Moscow at the 1979 World Championships. Lindbergh couldn't believe it when Philadelphia, *his* team, called in 1979 with the news that he had been drafted in the second round.

Pelle backstopped Sweden to a bronze medal

in the 1980 Olympics at Lake Placid. The following year, he was on the Flyers' farm in Maine learning that to survive in North America a goalie had to move towards the shot, not wait on the line for one last pass. He adjusted quickly, won an AHL championship and an MVP award in 1981, then chafed through a second minor-league season before Philadelphia traded Pete Peeters, opening up the No. 1 job.

Lindbergh carried the Flyers into first place until suffering a broken wrist bone in a Spectrum exhibition match against the Soviet national team, followed by a horrendous rookie-hazing haircut from his teammates just before the All-Star Game. His embarrassment at the event's banquet turned to mortification the following night when he was lit up for four goals by Wayne Gretzky.

Pelle struggled the rest of the season and through a first-round wipeout by the Rangers. The next year, his self-assurance bottomed out in a grotesque performance during a February 6-5 Spectrum loss against Vancouver. He kicked a puck that had caromed off the endboards into the net, then lost his balance in giving up the winning goal on a trickler.

Insecure to a fault, Lindbergh accepted far too much advice during "the year I spent sliding on a banana peel." But he offered no excuses and made no enemies. Although easily bruised, he was impossible to scar.

By the following season, Mike Keenan's opinion—that this goalies only needed a larger workload—was the only one that mattered. Lindbergh performed a marathon—83 games, counting regular season and playoffs—at sprint pace. He won 40 times as Philadelphia accumulated 113 points. In the playoffs, he slayed the Ranger dragon in three straight before finishing off the four-time champion Islanders in five games with a brilliant 1-0 shutout.

He was as good that night as he could be, yet only as great as he had been almost all season. Lindbergh might have enjoyed the best set of reflexes on any goalie in history. Shooters who assumed there was room between his bowed legs found out otherwise when the pads closed as quickly as a blinking eyelid. Pelle's balance was excellent, and his glove hand as soft as his personality.

All who knew and cheered him were left on November 10, 1985, with hearts as crushed as his car.

A guy who skated as quickly as anybody in Flyer history came even more rapidly out of nowhere to become their leader. Dave Poulin, who wasn't good enough to play major junior, to be recruited by an NCAA program or to play on an elite-level team during his year in Sweden, captained Philadelphia clubs that twice reached the Stanley Cup finals.

He grew up in Mississauga, Ontario, a Toronto suburb where it is impossible to play hockey with any skill and go unnoticed. Nevertheless, U.S. collegiate hockey powers did not look for prospects weighing 165 pounds. When a friend of Poulin's who had committed to Michigan State received a questionnaire from Notre Dame, he gave it to Dave. Poulin filled it out, got a call and won a scholarship.

When he came down with spinal meningitis, Poulin missed a third of his draft eligibility year and whatever chance he had of attracting interest from the NHL. But at Notre Dame he thrived, both in a mediocre hockey program and an excellent business curriculum. By his senior year, his 3.24 grade point average was tempting more recruiters than his 1.42 points per game.

Poulin, accepted into Procter & Gamble's prestigious management training program. Then, he received a call from Ted Sator.

Sator, a former player at Bowling Green State University, coached Rogle, a Swedish minor-league team. The rules allowed two American imports per club, so Sator phoned his friend, Ron Mason, coach at Michigan State, to ask if he knew of anyone with the wheels to thrive in the wide-open European game.

Three days after Poulin married Kim Kucera, a student at St. Mary's College, the newlyweds left on a six-month European hockey honeymoon before hubby was to join P & G. Poulin, by then beefed up to 180 pounds, thrived with Rogle. When Bob McCammon asked Sator, who had been a guest power-skating instructor at the Flyer training camp, if he knew of any potential stretch-drive help for the farm club at Maine, the coach recommended Poulin.

"It was just for the rest of the year," recalls Poulin, now head coach at Notre Dame. "I had

Poulin: Always in the right place at the right time.

nothing to lose." Neither did the slumping Flyers when they recalled him to Maple Leaf Gardens, the arena of his childhood dreams, for the next-to-last game of the regular season. Playing there turned out to be easier than it had ever been to get tickets. Poulin scored on his first two NHL shots.

A week later, he was taking a regular shift on left wing and recorded four points during the Rangers' three-game demolition of Philadelphia. Soon after, Poulin received a newspaper clipping of the match in Toronto and a letter from his boss-to-be at Procter & Gamble. "Obviously our paths are going different ways," he wrote. "I'm happy for you. Best of luck."

Next season, Poulin was centering the Flyers' No. 1 line between Brian Propp and Tim Kerr. Dave scored 76 points and won over Bobby Clarke who, as general manager, advised new coach Mike Keenan to make Poulin the team's captain in only his second season.

On the ice, Poulin knew how to be in the right place at the right time, and as captain he always knew what to say and when. His jump towards the puck and sense of when to commit made him an exceptional penalty killer, while his tenacity, intelligence, and command of the language earned him total respect in the locker room. "Dave was the best leader I ever played with," Mark Howe says today.

Poulin did not possess superior playmaking skills, but he was more valuable than many 100-point scorers. Among his qualities was pain tolerance. In 1985, after sustaining cracked ribs early in the semifinal series against Quebec, the captain sat out two games, then returned to score, playing two men short, perhaps the most electrifying goal in Spectrum history, putting the Flyers into the finals. In 1987, his ribs were again broken, but when his team faced a quarterfinal Game 7 after it had led the Islanders 3-1 in the series, Poulin donned a flak jacket and set up two goals that sparked Philadelphia's 5-1 victory.

In 1989 against Washington, a shot chipped the bone on the ring finger of Poulin's left hand, but he played the next night, scoring once to help the Flyers even a series they went on to win in six games. Two rounds later, Poulin suffered two broken toes which had to be frozen, yet he pushed in the Game 5 winner in overtime.

None of these injuries caused Poulin or the Flyer organization, as much agony as when coach Paul Holmgren, citing the need to transfer leadership to younger players, took the captaincy away in December 1990. Clarke, frustrated with Poulin's injuries and desperate for offense, then traded him to Boston a month later for Ken Linseman.

The deal was a disaster. Linseman was gone at the end of that season while Poulin, whose bowlegged skating style left him susceptible to lower abdominal pulls, underwent surgery to correct the problem and gave the Bruins and Capitals five more strong years.

Philadelphia got the best ones, though, to its incredible good fortune.

The kid from St. Paul, Minnesota, who joined the Flyers in March 1976 had big, strong shoulders that hinted at his promise, and sad, unconfident eyes that foretold his pain. At age 20, Paul Holmgren was shy in conversation, aggressive in playing style, and explosive in temper.

In his first NHL game, Holmgren charged onto the ice and knocked the immovable Phil Esposito onto his rear end. "Brushed him like a fly," said coach Fred Shero. "I thought to myself, there's the Stanley Cup." Thirty-six hours later, the rookie almost died.

Holmgren had reported to a team meeting in Boston with a right eye that was suddenly and dangerously swollen. Two weeks earlier, he had suffered a skate cut on his cornea while at the bottom of a pileup in an American Hockey League brawl. "I had just gotten there and didn't want anyone to be mad at me," he recalls. "I didn't tell anybody."

But the problem became too obvious to ignore. Bobby Clarke and Barry Ashbee took Holmgren to the Massachusetts Eye and Ear Infirmary, where doctors performed surgery the next morning to save his sight. While on the operating table, however, he suffered an adverse reaction to the anesthesia and went into convulsions.

His condition stabilized more quickly than his career. When struck in the same eye by a racquetball during the summer, surgery, prayer and exercise were again needed. Holmgren would cover his good eye and watch television with the other one, and doctors who first measured his vision at 20/300 were amazed when it improved to 20/30. But Paul's depth perception was permanently diminished. The right wing whose made a living going to the net for rebounds spent his career unable to distinguish whether the puck was on the ice or six inches off it.

He never let physical problems discourage him. In 1978, he suffered a chipped vertebra. Although declared out for the season, he was in the lineup for the next game. This strength of character was matched only by the strength in his upper body. "He ran into me one time at practice," Shero said, "and every part of me hurt. Even my hair. I didn't know hair could hurt."

Fearless and reckless, Holmgren threw his 210 pounds around rinks for nine Flyer seasons. His final statistics—144 goals, 179 assists in only 527 career games—suggest he was an average,

Holmgren: "All beat up he gave the Flyers all he had."

oft-injured, and penalty-prone performer whose penalty minutes (1684) more than tripled his final point totals.

Yet during his two peak seasons, 1979-80 and 1980-81, Holmgren scored 30 and 22 goals and was among the better right wings in the game. He protected his smallish, perpetually annoying linemates—Ken Linseman and Brian Propp—from physical harm, and cleared room for them and himself.

Holmgren's temper also drew the attention of league disciplinarian Brian O'Neill. He was suspended for 7 games in 1978 for cracking the Rangers' Carol Vadnais over the helmet with a stick, and for 5 games in 1982 for shoving referee Andy van Hellemond at the end of a fight with Pittsburgh's Paul Baxter. "I'm not proud of all the stupid stuff I did," Holmgren said. Only videotapes can confirm that this madman was the same soft-spoken, kind person who, off the ice, was always a perfect gentleman. When Clarke found out that Paul had two diabetic brothers—one of whom, Dave, had died in 1971 from complications associated with the disease—a bond was forged for life.

By 1984, Holmgren's shoulder was a wreck and his playing time diminished. He was traded home to Minnesota for prospect Paul Guay and a third-round draft choice. A season and a half and two operations later, the North Star called it a career at the too-young age of 29. He came back to Philadelphia as an assistant coach, succeeded Mike Keenan behind the bench for three seasons, and then coached the Hartford Whalers before returning to the Flyers in 1996 as the head of pro scouting.

Although the Cup Shero had predicted fell two games short of delivery in 1980, Holmgren's impact on the organization should not be minimized. While never a franchise player, he personified the club for which he played. "He was all beat up," said Clarke. "And he gave the Flyers all he had."

A fearsome sniper whose career was bittersweet.

The scoring left wing the Flyers coveted in the 1979 draft fell to them like manna from heaven. That always seemed appropriate of a player coming from the Brandon Wheat Kings, particularly one who was passed over by many NHL teams on the half-baked idea that his lifestyle was as bad as his brushcut. Thirteen clubs failed to select the sniper who went on to record 425 NHL goals.

Brian Propp, the preacher's kid from Lanigan, Saskatchewan, arrived at his first Flyer camp as quiet as a church mouse and as good at dodging eye contact as body contact. "When I have something to say, I'll say it," Propp said in a voice as low as his shot.

When Propp got the winning goal in his first NHL game, it was not such a big deal to someone who had scored 94 times the previous season. Philadelphia lost only one of the first 37 contests in which he played, which wasn't out of the ordinary for the 20-year-old gunner—his junior team had lost just five during Propp's final year.

"I was young and used to winning," he recalls. "I figured we would be winning for a long time." Indeed, the Flyers never recorded a losing season in the ten years the Brandon Bopper played for them.

Propp scored 40 or more goals in four different years, and amassed more than 90 points four times. He reached 97 points in both 1985 and 1986, when he missed 4 and 8 games, respectively, with injuries. Thus, the player as quick to pounce on a loose puck as any in franchise history left the loose end of never recording a 100-point season. It was symbolic of a bittersweet career in which he repeatedly fell just short.

When he scored only three playoff goals over three springs in the early 1980s and the Flyers went out in the first round each time, their best scorer became an easy and not completely undeserving target. Propp struggled in the early rounds of Philadelphia's 1985 redemption, and went goalless when the Flyers were upset by the Rangers in 1986.

He did, however, fully live down a choker's reputation with a brilliant Game 7 against the Islanders in 1987. "He played like he was possessed," said Mark Howe after Philadelphia, faced with blowing a series it had led 3-1, was dominant in a 5-1 victory. "It was probably the best I've ever seen him."

Propp scored 28 points in 26 playoff games that season and was also excellent in the 1989 semifinal run, right up until his head was rammed against the glass by Montreal's Chris Chelios. When Brian regained consciousness, he believed he was still playing in the previous round against Pittsburgh. It was probably the only time the winger ever lost his bearings on a rink.

Propp was always where he was expected to be, both offensively and defensively. His speed and sense of anticipation made him an excellent penalty killer and, when paired with Dave Poulin, a devastating shorthanded threat.

Careless at best and mean-spirited at worst with the use of his stick through much of his career, Propp eventually underwent changes in both his on-ice and off-ice personalities. He matured into an engaging conversationalist and even a showman, celebrating his goals with a "guffaw" hand motion popularized in the 1980s by comedian Howie Mandel.

Ironically, the player who broke into the NHL like he was born to win became one of hockey's greatest bridesmaids. Propp played five times for the Cup—three with Philadelphia and once each for Boston and Minnesota—without success.

"I guess some people will look at what I've done and say I wasn't a winner," says Propp, now the operator of a rink in Medford, New Jersey. "But I don't understand that. There aren't many players who get to the finals, let alone as many times as I did.

"Some of the greatest players never had the experience of the playoff games we did for ten years. It was a given we were always going to be a good team. Except for winning the Cup, you can't ask for anything more than that."

Rick Tocchet's nose indicates what kind of player he was for seven-plus seasons in Philadelphia. There seems to be a bump on it for each time he pushed his team over the hump during three valiant chases for the Stanley Cup in the 1980s. Just like the right wing they gambled on in the sixth round of the 1983 draft, the Flyers usually got farther than expected.

The third son of first-generation northern Italian immigrants who settled in the east end of Toronto was a nice kid with a passion for all games and an ambition especially suited for one where the rules allowed players to knock each other down.

When his mom, Norma, wasn't busy listening to Rick say over and over again how he was going to make it in the NHL, she created spaghetti sauce so spectacular that her son had to learn the recipe to avoid the bogus stuff served in restaurants.

Rick's dad, Nat, worked in an auto body shop and made the best wine Terry Crisp, Rick's junior coach at Sault Ste. Marie, ever tasted. "Mr. Tocchet always had some for me, too," recalls Crisp, "and that helped put Rick on the power play, no secret to that."

Crisp almost committed the culinary and coaching mistakes of his life by cutting Tocchet at his first camp. Fortunately the kid got hurt and, when healed, began knocking down too many players to be sent home. Nevertheless, the coach believed Rick would become little more than a tough guy and grinder until his second junior season, when he began doing something with the pucks he was bringing out of the corners. The winger figured that every play brought him closer to his dream.

"I always wanted one chance to play one game in the NHL, just to prove I belonged," Tocchet recalls.

On draft day, Sam McMaster, the Sault GM, told Flyers' GM/coach Bob McCammon that the kid's rough edges would smooth out. They did, rapidly. Tocchet went from 66 points to 108 the season following his selection, which guaranteed him a significantly longer look than just one game. Paul Holmgren, the hard-rock right wing of the previous Philadelphia generation, had already

A hard-nosed kid with a special touch for scoring.

been traded to make room for Tocchet when he arrived in Voorhees for the 1984 training camp.

New coach Mike Keenan put the rookie on a checking line that outplayed the opposition's top units all the way to the 1985 finals. Rick recorded 14 goals during each of his first two seasons and was pegged to eventually level off at around 20. Still, trapped inside that checker's body was a scorer's soul screaming to be released. "I accepted the role they wanted me to fill," recalls Tocchet, "but I told Mike that I thought I could do more."

Keenan, already blessed with Tim Kerr and Ilkka Sinisalo on right wing, filed Tocchet's confidence away for a rainy day. It came in the 1987 playoffs, as Kerr's shoulder gradually separated until he had to come out of the lineup. Tocchet stepped up with five goals in the Rangers series and two winners during the semifinals against Montreal. He finished the postseason with 11 as the Flyers came within one game of winning the Cup.

That fall, Keenan picked Tocchet for the Canadian team in the Canada Cup tournament and the winger proved himself capable of competing with the best players in the world. After sitting out the second contest of the three-game final against the Soviets with a bad knee, then begging Dr. John Gregg to dress for the finale, Rick scored to start his team out of its 3-0 hole and toward the championship of the greatest series ever played.

Tocchet's confidence surged. In 1987-88, he got 31 goals and established himself among the best right wings in the game, not merely the toughest. By 1988-89, Rick increased his total to 45 for coach Paul Holmgren and become the Flyers' best player as the bodies of Mark Howe, Tim Kerr and Ron Hextall began to break down.

The decline of the team, however, caused both the organization and Tocchet to confuse his proper role. For lack of a creative, 100-point performer, a player who had never reached 50 goals in a season became cast as the club's scoring star.

Holmgren, afraid of disillusioning Tocchet by passing over him for the captaincy, gave him the title for the 1991-92 season. When Rick got off to a bad scoring start, the additional leadership duties became his albatross. He grew bitter when singled out for the performance of a poor team he was incapable of carrying.

When he did not respond to coach Bill Dineen's attempts to boost his spirit, GM Russ Farwell traded Tocchet to Pittsburgh in a multiplayer deal that brought right wing Mark Recchi, four years younger and a better playmaker.

It was an unfortunate bitter end to what had been a perfect marriage of athlete and organization. Tocchet won a Cup with the Penguins and has moved on to productive years in Los Angeles and Boston with the character and skills developed in Philadelphia.

"He's a self-made player who deserves everything he's gotten," Keenan once praised. Included is the right to be recognized as a hard worker and clutch performer who reinforced what being a Flyer has traditionally been about.

Bobby Clarke always said that Brad Marsh's basic problem was his feet were as big as his heart. For seven largely happy and successful seasons in black and orange, Marsh used every ounce of strength from his helmetless head to his webbed toes to throw himself in front of shots, maul forwards, hug Philadelphia's goalies and make you care about the Flyers almost as much as he did.

None of the eight arms or sixteen hands he would place upon opponents proved useful on the rare occasions when Marsh would get into scoring position. But this ugly duckling of a player's lack of skill for the game only made his passion for it that much more endearing.

"When [the fans] see me out there, they see themselves playing on Sunday afternoon for their company team," Marsh once said. More than that, they saw a guy who only lit 23 red bulbs over 15 NHL seasons unfailingly illuminate the Spectrum with his enthusiasm. Whatever Marsh lacked in talent, he more than made up in people skills. When Miro Dvorak, the first European Flyer, came to training camp in 1982, Marsh put one of his ever-clutching-and-grabbing paws around the veteran Czech star's shoulder. For his three years in North America, Dvorak was never alone.

"Everybody would say I was a good guy for taking him everywhere," Marsh said. "But what it gets down to is I like him."

Marsh was also so fond of Pelle Lindbergh that six weeks after the goalie's death, he and wife Patty named their newborn son Erik, after Per-Erik. "It just seemed right," said Marsh.

Patty came from a family of eleven kids, most of them musicians, many of whom joined their father in the Quaker City String Band. In Philadelphia, that is about as down-home as one can get, so it wasn't surprising when Patty picked a husband absolutely without pretense or hidden agenda. Ten years into his NHL career, Marsh still was driving a truck with 185,000 miles on the odometer and wearing an old London Knights jacket that had been chewed around the collar by Ernie, his Rottweiler.

Atlanta made Marsh its first-round choice in 1978 and he became captain at age 22. In 1981, he was traded to the Flyers for Mel Bridgman because the Flames were convinced the defenseman had become a bassett in a game increasingly dominated by greyhounds. Marsh more than survived the sport's metamorphosis.

Helmetless Marsh was the goaltenders' fearless friend.

He thrived because he had so many of the qualities of his beloved dogs. Brad guarded his goalie with the fierceness of a trained German shepherd, yet interacted with his teammates like a friendly retriever.

The last guy away from the netminder before the face-off, Marsh would be the first to congratulate him at the buzzer, moving faster, it seemed, than at any point during the game. "If [my speed] was that bad, I would have been beaten to a lot more icings," he once said. "I just look big and clumsy, like a big oaf out there."

But a durable oaf, nonetheless. Challenged by Mike Keenan and assistant coach Ted Sator, to improve his conditioning, Marsh's pride and stamina grew. He thrived in Keenan's four-man rotation, reveled in the team's success over the next four years, and watched with considerable satisfaction as the ten players drafted ahead of him faded from the game.

When the NHL grandfathered a rule requiring helmets, Marsh was determined to be the last bareheaded player in the league. He paid a price for his stubbornness in December 1987 when a Ray Bourque–Cam Neely double-team check inadvertently smacked his skull against a Spectrum glass support. Marsh returned nine days later with reflexes still slowed by the trauma. Keenan cut the defenseman's ice time drastically, although for lack of anybody better, he was used regularly in the playoffs.

When the Flyers went down in the first round, Keenan was out. So was Brad the following year as GM Clarke, determined to make the defense younger, exposed Marsh in the waiver draft. He played four more seasons in Toronto, Detroit, Ottawa — for whom he now works as director of team and business development — and was loved in every city he played in, as fans recognized that what made Marsh so real was exactly what made him good.

The tears were barely dry when Ron Hextall miraculously appeared, like an even-up call from above. "You don't replace a Pelle Lindbergh," Bob Clarke said after the Flyers lost the reigning Vezina Trophy winner to an automobile accident. Yet there was one season later, Ron Hextall, a big (6-3, 192), quick, colorful, innovative, antagonistic and tireless 22-year-old rookie and sixth-round draft choice, who strapped Philadelphia to his back and carried it to within one game of the Stanley Cup.

The NHL had never seen anything like him. Hextall chopped at opponents' legs like young Abe Lincoln clearing a forest, played his stick against the goalposts like Lionel Hampton, and threw outlet passes like Kareem Abdul-Jabbar.

Grandpa (Hall of Famer Bryan Hextall Sr.) and Dad (Bryan Jr.) had been NHL centers, yet when young Ron watched his father practice, the kid's eyes were always focused on the keepers of the net. "Wouldn't you like to keep going?" his mother, Fay, asked whenever her roaming son had to stop at the red line—the goaltender's legal boundary. Resisting her wish that he become a defenseman, Hextall also turned a stone ear to the lectures from his Lady Byng–candidate grandfather who believed sticks were to be used on the puck, not against bodies.

Ron, however, was born with the feistiness of grandmother Gert and the drive of his hard-working journeyman father. The goalie's belligerence turned off as many talent evaluators as his 5.71 goals-against average when they dropped by Brandon, Manitoba, to watch him fight, a nightly battle for survival behind a bad junior team. "What I liked about him was what everybody else didn't," said Flyer scout Jerry Melnyk. "There were teams who thought he was loony."

Hextall refined his style but not his temper while working up from the low minors. Coach Mike Keenan, convinced Philadelphia needed an upgrade from Bob Froese, gave the rookie the same chance to run with the job that he had presented to Lindbergh two years earlier. Hextall opened the 1986-87 season against the Oilers at the Spectrum by stoning Wayne Gretzky on a breakaway and winning, 2-1. Ninety-two games and eight months later, he held off No. 99 and the greatest offensive machine in NHL history going into the fifty-seventh minute of the ultimate contest—Game 7 of the finals—until Glenn

Age has mellowed the fiercest goaltender in the league.

Anderson's goal put away a 3-1 win and the Cup.

That spring, when Hextall accepted the Vezina Trophy and announced he would try to become the best goalie ever, nobody laughed. He was never haunted by his declaration, even as expectations rose and the team in front of him declined. "I felt sorry for him," Mark Howe recalls, "because I knew no goalie could ever have a year like that again."

Ron struggled early in 1987-88 after serving an eight-game suspension for slashing Kent Nilsson during the finals. Then, after suffering an injury late in the season, he floundered during the Flyers' first-round loss to the Capitals. Nev-

ertheless Hextall, who became the first NHL goalie to ever shoot and score on December 8, 1987, still was named the team's MVP.

The following year he won the Bob Clarke Trophy for the third consecutive time and avenged the loss to Washington with an excellent performance. But his backup, Ken Wregget, became the hero of the semifinals when he stepped in for a gimpy Hextall and stoned the Penguins in Game 7 at Pittsburgh. Although Ron was back by Game 4 of the Montreal series, he was unable to turn either the tide or the other cheek when he had a chance to avenge a Chris Chelios' elbow that had sent Brian Propp to the hospital in Game 1. In the final seconds of the Canadiens' clinching victory, Hextall took the law into his own hands and his blocker to Chelios's head.

The goalie earned a 12-game suspension and more public scorn, neither of which discouraged him from asking the Flyers to renegotiate the eight-year contract (paid over twenty) that he had signed after his rookie season. When Clarke did not comply, Hextall hired the contentious Rich Winter as his agent and refused to report to training camp.

After being coaxed back in late October, Ron suffered repeated groin and hamstring pulls that caused him to subconsciously change what had been a near-perfect style. The 1989-90 season was effectively ruined and the next two centered around Hextall's up-and-down struggle to restore his lost promise.

The new, expensive contract the Flyers had begrudgingly given him, his inconsistency, and the organization's desire to make a new start punched the goaltender's ticket out of town in the Eric Lindros deal. Although Ron appeared to have found himself again during a strong regular season in Quebec, he suffered a poor playoff, then another after a trade the following year to the Islanders. His career was at

a crossroads when Clarke, back with Philadelphia as president/GM after an exile he had blamed on Hextall's holdout and subsequent struggles, found the Islanders desperate to move the goalie and willing to take Tommy Soderstrom in return.

Coach Terry Murray kept a lid on expectations of the return by declaring Ron an upgrade, but no savior. The goalie's balance, his primary strength in 1987, was a memory, so Hextall worked to reduce his crouch and better distribute his weight. Murray urged the 31-year-old to conserve energy by eliminating many of his pregame superstitious rituals. The Flyers' increased scoring capacity extended their goaltender's margin for error and reduced the temptation to try too hard. He stood up much more and began putting up the best numbers of his career.

Ron went 17-9-4 with a 2.89 goals-against-average during the lockout-shortened 1995 season, followed by a record of 10-5, with a 2.81 GAA in the playoffs. In 1995-96, he was 31-13-7, 2.17, then 6-6, 2.13 in the postseason.

The numbers, however, did not fully measure Hextall's role in restoring passion to a reassembled young team as it emerged from a five-year journey through a losing wilderness. "He added a lot of the ingredients I thought were missing on the ice and in the dressing room," said Murray.

Hextall is not the slasher who appalled audiences in his first run. While no less competitive, he is more capable of channeling his emotions. In the past, Ron seemed to gain strength after giving up a goal, but the low-level rage with which he played tired him more than he would admit.

Whenever he struggled, his frustration proved self-defeating. "I get upset when we lose now," he says. "But I don't let yesterday's loss affect me for the next game. I have a better balance than in the old days."

Despite an early-career as a villain, Hextall was always a much different person off the ice. A devoted husband to Diane, a former competitive figure skater, and a doting father to four children, Ron was also an exemplary teammate. Not only did he save comrades steps by coming back for the puck, he spared them his anger. Hextall has yet to allow a goal that he did not consider to be primarily his fault.

He never held a grudge against the organization, either, even though he had felt misled and exploited by the club and his former agent, Alan Eagleson, into accepting the twenty-year deferment of a large portion of his salary. The new deal he had sought was only to the going rate in a rapidly escalating market. It was strictly business when he walked out in 1989 and, although it turned into bad business for both the team and player, his stand was unfortunately taken for disloyalty by Clarke and Jay Snider.

Once settled, it was water under the bridge to the fiercest troll in the NHL who, despite it all, never wanted to do anything but guard the Flyers' net. It was distressing for a goalie as combative and innovative as the franchise he represented to participate in its decline. Thus, it seems particularly appropriate to watch Philadelphia's passion rekindled by the ever-escaping heat from under Hextall's collar.

ric Lindros sat up when he was four months old. He walked at seven and a half months, skated when he was a year-and-a-half, rode a two-wheeled bike at age 3, and waterskiied at 5. His parents enrolled him in hockey for the first time because they needed to tire out a busy child.

Eric was always a load, even before he became a hulk, then matured into a package of power and finesse unlike any the NHL has seen in its history. At no point during his 23 years has he paused to be normal.

"It's almost unfair," says Ron Hextall. "There is no one who can physically challenge Eric. He's so big and strong and skilled, he can hurt you in so many ways. Punch him in the head and he might skate away and score on the power play. Or he might turn around and knock you down."

Lindros is a steamroller that can do designs. He uses his 229 pounds and long reach to shield a puck delivered off either forehand or backhand with a touch that belies his brute force. One of the best wrist shots in the game rises from one of its quickest releases, and his vision of the ice and sense of anticipation, always above average, become more refined by the season.

"The guy," Craig MacTavish once said, "is just an absolute hockey machine."

After five years in the shop for major repairs, the Flyers are tooling along again, led by a player who is delivering on one of the most demanding warranties in sports history. Eric's mother, Bonnie, says she woke up in the middle of the night in a Buffalo hotel room trembling at the revelation that her 9-year-old, who had dominated a minor atom tournament that day, was extraordinary. "He wasn't even bigger than the other kids at that age," she recalls. "Just better." When Eric grew seven inches between age 13 and 14, the movers of the hockey world also began shaking like Mom.

At 16, Lindros was declared NHL-ready by Bobby Clarke in a *Sports Illustrated* profile. Eric became one of Canada's best-known athletes before he had performed in his first major junior contest, and the resulting obligations, pressures, and jealousies took away much from his teenage years.

Lindros was not allowed to have a bad game without being called overrated, or to play a good one without driving the unique standards to which he was being held even higher. The family's determination to plan Eric's development, both as a player and person, twice caused him to reject

The "absolute hockey machine" has the future in his hands.

drafts and became labeled as arrogant and selfish. But through painful times, he kept his feet on the ground and his heart in the right place, delivering on every level.

"I don't know any young player who could handle what Eric's handled so well," said Clarke. "He has no bitterness. Most of us would have come away scarred. But for all the demands put on him, how closely he's been watched, he's pretty uncomplicated. He just wants to play

hockey and enjoy his life."

Lindros was born in London, Ontario, where his father, Carl, had played football at the University of Western Ontario. When Eric was 9, his dad's accounting firm relocated the family to Toronto, where the backyard pool was removed so that Eric, younger brother Brett and sister Robin could have a skating rink.

Eric leaped to national attention on the celebrated Junior B team at St. Michael's College School. As he approached the Ontario Hockey League's draft age of 16, his parents, believing that his education would suffer, warned Sault Ste. Marie—the team with the first-overall pick—that they did not want him riding buses and planes to and from the league's most remote city.

When the Greyhounds called what they thought was a bluff and drafted Lindros anyway,

Eric boarded with a family in suburban Detroit, where he played in the top U.S. developmental league while completing high school and awaiting the trade of his OHL rights. They were acquired by Oshawa, forty-five minutes from Lindros's home, for three players, two draft picks and the unparalleled junior sum of $80,000. In one full season at Oshawa, Lindros scored 149 points in 57 games, added another 38 in 16 playoff matches and led the Generals to the OHL championship.

Quebec, where Lindros had no desire to play, made him the first pick in the 1991 NHL draft. He turned down a $50-million offer and spent the next year with Oshawa and three different Canadian national teams, including the Canada Cup club comprised of the top professionals. Lindros sparkled among established stars as Canada won the tournament, driving the desirability of the NHL's most-awaited prospect since Mario Lemieux to an unprecedented level.

At the 1992 draft, Quebec president Marcel Aubut conducted a frantic auction of Lindros's rights that led both the Flyers and Rangers to believe they had acquired the future megastar. League-appointed arbitrator Larry Bertuzzi validated Philadelphia's claim that it had made its deal first. In exchange for six players, two draft choices and $15 million, Lindros became a Flyer.

Already the highest-paid player in the league before putting on an NHL uniform, he was expected to make an instant impact on the stripped-down team that had acquired him. As always, he came through. Despite missing 23 and 19 games with knee injuries in his first two seasons, Lindros still scored 75 and 97 points, respectively.

In his third year, the defense-stabilizing acquisition of Eric Desjardins, and the addition of John LeClair to Philadelphia's top line with Lindros and Mikael Renberg, ended the losing. As the team emerged, so did Lindros, as both league MVP and a contented Flyer.

"I don't have my back up as much because people are not down my throat every time I turn a corner," he said.

Eric has benefited from associating with role models like Bob Clarke and Craig MacTavish, the veteran center acquired in July 1994 largely to set an example. As the few pre-Lindros Flyers moved on, the captaincy bestowed upon Eric at age 21 gave him official license to lead. After four years in the NHL, he has learned to concentrate more fully from night to night, as well as to safely

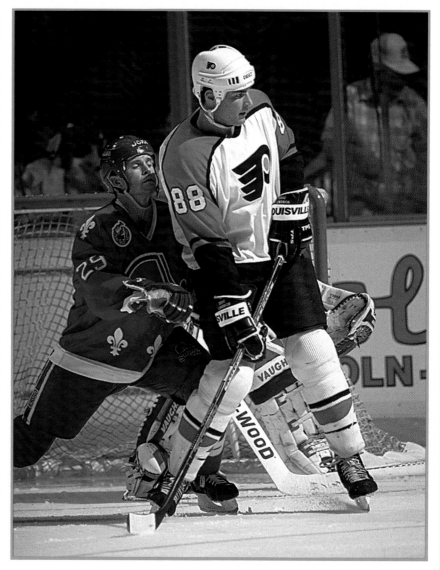

and effectively maximize his physical assets.

"My body can't go through the abuse I was giving it the first year or two," he says. "You can't just charge into the opponent's zone like a bull in a china shop, trying to cause havoc for fifteen years.

"The acquisition of John LeClair saved my career. I've got two big wingers with speed in addition to size, so I don't have to be as physical. I think I have the best job in hockey right now."

The choice seat in any NHL arena might be at the CoreStates Center, watching Lindros climb towards his peak. "What makes the best players great is that they don't accept anybody else's standards," says Flyers' coach Terry Murray. "They just keep on striving to be the best.

"One of the things that makes him truly great is that he's unpredictable. There are no patterns. He's also unselfish and that's really why his teammates love him. He's just one of the guys. He's got a half-ton truck. He's got a dog (a Great Dane named Bacchus). He's just so much like Clarkie, it's unbelievable."

That makes Lindros a perfect leadership fit for a franchise that risked the biggest trade in hockey history to restore its lost identity. As high as Philadelphia's expectations were, they were only the same as Eric's, which made the wedding perfect and the happily ever after intriguing.

t took a big man from the Green Mountain State of Vermont to get the Flyers out of a valley they had been wandering in for five years.

Ironic, considering Philadelphia traded for John LeClair with full knowledge that he might never amount to a hill of beans as a goal scorer. On February 9, 1995—the day the suffering stopped—president/GM Bob Clarke believed he was dealing Mark Recchi to Montreal for all-around defenseman Eric Desjardins plus a left wing of size (6-2, 215) and grit in LeClair. Basically, John was acquired to fortify Eric Lindros's line and perhaps score 25 goals.

"I thought he was a checker," said Clarke, who had every reason to feel as if his bank statement showed a higher balance than the checkbook. LeClair got 51 goals in 1995-96 and became an All-Star, an incredible achievement for a guy whose best previous performance had been 19 in a season with the Canadiens.

"They expected me to score more than 20 in Montreal, but I really was doing the best I had in me," he recalls. The lack of production, however, did not compute with the strength and skill LeClair had displayed to the world in recording two overtime winners during the 1993 Stanley Cup finals, when Canadiens' coach Jacques Demers announced him as the next Kevin Stevens.

"If you know Jacques, he says a lot of things," said LeClair. Indeed, Demers is almost as colorful as the multitude of swatches found at the paint store John's father manages in St. Albans, Vermont, but the winger's career had gone gray and his mood was turning increasingly black before being rejuvenated by the trade to Philadelphia.

Not only did it turn out to be the biggest thing to ever happen to LeClair, but practically the greatest event in his state since Ethan Allen and his linemates forechecked Fort Ticonderoga during the Revolutionary War.

The hockey culture gets clearance through customs to St. Albans, a community of 10,000

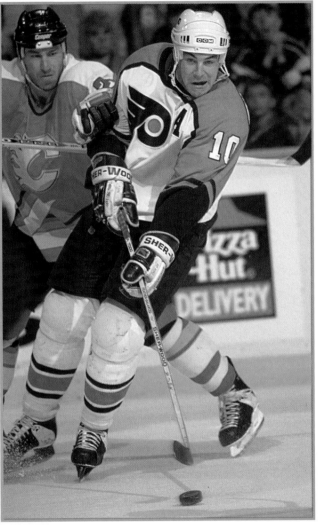

After a 51-goal season LeClair's offensive promise was realized.

residents only an hour from the Canadian border. John played soccer and baseball growing up, but at Bellows Free Academy the players on the ice received the most recognition. A state championship in LeClair's senior year helped relay word of his prowess to Boston and its high-powered NCAA programs. But a kid so low-key that he didn't drive the two hours to Montreal for his draft day in 1987, decided instead to attend the University of Vermont.

LeClair was taken thirty-third overall by the Canadiens before going off to campus. Underwhelmed by his own promise, he was surprised when Montreal approached him before his junior year about turning pro. "They really want me to play for them?" he thought.

While the Canadiens waited for John to complete his four seasons of eligibility, the goal-scoring touch had developed. As a senior, he recorded 25 in 33 games. But in the pros, he lost his balance too easily when hit and he fought the puck during long slumps. An attempted move to center was on its way to failure when he was rescued by the trade.

Since then it has been hard to tell whether Lindros has helped LeClair more than vice versa, but John has been too busy going to the net to waste time figuring it out. While not a punishing hitter, he is excellent at keeping the puck alive along the boards for Eric and Mikael Renberg. Eventually, opponents sag from having 652 pounds of forward line leaning on them.

"I don't know if it's all strength," LeClair says. "There are a lot of defensemen in the league who are stronger than I am. But I'm really getting in better position."

"The first thing John said [to me] when he came to town was, 'I'll take myself out of the play to allow you to come out in front of the net,'" recalls Lindros. "John will give himself up as a pick to make a play in the offensive zone. And his shot—he has a hammer. I think that's what surprised some of us. He can really bring it."

LeClair always could, which makes one wonder why his offensive promise remained dormant with the Canadiens. "In Montreal, the style we played was so defensive, I didn't get many open chances," he said. "We won a Cup, so that's not a complaint. I'm just saying that's why I didn't score much there.

"But never did I think I would score 51 goals. I'm just glad to know that all those people who always said I had potential were right."

Statues of Rod Brind'Amour can be seen throughout Athens. Years of weight training have given him the physique of a Greek god. And every coach Brind'-Amour ever had has wanted to mount his work ethic on a pedestal.

When Rod was 10 years old and a scrawny, two-time hockey dropout, his father, Bob, started him on ten-minute weight workouts that became a habit and grew into an obsession. A sixty-minute game has become a warmup for the session that follows.

Brind'Amour is rarely seen not dripping sweat, but when the Flyers hand him his paycheck they never have reason to feel soaked. He is dedicated and well-rounded in every skill except for one—the ability to put a bad game behind him and move on to the next one. At times, his hands have become as tight as the skin across his body, and finding the right linemates and position for the center/left wing has been an ongoing process.

Nonetheless, he has averaged more than a point a game for the Flyers even though scoring has never been his primary desire. In his last contract, Brind'Amour did not ask for bonuses for individual points. "I don't want to worry about stuff like that," he said. "If the team wins, I'll sleep at night."

His intensity has cost him more than a few winks, but rarely any ice time. Iron Rod has missed only three games in five Philadelphia seasons. "He's like a machine," defenseman Karl Dykhuis says. "He just keeps going. Penalty killing, power plays, five-on-five. Whenever you need an important face-off in the last minute of a game, he's out there."

Brind'Amour was born in Ottawa, but his family moved to Campbell River, British Columbia, when he was young. At age 15, he left home to attend the noted Notre Dame College in Wilcox, Saskatchewan, where he helped the Hounds to a national midget championship and earned a place on Canada's team with college-aged players competing at the Spengler Cup (world university) Tournament in Davos, Switzerland. When Canada took first place, a Swiss businessman bought the club a $1,000 bottle of champagne. Rod quietly sat drinking milk.

After St. Louis made him the ninth-overall choice in the 1988 entry draft, Brind'Amour played only one season at Michigan State, scoring 59 points in 42 games. "He was the most

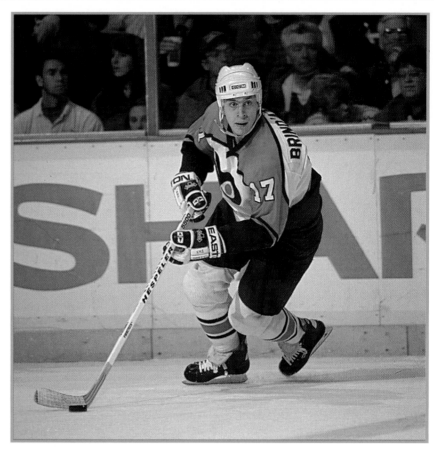

"I don't worry about bonuses. If the team wins, I'll sleep at night."

mature freshman I've ever had," said coach Ron Mason.

The Blues also praised Rod for his dedication during a 61-point rookie year, but began to see his devotion as fanaticism when he regressed by 12 points the following season. They saw him fighting long slumps by spending more time in the workout room and started to believe he was getting muscle-bound in the head.

Even the perpetually uptight St. Louis coach, Brian Sutter, thought Brind'Amour needed to lighten up. When the Blues signed free agent Brendan Shanahan, Rod and goaltender Curtis Joseph were offered as the compensation. Instead, Judge Edward Houston, the NHL-appointed arbitrator, awarded Scott Stevens to New

Jersey, leaving a big hole in St. Louis's defense as well as in the egos of two players. Flyers' GM Russ Farwell, who had been told Brind'Amour was untouchable a year earlier, tried again in September 1991, and GM Ron Caron accepted Ron Sutter—his coach's brother—and defenseman Murray Baron in trade.

Although the Flyers were several years from contention, Rod was happy to be where he was wanted and responded with 77 points in 80 games as the team's top center. When the Nordiques asked for everything short of Elfreth's Alley in the Lindros deal, Farwell and Jay Snider drew the line at Brind'Amour and Mark Recchi.

Before the arrival of John LeClair, Rod spent the second half of the 1993-94 season as Lindros' left wing and scored 97 points. The acquisition of Dale Hawerchuk moved Brind'Amour to the left side again, where the coaching staff feels he has been most effective.

Although preferring to play center, the club's most versatile member doesn't sweat the small stuff as long as he is perspiring someplace for the greater good of his team.

nyone still babbling the traditional nonsense about European players lacking gumption gets backed into a corner every time Mikael Renberg goes into one. Take it from the defensemen who play against him—there is no escaping this Swede's resolve.

Instead, we have a stereotype that works. Renberg is a classic, gritty Philadelphia winger right off the same assembly line that produced Gary Dornhoefer, Paul Holmgren and Rick Tocchet.

The newest model might be the deluxe one, too. Renberg is big (6-2, 218), unselfish, humble and, after only three NHL seasons, among the best players at his position in the league. He has all the traditional Scandinavian puck skills and is rapidly developing into one of the better packages ever to come in the plain brown wrapper of a fortieth overall (1990) pick.

Weighing less than 190 pounds when the Flyers selected him, Mikael needed only to add bulk, not courage. "I always felt I'd do better in the NHL than in Europe because over there they sometimes play around with the puck too much, just waiting for the big chance," he said. "Here, we shoot more, go to the net more, go after rebounds more. I like this way better."

For thirty years, so has Philadelphia, a city that discriminates against lazy, timid players regardless of nationality. A Flyers fan doesn't check green cards, only red lights, and Renberg has turned on the town with his willingness to do the little things that turn into big goals.

"He's a complete player," said Flyers' coach Terry Murray. "I have a lot of confidence in him defensively. On offense, one of the strengths he has is skating away from the puck, finding the seams, getting open.

"The defensemen have to back up to respect his speed, but his straight-ahead skating ability still isn't Mikael's main asset. He skates laterally so well to buy time, and when he finally makes a move, the defenseman might not adjust."

Bo Renberg's game was soccer, but he didn't

Renberg has Dornhoefer's grit with size and a flair for scoring.

kick when his only son turned to hockey. Dad ran a gas station in Pitea, a town of 20,000 in northern Sweden, where he pumped fuel into Volvos and sound values into Mikael and two daughters.

"I know that I'm not going to play good every game," said Renberg. "But at least I can work. You get nothing for free. You have to work for your chances."

The Flyers once tried to hand the right wing an opportunity before he was ready for it and got a "no thank-you." Depleted by the Eric Lindros trade and desperate to fill its holes, the organization had offered Mikael a contract for the 1992-93 season, but he chose to stay an additional year in the Swedish Elite League. "I wanted to be ready," he said. "Playing in the NHL has always been my dream and I had to make sure I was in the right condition."

When Renberg signed before the fall of 1993, it was immediately obvious that he was physically and mentally prepared. "I knew after I got drafted what happened to the Flyers," he said. "For years they missed the playoffs, so I knew I was coming to a team where I'd have a chance to play."

He was impressive from his initial scrimmage and coach Terry Simpson recognized the real thing when he saw it. "He'll play the same once the season starts," predicted Simpson.

Renberg actually proved a little slow out of the gate, but broke team rookie scoring records with and 82 points. Returning for his second year, Mikael pretended he was a rookie again to make sure he didn't get lazy, and with 57 points in the lockout-shortened 48-game season, seemed to convince himself.

Among Renberg's many gifts is the ability to recognize how fortunate he has been to land on an up-and-coming team with two of the best players in the game: Eric Lindros and John LeClair. "We're three big guys and we give each other a lot of space to do things," Renberg said.

After missing 30 of the last 36 contests in 1995-96 with a pelvic strain that defied rest and treatment, Renberg scored three times and had 9 points in 11 playoff matches despite rusty hands and a pulling sensation in his midsection. The problem was corrected with surgery during the summer, leading one to believe that the 87 goals he recorded in 181 Flyer games have been a mere warmup.

Continued from page 186
ever. And if I had my choice, I'd love to do it all over again."

"That ovation sent chills down my spine," said Craven who, along with other wide-eyed Flyers, provided Clarke with the best gift of all, a 6-1 victory. "It was like we were meant to win," said Poulin. Unfortunately, the new captain's personal destiny included a groin pull, putting him on the injured list with two other centers, Zezel and Hachborn.

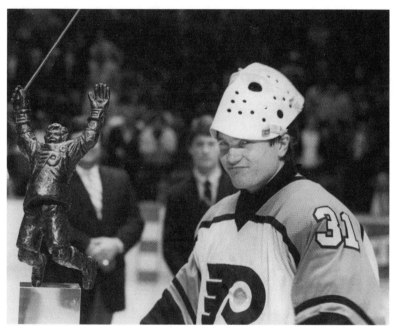

Keenan moved Craven over from the wing and double-shifted him. He contributed an excellent defensive job and the clinching goal in a 5-3 victory at Boston. The Sutter twins and Carson were also performing well in almost every game against their opposition's top line.

The young forwards, however, were not the only keys to Philadelphia's fast start. Marsh, no longer backing in, was clearing traffic and blocking shots. Brad McCrimmon, after ending a failed marriage, had restored his focus and elevated his play. The Beast, so nicknamed by teammates, was paired with Howe for twelve minutes of the third period as the club nursed a one-goal lead into a 4-2 victory in Buffalo on November 23. Eriksson, Dvorak and Doug Crossman had not gained Keenan's confidence and were spotted, but Hospodar responded to regular shifts with the best play of his career.

While amazing themselves, the Flyers also impressed the NHL. "Lindbergh's a little guy, but he looks as big as a house right now," said the Sabres' Craig Ramsay. "They're forcing you at every turn, and even with that kind of pressure, they're not giving you the three-on-twos and two-on-ones."

When Rich Sutter sustained a bruised shoulder, Tocchet was moved from the fourth to the third line and produced a pair of goals as Philadelphia rallied twice from two-goal deficits for a 4-4 tie in Hartford.

The Rangers jumped to a 1-0 lead on Jan Erixon's goal after only 21 seconds but, with Zezel returning to the lineup, the Flyers roared back to win, 6-2. "They were really psyched to play and we just totally shut them down," gushed Marsh as his team ran its record to 16-4-4.

Finally, they stumbled. Lindbergh, yanked after giving up four goals on December 11 at Winnipeg, had to go back in when Froese suffered a knee-ligament strain and surrendered the winning goal in overtime. Tocchet was on the ice for the first four in a five-goal Islander first period of a 6-2 loss at Uniondale, then missed his man on the game-winner as Philadelphia lost 3-2 to Montreal at the Spectrum.

Keenan took responsibility for poor preparation in the Islander debacle, but when Poulin gave up the puck, Propp was trapped and the Penguins' John Chabot blew a savable 40-footer between Lindbergh's pads for the winning goal in a 4-2 loss at Pittsburgh on December 21, the Flyer coach ripped away publicly for the first time. "You don't expect veterans to make a mistake like that," he said. "And if you want a comment on the goaltending, theirs played better than ours."

Kerr's hat trick spurred a 7-4 Spectrum victory over the Caps, who were neck-and-neck with Philadelphia for the division lead, and the delighted Flyers reported the next morning for a Christmas Eve practice and their traditional exchange of gag gifts and eggnog. Keenan played Scrooge, punishing them with a bewilderingly exhausting practice.

"I had pre-identified it as a conditioning day," re-

Pelle Lindbergh, the first winner of the Bobby Clarke Trophy as team MVP.

calls Keenan, "but we were starting to get noticed and I also wanted to reinforce the idea that expectations had been raised."

Indeed, Washington was psyched for the rematch three days later at the Capital Center, sending Philadelphia down to its 6th loss in 8 games, 6-0. "No Bobby Clarke," said Keenan, "no leadership." No Ray Allison, either, as the veteran right wing was farmed to Hershey.

On the strength of Carson's hat trick, the Flyers

Ron Sutter averaged 118 penalty minutes in each of his first three complete seasons.

bounced back to win in Vancouver, 7-4. And although Howe went out with a bruised knee in Inglewood, Lindbergh snapped back to form in a 3-2 victory. "I can't deny I wanted this one very much," said Pat Quinn, the Kings' new coach. Not half as much as the Philadelphia players had hoped to spend New Year's Eve in Los Angeles. But because Keenan desired a day without travel before the January 2 game in Edmonton, the Flyers rang in 1985 at Goose Loonies, a night spot in the cold north.

Keenan began the party by bringing a cigar onto the team bus, where smoking normally was punishable by death. He sat down next to Dvorak, a longtime chimney. "I bet you wish you had a cigarette," Keenan teased. When Dvorak opened his coat and showed the coach a whole carton, the bus roared. "I think it was the first time the players saw me laugh," Keenan recalls.

The coach's sense of intuition continued to prove better than even his sense of humor. In Edmonton,

Keenan moved Poulin to left wing, hoping to get his slow-starting captain untracked, and put Craven back at center. Poof. Craven set up three goals in a 5-2 victory, Philadelphia's second straight win over the champions. "Brad McCrimmon played a tremendous game," marveled Wayne Gretzky. "I couldn't get the puck to Jari (Kurri) all night."

Twenty-four hours later in Calgary, Howe returned on cortisone and Ron Sutter played heroically as the Flyers turned a 3-1 deficit into a 3-3 third-period tie. But Hakan Loob batted a deflected puck out of the air, giving Philadelphia a 4-3 loss that seemed unlucky to everyone but the demanding coach. "[The winning goal] wasn't completely undeserved," snapped Keenan. "Crossman gave the puck away. Kerr didn't do a thing for us."

He did in St. Louis, bouncing back for two goals in a 6-3 victory that closed a 4-2 trip. The Flyers were again tied for first place with Washington.

When Hachborn suffered a shoulder separation, the team recalled Todd Bergen. Poulin scored a goal and three assists, including setups of Bergen's first two NHL goals, in a 5-3 Spectrum victory over Vancouver. The rookie played again in a 6-1 romp over Chicago, then complained of pain in his abdomen. When tests failed to diagnose a problem, he was returned to Hershey.

Philadelphia, leading 3-2 at Uniondale with 3:15 remaining, lost both the game, 4-3, and Howe, when a Mike Bossy hit into the boards caused a cartilage tear near the Flyer's clavicle. His absence began to show. The Kings snapped a 0-17-4 Forum winless streak against Philadelphia with a 6-3 victory. As the Jets completed a three-game sweep of their season series with a 6-2 triumph in Winnipeg, Keenan lost confidence in Dvorak. The coach also found Crossman devoid of energy and detected little pulse from Eriksson. "Crossman and Eriksson simply need to improve at taking people out," he said. Keenan gave up trying to find ice time for Rich Sutter, who was sent to Hershey. "We waited because we were worried how it would affect Ron," Clarke told reporters.

The Flyers beat New Jersey 3-1 at the Spectrum on January 31, but needlessly lost McCrimmon. When he swiped the puck from Kerr during a pre-game drill, the winger took a frustrated swing with his stick and broke the defenseman's finger. Keenan, ever the control freak, was surprisingly unperturbed by the senseless injury. "These things happen," he said.

"Predictably unpredictable," was how the coach described himself. Indeed, with Froese still recuperating, Lindbergh played 24 straight games before Keenan curiously decided to give him the night off in, of all places, Uniondale. Philadelphia called up Darren Jensen, a free agent McCammon had recruited out of the IHL the previous spring, and the rookie lost 7-5, wasting Ilkka Sinisalo's hat trick.

Howe was back, but short of breath, as the Flyers' 4-0 lead turned into a 4-4 tie with Los Angeles at an unsettled Spectrum. Philadelphia was 12-12-2 since December 8, but Keenan was amazingly understanding. "We've been without key players and it all adds up," he said. "I do see signs of us starting to pay attention to details again."

The Flyers were eleven points behind Washington when they went to Landover on February 9. Despite the third four-goal game of the season by Kerr, the Capitals came back to force 3-3 and 4-4 ties. But in the final minute, Poulin and Propp worked the puck free from a goalmouth scramble and, as Poulin fell and tied up the sticks of Rod Langway and Darren Veitch, Howe threw the puck across the goalmouth. Propp scored the stunning winner at 19:58.

A 3-2 Spectrum victory followed over the struggling Rangers, whose GM, Craig Patrick, had gone behind the bench after firing Herb Brooks three weeks earlier. "I'm especially happy because all of us play really bad against the Rangers," said Lindbergh.

When Howe re-aggravated his torn cartilage, Marsh was chosen as a substitute for the All-Star Game. Unfortunately, his connecting flight in Toronto was snowbound and the Flyer did not make it to Calgary. Lindbergh, however, was present to confront a bad memory, his embarrassment by Gretzky two years earlier at Uniondale. This time, the goalie stopped four of five shots by No. 99 during the Wales Conference's 6-4 victory. Afterwards, the Great One noted that the Oilers had not beaten Philadelphia since Lindbergh's debacle. Four days later, Edmonton failed again, 5-4, at the Spectrum.

Froese returned from a conditioning stint in Hershey with an 8-2 Spectrum triumph over Pittsburgh, enabling the Flyers to creep within three points of Washington. Rich Sutter also was recalled and Poulin, coming on strong, had a goal and assist in a 4-1 Spectrum win over Calgary. "I think I was trying to keep everybody happy and not worrying enough about myself," said the first-year captain. Soon, consecutive losses at Boston, Quebec and New Jersey had the whole team fretting. The next three contests—at Long Island, and home-and-home with Washington—would be critical to the quest for first place.

The Islanders were eleven points behind the second-place Flyers and showing signs of age. But they had beaten Philadelphia three straight times and dwarfed Keenan's kids in big-game experience. The ex-champs scored twice in the third period to wipe out a 3-1 deficit. Even after the Flyers received a huge break when Carson's lob from the corner with 1:35 to play was misplayed into the net by goalie Kelly Hrudey, New York came right back. With Hrudey pulled, Bryan Trottier beat Kerr on a face-off and Bossy put in a rebound to tie the game, 4-4.

Just when it seemed like the old tortoises had again outfoxed the young hares, Propp picked up a broken pass and hit Poulin as he got a step on defenseman Paul Boutilier. The Flyer captain went in alone and stuck a wrist shot by Hrudey's stick side at 2:18 of overtime to give Philadelphia a thrilling 5-4 victory over a team that for four years had been impervious to failure in the clutch. "A win like that is invaluable," said Poulin.

Two nights later, the Flyers took the Spectrum ice against Washington with the confidence of a first-place team. After Caps goalie Pat Riggin gratuitously hung Zezel with a high-stick on Philadelphia's first possession, Kerr scored on the power play and Poulin cashed a Larry Murphy giveaway. Just as abruptly, Washington turned the game around, victimizing a shaky Froese with four straight goals. But Craig Laughlin quickly coughed up a windaround and Kerr scored his 50th goal of the season. He finished with Nos. 51 and 52 as the Flyers roared back for a free-wheeling 9-6 victory.

The following night in Landover, Kerr left the game with a sprained knee and McCrimmon was tossed for being the third man into an altercation. Nevertheless, Smith scored a goal and assist, lifting Philadelphia to a solid 4-2 victory. "It was the kind of game where you had to fight for every foot of space," said Rod Langway. "You had to be impressed with what the Flyers did."

Certainly the Spectrum fans were appreciative, giving their team a standing ovation when it came out against the Penguins two nights later. Kerr, saved from season-ending knee damage by the brace he had been wearing, would be out two weeks, but Philadelphia continued its surge without him. Bergen, back from Hershey and rehab for what was believed to have been a stomach muscle problem, scored a goal and Tocchet had four assists in an 11-4 rout that put the Flyers two points ahead of Washington. "We were lower than bleep when we took that bus ride to Long Island Monday night," said Marsh. "Boy, in your wildest dreams you never expected us to be sitting where we are right now."

Just before the March 12 deadline to set playoff rosters, Keenan urged his GM to sign himself to a playing contract. "It would have been great for my ego," recalls Clarke, "but when it's over, it's over." Instead of acquiring himself, he took a third-round pick from Vancouver for Cochrane.

Clarke had no reason for further changes. Philadelphia smoked the Rangers, 5-2, at Madison Square Garden and the Islanders, 5-3, at the Spectrum. "It doesn't seem to matter who's out there for them," marveled Trottier. "Every line keeps coming at you at the same pace. The only one who clutches and grabs now is Marsh. They aren't a dirty team anymore."

By March 21, the Caps had faded eight points behind, so Keenan began looking at Edmonton's schedule to ponder the Flyers' chances for a first-overall finish. "We're only four points back; we have a game in hand on them," he said. "If we're close, I'd like to go for it."

Kerr returned after 4 games and Crossman, used in a four-man rotation with Marsh, McCrimmon and Howe, responded well to the ice time. Philadelphia came from behind for 5-3 road victories at Pittsburgh and New Jersey and beat the Canadiens 4-3 at the Spectrum on Sinisalo's goal with 38 seconds remaining.

An 11-game winning streak ended with a 5-2 loss to the fired-up Blackhawks in Chicago. Keenan, never satisfied, unloaded on his players, who climbed all over Detroit the following night as they attempted to wrap up the division title. Goalie Corrado Micalef kept the game tied 1-1 into the third, until the Spectrum crowd rose in encouragement, Ron Sutter won a face-off and Smith put in Howe's rebound. Bergen walked out of the corner to score an insurance goal and the fans stood to count down the final happy seconds. The Flyers, eleven points behind on February

9, were ten ahead when they clinched their eighth division title in eighteen seasons.

"We're not drinking champagne tonight because this is just one step toward a larger goal," said Keenan. "Beer would be okay."

With another first-round series against the Rangers looming, Philadelphia completed its 7-game sweep of the season series by winning 2-1 on April 2 at New York. "They obviously have a lot of confidence, but that can shatter," said Anders Hedberg. "What if we win the first game?"

The Flyers had raced down the stretch like their streak of 9 straight playoff losses was ancient history. They won 16 of their last 17 games, finished with 53 victories and 113 points, claimed the Patrick Division by twelve and passed Edmonton to grab the overall points title by four. After being honored at the innaugural Bobby Clarke Trophy presentation as Flyer MVP, then shutting out the Islanders 3-0 in the home finale, Lindbergh was asked if the team's spectacular season seemed too good to be true. "No," he said. "Last year was too bad to be true."

Still, as bulletproof as the club's performance seemed, its players remained almost an entire generation removed from postseason success. Only Propp, Kerr and Eriksson had captured a playoff series in a Philadelphia uniform. Crossman, Marsh, McCrimmon and Hospodar had won rounds with other NHL teams.

"You know what I remember most about my four years here?" said Marsh the day before Game 1. "Not all the [regular-season] games we've won, but the feeling I had each year sitting in the locker room after we were eliminated. I want to erase that."

It didn't figure to be hard. In NHL history, only the 1977-78 Colorado Rockies had made the playoffs with a record worse than the Rangers' 26-44-10. But New York had lost so much that it went into the tournament with nothing to lose, unlike the Flyers. When Keenan walked into his locker room before the opener, he was shocked to find his team suddenly petrified.

"I could feel the nervousness," he recalls. "After all we had accomplished, as strongly as we had finished, they weren't sure they could win. I hadn't gone through those negative experiences with them, so I was really taken aback by it."

Fortunately, Game 1 at the Spectrum broke like regular-season clockwork for the orange. The disorganized Rangers gave up three odd-man rushes in the first seven minutes and Sutter put one of them off goalie Glen Hanlon's pads for a 1-0 lead. Bergen's 55-footer deflected off the stick of defenseman Grant

Ledyard and hit the top corner, and McCrimmon finished off a three-on-two from Propp and Poulin.

"It was 3-0 early, too early," recalls McGuire. "We started playing not to lose." After Kerr fumbled three excellent chances in the next ten minutes, Reijo Ruotsalainen's point drive went in off Sinisalo's stick. Lindbergh then lost sight of a shot that Marsh had blocked and Don Maloney put a flutterball into the unprotected net. At 1:17 of the third, Lindbergh bought Maloney's move after the veteran Flyer-killer had pounced on a rebound and New York had wiped out the lead.

Philadelphia promptly got back a goal as Bergen stole the puck from Hanlon, who had wandered almost to the corner, and fed Kerr for a gimme. "It helped," he said. "I was really fighting it out there." Reenergized, the team checked strongly. But when Sutter hit the crossbar with 3:20 remaining, the resultant clang was the chime of doom.

In the final minute, with Poulin trapped, the Rangers got one more rush. Marsh broke up Ledyard's centering attempt but Poulin, who had hustled back into the play, turned the wrong way looking for the puck. Hedberg jumped into the slot and fired a tying bullet past Lindbergh at 19:34.

The Spectrum was a collapsed lung. Fear of failure accompanied the Flyers back to their locker room, quickly followed by Keenan, who was not going to wait until the end of the rest period to peel paint from the walls. "They were being reflective," he recalls. "I wanted them angry, passionate, assertive."

When the players came out, they were determined to win, not afraid to lose. The fans, their hearts still in their throats, increased the noise level as their team picked up its pace.

The Flyers had outshot the Rangers 8-1 in the overtime when Sutter chased a McCrimmon dump and knocked Ruotsalainen off the puck behind the New York goal. Sutter carefully slid the puck out to Howe, who had moved up to the edge of the circle, with no Ranger within fifteen feet. As the crowd rose for the kill, Howe waited for Carson to obscure Hanlon's vision and blew a wrist shot between the legs of the hopelessly screened goalie. At 8:01 of overtime, in its tenth attempt over four springs, Philadelphia had finally won a playoff game.

"For those who were here and lived through that history, this helps," said Keenan, but his tone was more matter-of-fact than exultant. The on-ice celebration was almost perfunctory. The Flyers realized New York would not go down easily.

Indeed, the Rangers took a 1-0 lead into Game 2 when George McPhee deflected in a Ron Greschner shot. While the two teams exchanged hard checks and cheap shots, Bergen flitted around the ice almost oblivious to the war around him. Midway through the second period, the rookie flashed through the slot to redirect a Crossman point drive and tie the game. At 5:23 of the third period, Bergen pounced on a Marsh shot that pinballed off James Patrick and went upstairs on Hanlon to put Philadelphia ahead.

Propp and Kerr had nervous hands, but Sutter, getting extra shifts after Poulin sustained a slight ligament tear in his left knee during the first period, checked Mark Pavelich doggedly while the defense and Lindbergh were resolute.

With less than three minutes remaining, Sutter took defenseman Barry Beck wide and slipped a two-on-one pass into the slot. Sinisalo beat Hedberg to the puck and put it between Hanlon's legs to secure the Flyers' 3-1 victory.

"We'll be back here [for a deciding Game 5]," vowed Craig Patrick. The Rangers began Game 3 at Madison Square Garden as though they believed it, too. Ruotsalainen beat Lindbergh to the far side after Howe was not backed up on a center-ice pinch, then Ledyard scored through a Maloney screen with Crossman in the penalty box.

But New York quickly helped Philadelphia get back into the game. On the center-ice face-off following the second goal, Hedberg tripped Zezel, who scored on the power play through Kerr's legs to make it 2-1. Early in the second period, Hedberg tackled Marsh. With referee Bryan Lewis's arm raised for the delayed penalty, Crossman picked up a deep rebound of a Sutter shot, cut outside a crowd of bodies in the slot and sent a low drive past the needlessly flopping Hanlon to tie the game.

Willie Huber put the Rangers back ahead, going to the net for a wide-open rebound of a Ruotsalainen shot while Kerr was off for tripping. But with Mike Rogers in the box for taking down Zezel, Kerr reached back for a diagonal pass intended for Howe at the point and swept the puck past Hanlon.

The game was tied again. And Kerr was just getting warmed up. He pinched down the boards to pick off a Craven-forced backhanded clear by Hanlon, threw the puck in front, retrieved it off a skate, and snapped in a forehander. After Bob Brooke was called for holding Tocchet, Zezel retrieved a Howe drive and threw the puck into the slot, where Kerr used his backhand to redirect his third goal and make the score 5-3.

After Zezel made a smart pivot away from Tom Laidlaw to gain the zone, Kerr steamed up the middle to one-time the center's pass before a reeling Hanlon could set himself. The Flyers led 6-3 and Kerr had scored a Stanley Cup-record four goals in 8:16.

All Philadelphia had to do to wrap up the series was stay in the Rangers' way and out of the penalty box. But McCrimmon, giving Ledyard too much room wide, was forced to take him down at the second-period buzzer. John Vanbiesbrouck, who replaced Hanlon, stopped Sinisalo on a shorthanded breakaway early in the third, and on New York's next trip up ice, Sinisalo and Zezel failed to look for the trailing Pavelich. Maloney put in a rebound to make the score 6-4 and the Rangers were reenergized.

Hedberg stole an outlet pass from Tocchet, spun away from Marsh and shot into the post on the near side. Lindbergh tried to kick the puck away but accidentally booted it back off the far pipe and in.

The Garden werewolves were howling and the young Flyers, leading only 6-5, faced the longest 16:11 of their lives. Keenan called them to the bench and reminded them they still had the lead. He then put out Sutter, Carson and Tocchet, who jammed the puck into the New York end and created two quality chances. Zezel won draws and Bergen, backchecking for the first time in his life, tackled Ruotsalainen as he went to the net.

Philadelphia, becoming more composed with every shift, forced the Rangers to repeatedly dump the puck, and Howe and Crossman wheeled it out every time. Keenan showed surprising confidence in Joe Paterson, called up to replace the injured Poulin, and the Flyers controlled almost every one-on-one battle.

In the thirteen minutes following Hedberg's goal, Lindbergh only had to handle the puck twice, both times on lobs from center ice. Finally, after rookie Tomas Sandstrom stole from Sutter, Lindbergh came to the top of the crease to make a kick save. He needed attention from trainer Dave Settlemyre when rattled in the mask by Rogers's stick, but with two minutes remaining, he kicked away a Hedberg drive from the top of the circle.

Howe left his feet to deflect a Rogers pass that would have found Steve Patrick wide open at the goalmouth. And Sutter, with Vanbiesbrouck pulled, won three defensive zone draws before Craven finally rammed the puck through the right point with 8 seconds remaining.

Marsh, on the bench, lifted his arms in triumph as he watched the puck slide past him, then side-saddled the boards until a clock that had been running for four years finally ran out. As one of the Flyers who had suffered the longest, the big defenseman was the first to reach Lindbergh and celebrate Philadelphia's 6-5 victory and liberation from April hell.

"I don't know if the young guys appreciate it like we do or not," said Marsh in a radiant locker room. "Of course, it's been tough to deal with. This means a lot as many times as the Rangers have done it to us." As one Frankenstein was subdued, another suddenly staggered back into the Flyers' path. The Islanders rallied from a 2-0 series deficit to beat Washington.

The star-studded ex-champs had only forty-eight hours to prepare for Keenan's rested team, which was comfortably back into an underdog's position. Propp, whose three dry springs had continued into the first round, got pumping by setting up Tocchet's Game 1 opening goal, then blocking a shot and going the length of the ice so Kerr could knock in a rebound. Tocchet fed Sutter and Lindbergh recorded a 3-0 shutout. "You could see they were tired," said Marsh. "They didn't go to the net like an Islander team."

New York's legs recovered for Game 2, but after Hospodar's rebound goal opened the scoring, the Flyers killed three early disadvantages. Propp swept in a broken-down point shot, converted a Bergen setup and completed the natural hat trick through Dave Brown's screen. Kerr added a to his three assists and Philadelphia went on to a surprisingly routine 5-2 victory and a 2-0 lead in the series.

Sutter and Carson were handcuffing Bryan Trottier and Mike Bossy. "[Bossy] is gripping that stick tight, just like I do sometimes," said Kerr. Still, the Isles' extensive history of coming from behind left the Flyers anything but in control as the series shifted to the Nassau Coliseum.

Keenan relentlessly told his players that the Islanders were fallible. "Who the bleep is Mike Bossy?" the Flyer coach said. "Who the hell is Denis Potvin?"

Lindbergh wished he had never heard of Anders Kallur, either, after accidentally knocking in the winger's passout for a 1-0 New York lead. But Philadelphia kept up the pressure and the Islanders began taking penalties. Ken Morrow tripped Kerr, and Crossman scored on a four-on-three advantage to tie the game.

John Tonelli took a cheap shot at Propp and goalie Billy Smith tripped, then cross-checked, Brown. When penalized by referee Ron Wicks, Smith raged, then twice flopped on phantom penalties. With the continuously-victimized Dineen caught up ice, Tocchet took a two-on-one pass from Sutter and put the Flyers ahead, 2-1.

The Isles were self-destructing. "They played like we used to play," Kerr would say later. Early in the second period, Sutter rode off Tomas Jonsson and put the puck between Smith's legs. Propp, off a steal from Clark Gillies, got a shorthanded goal to make the score 4-1.

Brent Sutter cashed the power play to cut the lead to two and New York, feeling the series slip away, staged a desperate stand. The Islanders threw 27 second-period shots at Lindbergh and pulled

have to win one game, they have to win three," said Keenan. "Who has the psycholgical edge?"

He put no urgency on making the kill before the Islanders could gather more strength, instead pounding home his team's tangible advantages. With two of the Islanders' good young forwards—Greg Gilbert and Patrick Flatley—injured, Keenan reinforced carrying the puck wide on a decaying defense. "[New York] had to go with some older players longer than they really wanted to," recalls Sator. "We had the feel-

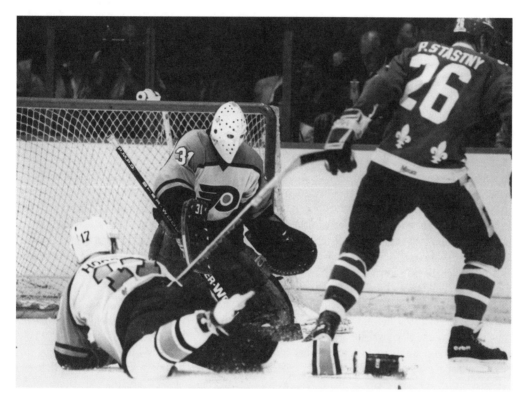

Lindbergh stops shot by the Nords' Peter Stastny.

within a goal in the final minute when Tonelli ran over Crossman to convert Lindbergh's missed pokecheck.

But New York's old limbs weakened and Philadelphia held the opposition to only 4 third-period shots. When Sinisalo scored into the empty net with 37 seconds remaining to wrap up the 5-3 victory, only the cheers from the Flyer bench pierced the silence at the Coliseum. The Islanders had always been at their best when cornered, but Philadelphia almost had them pinned.

In Game 4, New York picked corners on Lindbergh in racing to a 4-0 lead, but Keenan pulled the goalie before he could lose any confidence. Even after the 6-2 loss, the Flyers' first of the playoffs, the coach would not let his players be shaken. "We

ing that the Islanders had walked on land mines once too often."

Four Philadelphia bids for the lead in Game 5 at the wired Spectrum bounced off the post, but the team showed no sign of frustration. In the second period, Zezel gained the zone, dropped to Crossman and crashed into Hrudey. Sinisalo lifted Crossman's rebound into a wide-open net.

Carson and Howe limited Bossy to two shots but Hrudey continued to deny the relentless Flyers an insurance goal. The Islanders remained only one goal down through a tense third period. Lindbergh trapped a dangerous 20-footer by Tonelli with 6:46 remaining, then Howe dove to break up a two-on-one pass from Trottier. Strong forechecking by Carson, Sutter and Craven pinned the puck in the New York end for much of the final minute before Crossman deflected Tonelli's drive into the stands with 7 seconds left.

When Ron Sutter beat his brother Brent on the faceoff and Howe banked the puck to center, Philadelphia had earned a 1-0 victory and eliminated the Islanders in what Lindbergh called an "Unbeeeeelievable" 5 games.

"I admire the way the Islanders work, the way they have always found ways to win," said Howe. "It's one of the best teams of all time. And we beat them."

Quebec, which defeated Montreal on Peter Stastny's overtime goal in Game 7, had the extra home game in the Wales Conference final because Adams Division teams had accumulated more victories in head-to-head competition against Patrick clubs. But the deeper, stronger Flyers were still a favorite over the offensive-minded Nordiques.

Poulin returned for Game 1, but Kerr ran into Bergen and limped to the locker room with a ligament sprain of the right knee. The passionless opener remained scoreless into the third period, when Dale Hunter outwrestled Carson and redirected a Michel Goulet drive. Philadelphia tied the score six minutes later when Pat Price accidentally tipped in a McCrimmon shot, but goalie Mario Gosselin stoned Bergen and Poulin in overtime before Peter Stastny beat Lindbergh with a perfect 55-footer off the crossbar to give Quebec a 2-1 victory.

The Flyers announced Kerr's status as day-to-day, but feared he was lost for the playoffs. Despite his absence, Keenan took Bergen, the scoring specialist whose play had steadily deteriorated through the Islander series, out of the lineup and relied on his grinders.

Poulin suffered cracked ribs when sticked by Mario Marois, but before going to the locker room, the captain took a feed from Craven and gave his team a 1-0 lead. Goals by Craven and Sinisalo made it 3-0 before Zezel, playing superbly, lined up Hunter for a spectacular check that flipped the Nordique pest head over heels and shattered the end glass. The Flyers tied the series with a workmanlike 4-2 victory.

McCrimmon, driven into the boards from behind by Wilf Paiement in the first period of Game 3 at the Spectrum, was the next to go down. He was helped off the ice with his shoulder blade next to his ear. "[Dr. John] Gregg called it the worst separation he had ever seen," McCrimmon said later.

Hospodar took the injured defenseman's shifts and assisted on a Paterson goal that tied the game, 2-2. Sinisalo fired past Gosselin's glove, and Propp added an insurance goal as Philadelphia overcame

the absence of Kerr, Poulin and McCrimmon to win 4-2 and gain a 2-1 series lead. "I think we've shown a lot of guts," said Howe. "But we've also shown we have some depth."

Inevitably, Lindbergh showed he was human in Game 4, kicking at and missing Hunter's 65-footer that opened the scoring. Later, the goalie left too much of the short side exposed as Mark Kumpel opened up a 3-1 Quebec lead. Propp and Howe tallied to tie the game, and even after Eriksson fell down and Alain Cote put in Anton Stastny's rebound, 15:28 remained for another Flyer comeback. But after Hospodar high-sticked Paul Gillis, Lindbergh was again beaten to the short side, this time by Brad Maxwell.

"You can't be great every night," shrugged Lindbergh to the writers after the Nordiques' 5-3 victory squared the series. "You guys make it sound like I gave up twenty goals."

On the flight to Quebec City the next day, Lindbergh read *Mad* magazine. What, him worry? The goalie listened to relaxation tapes given to him by Dr. Stephen Rosenberg, a Philadelphia sports psychologist who was also counseling McCrimmon and Howe. "Pelle's gotten us this far," said Keenan as the series came to its fulcrum. "He'll respond."

For almost forty minutes of Game 5, Lindbergh was practically the only Flyer who did. After being beaten on a goal by J.F. Sauve, the goalie almost singlehandedly held his team in the game. Despite the return of the flak-jacketed Poulin, Philadelphia was lifeless. At the second intermission, the team was lucky to be trailing only 1-0.

"They were thinking if it ended here, they had still had a much better season than anyone expected," Keenan recalls. "The injuries were piling up. I could see the kids saying, 'Enough already.' But they could do more than they thought they could. We were in the twenty-first mile of a marathon. We needed the emotion to get through it."

The coach took a stick and knocked the juice bottles off the table in the middle of the locker room. "They were coming right at me, too," recalls Poulin. "It was the fastest I moved during the playoffs, even with bad ribs." Keenan climbed atop the table and accused the Flyers of quitting, then reminded them that they were still only a goal behind.

One minute into the third period, Howe pinched in on a Gosselin clear and fed Paterson, who jammed in his third goal of the playoffs to tie the game, 1-1. "Paterson was a guy just happy for the opportunity, with no fear of failure," recalls Keenan. "He was a big man for us that series."

Smith took an interference penalty and Stastny broke in alone, but Lindbergh followed the Quebec star across, forcing a shot into the side of the net. Philadelphia gained more strength. With five minutes remaining, Propp trapped two Nordiques with a pass up the middle to a breaking Craven, who fired off Gosselin's shoulder to put the Flyers ahead.

Philadelphia received a huge break with 2:10 left when referee Kerry Fraser waved off a goal that bounced in off Peter Stastny's foot. Propp took a needless penalty, Quebec pulled Gosselin and, with the Flyers hanging on desperately, Lindbergh was stung by a Marois drive in the back of his leg.

Keenan took every opportunity to stall, buying the hobbled Lindbergh, Poulin, Crossman and Howe recovery time as Philadelphia clung to its lead until the clock finally ran out. The Flyers raced for their plane like they were anxious to get out of town before the NHL challenged the validity of their 2-1 victory and 3-2 series lead. "It's like stealing," said Poulin.

Hospodar had practically commited murder in spearing Peter Stastny. Quebec coach Michel Bergeron summoned reporters to a VCR to replay the uncalled foul.

Back in Philadelphia, the Flyers did not need to look at video, only at each other, in a team meeting. "You just don't win the way we played those first two periods," said Howe. "It seemed like a good time to lay out everything, just in case people forgot."

The team was better prepared for Game 6 and the Spectrum was thoroughly wired. Lindbergh only had to make one good save in the first period—a stick stop on Kumpel—and Tocchet redirected a Howe drive for a 1-0 lead.

Early in the second, penalties to Paterson and Propp 37 seconds apart put Philadelphia down two men. Poulin lost a draw in the defensive end, then pounced between the points to pick off a telegraphed pass by Marois. The crowd roared as the captain raced the length of the ice on a breakaway, held its breath as Poulin closed to the hash marks, then went mad as the net bulged behind Gosselin's glove. The first three-on-five playoff goal in franchise history electrocuted Quebec.

The Flyers became more and more dominant as the game moved along, raising their play to an almost mystical level. They outshot Quebec 36-15 and outchanced them 19-2. Gosselin had to be spectacular to keep the final score to 3-0.

"I'll take a chance on overstating this," said McGuire. "By the third period, we would have been beating anybody. Edmonton, the Soviets, anybody. It was a coach's dream."

The youngest team in the league would now play for the championship. "I can't describe it," said Tocchet. "This is something I sat in my living room watching last year and now we're in it."

The Flyers had the legs to skate alongside the Oilers, who had eliminated Chicago in six games, but lacked the hands to score with them. Still, the return of Kerr, who was fitted with a specially designed knee brace, shortened the odds as a tingling Spectrum hosted its first Stanley cup final in five years.

Late in the first period of Game 1, Kerr was dragged down by defenseman Charlie Huddy, giving Philadelphia a two-man advantage. Bergen threw the puck across the slot to Kerr, who was stopped twice by goalie Grant Fuhr before Sinisalo stuffed in the rebound.

The score stayed 1-0 until the third period, when Sutter stole a Paul Coffey pass and soloed to flip in a backhander off Fuhr's glove. Later, the goalie tried to hand-pass the puck onto Glenn Anderson's stick after making a save, but Poulin stole it and fed Kerr at a half-empty net for the 3-0 lead.

Willy Lindstrom scored off the post to break the shutout before Poulin hit the empty net. Wayne Gretzky, who had 18 points in the Chicago series, was held without a shot as Keenan obsessively matched Howe, Crossman, Sutter, Smith and Tocchet against the Great One and linemates Jari Kurri and Mike Krushelnyski. As good as the Flyers had been in eliminating Quebec, they were even better in the finals' opener, outchancing Edmonton 17-4 in a 4-1 victory that extended Philadelphia's unbeaten streak over Edmonton to 9 games over three seasons. "It's scary how well we're playing," said Howe. "We were just all over them."

The choppy Spectrum ice, well-suited for Philadelphia's purposes, drew Oiler complaints the next day. So did the water bottles that Keenan had placed on the nets all season. "It's a great idea, especially when it's hot like this," said Edmonton coach-GM Glen Sather. "But let's not have any surprises when you get to the Stanley Cup finals. It wasn't discussed with everybody. Maybe we want a bucket of chicken on our net. Maybe hamburgers. I mean, if you have a water bottle out there, let's have lunch."

He decided on a change of lineup, not menu, replacing Krushelnyski with Esa Tikkanen, a newly-signed, 20-year-old Finnish left wing, on the Gretzky line. The Great One, meanwhile, stewed about one of

Al Morganti's lines in the *Inquirer*. "Unless they are total frauds, the Oilers should be able to play a lot better," Morganti wrote.

Halfway through the first period of Game 2, the insulted superstar followed a blazing Coffey down the right side, picked his own centering pass out of Howe's skates, circled the net and put in a backhander.

Kerr tied the score in the second period after Poulin had poked the puck free from Mark Messier and Carson had rattled Coffey with a body check. But Kevin McClelland rode Marsh off behind the net and neither Dvorak nor Zezel covered Lindstrom in front. His shot ticked off Lindbergh's pads to give Edmonton the 2-1 lead. The Flyers were held to only one good third period chance before Dave Hunter put the series-tying 3-1 victory away into the empty net. "They reminded me of the way we played in Game 1," said Keenan.

As the teams flew to Alberta for the next three games (to cut travel, the NHL had begun a 2-3-2 finals format in 1984), Keenan pondered dwindling options. Kerr's knee was giving out again, Sinisalo had a bad shoulder, and Poulin, on painkillers, was short of wind.

The coach kept his players functioning on Eastern time through Game 3 to lessen the effects of the time zone change on their body clocks. Unfortunately, Gretzky's alarm had sounded, making Philadelphia seem two hours late for the contest. In the first period, the Great One scored three goals in four-on-four situations. On the third, which came twelve minutes after Smith had tallied for the Flyers, Gretzky lifted his stick six inches off the ice to accept Messier's feed on the backhand, switched to the forehand, and went around Lindbergh for a deposit.

While the Oilers chased Hospodar, who had damaged three of Mark Napier's teeth with a high-stick, Keenan, down 3-1, attempted to scheme his way back into the game. He replaced Lindbergh with Froese to stall Edmonton's momentum during a five-on-three advantage, then reinstalled Lindbergh to begin the second period. After the Swede gave up a fourth goal on a Krushelnyski deflection, Froese was reinserted.

Kerr, his knee strength gone, came out of the game, so Keenan concocted a line of Craven centering Tocchet and Propp and played it every other shift down the stretch. Propp, a no-show in the first two games, woke up and hit Tocchet going to the net, enabling Howe to poke in a rebound. Propp then got Philadelphia to within one on a wide-angle drive off Fuhr's hip.

With 15 seconds remaining, Propp worked the puck loose along the boards to trap two Oilers and fed Craven, who feathered a crossing pass just a bit too softly for the streaking Tocchet. He reached back for the puck and stumbled, enabling Edmonton to hold on for the 4-3 victory.

The Flyers were in deeper trouble than the 2-1 series deficit suggested. Kerr was finished and Poulin gasping. Nevertheless, Ron Sutter picked off a Messier pass and shot the Game 4 opening goal off brother Rich's skate. Coffey one-timed a Huddy setup to tie the score but Bergen, playing only on power plays, detonated a 40-foot bomb over Fuhr's glove to put Philadelphia ahead. Ron Sutter, tackled by Messier on a clear-cut breakaway, was beaten by Fuhr on the penalty shot, but Craven took advantage of a fall by Huddy to score shorthanded and build a 3-1 lead.

The Oilers rallied. Huddy atoned with a goal while Hospodar was off for slashing, Anderson scored after stealing a Crossman pass and Gretzky put Edmonton ahead 4-3 by netting a backhander with Paterson in the penalty box.

The back of Lindbergh's knee, rattled by Marois's shot in Game 5 of the Quebec series, took another blast from a Krushelnyski drive, so Keenan went to Froese for the third period before Gretzky beat a flustered Crossman to a Coffey rebound. The shorthanded Flyers had skated with the Oilers but finished two fewer plays in a 5-3 loss that left the defending champions one game away from the Cup.

Before Philadelphia's last stand, Keenan put heat on Propp. "I expected more from him," the coach said. But he was whistling against thunder. Dr. John Gregg had diagnosed a partial tear in Lindbergh's quadriceps tendon and said it would be asking for bigger problems to use him for Game 5.

Froese, whose own knee had not completely recovered from its December trauma, became shark bait for Gretzky. No. 99 made a spectacular behind-the-back feed to Coffey, one of his three assists in a four-point night that keyed Edmonton's 8-3 rout.

After Brown had high-sticked Oiler defenseman Don Jackson in the final minutes, Sather made an obscene gesture and screamed at Keenan. But it would take more than one incident of ugliness to stain a beautiful season.

"I don't want to see anybody walk out of here with their heads down," Keenan told his players. "You had a good year."

It had been better than just good. Still, after speaking realistically about the power of the Oilers' machine to the media, Keenan cried on the plane ride home. "I couldn't stop," he recalls. "They had a better team, but I thought we were cheated by all the injuries of a chance to play them on an equal basis.

"Most clubs that reach the finals for the first time are pleased and proud and don't know what it takes to win. Maybe I was naive. I guess I expected the impossible at all times."

For setting such a standard and driving the Flyers to every goal but the ultimate one, Keenan was named coach

Clarke.

Sator, who had impressed New York GM Craig Patrick when they worked together for the USA Canada Cup team, was named head coach of the Rangers on June 19, creating a vacancy that Keenan tried to fill with University of Toronto coach Paul Titanic. Titanic accepted, then quickly changed his mind for personal reasons. So Paul Holmgren, retired from the North Stars because of shoulder problems and who had written Keenan to apply for the assistantship, was hired.

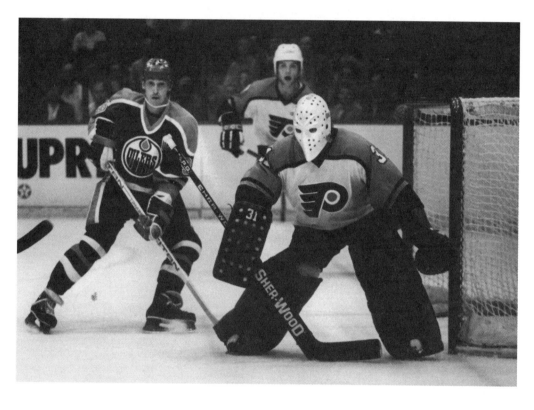

While Gretzky knocks on the door, Lindbergh focuses on the puck.

of the year by the NHL Broadcasters Association. The Sniders presented him with a leased Mercedes and a new contract.

Lindbergh was due for a salary bump, too, especially after he was handed the Vezina Trophy by presenter Bernie Parent on June 12 in Toronto. "The man I really want to thank is the guy standing next to me," Lindbergh said. "He taught me everything I know to play hockey in North America."

Clarke used the last pick of the draft's first round to select left wing Glen Seabrooke of Peterborough. The GM released Dvorak, with thanks, to a team in West Germany and signed center Per-Erik Eklund, an eighth-rounder from the astoundingly successful (Zezel, Smith and Tochet) 1983 draft. "We think if Eklund had been in this year's draft, he would have gone first overall," said

In August, Jay Snider announced that the Flyers would not participate in the following season's tour by the Soviet Central Red Army team or buy Soviet players. Said the team president: "We don't believe cultural or athletic exchanges or any policy of detente has had any real effect. It's a nation with a clear goal of trying to defeat us. Sports are used by them in an attempt to prove their superiority."

Barber, who had finished the season as interim coach at Hershey after a mental wipeout from his grueling knee rehabilitation, made his retirement official on August 22. The best left wing of his time wiped back a tear as he remembered his father Harry, who had died two weeks earlier. When asked to reflect on his statistical accomplishments, Barber spread his hands to show off two Stanley Cup rings. "None of those things were as important to me as these," he said. He was staying with the organization as a roving instructor.

Bergen, meanwhile, told Clarke that pursuing a career in golf was more important to him than playing for Keenan. The coach met with the 22-year-old center in Toronto and believed they had reached an understanding, but Bergen did not report to training camp. Clarke's calls to the player's Prince Albert, Saskatchewan, home were not returned.

Kerr, hospitalized during the exhibition season by an infection that settled into his brain lining, resumed skating one day before the 1985-86 opener and suited up. His two goals, and one by the debuting Eklund, still left the Flyers one short in a 6-5 Spectrum loss to New Jersey, but they rebounded with victories in Pittsburgh and Washington.

Telecasting rights to road games had been acquired by Channel 57, a new station unavailable on most cable systems, and Philadelphia's major newspapers were in the midst of a forty-six-day strike. Thus, hockey was almost as hard to find as Bergen. Reports drifting in, however, indicated the Flyers had picked up where they left off the preceding season. "They intimidate you with their work ethic," said Blackhawks assistant coach Roger Neilson after his team was beaten 4-2 at Chicago Stadium on October 20.

Trailing 4-3 in the third period at Montreal, Philadelphia failed on two power-play chances but Rich Sutter, playing regularly on a line with his brother and Tocchet, scored to tie the game and Propp's goal won it. "We never let up," recalls Poulin. "We didn't know any better than to succeed. We mirrored Mike's confidence."

With Froese the stronger goalie in the early going, Keenan went more to Lindbergh in an attempt to sharpen his skills. The Swede responded by beating Los Angeles 7-4 at the Spectrum (a game featuring three Brown bouts with Jay Wells), defeating the Rangers 5-2 in New York, and earning his team's third straight win as Kerr scored twice in a 6-2 swamping of visiting Chicago.

Two nights later on November 9, Kerr pumped in three more goals, giving him 16 in 13 games and helping Froese to a 5-3 success over Boston. The 12-2-0 Flyers had won 10 in a row, led the league in fewest goals against, were second in goals scored, and were systematically dismantling opponents. As Ed Snider left the Spectrum after the Bruins' defeat, he turned to his wife, Martha. "This is the best team we've ever had," he said.

The owner's telephone rang before seven the next morning, far too early for a Sunday. It was John Brogan, Jay's assistant.

"Pelle has been in a car accident," Brogan said.

Snider's heart pounded, jolting the sleep from his head.

"Sandy Clarke got a call from Murray Craven," Brogan continued. "He said it was serious. I don't know anything else."

"What do we do now?" Snider asked.

Sandy had already called Bob, who was in Boston on a scouting trip; Ed reached Jay, who was in Los Angeles for an NHL marketing meeting. While the words passed in phone calls on the morning of November 10, 1985, were stunning, the messages remained distressingly credible. Speed, Lindbergh's passion, had threatened to be his undoing.

One of the first things the goalie did after signing his contract in 1980 was to buy a new Corvette. Later, Lindbergh purchased a 1969 Porsche 930 Turbo and a speedboat that he kept in Stockholm. In 1983, he bought a new Porsche 930 Turbo in Germany for about $52,000 and sent it back to the Stuttgart factory for $41,000 worth of modifications.

The Porsche's speedometer went to 190 miles per hour. "It was the fastest car I ever drove," recalls Jack Prettyman, a Voorhees police officer who befriended many players. "Pelle told me he once took it up to 150 on the autobahn."

Lindbergh did not always drive like a maniac, but enjoyed showing off what the car could do. After taking his first ride, Clarke was never interested in another. "He scared me," said the GM. "We told Pelle he had to slow down. I guess when you're young and strong and full of life, you feel you're invincible."

Lindbergh had been quiet on the bench during the Saturday-night game against Boston, perhaps disappointed that Froese had gotten the start. His mother, Anna-Lisa, and brother-in-law Goran Hornestam, both visiting from Sweden, were being driven to the Spectrum by Lindbergh's live-in fiancee, Kerstin Pietzsch, when car trouble developed. By the time they arrived, the game had just ended. "Pelle's mom was very upset, the whole night was ruined," recalls Kerstin.

Following the Flyer victory, Keenan had told his team they would have Sunday off and only an optional practice on Monday. With five days until their next game, players had circled the night on their calendars for a long party at the Coliseum, which had an after-hours bar. Lindbergh went to his town house at The Moorings in Marlton, New Jersey, and at first didn't want to go out. "He thought he should be with his teammates," recalls Kerstin, "so he said he would go for an hour or so to be social. I said I would stay with his mom."

Shortly after midnight, the goalie drove alone to Bennigan's on Route 73. There he met several teammates and friend Ed Parvin, a part-time bartender at Kaminski's Ale House in Cherry Hill, New Jersey, who had visited Lindbergh the previous summer in Sweden.

According to witnesses, Lindbergh drank at least three ten-ounce drafts before 2:30 A.M. He asked Rich Sutter, who was with wife Rhonda and brother Ron, whether anyone wanted to go to the Coliseum. Rich, who knew how Lindbergh drove, turned him down. Parvin went instead.

The goalie gunned his Porsche up to 120 m.p.h. on Springdale Road towards the nightspot, where he and about a dozen teammates and friends drank. Close to 3 A.M., Cindy Volpe, a woman Tocchet had dated, and Kathy McNeal, her coworker and friend, arrived after completing their shifts as cocktail waitresses at Trump's in Atlantic City. McNeal had met many Flyers when she served drinks at the Airport Hilton and had dated Zezel for six months.

The group ordered beers and B-52s, a concoction of several types of alcoholic beverages. McNeal later testified she saw Lindbergh drink two of the mixed drinks, plus a beer. Tocchet also remembered buying Lindbergh two beers, but during the two-plus hours at the Coliseum, the goalie was often seen without a drink in his hand.

The club stopped serving at 4:45 and the lights went on at five. Parvin, drunk and tired, told Lindbergh at about 5:20 he would wait in the car and fell asleep in the front seat. The goalie walked to the parking lot only steps away from Poulin. "He wasn't falling-down drunk," Poulin recalls.

McNeal said she was hungry, so Lindbergh told Craven, who shared a house with Tocchet within walking distance of the Coliseum, that he would drive Parvin home to Mount Ephraim, New Jersey, then stop back for Craven and Tocchet so they could all go for breakfast. McNeal climbed onto the console of the two-seat Porsche. Neither Lindbergh nor Parvin wore a seat belt.

Tocchet and Craven were in the door less than twenty minutes when there was a knock. Two women who had been at the Coliseum said they had just seen Lindbergh's car hit a wall on Somerdale Road.

Lisa Garaguso and Kristina Trout, 19-year-old college students from Gloucester Township, New Jersey, had pulled out of the Coliseum's parking lot behind the Porsche. After it turned onto Somerdale Road, the sports car accelerated and swerved into the opposite lane before reaching the White Horse Pike stoplight, three-fifths of a mile away. At the intersection, Trout pulled her Chevette alongside the Porsche. McNeal was between Lindbergh and Parvin in the two-seat vehicle, her arms on the backs of both headrests.

"They were all laughing," Garaguso later told the *Inquirer*. When the light changed, the Porsche took off so fast that Trout said it looked like "the back wheels weren't on the ground."

Three-tenths of a mile past the stoplight, at the intersection of Somerdale Road and Ogg Avenue, Somerdale turns sharply to the right. Trout saw the Porsche continue instead straight towards the three-and-a-half-foot-high wall of the Somerdale Elementary School. Residents near the intersection heard the car roaring down the road and then a dull thud.

"Pelle just hit something," Trout said to Garaguso. From a distance, it looked like the Porsche might have merely jumped the curb and stirred up some dust. When the women got closer, they saw otherwise. The vehicle had impacted the wall just at the point where it parted for the front steps of the school. The driver's side was completely demolished and the passenger side rested against the steps. The windshield had been blown forty feet.

Parvin was slumped in the passenger seat with McNeal lying across him. Lindbergh was tilted up against the steering wheel, bleeding from the nose and mouth. "It's just amazing that someone with his kind of reflexes ends up like this," Somerdale police detective Charles Pope would say later. The skid marks indicated that Lindbergh did not apply the brakes until he was only ten feet from the wall.

Trout and Garaguso raced back to the mini market at Somerdale and the White Horse Pike and called the police emergency number. When ambulances arrived minutes later, McNeal was the only one of the three victims conscious. She complained of pain in her lower legs. "I told Pelle to slow down," she told one of the rescue workers. Later, she estimated their speed at 75 to 80 miles per hour. When the car's turbocharger kicked in, McNeal said it felt like the front wheels lifted off the road.

Rescuers could see Lindbergh's leg was broken, but his positioning made it difficult to tell whether he was breathing. Billy Lynch of the Magnolia Ambulance Corps was able to reach for a pulse. It still felt strong.

With the driver's side against the wall, pneumatic

tools could only free the victims through the passenger side. It took ten to fifteen minutes for the medics to remove Parvin and McNeal. By that time, Lindbergh's heart had stopped, making respiration a more immediate concern than spinal cord damage. Ambulance workers supported Lindbergh's head and neck as he was pulled out feetfirst. CPR was performed and his heartbeat revived.

One ambulance transported Parvin to Cooper Hospital in Camden, which had a specially designed

Patti Marsh had a hard time rousing her husband, who had just returned from the Coliseum, so Craven phoned Poulin. The captain's advice was to call Clarke and Keenan.

Craven and Tocchet were the first to arrive at Cooper Hospital, where they believed Lindbergh was being treated. They were asked to identify the critically-injured man who was about to undergo surgery. "Murray didn't have the stomach for it," recalls Tocchet. "I had a long walk down a hallway, afraid of

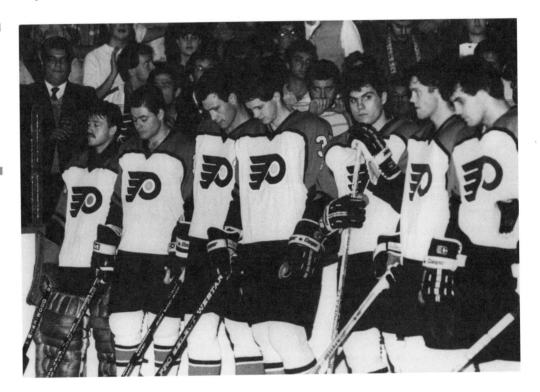

Grieving Flyer teammates line up for Pelle Lindbergh memorial service prior to game against Edmonton.

trauma unit to treat head injuries. McNeal was taken to John F. Kennedy Memorial Hospital in Stratford, only two minutes away. Because of Lindbergh's' grave condition, it was quickly decided to take him to JFK, too.

When Tocchet and Craven arrived at the scene, they saw their teammate covered with blankets, being placed in the ambulance. "I had seen players get carried off on stretchers and be fine," recalls Craven. "It was just getting light and I wasn't really close enough to see. I asked how badly hurt Pelle was. When the policeman said it was bad, I asked if he would be able to play hockey."

"He'll be lucky if he lives," said the policeman.

"It hit me hard," Craven recalls. He went home wondering whom to call first and decided on Marsh, with whom he had lived during his rookie season.

what I was about to see." He told the doctor it was Parvin.

Keenan and Poulin met in the parking lot of Kaminski's Ale House and drove together to Cooper, where Poulin called Parvin's parents, Jane and Ed Jr., with the hard news. When they arrived, Keenan spoke briefly to the father, a realtor for many Flyers who had purchased homes in South Jersey. Marsh got to the hospital soon afterwards and stayed with the Parvins while their son underwent surgery. Poulin and Keenan went on to JFK.

A Voorhees policeman at the crash site had recognized the Porsche and called Prettyman. The officer drove to the scene, then to JFK, where he was asked to identify the male crash victim who had arrived at the hospital with no brain activity. Prettyman stayed only long enough to observe the obvious—Lindbergh was in a life-or-death situation and his leg was badly broken—before leaving to tell Kerstin.

Lindbergh's fiancee had awoken earlier, wondering why Pelle had not come home. "But I knew he was with his teammates, so I didn't worry," she recalls. Kerstin went back to sleep until Goran awakened her to say a policeman was at the door.

As Prettyman told her about the accident, Anna-Lisa was coming down the stairs. Kerstin said a few words in Swedish to Pelle's mother and they both began to cry. On the way to the hospital, Prettyman told them that Pelle was in critical condition and, from what he had seen of the goalie's leg, would probably not play hockey again.

When Keenan and Poulin arrived at Kennedy, the coach went to the emergency room where Lindbergh lay. His eyes were closed and his chest rising and falling to the respirator's rhythm. "It was obvious he was finished," Keenan recalls. He leaned over his goalie. "We went through some good times together, didn't we?" the coach said.

Alone in the room with Lindbergh and McNeal, who was about to undergo surgery for the removal of her appendix and to repair her pelvis, spleen and liver, Keenan tried questioning the woman. "What happened?" he asked, but she was incoherent.

Lindbergh was undergoing a CATscan when Kerstin and Anna-Lisa arrived. "They put us in this terrible white room," Kerstin recalls, but she was unable to sit waiting for the news she dreaded. Keenan ran after her to the parking lot. "I want him to live," she said, "but I want him to be a person."

Keenan told her it was up to God.

"I'm not religious," recalls Kerstin. "I believed more in Pelle. I thought if anybody could pull through, it was him."

At about 9 A.M., the orthopedist spoke to the family, explaining the damage to Lindbergh's body—fractures to the hip and jaw, and two more in the lower leg. Al Morganti, the Flyers' beat writer for the *Inquirer*, had arrived at the hospital after getting an early-morning phone tip from a listener to the police-scanner. He stayed with Kerstin to help translate the doctor's words.

Almost an hour later, the neurologist informed family members of the complete hopelessness of Lindbergh's condition. The trauma to the brain stem had cut off the oxygen supply for too long, leaving him brain-dead. "They brought me Pelle's watch, necklace and his ring," recalls Kerstin. "When I saw those, it became real to me." She slumped in tears. Anna-Lisa rocked from side to side, her head in her hands.

The media, herded into the hospital cafeteria, were informed by Flyers' physician Dr. Edward Viner of Lindbergh's death just as Clarke, back from Boston, walked into the room. "Pelle is on a respirator, being supported fully," Dr. Viner said. "But it is essentially impossible for him to get better." The doctor said it would be up to Lindbergh's relatives to decide whether to donate his organs for transplantation.

Keenan directed Poulin to call teammates, most of whom were too drunk and sleepless to grasp their captain's words. Poulin had to persist to keep many from going back to bed. Bewildered, they dressed and came to the hospital. When Zezel arrived, he buried his head in Keenan's shoulder and wept.

Froese, who had not been at the Coliseum, was in church when he received a message to call Kim Poulin. "She was crying," recalls Froese. "She said Pelle was in an accident and it looked pretty bad, but as I recall, the only thing she knew for sure was that he had a broken leg. I'm not proud of the first thought that came into my head. I thought, 'I'm going to get a chance to play now.'"

When Froese pulled into the parking lot at Kennedy Hospital, Poulin was coming out. The captain got into Froese's car and stared straight ahead. "He's dead," said Poulin.

Outside the hospital, fan club president Evelyn Gross and member Kim Sparks sat on a bench, crying uncontrollably. The Flyers retreated to their Coliseum locker room with wives and girlfriends, where Dr. Viner repeated privately what he had told the media. One player still asked about Lindbergh's chance for recovery. "There isn't any," the doctor said. "Your teammate is dead. You have to understand that."

Flyers brass crowded into Keenan's office, where the coach sat on the floor and allowed himself one burst of anguish. "There goes the Stanley Cup," the coach said, before forcing himself back to reality. Heartsick players would need him to be strong. "I couldn't let those people down no matter how much pain I felt," Keenan said. "I probably needed to let myself go, but I didn't."

Late in the afternoon, the team went to Poulin's home and sat looking blankly at the food, football game and each other. "And then we went home," said Craven.

At Cooper Hospital, Parvin was still fighting for his life following a four-hour operation on a skull compression fracture. Ultimately, he recovered, although with permanent slurring of speech and a loss of some feeling in his right hand.

The last thing Lindbergh's friend remembered before the accident was falling asleep in the car. Among the first recollections afterwards was Kerstin standing at his hospital bed in early December questioning him about the crash. "Where's Pelle?" Parvin asked her.

On the day after the accident, Keenan gathered the Flyers for practice. "My instincts told me the only thing we knew was to work," he recalls. "We had to take the pain out in physical exertion. I don't know if it was good or bad or right or wrong, but the reality was we had no choice. The schedule was continuing."

Trainer Dave Settlemyre, who had become close to Lindbergh in Maine and nicknamed him "The Gumper" because of his bodily resemblance to Hall of Famer Gump Worsley, removed everything from Pelle's locker except for a small Swedish flag, which was mounted above the nameplate. During a one-hour emotionless skate, the net at the opposite end from Froese was functionally, as well as symbolically, empty. There had been no time to call up another goalie.

"Anger is one of the emotions," said Poulin, among the first players to comment publicly on his reaction to the tragedy. Marsh questioned why Lindbergh, going great places with an up-and-coming team, had thrown it all away in a car. "We're going to go on and win a couple of Cups," said the defenseman. "And Pelle's going to miss it."

After practice, the Flyers went to Keenan's house, where the coach encouraged them to expose their emotions. "I want my buddy back," said one player. When McCrimmon, the team stoic, broke down, they knew it was okay to cry.

"This is the first time I wept for me," said Howe. "I've cried at deaths, but always because I felt bad for somebody else's loss. We'll be okay, because we're a family. That sounds like a cliche, but it really is true. We're very close."

Eriksson, Lindbergh's countryman, had been Kerstin's shoulder at the goalie's bedside. "Everybody tells me how strong I've been," said the defenseman. "You do what you have to do. But seeing him there [in the hospital] has not prepared me for the fact that I'm never going to see him again. I'm just starting with that now."

So was Sigge Lindbergh, Pelle's father, who arrived from Stockholm on Monday night with stooped shoulders and a broken heart. The next morning, he and Anna-Lisa made the decision to allow Lindbergh's organs to be harvested for transplant.

Tests disclosed that the concentration of alcohol in Lindbergh's blood was .024 percent, a staggering amount equivalent to drinking ten and one half ounces of 80-proof whiskey within forty minutes on an empty stomach. "If he had a much higher reading than that, he would not have needed the car accident to kill himself," said John F. Vassallo Jr., director of the New Jersey Division of Alcoholic Beverage Control. Crusaders against drunk driving reacted with anger and condemnation, while those drinking with Lindbergh strongly disputed his lack of control. A second test of whole blood, rather than blood serum, indicated a .17 reading, still well above the .10 legal limit.

"People think we probably get drunk together all the time," said Howe. "We don't. Even four years ago, when I joined this team, it drank a lot more. This one, it's a couple of beers every once in a while and that's it."

"Pelle did what we have all done," said Clarke. "He got in a car when he shouldn't have."

The Flyers acknowledged that Lindbergh, who left no will, had never signed the new six-year, $1.7-million contract the team had announced on opening day. "I had talked to Pelle the day before the accident," recalls his agent, Frank Milne. "Monday was going to be the signing." The organization pledged to pay the full amount to Lindbergh's family.

The Oilers, opponents for Philadelphia's next scheduled game Thursday night at the Spectrum, offered a postponement. The Flyers considered it briefly, then decided to play. "We don't want to be disrespectful," said Clarke. "This situation has never come up before; we don't know what to do. But whether it's Thursday or Saturday or Sunday, we've got to start sometime. We've got to learn to live with what happened."

On Tuesday evening, after Sigge and Anna-Lisa had spent time at their son's bedside reconciling his death, doctors removed Lindbergh's organs and turned the respirator off. "Pelle's organs are going to save other lives," said Keenan. "It's appropriate. He died making one more save."

Ambulances left Kennedy Hospital for five locations. A liver transplant was performed on a 30-year-old Delaware man at Thomas Jefferson University Hospital and Lindbergh's kidneys were transplanted at Hahnemann Hospital. Dr. Irving Raber implanted one of the goalie's corneas into a 30-year-old Philadelphia-area resident at Scheie Eye Institute, while the other cornea was transplanted at Wills Eye Hospital.

John Keeler, 52, of Northfield, New Jersey, who had been gravely ill with cardiac disease at Temple University Hospital since October 22, was the recipient of a heart doctors described to his wife, Ann, as the most beautiful they had ever seen.

Medical science could not fix the hole in the Flyer net. "You don't replace a Pelle Lindbergh," Clarke said. "Goalies like that come along once in a lifetime."

The GM found one consolation. Froese, who had asked to be traded before the tragedy, had been offered to Los Angeles for defenseman Jay Wells. When the Kings had countered with Mark Hardy, Clarke had said no. Thus, his immediate dilemma

was only to find a backup.

Not wanting to burden top prospects Ron Hextall or Darren Jensen with becoming Lindbergh's de facto replacement, the GM made inquiries to other teams. The Penguins' Denis Herron and the Rangers' Glen Hanlon were both available, but Clarke decided not to meet the asking prices.

Instead, the Flyers called up Mike Bloski from Kalamazoo, who was on the ice at practice Wednesday when Froese got hit on the protective cup with a shot by Carson.

Froese finished the workout ("I was an idiot to stay in there," he recalls) but was in agony at a private memorial service for Lindbergh that afternoon at Philadelphia's Gloria Dei (Old Swedes) Church on Delaware Avenue. The guests, from inside and outside the game, entered solemnly and sat silently, some sobbing as Poulin delivered a eulogy.

"We'll always carry him with us and draw from his energy," said the captain.

"Pelle, we love you. We all love you."

When Froese arrived home from the service, he passed blood. The Flyers called up Jensen, who was in Sherbrooke, Quebec with the Hershey Bears.

A greater schedule maker than the NHL's had sent the Flyers a poignant first test following the tragedy: a game against the club that had defeated them in the previous spring's finals.

"Obviously you were concerned about whether we'd be able to concentrate, whether we could even skate and shoot," Poulin recalls. "We got it out in the open. If a player felt that way, he knew he was not alone."

Clarke and Jay Snider had privately discussed

Pelle Lindburgh's number 31 looms above the darkened Spectrum ice.

playing the upcoming Edmonton game without ceremony to facilitate a sense of normalcy. But the team was so inundated with tears and flowers, and even advice from faith healers and voodoo practitioners, that it decided the fans, who would have no opportunity to attend the funeral in Sweden, deserved a public chance to say goodbye. A memorial service would be held before the game, then the clubs would return to their locker rooms for fifteen minutes to compose themselves before the face-off.

"Can you believe that we're planning a *funeral?*" Jay said as the organization worked late hours to attend to the details. In lieu of flowers, and in light of the ongoing fight of Lindbergh's sister Ann-Christine against cancer, the Flyers asked for contributions to a research fund set up in Pelle's name. The only donation received from an opposing player came from Wayne Gretzky.

"If they had wanted more time [to resume the schedule] we would have understood," said Gretzky as the Oilers arrived in Philadelphia after losing to the Capitals in Landover. "Now that we're here, we'll do the best we can. But I just can't imagine how two teams can come out flying after something like this."

Keenan canceled the morning skate and told the players to go home and rest. Jensen spent the afternoon pacing in his hotel room.

By the time the fans arrived, the Spectrum's boards had been whitewashed of advertising. No Lindbergh souvenirs were sold. By coincidence, his picture had been printed on the tickets for the Edmonton game, so rather than tear them, the ushers marked a small *X* on the back and returned them to the patrons. Each fan also received a wallet-sized picture of the late goalie, surrounded by a black border. Written on the reverse side was:

In loving memory of Pelle Lindbergh
Our Goalie
Our Friend

A sign from the upper level of seats read: "Get Pelle's Name on the Cup. It's His Last Chance." More fans than usual gathered around the tunnel leading to the locker room and cheered as the players appeared. The Flyers wore embroidered patches with the number 31 on their shoulders and the Oilers wore black armbands. As Jensen warmed up, he pondered his predicament. "It occurred to me that there were easier teams to play against," he said later.

After the ice was resurfaced, the lights were dimmed and the Flyers returned to a minute-long standing ovation. The teams lined up along the blue lines as Sigge, Anna-Lisa and Kerstin watched from the owner's box. Behind a wreath of orange flowers in the shape of No. 31, Gene Hart set the ceremony's tone.

"What I would like to do this evening is make the theme ... not the mourning of a death, but the celebration of a life," said the announcer.

The Reverend John Casey, the Flyers' chaplain, recalled the effervescence of the little goalie's personality. "I tried to stay away from the maudlin and make sure everyone knew what kind of guy he was," Father Casey told Stan Hochman of the *Daily News.* "I was just trying to make sure God knew what was going on."

Lindbergh's stricken teacher, Bernie Parent felt as if he were addressing 17,000 members of a family, not strangers. Parent said he regretted never having told Lindbergh how much he admired him.

Hildegard Lindstrom, recommended by the Swedish consulate, sang Sweden's national anthem in celebration of one of her country's proudest sons.

Returning to the locker room, the players found themselves surprisingly ready to play. "It was not sad in there," Keenan would say later.

The game began tentatively, but after two minutes Hospodar showed business would be conducted as usual by roughing McClelland in front of the net. Howe then sent Poulin and Propp away on a shorthanded two-on-one and Jensen made a good pad save on Krushelnyski to kill off a penalty.

Late in the first period, Poulin beat Krushelnyski on a draw and Howe put a wrister off goalie Andy Moog's glove to give Philadelphia a 1-0 lead. Howe limped off with a groin pull in the second period, but Jensen looked composed.

He stayed on his feet as Gretzky tried a wraparound, came across to rob Kurri, then closed his legs on Hunter's shorthanded breakaway to earn a standing ovation. Larry Melnyk tied the game when he walked out from behind the net and caught Jensen flush, but after Coffey missed a wide-open net on a rebound, the goalie showed a quick glove on a Gretzky drive to keep the score tied.

With Hunter off for slashing Marsh and 2 seconds remaining in the second period, Messier went to his knees hoping to win a defensive zone draw from Kerr. When linesman Gerard Gauthier didn't drop the puck, the Edmonton center complained and was given an unsportsmanlike conduct penalty. Referee Don Koharski tacked on a delay-of-game call when the Oilers were late out of the locker room for the third period.

Sinisalo took a pretty diagonal feed from Eklund

and scored on the five-on-three, frustrating Moog into taking a slashing penalty that Propp cashed from the top of the circle. Coffey pulled Edmonton back within a goal during a five-on-three Oiler advantage, but Rich Sutter broke around Melnyk to extend the lead to two.

Again Edmonton came back when Messier roofed a shot after Jensen went down early, but Rich Sutter used a pick by his brother to get wide of Krushelnyski and fed McCrimmon for a goal to put

the game away with 3:10 remaining.

Kevin Lowe, livid with Koharski, used his stick to smash a light in the corridor on the way to the locker room, but the Spectrum suffered no loss of candlepower. The building glowed from the Flyers' courageous 5-3 victory. When the team left the ice to a huge, even tearful ovation, Keenan felt like leading the cheers. "Winning or losing was not a factor," the coach said. "I'm just so proud of the way they played."

"I was feeling everything at the same time," said Jensen. "Excitement, fear, sadness. I'm just glad it's over."

Two nights later the winning streak reached 12 games—the longest in Flyers' history—with a 5-2 victory in Hartford. Tocchet scored the first of his two goals to break a 1-1 tie late in the second and

Jensen was again superb. Keenan was so appreciative that he helped the flight attendants serve meals to the team on the charter flight home.

The following night at the Spectrum, the Islanders, whose lineup contained thirteen members of the 1981-82 team that set the NHL record of 15 consecutive victories, jumped to a 4-1 lead. With Howe still hurt and Eriksson on his way to Sweden for Lindbergh's funeral, the Flyers were short of bodies and appeared out of luck. But Craven put a shot in off Kerr's leg, then screened Billy Smith on a power-play goal by Eklund. With less than four minutes remaining, Propp knocked down Mike Bossy's clearing attempt and shot the tying score off Poulin's leg.

In the final minute of regulation time, Jensen came across to rob Bossy after Marsh had lost his stick. And in overtime, Ron Sutter forced a Gord Dineen giveaway and Billy Smith accidentally deflected Craven's centering pass into the net to give Philadelphia a 5-4 victory, the team's 13th straight. "I don't believe these guys," Keenan said.

The players had a hard time understanding it themselves. "We're just kind of living in here for ourselves with games and practices, oblivious to what's going on outside," said Poulin. "We're concentrating so well, it's like there was never a doubt we could come back. You know and I know everybody is waiting for a letdown. Psychologically, you'd be scared at the thought there wouldn't be one."

Two nights later at Nassau Coliseum, the Islanders jumped ahead 5-1 early in the second period before four Flyer power-play goals, two by Kerr, cut the lead to 6-5. Bossy, however, overpowered Jensen from the top of the circle before Hospodar scored shorthanded. Bryan Trottier hit the empty net to seal the 8-6 New York victory. "That's okay," said Kerr. "We'll just start another [streak]." Philadelphia had

Ron Sutter wasn't the first NHL player to look up to Wayne Gretzky.

learned there were greater losses than games.

The following day, more than eight hundred persons jammed Sofia Kyrka—a Lutheran church on a hill just a block from the South Stockholm apartment building where Lindbergh grew up—to pay final respects to a national hero.

Jay Snider, Clarke, Allen, Parent and Eriksson were joined by coaches and teammates from the two Swedish clubs—Hammarby and AIK—for whom Lindbergh had performed. Movie directors, actors (Lindbergh had once had a speaking part in a Swedish feature film) and representatives of Stockholm society shared the sorrow of the Soders, the city's south-side working class into which Pelle was born. So many people sent flowers, ushers had to place some at each pew.

The ceremony, planned by Kerstin, included the songs of Elton John, Pelle's favorite artist. The kids from Hammarby placed the club's green and white scarves on Lindbergh's closed casket. Later, at the wake in a restaurant, Kerstin looked over the decorations and plates of half-eaten food. "It is a shame," she told Mark Whicker of the *Daily News*. "This should have been a wedding."

Howe and Froese returned to the Flyer lineup the following night to shut out the Whalers 3-0. The goalie joked about his injury—"Too bad you guys don't write for *Penthouse*," he said–then somberly announced his intention of picking up where Lindbergh had left off. "We had become closer than people thought," he said. "But is you wallow in self-pity or are afraid of facing the challenge, you'll fail."

Bergen, meanwhile, reiterated that he didn't want to play for Keenan. "I play because I enjoy it," he said. "Mike made it a 9-to-5 job for me."

Clarke was not having much fun either, as he watched his coach rely on only four defensemen, so the GM took the best blueliner he could get for Bergen. On November 30, after the Flyers beat the North Stars 4-1 at the Met Center to run their record to 19-4-0, Clarke traded Bergen and Hospodar to Minnesota for defenseman Dave Richter and left wing Bo Berglund. Berglund's contract was being dumped on Philadelphia, but Clarke felt the 6-5, 220-pound Richter would provide a presence that was stronger and steadier than Hospodar's in front of the goal.

As December began, the Flyers finally slumped. When Detroit called up goalie Mark Laforest from Adirondack for a December 3 game at Joe Louis Arena, Jensen, who had seen Laforest play, gave the briefing: "He's a sieve, just shoot."

"Nice scouting report," Froese told Jensen after Laforest stoned Philadelphia 4-1 on 35 saves.

The Rangers, losers of 10-straight against the Flyers, broke through with a 3-1 victory at Madison Square Garden. But that didn't send nearly the chill down Keenan's back as the message he received following a 6-3 victory over New Jersey on December 19. Derrick Smith was at Our Lady of Lourdes Hospital in Camden, New Jersey, following an automobile accident. "You can imagine all the things I was thinking as I was driving over there," said the coach, who was relieved to learn the left wing had suffered only cuts and a sprained ankle after being rear-ended on the Walt Whitman Bridge.

Thus there were blessings to count at Christmas, such as the birth of Brad and Patti Marsh's firstborn, Erik David Marsh, named after Lindbergh, whose given name was Per-Erik. Philadelphia won six out of seven before the holidays but had hardly put Lindbergh's loss behind them.

"A couple of players are still having problems with it," said Poulin, "but they're getting help from the rest of us. More than bringing us together, this has shown us what we already meant to each other."

For Kerstin, a lonely figure at the team Christmas party, the ache continued. "It's difficult being here," she said, "but it would be harder not to be."

Several months later, she moved to Southern California, where she remained for two years. "It took me that long to come back to myself," Kerstin recalls. "I had healed and decided L.A. wasn't home." She returned to Sweden and met Kert Somnell, an airplane engineer. They married in May 1990. Today, she lives in Taby, outside Stockholm, with her husband and two daughters. "I am back to life," she said. "I am happy."

For the Lindberghs, time has not been as healing. Every Friday, Anna-Lisa and Sigge visit Sodra Skogkyrkogarden, the south-side Stockholm cemetery where two of their three children rest. "Pelle's older sister, Ann-Christine, died of cancer a few years after Pelle," Kerstin said. "His mom's a very strong person, but I don't think Sigge has ever gotten over the losses. He has become more and more bitter.

Lindbergh's heart gave John Keeler almost five additional years of life. He died at Temple Hospital on October 25, 1990.

The litigation from the accident proved complicated and contentious. Lloyds of London, which insured the Flyers' player assets, refused to pay the claim, arguing that Lindbergh's $1.7-million contract had never been signed and that the death had occurred during the commission of a felony—drunk driving. Eventually the insurance company settled with the team out of court. The Sniders, working around a Swedish inheritance tax of 70 percent, provided $300,000 for Pietzsch and $200,000 for Sigge and Anna-Lisa. "I didn't want to argue about money," recalls Kerstin. "I was satisfied."

A thorough examination of the car failed to prove that it had malfunctioned. McNeal, who later testified she had told Lindbergh he didn't have to speed

tlements from Lindbergh's automobile liability insuror.

As 1986 neared, the Flyers were still racking up victories. Kerr, seeing less ice time in five-on-five situations but benefiting from Eklund's setups, pumped a hat trick in a 6-1 win at Vancouver on December 27, bringing his goal total to 34 for the season. With 21 of them on the power play, Kerr was only 7 short of the NHL record held by Bossy and Phil Esposito.

When the team visited Edmonton on New Year's Eve, Philadelphia's 28-9-0 record did not surprise the Oilers at all. "The way they play, great goaltending isn't an absolute necessity every game," said Gretzky.

But it proved to be critical that evening. Froese gave the puck away on one goal and let Edmonton's 4-3 game-winner drop from his glove. Despite Froese's league-leading 2.64 goals-against average and .908 save percentage, goaltending was becoming an issue.

"Bob Froese or whoever gives us a better chance [at beating the Flyers than a year ago]," Caps coach Bryan Murray said, even after losing to Jensen 4-0 on January 9 at the Spectrum.

"Murray's no dummy, he's trying to psych me," replied Froese who, nevertheless, was beginning to look spooked by Lindbergh's ghost. On January 17, he allowed a short-sided score by Mark Hamway to start an Islander comeback that Trottier turned into a 4-3 victory by scoring with one second

"Iron Mike" Keenan makes his point.

to impress her and that she had warned him of the approaching wall, filed suit—as did Parvin—against the owners of the Coliseum bar and Bennigan's. McNeal, who had done sporadic modeling, claimed a surgical scar on her midriff eliminated her from consideration from certain jobs and that a bruised left cheekbone had caused her eye to droop. She also said she suffered from continuing hip pain and leg numbness and received an undisclosed out-of-court settlement. McNeal and Parvin also received set-

remaining in the game. The following night in Landover, Jensen allowed goals on the first two shots of a 5-2 loss.

Froese sensed the weight of Flyerdom on his shoulders. "I felt I couldn't make a mistake," he recalls. "Even if Darren had a bad game, I'd take it personally."

Keenan, not used to losing key contests, was all over Froese. "Once during a breakaway drill at practice, I dove out and tackled Dave Brown for laughs and Mike called me in and dressed me down," recalls Froese. "A lot of times I thought I was doing pretty good and he brought me down. Looking back, I see what he was doing, trying to make me stronger."

When the fans posthumously voted Lindbergh to the mid season All-Star Game, Keenan, the Wales Conference coach, picked Froese as a replacement, but with a backhanded compliment. "His statistics justify his selection," Keenan said.

Jensen finally answered for the embattled Philadelphia goalies with a remarkable 48-save, 1-0 shutout at St. Louis on January 25. "We realize we each failed to stop some big shots and a few games have gotten away," said the rookie. "But it's too early to panic. Look at the record. We're doing okay, aren't we? We're just trying to keep our sanity about this."

Keenan, however, was pushing his players toward the rubber room. In his first season, the coach had willed his team to perform beyond expectation. Now he believed so much in his own abilities that any loss was taken as a personal affront. Bad hops or bad nights were never acceptable reasons for losing; Keenan always felt there was another button he could have pushed. Determined not to to let the Flyers use Lindbergh's death as a cop-out, the coach would rage when players failed.

"Human nature wants comfort," says Poulin today. "Obviously, he thought anger at him would help us play better. You wanted to win just to shut him up."

Publicly, Keenan remained reasonably supportive of his players. Privately, he often belittled them. "It's like the guy who takes his wife out and tells everybody how wonderful she is, then goes home and treats her like dirt," recalls Froese. "How much does that praise mean to her?"

As Propp and Kerr slumped, Sinisalo became Philadelphia's only consistent scorer. Craven, Tocchet, Smith and Zezel—who had lost his spot on the first power-play unit to Eklund—were behind their paces of the previous season. Keenan, contemptuous of Richter's reluctance to hit, stayed with four defensemen who continued to get the job done. On most nights, the goaltending was adequate to win.

Froese, in fact, was excellent in handing Buffalo its first shutout loss at home in eight seasons, 4-0, on February 12. The following night at the Spectrum, the Flyers trailed 2-0 when Froese stopped Duane Sutter on a breakaway, keying a turnaround to a 6-3 victory over the Islanders. When the goalie beat the Capitals 3-1 at the Spectrum on February 22, Philadelphia was eleven points ahead of Washington.

But during a 7-4 loss at Calgary, Froese suffered an elbow injury when run into the boards by Gary Suter, and another goaltending crisis began. At Edmonton, Keenan was forced to use Jensen, who surrendered a bad overtime goal by Kurri in a disheartening 2-1 defeat.

Froese pronounced himself able when the Flyers returned to the Spectrum, but was yanked after waving feebly at two Buffalo goals. Eklund's four assists brought Philadelphia from its 4-0 deficit into a 4-4 tie until Adam Creighton's stoppable shot squeezed between Jensen's arm and body. Their momentum broken, the Flyers sagged to a 6-4 loss that cut the division lead over charging Washington to one point and placed Froese back in Keenan's doghouse.

"If he was unfit to play, I wasn't aware of it," said the annoyed coach. "If I say I can play, I'd better do the job," whispered the goalie.

Bill Barber was honored with a night on March 6, but Jay Snider made the decision not to hang No. 7 alongside Clarke's 16, Ashbee's 4 and Parent's 1. "We've had nights for only six players," said Jay Snider. "I think that says Billy Barber is among the six greatest players in our history. But retiring numbers is a very important and sacred thing."

Barber received a solid-silver puck, a new four-wheel drive truck driven onto the ice by Reggie Leach, and the joy of watching Howe's two-goal, four-assist night. "(Howe) is the best defenseman in the league and made this one of the most exciting moments of my life," said Barber after Froese's 7-4 victory over Toronto.

Jensen's confidence, however, had been destroyed by the bad overtime goal in Edmonton. He was beaten on 5 of the first 10 shots he faced on March 8 at New Jersey. Despite Kerr's NHL record-breaking 29th power-play goal of the season, the Flyers lost 7-3 to Chico Resch, furthering speculation that Philadelphia would acquire the New Jersey netminder prior to the approaching trade deadline. "Whether Bobby Clarke decides to deal for me or not," said Resch, the NHL's oldest goalie at 37, "I wanted to show him I could still play at a high level."

The following night at Madison Square Garden, Froese was back in commanding form as the Flyers won, 4-1. Keenan, however, had become convinced that his top goalie needed a veteran to push him. Clarke haggled with Devils GM Max McNab, refusing to meet the asking price of a third-round pick until Jay Snider saved an impasse. The Flyer president interceded with Devils owner John McMullen while convincing Clarke that a third-rounder was not too high a price for peace of mind heading into the playoffs.

The deal was closed minutes before the deadline, putting the longtime nemesis, critic and admirer of the orange and black into a Philadelphia uniform. "I've always wondered what goes on in that locker room," said a bubbly Resch.

At practice the following day, Keenan noticed a perkier Flyer team. "We picked up a guy who has really developed that sense of enthusiasm or charisma that energizes a team," said the coach.

With a 15-9-1 record and a 3.68 average, Jensen packed his bags for Hershey with a stiff upper lip. "I got 29 games in up here and I learned something," he said.

Froese was flawless as Philadelphia shut out Washington 2-0 to retake the division lead. Resch surrendered 5 goals of 12 shots in Toronto before being pulled after two periods, but the Flyers bounced back for a 6-5 overtime victory. Resch rallied, too, beating the Rangers 4-2 for his first Philadelphia victory.

Chico then failed to hug the post on the winning goal in a 6-5 loss in Landover, keeping the Caps' division-title hopes alive. But on April 2, Froese turned in his best performance of the season, winning 3-2 at Madison Square Garden. In Pittsburgh, the Flyers came from behind to win 4-3 on Sinisalo's overtime goal and returned home to face Washington in Game 80 needing a win or a tie to wrap up the Patrick championship.

Philadelphia started too cautiously and fell behind on goals 52 seconds apart by Jorgen Pettersson and Craig Laughlin. But Kerr got the team started with a goal and Propp spun away from rookie defenseman Kevin Hatcher to tie the game. McCrimmon then threw the puck past a flat-footed Scott Stevens, springing Poulin and Propp on a two-man shorthanded breakaway. Poulin lured goalie Pete Peeters, Propp hit a wide-open net, and the Flyers went on to a stirring 5-3 victory that seemed to reconfirm their infallibility under pressure.

Despite a season of anguish, Philadelphia equalled its previous year's total of 53 victories and earned a first-round series against the Rangers, a team the Flyers had defeated in 18 of their last 19 meetings.

Ted Sator had transformed New York, 36-38-6, into the third-best defensive team in the league behind Philadelphia and Washington, but his leading scorer, rookie Mike Ridley, had only 65 points. The division champion Flyers had more speed, more firepower and, after Froese had gone 12-0 down the stretch, no doubts they would have another long playoff run. "We're better than a year ago," said Howe. "We're healthier and our goaltending is just as good as it was last year."

Philadelphia quickly wiped out two one-goal deficits early in Game 1, almost as if it could score against the Rangers at will. But when New York killed off a 1:50 two-man advantage and Ridley cashed a Richter holding penalty, the game changed startlingly.

Ron Greschner had all day to pick the top corner after Froese steered Tomas Sandstrom's wide-angle drive up the slot and the shocked Flyers stopped moving the puck. Philadelphia's only response—a Brown cross-check that drove goalie John Vanbiesbrouck's head into the crossbar—brought back bad memories of undisciplined playoff losses to the Rangers.

"I wouldn't say we lost our poise," said Keenan, his voice as cold as the chill running up the spines of Flyer fans after the 6-2 loss. "We never had it. This was the worst game we played since I came here."

The following night in Game 2, the team responded positively. Ron Sutter spun away from Larry Melnyk behind the net and fed Rich for the game-opening goal. Only 16 seconds later, McCrimmon converted a give-and-go with Tocchet. But Vanbiesbrouck made 19 first-period saves and, after Pierre Larouche cut the lead to one on a two-man advantage early in the second, Philadelphia lost its offensive flow. The Rangers took restraining penalties, but set up a tight penalty-killing box that closed the passing lane between Eklund and Kerr.

Meanwhile, Froese, 0-4 lifetime in the playoffs, stood almost idly by as his teammates failed to provide a margin for error. But Derrick Smith, who had been scratched in the opener, dogged Sandstrom, Ron Sutter hounded Ridley, and New York was held nearly thirty-nine minutes without a quality shot in a series-tying 2-1 Flyer victory. "After last night, I didn't just have the monkey on my back," said Froese, "I had the whole zoo."

The rest of the club, unable to crush the Rangers despite a stronger effort, did not seem to share the goalie's relief. Still, Philadelphia managed goals by Kerr and Sinisalo to overcome Greschner's tally and take a 2-1 lead into the third period of Game 3 in New York.

Handling the puck like a hot potato and trudging barefoot across burning coals with another one-goal lead, Keenan's grim team was twelve minutes from squeaking through again when Melnyk saved the puck at the point, beat Ron Sutter down the boards, and fed an incomprehensibly wide-open Ridley for a tap-in.

Only 3:26 later, Smith unnecessarily tripped Bob Brooke as he moved laterally across the blueline. On the power play, Propp was caught too deep and Jim Wiemer jumped into the slot to backhand the go-ahead goal past Froese.

Keenan called his players to the bench, ordered the entire team onto the ice to face him and delivered an angry lecture. "It was a mistake," Keenan says today. "I should have been a calming influence."

Fourteen seconds after play resumed, Brooke beat Zezel on a faceoff and stepped around him to the puck. Brown mistakenly covered the point, Froese missed a diving poke check, and Brooke hit a wide-open net. Suddenly down by two, the Flyers gambled and Crossman was caught up ice as Greschner finished a two-on-one. The Rangers, 5-2 winners at a howling Garden, were one victory away from a monumental upset.

"Nobody in this room is down," said Tocchet defiantly to reporters. At the hotel, Keenan called a team meeting and allowed beer for a rare time with a game scheduled the following night. The players discussed their predicament rationally, reminding each other not to panic if they failed to score first in Game 4. Sure enough, with Kerr serving an early penalty, Sandstrom hooked Howe off the puck and Ridley fed Larouche for the 1-0 lead. Froese, however, refused to be rattled as New York went for a fast kill. Late in the period, McCrimmon intercepted the puck at the point and Zezel redirected Sinisalo's feed between Vanbiesbrouck's legs to tie the game.

Froese then made two sparkling saves on Larouche before Ridley took an interference penalty. Zezel, taking Eklund's spot on the power play to give Philadelphia more bulk against the aggressive Ranger penalty killing, put a shot through Kerr's screen and the Flyers, on their first power-play goal in 18 attempts, gained a 2-1 lead. "You could just feel the air come back into our lungs on the bench," Resch said later.

On the first shift of the second period, Poulin trapped Vanbiesbrouck's clear and scored off the skate of Greschner, who was trying to tie up the omnipresent Kerr. Less than a minute later, he picked up a Howe block, broke away and scored off Vanbiesbrouck's arm.

After Zezel completed a hat trick, Vanbiesbrouck was pulled for Glen Hanlon, who in Game 3 had taunted Tocchet following his fistic defeat at the hands of George McPhee. When Sutter rubbed out

Reijo Ruotsalainen at the blue line, Tocchet roared in alone to achieve vengeance and complete a five-goal second period. New York was routed 7-1 and both teams returned to the Spectrum for a deciding Game 5.

Marsh and Holmgren recalled the ill-fated euphoria after a similarly gutsy Game 6 victory at Calgary in 1981 and cautioned their teammates not to let down. "The Rangers are in a position where if they play the game of their lives, they can make their whole season," said Marsh.

Indeed, the pressure Sator's club had felt to avoid going back to Philadelphia was gone. And as the puck dropped, it was obvious the Flyers felt most of the anxiety. Howe had the dropsies, accidentally kicking a McCrimmon clear back in front of his own goal. On the next shift, he had to pick his own fumble out of Froese's skate to start a power-play rush.

Sandstrom twice beat Marsh to create New York chances, and Froese made twin stops on Kelly Miller before the winger intercepted a weak clear by the goalie and fed Pierre Larouche, whose shot caromed off the sliding Marsh's stick high into the net.

In the second period, Sinisalo chased down a long dump-out by Howe and beat Vanbiesbrouck off the far post to tie the game. But the Rangers were unfazed. They blocked a Howe shot to break out four-on-two, and when Ron Sutter chased behind the net instead of picking up Larouche in the slot, the New York sniper's rebound was converted by Willy Huber over Froese's glove. Only 1:11 later, Propp shoved Maloney into McCrimmon, allowing Mark Osborne to jump into a vacant left side, fake the challenging goalie, and slide the puck into the short side.

A four-man Ranger defense keyed by James Patrick protected the two-goal lead superbly until Zezel beat Brooke on a draw and McCrimmon's bouncer got by the butterflying Vanbiesbrouck with 8:24 remaining to make the score 3-2. When McCrimmon, following a broken-up Kerr rush, put a screamer through Poulin's screen, the captain was certain Philadelphia had tied the game. Instead, the team's last good chance was in Vanbiesbrouck's fully-extended glove. "I don't know how he saw it," Poulin said later.

In the final minute, Huber blocked a Howe shot and fed Miller for the first of two empty-net goals that sealed New York's improbable, yet impressive, 5-2 triumph.

As the fans departed in shocked silence, the Flyers sat stunned in front of their lockers. "We were mad that we lost," Tocchet recalls, "but I remember also thinking, 'At least it's over.' There had been a lot of pressure on us for a long time. I think it caught up with us."

Clarke expressed disappointment that the team's second-year players had not grown as expected. Keenan gave the Rangers, expertly prepared by Sator's intimate knowledge of the Flyers, the credit they deserved. "We came up against a team that rode on the confidence of its goaltender, had the advantage of playing in a short series, and did a terrific job," said the losing coach.

In time, Keenan came to feel he had pushed too hard through the regular season. "We had 110 points without an ace goalie but, having had success the first year, the team was a little more difficult to manage," he recalls. "I probably should have let them falter a little and learn their own lessons. They were a tremendously strong group. They deserved the opportunity to learn that on their own."

Froese, who had been superb during the slow Flyer starts of Games 4 and 5, but mishandled the puck before critical goals, was absolved of public blame by the coach. "Considering the pressures he was under, Bob Froese responded very well," Keenan said.

Privately, he was not sold. "I thought Froese was a great second goalie," recalls Keenan. "I just didn't think he was talented enough to be a No. 1 goalie. I knew we had to make a change."

As he spent the empty weeks that followed the loss watching Ron Hextall carry Hershey to the AHL finals, Keenan began to believe there was a viable option. "I can't say I was sure about what we had [in Hextall]," he recalls, "but I thought it was pretty good. I liked his competitiveness. I was going to give him every opportunity."

Keenan's pay was raised and his contract extended through 1988-89, the second extension in two years. "I think he did an even better job this year than he did a year ago," said Jay Snider.

Eriksson, who had never gained the coach's confidence, decided to return to Sweden to become a police officer. "Thomas was a good person," said Clarke. "I'm just not sure he wanted to be a good hockey player." Philadelphia used its No. 1 pick on a projected replacement, Kerry Huffman, then re-signed Hospodar, who had played out his Minnesota contract. But Clarke's biggest move during the summer of 1986 to strengthen his defense almost yielded a bonanza.

On June 6, the GM believed he had consummated a deal that would have sent Propp, Rich Sutter, Richter and a first-round 1986 choice to the Canucks for right wing Cam Neely, defenseman Jean-Jacques Daigneault, and Vancouver's first pick in the 1986 draft.

Clarke, who had been coveting Neely, a slow-to-develop 1983 first-round pick, for two years, was all but certain the trade was done. "Arthur Griffiths (the Canucks' assistant to the chairman) said they just wanted to talk it over one more time," Clarke recalls. Two hours later, Griffiths called and said Vancouver had decided instead to sign (Boston's free-agent center) Barry Pederson and offer Neely as compensation."

"I was sick," recalls Clarke. He begged Griffiths to go through with the Flyer deal, sign Pederson and then offer Propp to the Bruins, but Griffiths's mind was made up. He said if Philadelphia was still interested in Daigneault, Clarke should phone Canucks GM Jackie Gordon.

Later that day, Richter, Rich Sutter and a third-round pick were moved to Vancouver for a second-round pick and Daigneault. The 20-year-old defenseman, the tenth selection overall in 1984, was a brilliant skater who had lost confidence as coach Tom Watt preached defensive responsibility.

After the March signing of Scott Mellanby, a 1984 second-round pick who had been playing at the University of Wisconsin, Rich Sutter had dropped to fifth on the right wing depth chart. The Sutter family did not see opportunity for him in Vancouver, only red at the Flyers' audacity to split the twins. Mother Grace gave Keenan an earful when he phoned to wish Richie well. Father Louie publicly called the organization "backstabbers."

"I'm not worried about Louie," Clarke said. "I'm worried about Ron. He's the one who has to play for us." Indeed, familial considerations had had an impact on the decision. Clarke felt Ron's play was being hurt by his concern for his struggling brother. "I know that's what they're thinking," Ron said, "but every time he was playing well, he got yanked. I won't forget this."

Ron Sutter finished second to Chicago's Troy Murray for the Selke Trophy, awarded to the league's top defensive forward, and Howe, who had been beaten out for the Norris Trophy by Rod Langway in 1983, was again runner-up, this time to Paul Coffey.

Froese lost the Vezina by the heartbreaking margin of one second-place vote, but could not be angry when his speech was stolen by the winner. "There was an automobile accident in November," Vanbiesbrouck told the black-tie assemblage and Canadian television audience. "I would like to honor Pelle Lindbergh tonight in accepting this."

As if to complete the cycle of a painful season, in June 1986 the Flyers marked the passing of another beloved figure in their history. Kate Smith, who had been in ill health for ten years with problems associated with her diabetes, died at age 79 in Raleigh, North Carolina.

Clarke set high expectations for the coming season. "I think it's time for this team to do something," he said at a precamp press conference. At the same get-together, Keenan said he would heed the advice of his assistants and lighten up. "The players are mature enough now that the coaching staff can throw the ball to them and say, 'Let's have some fun,'" the coach said.

Keenan recalls. "It wasn't an emphatic discussion or an argument but I remember it clearly."

Clarke insists he also wanted Hextall to start in Philadelphia. But Keenan strongly assured the 22-year-old goalie both privately and publicly that a place on the big team was his to lose. "Evaluating him fits in with the overall philosophy of forcing myself to look more at the overall picture," the coach told the media.

Poulin received a doubled, troubled dose of per-

Ron Hextall won the starting goaltender's job with a strong training camp in 1986.

McCrimmon, unamused to be playing out his option for $160,000, sought a four-year deal at $250,000 per season. Clarke tried unsuccessfully to obtain Quebec defenseman Randy Moller for McCrimmon, who then rejected a four-year contract paid over six seasons that topped out at $225,000. After dressing for the first exhibition contest, McCrimmon refused to play until he had a new agreement. He was suspended and went home to Saskatchewan.

Although Hextall was outstanding, going 4-0 in his exhibition starts, the convenient move, with Resch re-signed, would have been to send the rookie to Hershey for another season. "I told Bob, 'No way,'"

spective four days before the start of the season. His wife, Kim, gave birth to twin daughters three months prematurely. Taylor and Lindsey Poulin weighed only two-and-one-half pounds each and faced a long, hard fight for survival.

Keenan, meanwhile, continued to incubate his scheme to make Hextall his top goaltender. On the morning of the opener against the Edmonton Oilers at the Spectrum, the coach told the kid that he would get the start. Hextall's afternoon nap was interrupted by calls from his agent, Alan Eagleson, and Clarke, who wanted a new contract signed before the option year of his old deal kicked in that night. Hextall agreed to the significant rookie salary of $200,000, then went out to play his first NHL game against the greatest offensive machine in league history.

Only 2:08 into the game, Kurri picked up a Coffey pass that had bounced off Esa Tikkanen's skate and went around Hextall for an easy deposit, but the goalie did not rattle. When Wayne Gretzky broke away, the Flyer challenged and made a stop by dragging his pad.

"Who the hell are you?" Gretzky said to Hextall.

"Who the hell are *you?*" Hextall shot back. When Tikkanen had a breakaway early in the second period, the 6-foot-3 wall moved to the top of crease, giving the Finn no view of the net. "You don't see it done any better than that," marveled Sather. In the third period, Sutter beat Grant Fuhr from a bad angle, Zezel put in a rebound, and Hextall protected Philadelphia's 2-1 lead. When the buzzer sounded, he celebrated with a leap into the air.

Froese, meanwhile, was not doing handsprings. "He'll get his chance in due time," said Keenan.

After Hextall beat Washington 6-1 in Landover, Froese got a start against Vancouver and won 6-2. But Keenan turned right back to Hextall, who stopped Hartford 6-3 and defeated Winnipeg, 3-1. The Jets' Hannu Jarvenpaa had two shots, no goals, and one question: "How old is that goalie?"

"[Hextall] is one of the best I've ever seen," raved Resch. "For a guy that size, he's really quick. The most impressive thing about him is his balance. He's always in control as he moves from side to side."

Clarke maneuvered to break the McCrimmon impasse, but could not get equal value in trade. The GM and defenseman agreed on a one-year deal plus an option that would pay the Flyer $190,000 for the team's remaining 71 games. "I could be a jerk and tell him to to sit out the entire year," said Clarke, leveraged by Philadelphia's 7-2 start. "But I'm not going to do that."

"They did their thing, I did mine," McCrimmon said. "It's time to play hockey."

When Froese asked Clarke when it would be *his* time to play, the GM had no answer. Hextall was roaming from the goal, firing breakout passes, performing rhythmic passages with his stick against the goalposts, and stopping the puck like a Hall of Famer. He also refused to be intimidated by an increasingly bitter Froese, who one day ordered the kid out of a seat on the team bus.

"That's where the No. 1 goalie sits," said Froese.

"I'll have that seat," said Hextall as he found another.

Froese tried to hold the Flyers to a promised upgrade of his $145,000-a-year contract. But a backup was not going to rate a raise, so Clarke agreed to search for a trade.

"I'm 28 and my time is now," the goalie said when revealing his request to the media on October 30. Keenan, who was planning to give Froese a start two nights later against Boston, was livid. "If I went ahead and played him, it would look like I was rewarding him for speaking out," the coach said. When Froese announced that he was mentally unprepared to play, Keenan refused to dress him.

On the whole, however, Iron Mike was keeping his training-camp pledge to be a kinder, gentler coach. When Philadelphia turned a 5-1 lead with ten minutes remaining into a 5-5 tie at New Jersey, Keenan left the arena without a word to his players. He even retained a smile after the Flyers lost twice within six days to the Rangers in early November. "Maybe this year they'll win all the games in the regular season and we'll beat them in the playoffs," he said.

Kerr, scheduled to walk to the altar with Kathleen Anzaldo on November 23, enjoyed a bachelor party at Chicago's expense, recording the fourth four-goal game of his career in a 5-1 victory. Tocchet wisely decided not to play tough guy when he skated away from the fistic challenge of Brian Curran and instead scored with 32 seconds left to beat the Islanders, 6-5. "I was more important on the ice," said Tocchet, whose 11 goals in 23 games left him only three short of his 1985-86 total.

Daigneault only sporadically flashed his offensive skills, so Keenan dug in again, rotating four defensemen. Propp, with 41 points in 27 games, suffered a fractured left knee during a 5-2 Spectrum victory over Edmonton and ruined his chance at a 100-point season. "I would have done it this time," said the disappointed winger, who would be out nine weeks.

The following day the Flyers announced that Froese was going into the net whether he was mentally prepared or not. "Like all other members of the team, he is expected to play," said Keenan, effectively reducing Resch, who had been in only two contests, to chopped liver.

"This is unbelievable," said Froese. "For two years, I've heard Mike Keenan give the same speech at the beginning of training camp. He said if somebody didn't want to be here, they would accommodate him. Now, somebody is speaking with a forked tongue."

Nevertheless, with Froese in goal, Philadelphia beat Vancouver, 6-3. Afterwards, the goalie said it was the hardest thing he ever had to do in his life. "Jay (Snider) called and told me to look at it as playing for myself, so that's what I did," said Froese. Nine days later, he was dealt to the Rangers for defenseman Kjell Samuelsson and a second-round pick in 1989.

Clarke assessed the 6-foot-6 Samuelsson, a second-year pro drafted at the advanced age of 25, as not only big, but annoying. The GM, however, had a hidden agenda as he pursued the trade with New York's new general manager, Phil Esposito, whose

Tim Kerr scored 50 goals for the fourth consecutive season in 1986-87.

fourth-place team was again looming as the Flyers' first-round opponent. Armed with a healthy respect for Vanbiesbrouck, Clarke hoped Froese's knowledge of the Philadelphia shooters would make him the logical playoff starter in the Rangers' eyes.

Esposito was bored with the conservative style New York had used during the Flyer and Washington upsets of the previous spring. He fired Sator and traded Bob Brooke to Minnesota for defenseman Curt Giles, thereby making Samuelsson expendable. "I've got a lot of guys like him," the Ranger GM said. Esposito immediately promised the Froese a new contract and half the starts. It was not the dream job the ex-Flyer wanted, but he was delighted to be freed

from Keenan.

Philadelphia fans and most members of the media were incredulous at the trade. Clarke had traded a goaltender with a 92-29-12 career record to the Flyers' archrival for a blueliner who had played 39 NHL games and looked like a flamingo.

Injuries began to take their toll. Sinisalo joined Propp on the sidelines, aggravating a left knee sprain on December 23 in Buffalo. The Sabres, playing their first game under new head coach Ted Sator, won 2-1. Sutter was lost to back problems during a comeback 5-4 victory in Boston and a 6-0-1 surge died with a 3-1 Spectrum loss to the Islanders on January 18. "There were just no more buttons to push," said Keenan.

Samuelsson, whose play initially upset only the fans, began crawling under opponents' skins. When he and Mel Bridgman pushed each other at the conclusion of New Jersey's 4-3 victory at the Meadowlands on January 24, the Flyers, noting the Devils were already on the ice to congratulate goalie Alain Chevrier, cleared the bench. Hextall, who had not played, made a beeline for Chevrier and pummeled him. "Maybe we aren't allowed to beat them," sneered Chevrier.

After Howe's back discs flared, Philadelphia faced the Sabres at the Aud on January 28 missing eight regulars. The Flyers won 7-4 thanks to a hat trick by Zezel.

Sutter's back didn't improve with rest and Dr. Robert Booth found a stress fracture in a vertebra, ordering the center off skates for at least six weeks.

Froese made a triumphant return to the Spectrum, slamming the door on a ragtag collection of Flyers and Hershey call-ups in New York's 3-1 win, but Keenan refused to take it personally. "This has been an exercise in self-restraint," said the coach. Propp returned after missing 27 games, but the Devils extended Philadelphia's losing streak to 4 with a 3-2 victory at the Meadowlands.

The five-day break created by Rendezvous 87—two games between the NHL All-Stars and Soviet national team in Quebec City—became a respite for a dragging club. It was also an opportunity for Poulin to strut his stuff with the sport's elite players. He redirected a Mario Lemieux feed with 1:15 remaining to give the NHL a thrilling 4-3 victory in Game 1. The Soviets bounced back for a 5-3 Game 2 win, but the captain, his mind clearing as his daughters grew strong enough to come home, was energized by the experience. When the regular season resumed, Poulin tallied twice as Philadelphia won 4-2 in St. Louis, then scored with 1:57 remaining to force a 4-4 tie with Pittsburgh that extended the Penguins' thirteen-year winless streak at the Spectrum to 0-33-2.

Howe returned from a 10-game absence on February 21 in Los Angeles and was instantly a major difference in a 4-2 victory. Sinisalo came back two games later in a 5-4 loss at Minnesota, leaving Sutter, as the sole disabled regular. The Flyers, only 12-13-3 since December 23, emerged from their injury onslaught with a 14-point Patrick Division lead.

As the playoffs approached, Keenan began cracking the whip with mixed results. Froese beat Philadelphia again, 6-1 at the Spectrum, but five days later in New York the Flyers got first-period goals by Propp and Poulin and solid goaltending from surprise starter Resch in a 5-2 victory. When the teams met for the third time in six nights, Kerr reached the 50-goal mark for the fourth consecutive year and Brown retaliated for a Tomas Sandstrom high stick of Howe by delivering a vicious cross-check across the antagonist's face shield. Philadelphia won 4-1, but lost Brown to a 5-game suspension.

A knee sprain sidelined Tocchet and the Flyers called up Craig Berube. In his debut, the free-agent signee collected 26 penalty minutes in three separate altercations during a wild 3-1 Spectrum victory over Pittsburgh.

Zezel sustained a torn medial meniscus in his left knee during a dismal 5-2 Spectrum loss to Los Angeles and Sinisalo limped off from a March 27 practice with a cracked bone in his left foot. Neither was expected back for a first round only ten days away.

The coach, willing to sacrifice the final few regular-season games, conducted brutal practices to increase the team's conditioning level going into the playoffs. Hextall, the lone consistent bright spot during the frustrating second half of the season, endured his worst game as the improving Red Wings ended a sixteen-year, 29-game winless streak at the Spectrum with a 5-1 victory. He bounced back sharply in a rematch at Detroit as Philadelphia

reached 100 points with a 2-1 victory. "What a goalie," marvelled Detroit coach Jacques Demers. "He got the puck out like a third defenseman. He controlled the game."

Hextall was named winner of the Bobby Clarke Trophy before the final match of the regular season, which the Flyers entered holding a three-goal lead over Montreal for the Jennings Trophy (lowest goals-against average). But after the Islanders scored four times on 7 shots during a 9-minute stretch of the third period and rolled 9-5, Philadelphia appeared vulnerable to a fifth first-round flop in six years.

"There are no excuses for that kind of effort," said Clarke. "The coach has to share some of the blame."

Clarke understood that injuries were the biggest factor in the Flyers' 15-15-5 record since January 17, but wondered if players were going cold on their demanding leader. The GM was annoyed how little ice time his additions of the last two seasons were receiving and cringed at Keenan's negative motivational techniques, particularly on Mellanby. "I still maintain it wasn't that bad an enviornment," said Marsh. "A lot of guys had their best years. But the expectations were higher and Mike hated losing so much that things became that much more tense."

Philadelphia (finishing 46-26-8) met the Rangers (34-38-8) in the first round of the playoffs for the seventh time in nine years. Only once during that stretch had New York accrued a higher regular-season point total, yet it won four of the six matchups.

"Every Ranger series had a surreal feeling to it," recalls Poulin. And the plot for this one seemed especially strange. Eighteen trades by Esposito had drastically altered New York's lineup since the semifinals of the preceding spring. Many of the club's hardest workers—such as Ridley, Miller and Brooke—were gone, and the league's third-best defensive team under Sator was now the third-worst.

Esposito, who had put himself behind the bench when coach Tom Webster developed an inner-ear problem, had twelve players aged 28 or older in the lineup.

The NHL had extended the first round to a best-of-seven to allow the better team more time to prove itself. But in Game 1 at the Spectrum, the Flyers looked like they would need more than seven games to get their act together.

After Daigneault hit a post early in a scoreless second period, Pierre Larouche stripped Crossman and beat Hextall between his legs. Ron Duguay's goal 27 seconds later put Keenan's team in a 2-0 hole and a state of disbelief that the Rangers could so suddenly have fixed their leaks. John Vanbiesbrouck's 3-0 shut-out was New York's first of the season.

Philadelphia tried not to panic. "I knew what they felt—that fear of losing to the bleeping Rangers again in the first round," recalls Clarke. The GM attended a postgame team meal and tried to stress Flyer strengths and Ranger weaknesses. "Mostly, we tried to stay calm," Clarke said.

Zezel returned for Game 2 as did the team's energy level. Brown ignited the crowd by pounding

Kjell Samuelsson got under the skin of the opposition.

George McPhee, but every rebound lay just out of Philadelphia's reach until late in the first period when Marsh's point shot through a screen broke Vanbiesbrouck's spell.

After Marcel Dionne tied the game, Mellanby scored to the goalie's glove side. With 1:09 left in the second period, Maloney held off Howe and redirected Kelly Kisio's pass to make it 2-2. But the Rangers, reverting to season-long form, gave the goal right back. Carson threw the puck past a daydreaming Larouche to Tocchet, who shot between Vanbiesbrouck's legs at 19:56 of the second.

Five minutes into the third, Kerr sneaked behind Larry Melnyk and scored off a pass from Howe. When Poulin made it 5-2 on a delayed penalty, Esposito

tapped Froese, who was beaten three times as the Flyers completed an 8-3 rout to tie the series, 1-1.

Before Game 3, Esposito, still angry that a replay of Brown's punchout of McPhee had been shown on ArenaVision, shoved a hand into Jay Snider's chest.

"You're a no-class bleep." said Esposito.

"Bleep you," said Jay.

When the puck was dropped, the Rangers were as riled as their boss, but Hextall dissipated the home team's early burst. Poulin forced a Tony McKegney giveaway, allowing Zezel to score shorthanded. Howe and Tocchet added goals in Hextall's 3-0 shutout.

Esposito apologized to Jay following the game, but ripped Keenan. "He sent Brown out after McPhee, plain as day," said Esposito. "It makes me think a lot of the rumors I've heard about him are true."

On these notes of mutual respect, Game 4 began. Philadelphia, positioned to gain a stranglehold on the series, was overanxious and paid for it. Zezel was caught up ice on Sandstrom's goal after only 1:03. Three minutes later, Ron Greschner connected with Pat Price coming out of the penalty box and Jeff Jackson converted a two-on-one. With Brown off for tripping, McPhee backhanded in a rebound to make the score 3-0.

Keenan tried to change the momentum by switching to Resch and, early in the second period, Propp converted Kerr's passout for the Flyers' first power-play goal of the series. But Carson ran over Froese, then hit him in the face as he went to the bench on the delayed penalty, earning an additional two minutes.

A wired Hextall returned to the nets to kill the disadvantage. Baited by Esposito, the rookie gestured back at the Ranger coach while hacking, whacking and kicking at every leg and puck in front of him. He kept Philadelphia within two goals until Mellanby unnecessarily tripped Larouche and Duguay converted on the power play.

As the Rangers pulled away, Keenan sent out Berube, who fought McPhee while Hextall gestured at Froese. "Ronald," Esposito taunted Hextall while making a yapping motion with his hand. "Ronald McDonald."

"This is hockey, not Wrestlemania," said a subdued Hextall after the 6-3 loss. But with the series tied at two, the Flyers had been lured into a steel-cage death match against an inferior foe. The pious New York complaints about Philadelphia's tactics were as old as many Rangers. Still, Keenan's team was begging for disaster.

Twenty-eight seconds after Samuelsson took a holding penalty in Game 5, Hextall accidentally cleared the puck over the glass, creating a two-man Ranger advantage. The rookie atoned with good saves on Sandstrom and Dionne. When James Patrick's drive ticked off Hextall's pads and trickled toward the line, Howe whisked the puck from danger.

Early in the second period, Tocchet knocked down Price's windaround, Derrick Smith kept a rebound alive, and Tocchet jammed in the game's precious first goal. Hextall won a race with Larouche, but missed a poke check, allowing the Ranger to score into an empty net. But the Flyers kept coming. Froese made a superlative stop on Zezel, but Eklund's centering pass hopped over the goalie's stick and Kerr flicked the puck into the net to give Philadelphia a 2-1 lead.

The Flyers were finally making the Rangers look tired, catching them continually in transition errors and forcing Froese to field 32 shots in the final two periods. But he gave his ex-teammates no margin for error until the final minute, when Tocchet tipped the puck out of the zone and Jackson threw his stick to keep Smith from scoring into the empty net. Referee Terry Gregson awarded the goal and Philadelphia, a 3-1 winner, was now one game away from avenging the previous spring's first-round loss. "After what we've been through, sure we're nervous," admitted Howe. "But I think we're handling the pressure much better this time."

While Samuelsson–the defenseman Esposito had termed generic–was responding to Keenan's increasing trust, the New York backline, minus Giles with an elbow injury from Game 5, was fraying.

A check by Duguay four minutes into Game 6 sent Poulin into the boards and to the hospital for Xrays of his ribs. But the Flyers, not disappointed by Esposito's decision to start Vanbiesbrouck, still had plenty left for the kill. Smith converted Tocchet's rebound and Crossman soloed off a McKegney giveaway to give Philadelphia a 2-0 lead.

In the second period, Patrick accidentally redirected a harmless Marsh throw-in past Vanbiesbrouck. "When you scored," said Keith Allen to Marsh after the game, "they knew to pack it in." Goals by Kerr and Carson finished up Hextall's 5-0 shutout.

Keenan lit up a cigar fatter than Esposito's head and Jay Snider couldn't resist gloating. "You want to beat any team to prove you're superior," said Snider. "But you want to beat the Rangers just to shut them up."

The Flyers eliminated the Rangers in six while the Islanders rallied to beat the Capitals—in eight. New York had played the equivalent of two seventh games before Pat LaFontaine's goal at 8:47 of the fourth overtime gave coach Terry Simpson's team a 3-2 victory. Forty hours later, the Islanders arrived at the Spectrum happy to be alive, but not exactly rested and healthy. Mike Bossy, Denis Potvin, Patrick Flatley and Brent Sutter were all out.

Philadelphia had players missing from its lineup as well. Poulin and Craven (who belatedly learned he had suffered a broken foot in the Ranger clincher) joined Ron Sutter on the injured list, necessitating the recall of Al Hill and Don Nachbaur from Hershey. Poof. Nachbaur scored a goal and Hill an assist as the Flyers rode Kerr's hat trick to a 4-2 victory.

The Islanders had their legs, plus Potvin, back for Game 2. Crossman's goal five minutes into the third broke a scoreless tie, but Potvin answered on the power play. Only one minute remained when Zezel jumped onto the ice during a change, even though Propp had already replaced Carson. Linesman Wayne Bonney counted seven Flyers and whistled a penalty.

On the power play, Tomas Jonsson twice spun away from Propp at the point and fed Mikko Makela down the side boards. Hextall challenged as the young winger wound up from above the face-off dot, but his perfect shot landed just inside the far post with only 3 seconds remaining. New York had tied the series with a stunning 2-1 victory.

Keenan took the heat for Zezel, who had mistaken the coach's reminder to be ready on the following shift for an order to immediately jump on the ice. "I take complete responsibility," said Keenan. But the coach was privately livid with Propp, who not only missed his check on the Game 2 winner, but had scored just once in Philadelphia's last 15 playoff games. Again the Flyers needed their best all-around forward to raise his level of play, but playoff pressure appeared to have him rattled.

"I never thought that was it," recalls Keenan. "I think it was just a matter of learning what it takes to succeed in the playoffs. [Propp] was a competitor, but he probably felt he couldn't stretch himself beyond a certain point and we needed that. To be fair, he wasn't a big man. A top player, but not a superstar."

Keenan had a long talk with Propp, dipped into

Hershey for 26-year-old AHL scoring champ Tim Tookey and matched him against LaFontaine, the emerging Islander star. The scoring in Game 3 opened when Howe's point drive was redirected by Hill just as he received a 40-stitch cut from Potvin's stick. The defenseman was not penalized, but justice prevailed when Potvin cleared a puck onto Tookey's stick and the awakening Propp rang up a rebound to make it 2-0. Eklund and Howe added goals as Philadelphia limited New York to one score—by LaFontaine—and two superior chances during a surprisingly easy 4-1 victory.

The return of Bossy and Brent Sutter gave the Islanders a stronger lineup for Game 4, but again the Hershey players came through. Tookey fed Hill for one goal, then forced a Rich Kromm giveaway before converting a goalmouth pass from Propp.

Kerr, set up by an increasingly shining Eklund, rammed in his second power-play goal of the night to put the Flyers ahead, 5-3. Brent Sutter scored on the advantage with 12:21 remaining but Hextall made a big stop on Sutter and Philadelphia diligently checked away the clock. In the final minute, Bossy stumbled over LaFontaine's setup in the slot and Tocchet soloed to the empty net to wrap up a 6-4 Flyer triumph.

The Islanders, who had also been down 3-1 in the Washington series, almost seemed comforted by their desperate situation. They did not concede Game 5, even after Carson blocked a Ken Morrow shot, raced the length of the ice and went backhand-to-forehand to put Philadelphia ahead. New York tied the score when Hextall tripped in a rut as he went to stop a routine Kromm shot, then went ahead early in the third when Morrow's dump from the side boards bounced in off Smith's leg as Randy Wood crashed Hextall. The Islanders jammed the middle, stayed out of the penalty box, and got good stops from Kelly Hrudey on Tocchet, Zezel and Eklund down the stretch to stay alive with a 2-1 victory.

When the Flyers returned to Uniondale for Game 6, Ron Sutter was in the lineup for the first time since January 10. But with Poulin still out, Zezel playing poorly, and Brent Sutter and Trottier getting stronger with each contest, Philadelphia was at a serious disadvantage up the middle. Although the Islanders' history of rising from the grave did not trouble the Flyers, Kerr's shoulder did. Throughout the series, the harness he was wearing had become increasingly ineffective and during Game 6's warmup, he could barely shoot.

While Philadelphia's top gun was now a mere de-coy, the Islanders' sniper, Bossy, was heating up. His power-play backhander opened the scoring and Trottier banked one in off Tookey before McCrimmon's shorthanded goal cut New York's edge in half.

Kerr did not come out for the third period, when Trottier redirected Ken Leiter's point drive to give New York a 3-1 lead. Propp's deflection once again pulled the Flyers to within one, but Jonsson stole the puck from Sinisalo and fed Bob Bassen, who put away a 4-2 victory that extended the Islanders' record in games in which they faced elimination to 22-8.

All of New York's key contributors were back for Game 7, while Kerr was finished for the playoffs. The Flyers would need an adrenaline burst to finish off their opponents, so Keenan tried to make sure his team did not waste any emotional energy on worry. At Clarke's suggestion, the coach and his boys spent the off-night at the Comedy Factory Outlet, where WMMR's John DeBella did a great Keenan, the kind of humor the players most appreciated.

Poulin's ribs still hurt when he laughed. "But when you could see it coming to a seventh game, I knew I was going to ask to play," he recalls. The captain took painkillers and wrapped himself in a flak jacket and bulky shoulder pads.

The Philadelphia fans, who had started to work themselves up several minutes before the Flyers hit the ice, roared at the sight of the captain. The Islanders did not like what they saw in their opponents' eyes. "After a few shifts you could tell there was just no way we were going to beat them," Trottier recalled later.

The visitors received a brief reprieve when Carson lifted the net off its magnets just as Tocchet was putting in Crossman's rebound. Referee Don Koharski correctly waved off the goal. But on the next shift, Poulin turned up inside the Islander blue line and hit Propp, who lifted a backhander that Brown, with position on Morrow, tipped between Hrudey's legs.

Three minutes later, with Carson off for hooking Bossy, Hextall came out to play a dump-in and fanned. McCrimmon, however, quickly wheeled the puck up to Propp, who was waiting with Poulin an unbelievable fifteen feet beyond Potvin and Leiter. Propp controlled a return pass from Poulin with his skate, and finished off the two-man breakaway.

The Spectrum was in a frenzy. On the next shift, Ron Sutter ran Jonsson off at the Islander line, enabling Marsh to jump up and shoot from near the left boards. The puck ticked off the short-side post and ricocheted off the far pipe and in. Philadelphia's two shorthanded goals within 44 seconds gave the team a 3-0 lead.

The Flyers forced eleven Islander giveaways in the first twenty minutes, held New York without a shot for 9:54 of the second, and were home free long before Sinisalo's two third-period goals made the score look as one-sided as the game. Potvin broke Hextall's shutout in the final minute, but the Islanders, the comeback kings, had succumbed to Philadelphia's will. The Flyers roared into a semifinal matchup against Stanley Cup champion Montreal with an overpowering 5-1 victory.

Marsh felt it was the most impressive accomplishment of the Keenan era. "We took the momentum away and sustained it in a do-or-die situation against a team that had been in this position many times before," said the proud defenseman. "That's the mark of a championship team."

Keenan praised Poulin's courage. "It was a tremendous gesture by a fabulous individual and a great leader," said the coach. Propp, who had played brilliantly, would never be called a choker again.

Big, strong Montreal, which defeated Quebec in 7 games, figured to be able to get to the net on Philadelphia's smallish defense. But the Flyers had more speed and a big edge in goal. Patrick Roy, who led the Canadiens to the 1986 Cup, had faltered against the Nordiques, and coach Jean Perron was staying with journeyman Brian Hayward.

Poulin's heroics had set back his recovery and he did not dress for Game 1 at the Spectrum, but Propp continued to take charge. He one-timed Crossman's pass for a power-play goal, giving the Flyers a 1-0 lead. Shayne Corson and Ryan Walter put Montreal ahead but Sinisalo, fed by Propp, tied the game 2-2 early in the third.

Bobby Smith scored on a backhander off the sticks of both Crossman and Marsh, the third Montreal goal to come on a deflection. But Eklund backed Chris Chelios off the Montreal line and dropped to Nachbaur, who came across his body with a remarkable pass into the high slot before being knocked down. Derrick Smith put the best shot of his life over Hayward's glove, sending the game to overtime.

Nine minutes into sudden death, Samuelsson pushed the puck down the boards and Zezel carried out front. Guy Carbonneau tackled the Philadelphia center as he jammed and Chelios, groping on all fours, tried to fall on the puck. It disappeared as Sinisalo took a poke, and emerged through the group grope just across the line.

Zezel, with the best view, leaped just before Terry Gregson's emphatic call. Like the scorekeeper, Sinisalo only guessed he had been the last Flyer to touch the puck but at 9:11 of overtime, all that mattered was that Philadelphia had won, 4-3.

The Canadiens leaned harder in Game 2, bringing the puck out of corners and establishing a stronger presence in front of Hextall. Tocchet could not take out Claude Lemieux, whose cross-crease pass was converted by Bobby Smith for a 1-0 lead. A tenacious Brian Skrudland fought off Marsh to redirect the puck to Sergio Momesso, whose backhander was chopped out of the air and between Hextall's legs by John Kordic. With the Flyers killing off Hextall's penalty for whacking the crease-strafing Lemieux, the irascible Montreal winger converted a Rick Green rebound.

Keenan went to Resch, and third-period goals by Smith and Crossman, cut the 4-0 lead in half. But Carbonneau fooled Crossman and put away Montreal's 5-2 victory.

The Canadiens had played steamroller hockey to tie the series, and as Hextall warmed up for Game 3 two nights later at the Forum, he sensed Philadelphia was still feeling the effect. "We're flat as a pancake, I can tell," Hextall whispered to Resch.

Sure enough, rebound goals by Chris Nilan and Chelios, both following excellent Hextall saves, put Montreal ahead, 2-0. The Flyers were outshot 17-3 at one point late in the first period and Hextall made 19 saves to get his team to the locker room down by only two. "I can't do any more than what I've already done," he quietly told his teammates. "You have to get going."

Keenan, who had been fearful of getting caught with Eklund in size mismatches, decided to use his speed to back off the Canadiens. Recalling a successful preseason line of Eklund, Propp and Tocchet, the coach arranged a reunion. It turned into a party. Eklund converted Tocchet's passout, then took a short feed from Tookey to beat Hayward through the legs and tie the game.

In the third period, Eklund raced outside Petr Svoboda, carried behind the net and set up Tocchet, who scored another goal through Hayward's five-hole. Tocchet was forced to take down Corson to prevent a breakaway and Mats Naslund converted a Chelios rebound to make the score 3-3. But four minutes later, Tocchet chased his own blocked shot and fed Propp at the hash marks. He hit the ever-present wicket between Hayward's legs and Philadelphia was back ahead.

Hextall nailed a Corson 30-footer, then dove across to get his chest in front of a Nilan shot. For sixty minutes the Canadiens bumped, taunted and blasted away at the Flyers' goalie, but in the end the rookie's arm was raised in celebration of his masterful 4-3 triumph.

Keenan was asked to consider the good fortune of finding Hextall only a year after losing Lindbergh. "Maybe somebody is looking after us," the coach said. Perron, meanwhile, was searching for the Roy who had made the Canadiens champions, but the slumping sophomore, who started Game 4, was betrayed by a rusty glove on goals by Sutter and Propp, the latter from outside the blue line.

Naslund cashed a Zezel retaliation penalty and Stephane Richer took advantage of a bad clear to tie the game. But Eklund split Svoboda and Larry Robinson, and one-handed the puck over Roy's stick to restore Philadelphia's lead. Just 14 seconds into the third period, Mellanby took advantage of Lemieux's giveaway to redirect Sutter's shot. Perron went back to Hayward but Eklund converted a Tocchet passout, then completed his first NHL hat trick on a breakaway sprung by Propp.

Considering the absence of Poulin, Craven and Kerr, the Flyers' 6-3 victory and 3-1 series lead hardly seemed real, but Eklund wasn't pinching himself. "I don't dream about hockey," he countered pleasantly to the media. "I just play it."

As the Canadiens prepared to make their last stand in Game 5 at the Spectrum, it was obvious Hextall had them shaken. "Average offensive players get upset when they don't score," said Perron. "You are haunted by a heartbreaker like we had in Game 3.

"Bobby Clarke told me Hextall was a franchise goalie, but I didn't believe it until now. He's a cocky son of a gun. He plays music against the posts and he comes to challenge our bench by banging the top of the boards during the warmup. I guess the Flyers stopped Lemieux. So we'll have to put somebody on our bench when Hextall comes by."

The Montreal coach was referring to Lemieux's end-of-warmup ritual of shooting the puck into the opposition net. With the encouragement of Reg Higgs, an advance scout for Philadelphia during the playoffs, Hospodar had schemed against Lemieux's pregame superstitions for most of the series.

Before Game 3, the Flyer defenseman had watched Lemieux out of the corner of his eye, intercepted his shot, and fired the puck back into the Canadiens' net. Resch joined the fun prior to Game 4, turning the net around before leaving the ice. When Hospodar and Resch again reversed the goal before

Game 5 at the Spectrum, Chelios swung it so Lemieux could feed his peace of mind.

What Montreal really needed most was not a turn of luck, but some saves. And after Bobby Smith and Derrick Smith traded early goals, Hayward finally gave the champions reason to be confident about their goaltending.

With Mellanby off for cross-checking Naslund, Lemieux screened Hextall, enabling Robinson to score the Canadiens' sixth power play goal in 12 tries. In the second period, Bob Gainey masterfully controlled the puck while his team was changing defense pairs and Philadelphia allowed Craig Ludwig to cut behind Hextall and redirect a Robinson feed. When Carbonneau threw a puck out of the corner that caromed in off Tocchet, Montreal had a 4-1 lead. The Canadiens kept their third forward high, cutting off the up-the-middle superhighway the Flyers had been travelling, and forced Game 6 with a solid 5-2 victory.

Poulin had dressed for the Game 5 warmup, but Keenan chose to rest his captain. With Philadelphia's series lead cut to 3-2 and Montreal's power play rolling, Poulin's time had arrived.

First, however, the evening's nonsense competition had to be settled. Hospodar and Resch waited by the goal until Lemieux, apparently giving up, went through the tunnel to the locker room. Satisfied, the two Flyers also left the ice. But when Lemieux and Corson suddenly reappeared with a puck and raced for the empty net, Resch and Hospodar came back out of the visiting tunnel in pursuit. Lemieux fed ahead to Corson, who deposited the last laugh of the practical joke.

Hospodar was no sport. He chased down Lemieux and started punching him. When the stick boy raced back to Philadelphia's locker room to tell them Hospodar was fighting on the ice, the team raced out in varying stages of undress. Keenan grabbed Hextall before he could get to the door, but Crossman ran onto the ice wearing shower slippers.

The Canadiens also poured from their room. As they paired off with Flyers, words were exchanged and several players took it from there. Brown went after Nilan, Nachbaur attacked Robinson, and Daryl Stanley fought with Kordic. It was several minutes until the officials, who were still dressing as the brawl broke out, could reach the ice to restore order, and fifteen minutes before both teams were back in their locker rooms.

"I've never seen anything like it," said Robinson. "I hope I never see anything like it again."

"I just thought he would try to stop the puck," said Lemieux. "I didn't know [Hospodar] would do anything like that. It was completely stupid."

"Maybe what I did wasn't right," Hospodar said. "but what [Lemieux] did wasn't right either."

Resch, a longtime pacifist and critic of Philadelphia's shenanigans, was embarrassed by his involvement. "I guess it was childish," he said. "But it was an emotional night."

The Forum crowd booed the U.S. anthem, then roared as Mike McPhee put a 40-footer through Naslund's feet and past Hextall only 59 seconds into the game. With Brown off for elbowing, the fans shrieked for another goal, but the shorthanded Flyers broke out three-on-three. Bobby Smith left Poulin alone and the captain took Crossman's pass, went around Hayward and tied the game.

Philadelphia, largely outplayed, was 4 seconds from the end of the period when Walter tied up Sutter on a face-off and Robinson scored off Hextall's far shoulder from a bad angle. In the second, with Derrick Smith off for tripping, Bobby Smith drew Hextall out of the net, used Naslund's screen to cut behind the goal, then beat the goalie to the far side.

With the Canadiens ahead 3-1, another Game 7 loomed, but the Flyers almost immediately bounced back. Mellanby, sent in by Sinisalo, was stood up by Chelios, but Marsh jumped on the puck and shot from along the boards. Hayward, screened by Sutter, couldn't control the rebound and Sinisalo hustled up the slot to score. Mellanby then split Lemieux and Walter and pushed the puck ahead to Crossman, who hung up Svoboda with a fake and went wide. Crossman slipped the puck back across the goalmouth to Mellanby, who controlled with his skate and put his stick on the puck just before it crossed the goal line. Only 2:40 after Montreal had opened a two-goal lead, the game was again tied.

With seven minutes elapsed in the third, Propp's quick hands knocked the puck off Chelios' stick after the Canadiens had won a center-ice draw and created a two-on-one against Robinson. Propp put a return pass between the defenseman's stick and body to Tocchet, who guided it into the net before Hayward could come across the crease. "I wanted to run down St. Catherine Street," said Tocchet later. Philadelphia had taken a 4-3 lead at 7:11, an omen of opportunism during a series in which the Flyers had been territorially outplayed.

Howe smartly foiled rush after rush. When Carbonneau got outside, Poulin hurried back to break up the pass. McCrimmon and Crossman were

splendid as the clock ticked down. "It was like an hourglass," said Tocchet, but the Flyers played with the wisdom of Father Time.

Bobby Smith jammed at the goalmouth after Lemieux pinched down the boards, but Hextall covered Montreal's last good chance with 3:18 remaining. Twice in the final minutes, Crossman smartly reversed the puck away from flooding Canadien forecheckers and Poulin blocked two Montreal attempts to get it on net.

With 20 seconds left, Tocchet iced the puck and the Canadiens took their time out. An exhausted Robinson sat against the boards drinking water. Sutter tied up Walter on the draw and Propp chipped the puck out of the Philadelphia zone. Howe batted away Montreal's last, desperate, long lead pass at the siren, then wheeled and raced to be the first Flyer to embrace Hextall.

"We're there," said the rookie goalie, quietly celebrating the 4-3 win. "We're in the finals." Philadelphia's success was due largely to Hextall, who strapped a crippled team to his back and carried it to victories in all three games at the Forum. "He's so tough that you think every goal he gives up is the last one they're going to get," said Tocchet.

Perron refused to shake the hand of Keenan, who snapped at reporters when the brawl drew more questions than the game. Brian O'Neill, the league disciplinarian, issued fines to both teams totaling $24,500 and Hospodar was suspended for the duration of the playoffs.

The punishment seemed a small price to pay for a second crack at the Oilers in three years. Edmonton, which had eliminated Detroit in a five-game Campbell Conference final, had grown more explosive than ever following trades for Reijo Ruotsalainen and Kent Nilsson, and was better defensively, too, with the free-agent signing of center Craig MacTavish.

The Flyers were still missing Kerr, but expected Craven back during the series, restoring their full complement of centers. Hextall and the experience gained in the 1985 finals gave the team confidence that it could somehow defuse the greatest offensive machine in the game's history.

Their chances immediately diminished on the initial shift of Game 1 at Northlands Coliseum, when Howe suffered a charley horse taking out Mark Messier. The defenseman stayed in the game, but could not accelerate.

Gretzky struck first but Propp handcuffed Grant Fuhr with a 55-footer to tie the game late in the second. Messier went right-to-left on Howe, retrieved his own blocked pass and circled the net to hit Glenn Anderson, who put in a one-timer off Hextall's skate.

Seven minutes later, Gretzky picked up Hunter's rebound and fed Paul Coffey, who blasted a bullet over Hextall's shoulder. Jari Kurri then chased a corner dump, and in one motion fired a puck in off the goalie's glove. Three Oiler scores in 8:23 had dropped the bottom out of a solid Philadelphia effort, sending it to a 4-2 defeat.

Craven came back for Game 2. So did the Flyers from Wayne Gretzky's early five-on-three goal. Sutter, getting stronger by the game, dug the puck loose from a goalmouth scramble so Derrick Smith could tie the score. Propp, left alone at the post, redirected Tocchet's drive and after two periods, Philadelphia led 2-1.

Including the playoffs, the 1986-87 Flyers were 45-1-4 in games they led going into the third period. But Sather went almost exclusively with his flamethrowers and eventually Philadelphia melted. Anderson steamed through center, poked the puck between Crossman's stick and body, and whipped a 20-footer past Hextall's stick side.

In overtime, Eklund didn't look for the late man and Gretzky dropped the puck at the point for Coffey. With four Flyers caught low, the Edmonton defenseman closed in, then whipped a diagonal pass to Kurri, whose one-timer beat Hextall before he could come across.

The Oilers had outchanced Philadelphia 16-1 in the third period and overtime of their 3-2 victory. "They were like a white wave coming at us," said the hobbled Howe. Still, the Flyers were not ready to give in to a team that had won only 3 of 17 games at the Spectrum.

The late, great Kate pumped the crowd for Game 3 through the magic of ArenaVision, but MacTavish blocked an off-balance McCrimmon drive and Messier soloed for a deflating shorthanded goal. In the final minute of the first period, Coffey ripped in a 25-footer through a crowded goalmouth. When Hextall, opening up as Anderson lost control pulling to his forehand, couldn't close his legs in time, the puck wobbled over the line for a 3-0 Edmonton lead.

The cool Oilers had chilled the Spectrum. Not even Philadelphia's first goal, scored on a power play when Craven used his stick shaft to bunt a Tocchet feed over Fuhr, suggested that the series would go past 4 games. But six minutes later, with Tikkanen off for slashing Poulin, Craven kicked the puck away from Lowe, and Tocchet walked out from the end boards. He passed through the goalmouth to Zezel,

whose return pass went off defenseman Craig Muni's skate and slid across the line. Muni quickly flicked his mistake out of the net, but not before referee Don Koharski signaled a goal.

Down only one, the Flyers were digging out of their grave like possessed gophers. Four minutes into the third period, Howe fed Mellanby, whose shot from the top of the circle ticked off the inside of Fuhr's pads to make the score 3-3. The thunder filling the Spectrum had hardly subsided when McCrimmon stopped Tikkanen's rush, fed ahead, then jumped into the play to take Mellanby's pass from the side boards. McCrimmon guided the puck off the falling Fuhr high into the net. Seventeen seconds after tying the game, Philadelphia was ahead.

The crowd roared throughout the third period as Samuelsson, a defensive octopus, forced the Oilers wide on rush after rush before Propp finished the 5-3 victory into the empty net. The Flyers had become the first team since 1944 to rally from a three-goal deficit to win a Cup finals game.

Disgusted with itself for blowing the lead, Edmonton bore down harder in Game 4 two nights later. Kurri batted an attempted Derrick Smith clear out of the air, then jumped into the slot to take a return pass from Gretzky to open the scoring. With Messier off for cross-checking Zezel, No. 99 pulled up inside the blue line and crisscrossed with Lowe, who got away from Propp and rammed the puck in before Hextall could come across.

Gretzky was serving a hooking penalty when McCrimmon one-timed Eklund's feed and beat Fuhr from 50 feet to cut the Oiler lead to 2-1. The fans came to life in expectation of another comeback, but Gretzky exited the box like a wet blanket. While Samuelsson was penalized for interference, the Great One led Randy Gregg perfectly on a give-and-go, enabling the Edmonton defenseman to tip the puck through Hextall's legs. Fuhr made two outstanding saves on Tocchet before Marsh gave away the puck to Krushelnyski, who soloed to build the lead to 4-1.

Hextall was seething. When he slightly juggled a wide-angle shot by Anderson, who followed to the net and jabbed at the puck, the goalie had an excuse to vent his frustration. Seconds later, as Nilsson skated past the crease, Hextall wound up and brought his stick hard across the back of the Oiler's right leg.

Nilsson crumpled but returned during an uneventful five-minute power play. Hextall escaped without referee Andy van Hellemond assessing a match penalty, but the Flyers were not spared their 4-1 loss or 3-1 series deficit. They drew respectful applause—a thank you for the great run—as they left the ice. Game 4 had been Philadelphia's 23rd game in the 1987 playoffs, an NHL single-season record, and a fresher Edmonton was going home for the kill.

The two clubs boarded separate all-night charters one gate apart at Philadelphia International Airport. The Oilers were smiling, joking and confident, while the depressed Flyers knew all their friends were staying behind. Hextall's slash had transformed Philadelphia's image from gutsy underdogs into vicious thugs.

The Northlands Coliseum crowd figured to be all over Hextall, who showed no remorse or fear. "Only one thing will bother me," he said, "and that's if we lose. That would bother me a lot."

Keenan knew his players, running on empty, needed an emotional jolt to push through another brick wall. At the morning skate, he commandeered the Cup from the room where it was being kept for probable presentation that evening and had it placed in the Philadelphia locker room. Someone else brought in a souvenir shirt already declaring the Oilers the 1987 Stanley Cup champions.

Victory parade plans had been published in Edmonton newspapers, giving the Flyers further inspiration. Yet when Game 5 began, they had no pulse. With Brown off for holding Messier and Koharski's arm up on a delayed penalty to Sutter, Kurri caromed a perfect shot through Krushelnyski's screen that clanked in off the far post. Marty McSorley pushed a Gretzky rebound through Hextall's legs for a 2-0 lead before seven minutes had elapsed. The fans, who had hung banners to catch the attention of "Hackstall," chanted for "Chico" and got ready to celebrate.

So did the Oilers, who turned up the heat one more notch, but Hextall stopped a Coffey breakaway, then another by Gretzky. The goalie kept his cool when run over by McSorley and got a break when referee Don Koharski lost sight of the puck and blew his whistle before an Anderson tap-in. A goal that should have counted was wiped out, leaving Philadelphia still down by two.

The overwhelmed visitors caught their breath when Jaroslav Pouzar was penalized for foolishly hooking Zezel behind the play. In the final minute of the opening period, Tocchet, playing with Propp and Eklund for the first time since the Montreal series, rapped a passout between Fuhr's legs.

McSorley deflected a Huddy drive out of midair past Hextall's right pad early in the second to re-store Edmonton's two-goal edge, but the Flyers had their equilibrium back. Tocchet buried Nilsson just as he took a drop pass from Anderson and Eklund fed a breaking Propp. Crossman jumped up to take the left wing's pass and closed to the edge of the circle before firing the puck over Fuhr's glove.

Four minutes later, Messier was called for slashing Sinisalo. Eklund dumped the puck, hurried Muni into a bad clear, and went to the front of the net. Fuhr stopped Propp's point drive and Lowe blocked Eklund's rebound, but the puck came right back to him with both the goalie and defenseman down. The little center lifted the puck into a wide-open net to tie the game.

The Oilers seemed more annoyed than impressed. They were all over Philadelphia as the third period began, but Hextall shrugged his blocker and stopped Anderson from straight up the slot. Six minutes in, MacTavish won a face-off in the Edmonton zone from Eklund, but Propp, playing like his life depended on the game's outcome, jumped ahead to lay his stick across Muni's hands as the defenseman went to fire up the boards. Muni fanned, allowing Propp to pick up the puck, walk in front and throw a backhand pass just past the glove of the sliding Lowe. Tocchet redirected the puck inside the post before Fuhr could come across, then clenched his fists in celebration. The Flyers, written off for dead, were leading 4-3.

There was a long 14:34 to go, but Philadelphia checked like demons. Samuelsson dove back to cut Anderson off on a partial breakaway and Hextall stood up on Kurri when he got inside Howe. Gretzky backhanded a passout through Samuelsson's legs to Kurri but Hextall got his shoulder in front of the puck.

In the final minute, Anderson's drive caromed off the endboards to Nilsson, who faced a half-empty net, but he had to dig the puck out of his skate, giving Howe time to slide back and cover. When linesman Kevin Collins allowed a phantom icing touchup by Kurri, the besieged visitors had to take two defensive zone draws during the final 18 seconds. The Oilers controlled the second face-off, but Crossman kept Anderson from centering and Howe lifted the puck off Gretzky's stick and over the glass as the clock ran out.

The Flyers—4-3 winners on guile, Hextall, and Propp's four assists—had amazed even themselves. "We're all kind of shaking our heads in here," said Howe. The victory had only upgraded the odds on winning the series from impossible to improbable, but as they flew home for a Game 6 that few had thought would be played, any chance at all was gratefully accepted.

As the roar accompanying the team's appearance on the ice drowned out the PA system and Starship's "Nothing's Going to Stop Us Now," the song's words became both unintelligible and believable at the same time.

Nevertheless, for the sixth straight game, Edmonton scored first. Gretzky, foiled on a breakaway, got the puck back at center, swung wide of Howe, circled the net and fed Lowe at the opposite post. Lowe kicked the puck in, but referee Dave Newell allowed the goal.

Craven was then beaten on a face-off by MacTavish and McClelland's rebound put Edmonton up 2-0. The Oilers dominated the rest of the period, but in the second, Hextall stopped a Kurri backhander and Marsh sprawled to prevent Gretzky—ever circling the net—from slipping the puck in front. A scramble resulted, Hextall rose to glove the puck and fate seemed to take his hand. Brown, a puncher, fed the puck ahead through the legs of Lowe, an all-star, so Carson, a plumber, could cut the lead to one at 7:12.

Edmonton, by now fully cognizant of Philadelphia's resiliency, was checking superbly. After forty minutes, the Flyers had only 13 shots. Still, Hextall and the Oilers' caution kept the score at 2-1 until Anderson, retaliating for a Zezel cross-check, cracked the Philadelphia center with a two-hander. Referee Newell gave the Flyers their sixth—and likely final—power-play opportunity.

Eklund gained the zone, then took a pass at the hash marks from Crossman. Propp jumped into the slot, accepted Eklund's feed, and held barely an instant before taking a half-windup and ripping a perfectly placed shot over Fuhr's glove to tie the game, 2-2.

The Spectrum walls were still shaking when Daigneault, taking a regular shift for most of the past two games, held off Kurri in front of Hextall. Philadelphia broke into the Oilers' zone where Kurri picked off Zezel's pass and without turning, tried to bank the puck off the boards and out. He did not get enough on the clear, which died as it approached the blue line.

Daigneault had come to the bench as the Flyers broke up ice, but Keenan, trying to buy time for a tired Howe, waved the kid defenseman to stay on. He reached the puck five feet inside the Edmonton zone and one-timed a skipping slap shot through Mellanby's screen and Fuhr's stick side.

Daigneault, his arms up, was spun by his teammates and pummeled. And the leaping, screaming and joy that surged through the Spectrum was uncontained for the final 5:32. "The loudest I ever heard the place," recalls Marsh. The stunned Oilers, challenged for every inch of space, were forced into low-percentage one-on-one rushes and easily savable shots. A Gretzky passout went off McSorley's skate with 2:30 to go, the best Edmonton chance until the final seconds.

After Propp missed the empty net from center, Hextall came out to clear an errant Messier pass intended for Coffey. The goalie tried to lift the puck up the middle, but Messier knocked the clear down with his glove, then tried to get the puck to lay flat as he cut for the net. By the time he could shoot, Hextall was able to scramble back and use his blocker, and Messier shot the rebound over the net. When Howe broke down a point drive at the buzzer, the Spectrum was bedlam. With a 3-2 victory, the Flyers had earned the opportunity to play the game of their lives.

"I guess we had a little more to give than everybody thought," said Brown. It was Philadelphia's third rally from two goals down during the finals, and fifth in the last 10 playoff games.

Gretzky called Hextall the "best goalie I ever played against" before the shaken Edmonton team boarded its charter. After being upset by Calgary the previous spring, there was enormous pressure on the favorites, whose character had become an easy target.

An additional day off (Northlands Coliseum had been previously booked for Saturday, May 30) would give the Oilers two days to compose themselves for the first Game 7 in a final series since 1971. Still, the Flyers, who could have flown to Alberta without a plane, refused to believe that anything could forestall them from their destiny. Jay Snider invited the members of the Cup teams to Edmonton at the organization's expense. "I think we're supposed to win now," Carson told the *Inquirer's* Ray Parrillo.

Sather railed to the media about the NHL's delay in disciplining Hextall for his slash of Nilsson, but to his players was nothing but supportive. Before Game 7, he told the Oilers that win or lose, he would be proud of them.

"I don't think we felt the pressure that they did," recalls Keenan.

As soon as Game 7 began on May 31, 1987, the anvil on Edmonton's back felt even heavier. Messier cross-checked Hextall, Coffey held Propp and Andy Van Hellemond whistled both fouls, giving Philadelphia a two-man advantage after only 1:13.

As Craven held the puck deep along the wing, Fuhr tried to cut off the passing lane by extending his stick. So Craven simply shot hard at the goalie's skate and got the intended carom between his legs. For the first time in the series, the Flyers had opened the scoring. And they still had 1:32 to exploit a man advantage.

Crossman took Eklund's pass, pulled around a sliding Lowe, and was about to make the score 2-0 when Fuhr charged out to poke the puck away. Edmonton killed the Coffey penalty, and Philadelphia survived one to Poulin before Anderson, flying through center, put the puck between the legs of the flat-footed Carson. Anderson fed wide to Nilsson, who had a speed mismatch against Brown and all the time he needed to feed back across the goalmouth to a flying Messier. A step ahead of Sutter, Messier tapped the puck just beyond the diving Hextall's glove to tie the game.

The breathtaking goal pumped oxygen back into the nervous Oilers, but the Flyers responded with three good chances. McSorley spotted Propp's rebound , which had dropped off Fuhr's chest behind him, an instant ahead of the Philadelphia winger and swept the puck away. Seven minutes into the second, Ruotsalainen atoned for a giveaway to Sutter by riding off the Flyer center, but Sinisalo followed up and was in alone. Fuhr brilliantly kicked the shot away with his right pad. When Zezel hurried Huddy and Smith fed the puck through the goalmouth, Sinisalo's redirection was gloved by the goalie.

But as the period moved along, Edmonton appeared to be getting stronger. Philadelphia cleared its zone with little difficulty, but was repeatedly unable to hit a man breaking through center. With Marsh off for holding Messier, Hextall stopped Coffey twice.

But less than a minute after the penalty expired, Randy Gregg lobbed the puck to the corner, where the hurried Crossman tried to reverse up the near boards, only to be bumped by Tikkanen. Gretzky came down the boards to pick up the puck as Sinisalo put his stick across Gretzky's chest, but the Great One saw Kurri move to just above the face-off dot and threaded a pass. Kurri quickly put a wrist shot between Zezel's legs and just inside the far post at 14:59.

With a 2-1 lead, the Oilers opened full throttle, separating the Flyer forwards from their defense and widening the skill gap between the two teams. Edmonton's best period of the series was the last one, when Philadelphia rarely had the puck. Hextall and

heaven were the only things that could help the Flyers now, but the rookie goalie refused to give into the inevitable.

Off one of the few face-offs Philadelphia won in the final two periods, Fuhr stopped a McCrimmon point drive and, later, Eklund tipped a Howe feed wide. They were the last real Flyer chances. Although the Oilers missed the net or were forced wide by Hextall on a number of scoring chances, they were flashing at and by the goalie at a dizzying pace.

Hextall had just thwarted Messier by coming across the crease when Craven fumbled a Howe outlet through center. Huddy headmanned to Anderson, who skated to within thirty-five feet and cranked a wicked, sinking slapshot off the inside of Hextall's pad. It went between his legs and into the net with 2:25 remaining.

Hextall, on his haunches, slumped forward as the Coliseum erupted. "I probably should have stopped it," he said later. "It would have still given us a chance to come back."

But there had been no glaring mistake or twist of fate in Game 7 to haunt the Flyers forever. The Oilers, 3-1 winners, were a superior team rising brilliantly to the occasion of an ultimate game. "When you're better in Game 7, you deserve the championship," said Keenan, as Edmonton paraded its third Cup in four seasons around the Coliseum. "We didn't get the break, but then the other team didn't give us a break either."

The Flyers shook hands with the champions, then used all ten minutes the league permitted before opening their locker room. It wasn't nearly enough time to come to terms with the pain. Howe buried his head under a running faucet in an attempt to plug and hide his tears. "I've never been shot with a bullet," he said. "But it couldn't hurt anymore than this."

Craven's eyes were also red, as he spoke to reporters. "We gave it everything we had, but that doesn't make me feel any better," he said. "Not now, anyway. We were just so close."

Hextall, brilliant to the end of his 92nd game of the season, composed himself enough to become only the fourth player from a losing team to accept the Conn Smythe Trophy. Then he, too, broke down. "I'm proud," he said. "But it's not a consolation. I've never been so disappointed in my life. All I can think about now is coming back and winning."

The coach plopped into his seat on the charter flight home and fell asleep. "I didn't cry as much as I had two years before," he recalls. "I was mentally and physically exhausted." While he slept, the players released the tension of 26 playoff games in 54 nights with alcohol. A group of veterans drank enough courage to ask Clarke to fire Keenan.

Two days later, the team met at the Coliseum to divide $378,000 in playoff winnings into 23 shares. "It's still hard," said Marsh, "but I'll always remember the time from right after Game 6 on Thursday until game time on Sunday. We were so excited. The Stanley Cup was right there."

The players cleared out their lockers and went to

Bobby Clarke's parents congratulate their son on his induction into the Hockey Hall of Fame.

a party that afternoon at Ed Snider's home in Bryn Mawr. The coaches had wanted to finish their final written player evaluations while the games were still fresh in their minds and so arrived over an hour late. "Ed came right up to me, very upset," recalls Keenan. "He thought I had snubbed him.

"I apologized, but I remember thinking, 'We just got to the seventh game of the Stanley Cup and the owner's mad at me because I'm late for his party?' I understand now. The season was over, the evaluations could have waited. The coach shouldn't have been that late."

For the third time in five seasons, Howe came in second, this year to Boston's Ray Bourque, for the Norris Trophy. But Poulin won the Selke and Hextall the Vezina. The goalie was a surprising runner-up for rookie of the year to L.A.'s Luc Robitaille. "Like a lot of people, I thought it would be the other way around," said Hextall. "But if I had a choice, I'd rather be recognized as best at my position. I'm striving to be the best goalie ever. It's a high goal, but I'm going to try."

One of the great try-ers of all time was inducted into the Hockey Hall of Fame at a dinner during the draft meetings in Detroit. "I believe Bobby Clarke

was the best leader ever in sports," said Ed Snider, placing the medallion around his GM's neck.

Clarke put the prized memento away for safekeeping and donned an albatross—Hextall had received an 8-game suspension for his two-hander to Nilsson. Resch was not offered a new contract so Philadelphia needed goaltending help. Clarke traded a second round 1987 pick to Detroit for 24-year-old Mark Laforest, who had made an impression when outdueling Hextall during the 1986 AHL finals.

Jensen, disappointing in Hershey, and Daryl Stanley were moved to Vancouver for goalie Wendell Young and a third-rounder.

The damage to Kerr's shoulder was so extensive, Dr. Gregg performed a two-stage operation to repair it. But when the 58-goal scorer went for a checkup on August 13 expecting to be cleared to begin off-season workouts, he learned that the pin Gregg put in during surgery had become dislodged. The following day, the doctor inserted a longer screw and described the setback as temporary.

McCrimmon was offered a four-year deal at $225,000 per season, but asked for $250,000, so Clarke pursued a swap with Vancouver for defenseman Michel Petit. When McCrimmon's agent, Herb Pinder, and the Canucks couldn't agree on contract terms, Clarke withdrew his offer in favor of a three-year deal for $210,000 a season, the minimum required to maintain the Flyers' equalization rights. Comfortable with Samuelsson and confident Kerry Huffman, his 1986 first pick, was ready for the NHL, Clarke traded McCrimmon to Calgary on August 26 for first- and third-round choices.

"I didn't like McCrimmon when I played with him," recalls Clarke. "He was a big boozer who I didn't think cared. He was a good player for Keenan, probably better than I gave him credit for being. Maybe there were some feelings from previous years, I don't really know. I was fighting with the agent, too.

"I should have gotten a player instead of a draft pick. But I never got a strong feeling from Mike that he thought it was important to keep Brad."

Keenan says he did not argue for McCrimmon because he thought it would be futile. "Bob and Brad weren't going to resolve their differences," recalls Keenan.

As coach of the Canadian team in the upcoming

Canada Cup, Keenan similarly rationalized his inability to prevent Poulin from being one of the final cuts. "We had let go of Roy to keep Hextall," recalls Keenan. "And I think I was due to lose one (to Montreal committee members Jean Perron and Serge Savard). After all Dave had done for me, I probably should have finessed a way."

Tocchet, who made the squad with Propp and Crossman, suffered a sprained left knee as Canada and the Soviets played to a 3-3 tie in the last game of the round-robin portion of the tournament, then limped through the Soviets' 6-5 victory at Montreal in Game 1 of a three-game final. Tocchet sat out Canada's classic 6-5 double-overtime win in Game 2 at Hamilton, Ontario then flew back to Philadelphia and successfully begged Dr. Gregg to play.

The winger scored to start Canada out of an early 3-0 hole, then forced a giveaway that allowed Propp, who had been benched by Keenan during Game 1, to cut the lead to 3-2. Canada came back to win the monumental series on Mario Lemieux's goal with 1:26 remaining. All three final games ended 6-5.

Propp and Tocchet, disappointed in the Stanley Cup finals twice in three years, quietly shared champagne in a corner of the dressing room. "I've been in that other locker room too many times. I know how much better it feels in here," said Propp. "It's something I'm going to have for the rest of my life, being on a championship team."

The Kings claimed Tookey, and the Sabres grabbed Hospodar in the waiver draft, but the losses appeared negligible to the Flyers, who figured to be back in the Oilers' faces the following spring. Problems in Edmonton—Coffey demanded a contract renegotiation and was being shopped for trade—made Philadelphia the favorite in many eyes.

Tocchet, foolishly used in 3 exhibition games in three nights, aggravated his knee injury and missed the 1987-88 season opener. His replacement, Swedish winger Magnus Roupe, a ninth-round 1982 pick, was an instant hit with the fans as Laforest tied the Canadiens 2-2 at the Spectrum. The Flyers won sloppily, 5-4, in Minnesota before being embarrassed by the Islanders 6-0 at the Spectrum.

Two nights later on Long Island, Keenan tried to snap his team to attention by benching Sutter. Helped by Tocchet's goal in his first game back, the Flyers won, 4-3. The following night, Sutter threw his usual blanket over Mario Lemieux, and Tocchet scored again in a 3-2 Spectrum victory over Pittsburgh. But after a dismal 4-1 home loss to Washington, Clarke had a round of meetings with key team members.

On October 26, an unrepentant Hextall rejoined his 3-4-1 club at Madison Square Garden. "I knew something had to be done and I did it," he said. "Kent Nilsson wasn't hurt and I think it definitely helped the next few (playoff) games."

With 7:21 remaining in the goalie's season debut, Hextall settled for a glare at Tomas Sandstrom when the longtime Philadelphia antagonist poked at a loose puck the goalie had just covered. But Brown snapped Sandstrom's head back with a vicious cross-check beneath the protective visor and on the side of his face, sending him to the hospital with a concussion and a feared broken jaw.

Brown received a high-sticking major and a match penalty for deliberate attempt to injure in his second attack on Sandstrom in ten months. The Flyers earned a 2-2 tie and as much contempt as they received for any incident in their history. "I don't even blame Brown," said John Vanbiesbrouck. "He's only doing a job assigned to him by Keenan. Keenan pats him on the head and says, 'Good job tonight. We'll put you in a cage and let you ride home on the team bus.'"

The Xrays of Sandstrom's jaw proved negative. So did the reaction the following night at the Meadowlands every time Brown touched the puck. But he was not the only Philadelphia player worthy of disdain in a low energy 4-0 loss to the Devils.

Keenan benched only Zezel, even though Eklund, Sinisalo and Crossman were equally lethargic. Tocchet dragged and the Flyers obviously missed Kerr. Suffering shoulder soreness, weight and energy loss and hot-and-cold flashes, he returned to the hospital for tests. Dr. Gregg and two other specialists concurred the screw had probably become infected and should be removed.

When Gregg performed the procedure, he was relieved to find the bone block had fused to the point where a new screw was not necessary. Kerr's overall health improved quickly, but he was not expected back in the lineup until at least March. "I've had no problems with the handling of this by John Gregg," said the luckless winger.

Propp's 300th career goal and three points by Craven got Philadelphia past Los Angeles, 4-1, at the Spectrum, but the burst of energy seemed to quickly exhaust them. The 15-game suspension Brown received on November 2 was certainly nothing to rally around but Keenan, at least publicly, stayed calm and supportive after the Flyers were bombed 5-1 the following day in Pittsburgh. "The thing I've found works best during a slump is to work on fundamentals," said the coach.

His team, however, remained incapable of sustaining an effort for an entire contest. Philadelphia lost a 2-0 lead to Vancouver within the first minute of the third period, then rallied back to tie 3-3 on Tocchet's power play goal with 1:02 remaining. Samuelsson and Propp then blew a coverage and Greg Adams's backhander between Hextall's legs at 19:49 won the game, 4-3.

"Surreal," was how Poulin described the loss. But there were tangible factors for the slide. Howe, playing with a chipped vertebra, was unaccustomed to Samuelsson after being paired for so many years with McCrimmon. There was also an undercurrent of disillusionment with management. The Flyers had entered the season feeling they needed another good player to get over the top against Edmonton, only to see McCrimmon subtracted over a refusal to give him a modest raise.

"More than being a big part of our defense, he was really good with the young players," recalls Marsh. "The [organization] underestimated his value that way.

"We weren't given individual bonuses in our contracts, only team ones, and we believed in that concept. If they were letting one of the team leaders go over $25,000 a year, this wasn't the family we had been led to believe it was. We weren't in the slump for that reason, but overall, I think it made players think more selfishly."

Keenan was kicking himself for taking a week's rest following the Canada Cup and sending a too-relaxed signal to the club. But he understood that the Canada Cup participants were still coming down from a high and that the season-long wait for another shot at the Cup probably was boring the entire team. "They geared themselves up for the opener," said Keenan, "but after that it was, 'My God, we've got 79 games to go.'"

As Philadelphia's skid reached 1-9-1, there was a presumption that some players were trying to get the coach fired. "I don't think that was the case," Poulin recalls, but some of the more embittered Flyers saw Keenan, and not the mounting losses, as the primary source of team tension. Crossman, turned off by four years of the bench boss's pyrotechnics, was merely going through the motions. Increasingly, team members talked back when Keenan got on them at practice, sometimes within his earshot. "Almost everybody did at one point or another," recalls Tocchet. "You did it to keep your self-respect."

Ed Snider, who had suggested to Keenan the previous summer that he be more positive with his play-

ers, was losing confidence in his coach. But as rumors of a change gained momentum, Clarke denied it was being considered. "It's a lie," the GM said.

Certainly somebody wasn't telling the truth on November 10, when Tocchet was benched during the second period of a desultory 5-2 loss at St. Louis, then told the media it was because he had refused Keenan's orders to start a fight. The coach denied the charges, then blistered Tocchet for selfishness. "There are players who have their personal priorities ahead of the hockey club's," Keenan said. "They are thinking about their own needs rather than the team's."

Members of the team said they heard neither a blatant order by Keenan to fight nor a refusal by Tocchet. The clash was largely a red herring on a club whose performance smelled like old fish. "We were a disgrace to the uniform," said Hextall, "and I'm a lot of what's going wrong right now."

The goalie had just agreed to an eight-year, $500,000-a-year contract ($300,000 per season was to be deferred) and felt so responsible for the team's slide that he was sleeping only three or four hours a night. Still, he was hardly the only Flyer fearing a management wake-up call. "You can't continue losing like this and not have changes," said Howe. "I can't believe there hasn't been a trade yet."

Instead of holding a scheduled practice the next morning in St. Louis, Keenan called a team meeting. When he moved the table away from the middle of the locker room, Poulin whispered to Carson that the coach was going to challenge him physically. "Go for it," said Lindsay. But Keenan wanted only eye contact, not fisticuffs. He went player to player, asking them to discuss their contribution to the team. Then he left the room and allowed the players to complete the session themselves.

"We talked about whether we should just come out and say we'd had enough of Mike," recalls Marsh. "But we decided we were pros. We would play for ourselves."

Meanwhile, back in Philadelphia, Clarke refused to overreact. "Rick's emotional and he may have taken something the wrong way," said the GM. "I'm not trading him and I'm not firing the coach. To tell you the truth, I was glad to see somebody expressing some amount of emotion or frustration after a loss. That's been missing."

Keenan had long talks with Poulin and Tocchet on the flight home. After Philadelphia beat the Lemieux-less Penguins 5-2, the captain attempted to diplomatically acknowledge the player-coach problems. "Certainly there have been some differences," Poulin said. "We've got to be above that, though, and I think both sides are working toward that."

Together, they sank even lower two days later in an unbelievable 6-0 Spectrum loss to sickly Toronto. "We've been thinking that the whole season's going to go down the drain if we don't get it turned around right away, and that puts even more pressure on ourselves," said Tocchet.

Keenan, however, showed no trace of paranoia about his job and continued to stress the concept of concentrating on one game at a time. But the team could only handle two periods at a time. At New Jersey, they took a 3-2 lead into the final stanza. But Hextall cleared a rebound right to Patrik Sundstrom, then defenseman Jeff Chychrun, a 1984 second-round pick called up from Hershey, took a penalty that was cashed by Pat Verbeek and the Flyers went down again, 4-3.

Brown tried to lighten the mood by getting on stage at the Comedy Factory Outlet and telling high-sticking jokes. "I guess I should have used different material," he said after being admonished by Clarke. Philadelphia slopped past Los Angeles 7-5, then flashed its best form since opening night in building a 4-1 lead over the Islanders. But Zezel missed a check on a goal by Randy Wood, and Young, given the start so Hextall could clear his head, gambled and lost twice on poke checks as the Flyers collapsed to a 6-4 loss at a howlingly angry Spectrum.

Philadelphia's record had sunk to 6-13-3. Yet, Clarke refused to make a change just for change's sake. When his best offer for Coffey (Sutter and Crossman) failed to satisfy Sather (who wanted Tocchet), Clarke watched the Oilers trade the superstar defenseman to Pittsburgh, an improving divisional rival.

The Flyers, their trade anxieties temporarily put to rest with Coffey off the market, reminded themselves that they had played two encouraging periods against the Islanders. On Thanksgiving Eve at the Spectrum, they finally played three. Although the Sabres scored twice in the second period to erase a 2-0 deficit, Philadelphia didn't fold. Berube scored his first NHL goal and Poulin added two as the club pulled away to win, 5-2.

When a 6-3 success followed in Quebec City, Keenan declared the corner turned, but did not cancel a three-day minicamp he had scheduled in Lake Placid. Craven came out of the retreat still in full charge. The one player who had scored consistently throughout the slump had three assists in a 5-2 victory over Hartford.

The Bruins came to town on December 8, a good test of whether the Flyers had buried their confidence problems. For a scary moment, the team thought they might have to bury Marsh. He was nailed with concurrent, clean body checks by Neely and Bourque just outside the Philadelphia blue line, tumbled backwards, and hit his helmetless head on the glass-supporting rod at the corner of the visitors' bench.

Marsh was unconscious even before his head bounced off the ice, where he lay motionless, his arm twisted awkwardly behind him. "I really thought he was dead," recalls Keenan.

As trainer Dave Settlemyre reached the defenseman, he went into a jaw-locking seizure. The trainer inserted a clamp into Marsh's mouth to maintain an air passage while Dr. Gregg and internist Dr. Jeff Hartzell supervised the stabilization of his head and neck. Marsh was awake and jokingly asking for his chewing tobacco as the ambulance sped him to Pennsylvania Hospital.

"He's a teammate and like a brother," Hextall said later. "It was really hard getting back into the game."

The Bruins scored goals 1:42 apart to carry a 2-1 lead into second intermission. "I think we sensed that we had a real opportunity to make this a turn-around game," Poulin said. In an overwhelming third period, Zezel tied the game off a Mellanby feed and redirected Craven's wrist shot to put Philadelphia ahead.

Propp then put in his own rebound for an insurance goal at 17:33, sending a number of unfortunately impatient fans to their cars. For the sake of beating traffic, they would miss witnessing NHL history.

When the Bruins pulled goalie Reggie Lemelin with 1:43 remaining, Hextall eyed the empty net.

In 1979, Billy Smith became the first NHL goalie to be credited with a goal when he was the last Islander to touch a puck that a Colorado player had accidentally shot into his own net. Michel Plasse of the CHL Kansas City Blues was the first minor-league goalie to actually shoot and score in 1971 and Rochester's Darcy Wakaluk had repeated the trick three days before the Boston goal winked at Hextall.

Although he had announced his intention of performing an NHL first in his rookie season, Hextall had always waited for two-goal leads so as not to risk a game-threatening icing call. His one attempt in a game against Washington, had been gloved down by Scott Stevens before it left the Philadelphia zone.

When Bourque rimmed from center ice, the forecheckers were in too close, so the goalie played it safe and cleared. Bourque went cross-ice to Gord

Kluzak, who dumped again. Hextall bolted to the back boards, dropped to one knee and laid his stick down to stop the puck. As he rose, the closest Bruin, Lyndon Byers, was fifteen feet away. Hextall took aim and wristed the puck twenty feet into the air. It came down a foot from the Boston blue line, bounced and slid towards the goal.

There was no doubt that the shot had ample power and that Bourque, the closest Bruin, could not reach it. Only the course was in question. "The way I

On December 8, 1987, Ron Hextall became the first NHL goalie to score a goal by shooting the puck into the opposing team's net.

shoot it, the spin I put on it, the puck always curls off to the right," said the goalie later. This one, on a mission to the Hall of Fame, hurried across the line just inside the right post.

Hextall leaped into the air as archivist Derrick Smith fished out the memento. The goalie's teammates jumped off the bench to mob him, forcing a smiling Andy Van Hellemond to call an obligatory delay-of-game penalty.

"It doesn't seem real yet," Hextall said after the 5-2 victory. "But when you think about it, it's really surprising that nobody has ever done it before. It's not the biggest thrill of my career, but it is pretty great. And I may even get a few more."

The Flyers, unable to do anything right for two months, could suddenly do no wrong. On December 13 at Winnipeg, they squandered a 3-1 lead within 39 seconds of the third period before Hextall took consecutive penalties for tripping and clearing the puck over the glass. But on the five-on-three, Cra-

ven stole the puck from Marois, shot from the blue line to avoid being trapped and was astonished to beat goalie Pokey Reddick's catching hand. Philadelphia hung on to win, 4-3, and reached the .500 mark in the next game with a 5-2 victory in Pittsburgh. "I can't believe how fast we made this up," said Hextall.

Marsh, ordered to wear a helmet by Dr. Hartzel, returned after nine days for a 4-3 victory over the Islanders. "I wanted to be the last player in the league without a helmet, but my real objective has always been to play as long as I can," said Marsh.

Mellanby, one of Keenan's favorite punching bags, scored twice as the Flyers completed a home-and-home sweep with the Islanders, winning 5-4 at Uniondale. "There's been some bitterness between us," said the second-year right winger. "Maybe it's improved me, I don't know."

Propp suffered a sprained left knee ligament during a 6-4 victory December 22 at Madison Square Garden, but the team had no time for the pain. The following night they completed an astonishing thirty-day ride from last place to first with a 5-3 Spectrum victory over Minnesota.

"This wasn't in my wildest dreams," said Hextall. Jay Snider celebrated the 13-game undefeated streak by jumping fully clothed into the sunken whirlpool in the dressing room. The night after Christmas, the streak went to 14 when Sinisalo chased down a Howe lob over Stevens's head and soloed to beat Washington 3-2 at the Capital Center.

The flu bug caught Hextall, who missed two days of practice, then missed six pucks when Philadelphia lost for the first time in thirty-nine days, 6-0 in Edmonton. "Boy, there's a lot of bad memories in this room," said Mellanby, looking at the visitiors' lockers in Northlands Coliseum. The following night, Laforest lost a heartbreaker in Calgary on Gary Suter's power play goal with 8 seconds remaining. Still, the Flyers bounced back with Hextall's 4-1 victory in Vancouver and started the New Year having regained control of the Patrick Division.

Control was fleeting, though. On January 10, Hextall was ejected for exchanging insults with referee Don Koharski, forcing Laforest, who that morning had undergone extensive dental surgery, into goal. The improving Devils extracted a 7-5 victory through the novocaine-numbed Laforest. Meanwhile, Huffman who had been justifying the McCrimmon trade, tried to play with a charley horse, altered his stride, stretched knee ligaments and developed a calcium buildup in his thigh. Daigneault, getting little ice time, was sent to Hershey, and Marsh, his reaction time slightly dulled by his concussion, was used mostly on spot shifts and to kill penalties. "Looking back, I was getting hit more. But I was getting madder and madder and guys were saying what a *bleep* Keenan was to do this to me," recalls Marsh.

According to Keenan, "It took him longer than he would admit to bounce back."

After Howe and Samuelsson, the defense was as thin as Philadelphia's margin for error without Kerr. But Hextall, who stoned the Rangers 2-1 in New York on January 17, continued to be superb.

Berube took Carson's ice time and, eventually, his job. The seven-year veteran was traded to Hartford on January 22 for left wing Paul Lawless, a failed Whaler top pick. "Lindsay hated Mike," recalls Clarke. "He thought he was ruining his career. I told him there were a lot of players like him in the league and he would be better off staying where the GM knew him. But he wanted out."

Clarke, who had tried packaging Carson with Daigneault for Minnesota center Keith Acton, hoped the speedy but undisciplined Lawless could pump up the Flyers' anemic offense. Keenan instead sat the pudgy 23-year-old on the exercise bike and dug in with his reliables, almost to the point of obsession. Hextall, bent over in pain after being hit on the right shoulder by the Rangers' Michel Petit on January 28, remained in the game. Obviously having trouble moving his stick, the goalie allowed four goals before finally being pulled before the third period.

"[Hextall] was impaired at handling the puck, but not stopping it," snapped Keenan to the media after New York's 5-2 victory. He left the Spectrum before realizing the anger of Ed Snider, who unloaded on the assistant coaches. "How could [Keenan] risk the career of a franchise goalie?" he asked. Hextall's Xrays were negative. But so, increasingly, were the owner's vibes about his coach.

Kerr's rehabilitation proceeded steadily towards March but, in the meantime, every game was a one-goal battle. Kelly Miller scored with 1:34 remaining in overtime to beat Hextall 1-0 at the Capital Centre.

Clarke, scrambling for defensive help, picked up veteran Gordie Roberts from Minnesota for a fourth round draft choice. Keenan showed the same appreciation for this acquisition as he had for Lawless and Laforest. Before Philadelphia opened a six-game trip in Detroit, a virus-ridden Hextall vomited in the locker room. But when he told Keenan on the bench he felt well enough to play, Laforest was yanked only 45 seconds into the game.

Hextall, who could barely raise his head, gave up three goals before he was pulled. The Flyers fell behind 5-1 in the second period, then, with considerable help from Detroit goalie Glen Hanlon, rallied for a wild 11-6 victory.

Five nights later, Tocchet scored four goals, including a bank shot off the glass that rolled into the empty net, and Philadelphia outlasted the Kings, 8-6. But Howe, the catalyst to this sudden offensive explosion, was forced to fly home after his back pain recurred, leaving Keenan appealing to Snider over dinner at the owner's Malibu home for another skilled defenseman. "If we get one, we can win the Stanley Cup," the coach said.

Three days later, as the Flyers prepared to play in Vancouver, Clarke traded Lawless, who had performed in only eight games, plus a fifth-round draft choice to the Canucks for defenseman Willie Huber.

"He was the only thing available," recalls Clarke. "He had size and skill and had played well against us when Teddy (Sator) coached the Rangers."

"Willie's work habits might not be up to the expectations of the Flyers," warned Canuck GM Pat Quinn. It took only hours to see what their former coach meant. Lawless played for the Canucks, but Huber asked to be excused to get his personal effects together at his Vancouver home.

He wasn't missed, thanks to Tocchet. The winger's third hat trick in four games gave him a career-high 30 goals. Philadelphia won 7-3, but two nights later, in a 6-3 loss at Calgary, Tocchet's left shoulder was strained while checking the Flames' Jiri Hrdina. After Huber debuted by scoring one goal and giving away another, Tocchet followed Howe, Poulin (groin pull) and Eklund (hip flexor) on flights home for treatment.

The next evening, Sutter's shoulder was separated in a 7-4 loss to Edmonton. The Flyers were down to one regular center, Zezel, when they closed the trip by coughing up a 2-1 third-period lead into a 4-2 loss at New Jersey. Marsh "forgot" to put on his helmet for the game and looked like his old self, so Clarke passed up an opportunity to recycle the veteran defenseman to St. Louis for draft choices. Instead, Roberts was moved to the Blues for a fifth-rounder.

Kerr, a sight for the sorest eyes, returned March 10, just in time to face Washington, which he had tortured for 20 goals in the last 21 meetings. The Caps rushed panic-stricken towards their old tormentor, leaving a reenergized Propp open for two goals in a 5-2 victory. "It was so long, you forgot just what Timmy meant to us," said Craven.

Howe was also in the lineup for the Washington

triumph, which put Philadelphia back into first place and appeared to trumpet the start of a strong stretch run. But two days later, as Kerr warmed up for an afternoon game at the Spectrum against New Jersey, the strength in his arm vanished completely. He struggled through the 6-5 loss to the Devils, pushed eight weak shots at the Blackhawk goal in a 5-4 overtime loss in Chicago, then went back to see Dr. Gregg. Kerr was told that muscle fatigue was a natural consequence of his long layoff. He left the lineup to go on a revised strengthening program, designed to simulate the shooting motion.

Hextall, accidentally kneed by Mario Lemieux, suffered a mild shoulder separation in a 7-0 defeat in Pittsburgh as Keenan's patience with Crossman's season-long indifference finally ran out. After repeated warnings, the coach benched the defenseman when the Penguins came to the Spectrum to complete the home-and-home weekend series.

While only four points out of first, the Flyers were merely six ahead of the fifth-place Penguins and suddenly fighting for their playoff lives. Nevertheless, Crossman sat in the press box while Huffman, who had struggled since his return from a 23-game absence, and Greg Smyth, spot-shifted since his December recall from Hershey, took regular turns. "There are a lot of talented people in the world who don't want to apply themselves," Keenan said. "The coach's responsibility is to the team. We don't have time to waste anymore."

The players had become even less tolerant of Crossman than even Keenan. Three weeks earlier, Poulin had begged the defenseman to pick up his pace. "I think it was just a cumulative effect of four years of playing for Mike," recalls Poulin. "Dougie was down on Mike for the way he treated other players more than for the way he was treated himself."

The Penguins, carrying a 0-36-0 Spectrum winless streak, jumped to a 2-0 lead. But Laforest was stellar and Philadelphia machine-gunned four goals in a 9:29 stretch of the second period to record a gutsy 4-2 victory.

Crossman did not seem embarrassed. "I see this happening to different guys here at different points of every year," he told the media. "It's my turn. I'll try to put more work into it, I guess."

Clarke appealed to the defenseman's pride in a heart-to-heartless talk, but Crossman failed to be inspired by the inductions of the first two members—Clarke and Parent—into the Flyers' Hall of Fame. The ceremony went better than the game that followed. Crippled without Hextall, Kerr, Poulin and

Sutter, Philadelphia was blanked 3-0 by the Bruins.

One game later, Keenan pretended Crossman was working harder and reinserted him for a game at the Capital Center. Poulin, Craven and Tocchet had healed enough to return, too. But Tocchet's shoulder was reseparated as Washington rallied from a 3-2 third-period deficit to a 5-3 victory. The following night, Kerr, convinced the pulley contraption trainer Pat Croce had rigged up to strengthen his shoulder was working, came back with a hat trick during Laforest's 6-0 Spectrum shutout of Winnipeg. But Huber, who had been in and out of Vancouver's lineup with a knee sprain, proved to be damaged goods, needing further rest and rehabilitation.

"I called Pat Quinn and said, 'You bleeper, you sent me a guy with a bad knee,'" recalls Clarke. "He said, 'You bleeper, you sent me a guy (Lawless) with a lobotomy.'"

The injured were all expected back within two weeks, but the Flyers were running out of time to set their lineup and build intensity for the playoffs—provided, of course, they even made the playoffs. On March 26, the teams of the Patrick Division were separated by only twelve points from first to sixth place.

Philadelphia's 5-3 loss at Uniondale, the team's 8th defeat of the season in which it held a third-period lead, all but gave the division title to the Islanders. With three games remaining, the Flyers still needed two points to secure a place in the postseason. Against Quebec, Poulin did his best, scoring twice, but Hextall, playing for the first time in 6 games, surrendered a short-side goal to Michel Goulet as Philadelphia settled for a 4-4 Spectrum tie.

The following night, the Flyers slipped into the playoffs through the back door when the Rangers tied at Winnipeg. The winner of the regular-season finale between Philadelphia and Washington would determine home-ice advantage for the two clubs' upcoming first-round series.

Hextall, honored with his second consecutive Clarke Trophy in pregame ceremonies, led 2-0 until Garry Galley's passout went off the goalie's stick and between his legs. Only 3:09 later, Galley went undetected coming off the bench on a line change and ripped a 45-footer off Hextall's shoulder, enabling the Caps to claim a 2-2 tie and the right to go home for Game 1.

Washington, 1-5-3 to finish the season, was sputtering as badly as the Flyers, who were 4-11-2 since March 1. Tocchet was not expected back until Game 3 and Kerr would miss the opener after taking a glancing stick blow in the eye during the regular-season finale. His larger problem, however, was the arm hanging lifelessly by his side.

Two rebound goals by Zezel braced Philadelphia to a 2-0 lead in Game 1, but Michal Pivonka, then Dale Hunter, scored on power plays and, for the 17th time in 1987-88, the Flyers had been caught from behind in a third period. They were saved when Lou Franceschetti tripped Howe behind the net, Poulin tied up Bobby Gould on a neutral-zone face-off, then

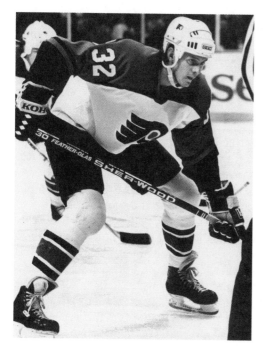

finished off a two-on-one with Sinisalo. Sutter hounded Larry Murphy into a giveaway and Craven hit the empty net to give Philadelphia a 4-2 victory.

In Game 2, Kevin Hatcher scored in the first minute, but the Flyers bounced back to take 2-1 and 3-2 leads. Unfortunately, Howe and Samuelsson could each play only thirty to thirty-five minutes a game, not the full sixty, leaving Keenan spotting Huber mostly on power plays and going more with Marsh and Crossman. Marsh, on for four goals against, was stripped by Steve Leach, who fed Kelly Miller to put Washington ahead, 5-3. Propp's score rekindled Philadelphia's hopes in the final minutes, but Caps' goalie Pete Peeters squeezed his pads on a good chance by Howe.

"There are about ten guys on Washington that I feel like killing," said Tocchet from the press box during the series-tying 5-4 Caps' victory. On his first

two shifts of Game 3, he threw four body checks, setting the tone for a furious first period. Propp beat Peeters after only 40 seconds, but Hunter tied the game just after he had been bloodied by a Tocchet high-stick. While the Flyers served his major penalty and Crossman was off for holding, Bengt Gustafsson cashed the two-man advantage.

Sinisalo made it 2-2 on the power play, then Howe sprung Poulin for a breakaway goal. Hatcher, persona non grata in Philadelphia after having cross-checked Propp in the back of the neck during Game 2, tied the game, but Samuelsson went to the slot to score off a pass from Tocchet, then reached out his long arms repeatedly to foil Washington in the third period. The Flyers, zealously guarding a less-than-sharp Hextall, hung on for a 4-3 victory and a 2-1 series edge.

Keenan had his full lineup for the first time all season in Game 4, while injured Caps Scott Stevens and Rod Langway watched in street clothes. The Caps defense had to be anchored by Murphy, who was playing so shakily that he had been scratched the previous night. But after Sinisalo's unassisted goal gave Philadelphia a 1-0 lead, a 40-footer by Pivonka went in off Hextall's stick and Gustafsson scored off the increasingly struggling goalie's blocker. The Flyers, forced to gamble in the third period, were then caught up ice on goals by Mike Gartner and Hunter. Trailing 4-1 and trying to save what was left of Hextall's confidence for Game 5, Keenan went to Laforest.

The clock had ticked under nine minutes when Eklund forced Murphy, Propp poked the puck loose from Peter Sundstrom, and Howe put in Samuelsson's rebound to make the score 4-2. With five minutes to go, Samuelsson gloved down a Murphy clear and Tocchet cut off the boards to feed Propp for a tip-in. There were only :53 remaining—and not a sane patron left in the Spectrum—when Craven pushed a passout through a mass of humanity and Samuelsson jammed the tying goal between Clint Malarchuk's legs.

"The first five minutes [of the break before overtime] we were real quiet, almost like we couldn't believe it," said Tocchet. "Then Brownie said, 'We just tied this game, let's start sounding like it.' Then we really started to get excited."

On the second shift, Malarchuk cleared a Philadelphia dump to Yvon Corriveau, whose hurried outlet pass for Hunter hit Poulin's skate. The Flyer captain wheeled a backhander past Murphy to Tocchet, who was preparing to shoot when he heard Craven yelling for the puck. Tocchet fed across the slot and

Murray Craven scored 30 goals in 1987-88.

Craven lifted the puck beyond Malarchuk's frantic dive at 1:18 of overtime. Craven and Tocchet hugged each other from their knees, celebrating a mind-boggling 5-4 victory. "We play that game 250 times, we win it once," said Howe.

Of course, the Caps, who in the previous three springs had blown leads of 2-0 (in a five-gamer), 2-1 and 3-1, no longer surprised anyone in case of a collapse. "They're telling themselves they can't win," said Tocchet. "If you are playing a team that doubts itself, then you take advantage of them."

Washington GM David Poile challenged his players to finally rise to an occasion. "[Game 5] is the most important in the career of a number of Washington Capitals," he said. Stevens's return gave Washington a boost, and Hextall could not repel a first-period burst of desperation. Mike Ridley got away from a strangely passive Ron Sutter to take a pass from Greg C. Adams and put the Caps ahead. Thirty-six seconds later, Hextall left his feet unnecessarily, allowing Gustafsson to put in a rebound.

Philadelphia cut the lead to 2-1 on a gift—Sinisalo had clearly kicked in his own rebound—but Hatcher's shot from the boards went over Hextall's shoulder to restore a two-goal cushion. Hextall then missed a poke check on Gould's shorthanded breakaway and Washington went on to a 5-2 victory.

The Flyers chastised themselves for not throwing enough body shots while the Caps hung on the ropes. But in reality, Hextall had not played well enough to give his teammates any chance. Thus Keenan, not surprised that Washington had stayed alive ("I was never comfortable, even leading 3-1," he recalls), faced a tough decision. Laforest, who had made a huge stop on Ridley during Philadelphia's rally in Game 4, was a viable alternative. But Hextall was proven in the clutch and, because of his puckhandling, was also the Flyers' third-best defenseman.

Keenan asked for advice. Clarke and Parent both felt the coach should go with Laforest, then, if necessary, come back with Hextall in Game 7. "Laforest wasn't that bad, he could have beaten them," recalls Clarke. "If not, Hexy would have had a chance to regroup.

"But Mike went with Hextall. I wondered why he had even asked. It was like that a lot with Mike. You never felt you were working with him, only for him."

Ridley blew the Capitals' first shot of Game 6 through Hextall's pads. Early in the second period, Gustafsson blocked a Marsh point shot and Dave Christian beat the goalie to the glove side on a breakaway to make it 2-0. As the light went on,

Brown, interfered with by Gould on the play, chased him down and pummeled him with left hands.

Gould turtled and Brown went to the penalty box for five minutes, enabling Gustafsson and Hatcher to cash power-play goals 38 seconds apart. The Spectrum faithless mocked Hextall as Washington, helped along by six savable goals, tied the series with a 7-2 victory. "I don't know what's wrong," the goalie said. "I'm letting a lot of people down."

Keenan refused to join the lynch mob. He told the team minutes after the loss that Hextall would start Game 7. Pumped up after watching a video of his playoff triumphs of 1987, Hextall was ready, too. The Caps, suddenly and unexpectedly on the brink of victory, nervously squandered four consecutive first-period power-play opportunities before Adams was caught holding and Grant Ledyard was penalized for spearing Tocchet. Kerr, fed by Craven at the side of the crease, scored off Peeters's blocker just as the two-man advantage expired.

Playing four-on-four early in the second, Propp swept in Samuelsson's rebound and, 1:24 later, Howe came out of the penalty box to beat Peeters with a perfect wrist shot just under the crossbar.

But Philadelphia, up 3-0, couldn't tighten the screws. Sutter failed to look for a trailer, enabling Garry Galley to take a Hunter drop pass and beat Hextall to the stick side. Less than a minute and a half later, Hextall missed a sweep check and Miller, outmuscling Crossman, poked the puck between Hextall's legs. The two goals put Washington back in the game and Hatcher tied it before the end of the period by gloving down Propp's attempted clear and beating Hextall to the short side.

With Samuelsson off for tripping, Hunter intercepted Galley's point drive and shot before Hextall could reset himself, putting the Caps ahead, 4-3. The reeling Flyers quickly righted themselves, however. Zezel won a draw cleanly from Hunter, Craven took Hatcher to the net, and Marsh's drive went through the legs of the screened Peeters to tie the game.

Philadelphia had the better chances through most of the third period, but a Propp giveaway in the final minute forced Hextall to stop Mike Gartner. As sudden death began, Washington dominated. Samuelsson slid to block a Christian attempt at an open net and Christian, then Gartner, hit crossbars. With Crossman trapped by a Ridley pass, Hextall slid across to make a spectacular pad save on Peter Sundstrom. After backing the Flyers to the cliff, the goalie was saving them from the abyss.

Howe took a penalty to stop Gartner, and Poulin

sprung Propp shorthanded. But when the winger was cut off at the top of the circle, the first Flyer chance in overtime turned into a routine save. The Caps continued to carry the play. Hunter dug a puck off the end boards and fed Gould point-blank, but Hextall came up big again.

A minute later, Craven tried to dump the puck at the Washington blue line for a line change but Murphy intercepted, put the puck between Stevens' skates, and started the other way. Hunter turned more quickly than Tocchet, took Murphy's pass, eluded the winger's desperate hook and blew between the slow-to-close Crossman and Marsh. The center got Hextall to open up by faking to the backhand, and shot between his legs. The puck ticked off the goalie's skate and went across the line at 5:57, giving the Capitals a 5-4 victory and the series.

Sutter put his hand on Hextall's head as he slumped against the net. But the goalie was not consoled by his strong last-ditch effort to save the season. "If I would have played better, we might have won it in the fifth or sixth game," he said.

In becoming only the fifth team in NHL history to squander a 3-1 series lead, Philadelphia had shown signs of weariness. Tocchet, Sutter and Poulin, who had rejoined the lineup with little time to prepare for the playoffs, ran out of gas and Kerr played with one arm. Still, management projected the forwards as the team's strength. It was the defense that needed an overhaul.

So, in Clarke's view, did the relationship between players and coach.

During the playoffs, Jay had denied rumors Keenan would not be back. "We think we have the best coach in the world," he said. "We intend to keep him happy." Clarke had said he "absolutely" intended to negotiate a new multiyear deal with Keenan, who had one year left on the old contract. Preliminary negotiations with his agent, Alan Eagleson, had begun.

But Clarke was particularly frustrated by Keenan's impatience with players added to the team over the previous two seasons. "I may have been too hard on Scott Mellanby," recalls Keenan, "but I thought he was handed a spot when he should have been in Hershey. The rap on me was not playing the kids, but I didn't think the kids were ready to play for us."

Some of those young players privately told Clarke they did not want to come back if Keenan did. The GM believed the lackluster playoff perform-

ance of some veterans could be traced to the coach, too.

As Clarke considered a change, he received only encouragement from Ed or Jay Snider. "We wanted hard work and discipline and a lot of the great things that Mike brought," Jay Snider says today. "But we also wanted an atmosphere that showed he cared about them as people."

During the first week of May, Eagleson called Clarke to schedule negotiations. "Clarke said, 'Al, it's going to be tough to do a long-term deal,'" Eagleson later recalled. "Although Clarke did not say what his plans were, my gut reaction was, 'It's over.'" Eagleson relayed his thoughts to Keenan, but the coach clung to the belief his track record would save him.

A trickle of clues suggested otherwise. Clarke told the *Daily News* that the Flyers first-round defeat was caused by a "lack of enthusiasm as much as a lack of anything else." Five days later, on Tuesday, May 10, Eagleson called Clarke again requesting clarification of Keenan's status. The agent was invited to Philadelphia for a Thursday meeting.

The following morning, the *Rochester Times-Union* strongly speculated a firing was about to take place. Clarke, who indeed had already made that decision, was angered by the story, believing the coach to be its source. The GM decided not to wait for Eagleson. Keenan was asked to come to the Coliseum.

In his office, the coach was told that because the Flyers were no longer playing up to their capabilities, a change was being made. Keenan replied only that he disagreed with Clarke's assessment. After only a few minutes, the GM left the coach alone and went to the locker room. "It's an awful thing to do to anybody," says Clarke. As he exited the Coliseum, Keenan was standing by the boards, staring out at the rink.

"I couldn't stop crying," recalls Keenan. "I couldn't even talk."

He drove to McGuire's house in Haddonfield, where he listened to Clarke's press conference on WIP. The GM conceded that Philadelphia had played well when its lineup had been healthiest through the middle 40 games of the season. "But I never sensed there was a lot of happiness there," Clarke said.

Most of the media and fan reaction to the firing was negative. Still, Jay vehemently insisted Clarke was doing the right thing. "We've been backing Mike up completely for two years," said the Flyers' president, "but the team was not playing the way it did earlier for him. If you look at some of those home games, they were disgraceful."

Keenan listened to the press conference impassively, then drove home, dodging a car chase by KYW-TV's Michael Barkann and refusing comment when the reporter knocked at the door. Instead, the ex-coach called a press conference the following day at the Coliseum.

"The thing I'd like to stress is that I changed," Keenan told reporters. "I came into the NHL with the youngest team in the league and was not coaching it the same way in the end. I wasn't nearly as tough on them this year as I was in the past. I found out in the playoffs last year that the team had grown up. I learned a lot working with elite players in the Canada Cup.

"How much happiness is there on any team? If that's the No. 1 priority, we could have the happiest group in the league, but not be as successful as we were. On all the great teams in the history of the game there were always unhappy players. You can't tell me those Montreal teams (under Scotty Bowman in the seventies) were happy.

"I thought it was a trying year. We had our goaltender suspended. We had our 50-goal scorer out of the lineup. We had a stretch where we had the best record in the NHL and then we ran into injuries."

Most of the Flyers were surprised by the firing. Only two, Derrick Smith and Marsh, made a point of visiting the ex-coach at his home to thank him, and only Hextall came strongly to his defense. "Mike is a win-at-all-costs kind of coach," the goaltender told the *Inquirer*'s Ray Parrillo, "and not every player is a win-at-all-costs kind of player. [But] that is no excuse. You still play for your teammates."

Poulin told reporters Clarke's concerns were justified. "I think management had a finger on the situation," he said, but added he felt it was too easy to blame Keenan for the team's slide backwards. "I don't believe it reached a point where he was no longer an effective coach," said the captain.

Tocchet acknowledged the negativism took its toll. "There are times you need a pat on the back when you're down." said Tocchet. Howe added that "Mike had a way of cutting the heart and soul out of a player."

In the end, Clarke had returned the favor. "I was crushed," Keenan recalls. "I had given so much to the organization. I felt like a Flyer through and through. And of course my ego was involved.

"I tried to get closer to the players my final year. I don't know if they ever acknowledged they went home with a helluva lot more cash every spring or had a chance to play in the Canada Cup because of

our relationship.

"But looking back, I don't blame them for firing me. It was time for a change. I pushed those guys pretty hard and it would have been difficult to change as many players that needed to be changed. I'll be the first to admit I made mistakes. There were times I should have taken a loss to win others along the way, but I didn't want to compromise the aspects of a program I believed in.

"Those teams were built with intensity and hard work. Unless we played at a higher emotional level than our opponents, we weren't going to challenge for the Cup.

"The players wanted to demonstrate they were more talented than they really were. That's where we ran into disagreements, why they became an increasingly difficult group to manage. One day, I don't remember when, Ronnie Sutter made fun of me on the ice.

"If I had expressed to them I trusted them, it probably would have worked out a lot better. But at the time, I didn't think I could afford to change. If you are a nice guy, you can't get tough all of a sudden. If you're tough, you can occasionally be nice, but you can't be something that you aren't.

"A lot of people, Mr. (Ed) Snider included, tried to be helpful by asking me to let up, but I was insecure. Mr. Snider saw me in a different light, that I could now live on my reputation without forcing it as much as I did. A few kind words from time to time would have been just what the doctor ordered. I didn't have to show the intensity I did. I could have delivered the same message without saying a word and probably have been more effective.

"But I started out knowing that I wasn't a former player and that the [longevity] of coaches is not very good. I wanted my career to last a long time, so I pushed. I always felt I had to prove myself."

Beyond any question, Keenan did. So did his teams. The 1984-88 Flyers were stricken by tragedy and suffered ill-timing. They peaked at the same time as Edmonton clubs that were among the finest in NHL history. Twice Stanley Cup finalists, Keenan's teams were good enough to have won a championship in many eras. They were ferociously driven, superbly organized, colorful and, ultimately, heroic.

"We reinforced the Philadelphia identity," recalls Marsh. "We weren't the Broad Street Bullies, but we had a bunch of talented, hard-working guys who had a lot in common with the Flyers' Cup teams. It's unfortunate we didn't win. With a break, we could have. We came so close."

Chapter 10

♦♦♦

No One Monkey Stops the Show

The only two candidates Bobby Clarke considered to replace Mike Keenan came from within the organization. John Paddock had just coached Hershey to a 12-0 playoff record in winning the AHL Calder Cup, but Clarke leaned all along towards Paul Holmgren, Keenan's assistant for the past three seasons.

"I thought the players had been verbally abused pretty badly by Mike," recalls Clarke. "And while Mike was doing that, a lot of the players turned to Homer.

"He didn't have head coaching experience and that was a consideration. But I felt we were still a good enough team that we could get back to where we should be as long as the players were happy and working hard. John was ready to coach an NHL team, but Paul had a good feel for those players. I thought they would respond to him. He was strong enough, too, that I didn't think they would take advantage."

Both interviewed with Clarke and then Jay Snider. "I was at Jay's house for about three hours," recalls Holmgren, where the two talked philosophy. Holmgren was hopeful, but believed Paddock might be more qualified He recalled telling Snider, "If I don't get the Flyer job because of my lack of head-coaching experience, then I want to coach at Hershey."

The interview process concluded when Paddock met with Snider on Friday, May 27. Clarke, prom-

ising a decision after Memorial Day, spent the long weekend at his Ocean City condominium. On Tuesday morning, May 31, he called Holmgren at his Laurel Springs, New Jersey, home and asked him to come to the Spectrum at noon.

"When I drove into the parking lot, I thought I saw John Paddock's car," Holmgren recalls. "I thought, 'Well, at least I'll be head coach at Hershey.' I was walking down the corridor to Clarkie's office when I saw [assistant public relations director] Mark Piazza.

"I whispered to him, 'Paddock got the job, didn't he?' He looked at me funny. I said, 'Well, who got the job?' He said 'I think you did.'

"I went into Clarkie's office and closed the door. He said, 'Do you still want to be the coach? The job's yours.'"

Clarke and George Lyon, Holmgren's Minneapolis-based financial advisor, had already okayed a three-year deal starting at $100,000 per season.

Holmgren went home and laid low, awaiting the announcement at a 1 P.M. press conference the following day and instructing his wife Doreen to tell the media that her husband had gone "night blue fishing." It wasn't a complete lie: the new coach was in his den with E.J. McGuire, trying to reel in an assistant. Holmgren offered McGuire increased responsibility if he would stay. McGuire, promised a job by Keenan wherever Mike landed, said he would think it over.

Clarke waited until morning to inform Paddock

of his decision, not wanting to put him in the position of having to lie to reporters or spoil the press conference. When Clarke phoned, the Hershey coach was not home and so wasn't officially informed until a half-hour before the press conference.

Paddock refused to be angry. "I've had a good relationship with the Flyers," he said later that day. "I love coaching [in Hershey] and the support they give me and I'm not going to let this damage anything."

Indeed, Paddock remained Clarke's fallback in case Holmgren proved to be in over his head—a concern the media raised often at the press conference, wanting to know if firing the stern schoolmaster would create a recess atmosphere in the classroom.

Clarke disagreed, describing Holmgren as "firm but fair" and having the "ability to create a good working environment." The seventh coach in Flyer history then reiterated that he would praise more and criticize less than his predecessor. "I think positive reinforcement goes a long way with the players of today," Holmgren said.

Players insisted that they did not expect Holmgren to be easier than Keenan, only more positive. "I don't think Paul is going to be our big friend as everyone else seems to be implying," said Poulin. "I don't think it will be buddy-buddy at all."

"There's absolutely no question in my mind that he'll be tough enough," said Hextall. "Paul gave out his share of bleep when somebody deserved it. I don't think there's a guy in the room who doesn't respect him."

Paddock turned down Holmgren's offer of an assistantship to remain with the Bears. Six days later, McGuire told Holmgren he would follow Keenan, who was being wooed by the Blues and Blackhawks. As both teams readied offers, Keenan's agent, Alan Eagleson, negotiated a settlement of the $150,000 the Flyers owed their former coach for the final year of his contract. In the wee hours of Thursday, June 9, Keenan accepted a five-year deal with Chicago which called for him to serve two years as coach before adding GM duties.

Unable to land his first two choices for assistants, Holmgren brainstormed for other candidates. George

Lyon suggested Mike Eaves, the former Flame and North Star center who had been particularly close with coach Bob Johnson at the University of Wisconsin and in Calgary. Holmgren, who had attended the 1981 Team USA Canada Cup camp, remembered Johnson had Eaves teach other players the power play. "I remembered how gung-ho he was," recalls Holmgren.

Johnson happily put Holmgren in touch with Eaves, who was an assistant coach at Minnesota's

St. Cloud State University. Eaves believed college coaching provided more security than the pros, but Clarke convinced him that professional experience would enhance his resume.

Having found an instructor-motivator, Holmgren now sought an experienced head coach for the other assistant's post. A month earlier, Holmgren had helped Andy Murray run a Bears practice. Murray, an old teammate of Paddock's, had seven years' experience in Switzerland and had been coming to

Hershey to help his friend after the completion of Swiss seasons.

Murray impressed Holmgren, who invited him to the NHL entry draft in Minneapolis for an interview. Although he had just signed a three-year deal with his Swiss team for triple the money the Flyers would pay an assistant, the contract had an escape clause should he receive an NHL offer.

Murray's hiring completed the revamped coaching staff. There were changes in the Flyer hierarchy as well.

Jay Snider had become busier in his role as Spectacor chairman and he felt too many Flyer decisions were falling on Donn Patton, the team's chief financial officer. "It wasn't Donn's area," recalls Jay. "I was looking for a CEO type for administration and business.

"I was telling Howard Baldwin [the Whalers' managing partner] at an [NHL] advisory committee meeting what I was looking for. He said, 'Ron Ryan is just the guy for you.'"

A former coach and GM of the New England Whalers and later executive director of the WHA, Ryan had been instrumental in the creation of SportsChannel New England and was now presiding over the fledgling SportsChannel Florida. But the opportunity to get back into hockey was appealing and he was appointed the Flyers' executive vice president.

There were changes in the broadcast booth as well. Mike Emrick and Bill Clement became the Flyers' television voices while Gene Hart and Bobby Taylor moved exclusively to radio.

Practically the only aspect of the organization not overhauled during the summer of 1988 was the team itself. Clarke's attempts to move up in the draft involved only fringe players and picks. He tried to interest St. Louis in one of Philadelphia's two first-round picks, plus some lower picks, in hopes of drafting center Rod Brind'Amour, but the Blues selected the center from Saskatchewan's Notre Dame Academy ninth overall. Five selections later, the Flyers chose Claude Boivin, a hard-nosed left wing from Drummondville.

"The Flyers are my style," said Boivin, the first Quebec league player the organization had taken in the opening round since Clement in 1970. Clarke decided to wait until the following June to exercise his option on Calgary's top pick, twenty-first overall, which had been acquired for Brad McCrimmon.

By not attempting to trade for veteran help, Clarke offered most Flyer incumbents the amnesty

of a fresh start under Holmgren. "Crossman was the only guy I was unhappy with," said Clarke. "He didn't play to his capabilities and I think I know why. There was obviously a conflict between him and Mike.

"A guy like Peter Zezel looked like he was going to be a tremendous player for quite a while and then, all of a sudden, he's struggling. The roles Keenan assigned to these guys, Paul might not. Some guys who didn't play much might play a lot now and have more value."

Although Clarke thought his blueline corps needed some freshening, he figured Crossman would see more action now that Keenan was gone. But in late August, agent Ron Salcer informed the team that the defenseman—upset that management didn't back him in his tiff with Keenan and unhappy about his treatment in the press—would not report.

"I'll trade Crossman when I can get equal value," said Clarke. "I think he's one of the top twelve defensemen in the league."

Clarke felt Greg Smyth, annually overweight when he arrived at camp, was no longer worth the time and effort. Given the chance to trade Smyth and a third-round choice to Quebec for defenseman Terry Carkner, Clarke jumped. He had coveted Carkner, a late-blooming 1984 top pick of the Rangers, for several years. "I almost had him [in 1986]," recalls Clarke. "Phil [Esposito] was going to trade him to me, but then Carkner beat the crap out of [tough Flyer farmhand] Steve Martinson in an exhibition game and Phil changed his mind."

Esposito eventually traded Carkner to Quebec, where he became a spare and then a free agent with compensation. Clarke was ready to offer Daigneault, feeling confident an arbitrator would consider it a fair swap. When the Nordiques insisted on Smyth, Clarke happily threw in the third-round pick to close the deal.

Clarke took time out from the Crossman question for the happier task of hanging a Hockey Hall of Fame medallion around Ed Snider's neck. Clarke and Bernie Parent, the two Flyers already enshrined, presented the Flyer patriarch for induction on September 7 at a Metropolitan Toronto Convention Centre dinner.

"The success of the Flyers has been achieved because Mr. Snider cared for all of us who played for him," Clarke told the assemblage. "The Flyers have fourteen ex-players working for them at this time. I think that says more for the man than anything else I could say."

Snider called his 1969 decision to make Keith Allen general manager "the best I ever made in hockey," and specifically thanked Clarke and Parent. "Without you both, I wouldn't be here today," he said. But the Flyer owner also expressed his appreciation for "the 211 players who have worn the black and orange. In choosing to honor me tonight, you have really chosen to honor them."

One of the 211 didn't feel particularly blessed. Willie Huber was offered a $100,000 pay cut by Clarke. "I thought I played well for them," said Huber, who had, in fact, barely played at all. But he took the hint and retired.

Gord Murphy, a 1985 ninth-round pick who had keyed Hershey's championship, was wearing Crossman's No. 3 when the Flyers began exhibition play. Jeff Chychrun and Carkner also received considerable ice time during the pre-eason while Kjell Samuelsson's herniated lower back disc and Brad Marsh's slight stomach muscle pull healed.

Fortunately, Tim Kerr, who had given his shoulder complete rest until August, then gradually built up strength with shooting repetitions, felt hale and hearty. The Flyers' top gun had a new contract—a four-year deal that started at $400,000 a year—and reason to believe he could earn it. "I don't know how I got through last year," he said. "I don't think I could do it again."

Clarke talked to a few clubs about dealing Crossman. Seven months earlier, the Kings had offered 29-year-old defenseman Jay Wells for Crossman and tried again, but Clarke still believed the tougher but less skilled Wells was not enough. The Flyer GM expanded the offer to include Propp and Crossman for Wells and center Bernie Nicholls, but the Kings, reborn after the summertime acquisition of Wayne Gretzky from Edmonton in hockey's most momentous trade ever, decided against moving Nicholls.

On September 29, Clarke finally accepted the straight Crossman-for-Wells swap. "Wait too long and [Wells] might not be there," said Clarke. "He's strong, he can move the puck and he has lots of experience."

Clarke then savaged Crossman. "You see kids working their rear ends off to make this team and you see a player with all that ability who doesn't want to play. It makes me sick."

Today, his contempt of Crossman remains. "He didn't even try to stop [Dale] Hunter on the [Game 7 overtime] breakaway." Clarke says. "He just wanted it over. His teammates knew that and that's why he didn't want to come back. He couldn't face them."

Wells tried to be brave, but still wanted to be a King. "Sometimes players fantasize," he said. "Philadelphia was always a place you'd want to play," he

said. "But with the big change [Gretzky's arrival], the chances of winning and glamour were all looking up in Los Angeles. I've never really wanted to leave and it's even harder to go now."

Few departures in sports have ever been as difficult, though, as Marsh's. Told by Holmgren that he would be scratched from the opener, Marsh replied he didn't want to stay if it meant not being a regular. Holmgren asked the 30-year-old defenseman to give the matter some time. But that very afternoon Clarke claimed 29-year-old winger Doug Sulliman in the waiver draft from New Jersey, making it necessary to drop a player from the protected list. Clarke removed Marsh, who was claimed by Toronto. "Sulliman is a useful player and we have to turn over our defense some time," said Clarke.

Marsh felt humiliated by his departure. "I was hurt by the way it happened," he recalls. "I was let go for Doug Sulliman. Who the hell is Doug Sulliman? It became really important to me to play longer than Sulliman and show the Flyers made a mistake."

"I feel awful," said Clarke. "You represent an organization where loyalty and character have always been stressed and then you have to make a miserable decision like this."

The 1988-89 season opened with Samuelsson, bothered by back spasms, hanging in anti-gravity boots and four new faces—Wells, Chychrun, Carkner and Murphy—on defense. Murphy, paired with Howe, killed off a 1:08 two-man advantage, set up Tocchet to erase a 1-0 New Jersey lead, and added another assist in a 4-1 Spectrum victory.

"I think Gord Murphy is going to be outstanding," Holmgren told the media. The rookie coach marked his first NHL victory by writing "Good Job!" on the locker-room blackboard. His praise pumped fresh air into the Flyers' lungs.

Zezel deflected in Howe's drive with 30 seconds remaining and, in overtime, Sutter fought off Phil Housley to score for a 4-3 Spectrum victory over Buffalo. The young coaching staff made the power play a priority—it had clicked at only 17.3 per cent in the 72 games Kerr missed in 1987-88—and the Flyers tied a club record with six power-play goals in a 7-6 victory at Minnesota. Then, bolstered by the return of Samuelsson, they shut down Gretzky's new-look Kings 4-1 at Los Angeles.

"I'm excited," said Hextall. "not because we're 4-0, but because of the atmosphere around here. We're a lot better on the backline with the changes we've made and a lot of guys have their enthusiasm back."

The Flyers, who had stumbled to a 6-13-3 start

the previous season, were bolting from the blocks. "We were so bad [early] last year that when you look back it doesn't seem real," said Craven. "I don't believe it happened and I don't think it will ever happen again."

But it did. Mario Lemieux's hat trick handed the Flyers their first loss, 4-2 at Pittsburgh, then Laforest's 8-6 loss in Hartford exposed the team's inexperienced defense. Against powerful Calgary at the Spectrum, Hakan Loob scored with 1:21 remaining in regulation and Jim Peplinski beat Hextall with only 37 seconds left in overtime to deflate the Flyers, 5-4. Then, at Madison Square Garden, Mellanby missed a check on Tony Granato and Hextall surrendered a goal between his legs to Brian Leetch as a 3-2 third-period lead evaporated into a 4-3 loss.

During a 5-2 Flyer victory the following night at the Spectrum, Tocchet answered two uppercuts from Islander rookie Dean Chynoweth with several rights and held Chynoweth by the back of the neck as he went down. As the Islander folded to a turtle position, Tocchet's hand reached around to his adversary's face.

Linesmen Pat Dapuzzo and Gordie Broseker heard Chynoweth scream. When they pulled Tocchet off, they saw why: Chynoweth's left eye had been gouged. "It was above the eye, outside the eye, underneath the eye and in the eye itself," Islander GM Bill Torrey said. "A thorough, complete job."

Chynoweth suffered from contusions and internal bleeding, and a Long Island specialist ordered him off skates for two weeks and away from contact for four. Tocchet denied an intentional gouging. "When you get punched, you're dazed and swinging and just trying to survive," said Tocchet. His match penalty made him subject to indefinite suspension, pending a league hearing.

Two nights later at the Spectrum, the Rangers led the Flyers 6-5 with three minutes remaining when James Patrick's stick caught the jaw of the forechecking Sutter, dropping him to all fours. Referee Don Koharski called a minor penalty and Sutter played one more shift, but after the Rangers hung on to win, the confused Flyer center asked trainer Dave Settlemyre how he had played and then complained of pain in his jaw.

Xrays taken at Pennsylvania Hospital revealed compound fractures. "It was a bad one," said Dr. Everett Borghesani. "It would take a tremendous blow under the jaw to cause damage like that."

Sutter, expected to be out for at least four weeks, underwent surgery on Monday, the same day Tocchet was suspended for 10 games. The Flyers, who had lost five of six, were now without two of their best forwards.

Given a more offensive role by Holmgren, Sutter was leading the team with 14 points in 10 games. His loss, and a rare opportunity to turn the tables of prosecution on the Rangers, had the Flyers screaming for league justice against Patrick. "If it was hard enough to cause a concussion and broken jaw," said Clarke, "you have to believe it was an attempt to injure."

"Typical Bobby Clarke style," sniffed Ranger GM Phil Esposito. "Throwing the emphasis on something else and away from the Tocchet thing."

Tocchet called his suspension "a nightmare." It would be a long time until dawn for the Flyers. In five consecutive games they entered the third period leading or tied and managed only one win. As the frustration mounted, a 3-2 loss at New Jersey had Holmgren sounding like Keenan. "Good efforts don't matter," he snapped. "They're paid to win hockey games."

But when the catatonic Flyers were bombed by Vancouver, 5-2, at the Spectrum, Holmgren administered positive reinforcement. "I don't think we're getting the return on the investment we're putting in," he reasoned. "We're working hard and just not scoring."

The Flyers were getting their faces bashed in. Literally. The following night in Detroit, after Steve Yzerman had wiped out yet another late Flyer lead in the last minute, Craven fired a breakaway goal in overtime, an instant before Mirko Frycer crashed his stick into the side of Craven's face and his eye. It sent the Flyers to a 4-3 victory and the traumatized hero to Ford Hospital.

Just before the game, the club learned the league had exonerated Patrick. "There was no deliberate attempt to injure," said Brian O'Neill. The Flyers went ballistic about Frycer. "What kind of a person would crack another one in the face with a stick?" steamed Clarke. "I wonder if this is going to be called unintentional, too."

It wasn't. Frycer, who had attempted to hook Craven's shoulder, was suspended for 10 games. Craven, meanwhile, suffered only a severe fright and was expected back in five days.

Laforest followed up with his second straight victory, 5-4 over Pittsburgh, but the rest didn't help the struggling Hextall. When he continued to kick at and miss shots in a 5-3 loss at Madison Square Garden,

Holmgren went to Laforest the next night at the Spectrum against Calgary. He played his heart out, as did the undermanned Flyers. But a Zezel mistake led to Joe Nieuwendyk's redirection and a 3-2 defeat, their second overtime loss at the Spectrum in eighteen days.

Poulin was next to go down, suffering a separated shoulder as the Flyers settled for a 3-3 tie with the Rangers on November 15. The Flyers continued to beat themselves with bad decisions at the worst possible times. Carkner was committing mind-boggling giveaways and Wells, who had missed five games with a bruised shoulder, had started terribly.

The Flyers were competitive, however, until the Blues ended their 34-game (0-31-3), sixteen-year winless streak at the Spectrum with a 3-1 victory on November 17. "The worst game I've ever seen the Flyers play," said Ed Snider after his team managed only 15 pitiful shots. A distraught Holmgren, feeling he was letting Clarke down, privately volunteered his resignation to the GM. "If you're getting heat, I'll quit," he told Clarke. But Clarke told Holmgren that things would still work out.

Jay Snider also backed the coach. "We are committed to Paul Holmgren," the team president said. "He's going to make mistakes like any rookie but he's going to get better and better."

Tocchet returned to contribute both a hat trick in a 7-1 victory over New Jersey and another vote of confidence for the young coaches. "I don't think there's a better staff in the league right now," he said. "Every morning you see the stress on their faces, but they're sticking by us and we want to win for them. When we get Ron Sutter, Dave Poulin and Murray Craven, it'll be like the cavalry coming back. The horn's going to be blowing pretty soon."

F Troop, however, was still short of horses–and confidence. The Kings' 6-1 embarrassment of the Flyers at the Spectrum had the fans screaming at Clarke in the press box, Holmgren blasting the players in the locker room and Crossman smugly commenting on Philadelphia's problems. "The fans tend to believe everything that's said and written about the team and there's always going to be one or two [scapegoats] every year," said the disillusioned former Flyer.

Clarke admitted that he "misjudged some players." One of them, Zezel, took the wrong man on a face-off in overtime on Thanksgiving night in Boston. Bob Sweeney scored for a 2-1 Bruin win, the second sudden-death goal of the season resulting from a Zezel mistake.

As in the previous year, Zezel was the Flyers only

healthy regular center and, again, he was failing to meet the challenge. "He hasn't played as well as we had hoped for a guy who has been in the league as long as he has," said Holmgren. The coach also tore into the 23-year-old in the locker room after Zezel forgot about an appointment for a coach-player chat and left Holmgren waiting three hours.

On November 26 in Pittsburgh, Zezel was caught up ice on a Penguin power-play goal, then gave the puck away on Kevin Stevens's bad-angle third-period winner. The camel's back broke in Buffalo the next evening. The Flyers carried a 3-2 lead into the third period, only to see it explode into a 7-3 loss, their 10th in 11 games (1-9-1). "I'll do something if I can," said Clarke at the buzzer.

Needing a playmaking center, Clarke had explored trading Poulin to Minnesota for slumping Neal Broten, but the North Stars backed away. Zezel, who in massive amounts of ice time had 13 points in 23 games, became the player Clarke most wanted to move. He swapped Zezel for Blues center Mike Bullard.

The 27-year-old Bullard's character and living habits had been questioned even before he arrived in St. Louis from Calgary. But in 1987-88, his one full season with the Flames, he recorded 103 points and blended well into a powerful lineup. Burdened with being the No. 1 center on an average St. Louis team, however, Bullard had gotten off to a poor start.

"He wasn't a secret to us," recalls Clarke. "It's an act that gets sour, but we needed a scoring center, so I thought it was the right thing to do at the time. I didn't think Zezel would ever take much responsibility. Mike [Keenan] got a lot out of Peter."

Clarke called Zezel to his office the morning of the Flyers' November 29 Spectrum game against Boston. Zezel left fighting tears, a sentiment hardly shared by Holmgren. "I jumped for joy when Clarkie told me," recalled the coach. "Literally. We really needed a scorer."

The Flyer switchboard received about thirty calls protesting the trade of their heartthrob center. Predictably, most of them came from females. "The men that called all liked the deal," said John Brogan, the Flyers' vice president of communications.

Bullard was in a Philadelphia uniform that night. Leading Boston 3-1 early in the third period, the Flyers were at their usual cave-in point when their new acquisition took a drop pass from Propp and beat goalie Andy Moog. The club, also helped immeasurably by Poulin's return, pulled away to win, 5-1.

"In the last four years I've matured a lot and done

everything asked of me and I seem to get traded all the time," said Bullard. "I'm really happy about this trade, though. And it takes a lot of the pressure off getting [a goal] right away."

Two nights later, Bullard's goal and assist brought the Flyers back from a 2-0 hole for a 2-2 Spectrum tie with Montreal. When Hextall came down with a virus, Laforest swept a weekend home-and-home series with New Jersey and the Flyers began to roll.

At the nadir of the slump, Andy Murray had suggested limiting the defensemen's pinching options, which cut down on mistakes. Simpler proved better and the defense settled down, even after Howe was lost with a groin pull in a 4-3 loss at Landover on December 6. Two days later, the team acquired 27-year-old defenseman Moe Mantha from Minnesota for a fifth-round choice, then rallied from a 2-0 deficit to beat Pittsburgh 4-3, extending their uncanny home-ice unbeaten streak against the Penguins to 42 games.

The Flyers had fully regained their confidence by the time Keenan's struggling Blackhawks came to the Spectrum for the first time on December 10. Most of the fans already in their seats stood and applauded as the ex-Flyer coach walked along the boards to the bench before the game.

"I think it was an acknowledgment that we played a lot of good hockey here," Keenan said. "I really appreciated it." One of his prize pupils, Derrick Smith, had a hat trick as the Flyers sent the goaltender-poor Blackhawks down to their 19th loss in 29 games. An angry Keenan knocked water bottles off the table in the visiting locker room between periods. "I seen that act," grimaced Dave Brown, "and it ain't purty."

The Flyers farmed the virtually unused Magnus Roupe to Hershey, pending his release to resume his career in Sweden. Meanwhile, Sutter returned wearing a face shield and scored 5 goals in his first 7 games. Bullard continued to find the net, Hextall had come full circle back to his Vezina form and Wells and Carkner stopped making game-killing mistakes.

The Flyers bombed struggling Toronto goalie Ken Wregget 7-1 at Maple Leaf Gardens and sent the Islanders, winners of one in their previous 15, down to a 4-2 defeat at Nassau Coliseum. When Bullard scored the winning goal with 29 seconds left to beat Hartford 5-4 on December 23, the Flyers — 10-1-1 in their last 12 games — roared into Christmas like an open fire.

Howe reinjured his groin after three games back, leaving the lineup again, and Kerr, who had 27 goals in 39 games, stretched a shoulder muscle in a 4-3 loss December 27 at Washington. But even as their best defenseman and top scorer rested, the Flyers motored on.

Samuelsson's long arms masterfully frustrated Mario Lemieux as Philadelphia set the Penguins down 3-2, only Pittsburgh's third home loss of the season and first with Lemieux in the lineup. Howe returned and Hextall was brilliant at Long Island on January 3 when Bullard threw a beautiful backhand goalmouth pass to Propp for the lead goal in a 4-1 victory. The practical-joking Bullard, with 8 goals and 12 assists in his first 16 Flyers games, was torturing both goalies and teammates. "He makes a team that has grown up being tense, very loose," said Holmgren. "And he's worked as hard as anybody."

The Flyers, 13-2-1 since their turnaround, had surrendered only 37 goals in those 16 games. They closed a six-game trip with losses in Minnesota and St. Louis, but Kerr scored a goal on his return as the Flyers beat the North Stars, 3-2, at the Spectrum. The big guy's shoulder ached, but it was impossible to tell from watching him. His hat trick in a 7-3 win on January 21 at Winnipeg gave him 32 goals in the 45 games for which he had dressed.

"I can play all year with one shoulder if that's the way it's going to be," Kerr said. "That's what I want to know. If they tell me it's going to be sore the rest of my career, then I'll just have to accept it." Kerr went for another opinion from Boston specialist William Southmayd, but remained in the lineup.

On February 2, two Pittsburgh disc jockeys did a pregame broadcast from the Spectrum press box dressed as witch doctors, attempting to ward away the evil spirits that had kept the Penguins winless at the Spectrum for fifteen seasons. Indeed, the haunted visitors came out like it was voodoo or die.

With the Penguins leading 2-1 in the second period, a Chris Dahlquist hip check flipped Howe, who then went to check Lemieux and discovered he had no acceleration. The Penguin star raced to the net to set up a goal by Bob Errey and Howe went to the locker room to see a doctor, John Gregg, who did *not* wear a grass skirt. By period's end, Pittsburgh led 4-1.

After Bullard scored early in the third period, the Flyers began acting as if they believed the Penguins had not suffered long enough. They forced goalie Wendell Young to make superlative saves before Smith hit the post. Pittsburgh hung on until Dan

Quinn slipped behind Carkner for a breakaway pass and scored the knock-out goal in a 5-3 victory. The 15-year, 42-game streak was finally over.

Two games over .500, the fourth-place Flyers comfortably led New Jersey by ten points, but their momentum was fading. Sinisalo, who had played only twice since November 20 because of a severely sprained ankle, returned and immediately suffered a broken wrist. Joining him in the training room was Howe, diagnosed with a sprained knee, and Craven, bothered by back spasms.

Propp's mediocrity made Clarke nervous about the Flyers' left side, so at the All-Star break he picked up 30-year-old Al Secord from Toronto for a conditional middle-round pick. Less than twelve hours later, Clarke traded the little-used Dave Brown to Edmonton for 30-year-old center Keith Acton and a sixth-round pick.

The fighting skills of Carkner and Chychrun had rendered Brown less essential and Clarke felt Acton would upgrade team speed. With the Oilers visiting the Spectrum only two nights after the deal, the disappointed Brown said he was in no mood to play against his ex-mates. But he changed his mind and skated uneventfully, as did Acton, in the Oilers' 3-1 victory.

Kerr came out of the lineup to gulp quantities of aspirin in a doctor-supervised attempt to desensitize his allergies to anti-inflammatory drugs. Bullard's play tailed off and the defense, chafing at the restrictions that had helped the Flyers right themselves in December, began leaking again. When Acton fed Secord for the insurance goal in a 3-1 Spectrum victory over the Rangers on February 14, it was the Flyers' only win in a six-game stretch — and a lengthy road trip loomed ahead.

Kerr's aspirin program worked, however. He stuck three pills past Bob Froese as the Flyers, also bolstered by Howe's return, beat the Rangers 6-4 on February 22 at Madison Square Garden. "It's just a pleasure to be able to play without pain," Kerr said.

The healthy Flyers were obviously still a good team, especially when they had their leading goal-scorer and best defenseman. With the fifth-place Devils trying to muster a run at the fourth-place Flyers, Kerr tipped the puck away from Tom Kurvers and soloed for the game-turning goal in a dominating 6-2 victory at the Meadowlands.

But key scratches again thwarted the club's attempt to build momentum. Craven, his season already interrupted five times by injury, suffered a broken wrist against New Jersey, then Howe hurt his knee again in a 6-3 loss at Calgary. Although Tocchet, who was finessing too much for Holmgren's taste, scored in the final two minutes to save a 4-4 tie in Winnipeg, Gretzky took advantage of Howe's absence with four assists in a 6:27 second period stretch as the Kings routed the Flyers 6-2 to close the trip. "Earlier in the season everybody was playing so well we were able to compensate (for Howe's absence)," said assistant coach Mike Eaves. "Now, guys are looking over their shoulder."

Unable to acquire a settling influence, Clarke instead did some commodity dealing at the trading deadline. He moved his two first round picks in the 1989 draft to Toronto for goalie Ken Wregget.

"He's a No. 1 goalie, not a backup, who we'd be comfortable with if something ever happened to Hexy," said Clarke. In truth, Clarke was hoping to use Wregget, who had been out of the Leafs' lineup for five weeks with mononucleosis, as summer trade bait, ideally in a package for Minnesota left wing Brian Bellows.

Most scouts assessed the 1989 draft crop as a poor one, so Clarke felt the 24-year-old Wregget had more trade value than two middle-to-late first-round picks. Nevertheless the deal was controversial, especially considering the dwindling Flyer supply of prospects. Their last three No. 1 picks — Glen Seabrooke, Kerry Huffman and Darren Rumble — weren't playing like top prospects at Hershey, an ominous sign for a team that had twelve players age 28 or older.

Laforest, bombed by Detroit 8-4 in his only start in three months, was ticketed for Hershey as soon as Wregget recovered. But when Hextall felt a tug in his hamstring and proved too sore to play at Long Island two days later, Holmgren was forced to play Laforest, who made 34 saves, several of them impressive, as the Flyers pulled out a 4-4 tie on Kerr's goal at 19:56 of the third.

"I just wanted to show that if they would have given me a chance, I could have been doing this all along," said Laforest, who then held off an early Chicago flurry in a 7-2 Spectrum victory and helped the Flyers to their fourth tie in six games, 4-4 in Hartford.

They were scrambling with Hextall and Howe still out, but the Flyers had rallied in the final four minutes to create three of those ties, an indication that morale was still good. "I think you can credit that to Paul," said Poulin. "He's kept the yelling to a minimum and come back with people after they've made mistakes."

Still holding an eleven-point cushion over New Jersey, Holmgren could afford to emphasize form rather than results. The players, tired of the pressure of going into the playoffs as favorites year after year, were not uncomfortable lying in the weeds in fourth place. "If we move up a place or two, fine," said Tocchet. "But I'd rather have the injured guys wait and come back at 100 percent [for the playoffs] than to win a few more games now."

Thanks largely to Kerr's health, Eklund's more relaxed and consistent play, and the X's and O's drawn by Andy Murray, the Flyers had the league's leading power play and the fourth-best penalty-killing record. Despite their inability to climb any distance over .500, they weren't losing confidence. "A lot of the things you need to have success in the playoffs are there," said Holmgren. "I've never gotten down. I believe that when we're healthy, we're still a good team."

Some nights, the Flyers tested that belief. On March 16 at the Spectrum, Laforest, prone to knee problems, couldn't hold three one-goal leads over St. Louis. Greg Paslawski tied the game in the final minute, then an unchecked Brett Hull drilled in Sergio Momesso's rebound to give the Blues a 4-3 overtime victory.

Holmgren turned to Wregget, pronounced cured of mononucleosis, but he gave up five goals in two periods of a 6-3 loss at Boston. Emergency recall Marc D'Amour finished up but he, too, was suffering from a groin pull, leaving Holmgren little choice but to come back with Wregget the following night at home against Toronto. Wregget blew a 4-1 first-period lead but the Flyers pulled out an 8-6 eyesore of a victory on late goals by Propp and Tocchet.

A growing number of critics suggested the Flyers were going nowhere but down. And for several terrifying seconds on a March 21 flight to Chicago, the team even agreed. Their trip was aborted seconds after takeoff when a fuel line burst. The pilot announced a tire had blown, but fire trucks on the runway when the plane landed twenty minutes later back at Philadelphia International Airport suggested otherwise. "I told Homer he was almost the first coach never to get fired," said Blackhawks assistant E.J. McGuire after the Flyers, who waited with extreme patience for another aircraft, finally made it to Chicago.

Happy to be alive, let alone celebrate the return of Howe and Hextall, the Flyers played like champions in rallying from a 2-0 deficit to a 3-2 victory over Keenan's improving Blackhawks. It was the only sweep of a season series that the Flyers would accomplish in 1988-89.

"I'd say [Howe] makes a wee bit of difference," said Poulin afterwards. "I don't think you can give a player a higher compliment than to say he lifts everybody else's game." Even Mellanby's. With only three goals in 33 games, the slumping right wing drew a penalty leading to Carkner's tying goal, then set up Poulin's rebound winner with only 1:54 remaining.

Thus, the Flyers looked very much alive and well, even though an airplane again gave them reason to ponder their ultimate fate. As their flight to Washington landed, a wind shear caused the right wing to dip within a few feet of the ground. The pilot took the plane up again, circled and landed safely. "It was terrible," said Poulin, "you can't even joke about it."

The shaken Flyers ran into a buzz saw the next night. The division-leading Capitals, surging since they acquired defensemen Bob Rouse and Calle Johansson and winger Dino Ciccarelli in separate trade-deadline deals, overwhelmed the penalty-prone Flyers. Hextall, cheating out to play what he thought was going to be a dump-in, surrendered a 75-foot goal to Geoff Courtnall and three others between his legs. The 6-1 Caps victory was their 7th in a row and 9th in 10 games.

"This game was an aberration," insisted Holmgren. Sure enough, the Flyers bounced back the following night with a 6-1 smashing of the crippled Rangers. Poulin had three points and addressed off-the-record front-office criticism he had received for allegedly allowing his off-season work as a stockbroker to distract him. "I think it's very unfair," said the captain, who had been used in more of a defensive role than in past seasons. "I think it's unfortunate that my production is down in a year where this could come up."

With the season in its final week, the Flyers were running out of time to establish consistency heading into the playoffs. As good as they looked against the Rangers, the Flyers were equally horrible two nights later at New Jersey, when Craven's return could not prevent them from blowing a 2-0 lead into a 5-3 loss.

"Discipline has been a topic of conversation a lot," said Holmgren after the Flyers gave the Devils nine power-play opportunities. "Kjell Samuelsson wraps his stick around a guy's neck when we're already shorthanded. Brian Propp takes a slash in the same situation, Sutter retaliates right in front of the referee. Maybe I have to sit some people on the bench."

After their Hydes were burned at the Meadowlands, the Flyers again became Dr. Jekylls two nights later at the Spectrum. Washington, with its first regular-season Patrick Division title locked up, rested Rod Langway and Bengt Gustafsson and the Flyers dominated the contest more than the 5-4 final suggested. Kerr scored goals 46 and 47 in his 67th game and pronounced himself finally healthy on the eve of a playoff. "After having so little hope at this time of year so many times, this is a great feeling," he said.

When the Flyers followed up two nights later in Montreal with another solid effort things were indeed looking up. The Canadiens, challenging Calgary for first place overall, were matched stride-for-stride by the Flyers into overtime. Then the Flyers' playoff chances flashed before their eyes. When Tocchet gave Mats Naslund a stick tug at center the Canadien winger fell into Howe, who collapsed and writhed on the ice with a reinjured left knee.

"I looked back and saw it was Mark," said Tocchet. "Then my eyes locked with Brian Propp's and we both shook our heads at the same time. Not him. Not now." Howe had to be helped to the locker room before the Flyers played out the tie.

Having learned to assume the worst, the Flyers were surprised the next day to learn that Howe's knee damage was far less severe than originally believed. Dr. Gregg said the first-degree medial collateral sprain might take only seven to ten days to heal. Conceivably, Howe could return by Game 4 of the opening round.

"We lit a candle," recalls Holmgren. On the last day of the season, this was better than cursing the potential end of a remarkable streak: the Flyers, 36-35-8, needed only a tie against Pittsburgh at the Spectrum to record their seventeenth consecutive winning season. A win would give Philadelphia a chance to finish third and avoid division champion Washington in the first round. The game also had meaning for the Penguins, who preferred an opening-round match with the reeling Rangers to their old Flyer nemeses.

After Hextall, a tower of consistency since his December turnaround, was presented his third consecutive Bobby Clarke Trophy and Samuelsson won his first Barry Ashbee Award, the Flyers jumped ahead on Tocchet's career-high 45th goal and another score by Propp. But then they played as scatter-brained as ever without Howe, continually giving up outnumbered breaks.

The Flyers were also unlucky on three goals that came off caroms, one by Kevin Stevens in the final 5 seconds of the second period, which gave Pittsburgh a 5-2 lead. But Murphy made a smart play at the point to set up a Propp goal, and Poulin fed Smith

who cut the lead to one. With 2:27 remaining, Kerr backhanded in his 48th goal of the season to even the game.

A tie would have kept the consecutive winning-season streak alive. But Holmgren went for the win and third place by pulling Hextall with two minutes left in overtime, and Lemieux, avoiding Kerr's sweep check, put his 199th point of the season into the empty-net from center ice.

To the Flyers' fans, the 6-5 regular season-ending loss seemed typical of an inconsistent, fourth-place, .500 team. Nevertheless, the Flyers were determined not to get down. "That's okay, we have a better goalie than Washington," said Tocchet, "and that's going to be the difference."

For the first time since the pre-Bully days, the Flyers were a clear underdog going into a first-round series. After the pressure-packed Keenan Era, this role seemed refreshing. "We're not going to lose," vowed Hextall privately before the team bused down I-95 for the opener. "You can be sure of that."

When Howe, who checked out his knee in the morning skate the day of Game 1, miraculously felt well enough to play that night, the Flyers believed in themselves more than ever. "There was no swelling and no pain," said Pat Croce. "I'm really surprised. I thought when he skated today, he would feel good enough that we'd feel better about getting him in there this weekend."

Propp put the Flyers ahead, then Kerr scored on a five-on-three. With a 2-0 lead and a still on the power play, Kerr was called for high-sticking Rod Langway during one of their titanic struggles in the slot. After Acton slashed Scott Stevens, Geoff Courtnall cashed the two-man advantage, banking the puck in off Hextall's skate.

Pete Peeters robbed Craven on two superior shorthanded chances 45 seconds apart just before the Flyer winger jammed his wrist again and had to leave the game. The Flyers lost momentum when they took two more penalties and a Tocchet giveaway enabled Michal Pivonka to put the tying goal through Hextall's legs. Only 1:35 later, Lou Franceschetti gained a step on Poulin, caught Hextall flush at the post and jammed in the winning goal.

Peeters had been the better goalie in Washington's 3-2 victory, but Holmgren assured his team it had established a standard of play that could win the series. Noting Mike Ridley and Kelly Miller's past successes against Howe and Samuelsson, the Flyer coach instead matched Carkner and Chychrun against the two longtime Flyer-killers. The young defensemen were also answering the physical challenge of Kevin Hatcher, who had dominated the Flyers during Washington's first-round victory the preceding spring.

The Flyers could not afford excessive penalties, but after taking ten in Game 1, they continued on the same self-destructive path. With Game 2 scoreless late in the second period, Hextall slashed Miller. Dino Ciccarelli got a step on Howe and controlled Courtnall's pass with his skate before either kicking or sticking the puck past Hextall just one second before the buzzer. The Flyers screamed but TV replays neither confirmed nor refuted referee Rob Shick's call.

Early in the third period, Mellanby, who took a bad retaliation penalty late in Game 1, made a foolish lateral pass that Courtnall cashed by beating Hextall to the stick side. With Secord in the box for bumping Peeters, the Caps had an opportunity to lock up the game.

The Flyers killed the penalty, however, then scored their first goal in five periods. Wells pinched down the boards to free the puck for Bullard, who quickly threw it goalward. Peeters could not control the bad-angle rebound and Acton cut the lead to 2-1.

Hatcher high-sticked Bullard with 8:35 remaining and Propp tipped Gord Murphy's shot out of the air on the power play to tie the game. There were less than two minutes remaining in regulation time when Dale Hunter's stick came up on Hextall as the goalie cleared the puck. On the power play, Kerr cut in off the left wing at a deep angle and shot just as Propp, going to the net as he had not done all season, took a cross-check in the back from Neil Sheehy. The puck caromed off Propp's skate and into the goal at 19:09, giving the Flyers a dramatic 3-2 victory and a split in the two Landover games.

"I think coming back after being down two is a pretty big feat," said Holmgren. "I think my team is a very determined team."

The Spectrum fans, now believing that the Flyers had a chance, were rocking as Game 3 began. Rouse and Hatcher took penalties 1:30 apart and Tocchet redirected Howe's feed to give the Flyers a 1-0 lead. But Washington, buoyed by the return of Bengt Gustafsson from his father's funeral in Sweden, shook off the initial Flyer burst and began carrying the play.

The Flyers hung in the game with Hextall and opportunism. Sutter set up Mellanby to answer a Bob Rouse goal, and when Steve Leach again tied the game for Washington, Tocchet beat Gustafsson out of the corner and fed Propp to restore the Flyers' lead early in the third.

Without Poulin–forced out in the second period after Stevens's shot cracked his finger–the ice was still tilting the Caps' way. When Mellanby cross-checked Fransechetti in the slot, Gustafsson put in Johansson's rebound to tie the game.

Overtime lasted only 51 seconds. Hextall stoned Pivonka's breakaway but Miller retrieved a Ridley rebound, crossed in front of the net and fired back across Hextall's body. The puck deflected off Samuelsson's stick and landed just under the crossbar, giving Washington a 4-3 victory and a 2-1 series edge.

With Poulin's finger broken and Gustafsson playing strongly, the matchups had swung back in Washington's favor. But the next morning Poulin was surprised by his pain tolerance. He lathered the finger with DMSO and found his hand encouragingly functional during the warmup.

When Holmgren asked his captain if he preferred to merely kill penalties or take a regular shift, Poulin wanted it all. "It's not like I have to stand there one-timing pucks on power plays," he said. "In my role, I could get by."

Out of radiology and into battle the captain rode, just as he had come to the rescue—cracked ribs and all—during the 1985 and 1987 drives to the finals. Hextall made a big glove save on Geoff Courtnall and stood tall against a five-on-three in the first period, keeping the game scoreless until the Flyers caught a break in the second period.

With Dale Hunter in the penalty box, a Howe windaround hit a glass support and bounced away from Peeters into the slot, where Kerr easily converted. Five minutes later, the jet-lagged Gustafsson dropped a pass at the Flyer line out of Ciccarelli's reach and Poulin took off with the puck. His shot from the top of the circle clanged off the crossbar, bounced off Peeters's rear end, and in.

Murphy, a steel trap at the point, intercepted a panic-induced clear by Hatcher and fired back off the Caps' defenseman to make it 3-0, and Bullard set up Tocchet on a power play, completing a four-goal second-period barrage. Mellanby, still playing despite a trail of bad penalties and giveaways, soloed off a steal during the third and the Flyers, 5-2 victors, squared the series and turned it into a virtual toss-up.

"They were twelve points back [in the regular-season standings], but they're healthy now," said a worried Bryan Murray. "They're big at the blueline, and when they make rookie mistakes, Hextall saves them. They have some high-level players—Kerr, Eklund, Propp and Tocchet. We're well aware of what they can do."

Still, after giving the Caps nine power-play opportunities in Game 4, would Philadelphia give itself a fair chance? The Flyers took a 2-1 lead in the first period of Game 5 on goals by Tocchet and Bullard, but then quickly put themselves two men down. With both Kerr and Chychrun penalized, Dave

Hextall celebrates his goal in the playoffs.

Christian retrieved his own centering pass and tied the score before Hextall could reset himself.

Pivonka, set up when Ridley and Christian double-teamed Carkner in the corner, put Washington ahead by surprising Hextall from the right side boards. But Howe's shot from the point was redirected out of the air by Kerr to create the game's third

tie.

Again, the Flyers handed the Caps a power play when Tocchet held Hatcher, and again Washington took the lead on a power-play goal by Ciccarelli. But the Caps' discipline also began breaking down as Courtnall took a charging penalty and Hatcher slashed the industrious Eklund, giving the Flyers a two-man advantage. Eklund fooled Stevens into thinking he would walk out the far side of the net, passing instead to Kerr, who tied the game 4-4.

Early in the third, with Chychrun in the box, Courtnall tripped up Poulin but play went on, giving Calle Johansson the room to close in from the point and beat Hextall, and again the Caps had a one-goal lead.

But Hextall kept Philadelphia from falling off the seesaw, making several key stops. Right after his fine save on Ridley, the Flyers broke back up ice. Tocchet tried to feed through Hatcher, but the Caps' defenseman deflected the puck high into the air. It landed on Ridley's helmet, then dropped conveniently at the feet of Propp, who promptly whipped a backhander past Peeters. With 11:57 remaining, the Flyers had knotted the score 5-5, the game's fifth tie.

Derrick Smith embellished Courtnall's interference with a dive, giving the Flyers a fifth power play. Eklund's brilliant move at the point kept the puck in the zone, and he finished the play a few seconds later when left alone in front of the net to score off Propp's passout.

With 6:08 remaining, a one-goal lead hardly looked airtight, but Peeters was now leaking worse than the Flyers. Samuelsson picked off a soft lob by Johansson, carried into the Washington zone and shot a wobbling, perfectly-placed shot under the crossbar on the goalie's glove side to make the score 7-5.

With 2:33 left, Chychrun was called for hauling down Ciccarelli, so when the Caps pulled Peeters and Stevens wound the puck into the Flyer end, Hextall did not have to worry about an icing. He bolted from the crease and trapped the puck along the end boards. Turning, Hextall eyed the emptynet and let fly from the goal line.

The puck headed straight for the net, hitting the ice halfway between the red line and the Washington blue line. Hextall had his arms in the air even before his shot slid two feet inside the right post. The only goalie to ever shoot and score a goal in an NHL game had repeated his feat in the playoffs.

"Somebody told me the other day that it had been over 100 games since I had scored," smiled Hextall after the Flyers' 8-5 victory. "I guess it was time."

Philadelphia had been shorthanded thirteen more times than Washington over five games, but Hextall's saves and puckhandling had put his team into a 3-2 lead going back to the Spectrum.

The sky—and series-turning pucks—were falling on Washington's seemingly ever-luckless playoff heads. Peeters was tiring and backup Don Beaupre was too cold for a season-saving situation. Still, the Flyers had shown so little game-to-game consistency prior to the playoffs that their being so close to advancing seemed surreal. And in the same situation against the Capitals the previous spring, they had not gotten the job done.

Game 6 began ominously, too, with Kerr receiving a major and a game misconduct for a stick joust with Rouse. Hatcher cashed the power play with a point drive, but Hextall made three big saves during the remaining 4:35 of the penalty to keep the Flyers within a goal.

The Flyers continued to flirt with disaster when Chychrun was called for elbowing Ciccarelli, but Propp stole the puck and Howe led a two-on-one against Stevens. The Caps defenseman shut off the passing lane, so Howe carried behind the goal line, sending the surprised Stevens sprawling. Meanwhile, Courtnall mindlessly skated by Propp, leaving the Flyer winger alone to take Howe's passout and rip his sixth goal of the series past Peeters's glove.

Murphy then batted down Doug Wickenheiser's clearing attempt and cranked a 45-footer through Tocchet's screen, and the Flyers led 2-1. But from behind the net, Ciccarelli fed Stevens, who tied the game 3:28 into the third period.

The Caps carried the play, but the Flyers took another lead. Pressured by Tocchet, Langway's clear was picked off by Carkner, who fed Propp. Propp tipped the puck ahead to Tocchet, who fired and beat Peeters, and the Flyers, leading 3-2, were 12:33 away from taking the series.

Still, the Caps came back when Gustafsson worked a give-and-go to the net with Johansson. Hextall extended almost fully to glove the puck down, but Gustafsson kicked the rebound high into the net. A hopping-mad Hextall failed to convince referee Denis Morel that Gustafsson had punted the puck and he had booted the call.

For the second time, Washington had erased a one-goal third-period lead, but lost momentum when Ciccarelli carelessly high-sticked Tocchet. When the penalty expired, Ciccarelli missed a pokecheck on Chychrun at the right point. The Flyer defenseman

jammed the puck down the boards where Bullard, pinned against the wall by Langway, deflected it to Tocchet in the corner.

Tocchet's pass through the crease for Mellanby hit the stick of Peeters as he stood flush in the net. The puck trickled between his legs and settled just over the line. With 3:19 remaining, the Flyers had gained another one-goal lead.

With Peeters pulled, the Caps forced five face-offs in the Flyer end. Sutter was not beaten cleanly on any of them, but each time the Caps' extra man jumped up to take control. Three times, Hextall bailed the Flyers out with clutch saves. "I wet my pants," said Holmgren.

After the fourth face-off, Pivonka jammed a backhander that might have gone in had it not hit his own skate. Howe dislodged the net—and the incredible pressure—with 19 seconds remaining. When Gustafsson pushed past Samuelsson and shot from a bad angle, Hextall, hugging the post, blocked the puck and Sutter finally rammed it out of the zone to a cathartic roar. As the clock expired, Hextall pumped his arms into the delirious Spectrum air.

Holmgren walked to the Caps' bench to shake hands with the coaches, then went directly up the runway. As the players exchanged handshakes and the fans celebrated, the coach locked the door of his office and cried.

"It was one of the best feelings I have ever had," he recalls. His eyes were still welling up as he spoke to the media and his players felt like shedding a few tears, too. "This is for Paul," said Tocchet, "more than for ourselves."

"I think Mike Keenan gave us the freedom to have fun," added Sutter. "But when things were going tough, I think Homer might have been somewhat more supportive. If we made a mistake, he put us right back out there."

Almost lost in the joy of the Flyers first true upset victory since the 1974 final win over Boston was the satisfaction of avenging their excruciating loss to the Caps the previous spring. Hextall, greatly responsible for that failure and so clearly the primary reason for the redemption, downplayed the turnaround. "I don't look back," he said. "I knew we were going to win.

"That's not a knock on the Capitals because they played a great series as well. But I just thought our team was underrated all season. We have a lot of talented players and I just knew they were going to come up big when they had to."

Among the heroes were Kerr, whose arm had rendered him virtually useless the previous spring, and three young defensemen — Carkner, Chychrun and Murphy. "Defense was the weakest part of their team," said the Caps' Stevens. "But in this series their defense really pulled together."

The first Philadelphia-Pittsburgh series in the twenty-two seasons since the teams joined the NHL began three days later at the Civic Arena. Although outscored by their opponents over 80 games, the second-place Penguins, a playoff participant for the first time in seven years, had smoked Phil Esposito's Rangers in four straight. The Penguins had broken their Spectrum jinx with victories in their last two visits, but going into the Patrick Division final, the Flyers felt deeper, stronger and more battle-tested.

"Let's face it," said Tocchet, "their defense is suspect." The Flyers also had Samuelsson's long arms and Howe's speed and smarts with which to contain Mario Lemieux, plus three good defensive centers —Poulin, Sutter and Acton — to match against the superstar.

In Game 1, Poulin's shorthanded goal, Kerr's power-play rebound and Propp's redirection gave the Flyers a 3-1 second period lead, but Dan Quinn and John Cullen tied the game. It remained tied and relatively passionless until the 13-minute mark of the third. Kevin Stevens got wide of Howe, and Eklund failed to look behind himself as Robbie Brown came up the slot. Howe recovered in time only to deflect Brown's drive over Hextall's glove.

The Flyers bore down harder. Propp's late try at a wide-open net was thwarted by Zarley Zalapski's stick check, and the Penguins held on for a 4-3 victory. "I think we realize we have to take charge more," said Tocchet. "Don't worry, we're going to win."

Game 2 was delayed seventy-four minutes by a blowout of a Civic Arena transformer. After power was restored, Kerr personally tested the red bulb behind the Pittsburgh net. He lit it three times in 11:23, proving the light to be in better working order than Penguin goalie Tom Barrasso, who left the game trailing 3-1. Coach Gene Ubriaco later reported Barrasso to be suffering from a "touch of the flu."

"Yeah, the Philly flu," mocked Kerr, who had exchanged insults with Barrasso during play and

couldn't pass up the chance to accuse the goalie of bailing out on a bad night.

Lemieux picked off Carkner's pass between the points and soloed for a shorthanded goal that cut the lead to one, but the Flyers toughened. "There must have been ten guys on the bench yelling 'We're alright. Let's just keep playing the same way,'" said Sutter. With Randy Cunneyworth coming out of the penalty box, Propp took a pass from Poulin and restored a two-goal lead.

"Experience teaches you to stay relaxed when the pressure is on," Sutter said later. He, Poulin, Howe and Samuelsson were all over Lemieux as the Flyers, possessing fourteen players with Stanley Cup final experience compared with only Coffey among the Penguins, patiently checked away their 4-2 victory to even the series.

Barrasso's problem was later reclassified as double vision. Not only was he healthy for Game 3 at the Spectrum, he became scarier to the Flyers than a cyclops. After two early goals by Lemieux and Quinn, the Flyers threw everything they had at the Pittsburgh goalie.

Kerr's work behind the net evened the score. He

Playmaking center Keith Acton heads up ice.

first passed out to Acton, whose shot beat Barrasso to the stick side. Then his bullish work got the puck to Carkner, who fed Propp for a shot that snuck under the goalie's glove. Jock Callander restored Pittsburgh's lead, then Poulin went to the net to put in a Sutter carom at 2:51 of the third period, tying the game, 3-3.

Barrasso, spectacular in the third period and overtime, was saved once when Gord Dineen hooked Tocchet's stick just before he was about to put the winner into a wide-open net. Propp missed a breakaway, then a backhander off a golden setup from Sutter before Cullen got a piece of a pinching Samuelsson, forcing the Flyer defenseman off balance. Brown broke out with a full head of steam, fought off Howe, and fed the puck past Poulin to Phil Bourque, who jammed home the Penguins' only good chance in 12:08 of overtime.

"We play this same game ten times, fifteen times, we lose once," said Hextall. The Flyers had outshot the Penguins 47-32 and outchanced them 26-15, but trailed the series 2-1. "If you don't beat a goalie when you have 47 shots," Howe said, "you can begin to think you need 85. You start gambling and get away from your game plan."

Holmgren reminded his team—who learned after Game 3 that Tocchet was lost indefinitely with a hyperextended knee—that they had beaten Washington by patiently forcing neutral-ice turnovers. Of course, Philadelphia had also gotten saves at key times from Hextall, who came up big again early in Game 4 when Lemieux broke in alone. Hextall followed the deadly Penguin across the crease and used his stick to close the five-hole. Thus, when Bullard fumbled the puck and Cullen converted a two-on-one, the Flyers were down only one goal, not two.

Derrick Smith got outside Jim Johnson and fed Poulin, who tied the game, then Kerr scored on a power-play deflection of Murphy's point shot, and again on a one-timer off Eklund's feed, to produce a 3-1 lead. When Lemieux hit his head on teammate Randy Cunneyworth's shoulder and had to be helped from the ice, the Penguins resolve exited as well. In the third period, Poulin broke out shorthanded and Carkner converted the rebound, putting away the Flyers' series-tying 4-1 victory.

Lemieux's cobwebs cleared, but his neck remained stiff, leaving him questionable for Game 5 in Pittsburgh. Despite vigorous treatments, he couldn't look to his left, only to the right or straight ahead. Nevertheless, after he skated onto the ice to tumultuous cheers, the Flyers were the ones who

wound up being blindsided.

After only 10 seconds, Secord took another in his playoff-long series of undisciplined penalties. He was back on the ice, but not in the play, when Lemieux electrified the crowd by getting behind Chychrun and scoring on a breakaway. The Grand Penguin, held to 5 points in the first 4 games, then shucked Sutter to tap in a feed from Bob Errey. When Lemieux followed up with a 30-foot screamer after a Cullen steal from Sutter, the Penguin shark was in a feeding frenzy. "A snowball with No. 66 on it," Holmgren would say later.

A rattled Hextall started out after a dump-in, then was trapped after losing the race to Brown. Errey scored into the empty net to make it 4-0. Bullard got a goal back, but when Hextall came behind the net to play a reverse pass from Howe, the goalie had his stick lifted by Lemieux, who wrapped the puck into the empty net. Hextall was wild now, foolishly coming way out of the net in an ill-conceived attempt to beat the less than dangerous Troy Loney, who completed a six-goal Penguin first period.

Eklund converted a two-on-one pass from Kerr 6 seconds into the second period, but Howe got trapped on a Lemieux pass that fed Stevens for a breakaway goal. Flyer heads were rolling all over the Civic Arena. Still, when Propp walked in from the point and scored under the increasingly vulnerable Barrasso's arm, they were back to within four goals with still more than half the game remaining.

Nevertheless, they were absolutely powerless to stop Lemieux. He fed Brown, who scored his second goal of the game and began his trademark celebratory windmill motion with his right arm, only to run towards center ice when he saw the enraged Hextall coming at him. "I mean, enough is enough already," Hextall said later. He was restrained, then replaced by Wregget.

After forty minutes, Holmgren repeated the same message he had delivered after the first twenty: use the new period for a start towards Game 6. This time, the concept sunk in. As the Flyers gambled, Wregget made a number of good saves and they crept back into the game.

Derrick Smith and Eklund scored goals, then Kerr added two more as the Flyers worked the lead down to 9-7. Bullard missed a tip on a half-empty net with two minutes remaining, making Ubriaco nervous enough to leave Lemieux on the ice for the final minute. He scored his Stanley Cup record-tying fifth goal–and eighth point–of the game into the empty net.

"I felt like the longer we did fairly well without him having a game like this, we'd be all right," said

Ubriaco. "It had to happen. You can't keep him down too long."

Still, as devastating as Lemieux had been in the 10-7 victory, the third-period Flyer rally actually seemed more relevant to the flow of the series. It may have been a rally of garbage goals, but the Penguins, deteriorating in their own end as the series progressed, were like Hefty bags sitting on the curb waiting for pickup. "Barrasso is a helluva goalie, but we're not having any trouble scoring goals on him,"

Goalie Ken Wregget makes the save.

said Kerr. "We have to win two games, that's all. We can do that."

Holmgren apologized to his players for not having them prepared to play. "I thought I would take them off the hook," he recalls, "but I think it made them feel guilty."

Holmgren had more than the Flyers' emotions to play with in Game 6. Sinisalo, out since January 17 with a broken forearm, suited up, as did Tocchet, whose knee was deemed ready for action following a two-game absence. He juiced the crowd with some early hits before a wondrous 35-footer by Kerr over Barrasso's glove opened the scoring.

Lemieux soloed off a steal from Eklund, but Hextall followed him across and forced a shot wide. "In the last game my scoring lifted everybody," said

Lemieux. "I wanted to do it again." Frustrated, he took a penalty and Kerr tipped his eighth power-play goal of the playoffs.

Cunneyworth tallied twice around a Derrick Smith goal to cut the Flyer lead to 3-2 but only the score, not the play, was close. Sutter ran over Zalapski and put a backhander in off defenseman Rod Buskas, then Smith's goal opened up a 5-2 lead. Like Scarlett O'Hara, the Penguins figured tomorrow—a Game 7 at home—would be another day.

Pittsburgh took only three third-period shots, which was fortunate for a hobbled Hextall. He had hurt his right knee when Phil Bourque fell on him in the second period and had received anti-inflammatory medicine at the intermission. Hextall wasn't the only concealed casualty, either. Kerr did his postgame interviews with a towel hiding a thumb broken by a Jim Johnson slash.

The next day, Hextall was excused from the optional practice and reexamined by Dr. John Gregg in Pittsburgh. Gregg diagnosed a first-degree medial collateral ligament sprain, but Hextall hoped a night's rest and another needle would enable him to play Game 7. The Flyers recalled Mark Laforest from Hershey as a precaution.

The next morning, it took the hobbled Hextall 15 minutes to cross the street from the Flyers' hotel to the Civic Arena. He begged for a shot that would enable him to play, but Dr. Gregg refused. During the morning skate, Holmgren told Wregget he would be playing. "If he was scared," recalls Holmgren, "he hid it pretty well."

Wregget was hiding it pretty well. He spent much of the afternoon looking out his hotel room window at the arena, pondering his predicament. Wregget had played only four games in three months, completing only one of them, and now the Flyers were asking him to save their season. He told himself that he had lost his two previous seventh-game starts, both with Toronto, and that he was due to win one. Wregget had played well in Game 5 but, with the Flyers getting bombed, that had been a virtually pressure-less situation.

"Geez, I'm nervous," Wregget confided to Kurt Mundt, the assistant trainer, as they shared a pre-game cigarette break under the stands.

"You wanted to be a goalie," Mundt said. "You've prepared your whole life to play a game like this. This is it, your chance."

Wregget nodded. "I think that helped," he recalls. "Then again, maybe I was so nervous that I was actually calm. I know that when the game started I felt pretty good."

He looked even better. Four minutes into the contest, Lemieux fed Quinn in the slot, but Wregget made a pad save. Later, Cullen aimed for the far corner on a three-on-two, but the goalie flashed out his left leg. Johnson, crashing the goalie just as a Lemieux shot arrived, tried to tuck in the rebound, but Wregget deflected the puck away.

The Flyers, taking their chances on Coffey and Zalapski point drives, packed their penalty killers low to choke off Lemieux's passing lanes. They had just killed a penalty flawlessly when Tocchet led a rush up ice. Barrasso stopped Tocchet's drive and another from Samuelsson, but Sutter got to the rebound and threw the puck across to an untended Propp. He carefully backhanded the game's precious first goal high into an almost empty net.

Almost three minutes into the second period, Propp's high-stick gave Pittsburgh its fourth power-play opportunity. Lemieux closed ten feet inside the outer edge of the right circle and fired as Samuelsson, tangling with Brown, inadvertently took Wregget's feet out from under him. The puck got through the maze to tie the score.

The Civic Arena surged to life as Wregget thwarted Cullen's one-timer. A cross-check by Chychrun left the Flyers shorthanded again and the Lemieux shark smelled Flyer blood, but their penalty killers were superb. And fortunate. Poulin got away with a chop on Zalapski, and when Coffey fired from the point, Propp blocked the shot and tackled Johnson in the race for the puck.

Replays later suggested the play was offside at the Flyer blue line, but linesman Ron Finn waved it off and referee Don Koharski did nothing about Propp's blatant hold. Poulin fed ahead to Howe and went straight up the slot to wait for the return feed. Coffey lunged for the pass, but lost his balance and slid backwards as Poulin one-timed the puck between the sliding Barrasso's legs to put the Flyers back ahead.

Outraged by the uncalled foul, the fans littered the ice with garbage. And the Flyers resumed checking like starving dogs going through trash cans. With Carkner off for hooking Bourque, Wregget trapped Coffey's shot against his shoulder and made a quick stick save on Lemieux.

In the first minute of the third period, with Coffey serving a penalty, Johnson bumped Howe from the puck and fed ahead to Lemieux. He backhanded a spectacular pass that put Bob Errey in alone with a chance to tie the game. But the Penguin winger shot over the net and the Flyers broke back up ice. Murphy chased down a rebound in Pittsburgh's zone, circled out of the corner and saw Bullard cutting for the slot. Lemieux, cheating for another shorthanded chance, was caught too high and Bullard gleefully swept Murphy's pass into the goal before Barrasso could come across.

Up 3-1, the Flyers had a working lead and the experience to know what to do with it. Murphy, Howe and Samuelsson, with lots of help behind them, repeatedly blocked passouts. Poulin glued himself to Lemieux as he tried to bull his way through the slot, and the Flyer captain finally cleared the puck while on his stomach. Coffey, forever open at the point, was arm-weary and missing the net. When Troy Loney's dump-in took an unexpected carom into the crease, Wregget jumped out of the way before the puck could bound in off his legs.

Coffey and Stevens held Mellanby from getting to the empty net with just over a minute to play keeping the game within the long reach of Lemieux. But one face-off later, Howe banked the puck past the exhausted Coffey to Mellanby, who had a 20-foot lead on his pursuers. Mellanby went right to the goalmouth before putting in the clincher, then mockingly performed a Robbie Brown windmill as he skated past the Penguin bench.

Wregget, who gloved a center-ice drive by Dineen in the final seconds, appropriately held the puck as the buzzer went off. "It seemed like a real long day," he said into the microphones after sneaking away for a cigarette, "but it was make-or-break time." The older, wiser Flyers had made their own breaks and advanced to their third Wales Conference final in five years with a masterful 4-1 road victory.

"Very sweet," said Poulin. Especially so for Bullard, the ex-Penguin who, after completing the handshake line, stood in front of the end seats gesturing at fans who had heckled him throughout the series.

The Flyers entered the semifinals against Montreal, the league's best defensive team, in typically battered condition. Acton, lost early in Game 7 after being sticked in the ribs by Coffey, joined Hextall as scratches. Tocchet's knee was on borrowed time and Kerr's broken finger prevented him from shooting.

Nevertheless, as Game 1 began at the Forum, the Flyers were still flying on the adrenaline of the Pittsburgh victory. Meanwhile, the Canadiens, who had needed only nine games to eliminate Hartford and Boston, looked rusty. Thirteen minutes into the first period, Chris Chelios batted a Flyer clear directly onto the stick of Derrick Smith, giving the Flyer winger a shorthanded breakaway. Instead of a head-down blast from the usually uncreative Smith, the winger faked to his backhand and goalie Patrick Roy went sliding, leaving the net wide open on the game's first goal.

About midway through the second period, Propp tried to clear the puck from along the left-wing boards and took a vicious elbow from Chelios, who drove the Flyer's head into the glass. Propp was unconscious even before his skull took another hard bounce as it hit the ice. He lay motionless for three minutes, blood coming out of a cut in the back of his head, before being carried on a stretcher to the Forum's infirmary. There, Propp claimed still to be in Pittsburgh, although he did remember his telephone number, just as Tocchet had memorized the one on Chelios's back. At the first opportunity, Tocchet retaliated, drawing a cross-checking penalty.

Holmgren warned the Flyers to concentrate on the game. Sutter was off on a necessary penalty—he took down Chelios to cover up for a Chychrun giveaway—when Poulin fed Sinisalo. As he crossed in front of Roy, Sinisalo lifted a backhander, which hatched under the goalie as he dropped down. The puck dribbled across the line to give Philadelphia a 2-0 lead.

With Sutter still penalized, Shayne Corson's second swing at a rebound made the score 2-1. But a minute later, Secord outmuscled Petr Svoboda behind the net and fed Tocchet at the left post. Tocchet, catching the goalie flush in the net, hit the far side. The 3-1 final handed Roy his first loss in 34 home starts.

The next day, the Flyers delivered a videotape of the Chelios hit to Brian O'Neill, who ruled the unpenalized Canadiens defenseman should have received a major, but was not deserving of a suspension. The Flyers chilled out. "There's not going to be any talk of retribution on my part," said Holmgren. Even Propp, feeling surprisingly chipper upon his release from the hospital in the morning, said venge-

ance was unnecessary. "These things happen in hockey," he said.

The Canadiens, who had lost back-to-back games only once since October, were much more focused for Game 2. After Berube high-sticked Russ Courtnall and Wregget cleared the puck over the glass, Stephane Richer cashed the five-on-three by putting in his own rebound. With Chychrun penalized, Carkner was bumped off the puck by Corson, enabling Chelios to feed Eric Desjardins for a 2-0 lead.

Coach Pat Burns's Canadiens controlled center ice and sealed off the slot, leaving the Flyers, who had 20 power-play goals in their previous two series, unable to work the puck to Kerr. Guy Carbonneau, fed by Mats Naslund, put away Montreal's series-evening 3-0 shutout.

"They raised their play a notch and we didn't have the spark to do the same thing," said Clarke. He hoped the return of the incendiary Acton and Propp, who passed a battery of tests at the University of Pennsylvania Hospital, would pierce the Montreal wall.

Indeed, the Flyers threw their bodies furiously into the Canadiens for the first fifteen minutes of Game 3 at the Spectrum, but still could not muster a serious scoring chance. When Philadelphia's adrenaline surge ebbed, the Canadiens made good on one of their first opportunities. Ryan Walter knocked the puck out of Mellanby's skates and fed Guy Carbonneau, who beat Wregget to the short side.

Though down only 1-0, the Flyers knew they were already in trouble. "They're so good defensively it's really important to get a lead against them," said Sutter. Corson scored on a two-on-one while Acton was in the penalty box, then Kerr lost Bob Gainey at center, enabling the Montreal veteran to tip in a Chelios feed.

Propp banged in a Carkner rebound to avoid a second consecutive shutout, but the stony silence at the Spectrum reflected how completely Montreal had suffocated the Flyers in winning 5-1 and taking a 2-1 series lead.

Kerr had tried not freezing his thumb in Game 1, but with or without medication he had no control of his hand. "If the puck ever got to me, I probably wouldn't be any good," he said. In fact, the Flyers had few power-play opportunities, let alone chances to score, against a disciplined Montreal team that had been shorthanded an average of only 3.6 minutes per playoff game.

The Flyers came into Game 4 so desperate to get ahead and make Montreal open up that the contest began in virtual sudden-death. Hextall was back and looking sharp, stopping Courtnall on a power play during a scoreless first period. Philadelphia pulled its forwards out higher on the breakout, trying long passes to loosen the Canadiens' total control of center ice, but Montreal began to pinch down lower and the Flyers' outlet passes were stopped.

In the attacking zone, the Flyers sent forwards right at Montreal defensemen, hoping to create room for a fourth or fifth attacker to come behind the play.

goalmouth pass, used Roy's head to break his momentum, drawing a penalty. Hextall then put a clear over the glass and Chelios cashed the five-on-three with a stickside blast.

After Carbonneau went around Hextall to score shorthanded, the Spectrum fans, with virtually nothing to cheer about for two consecutive games, became ugly, pelting the Montreal bench. Burns retaliated by spritzing a patron with a water bottle and Eric Desjardins and Claude Lemieux broke their sticks banging on the glass. It was the only breach of discipline by the Canadiens in three games.

After Roy completed his second 3-0 shutout of the series, Montreal had given up one goal in 186:51 of playing time. "I never thought they'd be able to play like this for three straight games," said Holmgren. "I just didn't think it was possible."

He told his team the Canadiens couldn't keep it up. He wanted the Flyers to be loose, but Bullard took him too literally, seeking relaxation in the Montreal night. When Pat Croce saw Bullard come in well after curfew, Holmgren took the opportunity to make a point. As he charged up his troops the next day, the coach suddenly wheeled around on Bullard, and picked him up by the throat.

"You, out late drinking the night before a playoff game!" said Holmgren.

Tim Kerr battles for the puck.

But the Canadiens played an arm's length off the Flyers, using positioning and strength to remain virtually impenetrable. Montreal's play away from the puck was almost perfect. "It is so unselfish, it is almost utopian," said Mike Eaves. "They are a chain without a weak link."

The Flyers rusted first. Corson blocked a Mellanby shot, trapping Poulin and Smith, and went to the net to tuck in his own rebound. Less than three minutes later, Acton, unable to reach a

"Urrrgh," said Bullard.

"One of the scariest things I've ever seen," Howe would say later.

Clarke talked Holmgren out of benching Bullard. The veteran center felt lucky to be alive and Holmgren wanted the Flyers, trailing 3-1 in the series, to feel the same way. So to ease the tension, the coach had his video guys, Leon Friedrich and Steve Romanowksi, do some editing of the positive-reinforcement video the players watched before every playoff game. "We got tired of showing them the same damn [Flyer] goal," said Holmgren. Spliced into the video were scenes of couples in amorous embrace followed by Derrick Smith sitting on the bench with a big smile on his face, and bouts between alien creatures interrupting a Chychrun-Claude Lemieux slugfest.

The Flyers entered Game 5 laughing. "Loosest warmup we ever had," said Kerr. Poulin, who had been taking painkillers for two broken toes, missed the hilarity, having to wait in the locker room for the flight-delayed Dr. Gregg to show up with the novocaine. Gregg arrived in time to send Poulin into battle, but had no magic needle for Tocchet, whose hyperextended knee finally took him from the lineup.

The game began almost as tightly as the previous three, but the Flyers finally grabbed a lead. From behind the net, Sinisalo passed to Smith, who had rare position on Ludwig. Smith shot back across Roy's body for the Flyers' first goal in 96:57.

In the next ten minutes, they had more scoring chances than in the previous three games combined. Roy stopped a noticeably more active Bullard on a breakaway and a two-on-one setup. But Hextall was even better in stopping a Mats Naslund breakaway and twice foiling Russ Courtnall. "If you're down to your last straw," said Howe, "it's good that the straw is Hexy."

The Flyers, who finally had a lead and the opportunity to play Montreal's game, nursed their one-goal edge deep into the third period. But with less than five minutes left, Carkner's clearing attempt was saved by Robinson as Chychrun lost his stick. Robinson fed a backhand pass to Bobby Smith in the slot and when Hextall dropped down to cover the bottom half of the net, Smith put the puck over his glove with 4:14 remaining.

The Forum shook in anticipation of another Montreal goal and the end of the series, but Hextall coolly erased chances by Carbonneau and Mike Keane in the final minute of regulation to send the game to sudden death.

The Flyers had not won in 15 consecutive overtime games, going 0-7-8 counting the playoffs. Yet they faced the end of their season coolly. On the sixth shift, Wells lobbed a long diagonal pass through center, where the puck deflected to Sinisalo. Instead of trying to get around Robinson, Sinisalo pulled up and dropped the puck to Murphy, who took one step and fired. The puck bounced off the leg of the screening Derrick Smith to Poulin, who was arriving late

after being tripped up ice by Bobby Smith. Roy, committed to stopping Murphy's drive, had no chance as Poulin slid in the stunning winner at 5:02 of overtime.

"Everybody wrote us off," said Kerr. "And now we feel we have nothing to lose." Indeed the 2-1 victory, forged under circumstances similar to Game 5 in 1987 at Edmonton, had the Spectrum thoroughly wired two nights later. When Mellanby scored as a Brian Skrudland penalty expired, he gave the Flyers an early lead and the opportunity to show the same patience that had paid off in Game 5.

But Jay Wells took Skrudland down, despite the fact that the puck had already rolled harmlessly off the Montreal center's stick, and Chychrun, attempting to whisk a power-play drive from the goalmouth, accidentally put the puck in his own net to tie the score.

In the second period, Sutter was off for interference when Smith deflected Chelios's drive over Hextall. Seven minutes later, Chelios took Gainey's drop pass on a three-on-two and shot through a falling Murphy and a screened Hextall, giving Montreal a 3-1 lead. The Flyers, forced to gamble, were burned when Ryan Walter converted a two-on-one.

Propp scored with 6:05 remaining to cut the lead to 4-2, but whatever slim chance still remained for the Flyers was effectively cancelled when Sutter went headhunting on Chelios. The Flyer center left his feet to high-stick the defenseman, who raised his own stick in time to defend himself. "It wasn't planned," recalls Sutter, "I just saw who it was, remembered what he had gotten away with on Proppie and did it."

Sutter's minor penalty unfortunately jogged Hextall's memory, too. When Chelios took the puck in offside during the final two minutes, the goalie raced out towards him. "I'd been thinking about it for the last 10 or 15 seconds," recalls Hextall. "Obviously, I wasn't thinking too clearly."

Chelios saw the goalie coming at the last second, but could not cover up in time to avoid being crowned by Hextall's blocker. A pileup ensued and when the enraged, sweaterless Hextall was finally pried away, linesman Gerard Gauthier tried to guide the goalie to the locker-room tunnel. But Hextall began screaming at Roy, who had come to his own blue line to shout at the Flyer goalie. "I never had any respect for Hextall," Roy would say later.

Meanwhile, the fans threw garbage, including a bottle, onto the ice, forcing public address announcer Lou Nolan to twice plead for calm. Bobby Smith, who received a misconduct for his part in the melee, skated off with his index finger raised in a No. 1 salute as the fans chanted "We want Chelios!" Philadelphia's public enemy No. 1 dashed for the visiting team's tunnel as trash rained down on him. He obeyed Burns's orders not to come back on the ice for the handshake line.

"You never know what to expect with Hextall," Chelios said after the ice was cleared and the Canadiens closed out the Flyers with a 4-2 victory. "But I saw him and was ready. I was fortunate I didn't get a skate in the head or anything."

Hextall refused to be contrite. "Did you see what he did to Brian Propp?" he said. "Come on, I think we owed him something. God Almighty, he just about took [Propp's] head off. I think that's good enough reason."

Some fans were ejected, but there were no arrests and no apologies from the Flyers for Hextall's behavior. "I don't think you like to see a series end on that type of incident," said Clarke. "But we like the fact that a player will stand up for one of his teammates."

Hextall was suspended for 12 games, the fourth most severe penalty in NHL history at the time. The Flyers seethed. "We've worked hard as an organization to try to be more disciplined," said Jay Snider. "Something like this sets us back. But when you look at all the incidents that have happened in the National Hockey League, I defy you or anybody else to tell me that this is one of the most heinous that ever happened."

On May 25, the Flyers announced the resignation of assistant GM Gary Darling. A holdover from Bob McCammon's regime, Darling had received a clean bill of health following cancer treatments, but had never gained Clarke's confidence.

A long-standing personality conflict between Darling and head scout Jerry Melnyk was adversely affecting Flyer drafts. "Gary was making some choices of players he hadn't seen [as often] as Jerry," recalls Clarke. "And after a while, Jerry would just say, 'Take who you want. You'll see' It's unfair to blame Gary for all the picks that didn't turn out, but it created friction. I should have handled it differently, but I didn't know how."

Clarke offered Darling's position to Hershey coach John Paddock. Paddock, whose ambitions remained in coaching, reluctantly accepted. "Between Clarkie and Jill [Paddock's wife], it was hard to say no," recalls Paddock. "In coaching you never know from year to year what can happen. And what could

have seemed more stable than working in the Flyer front office under Bobby Clarke?"

After successfully turning over half the Flyer defense during 1988-89, Clarke made the pursuit of offense his main off-season priority. He was counting on healthier years from Craven and Sinisalo, who was coaxed back from IFK Finland when the Flyers upped the ante on a one-year-plus-an-option contract.

Clarke still had his eye on Minnesota winger Brian Bellows, however. And when Washington allowed Pete Peeters to become a free agent, Clarke saw an opportunity to acquire the goaltending depth that would enable him to move Wregget. Just before the entry draft in Minnesota, Clarke offered Peeters a contract which called for a salary cut from $325,000 to $285,000, but provided the 31-year-old veteran with a two-year deal plus an option on a third. Peeters knew he would be returning to Philadelphia strictly as a backup, but jumped at the opportunity.

Trade talks with the North Stars cooled.

Their two first-round picks had been traded to Toronto in the Wregget deal, so the Flyers used their first selection, thirty-third overall, on Greg Johnson, a U.S. Hockey League center headed for the University of North Dakota. In the second round, the Flyers drafted Swedish left wing Patrick Juhlin, even though none of their full-time scouts had watched him play. Clarke took Juhlin on the recommendation of Inge Hammarstrom of the NHL's Central Scouting Bureau.

Hammarstrom, the former Toronto winger, had worked for Central Scouting on the side while selling real estate in his hometown of Gavle, Sweden. He occasionally traveled with Melnyk when the Flyer head scout visited Europe. Clarke, impressed with Hammarstrom's intuition, decided to make it worth Inge's while to give up his real-estate business. He became the Flyers' first full-time European scout.

Kerr's comeback season earned the Bill Masterton Trophy, the NHL award for perseverance, sportsmanship and dedication. "Getting back to the playing standards I was used to was gratifying. This was the most satisfying season of my career," said Kerr. "Now, I'm confident I should be able to play as long as I want."

Kerr wasn't the only Flyer honoree at the NHL meetings. Darryl Sittler joined Clarke, Parent and Allan Stanley (who finished his 21-year NHL career with the 1968-69 Flyers) as the fourth player from the organization to be voted into the Hockey Hall of Fame. Barber missed election by one vote.

The Flyers, who had plans drawn for a new practice facility at the Main Street complex in Voorhees, instead spent approximately $1 million to renovate the Coliseum. While that work proceeded during the summer of 1989, the seeds of a far larger construction project were being sown.

The previous November, Sixers owner Harold Katz had contacted Bob Mulcahy, head of the New Jersey Sports and Exposition Authority, and asked about the feasibility of a new home for the NBA team across the Delaware River. Realizing no income from Spectrum suites and concessions, and unhappy with his yearly rent of approximately $1.5 million, Katz envisioned an arena at Garden State Park, already operated by the NJSEA.

Mulcahy, who had lured the New York Giants to New Jersey with the development of the Meadowlands complex, had another idea. He told Katz that Camden officials, anxious for urban renewal, might present a better deal than Garden State Park.

The Spectacor brass was hardly surprised when it got wind of Katz's desires. Their own feasibility studies to expand the Spectrum, which had only fourteen suites, estimated the cost of raising the roof and adding skyboxes at about $60 million, roughly two-thirds the cost of a new arena.

Still, Katz–cognizant of the $11 million in annual suite revenues being generated by the NBA's Detroit Pistons at their new Palace at Auburn Hills–would not be placated by a cut of skybox income from a refurbished Spectrum. He wanted his own, new home for the Sixers.

Obviously, the Spectrum did not need competition from a new building. And the Flyers, also facing rising player costs, saw an eventual need for more luxury seating. When Ed Snider, honored on May 4, 1989, by the Philadelphia Police Athletic League, mentioned Katz's overture to his dais companion Wilson Goode, the Philadelphia mayor responded competitively. "He said we'd have a deal for a new arena in the city in five days," Snider recalls.

Encouraged, Snider called Katz, told him it made no sense for their teams to play in two different buildings, and suggested a partnership on a new arena. Katz had already met with New Jersey Governor Tom Kean and toured two potential sites along the Camden waterfront, but he worried about selling sixty suites for a one-tenant arena and the certain legal entanglements involved in breaking his Spectrum lease. Katz responded to Snider's suggestion with interest.

Snider was relieved. To him, moving across the river was like selling Philadelphia down one. For over twenty-three years, the corner of Broad and Pattison

had proved an ideal spot. "We were in the best location in the Delaware Valley," recalls Snider. "The subway and I-95 are right there. I was reluctant to go to another location that I thought was less desirable."

With plenty of land adjacent to the Spectrum at the crumbling, little-used, 63-year-old JFK Stadium, Goode suggested the site to Katz when they met. On June 15, Katz invited Ed and Jay Snider to his Huntingdon Valley home, where they shook hands and verbally agreed to collaborate on the project. Spectacor took the lead in negotiations with both the city and the NJSEA.

On July 13, city inspectors found structural problems at JFK Stadium, causing Goode to cancel a September Rolling Stones concert and padlock the doors. In announcing his decision the next day, Goode also made public the news of Katz's nine-month-long flirtation with New Jersey. The mayor said the city was determined to build a new arena on the site of the old stadium and keep its hockey and basketball teams.

New Jersey had promised Katz it could finance $65 million of the arena project's cost, approximately $100 million, through a bond issue—an offer the nearly bankrupt city of Philadelphia could not match. But Snider and Spectacor were willing to obtain private financing as long as they were assured tax breaks similar to those that had helped make the Spectrum profitable.

The Spectrum's tax-exempt status had twice been legally challenged, and upheld both times by Leon Higgenbotham, the U.S. District Court judge who had presided over the 1971 bankruptcy hearings. Nevertheless, the concept of a privately owned arena sitting on city land paying no property taxes was ripe for political challenge.

Those concerns and the city bureaucracy bogged down the negotiations. "The people we were dealing with were well-intentioned," recalls Carl Hirsh, Spectacor's chief negotiator, "but when they would take it to the next step, they had to interpret what they'd done and that often resulted in frustration.

"I don't think there was a specific point where we said 'this is it, we're going to Jersey.' I would say we always went back to them to see where we were. But I don't think there is much question that if Ed hadn't felt the way he did [against moving], the rest of us probably would have packed it in."

Ed Snider did meet with Governor Kean, and Jay and Katz again studied the New Jersey site. "The site they had picked [just north of the base of the Walt Whitman Bridge] had little access," recalls Ed.

"They were planning to put roads in, but the costs were going to be astronomical. It scared me."

Nevertheless, New Jersey had an offer on the table and Philadelphia did not. At Goode's request, Pennsylvania Governor William Casey entered the negotiations.

While the arena story made headlines, Andy Murray was quietly sneaking defenseman Jiri Latal out of a Czechoslovakian training camp in Nuremberg, Germany. Clarke had traded a conditional seventh-rounder to Toronto for the player's rights. Still, the Flyers were losing more players than they were gaining. Secord rejected a modest Flyer contract offer to sign with Chicago, where he had enjoyed his best seasons.

Then, Mellanby's left forearm was severely injured during a hotel bar fight in a cottage region north of Toronto. Hit by a beer bottle while coming to the aid of a friend who angered a bar patron by asking to dance with his girlfriend, Mellanby's ulnar nerve, ulnar artery and five tendons were severed. The Toronto doctor who performed surgery predicted a full recovery, but the winger would be lost until December. "The outcome was terribly unfortunate," said Clarke. "But we trust Scott's judgment."

The GM was not as magnanimous towards Hextall, who asked for a contract renegotiation. The goalie had become convinced he had received bad advice from agent Alan Eagleson in 1988, when Hextall signed an eight-year deal that deferred $300,000 of his annual $500,000 salary over a twenty-year period.

Hextall met with Clarke and Jay Snider and asked that the contract be revised. "I told them I thought the contract was unfair," recalls Hextall. "Clarke said it wasn't and that he wouldn't do anything about it. At the end, Jay said something like, 'Despite what Bob said, we'll take a look at it and see where we can go.'"

Hextall hired Rich Winter, an Edmonton-based lawyer with a history of contentiousness, whom Ron had met at the 1987 Canada Cup. "I knew Grant Fuhr used him," recalls Hextall, "and I really didn't know anybody else." The goalie's version—that he brought in Winter only after hearing nothing from the Flyers regarding his request—differs from that of Clarke and Snider, who recall that Winter was a gun to their heads from the beginning.

Snider recalls Winter flew to Philadelphia for a meeting that "started badly and veered off into horrible. He walked in and immediately stated that we

had made $13 million the season before and presented all these rationalizations for how much of it we owed Hextall. His figures were completely far-fetched. He attacked us like we had never been attacked."

The Sniders and Clarke resented what they considered Hextall's ingratitude. They felt they had treated him well, signing him to a high rookie contract and then tearing it up to make him the second-highest paid goalie in the league. The Flyers had also presented him with a boat after his spectacular rookie season and a car following his first goal. They believed Hextall had been pleased with the security of an eight-year deal when he signed it.

But Hextall felt a gift was a gift–gratefully accepted, but no excuse for the Flyers to defer two-thirds of his salary for six prime years of his career. He was losing considerable investment income in return for smaller payments over twenty years. "If they had just stopped deferring the money, that likely would have [solved the problem]," Hextall recalls.

On September 1, Snider and Clarke told Hextall they would no longer deal with Winter. One day before Hextall was scheduled to report to training camp, he called a press conference at the Cherry Hill Hyatt and tearfully announced he would not report. "If everybody knew what I knew [about the contract ...]," he said. "I don't think I'm being unfair." According to his information, Hextall said he was the 71st-highest-paid player in the NHL. He reiterated his desire to remain a Flyer, saying he would accept $100,000 a year less to stay in Philadelphia than play somewhere else.

Hextall went home to Brandon, Manitoba to wait out the siege. "Look," said Clarke. "Ron Hextall doesn't have to play hockey for a living. It's a free country."

With both Peeters and Bruce Hoffort, a free agent from Lake Superior State, under contract as backup protection behind Wregget, Mark Laforest was moved to Toronto for sixth- and seventh-round draft choices. Nevertheless, Clarke still had more players than he could protect in the waiver draft. He lost winger Nick Kypreos to Washington and Moe Mantha to Winnipeg, but saved Peeters and Acton by "trading" them to the Jets for "future considerations," then "reacquiring" them after the draft. The Flyers paid Winnipeg a stashing fee by waiving a fourth-round choice the Jets owed Philadelphia for minor-league defenseman Shawn Cronin. Two months later, both teams were fined $10,000 by the NHL for circumventing the draft.

While Hextall was skating with the Brandon Wheat Kings and running the steps of their arena,

Holmgren expressed confidence in Wregget. "I'm ecstatic about our goaltending situation," he said. But on opening night, the Devils introduced Viacheslav Fetisov, one of five older Soviet national team stars who had won releases to join the NHL, and clobbered Wregget 6-2 at the Spectrum.

The next night, the Flyers lost more than a 5-3 game at the Capital Center. Kerr left with a strained left shoulder. Peeters, who had come to camp with a bad tennis elbow, re-debuted with the Flyers in a 5-3 loss in Winnipeg, giving the Flyers their first 0-3 start in team history. Though they beat lowly Quebec, 4-2, at the Spectrum, it would be the only victory in their first 8 games. Carkner was lost for the first month with torn knee cartilage, Tocchet missed three games with back spasms, and although Kerr returned after four games, his shoulder ached.

Poulin's calls to Hextall reassured the goalie that his teammates were not angry with him. But the captain nevertheless urged Hextall, who was under league suspension for the Chelios incident until November 4, to rejoin the team. On October 19, Hextall returned Clarke's phone call of three days earlier and agreed that it was in his best interest to be playing hockey.

The goalie arrived in Philadelphia the next day and met with Ed Snider and Clarke, who agreed to drop the salary deferment. The goalie dropped his threat of a lawsuit charging collusion between Eagleson and the Flyers, and says he was told the team would renegotiate his contract at the end of the season. Neither Jay nor Ed Snider recall definitively promising a renegotiation. Temporarily, however, Hextall's unhappiness was resolved.

"I think management and myself got one point each," Hextall told the media after his first practice. "Look, I did what I thought I had to do at the time. It's over with."

When Wregget suffered a hamstring pull in a 5-5 tie at Detroit, Hextall's return to eligibility three nights later in Toronto seemed perfectly timed. But midway through the first period the goalie did a split, felt a pull in his groin and, at the warnings of Settlemyre, Poulin and Holmgren, left after forty minutes.

Peeters wrapped up the 7-4 victory. But he in turn was injured in a collision against the Islanders and Hoffort preserved the 3-2 win. Hextall returned with a 5-4 victory on November 14 at Long Island, but sustained a strained hamstring in practice the next day and was lost again. And Kerr, whose shoulder problems had taken him from the Long Island game,

was forced to undergo an operation.

Noted Birmingham, Alabama, specialist Dr. James Andrews removed two bone chips, decompressed a bone spur and repaired a tiny tear in the biceps tendon. Kerr, who had feared more severe rotator cuff damage, was relieved he would only miss four to six weeks, but his loss to the Flyers was coupled with Propp's, who needed surgery on a blood clot in his left hand. The Flyers' two best offensive players would be out until January.

Wregget returned, losing 1-0 in overtime to Winnipeg, but seeming to find himself in the process. A line of Craven, Sutter and Tocchet picked up for Kerr and Propp and the Flyers surged. Craven had two goals and two assists as the Flyers marked Mellanby's early return in a 5-1 Thanksgiving Eve Spectrum victory over Montreal. Two days later, Craven scored twice more in a 5-1 home rout of Edmonton.

Howe celebrated his new three-year, $1.9-million contract with two goals as the Flyers completed a home-and-home sweep of Pittsburgh, and when Bullard's last minute goal beat Washington 3-2 in Landover, Philadelphia was on an 11-3-2 tear and only three points behind the division-leading Rangers.

"I think our leadership during this stretch has switched to younger guys like Tocchet, Carkner and Ron Sutter," said Holmgren. "With so many people out, I think they realize they have to lead."

Things were looking up on the arena front, too. Michael Hershock, the Pennsylvania state budget secretary, devised a law that permitted the city to cap real estate taxes for the project, allowing for breaks similar to those that had helped create the original Spectrum. The state also committed $8.5 million in aid for public projects and parking at the proposed JFK site, clearing the way for further negotiations between the city and Spectacor.

"Hershock got the city, the state and us back to the table at a point where it was leaning New Jersey's way," recalls Carl Hirsh. "He made it happen."

When December turned, the Flyers cooled like the weather. After losing consecutive one-goal Spectrum contests to Boston and Washington, they were leading 6-4 in Quebec City with 23 seconds remaining when Wregget ended a goalmouth scramble by dislodging the net. Joe Sakic scored on the penalty shot, then Wregget foolishly played an icing when the Nordiques dumped the puck off the ensuing face-off. Craven missed picking up Lucien DeBlois, who scored at 19:53 to create a maddening 6-6 tie.

The following night at Madison Square Garden,

the Flyers ground out a 4-2 victory over the slumping Rangers to pull back within a point of the leaders. Nevertheless, a 3-2 Spectrum loss to Hartford on December 15 left Holmgren believing his 15-13-4 team was suffering a leadership crisis. The day after the game, the coach announced he was removing Poulin as captain and replacing him with Sutter. Carkner would replace Howe and join Tocchet as one of the two alternates.

"There comes a time when the torch has to be passed to the younger players," Holmgren said.

Poulin felt burned . "[Holmgren] just told Mark and I he was going to make a change in the leadership of the team," recalls Poulin. "That was his prerogative, but I don't think changing captains really changes leadership. As I recall, the one who was most upset was Carkner. He didn't want it, especially the way he got it."

Sutter, too, recalls feeling the move was unjustified. "I don't think any captain on any team I ever played for has even been close in leadership ability to Davey," Sutter says today. "I didn't care if I got [the captaincy] or not, but I think it was really unfair to him."

Poulin tried to hide his hurt. "I can understand the reason for [the change]," he told the media. "I'm a little stunned because I really loved the role and thought I did a good job at it." Typically, he played well the next night, blanketing Wayne Gretzky in a 5-2 Spectrum victory over Los Angeles that temporarily lifted the Flyers to the top of a jumbled, mediocre Patrick Division.

Holmgren came to regret his decision. "It was a mistake," he now says. "It was a flippant response by me to losing that game. I thought the young guys should be put in leadership roles, but to do it the way I did was wrong. I underestimated Poulin's leadership and I overestimated the young guys' readiness."

The Flyers, 2-3-1 in the games prior to the change, accelerated their slide. Latal, who was starting to do promising things, was lost with cracked ribs and Hextall's absence was crippling. The goalie agreed to a short AHL conditioning stint, joined Hershey in New Haven, and reinjured his groin muscle in his first game.

Hextall was in agony on the limousine ride back to Philadelphia and screamed out loud through the night. At 6 A.M., he called Dr. Gregg, who gave the goalie painkillers and put him on crutches. Nothing, however, could cure Hextall's case of third-degree frustration. Three times now he had failed to

make it past his first game. "I thought you were supposed to be asleep for a nightmare," he said.

Wregget began to average a bad goal a game, one too many for a team having trouble scoring. An astonishing three-goal burst by fourth-liner Tony Horacek gave the Flyers a 6-3 win in Los Angeles, but Howe's back pain resurfaced in a 2-2 tie in Vancouver and forced him from the lineup.

Propp returned in Calgary on January 2, but leads of 3-1 and 4-3 faded into a 4-4 tie with the Flames. When a 2-0 second period edge in St. Louis exploded into a 4-2 deficit and ultimately a 5-4 overtime loss, the Flyers' confidence seemed to break. They completed a 2-3-2 trip with an 8-5 bombing at Chicago, then lost again to the Blackhawks, 5-4, at the Spectrum when Wregget missed Secord's volley from the neutral zone.

As if the Flyers did not already have enough broken bodies, Clarke picked up another on January 5. Right wing Norm Lacombe, acquired from Edmonton for a fourth-round pick, arrived with a condition that caused his tissue linings to inflame after exercise. While the Flyers appealed to the league to reverse the trade, Lacombe sat in limbo.

Jay Snider blamed the Oilers for peddling damaged goods, but saw Lacombe as part of a disturbing pattern. Snider felt Clarke was only adding marginal players and losing sight of the bigger picture.

Tension was building throughout the organization. On January 14, after Wregget allowed Brian Mullen's soft goal to ignite a Ranger comeback from a 3-1 third-period deficit to a 4-3 overtime victory at Madison Square Garden, Holmgren boiled. "Sometime pretty soon we're going to have twenty-seven players," said Holmgren. "It'll be easy for them to focus, because if they don't, they won't be in the lineup."

Jay Snider, however, had grown even angrier. The next day, he met with Clarke at the Coliseum offices and shouted loudly enough for reporters in the hallway leading to the press room to overhear him. "I want to know where this organization is going," he asked his GM. Snider told Clarke that the Flyers had to get younger and, even if it meant missing the upcoming playoffs, they should get what they could for their older players.

Clarke was shocked and resentful. The next day, he forcefully replied to the team president that he was being unrealistic about the recycling value of the veterans Snider wanted moved. Clarke had, in fact, already discussed Poulin with Bruins GM Harry Sinden at a recent general manager's meeting in Phoenix, but the Bruins wouldn't trade young talent or a first-round pick for a 31-year-old player. Clarke decided to go for what he felt would be equal value for Poulin in a veteran. He asked about ex-Flyer Ken Linseman, who had fallen into new Bruin coach Mike Milbury's doghouse.

"Linseman had over 80 points [actually 72] the season before," Clarke recalls, "and we needed some scoring desperately." He called Holmgren, who was with the team in Pittsburgh, and asked his opinion of a Linseman-for-Poulin swap.

Mark Howe was hobbled with a bad back.

Holmgren recalls telling Clarke he did not like the deal. "I was open to moving Dave," recalls Holmgren. "But I wasn't really down on him. And I knew I didn't want to trade him for Linseman.

"Clarkie told me to get [assistants] Andy and Mike to talk it over, but I couldn't get them right away. About an hour later, Clarkie called me back and told me the deal was done."

Tocchet, Poulin's road roommate, answered the phone in their room at about 3 P.M. "A funny look came over his face," recalls Poulin, "and he told me it was Bob Clarke."

Poulin did not ask Clarke whom the Flyers had received in the trade. "That didn't really matter to me," he recalls. "I was stunned and hurt and wondering about my future.

"Kim was pregnant, and after what we'd gone through with the twins, she was considered high risk and couldn't travel. I had worked towards setting something up off-ice [as a stockbroker] and wondered if I would have to give that up. I wondered if the Bruins had just gotten me for the rest of the year."

Poulin assembled his things and went to the lobby, where traveling secretary Joe Kadlec gave him a ticket to fly back to Philadelphia. Only after Poulin landed did he learn from a newsman's question that he had been traded for Linseman.

The Flyers were not shocked by the deal, which came only one month after Poulin's captaincy had been stripped, but they were saddened. "I don't think I've ever respected anybody as much as I have Dave Poulin," said Mark Howe. His heartache, however, was dwarfed by his backache when he returned to the lineup that night. The Flyers winless streak went to 8 in a 4-3 loss to the Penguins.

Holmgren tried to put a good face on a deal he did not want. "We're lacking offense and that's the reason we had to trade a guy like Poulin, a guy that's given everything he's had for the last six years," said the coach. "Kenny was a real rebel in his early years with us. He has a wife and family now and has settled down with each year."

Linseman had missed the start of the season with a blood clot in his arm and been relegated to third- and fourth-line duties. He was out of shape and surprised the Flyers wanted him back, but was happy to go to a team that figured to use him more than Boston had. In his first Flyers game in eight seasons, Linseman assisted on Murphy's tying second-period goal, but Vancouver's Dan Quinn scored to beat the Flyers 3-2 in overtime. The pall that had descended over the Spectrum thickened.

"It was like the Flyers had exploded by the time I got there," recalls Linseman. "The team was confused and everybody was worrying about himself. There was still some talent there, but the fundamental character of the franchise—like along the boards—was gone. It was really sad to see."

Poulin, reassured about his future by a three-year contract offer, went happily off to Boston, leaving the fraying Flyers behind. Howe, who received an epidural block, and Kerr, who scored on a whirling assist by Linseman, both returned January 23 against Buffalo, but the Flyers lost 3-2 when Wregget fumbled a bad-angle shot by Rick Vaive into the net at 19:45 of the second period.

The agony of a 10-game winless streak—the franchise's longest since 1971—moved Sutter to guarantee a victory two nights later against Winnipeg. Twice in the third period, the Flyers surrendered one-goal leads but the captain's rebound goal with 6:11 remaining put the Flyers ahead for good, 7-6. Tocchet capped a four-goal, two-assist performance with an empty net tally and Philadelphia interrupted its agony with an ugly 8-6 victory.

"I said last year before Rick came back from his 10-game suspension that he's not Jesus Christ," said Holmgren. "Maybe he is. He gave the team a big lift tonight."

Howe tried out his back two days later in Boston, but felt numbness in the right foot and pain down his legs. After scoring a second-period goal, he had to leave the game. "We're going to have to find out what can be done," he said discouragingly after the Flyers played just well enough to lose, 2-1, on a late goal set up by Poulin. "As far as I'm concerned, Mark might be done," said Holmgren.

The reeling Flyers were blown away 7-2 in Washington the following day. Two Kerr goals produced a 6-3 victory in Pittsburgh, but the Flyers kicked a 6-2 lead over Minnesota into a 6-6 tie before Bullard scored with 9 seconds remaining in overtime to rescue a bizarre victory.

When the Flyers blew a 5-3 third-period lead over the Islanders into a 5-5 tie, Holmgren benched both Propp, who had only 24 points in 36 games, and Linseman, whose 9-game Flyer output totaled 1 goal and 4 assists.

Though disappointed with Propp, Clarke did not approve of the benchings. He told reporters he did not believe sitting out veteran players served any valid motivational purpose. Holmgren replied publicly that the lineup was his responsibility, and the exchange drew a big headline in the *Inquirer*, caus-

ing Holmgren to state publicly that his working relationship with his longtime friend had not been strained.

When Clarke requested a meeting with Holmgren, the coach started to tell his GM that there was no problem between them. "I told him, 'It's a bunch of bullbleep stirred up about nothing,'" recalls Holmgren. He said, 'No, it's not about that.' He asked if there was some place we could talk. He came to my house and told me he had had a disagreement with Jay. Clarkie was in tears."

The Flyers goaltending alone was enough to make grown men cry. Wregget missed 4 of the Penguins' first 15 shots in a 4-1 Flyer loss at the Spectrum. The reinstatement of Propp for the following game failed to prevent a 4-3 Spectrum loss to the Rangers.

Peeters, 0-8-4 in 12 games, shut out Toronto 3-0 but exhausted himself in the effort. The next night, he was bombed 9-6 in Detroit. Thus did the curtain part for another return by Hextall, who backstopped the Flyers to their best game in two and a half months, a come-from-behind 3-2 Spectrum victory over the Islanders. The Flyers, though tied for fifth place with Washington, were nevertheless only five points behind the first-place Islanders in the stumbling, bumbling, Patrick. "Everyone has nine lives," said Craven. "This is the cat's division."

Predominantly black cats, however. Hextall reported some hamstring tightness the next day at practice, but when Wregget was beaten in Pittsburgh, 6-4, Holmgren turned back to his savior. Hextall won 7-4 in St. Louis, but when the Flyers dragged through a 4-1 loss in Chicago, the goalie publicly ripped his teammates.

On the ice and in the training room, the news remained relentlessly bad. Howe was advised to rest, but after a month off the ice, he could only leave his bed for an hour at a time. "I can't even kick my legs in the pool," he said after his first rehab session. "I can't walk right and I can't get any rest. I'm going crazy."

In his absence, the defense was going cuckoo, too. The Flyers were in almost every game until somebody would pass up a simple, safe play and make a game-killing error. Hextall, hitting the wall from his inactivity, surrendered seven goals in Vancouver, where Eklund and Kerr scored in the final minute to pull out a 7-7 tie.

For Propp, yearning to depart Philadelphia for a long-term contract elsewhere had become an almost full-time preoccupation, causing Holmgren to sour on him. Clarke decided to scratch another name off the list of veterans Jay Snider wanted recycled.

"It was time to get a little younger and Proppy wasn't doing much for us," recalls the GM. When Sinden, seeking experienced help for the Bruins' playoff drive, offered a second-rounder in the upcoming draft, Clarke felt it was the best he could do for both the Flyers and Propp.

"It was the right time for Brian," Clarke says today. "And I was glad it was Boston. He was a good player for this organization for a long time and I thought sending him to a good team might salvage his career."

On March 1 in Calgary, Propp played one of his best games of the season, scoring a goal and an assist as the Flyers and Wregget surprised the defending Stanley Cup champion Flames, 4-2. Sinden recalls wondering the next morning whether Propp's performance would cause the Flyers to call off the deal. But Clarke didn't flinch.

Propp was having breakfast in the hotel coffee shop with his parents when he got a message to call Holmgren in his room. The coach told Propp to call Clarke. "I knew something had happened," recalls Propp. "I was just anxious to find out where. When he said Boston, I was excited. Poulin was there and they had a chance to win the Stanley Cup. I knew I wasn't going to get a new contract with the Flyers."

He was on a flight east before the Flyers gathered for the trip to Edmonton. Propp left behind eleven seasons, 369 goals, 480 assists, and very few regrets. "I was thankful for the opportunity [in Boston] and to the Flyers, too," he recalls. "Those years in Philadelphia were the greatest part of my life.

Just as they began a desperate drive to salvage an 18th consecutive playoff spot, the Flyers gave up their third all-time scorer for a draft choice. But Propp's mediocre season caused none of his ex-teammates to question the deal. "I don't think anybody is really shocked," Tocchet told the media. "I'm sure they want to get a youth movement in."

Clarke, indeed, was trying to think ahead, but still didn't believe he was sacrificing the current season. "I couldn't give the players the idea we weren't trying to win," he said. "We had to keep some players."

Believing he had two more young defenseman who could play—Latal and Murray Baron, an eighth round 1986 pick called up March 1—Clarke tried to move Kerry Huffman to Buffalo for promising winger Darrin Shannon and muscleman Kevin Maguire. When the Sabres, nervously watching divisional rival Boston stock up on Flyer veterans, countered with

an offer of a second-rounder and Maguire for Jay Wells, Clarke closed the deal on eve of the trading deadline.

"If we were going to be at the top, we'd stay with our veterans," the GM explained. "But as the season progressed, we didn't win enough. I blame most of it on injuries, but we've got to bring our young players in and see what they can do."

The following night, Maguire scored against Boston in his Flyer debut. But the unsettling presence of Propp and Poulin in Bruin jerseys turned the Spectrum faithful into a seething mob. After the two ex-Flyers, clearly rejuvenated by joining the NHL's overall points leader, played well in a Boston victory, fans stood in front of the press box screaming epithets at Clarke.

Two nights later, Hextall suffered a groin pull kicking at a goal by the Rangers' Normand Rochefort and was lost for the year.

When the Caps scored two late goals to beat Wregget 4-3 at the Spectrum on March 10, Philadelphia lost its 20th one-goal game of the season. Holmgren tried Wregget again and Sinisalo's late goal got the Flyers past the reeling Islanders, 5-4. But two nights later, Peeters was beaten 6-3 in Quebec City by the 11-53-7 Nordiques, assuring the Flyers of their first losing season since 1971-72.

Nevertheless, Philadelphia remained only four points behind fourth-place Washington. And when the Flyers bounced back the night following the Quebec debacle to score four in the third and beat Los Angeles 7-4, they began a last-ditch run. The league had validated the Lacombe deal, so he was used on an effective line with Acton, who now got more ice time than the defensively-suspect Linseman. With Propp gone, Mellanby's hand increasingly numb and Kerr's shoulder forcing him from the lineup again, Holmgren felt the Flyers' only chance to make the playoffs was to grind their way in.

They erased a 2-1 deficit and checked their way to a solid 3-2 victory at New Jersey. And two nights later, the Spectrum tingled with renewed hope and reminders of past glories.

"Once a Flyer, always a Flyer," said Fred Shero as he and Rick MacLeish were inducted into the Flyer Hall of Fame. Back from a battle with cancer, four years in the Devils' broadcast booth and a season coaching in Holland, Shero had written Keith Allen a letter asking the Flyers for a job. "I knew the day I left [in 1978] I had made a mistake," Shero said. Better late than never, the Flyers had invited him back as a consultant.

Keyed by three goals from a line of Acton, Lacombe

and a heretofore disappointing Derrick Smith, the Flyers beat the skidding (6-10-1 since Lemieux's back problems forced him from the lineup) Penguins 5-3 to climb within a point of a playoff spot.

Two days later, however, another raft of injuries flooded the Flyers' chances of improving. Acton's back spasms and Bullard's pulled groin kept them from a Spectrum game against New Jersey. Wregget then pulled a hamstring in warmups, forcing Holmgren to tap Peeters, who gave up two soft goals

experience and Peeters responded with a strong game. The fans, watching ArenaVision highlights of Pittsburgh's game in St. Louis, warmed to the Flyers' effort with lusty cheering for the Blues as well as Peeters. Kerr returned to score a goal and Sinisalo gave Philadelphia a 2-1 lead. But the Caps' Geoff Courtnall answered midway in the second period and the Flyers settled for a hard-fought 2-2 tie.

While the Flyers watched from their locker room, the Blues pulled out a late 5-4 victory. Holmgren's

Rick Tocchet in action: "Sometimes these things have a positive side."

in a 5-2 loss. Murphy's hip pointer and Craven's rotator cuff made them scratches the next afternoon at Madison Square Garden. After Tocchet was ejected early for an accidental high-stick, Peeters was bombed 7-3.

Still, the Penguins and Islanders also stumbled, leaving the Flyers in position to control their destiny. When Washington came to the Spectrum for Game 78, Philadelphia trailed fourth-place Pittsburgh by three points, the fifth-place Isles by two, and had a game in hand.

Holmgren had the choice of Bruce Hoffort, who had not continued his early-season Flyer success at Hershey, or the 1-12-4 Peeters. The coach went for

team still had a chance. If the Penguins lost or tied their final game against Buffalo and the Flyers defeated or tied the Islanders Saturday night at Nassau Coliseum, Philadelphia could make the playoffs by beating Detroit on Sunday night at the Spectrum.

"We had two games that were winnable," recalls Holmgren. "I was still confident." Indeed, the Islanders, who stayed alive on Thursday night with a 6-3 win in Toronto, had won only twice in their their previous 21 games.

Kerr put the Isles behind 1-0 after only 40 seconds and a power play gave the Flyers an opportunity to seize early control, but Carkner coughed up an unassisted shorthanded goal to Brent Sutter, who added a power-play goal shortly thereafter to put New York ahead.

In the first minute of the second period, Tocchet's 36th of the season made the score 2-2, but Jari Gronstrand's backhander over a prone Peeters restored the Islanders' lead. Trailing 3-2 and with the season slipping away, Holmgren switched to Hoffort, who 1:14 later gave up a top-shelf goal to David Volek.

The out-of-town scoreboard showed Buffalo ahead of Pittsburgh 2-1, announcing a playoff spot was still available. But early in the third period, Pat LaFontaine's power-play goal opened a three-goal lead and doomed the Flyers to the longest third period of their existence. Just after they trudged off as 6-2 losers, they heard the Nassau Coliseum erupt. Uwe Krupp's overtime goal in Pittsburgh had given Buffalo a 3-2 victory to put the Islanders into the playoffs.

After being at the end of their rope for three months, the Flyers were neither surprised nor devastated when the end came. "I've never not made the playoffs before," said Tocchet in the quiet locker room. "But I've learned a lot about myself and my teammates this season. I hate to say it, but sometimes these things have a positive side."

Indeed, a high pick in the entry draft was a considerable consolation prize for an aging team following a season obliterated by injuries. But Clarke had never felt the opportunity to draft a blue-chip player was worth the pain of seeing the Flyers' 17-season streak of making the playoffs, second only to Boston's 23, come to an end. "I think it was about the worst thing that ever happened to me," Clarke recalls.

When the Flyers completed the season the following night against Detroit at an eerily-subdued Spectrum, it was their first game ever in which they were playing out the string. In the other two seasons that the franchise missed the playoffs, 1970 and 1972, the Flyers were eliminated on the final day of the season.

For the Flyers and Red Wings, the only real accomplishment in Game 80 could come from losing. The winner would get fourth pick in the entry draft; the loser, third pick. Steve Yzerman's goal off Hoffort with 3:20 remaining pulled Detroit into a 3-3 tie. But with the managements of both organizations perversely, silently, rooting against their own clubs, neither the Flyers nor the Wings could give the game away in overtime. The 71-point Flyers would have the fourth pick behind Quebec, Vancouver and Detroit.

Tocchet and Murphy had been presented the Bobby Clarke and Barry Ashbee Trophies in ceremonies before the game, but the 1989-90 season had been one of minimal accomplishment. In his public assessments, Clarke blamed Hextall and injuries. "The holdout screwed things up right from the start," said the GM. "And every time we got something going, another key player would get hurt."

He groused about the new-age emphasis on off-ice conditioning. "Some of these guys look like Greek gods but they can't carry the muscle around the ice," he said. "They're better off being ten or fifteen pounds lighter, even if it is fat. I think we stretch too much."

Clarke also felt discipline had broken down. "Some of the players bleeped on Paul," Clarke said. "He's got to get tougher." Nevertheless, the GM said his coach's job was not in jeopardy. "Considering all the adversity he faced, I thought Paul did a pretty good job," said Clarke. "One thing we learned is which players hung tough when things went bad and which ones didn't. It wasn't much fun to go through this kind of season. But we'll bounce back."

The Poulin trade, Clarke admitted, had been a flop. "But no one's going to give you a high draft choice or a young player who can do the same things as one of your 31 year-olds." he told Ray Parrillo of the Inquirer. "Our only excess was in our goalies and that was no longer an excess when Hextall held out and then got injured."

Nevertheless, Clarke felt he was fulfilling his mandate to turn the team over. The second-and-third-round picks from the 1988 draft, Michigan State winger Pat Murray and University of Miami center Craig Fisher, were expected to contribute the following season. The second-round picks acquired for Propp and Wells went into a pool with three previously-obtained third rounders. The Flyers would have eight of the top 52 selections in the upcoming draft.

Among the questions a troubled Jay Snider was asking himself, however, was whether those picks would be put to good use. From the Flyers' 1985 through 1987 drafts, only four selections—Murphy, Huffman, Baron and Horacek—had become NHL players.

"We didn't have high first-round picks in those years," Snider recalls. "But we didn't have players like [Brian] Leetch and [Jeremy] Roenick rated nearly as high as they were taken. We weren't taking many American players and Claude Boivin [No. 1, 1988] had been our first French-Canadian pick in [18] years."

The Snider family's moral decision not to select

Soviet players had also diminished the pool of players their scouts could consider. So Jay did not specifically blame his talent evaluators. He felt Clarke's administration of the scouting operation was the Flyers' real problem.

Snider liked Paddock, but felt that if he wanted to coach, it had been a mistake to put him in an office. The Flyers had an assistant GM with a disinterest in paperwork, leaving Clarke less time to scan the big picture. When drafting, Clarke was sometimes allowing the scout with the best book on a player to be overruled by stronger personalities. Snider felt his GM had also become insulated with a select few confidants who discouraged input about potential moves. Snider was outside the circle, leaving him to believe Clarke did not respect his hockey knowledge.

"It wasn't the deals," recalls Snider. "I don't make the deals. Where I came in, or wanted to come in, was with the question, 'What are we trying to accomplish?' Let's agree where we have to go. What is the game plan for winning the Stanley Cup?

"A lot of our [differences] had to do with turning the team over. The art of being a GM is rebuilding before it's necessary. Making cut-your-losses decisions like trading Behn Wilson for Doug Crossman keeps you a top team. That didn't happen for the Flyers in the late eighties.

"Bob's philosophy is that if you get to the playoffs, anything can happen. My dad's philosophy from Day One was to measure everything against winning the Cup. I'd much rather go into the playoffs with a 100-point team than an 80-point one because by and large, I'll have a better chance of winning the Cup. Bob agreed the goal is to win the Cup, but to do that you have to make sure you get in the playoffs every year. In my mind, that leads to short-term deals.

"That was our fundamental difference. I felt the organization was deteriorating. I have to be convinced that there is a game plan that works, and that's where things broke down between Bob and me."

Jay refused public comment in the immediate aftermath of the season, but Clarke did not necessarily think the club president's silence was ominous. When he and Snider met about a week following the Flyers' elimination, the president asked the GM to write down what he thought had gone wrong and his plans to rebuild the team.

When Snider called Clarke to the Spectacor offices in center city on Monday, April 16, the GM had prepared his notes. "I never got a chance to use them," Clarke recalls. Snider told Clarke he could

not continue as GM, but asked for time to create another meaningful position for him in the organization. Clarke said he wasn't interested and wanted the move announced as a firing, rather than a resignation.

"It wasn't a long meeting," recalls Clarke. "I reminded him he had a lot of draft picks and left." He called Sandy from his car phone, cleared his office at The Coliseum and threw the notes he had prepared for Snider into the trash. "It was almost a dead feeling," he recalls. "I wasn't angry. That comes later. My training as a player was to fight back. But I had no way of fighting back against this."

In the early evening, Clarke went to Holmgren's house in Laurel Springs, New Jersey, where he and the coach drank beer and listened to Jay Snider's press conference on WIP.

Snider refused to publicly detail the specific nature of the differences, resulting in unfounded media speculation that Clarke had been let go for refusing to fire Holmgren. Few knew the real story. The *Daily News*'s Les Bowen had speculated the day of Clarke's firing that his job might be in jeopardy, but otherwise there had been no preparation for the unthinkable: the Flyers without Bobby Clarke.

"When you mention Bob Clarke," Mark Howe said, "you mention the Flyers in the same breath.

"But I've seen things like this happen to my dad [Gordie] when he retired. It's unpleasant, but things change."

Ed Snider says he had tried to encourage more communication between his son and Clarke. "I thought things were better when I left town," he recalls. "Next thing I knew, Jay had fired him. It was my fault for letting it get to that stage."

From his home in Malibu, Snider reached Clarke at his house late on the night of the firing and offered to create a position for Clarke somewhere in the Spectacor hierarchy. Snider told the media it made him sick to think about Clarke working for another team, but the Flyer patriarch did not disagree with his son's reasons for wanting the change.

"We talk about things all the time," said Ed, "but Jay runs the team. The two had different blueprints and when they couldn't come to a compromise, it came to this. It was just impossible to continue."

Clarke, like Jay Snider, refused to publicly detail the differences that led to his firing. His children were devastated, refusing to wear any of their Flyer shirts or jewelry items, but Clarke bit his tongue at a Coliseum press gathering held three days after his dismissal.

"I won't let one day spoil 21 years," Clarke said. "Jay Snider treated me well. He was good to my family and I like him as a person. Some of our views differed, but I think that's understandable. We've come up differently. We've been through different things."

Clarke had already been offered a job in the Vancouver organization by Canucks' president Pat Quinn, but said he wanted to get another managing job as soon as possible. "That's my life," he said. "That's all I know."

When he was named GM of the Minnesota North Stars on June 8, Clarke allowed his bitterness to become public. "It's been brutal," he told Ray Didinger of the *Daily News* at the press conference. "How would anyone feel to put that many years into something you love and then be let go like that?

"I thought I'd always be a Philadelphia Flyer. I helped build that club. I loved it every bit as much as Jay does. When I was playing, we felt like it was our team. It was like a family. There was tremendous loyalty. That's not there anymore. What happened to me is proof of that."

Eventually, Clarke's anger faded and he conceded that better communication might have saved his job. "The last few moves I made, I was trying to maintain a competitive team while picking up draft choices," he says today. "I was doing it because I wanted to, not because I was ordered. So I don't really think that, philosophically, my differences with Jay were that great. We just didn't talk enough about it. If I had to do it over again, I probably would have started moving guys earlier."

Jay Snider says today that he erred in not having a specific job proposal for Clarke on the day of their final meeting. Snider also says he underestimated the vilification and ridicule he would endure by taking down the franchise icon. "I knew it would be tough," Jay says, "but I don't think I realized the full impact of it.

"Still, Grandma Snider, my father's mother, had this expression, 'No one monkey stops the show.' And that includes me or anybody else. The Flyers were the primary concern, not Bobby Clarke, not myself. That's been the family's philosophy."

Holmgren met with Jay the day after Clarke's firing and was told his fate would be in the new GM's hands. "Jay said something to me like, 'It's hard for me to tell whether you're a good coach or not, with all the problems we had last year,'" recalls Holmgren.

At a later meeting with the coach, Snider said he would recommend Holmgren's retention. But with

no guarantees, Holmgren hung helplessly, awaiting the naming of the new GM.

In his public statements, Holmgren was pragmatic. Privately, however, Holmgren was miserable. "When the guy who hired you is one of your best friends and he gets fired, it's not a great position to be in," he recalls.

Snider outlined the prerequisites for the new general manager to Gary Miles of the *Inquirer*. "He has to be a good manager of people," Jay said. "He has to be able to plan ahead ... make tough decisions and stay level. My father is emotional and I'm emotional. I need someone who can keep their composure in tough situations."

Jay solicited Keith Allen's advice and compiled a list of four primary candidates who were invited to Philadelphia for preliminary interviews: Western Hockey League president Ed Chenowyth (to whom Bob McCammon had offered the Flyers' assistant GM job in 1983), Vancouver assistant GM Brian Burke, longtime Toronto-based player agent Bill Watters, and Russ Farwell, general manager of the Western league Seattle Thunderbirds.

Though only 34, Farwell had won two Memorial Cups in six seasons as GM of the Medicine Hat Tigers before moving to Seattle in 1988. He had ties to the Flyers going back a decade.

Melnyk had enlisted Farwell, then GM of the Calgary Canucks of the Alberta Junior Hockey League, to work for the Flyers on a per-game basis. Farwell continued scouting, as his time allowed, for six years, until the NHL ruled that junior team employees doubling as scouts were in a conflict of interest.

Even after Farwell left the payroll, however, he remained a source of information for Clarke. It was partly on Farwell's recommendation that the Flyers traded for Craven, who played for Farwell at Medicine Hat. "When Bob or Jerry [Melnyk] or Keith [Allen] were out west, we'd sit in the office talking until 2:30 or 3:00 A.M.," recalls Farwell. "I always felt close to the Flyers."

Allen invited him to a first interview with Jay, but Farwell flew to Philadelphia not knowing how seriously to take his candidacy. "I had always thought that when I made the jump to the NHL, it would be as an assistant GM," Farwell recalls.

In light of Clarke's firing, Farwell also shared the doubts of many in hockey as to how much autonomy a Flyer GM could enjoy. So his first meeting was over breakfast with Clarke at a New Jersey diner. "Bob was the guy I knew best here," recalls Farwell. "He didn't go into any details of why he was fired and he didn't try to discourage me. He said, 'Someone's going to take the job. It might as well be you.'"

Later that day, Farwell met for several hours with Jay, then left for the Memorial Cup tournament in Hamilton, Ontario. Of the other three candidates, Watters and Chenowyth interviewed more unobtrusively than Burke, who on the eve of his meeting with Snider told Bowen of the *Daily News* that Clarke should not have been fired.

Farwell emerged as the top candidate, not only because of his impressive first interview, but also his proven record in talent evaluation. "That's was our Achilles' heel over the last five or six seasons," Jay recalls. "When I ranked what a GM has to do, scouting came first and that was clearly Russ's forte."

Snider faxed Farwell a list of questions/theories that he should be prepared to speak about when he returned to Philadelphia on May 21. Over two days, Farwell met with Jay, Spectacor president Fred Shabel, Ron Ryan, the coaching staff, and a representative of an executive headhunting firm Snider had hired. Snider talked Farwell through hypothetical situations to see how the candidate might handle them.

"His evaluations were always sensible and logical," Jay recalled later. "It consistently came back to me that he had that innate feeling. He was quiet, but he exuded confidence and I had the feeling he had the guts to make a tough decision. He reminded me of Keith Allen in that regard, very much."

Farwell, too, came away with a good impression of Snider. "He was thorough, very well prepared, and made it very clear he wanted a structure that would insure he would be included," Farwell recalls. "Jay wanted to know what was going on."

By now, Farwell was convinced the position would give him enough autonomy to make it desirable. "I must not have given him the impression right away that I definitely wanted the job," recalls Farwell, "because Jay asked me if I did."

Snider believed he had found his man. There was one loose end, however. "Somebody, I don't remember who, suggested I really should talk to Bryan Murray," Snider recalls. "Maybe it was because of our rivalry with Washington, but I had never really liked him or thought I'd ever want to hire him. But he had a good track record and was available so I thought I should call."

Murray, fired in January after over eight seasons as coach of the Capitals, was surprised to hear

from the enemy. The next day he drove up I-95 to meet with Jay. "The lunch lasted six hours," Murray recalls. "We really had a good rapport."

Snider became intrigued. Murray, who used to bait the Flyers from the Capitals' bench, came across one-on-one as bright and personable. He had drawn up a Flyer depth chart and conveyed to Snider strong ideas on what changes should and should not be made. Obviously, Murray could start the job with a better book on the team he inherited than Farwell.

"He had hands-on experience in the NHL," recalls Snider. "Something Russ didn't. Bryan had experience in the family [inn] business [in Shawville, Quebec], had taught school and had experience on all levels of hockey."

Murray returned to Philadelphia late the following week to meet the same people who had talked to Farwell. In the evening, he and Snider shared pizza at the Coliseum while watching a Bruins-Oilers Stanley Cup final game on television. The next day, Snider drove through South Jersey with Murray showing him where past and present Flyers lived. He asked the candidate who would represent him in contract talks. Murray left thinking he had the job. And at that point, he practically did.

"When I left work Friday evening, I was leaning to Bryan," recalls Jay. "But as I slept on it through the weekend, I just started believing Russ was the right guy.

"I had a great feeling about both of them, but Russ's scouting background really made up my mind. To me, Bryan was a proven commodity just as a coach. It was really close, but I just thought Russ's strengths would be more evident in the long run."

Snider called Farwell on Sunday, June 3. "We talked for a little bit before he asked me if I wanted the job," Farwell recalls. "My mind was racing."

"Russ said something like, 'Okay,'" recalls Snider. "And that was about it." He asked Farwell to fly to Philadelphia the next day so they could discuss a contract on Tuesday.

When news of his imminent appointment leaked, Farwell was met at Philadelphia International Airport by reporters. "Obviously I'm interested or I wouldn't be here," he told them. Meanwhile, a very disappointed Murray got a phone call from Snider late Monday afternoon. "I had felt very good about my chances," Murray recalls.

A few weeks later, when Murray became a candidate for the GM-coach vacancy in Detroit, Snider called Red Wing owner Mike Ilitch to let him know how impressed he had been with the former Caps coach. Murray got the job.

Farwell and Snider agreed to a three-year deal. On Wednesday morning, before the official press conference, Farwell met with Hextall and his agent Rich Winter, then with Holmgren. The Flyer coach, his fate hanging on the new GM's decision, said he doubted he could coach effectively on the upcoming final year of his contract. If Farwell wanted to retain Holmgren, he wanted a contract extension that would remove his lame-duck status.

Holmgren was invited by Farwell to fly to Seattle on his way to the entry draft in Vancouver so that he and the new GM could drive and converse the rest of the way together. The incumbent coach was slightly encouraged after his talk with Farwell, but decided it would be awkward to attend the coronation that afternoon.

Farwell faced cameras at the Four Seasons Hotel as the first junior GM to be promoted directly to the NHL since Oshawa's Wren Blair was hired by the North Stars in 1967. The Philadelphia media was introduced to a bespectacled fellow who looked more like a graduate student than a career hockey man, but Brenda Farwell said her husband had only one scholarly pursuit. "(When) I was asked what kind of hobbies he has, it took me a minute to think, and then I realized he hasn't any," she said. "Hockey is his life."

Predictably, among the first questions asked of Farwell at the press conference was about his projected compatibility with his new boss. "I've talked to Jay, I think we're very much in sync philosophically," Farwell replied. The fifth GM in Flyers history rejected prevailing media theories that the team would undergo a quick and massive overhaul. "Whether you are going to take a run at [the Stanley Cup] today or you are going to bring in young guys and build, you need character and strength in older players," he said. "I think we have that, so I don't think sweeping a great number of guys out would be my plan right now."

Farwell's knowledge of the Western league was obviously going to be a Flyer advantage in the draft. His best player in Seattle, center Petr Nedved, was expected to be among the first picks.

"The Flyers hadn't had a star in a long time," recalls Farwell. "And Keith was supportive of the idea of trying to trade up." But neither Quebec, which would take Cornwall right wing Owen Nolan with the first pick, nor Vancouver, to whom Farwell offered Mellanby and Carkner, would budge.

To hometown cheers, Canucks GM Pat Quinn chose Nedved, leaving the Flyers with a difficult choice. Czechoslovakian winger Jaromir Jagr was the purest talent in the draft, but Peterborough center Mike Ricci was skilled, smart, gutsy, and a proven leader. Ricci, who started the season favored to become the top pick in the 1990 draft, had captained Canada to a gold medal at the World Junior Tournament. A shoulder injury, however, limited Ricci to 60 games in the Ontario Hockey League and crushed his final opportunity to convince the scouts he could overcome his one liability: he was only an average skater.

"Jerry (Melnyk) had been over to see Jagr," recalls Farwell. "He had him rated best overall, but at that point, there wasn't really a history of success taking Europeans with that high a pick. We just didn't know how good Jagr would become how quickly.

"The Flyers had just missed the playoffs and we were really impressed that Ricci could play right away. I hadn't seen Jagr personally. All things considered, I guess we didn't have the courage to pick Jagr."

Immediately after the Flyers picked Ricci, Jagr was taken by Pittsburgh. "He was a tough guy to pass up," Jay Snider told reporters on the draft floor. "But we've been dying for [Ricci's] type of leadership."

Minutes after putting on a Flyer jersey for the first time, Ricci was asked about the "disappointment" of being selected the fourth-best player in his age group in the world.

"In four or five years, nobody remembers who went first, second or third," said the Toronto native. "It's what you do on the ice. I'm sure the Flyers want me or they wouldn't have taken me."

With the twenty-fifth selection, the Flyers debated selecting Chris Simon, a hulking left wing from Ottawa, or Swedish winger Mikael Renberg. They tabbed Simon, but Renberg, recommended by Inge Hammarstrom, became a Flyer on the fortieth pick.

Farwell used four of the next six picks on Western leaguers, but none of those selections caught nearly the attention of the sixth-round choice: center Vyacheslav Butsayev of the Central Army hockey club became the first Flyer draft from the Soviet Union since Jay Snider's 1985 declaration that the organization would do no more business with the Russian Bear.

"I thought (Butsayev) was a Czech," joked Jay, but he explained that the world had changed and so had his mind. The major human-rights organizations are changing their position [about the Soviet Union]," Snider said. "And we've always said we would take a defector."

New beginnings for the Flyers thus selected, one of their oldies and goodies next received the game's highest honor. The day after the draft, Bill Barber became the fifth Flyer named to the Hockey Hall of Fame. "It's the thrill of a lifetime," said the Flyers' second all-time leading scorer, who had missed by one vote the previous year.

Holmgren's talk with Farwell on the way to Vancouver resulted in a contract as long as the GM's. "We're looking to make plans for more than one season," Farwell told the media on June 28 when announcing the extension. "Paul has to feel like he'll be a part of the team for that time."

With changes coming, Farwell felt continuity behind the bench would be an asset. "(Holmgren) wanted to be here," Farwell recalls, "and with so many things new, I thought it would work. I talked to some players and didn't hear anything that set off any warning signs.

"As I look back on it, I think Paul gave me what he thought were the right answers, rather than specifically what he thought. But from a standpoint of discipline, teaching, and his ideas of how a team should be run, I was satisfied with what I heard."

Farwell insisted, however, that Holmgren make at least one change among his assistants. "The people I talked to [in the organization] felt something wasn't quite right with the coaching," Farwell recalls. "I wanted to have some impact and I just did not feel comfortable with keeping things exactly the same coming off a year like that. Paul didn't disagree."

Andy Murray, who was outspokenly loyal to Clarke, was relieved of his position and would ultimately rejoin Clarke as an assistant coach in Minnesota. With both an assistant's position and a head coaching job in Hershey available—Kevin McCarthy was leaving the Bears' bench to become a pro scout with the Flyers—Farwell interviewed candidates for both positions.

Farwell contacted Terry Simpson, the former Islander coach who had been a longtime Western league rival of Farwell's at Prince Albert, but the veteran coach had an assistant's offer from Winnipeg and no desire to return east for anything less than a head coaching opportunity. Also interviewed were Craig Hartsburg, Holmgren's former Minnesota teammate, Washington assistant Doug MacLean and Kamloops coach Ken Hitchcock.

Hitchcock, a WHL competitor of Farwell's, had produced five division winners in six seasons, but steps up the hockey ladder—or any ladder for that matter—had been made difficult by his 430-pound frame. Hitchcock tied a diet into a fund-raising campaign to pledge for a new Kamloops arena and lost more than 120 pounds.

When MacLean rejoined Murray as an assistant in Detroit, Farwell decided to hire Hartsburg and Hitchcock. "I wasn't sure whether I wanted Hitchcock for Hershey or here," recalls Farwell. But Eaves, wanting to add head coaching experience to his resume, solved the dilemma by volunteering to go to Hershey.

"Hitchcock was already hired," recalls Holmgren. "It was my decision whether he would be in Philly or in Hershey. I was impressed with him. He was personable, knowledgeable and enthusiastic."

As the coaching staff underwent changes, so did the scouting department. Melnyk was upset by Clarke's firing, but the head scout had time left on his contract and a good feeling about Farwell. However, eastern scout Dennis Patterson and Manitoba scout Doug Overton followed Clarke to Minnesota, creating two openings.

Former Flyer Simon Nolet, Quebec's director of pro scouting, was hired to fill one vacancy. Meanwhile, Barry Melrose, who had coached for Farwell at Medicine Hat before becoming coach of Detroit's AHL Adirondack farm club, told the Flyers' GM that Bill Dineen, Melrose's predecessor at Adirondack, had become unhappy about his reduced role in the Detroit organization. Dineen had stepped upstairs in favor of Melrose, considered a rising star by the parent Red Wings. "They had a management contract to run the building there," recalls Dineen. "So, except for a little scouting in Quebec, there was really nothing for me to do."

Dineen accepted Farwell's offer of a four-year contract as a Flyer scout. Farwell also hired John Blackwell, the 41-year-old director of AHL operations for the Edmonton Oilers, as assistant general manager. "He'd done a lot of different jobs for the Oilers," recalls Farwell. "I had no idea what it would cost to run an NHL team and John had done a lot of special projects for [Glen] Sather. He came to mind as someone who could fill in the blanks."

Farwell got busy with contract negotiations, planning to get most of his renewals settled within a few weeks so he'd have time to study video of his new team. He was set back, however, by an economic revolution in the game. Aggressive ownerships in Los Angeles, Detroit and St. Louis, combined with an NHL Players Association decision to disclose salaries, were causing player costs to spiral upward.

The Blues threw open the $1-million-a-year threshold that had been reserved exclusively for Gretzky and Lemieux when sniper Brett Hull signed for $7 million over four years. St. Louis further rocked the structure by signing free-agent defenseman Scott Stevens away from Washington (compensating the Caps with five first-round draft choices) for $5.45 million over four seasons.

"We had to do three different budgets that summer," Farwell recalls. "I'd figure we would get guys signed for $50,000 increases. It became clear to me it would take $250,000 to $300,000."

Personalities, not just cash, had gotten in the way of making Hextall a happy Flyer again. Rich Winter insisted that the goalie had returned the previous November on a verbal promise his contract would be renegotiated. The Flyers maintained they had made no such pledge. On July 7, another impasse became public. "I have no use for Rich Winter," Snider told Ray Parrillo of the *Inquirer*. "He's not out for the player's best interest. He's out for his own best interest.

"We absolutely will not renegotiate Ron's contract. I have nothing to talk to [Winter] about. [Hextall's] getting $500,000 a year. We didn't get our $500,000 worth from Ron last year."

Hextall initially refused to change agents. "Why should Rich Winter be the issue?" the goalie asked. "He's basically a middleman."

But Hextall grew frustrated with the lack of progress. "I just think it was a case of [Winter's] reputation preceding him, the Flyers getting their backs up, and nothing getting done," the goalie recalls. "I felt I had to make a move."

Late in July, Hextall paid off Winter and hired Steve Mountain, the Philadelphia-based agent who represented other Flyers, including Tocchet and Kerr. Tense negotiations between Mountain and the Flyers finally led to new contracts for both Hextall and Tocchet. "Both players are among the best in the NHL at their positions," said Farwell in announcing the deals on the night of the exhibition opener. "They will be a big part of our effort to reestablish the Flyers among the elite teams in the NHL."

Tocchet signed a four-year deal, plus an option, that started at $750,000 (a raise from $250,000) and reached $1.05 million in its final season. With incentives, Tocchet figured to earn about $1 million per year over the course of the deal.

For Hextall, Mountain and Farwell negotiated a five-year agreement laden with incentives. The goalie's base salary was increased from $500,000 to $760,000, but he could top $1 million with 30 victories. Accomplishments comparable to Hextall's spectacular rookie year would earn the goalie up to $1.4 million a season.

"If I jumped for joy," Hextall smiled, "I might hurt myself. I'm just happy to be part of this organization and hopefully, I'll be here for a long time."

Farwell also began clearing out deadwood. Bullard, told even before Farwell's hiring he would not receive a new contract, left to play in Switzerland. On Holmgren's advice, Farwell jettisoned Linseman, who signed as a free agent with Edmonton. "Kenny's attitude was good," recalls Holmgren. "I just didn't think he could do it anymore."

The coach felt Sinisalo was worth saving, so with Farwell's blessing, he attempted to talk the veteran winger out of signing with Clarke's North Stars, an attempt that ultimately failed. "Here we were talking about adding speed and letting somebody like that go," recalls Holmgren. "I think Ilkka was bleeped off and hurt and I called too late."

The quiet Finn thus departed with the same minimal fanfare that marked his nine-year Flyer career. Sinisalo, who ranks behind only Kerr and Poulin on the list of the organization's best-ever free-agent signings, contributed 199 goals and 210 assists. "We didn't think anyone would pay him what the North Stars did," Farwell told the media.

Keith Acton received a one-year termination contract that gave him thirty days to sign with any club. Acton, however, called Jay Snider and argued that the Flyers could still use him.

"He made a compelling case," recalls Farwell. "And Paul wanted him back. I think we realized that maybe in the eagerness to sweep things out, this may have been a mistake." Acton was re-signed for one year, plus an option.

For the Flyers to bounce back from their 1989-90 disaster, Hextall's body wasn't the only one requiring the team to cross its fingers; the health of Howe and Kerr remained crucial as well. So it was a bad omen when the big right wing missed the first 8 exhibition games with his recurring shoulder problem.

Nevertheless, Ricci's strong camp confirmed he could contribute immediately at age 18, and Farwell hoped that two rookies—left wing Pat Murray and Czechoslovakian center Martin Hostak—would fill some of the offense lost in the departures of Sinisalo, Bullard, Linseman and Propp. Having rid themselves of players whose skills had eroded ahead of their egos, the Flyers went into 1990-91 counting on improved morale, tighter checking, and a less than daunting

Patrick Division, which had been won the previous season by an 85-point Ranger team.

"We have a bitter taste in our mouths from last year and we're out to change it," said Holmgren. "I think enough guys had really off years that if they can get back to the level at which I believe they can play, I don't think we're going to have a problem."

However, the season began as unluckily as the previous one had ended. Seven minutes into a 4-1 opening-night loss at Boston, Ricci suffered a fractured index finger blocking a shot. Ricci was joined by Kerr on the absentee list when the Flyers also lost their second start, 3-1 at New Jersey. Kerr had a happy excuse, though: his wife, Kathy, was giving birth to a daughter, Kimberly. When the proud papa returned the following night for the home opener against Detroit, he whipped Steve Yzerman on an offensive-zone face-off and banged in Latal's rebound to start the Flyers back from a 2-0 deficit to a 7-2 victory.

Bill Barber, who had been given a night at the Spectrum in 1986, was again honored on October 11 in recognition of his Hockey Hall of Fame induction. "It was worth the wait," said Barber, as the Flyers finally retired his jersey. Keith Allen, Barber's handpicked Hall of Fame presenter, termed Barber "the best left wing of his time."

In the game that followed, memories of better Flyer days were being dutifully rekindled until Hextall, leading the Devils 4-2, was again the victim of a strained groin. As the beleaguered goalie was helped off the ice, there were scattered boos. "I'm telling you I'm going to win this battle," said Hextall of his recurring leg problems.

Wregget, who finished up the 7-4 victory, figured his paycheck should expand proportionately to his role. The goalie was asking an arbitrator for $500,000 a year, more than $200,000 above the Flyers' offer. "It doesn't seem like they want me," Wregget told PRISM's Ken Adelberger.

Believing that cashing his checks would jeopardize his arbitration claim, Wregget held them until his agent Rick Curran informed him the additional amount would be awarded retroactively. The relieved goalie beat Winnipeg 4-3 at the Spectrum. The Flyers flew to Pittsburgh two nights later with a three-game winning streak and fuel for their badly-needed fresh start.

Tim Kerr was awakened the next morning by a shaken doctor on the line saying something about complications. As adrenaline jolted him from his sleep, Kerr's mind raced ahead of the caller's words.

He couldn't tell if something had happened to ten-day-old Kimberly, or his wife, Kathy.

"What are you trying to tell me?" he asked.

"I'm telling you that Kathy passed away this morning," the doctor said.

This was incomprehensible. Kerr's wife had remained at Pennsylvania Hospital for ten days receiving treatment for a post partum pelvic infection. But when her husband left Philadelphia with the team the previous evening, Kathy believed she was going home the next day. When the couple talked twice after Kerr's arrival in Pittsburgh, her mood was buoyant. But during routine morning rounds, she had been found still in her bed, dead of what the hospital announced as a "sudden cardiopulmonary complication."

Holmgren was asleep when the phone rang in his room. The voice on the line was raspy, desperate, almost unintelligible. "Homer, I don't know what I'm going to do," the coach thought he heard.

"Who is this?" he asked.

"It's Timmy. My wife is dead. What am I going to do?"

Holmgren cringed, dressed, and went to Kerr's room. As he waited for Jay Snider and Farwell to come for him in a private jet, the reeling widower cried to Holmgren for almost three hours.

The coach made the necessary calls and struggled for some helpful words. "You have to be strong," Holmgren said. But Kerr's thoughts whirled from a funeral to Jackie, his 7-year-old stepdaughter, whose father would now want her to come live with him, to the fear of not being able to care for the infant Kimberley and his 10-month-old adopted daughter Kayleigh, to a life without Kathy.

The Flyers' assistant coaches told the players the numbing news as they got off the hotel elevators on their way to the morning skate. In the locker room, Acton said a prayer for Kathy and her daughters. Penguins GM Craig Patrick ordered all the doors of the Civic Arena locked so that the Flyers could have privacy.

That night before the opening face-off, the Penguins asked their fans to observe a moment of silence. "That was the hardest part," Craven said, and indeed, the Flyers found themselves amazingly focused as the game began. Two goals by Mellanby spurred a 5-1 victory. "It was a tough day for everybody," said Hartsburg. "We're all proud of the way our guys played."

"If there's any place you can forget it," said Craven, "it's out on the ice, in practice or in a game." The most difficult part was still to come, when the Flyers flew home the next day to devastated wives and girl-friends. For two years, Kathy had been a tireless chairwoman for the Fight for Lives Carnival. To a crushed Fran Tobin and the Flyer ladies, Kathy Kerr's leadership was only a fraction of the loss.

"She would just do anything for you," Margo Sutter said. "She brought a lot of spark to everyone on the team and in the wives' lounge. She was as big as life."

The following night, in a hushed, darkened Spectrum, Kathy's face looked down from the ArenaVision screen while the Reverend John Casey said a pre-game prayer. The Flyers, appearing more distracted than they had in Pittsburgh, blew an early 3-0 lead to the Nordiques but pulled out a 5-4 victory on a third-period goal by Lacombe.

The next morning, the Flyers attended a private wake for Kathy at a funeral home in Upper Darby. Kerr seemed buoyed by his teammates' company, jok-ingly warning Sutter, Kerr's replacement on the power play, that he would not have his job for long. Pat Croce told Kerr he would pick him up two days hence to go to the gym. When the Flyers' condition-ing guru showed up, Kerr went. He was more sol-emn than usual, but at the end of the forty-minute workout, he told Croce he would come back.

Croce, Jay Snider and Steve Mountain took turns staying with Kerr through the long evenings of the next several weeks. Terry Snider, Jay's wife, organ-ized, hosted, and cleaned at the Kerr home. Tim's parents, Eileen and Earl, moved from Tecumseh, Ontario, to help with the babies.

On the ice, the team responded exactly as it had following the Lindbergh tragedy five years earlier. Third-period goals by Mellanby and Eklund gave the Flyers a 6th straight victory, 5-3 in Montreal.

Inevitably, Howe's back discs flared again, forc-ing him out before a streak-snapping 6-2 loss to Washington at the Spectrum. And incredibly, for the fourth time in two seasons, Hextall did not survive his first game back in the lineup. This time, in Uniondale, the goalie was victimized by Latal's bad decision to foil a breakaway by the Islanders' Randy Wood by jumping on his back. Both players crashed into the crease, wrapping Hextall's left leg around the goalpost and partially tearing his medial collat-eral ligament.

"I'm going to get a break somewhere along the way," said Hextall after the Islanders' 5-2 victory. "I don't know where yet, but I will."

Frustrating as they were, the goalie's problems still seemed trivial next to Kerr's. An autopsy re-vealed his wife had been killed by the infection for which she was being treated, but that gave him lit-tle explanation and no consolation. His stoicism was read by many of his friends as a sign of lingering shock, so they advised him not to rush back. But two weeks to the day of Kathy's death, Kerr climbed over the Spectrum boards for the second shift of a game against the Penguins.

As the ovation swelled, Kerr leaned on his stick and stared at the ice. Finally, he looked up at Ron Asselstine, silently asking the linesman to please drop the puck so that he could get on with his life. The Penguins rolled to a 6-2 victory but two nights later, Ricci returned to the lineup to score his first NHL goal as the Flyers beat Clarke's North Stars 6-3. "It's not awkward," Clarke insisted of his first visit back to the Spectrum. "I didn't like [getting fired], but I didn't die."

A daytime visit to Cooper Hospital had helped Clarke put his pride into proper perspective. Fred Shero, who had barely begun to fulfill his Flyer ad-visory duties before a recurrence of stomach cancer, had only weeks to live.

Meanwhile, Peeters, who had elbow surgery af-ter enduring a 1-13-5 season, wanted to prove he could still play, so he asked Farwell for some work in Hershey. In two AHL games, Peeters gave up 11 goals, then rejoined the Flyers in Toronto. He was enjoying the night off when Wregget, laboring with a slight hip-flexor pull, had to leave the game. Peeters climbed into the crease, made a fully ex-tended glove stop on a Gary Leeman penalty shot and the Flyers went on to a 7-1 romp.

Howe, back in the lineup for six games, felt a sharp back pain in Toronto and missed the game in Winnipeg two nights later, but Peeters won again, 4-2. Fatigue and the Flames blew the veteran goalie away 8-2 at the Spectrum, but Peeters won 5-2 in Quebec, then was outstanding in a 2-0 Spectrum shutout of Vancouver.

Though Kerr was lost again with torn right-knee cartilage, the Flyers stayed hot, thanks largely to the resurgent Peeters. He held the Rangers to a 1-1 tie, then beat Montreal 4-1 at the Spectrum. "We're mentally tougher now at critical times than we were last season," said Acton. Indeed, the Flyers bounced back from two weekend losses to New Jersey and recorded their second straight victory in Pittsburgh, 5-4. The team seemed reborn as the man who coached the franchise to its two Stanley Cups passed away.

Fred Shero died at 5:30 A.M. on Saturday, Novem-ber 24, 1990. "He was a saint," said Clarke from Minnesota. "He understood the players and the game better than anybody."

The following night, before the Flyers beat the Islanders 4-1 at the Spectrum, the Flyers marked the passing of both Shero and Wayne Hillman, a Flyer defenseman from 1969 to 1973 who had died of cancer over the weekend in Cleveland.

Three days later, Shero was memorialized at the Church of St. Mary's in Cherry Hill. Members of the Stanley Cup team carried their coach's casket and remembered his enormous role in the happiest years of their careers. Clarke eulogized Shero as a "complex and simple man" and remembered the words he had written on the blackboard during the 1974 finals: *Win and we will walk together forever.*

"Forever didn't stop on Saturday," said Clarke. "Freddie left a piece of himself with every one of us."

That night at the Meadowlands, the Devils chased Peeters and led 5-2 with less than four minutes remaining. But with three late goals, the last one at 19:11 when Tocchet blindly deflected in Ricci's centering pass, the Flyers pulled out a 5-5 tie.

Wregget lost his arbitration hearing, receiving $300,000 of the $500,000 he had requested. "It makes you wonder what [the Flyers] think about me," the disgruntled goalie said. In fact, Wregget was largely out of mind as Peeters beat the first-place Rangers, 5-1, to pull the 17-10-2 Flyers within one point of the division lead. "He's the reason why we're here," said Holmgren. The dusted-off veteran was now 8-3-1 with a 2.21 average.

Huffman, frustrated by a lack of playing time, walked away from the team for 12 games, but ultimately decided he wanted to play and accepted a demotion to Hershey. Howe, too, missed hockey but remained in agony every time he tried to play it. "I can't even breathe when I try to practice," he said.

Peeters finally ran out of air, too, after Edmonton punctured him 6-3 on December 2. The veteran goalie had to be yanked from the next two games. Wregget, seeing his first action in thirty-four days, relieved Peeters by giving up four goals in a 7-0 embarrassment at Minnesota. A few hours later, on a charter flight to Chicago, Hextall came to Holmgren and said he was ready to return the following night. The coach wasn't about to argue on the side of caution.

"He's a very intense player and he means a lot to us in the room," said Holmgren. Sure enough, the reenergized Flyers jumped to a 4-1 lead and, thanks to a well-timed five-on-three goal by Eklund, sur-

vived a third-period Chicago rally for a 5-4 victory. "I was as tired as I've ever been tonight," said Hextall after finally lasting an entire game. "But I can honestly tell you the thought of getting hurt did not go through my mind once."

Indeed, the only injury incurred was to Wregget's feelings. "I guess this is what they've been waiting for," he said. Nevertheless, as Hextall scraped off what was practically a year and a half's worth of rust, Wregget recorded the Flyers' only victory in their next 8 games. On December 23 at the Spectrum, they blew a 4-0 lead into a 4-4 tie with Montreal, but Kerr returned to score a goal as the Flyers opened up their usual western holiday swing with a 7-5 victory in Los Angeles.

Hextall seemed back to his old form in a 3-1 victory in St. Louis, but gave up five goals New Year's Eve in Buffalo and slipped backwards. Three times in three games, the Flyers blew one-goal third period leads. To add to their misfortune, Kerr's cranky knee again forced him from the lineup. Nevertheless, the Flyers snapped a 4-game winless streak with a solid trip-closing 3-1 victory in Boston. "Biggest win of the year," said Carkner. Again, just at a point where the Flyers appeared to be sinking, they managed a buoying road victory.

Only Eklund, having an outstanding year playing with Ricci and Tocchet, provided the Flyers with quickness, and their goaltending remained spotty. But despite their shortage of hares, the Flyers were playing like smart tortoises, and staying in playoff position.

Meanwhile, the prolonged bureaucratic wrangling over a new home for the Flyers and 76ers continued. Over the previous summer, Sixers owner Harold Katz, having extended several deadlines he had set for movement on the project, signed a thirty-year lease with Spectacor that lowered the game-night costs the basketball team had been required to pay at the Spectrum by $1 million a year, while giving the Sixers a share of parking, concession, luxury box, and advertisement revenues to be generated in the proposed new arena.

If ground on a new arena was not broken before August 23, 1993, Katz would have until February 1, 1994, to notify Snider he was canceling the lease, effective at the end of that season.

Carl Hirsh, Spectacor's chief negotiator, and the city reached agreement on a workable deal for a new 21,000-seat arena. But while lawyers had haggled over what-if scenarios, New Jersey raised its offer. The state pledged to pick up 75 to 80 percent of the growing tab for the new facility, up from the state's original offer of a flat $65 million.

A frustrated Katz and a majority of high-ranking Spectacor officials wanted to move across the bridge. But Ed Snider still didn't want to give up so the snail-paced talks between Philadelphia and Spectacor continued.

The lawyers eventually sorted things out. But with the city nearing bankruptcy, sensitivities were running high over any tax breaks given to private enterprises. The Sniders agreed that formal presentation of the deal for city council approval should wait. It was not until January, when the State of Pennsylvania appropriated a bailout package for Philadelphia, that Spectacor and the city announced the agreement had been concluded.

Former mayor Frank Rizzo, running to regain that office, quickly made a campaign issue of one particular facet of the deal—a city gift of $6.5-million to Spectacor for it to build a multi-tiered parking facility. That amount represented half the cost of the 1,000-car garage, and Spectacor was slated to receive all the parking revenue. As Spectacor and city officials returned to the table for one more restructuring of the deal, Governor Jim Florio of New Jersey took his state out of the running.

The negotiations had become almost as numbing as the sensation running down Howe's right leg. The frustrated defenseman finally submitted to back disc surgery on January 18. "He thinks he can play a number of years more," said Jay Snider. "I think we do as well."

With Murray and Hostak having fizzled and been sent to Hershey, Ricci had become the only tangible manifestation of the Flyers' intended youth movement. The team desperately needed another scorer to ease the burden on their one effective line. When St. Louis inquired about Ron Sutter, Farwell asked for Rod Brind'Amour, the Blues top pick in 1988. General manager Ron Caron insisted Brind'Amour was untouchable and the Flyers plodded on.

"It's been frustrating watching this team play hard every night and lose by a goal," he told the *Inquirer's* Ray Parrillo. "Still, I'm not getting frantic. I try to be patient and sometimes that can be confused with inactivity."

Farwell's mandate was to build a long-term contender, not make stopgap deals for mediocre veterans. "So maybe we're being fussy," the rookie GM said. Sports talk-show callers, most of whom had pegged Farwell as Jay Snider's do-nothing puppet, were screaming for another scorer. But again, just

as the talent shortfall appeared to doom the Flyers, they found life.

Hextall, nasty and dominating as ever, bopped Nick Kypreos and kicked Alan May during a 6-1 Spectrum rout of Washington on January 24. The Flyers (26-21-6) moved to within two points of the division-leading Rangers and twelve ahead of the fifth-place Caps.

Although Tocchet tore a groin tendon in a 5-3 loss at Hartford, Kerr returned the following game and the Flyers beat Pittsburgh, 4-2. But five nights later at the Spectrum, the big right wing pulled a muscle stepping on a puck during warmups for a game with Los Angeles and by the third period was completely immobile.

A 5-2 loss at Landover brought the Flyers' latest losing streak to 4, while a cheap hit by the Caps' Dale Hunter bulged the veins in Holmgren's neck. After Gord Murphy, elbowed into the glass by a hard-charging Hunter, slumped to the ice, the enraged Flyer coach verbally threatened his counterpart, Terry Murray, then picked up a stick and smacked it against the glass. Later, security guards moved into the press box between taunting Caps' fans and the injured Tocchet.

Tocchet vowed vengeance even after the elbow was deemed vicious enough by Brian O'Neill to earn Hunter a 4-game league suspension. "It's not over," said the Flyer winger. In his first game back he took out his frustration on the Leafs, scoring twice in a 6-3 victory. Following Hextall's shaky 3-2 loss at New Jersey, Wregget stepped in and beat Chicago 5-3 at the Spectrum.

Hextall, however, bounced back to sweep the Islanders in a home-and-home series. And when late goals by Berube and Eklund enabled the Flyers to rally for a 4-4 Spectrum tie with St. Louis on March 2, they were solidly positioned for the stretch drive.

A six-game road trip lay ahead, but if the second-place Flyers could play .500 in their final 13 games, the fifth-place Caps would need to play at a .750 clip to knock Philadelphia out of the playoffs.

Tocchet, his groin still bothersome, did not play two nights later at Madison Square Garden, where Wregget was yanked after giving up three first-period goals in a 6-2 loss. As the Flyers flew to Calgary on the day of the trading deadline, Farwell finally made his first deal. Left wing Mark Pederson, a failed Montreal first-round pick who had played for Farwell at Medicine Hat, was acquired from the Canadiens for a second-round choice in the 1991 draft.

Farwell attempted to pull off more substantial deals at the trade deadline with Hartford and Edmonton. Whaler GM Ed Johnston dangled one-time 45-goal scorer Kevin Dineen to snag either Wregget or Mellanby and Farwell had approached Glen Sather about trading the rights to Jari Kurri, who was playing for Milan of the Italian league. The Oiler GM wasn't interested in moving Kurri for the grinders Farwell offered—Mellanby and Craig Berube. But Sather said he would move left wing Joe Murphy and right wing Dave Brown, who was not going to get the contract he wanted in Edmonton and desired to return to Philadelphia.

In Farwell's mind, he needed a replacement for Mellanby on right wing before moving him for Murphy, a left wing. "Looking back on it, that sounds silly," says Farwell, "but at the time Murphy hadn't had that big year [he would score 82 points the following season]. Murphy was a question mark and Mellanby was a solid third-line right wing."

Johnston was also shopping Dineen to Sather, but as the the 3 P.M. deadline came and went, the three GMs could reach no agreements. Farwell was frustrated, but reasoned Dineen and Murphy would likely be available over the summer. The Flyers' comfortable playoff position enabled their GM to maintain a long-term view.

"I wasn't upset either," recalls Holmgren. "I hoped Pederson could score some goals. You looked at the lead we had and it looked pretty good for us."

Some veterans privately grumbled about Farwell's failure to juice up the Flyers for the stretch drive. Sutter doesn't recall feeling that way, however. "I guess I was hoping, but our morale was really good and I knew you'd have to give up something to get something," he recalls. "I thought we'd be okay."

Anxious to establish himself in the NHL, Pederson debuted in Calgary with an assist on Craven's second-period goal. But with less than five minutes remaining in a 2-2 tie, Gord Murphy failed to completely tie up Sergei Makarov, who freed his stick to deflect Frantisek Musil's centering pass for the go-ahead goal. Joe Nieuwendyk then blew by the struggling Murphy and beat Hextall, who allowed his second short side goal of the game as the Flyers went down to a deflating 4-2 defeat.

"We limited their chances and got the puck deep," said Holmgren. "Unfortunately we didn't get the goaltending we needed."

Neither did they get it from Wregget the following night in Edmonton. Presented with an early 2-0

lead, he gave up consecutive weak goals to Petr Klima. Wregget also gambled and lost trying to pokecheck a Craig MacTavish breakaway. Pederson's first Flyer goal and another by Lacombe cut a 5-2 Oiler lead to 5-4 midway through the third, but the Flyers fell short. When Washington followed Philadelphia to Northlands Coliseum and won, the gap between the clubs was down to three points.

The Flyers waited in Los Angeles for three days while the Kings finished a road trip, but the rest did not slow Philadelphia's bleeding. The Kings dominated from the first minute, throwing 17 first-period shots at Hextall and racing to a 3-0 lead. The score was 5-0 in the third when, moving laterally, Hextall felt his groin pop. The goalie could not get off his knee as Marty McSorley scored.

The Flyers would now be without their No. 1 goalie for the stretch drive. "I think this is the most disappointing injury I've ever had," said Hextall after the 6-0 rout. Holmgren was pale as he spoke to the media. "The whole thing just blows my mind," the coach said. "We got killed tonight. They should be embarrassed for themselves. We failed to compete."

With Washington home for 7 of its last 10 games, the walls were closing in on the Flyers as they took the ice the following night in Vancouver. Chris Jensen gave them a 1-0 lead, but Wregget was beaten twice through screens, then on a Trevor Linden breakaway. An unchecked Rob Murphy made the score 4-1, but Eklund's power-play goal, and Lacombe's wraparound 11 seconds later drew the Flyers to within one.

Suddenly, there was a light above the collapsing mine shaft. The Flyers made a run for it. Early in the third, Mellanby banged in a Chychrun rebound to tie the game. Then, in overtime, Murray Baron followed Craven up the right wing, jumped on a broken play and beat goalie Troy Gamble between his legs. The Flyers thought they had just won their biggest game of the year. "It feels like 200 points instead of two," said Hitchcock.

In reality, however, the game three nights later in Landover was even more critical. Early roughing penalties by Wregget and Lacombe led to Cap power-play goals that shoved the Flyers into a quick 3-0 hole. Holmgren yanked Wregget after Mikhail Tatarinov blew down the middle and deked the goalie to make it 4-0, but the game was already gone, along with the the Flyers' chance of holding off Washington's playoff surge. Tocchet's groin popped again before the Caps completed a 6-0 clubbing that pulled them into a fourth-place tie with New Jersey, a point behind Philadelphia.

"To not make the playoffs this year would be devastating," said Craven before the reeling Flyers bused home. Five of the 7 remaining games were at the Spectrum, but the Flyers' edgy fans did not figure to provide much inspiration. Neither did the sore-groined Tocchet, nor Ricci, who had shoulder problems on top of the knowledge that his father, Mario, had been diagnosed with cancer.

Kerr, however, was ready to go. The big guy, who invariably scored in his first games back from injuries, deflected an Eklund shot past Bruin goalie Reggie Lemelin to create a 1-1 tie. In his first start since January 15, Peeters played well, but the Flyers' offensive confidence was nearly depleted. Petri Skriko, whom Farwell had declined to pursue before Vancouver traded the Finnish winger to Boston in January, broke the tie with a 25-footer between Peeters's legs and the Bruins went on to a 3-1 victory.

The induction into the Flyers' Hall of Fame of two of the franchise's all-time workhorses—Gary Dornhoefer and the late Barry Ashbee—failed to inspire their free-falling heirs. Three St. Louis goals on the first 7 shots against Wregget kept Philadelphia tumbling down what now seemed like a bottomless pit. With the 4-1 loss, the Flyers, losers of 7 of their last 8 games, dropped to fifth place, two points behind the third-place Devils and one behind the Caps.

The situation was desperate enough for Tocchet, who had not skated in six days, to return to the lineup when the Rangers brought a 7-game losing streak to the Spectrum. Finally, the Flyers had found a team playing even worse than they were. Tocchet scored his first goal since February 18 and Ricci, who would later reinjure his shoulder, scored his first in 8 games. Eklund danced to a hat trick and Peeters got his body in front of 22 Ranger shots as the Flyers kept their playoff hopes flickering with a 7-4 victory.

However, the exhausted and dehydrated Peeters told Holmgren on the flight to Buffalo after the game that he didn't think he could play again the next afternoon, leaving the coach no choice but to go back to the shattered Wregget. The last of three bad goals on the Sabres' first 9 shots floated in from the blue line off the stick of Dean Kennedy, forcing Holmgren to put in the pooped Peeters, who surrendered three more goals in a dreary 6-2 loss. Fourth-place New Jersey now led the Flyers by a point with four games remaining to Philadelphia's three.

"We still have a chance," said Tocchet, but the Flyers were grasping desperately at their final straws. Philadelphia pumped 49 shots at Tom Barrasso, but the Pittsburgh goalie and two Lemieux breakaway goals produced a 3-1 Spectrum victory that put the Penguins within one point of their first division title.

The help the Flyers would need to salvage a playoff spot with victories in their final two games seemed irrelevant to a team that had become incapable of helping itself.

"When the chips are down, there is an element missing," Farwell told reporters the day before Washington came to the Spectrum for Game 79. "We played as well as we did all year in Calgary [on March 7] and that was the last time until [the Pittsburgh game] that we had that really good team effort.

Farwell said Holmgren would not be blamed for the collapse. "I think our team has been coached just as well in the last [13] games as we were in the first 65. Had we maintained even close to our standing at the trade deadline, people would be raving about the job that was done. I don't think [coaching] is our problem at all."

The fans agreed, at least for the moment. They came to the Spectrum the following night ready to blame management.

The Flyers were so desperate for offense that they called up 19-year-old Kimbi Daniels and played him with Eklund and the crippled Tocchet. Only minutes after Eklund was presented with the Bobby Clarke Trophy and Samuelsson won the Barry Ashbee Trophy, Peeters went down with a knee sprain. Wregget surrendered a Hatcher howitzer that gave Washington a 1-0 lead, then played his best game since the Flyer slide began. But it was far too late to make any difference.

John Druce's breakaway goal midway through the third period removed the last vestiges of hope that the flailing, failing Flyers could still salvage the season. Fans chanted "Jay Must Go" and screamed insults at Farwell as they passed in front of the GM's box on their way out of the Spectrum.

The 3-0 defeat differed little from the others the Flyers suffered in their 2-10-2 collapse. During those 10 losses, they scored only 13 goals.

"I thought last year was a fluke thing," said Craven. "It's tough to swallow this time. It's a really bitter thing."

Veteran Flyers snapped back at Farwell for blaming the collapse on their failure to provide leadership. "It's easy to start criticizing the guys now," Tocchet said. "Why didn't they do something before the trading deadline? Guys worked hard. They're not great goal scorers, but they worked hard. I'll back every guy on the team."

Holmgren also felt the crippled, punchless Flyers had not given up. "They tried, they just couldn't get there," he said after the game. "Right now, there are some guys that I think have probably been here too long, that's all."

After the Flyers closed the season with a meaningless 4-4 tie in Pittsburgh, Sutter echoed Tocchet's criticism, suggesting management-player communication was lacking. "We're used to having a guy like Bobby Clarke who was always around," he said. To this day, Sutter believes Farwell's criticism caused some players to quit in the Washington game.

"It had some guys saying, 'Bleep him, if that's the way he feels,'" recalls Sutter. "They thought they weren't going to be here next year anyway. Some guys were just playing the year out. They packed it in when they read that."

Jay Snider did not speak to the media about the collapse and his vilification by the fans. Farwell, no conquering hero himself, leaped to his boss's defense. "I've only been here one year, but I know if it's rebuilt, he'll play a part in it because he has never been short on encouragement to get better. I'm in a very good situation. [I'm] not restricted by what [a move] is going to cost or by having to do safe things."

Jay had been realistic about the 1990-91 Flyers' capabilities, but still found the collapse devastating. "We knew with our talent we weren't going to win the Cup," he recalls. "But we thought we could reestablish the work ethic and give Russ some time to get the operation back on solid footing. At least we were arresting the decline. To collapse like that was a big, big blow."

Today, Holmgren believes he made a mistake allowing Peeters to become so cold and subsequently ineffective in the final weeks. "I really don't think Paul had much choice on that part of it," Farwell says today, but despite the public absolution he gave Holmgren, the GM did fault the coaching the Flyers received down the stretch.

"Technically, there was no problem with it," recalls Farwell, "but I don't think we tried anything different to pull ourselves out of it." In retrospect, he regrets having blurted out his criticism while the Flyers still clung to a ray of hope. "It was a response to a question, not calculated at all," Farwell says. "But from a timing standpoint, it was a rookie mistake.

"Still, I have to say I stand by what I said. We were looking for excuses, and nobody looked at themselves. We needed a trade, but people were trying to rob us, maybe as a result of the perception of my inexperience. I can't think of a deal we passed over that would have made a difference for us.

"The players all wanted a trade just to see a trade, but none of them thought it would be them that would go. We had guys who thought they were better than they were, who wanted more ice time and big money. We just weren't going to get it turned around with that group."

Farwell took the job knowing that the Flyers needed to upgrade their skill level, but the collapse convinced him they had to replace some of their grinders, too. "The first time you miss the playoffs, it's a

Steve Duchesne was acquired to fill the Flyers' immediate need for an offensive defenseman.

big surprise and shock," he says today. "This contributes to the sense that it's just a year where a lot of bad things happened.

"But when it occurs a second time, the reality hits home. For a successful team, missing the playoffs is unfathomable, and the fear of missing becomes a big, guiding force. Once a team starts to stumble, the weaker guys start to think, 'Well, it didn't hurt so bad after all.' And when you have a few guys thinking like that, it grows within your team. That's why

Dave Brown was thrilled to be back with the Flyers.

it's so hard for chronically losing teams that seem to be adding talent to get it turned around.

"The other thing about missing the playoffs is that it reduced the trade value of our players. Teams always had an attraction to Flyers because they were perceived to be winners."

Just another team now, the Flyers were heading into their 25th season with only a past to celebrate. Their immediate future looked dreary. The only full-time NHLers, let alone Flyers, who had come from Clarke's 1984-89 drafts were four average players

— Chychrun, Murphy, Mellanby and Baron. Ricci was the only block of a new foundation in place. The talent had worn so thin, Farwell was going to have to become creative to maximize his still-tradable assets.

The Flyers' most immediate needs were a sniper and an offensive defenseman. Farwell targeted the Kings' Steve Duchesne, but L.A. wanted a player whose rights belonged to Edmonton. "Rogie [Kings' GM Vachon] told me, if you can get Kurri, then I think we could do a deal," recalls Farwell.

Farwell had continued his pursuit of Jari Kurri at the World Championships in April, but the Finnish right wing's agent, Don Baizley, told the Flyers GM his client preferred to return to the NHL with a club that had a top playmaking center. What Kurri wanted most was to rejoin Gretzky in Los Angeles.

With an eye towards working a three-way deal, Farwell renewed talks with Edmonton about Mellanby and Berube, two Flyers who had almost become Oilers at the previous trading deadline. Sather still liked Mellanby and was willing to take Berube for Dave Brown. But the Oilers also needed a center. Farwell wasn't parting with Ricci, and Sutter was too valuable to use as a throw-in, so Farwell offered Hershey's Craig Fisher, who had fallen off a very short list of promising Flyer prospects.

Fisher had scored at a point-a-game pace in Hershey, so Farwell wanted an Oiler prospect in return. He and Sather settled on defenseman Corey Foster, a 1988 first-round pick by New Jersey with one superior asset—a blazing shot.

The Flyers and Kings each agreed to pay $250,000 to the Oilers, who were insisting on receiving cash in every major deal they made. Sather also dickered with Detroit, which had pledged more money than the Flyers but couldn't match the players Philadelphia offered. The Flyers also satisfied the Kings' wish for a physical defenseman by surrendering Chychrun.

With Philadelphia willing to surrender Kurri and Chychrun in the Los Angeles part of the deal but receiving only Duchesne, Farwell asked for more in return. The Kings countered by offering either a third-round pick or a fourth-round pick plus 29-year-old center Steve Kasper. Farwell felt Kasper, once one of the league's premier defensive centers, could still be useful.

Kurri's Italian league team had set a buyout deadline, and the Flyers were working against another: all NHL rosters were to be frozen for a June expansion draft. Both the new San Jose Sharks and Clarke's North Stars—who had surrendered a portion of their roster to the Sharks as part of the complex settlement in which the Minnesota owners, George and Gordon Gund, took control of San Jose — would receive players.

Farwell had decided not to protect Kerr in that draft. After eleven seasons and 363 goals, the most consistent scoring machine in Flyer history had worn out.

Farwell shopped Kerr around, but didn't generate any worthwhile offers. This left the choice of letting the veteran go in the expansion draft or honoring the upcoming option year on Kerr's $500,000-a-season contract with a one-year termination offer. In the latter case, Kerr would be free to shop himself for thirty days. "Then we might have lost him for nothing," recalls Farwell. "We decided to use him to satisfy our expansion obligation."

Steve Mountain quickly sprung into action, trying to fulfill Kerr's wish to play with an East Coast team. Both Keenan in Chicago and Clarke indicated interest but San Jose accepted an offer from the Rangers of winger Brian Mullen, on condition that the Sharks select Kerr. Indeed, Kerr was chosen with the first pick of the forwards' phase of the draft and immediately traded to the Flyers' bitterest rival.

His ego wounded, Kerr lashed out at Farwell during a media conference call arranged by the Rangers. "To put me in the draft and think I'm not going to be picked is ludicrous," Kerr said. "Whether Russ Farwell is not a very smart man or he couldn't figure that out, I don't know."

Later in the evening, however, the stoic, tragedy-stricken man-mountain whose four 50-plus goal seasons were only a glimmer of what he could have done with better health, was more conciliatory. "I felt like I put my life on the line for the Flyers when I went on the ice," he told *Daily News* columnist Rich Hofmann. "And I can say that Jay Snider went beyond the call for me.

"I've had some really bad hands dealt to me in the last few years, but you've got to get up every day and not dwell on the bad things. I'm a positive guy, even tonight. This is not the end I wanted, but you've got to get up every day and keep going. It's nice to be wanted by somebody."

Late that evening, when rosters were unfrozen with the completion of the expansion draft, the Flyers announced their three-way deal with Edmonton and Los Angeles. Fisher, Berube, and Mellanby went to Edmonton for Brown, Foster and the rights to Kurri. Chychrun and Kurri were then sent to Los Angeles for Duchesne, Kasper, and the Kings' fourth-round choice in the 1991 draft.

"We're making a big change in style," Farwell told reporters. "Getting an offensive defenseman was important."

Brown, who had never sold his South Jersey home, was thrilled to be back. Mellanby recognized it was best he move on.

Meanwhile, a state appropriation had eased Philadelphia's financial crisis. The climate had thus improved for the finalization of an arena plan to be announced, but the controversy that had developed over the city's only outlay of cash towards the project — the $6.5-million gift towards construction of the parking facility — had to be defused.

"The garage was the city's idea, not ours," recalls Carl Hirsh. "We were actually gaining 2,000 [ground-level] parking spaces even without the garage because the arena would cover less ground than JFK Stadium did. The city wanted the garage to ease the burden on the neighborhood for sold-out [Veterans] Stadium events."

Spectacor agreed to accept a low-interest loan from the city, repayable over twenty-four years, rather than have Philadelphia pay for half of the garage. The way was cleared for the grand announcement. On June 10, at a Hershey Hotel press conference, schematic drawings of the proposed 21,000-seat palace were unveiled. "After twenty-five years, it just didn't seem right to move," Ed Snider told reporters. "Broad and Pattison has been very good to us."

The arena, soon given the working title of Spectrum II, was designed by the Kansas City architectural firm of Ellerbe, Becket. The plans called for a capacity of 19,000 for hockey and included seventy-eight luxury boxes. Scheduled for completion in the fall of 1994, the project included a store-lined concourse connecting the new arena with the old Spectrum, which would house events requiring a smaller seating capacity. Ed Snider estimated the total venture would cost up to $200 million, about half of which would go toward construction of the arena itself.

Spectacor agreed to pay all construction fees for the new building, which would rest on land leased from the city at a base of $100,000 a year, increasing by $5,000 per year through 2057. Spectacor would also receive from the city a five-year abatement on property taxes for the arena. Starting in the sixth year, the company would pay $2 million a year until 2024, when that payment would increase by $100,000 a year to a cap of $4 million.

Annual rent for the land on which the old Spectrum sat would remain at the current $15,000 until 2017, when it would increase to $100,000. Spectacor retained the right to demolish the old Spectrum and redevelop the land should operating the building prove not viable.

The state would pay $2 million toward construction of the $13-million garage, plus $5 million to demolish JFK Stadium and prepare the site for construction. Pennsylvania would also foot the $1.5-million bill to relocate the Eagles' bad-weather practice bubble sitting inside the old stadium.

Spectacor estimated that for its first thirty-one years, Spectrum II would generate $3.2 million more a year in tax dollars than Spectrum I. Weighing that amount against a loss of tax revenue should the Flyers and Sixers move to New Jersey (and take other attractions with them), the projected net gain for the city on a new arena was $11.84 million a year for thirty-one years. For this, the city's only investment was a one-time $6.5-million loan, to be repaid over twenty-four years by Spectacor.

At the press conference, Mayor Wilson Goode proudly pointed out that Philadelphia and Chicago were the only two U.S. cities to have all its teams from the four major leagues playing within the city limits. Nevertheless, residents of the blocks just north of Veterans Stadium, represented by councilwoman Anna Verna, felt betrayed because a promise for open discussion before the arena deal was officially announced had not been kept. Mayoral candidate Frank Rizzo announced he would continue to oppose giving taxpayers' money to "zillionare owners."

But Spectacor did its homework, briefed all the affected parties, and reminded council members about the benefits of the new arena by inviting construction labor representatives to sit in council chambers during the July 7 vote. The deal was approved unanimously, without a peep of dissent. Spectacor officials celebrated at their Rittenhouse Square headquarters. The drawing of blueprints could begin. The investment banking firm of Goldman Sachs was hired to obtain financing before a deadline of July 11, 1992, one year hence.

Meanwhile, the big news at the 1991 entry draft was not the Nordiques' selection of center Eric Lindros—considered the best prospect since Lemieux

— with the first pick, but his reaction to Quebec's claim. The 6-4, 235-pounder did nothing to dispel media rumors that he would not play for the Nordiques. Lindros refused to put on their sweater after they called his name.

"I wouldn't say Quebec isn't an option, but putting on the jersey would be a commitment," said Lindros. While he was being pressed by a crush of reporters, the Flyers were surprising draft prognosticators by using the sixth pick overall on center Peter Forsberg from MoDo of Sweden. Central Scouting had rated Forsberg the 18th-best prospect available.

The Flyers weighed Forsberg against defenseman Richard Matvichuk, who was taken on the next selection by the North Stars. "It scared even me to use the sixth pick in the draft for a European player, but all our scouts loved him," recalls Farwell. "He was very highly skilled, a tremendously hard worker, and we didn't have one guy who had a negative thing to say about him."

Farwell also took a run at a free agent who could not only skate, but score. Pittsburgh right wing Mark Recchi, a 113-point scorer the previous season, was having trouble reaching contract agreement with the Stanley Cup champions. So Farwell, prepared to offer Tocchet as compensation, overbid the Penguins by approximately $250,000 on a four-year package for Recchi.

Farwell felt the younger Recchi was more of an offensive catalyst than Tocchet, who could certainly finish plays but needed a skilled center to get him the puck—something the Flyers lacked.

Recchi's agent, Rick Curran, went to the Spectrum on a mid-August morning intending to close the deal. "Mark had a good feeling about the Flyers and was excited about Ken Hitchcock [his junior coach] being there," recalls Curran. "But Mark had friends and popularity in Pittsburgh and I told him to consider whether giving that up was worthwhile." Curran phoned his client from the Spectrum parking lot just before the meeting with Farwell. Recchi informed his agent that he had decided not to leave Pittsburgh and later signed the Penguins' four-year, $3.55-million offer.

Tocchet, blissfully unaware that he had almost become a Penguin, was the only Flyer representative on a Team Canada which labored mightily in the one-game Canada Cup semifinal to get the puck past Tommy Soderstrom, an unknown, 22-year-old Swedish goalie drafted in the eleventh round by the Flyers the previous summer. High-powered Canada eventually defeated Sweden 4-0 and, with the 18-

year-old Lindros playing like a man among the NHL's giants, swept a two-game final from Team USA.

Eklund, coming off a 69-point season, signed a three-year contract that averaged $550,000 per season. When Farwell refused to make similar commitments to Craven and Sutter, it was obvious their Flyer days were nearing an end.

Craven, making $200,000, asked for a deal starting at $450,000 and ending at $500,000, but the Flyers' offer started at only $400,000. Sutter, who made $250,000, called an offer of a raise to $300,000 (what the Flyers had paid free agent Brad Jones, a fleet, 26-year-old who had scored 9 goals the previous season with the Kings) an "insult." Sutter, headed into his option year and coming off off a 17-goal, 28-assist season, exercised his right to report a day late for training camp. And when the Flyers began their exhibition season, the *C* had been taken off his jersey.

"We [Sutter and Craven] certainly seem to be two guys they're thinking of trading," Sutter told Les Bowen of the *Daily News.* "You don't have to be a brain surgeon to figure that out."

Indeed, Farwell had resumed efforts to deal Sutter to St. Louis for Rod Brind'Amour. The 21-year-old former first round pick had been an untouchable nine months earlier, but the Blues decided that his tendency to press too hard would keep him from reaching his potential. Brind'Amour and goalie Curtis Joseph had been offered to New Jersey as compensation for the Blues' signing free-agent winger Brendan Shanahan away from the Devils, but Judge Edward Houston, the NHL-appointed arbitrator, instead awarded Scott Stevens to New Jersey.

The Blues were thus left with a huge hole on their blue line, one Farwell offered to partly fill. The additions of Duchesne and Foster left Murray Baron expendable, so the 24-year-old defenseman was offered with Sutter, whom St. Louis GM Ron Caron wanted to reunite with twin brother Rich and older brother Brian, the Blues' coach.

Caron sent Blues scout Paul MacLean to a Flyer-Red Wing exhibition game in Orlando to watch Baron, who played shakily. "I was sick," recalls Farwell. "I thought they would pull out for sure." But when he arrived in Miami for another Flyer exhibition the next day, Caron said he still wanted to do the deal with an added condition. The Flyers would have to take Dan Quinn. Farwell tried to get Caron to substitute other Blues, but Caron was insistent on unloading the final year of Quinn's contract.

"I called Jay and told him Brind'Amour still made it a good deal for us," recalls Farwell. "He said to go ahead, that if we wound up having to eat Quinn's contract, we would."

Sutter, an uncharacteristic victim of a rare Holmgren tirade following the first period of the game in Orlando, was feeling abused and resentful when he was called by Farwell to his hotel room. "It was pretty obvious the screws were being put to Paul," Sutter recalls. "I knew it was only a matter of time until I was gone."

Nevertheless, as the veteran center rode the elevator he still wanted to remain a Flyer, despite it all. "I had never asked to be traded," he recalls. "Deep down, I was hoping [Farwell] would say [a new] contract was done."

Instead, Sutter was told he was gone. "I think I laughed when he told me," recalls Sutter. "I guess I was in a fog. Margo [his wife] had told me a couple hours earlier there were rumors in St. Louis I was going there, but when I called her back to tell her it really had happened, she didn't believe it. She thought I was [twin brother] Richard playing a joke. I told her, 'I'm coming home. When I walk into the house tonight, then you'll believe me.'"

Holmgren says today that even in Sutter's final unhappy days as a Flyer, his effort was irreproachable. "He came back with a broken jaw and scored 26 goals for me my first year," the coach said. "He wasn't a real skilled player and we were so short of offense we had to depend on him to get some points. I think everybody's expectations got a little high."

Brind'Amour was told of the trade hours before an exhibition game in Chicago. The long faces of the Blues' officials when they had lost the arbitration hearing were still vivid in his mind, and he was cheered by the news. "It was just a relief to be out of there," he said. "I didn't really care that much where."

Holmgren, who had thought Brind'Amour would be a younger version of Sutter, was surprised when the new Flyer skated with the team for the first time. "I didn't realize he was that skilled," said the coach. He immediately put Brind'Amour in Ricci's place between Tocchet and Eklund.

Brind'Amour, criticized for his bodybuilding obsession in St. Louis, acknowledged the Blues had a right to be disappointed with him. "I put a lot of pressure on myself, and didn't play as well as I could have," he told reporters. "I didn't come out of the gate very well, then [the Blues] stuck me in a third-line role."

He debuted with a goal and an assist in an exhibition victory over Hartford at the Spectrum and got off to a good, relaxed, start.

Holmgren gave the captaincy to Tocchet, the Flyers' best player, despite the coach's concern for the 27-year-old winger's lack of diplomatic skills. "If we didn't give it to him, we'd lose him," the coach recalls thinking.

Tocchet took the C, agreeing he would have to learn to say the right thing at the right time. "Some stuff has to stay in the the room," he said. "We have a lot of young guys on the team now and [criticism] has to be constructive."

Hextall, eager for advice on how to break his two-year cycle of groin and hamstring pulls, worked out a strengthening program with Pat Croce and William DeGregory, a dancer with the Pennsylvania Ballet. Farwell didn't quite share Holmgren's faith in Hextall, but still felt he should receive the majority of starts. At 27, Hextall was probably too old to be part of the young nucleus the Flyers were trying to assemble, but if he stayed healthy, Farwell felt the veteran could reestablish his trade value.

There would, however, be another delay in that process. Hextall, who had slashed Detroit winger Jim Cummins in the Miami exhibition game, drew a 6-game suspension. The Flyers used up their allotted seven days before deciding not to appeal, allowing Hextall to play the season's first two games before serving his punishment.

Farwell worked to clear room in the nets for Dominic Roussel, a third-round pick in the 1988 draft coming off a promising year at Hershey, by trying to trade Wregget for Detroit winger Brent Fedyk, a failed 1985 first-rounder recommended by Bill Dineen, who had coached Fedyk at Adirondack. Detroit was willing to move Fedyk, but was apathetic towards Wregget. Similarly, Farwell could find no takers for Peeters, so the option year of his contract was bought out at the end of training camp.

The day before the opening game of their twenty-fifth season, the Flyers officially announced the signing of 27-year-old Andrei Lomakin, the 1991 seventh-round pick who would be their first player from the dissolving Soviet Union. With the world changing, so were attitudes. "The guys don't care if they bring a Martian in here if he's going to bring us closer to winning the Stanley Cup," said Tocchet.

The addition of the Russian winger brought the number of new Flyers on the opening-night roster to eleven. With the likes of Brind'Amour, Lomakin and

Quinn, Philadelphia significantly bolstered its speed up front, while Roussel, recalled from Hershey when Hextall began serving his suspension, pumped fresh blood into their crease. Duchesne added mobility on defense and although, technically, Dave Brown's face was not new, opponents were still likely to need one after being reacquainted with his fists.

Even with all those changes, the Flyers' most important off-season acquisition was Mark Howe's new body. Offered only a one-year termination contract because back problems had limited him to 19 games in 1990-91, the 36-year-old defenseman reported to camp with two surgically repaired discs and none of the pain that had been shooting down his legs for two seasons.

"I want to play until the team says I'm done or unless I go down and can't play anymore," Howe said. Alas, when he could not get through the second period of an opening-night 5-2 loss in Landover, it looked as if that time had come, but Howe decided to see if more rest would help. He was again joined on the sidelines by Hextall, who looked sharp in a 2-2 tie at Pittsburgh, then started his suspension.

The Flyers began the home portion of their silver- anniversary season with pregame introductions of players from their original team. The Penguins, 1-0 losers on dedication night in 1967, had grown up twenty-five years later to be Stanley Cup champions. They buried Wregget, 6-3. He bounced back to get the Flyers into the win column with a 4-2 Spectrum victory over New Jersey, but when Roussel beat Quebec 5-3 in his first NHL start, Holmgren decided to take a longer look at the rookie.

Roussel was beaten only by a deflection in a 1-0 Spectrum loss to the tight-checking Canadiens, so he started again five nights later in Minnesota. A plus-5 performance by Howe in his return sent the Flyers to an impressive 5-2 victory over Clarke's team. The following day the ex-Flyer GM snatched Derrick Smith, whose aggressiveness had diminished as his role became less clear, from the waiver wire.

His debt to society paid, Hextall returned to beat San Jose 5-2 in their first visit to the Spectrum, but when a 4-2 Spectrum loss to the Rangers followed, Holmgren felt the time had come for a talk with an unproductive Craven. The veteran winger, campaigning publicly for a trade, left his meeting with the coach before the November 5 game in St. Louis thinking the air had been cleared. On the contrary, Holmgren felt Craven's attitude was polluting the Flyers' fresh start. Scratched from the lineup, he returned to the hotel before the end of Philadelphia's

4-3 victory.

"I think I'm saying not just to Murray Craven but to everybody else, 'You play to the standards the coaches set,'" said Holmgren. "[He] admits he sulks when he's not on the power play. He's not mentally prepared to help the Flyers at this time."

"They usually want everybody to toe the line here," Craven said. "When you don't do it exactly how they want it, you're dealt with the way I've been dealt with. I saw it with Brad McCrimmon and

Brian Propp and Dave Poulin and Ron Sutter. I see no light at the end of the tunnel. The only light I see is a move." It came one week later when Farwell sent the 27-year-old to Hartford for 28-year-old right wing Kevin Dineen.

Dineen, like Craven, was a good player, but not capable of being a star for a franchise desperately needing one. Each winger had become symbolic of his team's stagnation and was now trade bait for new managements determined to make major changes. A two-time 40-goal scorer and son of the Flyers' eastern scout, Dineen had managed only 17 goals in 1990-91, when he was hospitalized for a flare-up of Crohn's disease, a bowel affliction.

Hextall's return meant Roussel was returned to Hershey for regular work, but when the veteran wasted a 38-shot Flyer effort in a a 5-2 loss at New Jersey, Holmgren decided to go with Wregget. He responded with a 3-1 win over Edmonton—a victory marred by the loss of Kasper for the year with torn knee ligaments—then followed up two nights later in Montreal with another strong effort. Mark Pederson scored a late, sweet, goal against his former team and the Flyers went on to a 3-1 victory.

In light of a slow start by Tocchet and the massive roster turnover, the Flyers' 8-8-1 record seemed encouraging. Lomakin had tailed off after scoring 4 goals in his first 8 games, but Duchesne had injected 3 goals and 12 assists in 17 contests. Most promising of all, Howe had played seven consecutive games.

But the following night at the Spectrum, an unforced Murphy error gave a goal away to Winnipeg's Mike Hartman, then Fredrik Olausson cashed a five-minute high-sticking penalty to send the Flyers to a 2-1 loss. They played like strangers in a 5-2 loss in the next game at Pittsburgh, and when a slash broke Howe's thumb in a 5-5 Spectrum tie with New Jersey, the wheels began to fall off the Flyers' redesigned cart.

Two extremely raw rookies, Foster and Dan Kordic, were making glaring errors on defense. Duchesne was gambling, often foolishly, and his increasingly nervous hands weren't getting back the many goals he was giving away. When the Flyers were blown away 7-3 on Thanksgiving Eve against a Hartford team that had gone 4-9-2 in its previous 15 games, the Spectrum fans began chanting, "Paul Must Go."

Holmgren, meanwhile, resisted the urge to tell his players where to go. "I'm thoroughly disgusted with the way the team played tonight," announced the coach, who then walked out of his postgame press conference without taking questions. The Flyers had gone only 4 games without winning, but their 1-6-2

Dave Brown added toughness to the Philadelphia blue line.

divisional record already placed them 8 points out of the fourth and final Patrick playoff spot.

"We gotta get this thing going a little better," Farwell told Holmgren after the game.

"I know," the coach replied.

The changes had raised the Flyers' expectations, which had increased the pressure on Holmgren. "You can't blame Paul," said the slumping Tocchet. "I'm not scoring and we're not getting goals."

Panic was showing in the Flyers' disjointed play. "We come in here after the game and we all feel like we just worked our behinds off," said Brind'Amour after the Flyers' brisk 90-minute Thanksgiving-morning workout. "Maybe we're just not working smart."

Contrary to the popular perception of Holmgren as a player's coach, Farwell was becoming increasingly concerned about what he perceived as a shortage of coaching positivism. "You can't write guys off, and Paul did that all the time," recalls the GM. "Once Paul didn't like them, that was it. With Derrick Smith, he wanted him out of here in the worst way and just stopped playing him. As a result I had no market for him at all.

"That's just one example. Paul wasn't trying to change players' thinking or get more from them, and that's what coaching is. Tocchet was just playing awful and there was no sign of him pulling out of it. Now, I didn't blame Paul for Rick getting into that condition. But I don't think he was doing anything to help him out of it, either.

"I know he did that with guys like Sutter and Eklund after taking over from Keenan, but I didn't see it after I got here."

Nevertheless, on Thanksgiving Day, Farwell denied his coach was cooked. "I don't think we're at that point at all," the GM told reporters. "Outside of three, maybe four, games, I'd say we've played pretty well. I think our spirit is good and our attitude is good ... Especially when you're piecing things together, sometimes you try and it turns to bleep."

The bleep was deep the following afternoon, when the Penguins came to the Spectrum to open a home-and-home series. Acton, who had suffered a broken wrist against Hartford, joined Kasper on the sidelines, leaving the Flyers without either of their experienced checking centers. Hextall sat out with shoulder tendonitis that had worsened in the Hartford debacle, and Wregget misplayed two early Penguin goals.

Holmgren switched to Roussel, who received no help from his distraught teammates. Tocchet limped off with a knee sprain and the Penguins raced to a 6-

0 lead. "Everybody's scared to make a mistake," said Duchesne, who was making many. "You're not sure if somebody's behind you or not."

The volume of the anti-Holmgren chants grew louder as the Penguins rolled to a 9-3 victory. "I knew after that game that I would never coach another one at the Spectrum," recalls Holmgren.

When the Flyers arrived at their Pittsburgh hotel several hours later, the general manager asked the coach if he wanted to get together. Holmgren said he would phone. By Farwell's recollection, he did not hear from the coach until 10:30 P.M. It troubled Farwell that Holmgren had not called a team meeting to deal with the worsening crisis. The GM wondered if the coach had become too resigned to his fate to reenergize the team.

Although Holmgren had always said he had a good working relationship with his GM, Farwell never shared that feeling. "I never felt I gained Paul's confidence or trust," recalls Farwell. "We never had any disagreements, but if being on the same wavelength means you were honest and open and exchanging thoughts, I didn't feel that was happening.

"I never could crack it. He played it very safe with me. I felt he was telling me what he wanted me to hear. A lot of times, I don't think I got his true feeling."

By the next morning, Farwell was leaning towards making a coaching change. He felt his best option to get through the rest of the season was Bill Dineen.

Dineen, 59, had thirteen years' head coaching experience with Houston and New England of the WHA and with Adirondack. He had not run a bench since 1989. But Farwell thought of Dineen as a wise old hockey head whose grandfatherly approach had always seemed to restore players' confidence.

The GM called Dineen in Seattle, where he was scouting juniors, and asked him to come to New York on Monday to see the Flyers play the Rangers. Farwell told Dineen, who had already been scheduled to fly home to Lake George, New York, on Monday, that his opinion on the slumping team was needed.

In Pittsburgh, the Flyers fell behind 3-1, then began to outplay the Penguins. Typically, just when it appeared they were coming on, the Flyers became confused on a player change. When Carkner stepped out of the penalty box, Ricci and Huffman both rushed to cover Jagr, leaving Gordie Roberts open to fire an insurance goal over Wregget's blocker. The Flyers outshot the Penguins 34-28, but lost 5-1. In their last three games, they had been outscored 21-7.

Because the game in New York would be the Flyers' third contest in four nights, Holmgren stuck to his usual schedule on the off-day, making the practice in Pittsburgh optional. When Holmgren didn't attend the workout, Farwell became more convinced than ever that his coach had become too depressed to get the Flyers turned around.

Tocchet, who had limped in Pittsburgh, joined the scratch list for the game at Madison Square Garden. Nevertheless Dineen watched a team that seemed curiously reenergized. After Lomakin's backhander through John Vanbiesbrouck's legs tied the score 2-2 in the third, the Flyers carried the play.

Brind'Amour, with an excellent opportunity off a two-on-one with Kevin Dineen, shot the puck over the net and the Rangers came up ice on an outnumbered break. Duchesne missed breaking up Paul Broten's goalmouth pass to Mark Hardy, who had an easy tap-in to put New York back ahead. "Typical of the way things have been going the whole year," said the self-flagellating Brind'Amour. The Rangers went on to a 4-2 victory that extended the Flyers' winless streak to 0-6-1.

"Everybody's frustrated," said Holmgren. "We've played some bad games lately, but tonight I thought we played a good game against a very good team in our division.

"We still came away with no points. We're eleven points out of a playoff spot now. I think they [management] have been fair about it, but you can only be fair for so long. This can't go on before changes are made. Sooner or later, we're going to have to win."

At dinner after the game, Farwell and Dineen discussed the team the scout had just watched for the first time that season. Afterwards, as they sat in the lobby of the Paramount Hotel, the GM told the scout he was thinking of making a coaching change. Dineen asked if Farwell was considering going after Barry Melrose, who had coached for Farwell in Medicine Hat prior to replacing Dineen in Adirondack, or was contemplating promoting either of the assistants—Hitchcock or Hartsburg—or Hershey's Mike Eaves. The GM replied he didn't think any of them were ready.

"He kind of dropped it and went on to something else," recalls Dineen. "About ten minutes later, he said something like, 'What would you think about coaching yourself?'

"It just slammed me. I didn't have any awareness he was thinking of me at all. I said, 'Was there something in that water you were drinking at the restaurant?'"

Dineen began grilling Farwell. "It was like he was sounding me out if I was serious or not," recalls the GM. "He saw that I was. When we met for breakfast the next morning, he said if that was what I wanted, he would do it."

Dineen was intrigued by the opportunity, but worried about having been out of coaching for two and a half years. He also knew little about the team he would be taking over. Thus, when Farwell asked if Dineen wanted to bring in his own assistants, he said he preferred to have Hitchcock's and Hartsburg's input. Farwell told Dineen he was going home to consult Jay Snider before making a final decision, but to expect a call that night.

After flying home to Lake George, Dineen did not inform his wife, Pat, about the pending offer. "There was no sense getting her riled up if it wasn't going to happen," recalls Dineen. "Besides, after being a coach's wife and a player's mother for so many years, she would accept that I would do what I wanted."

Farwell called Dineen to confirm the offer at around 8:30 P.M. He asked for half an hour to talk to Pat, then went to the basement and brought up the skates he hadn't worn since leaving the bench. "Pat, do you think we can get the rust off of these?" he asked.

"Don't tell me," she said.

Holmgren returned home from a run early the next morning to find a message that Farwell wanted a meeting. He drove to the Coliseum, where Farwell closed his office door and told Holmgren he didn't see much hope for turning the team around without making a coaching change.

Holmgren almost immediately got up to leave. "Wait a minute," said Farwell. He asked the fired coach if he wanted to stay on in some capacity, perhaps as a scout to replace Dineen.

"He wasn't hearing me," recalls Farwell. "And I didn't blame him." Scouting had never appealed to Holmgren, but he shrugged and said he would think about it. He walked downstairs to his Coliseum office to clean out his desk, then proceeded to the Spectrum to do the same at his office there. Holmgren stopped at home, called Clarke with the news, then got drunk.

Farwell announced the coaching change at a late-morning press conference at Ovations. "Unfortunately, because of the class of the guy involved and as loyal as Paul's been in the past, it makes the decision much tougher," Farwell said. "But once I reached the decision, I felt the quicker the better.

"Bill has a very proven track record. He's always won and he's always gotten the most out of what he has. He's a tough guy not to play hard for. He sits down and if it doesn't go right, he's going to talk to you. And if it still doesn't go right, he's going to talk to you tomorrow. He's ideal for the job."

Kevin Dineen came to the Coliseum that morning to learn from Kjell Samuelsson that Holmgren had been fired and practice set back several hours. "When Billy gets here, he's going to have a meeting first," said Samuelsson.

"Billy who?" asked Dineen.

"Your dad," said Samuelsson. "He's the new coach."

"It just floored me," recalls Kevin.

His father, scheduled to take a 7:30 A.M. flight out of Albany, changed his mind as he approached the airport and decided to continue driving to Philadelphia. He listened to Farwell's press conference on WIP on the car radio. At the Coliseum, Dineen briefly addressed his players, telling them he knew they had talent and that they should look forward to a fresh start. Then, Farwell asked the trainers for a list of the players' uniform numbers so he could tell who they were while they practiced.

After an hour-long workout, the stoop-shouldered, gravelly-voiced grandfather and rookie NHL coach told the media that his nickname, "The Fox," stemmed from "missing the odd curfew" in his playing days. Dineen agreed that he had a knack for fixing team's problems, but confessed he wasn't exactly sure in this case what had to be fixed. The one game he had seen the Flyers, they had played well.

While Howe, who had played for Dineen in Houston, confirmed the new coach's likability, the rest of the Flyers voiced the standard hate-to-see-it-happen rhetoric that accompanies any coaching change. Still, most of the Flyers sincerely felt they had betrayed a good man. "I don't think anyone wanted Paul fired," said Ricci, "It's not right when someone has to take the punishment for what somebody else has done."

Contrary to any impression he may have given his team and bosses in the final days, Holmgren felt anything but left off the hook. "Right now, I'm confused," he said when he met with the media at the Cherry Hill Hyatt the day following the firing. "I'm hurt.

"I think with patience, they're going to be a very good team. I don't think 24 games is enough time."

At the time of his firing, Holmgren was tied with Montreal's Pat Burns as the NHL's longest-serving coach. In three-plus seasons of Flyer transition and

decline, Holmgren had gone 107-126-31, but in his only playoff experience he guided his team to the Stanley Cup semifinals.

In time, Holmgren came to question whether he set off wrong signals as his reign was crashing down. "I didn't think it was a big deal that I didn't go to the optional practice [in Pittsburgh]," he says. "Maybe I should have." But he believes his relationship with the general manager was undercut by Hitchcock, who Holmgren believes was second-guessing the coach's decisions directly to the GM.

"It got back to me that there were times he was criticizing the way I handled certain things," said Holmgren. "I wasn't riding with Russ to Hershey all the time like Hitchcock was."

Hitchcock denies he ever criticized Holmgren to Farwell. "Russ would ask me about players that I knew from the Western League that he was thinking of getting, but not about Homer. The part about driving to Hershey bothers me. I went there a lot, sometimes by myself, sometimes with Russ or Bill Barber or Bill Dineen or whoever was going because I wanted to watch hockey.

"Look, I thought if Homer got fired, we were all going to get fired. I didn't turn on him. There was a lot of pressure on Paul, not just from Russ, but from being part of that organization. A lot of people around the team, some of whom played for it, have an opinion and they give it. I don't even think it's sniping, I think they're trying to help, but that adds to the stress level."

Farwell, who hired Hitchcock, denies he was used as an informant. "I didn't know Hitchcock better than I knew Holmgren. I knew him as an [WHL] adversary [when Hitchcock coached at Kamloops]. I might have golfed with him at a league meeting or something, but he certainly wasn't a friend of mine. I never went to him and asked him anything [about Holmgren]."

The Flyers began the Bill Dineen era in much the same scatterbrained way they ended the Holmgren one. Penalties in the first 1:37 gave Washington a two-man advantage. Ricci, however, promptly stole the puck and fed Carkner, who so startled the Caps by going to the net that he even had time to put in his own rebound.

It was the Flyers' first three-on-five goal since Poulin's dramatic 1985 series-breaker against Quebec and it electrified the Spectrum but only until Hunter banked in a shot off Huffman as the first penalty expired. Then goals by Randy Burridge and Kevin Hatcher put Washington ahead 3-1 before seven minutes had been played. Ricci cut the lead to one, but an ever-gambling Duchesne gave the puck away at the Washington line and Burridge blew past Eklund and Foster for a breakaway goal on Wregget. "You believe that your guys are behind you and helping you out," said Duchesne.

The fans, without Holmgren to kick around anymore, chanted for Dave Brown as the Caps extended the Flyers' winless streak to 0-7-1 with a 6-3 victory. "I don't know what to tell you," said Dineen at his postgame press conference. "We'll work on our defensive coverage. That's our No. 1 priority right now."

Asked to grade his own performance, the coach admitted he had struggled. "I was having a little problem, especially when guys were going off for penalties," he said. "Certainly, I'm going to have to do a little more homework. In fairness, I haven't really had a great deal of sleep in the last three days."

Two nights later in Boston, Dineen juggled his combinations, putting Brind'Amour, the only consistent Flyer during the skid, with Lomakin and Brad Jones. Brind'Amour scored twice and Jones once as the Flyers broke two third-period ties and posted the new coach's first victory, 5-3.

"The difference was that twenty-one guys gave a special effort and finally some bounces went our way," said Dineen. In truth, the coach was very thankful for some large favors from shaky Boston goalie Reggie Lemelin. "Getting a win in my second game, on the road against a good team, took a lot of the pressure off," Dineen recalls.

His team began to relax, too. The following night the Flyers blew a 2-0 lead in the final 4:33 into a 2-2 Spectrum deadlock with New Jersey, but Quinn's goal with 1:27 remaining gave them a buoying 1-1 tie with the Blackhawks. The following afternoon in Chicago, three third-period goals and a four-point game by Lomakin gave the Flyers another deadlock, 4-4. They seemed to be responding to the coaching change.

"It has no bearing on Homer at all," said Hextall, still out of the lineup with tendinitis. "When you change a coach, it takes the pressure off for a while. And we felt a lot of pressure because we didn't want Homer to lose his job."

Still, the absent-minded grandfather behind the Flyer bench was providing the exact touch Farwell had expected. No NHL coach had ever, on first impression, appeared as dumb as this Fox. The amiable Dineen shuffled around the Spectrum and Coli-

seum warmly greeting everybody, while considering any and all theories about the Flyers' difficulties. Except for his son, whom he made a point of avoiding for fear of charges of favoritism, Dineen asked the players how they were and really listened to their answers.

Devils coach Tommy McVie, a longtime friend and adversary from the bus leagues, referred to Dineen as "Lieutenant Columbo." Indeed, Dineen's seemingly bumbling investigation had quickly gotten to the bottom of the Flyers' confidence problems.

Holmgren, with nothing better to do, decided to try scouting. Hextall returned with a 3-0 shutout in Minnesota then, after a long flight home and a short night's sleep, the Flyers tested their progress in a Spectrum matinee against a Washington team that three weeks earlier had outclassed them in Dineen's debut. This time Philadelphia took a 3-2 lead into the final minute before a mix-up between Wregget and Carkner behind the net enabled Kelly Miller to stuff the equalizer into an empty net. But Jones banged in a Tocchet rebound in overtime to give the Flyers a 4-3 victory and the Spectrum its first afterglow in a long time.

After a sharp Hextall opened a four-game trip by holding the vastly improved Canucks to a 1-1 tie, the Flyers sputtered in Calgary the next night, losing 5-1. Dineen, despite the unhappiness of some players, brought the team home during a five-day break in the western swing, but at least one Flyer, Gord Murphy, was saved further jet lag by Farwell. On the morning of January 2, as the Flyers were boarding a flight to San Francisco the GM showed up to tell the 24-year-old defenseman he had been traded to Boston. The Flyers were sending Murphy, right wing Brian Dobbin, and a third-round 1992 draft choice to the Bruins for defenseman Garry Galley and center Wes Walz, a former high-scoring junior.

"We had talked about Walz with the Bruins before, then [assistant GM] Mike Milbury called out of the blue and asked if we'd take Galley and Walz for Murphy and a draft pick," recalls Farwell.

"Eighty to 90 percent of the players in the NHL were high picks and, if you look at their records, most of them have been traded at one point. A Mark Pederson or a Wes Walz might or might not pan out, but you gotta go for it."

The Bruins anticipated the veteran Galley would seek a larger contract when his present one ran out. Murphy, who had slumped—probably from overuse—during the 1991 collapse, had never played as well as he had during his rookie year, but the Bruins sought him as a fair exchange for Galley.

"I liked Galley a lot. I thought he really stood up for them one year when [Ray] Bourque got hurt," recalls Farwell. "We wouldn't have gotten him if they hadn't reached a frustrating position on a contract."

To the media, Farwell had to justify giving up a 24-year-old defenseman for a 28-year-old while in the midst of a rebuilding program. "We're getting a gung-ho guy [in Galley], a leader," the GM explained. "We weren't going to get anything with that third pick that would have the potential of Walz."

Farwell, who sent Walz to Hershey, telephoned Galley in Boston at midmorning, welcoming him and informing him that the Flyers had a game at the Cow Palace the following night. "I said, 'Whoa, I have a 2 year-old daughter and a 2-week-old boy and a wife who's hysterical,'" Galley recalls. "Russ said, 'Well, if you can make it, the ticket will be at the airport.'

"I spent about three hours with Terry to make sure she was settled and strong. She encouraged me to go. She wanted me to get there and start fitting in."

Galley stopped at Boston Garden on the way to the airport to get his equipment. Murphy, who after talking to Farwell had walked to another ticket counter and caught a flight to Boston, was in the Bruin locker room, his name already on Galley's No. 28 jersey. They wished each other luck. Before leaving, Galley asked Dave Poulin about Philadelphia and the state of the Flyers. "He told me the Sniders cared too much and had too many resources not to get things turned around again," recalls Galley.

In his Flyer debut the following night, the Flyers lost 2-1 to the expansion Sharks. Galley was taken aback by some of his new teammates' attitudes. "There were guys more worried about when we were getting to L.A. than losing to the bleeping Sharks," he recalls. "I wasn't the only guy who was frustrated, but you could see that there wasn't the fear of losing there had been in Boston."

The next night the Flyers were bombed 7-3 in Los Angeles. The adrenaline burst from the coaching change was fading. And when the Flyers came home, the natives were growing restless again. Hextall was booed viciously when he accidentally gloved a wide, 70-foot drive by Buffalo's Gord Donnelly into his own net during a 5-5 tie with the Sabres.

Eklund, with only 19 points in 37 games, was forced out of the lineup with a sprained knee during a 4-3 victory on January 12 against the Islanders. The Flyers had won only two of their last 10 games when the NHL came to the Spectrum for the 1992 All-Star Game.

The organization had hoped the weekend, the apex of the club's twenty-fifth Anniversary celebration, would herald a turn-around season. Instead, the Flyers were in last place in the Patrick Division, fourteen points and three years removed from a playoff spot. The exiled Bobby Clarke drew the biggest pregame ovation when he was introduced as honorary Wales Conference captain–yet another depressing reminder of the franchise's faded glory.

Behind the scenes, however, a reconciliation between Clarke and the Flyers was already in the works. Ed Snider, who had stayed above the problems between his son and Clarke, had dined with the North Star GM on visits to Los Angeles. Jay and Clarke had also begun to speak again at various league meetings and functions. John Brogan, the Flyers' vice president of communications, had pushed Jay to invite Clarke to return. "I told Bob that weekend that he was welcome if he ever wanted to come back," recalls Jay. "This was his home."

The second-biggest cheer during the All-Star weekend was for a Flyer who had been with the team less than one season. Brind'Amour, the Flyers' lone representative, had also become their lone bright spot. With 20 goals and 36 assists in 44 hard-nosed games, Brind'Amour was proving to be a team cornerstone. "He's been given an opportunity here and he's really standing up and grabbing it," said Bill Dineen.

Much of the responsibility Brind'Amour seized had been intended for Ricci, whose sophomore blahs were exacerbated by the ordeal of his cancer-stricken father, Mario. Dineen tried to make the excuse of having to use Ricci in more defensive situations with Acton and Kasper still out, but the kid admitted his concentration was wavering. "Losing takes a lot of fun out of the game," Ricci told the *Inquirer's* Ray Parrillo. "My head starts to wander when I get frustrated. I can't let it get me down."

Whatever pep talks Tocchet had tried to give himself had failed. A lousy season turned worse when X-rays of a bruised heel revealed a stress fracture and took him from the lineup for 10 games. The Flyer captain, who had only 11 goals, resented the fact that too much of the blame for the season was being placed on him and he became increasingly heartened by trade rumors. "Last year I scored 40 and we still didn't make the playoffs, so I don't know what it all means," he said. "I just don't think I should be singled out as much as I have been. Let's put it this way, I won't be devastated [by a trade]."

Farwell, convinced that Tocchet was too disillusioned and too far into his prime to outlast the re-building process, hoped to accommodate his sour winger's wishes. The captain was offered in a pack-age to Quebec for Eric Lindros, who had refused to sign with the Nordiques and, after making an im-pact in the 1991 Canada Cup, was spending the sea-son playing with various Canadian national teams. Farwell, who had questioned Lindros's desire when he had refused to sign with Quebec, became con-vinced that he was the game's next great player.

Jay Snider didn't have to be convinced of the revitalizing effect a young superstar would have upon the Flyers. So at a January meeting of the NHL advisory committee, Snider approached Nordiques president Marcel Aubut about dealing the rights for Lindros. Aubut insisted, as he had to all suitors, that his team would not trade the prospect. Snider said he was going to make an offer anyway. "I wanted to show him we were serious," recalls Snider.

In consultation with Farwell, Jay had designed a proposal structured like a Chinese-food menu. From a Category A list of Tocchet, Hextall, Duchesne and Terry Carkner, Quebec could pick two players. From a Category B list, the Nordiques could also choose two of the following: the Flyers' first pick in 1992, their first pick in 1994, Kimbi Daniels, Walz, or Greg Johnson.

The Flyers would pay the Nordiques $15 million in three installments $6 million upon signing, and $4.5 million in August of the two subsequent years. If Lindros refused to sign with the Flyers, Quebec would return the $6 million, the Category B assets, plus star center Joe Sakic and goaltending prospect Stephane Fiset.

As Snider recalls, he never laid out the contin-gency plan to Aubut. But the Nordique boss lis-tened to the offer before restating that his goal was still to sign, not trade, Lindros. "I don't think [Aubut] considered it," recalls Snider. "But I think he knew we'd be a player if and when they decided to trade Lindros. In fact, I think our offer set the standard."

Howe, his broken thumb healed and his back strengthened from the additional rest, returned from a two-month absence on January 21 in Detroit, and instantly, the Flyers' oldest defenseman re-sumed being their best—a reflection upon the play of Duchesne and the kids the Flyers had been count-ing on. The Flyers trailed the Red Wings 2-1 when Dineen and Carkner took foolish penalties. Duchesne then gambled up ice and when the puck was turned over, Hextall was left alone for a suc-cessful Sergei Fedorov breakaway. Detroit tough guy

Bob Probert completed a 7-3 humiliation by taking three pokes at Hextall with his gloved fist until Huffman finally stood up for Hextall while praying for fast intervention by the linesmen.

"I didn't want help," said the enraged Hextall. "I'd have taken [Probert] myself. I'd have gotten killed, but I would have taken him.

"We played a bad hockey game. Taking penalties, making absolutely disgraceful decisions like defensemen jumping up five-on-three. It's a disgrace. If I'm the GM, I'd look at our position right now and take a long look around the room."

More lockers, indeed, needed cleaning. Jiri Latal was released, the pain in the talented Czech's left knee defying diagnosis by both Flyers' orthopedist Dr. Arthur Bartolozzi and a doctor of Latal's choosing.

Meanwhile, Eklund and Tocchet remained on the sidelines, but in a relentlessly bleak January, the in-juries did not draw as much attention as a WPVI-TV report that Bobby Clarke was coming back to the Fly-ers as team president. The station said Jay Snider would bow out to devote his full attention to building the new arena.

"It's totally ridiculous, and it's hardly worth a com-ment," an angry Jay told reporters between periods of a January 21 Spectrum game with Winnipeg. "There will always be a place for Bobby Clarke here ... [but] not to replace me and not to replace Russ Farwell either.

"I'm going to be here and I'm going to see this thing through. And I'm not going to be run out of here by anyone. Our fans are frustrated and they're taking it out on me. I can live with that. At least they're here and at least they're emotional and they care.

"It's very popular to say these days that as soon as I took over the Flyers, the thing has gone downhlll. That's not true. I got involved in 1983 and we were going downhill then. The fan base was off, we built it back up with an exciting product and had a heckuva run and we're going to do it again."

As Snider's anger grew, he sounded very much like his father had twenty-one years earlier, when a non-descript Flyer team was losing ground in the 1971 playoff race. Ed Snider had exploded at the fans and media's short-term preoccupations and insisted the goal was to win the Stanley Cup.

"We can trade away our best young guys, make the playoffs, and make everybody happy," said Jay Snider. "Or we can try to rebuild this thing for the next fifteen years.

"It's painful. I made mistakes. Everybody in the organization made them, but we've learned from them. We know the problems we have, we see the same games, but there isn't some magic wand you can wave. I'm kind of fed up with all the cheap shots. Everybody says we don't spend money. We're third from the bottom [of the standings] and we've got the ninth-highest payroll.

"We're down now and it's easy to kick us. We're trying hard. We're not a bunch of idiots here."

The Flyers, looking considerably cooler under the collar that night than their team president, were locked in a scoreless embrace with the Jets until Phil Housley banked the puck in off Hextall from behind the goal line with 3:55 remaining. The 1-0 loss dropped the Flyers' record to 14-24-9.

As the injured players came back, however, so did some hope. Acton returned on January 28, yakking and attacking and setting up Quinn's game-winning goal in a 3-2 victory over Washington. Howe, who scored twice in a 5-3 victory over Minnesota, provided his usual settling presence, causing Farwell to suggest the 36-year-old defenseman might survive the youth movement. "I don't think there's a better guy to teach people to play and to build with," the GM said.

As February began and the wrecking ball crashed into JFK Stadium, the Flyers briefly recalled Walz, who scored a goal in a 5-1 Spectrum victory over Boston, the team that had given up on him. Back-to-back Hextall victories over Quebec extended a winning streak to four games and pushed the Flyers to within six points of the slumping Penguins and a playoff spot when Pittsburgh visited the Spectrum on February 16. Tocchet, who had been back for three games, scored in the third period to create a hard-fought 3-3 tie.

Two nights later, after arriving home in the wee hours following a 4-3 overtime loss at New Jersey, Tocchet received a phone call from the Penguins' Paul Coffey, his old Canada Cup buddy. Coffey told Tocchet that they were both involved in a three-way trade that would land Tocchet in Pittsburgh and Coffey in Los Angeles.

The deal was announced the next day. The Flyers were sending Tocchet, Samuelsson, Wregget and a third-round pick in the 1993 draft to Pittsburgh for Recchi, defenseman Brian Benning and a first-round pick in the upcoming 1992 draft. The Penguins had first sent Coffey to Los Angeles for Benning, Chychrun and the first-round draft choice they were moving on to the Flyers.

"It actually started with us inquiring about Coffey," recalls Farwell. "We heard he might be avail-

able and we wanted any talent we could get."

Coffey, a greater defensive liability than ever, had gotten into the doghouse of Pittsburgh coach Scotty Bowman, who had taken over after Bob Johnson was diagnosed with what would prove to be a fatal brain tumor. A frustrated Recchi, losing ice time to the rapidly blossoming Jaromir Jagr, had exchanged angry words with the Penguin coaches. He still had 70 points in 58 games and Coffey remained the league's top offensive defenseman. But the goal-happy defending champions wanted more grit, a commodity the Kings could not provide.

"Rogie [Vachon] offered that if he could get Coffey, then he would give up Benning and the number one," recalls Farwell. "Samuelsson came into it on the last day." The Flyer GM hoped Benning, 25, would be a passable substitute for Samuelsson, still an effective player but at 32 too old to fit Philadelphia's long-range plans.

The Flyers, who maintained an outside shot at a playoff spot, were helping one of the teams they were chasing. Nevertheless, they were making the same Recchi-for-Tocchet exchange they had wanted the previous summer.

In the exchange of right wings, the Flyers were gaining four years and considerable playmaking ability while clearing the locker room of an unproductive, alienated captain. They were also picking up a second first-round pick in the upcoming draft, while making room to give Roussel a substantial trial in goal.

"Recchi is a legitimate 100-point scorer, something the Flyers haven't had in a long time," Farwell told the media. "Sure, trading within your division is not done much, but maybe I haven't caught on to that."

Recchi although frustrated never wanted to be traded. After hearing of the deal from Rick Curran, Recchi told reporters he was "really shocked and a little upset." But he says he never was depressed about leaving a contender for a team facing a long rebuilding process. "I was excited about it," he recalls. "I thought a lot of the organization and I knew I'd get to play a lot."

When he joined the Flyers for practice the next day, Recchi was surprised to see how much harder they worked than the team he left behind. The workout was crisp and the atmosphere rejuvenating, now that the unhappy Tocchet was gone. "Morale was pretty ugly the first few months I was here," recalls Kevin Dineen. "There were guys on the team who had come to feel the way I had at the end in Hartford. They wanted to leave."

Recchi, too, was encouraged by how excited his new teammates seemed about acquiring him. "They weren't acting like a team that was out of the playoffs," he recalls. "I remember looking at Hexy before my first game [February 22 in Landover]. I'd never seen anyone psych himself up like that."

Recchi's first shot as a Flyer beat the glove of Washington goalie Don Beaupre. In the second period, Recchi's breakaway goal tied the game, 3-3. "I remember him making a play out of the corner that right away told me we did the right thing," recalls Bill Dineen.

Nevertheless, two giveaways by Hextall helped send the Flyers down to a 7-5 loss, causing the coach to try Roussel the following night in New York. The rookie's superb 35-save effort was ruined on a third-period goal by Tony Amonte that gave the Rangers a 2-1 victory.

Roussel bounced back with two victories over the Islanders, then a shutout at Calgary. Hextall followed by blanking the Sharks at the Cow Palace. Recchi, the Flyers' most creative playmaker since Clarke, had rekindled a spark in Ricci. Brind'Amour became an effective complement for Kevin Dineen, and a checking line of Acton, Claude Boivin and Al Conroy, a 5-foot-8 free-agent signee recalled from Hershey in late January, provided spunk. Pittsburgh, thanks in part to a revitalized Tocchet, had pulled away from the Flyers in the standings, but as playoff hopes evaporated for a third straight season, there were signs of improvement.

Howe, able to play 17 of the last 21 games, made his usual, huge difference. On March 18, his perfect goalmouth pass set up Pederson's second game-winner at the Montreal Forum that season. Two nights later, Howe sprung Recchi for a breakaway goal that completed a spirited comeback from a third-period three-goal deficit at Landover. The Flyers' 7-6 victory against the Caps was their first divisional win on the road in 19 tries over two seasons.

Behind Roussel, the Flyers rallied for a 4-3 Spectrum victory over Detroit that pushed a winning streak to five games, three of which were against divisional leaders. As the Flyers took the ice in Pittsburgh in the final hours before a threatened April 1 strike by the players, the team was an encouraging 16-8-2 since January 25.

Tocchet, playing with a broken jaw, said he hoped to beat his ex-mates by "10 goals" when he faced them for the first time. He settled for one-goal margin in a come-from-behind 6-5 Pittsburgh victory.

"We're more of a team now than when *he* was here," huffed Galley, but most NHL players were holding deeper grudges against management.

Having played all season without a collective bargaining agreement, disturbed by perceived restrictions on free agency and angered at the owner's insistence on obtaining a share of rapidly escalating royalties for trading cards and other forms of licensing, the players carried out their threat and struck the next morning.

With talks broken off and no new ones scheduled before the league's April 9 deadline for cancellation of the playoffs, the postseason seemed doomed. But several influential player agents relieved some of the concerns of several high-profile players, who feared they were setting themselves up for a lockout if they agreed to a proposed contract the owners were insisting upon that would expire at the conclusion of the following season.

Negotiations secretly resumed the morning of the 3 P.M. final deadline. The two sides agreed on a formula for dividing the card money and the players gained some liberalizations of the free-agency compensation formula. An agreement, which would expire at the end of the 1992-93 season, was struck at 11:45 P.M. on Friday, April 10, the 11th day of the strike.

Carkner, the Flyer player representative, recalled the troops, many of whom had gone home in anticipation of the season's cancellation. All but four of the Flyers were on the ice by the end of an afternoon workout the day after the settlement and the next night the Flyers lost the first of their three rescheduled games, 4-2 in Hartford. They beat Toronto 6-2 and closed the season with a 4-3 overtime loss to the Whalers at the Spectrum.

The Flyers, 24-23-9 after Holmgren's firing, achieved one less victory and point than they had the previous season. Nevertheless, there was no question they had become a younger and better offensive team. Only four of the twenty players who had dressed for the final game the previous April remained, rendering laughable the preliminary assessment of Farwell as a do-nothing. Recchi had 27 points in his 22 Flyer games and Brind'Amour, who won the Bobby Clarke Trophy, and Ricci were two centers the team could grow around. "We were really positive about what was happening," recalls Farwell.

But he was also realistic. Size, grit and depth were still lacking, and though Duchesne's performance had improved over the second half, his refusal to play the game according to the clock and score had all but convinced Farwell the defenseman wasn't worth anywhere near the $1 million a year he would seek when his contract expired over the summer. The Flyers, despite their efforts to rebuild, were still dependent on the 36-year-old Howe's presence in the lineup. They were a respectable 21-18-3, when Howe played, and a poor 11-19-8, when he did not. It indicated they had made little progress in rebuilding their backline.

The players believed they could compete for a playoff spot in 1992-93, but the Flyers were still far from being Stanley Cup contenders. The organization had worked hard with season-ticket relocations and innovative pitches to maintain its fan base and had not suffered more than 750 empty seats at any home game during the 1991-92 season. Still, the Spectrum had been sold out for only 11 of the 40 dates and management feared the recession and a third straight failure to qualify for the playoffs made an attendance slide inevitable.

Only the acquisition of a dominating offensive player, a commodity the team had not possessed since Clarke's heyday, could immediately arrest the ticket drain and help sell the suites for Spectrum II. Lindros was still waiting to be traded and the Flyers had the cash to obtain and pay him. But how many of the building blocks already in place would have to be sacrificed in a deal to obtain the league's next dominating player? And how long would it then take to reassemble a winning team?

Chapter 11

◆◆◆

The Second Coming

A year after drafting him No. 1 overall, the Nordiques had reluctantly concluded they could not sign Eric Lindros. "The family said from the very beginning he would never play for Quebec," recalls Pierre Page, the GM who made the selection in the 1991 draft. "I'm sure we said some things after drafting him that offended them, too, but that didn't really matter. Their minds were already made up.

"They had worked very hard all those years to make the kid into a marketing giant and then he gets drafted by a small market. With the possibility of the province's separation [from Canada], they also wanted a place [that was] not as controversial. "Marcel [Nordique president Aubut] felt the deadline to trade Lindros would be the [1992] draft. A lot of teams wouldn't want to give up too many players to get one, so draft choices would be a critical part of the deal."

Because an unsigned Lindros would reenter the pool for the 1993 draft, Quebec would lose leverage by extending the auction into a second year. A fifth consecutive last-place finish in the Adams Division had also intensified a desire to start moving up in the

standings. The Nordiques had been collecting promising players with high first-round picks, but the team was still a big loser.

"We were way too young," recalls Page. "We had to get some veterans who could help us right away. But we also had to get young guys and draft picks who would counterbalance Lindros when he became a star for ten years. We studied the Minnesota-Dallas trade and how it had enabled Dallas to rebuild in a short time."

In 1991, the NFL Cowboys had acquired five Vikings and eight draft choices in the first three rounds for running back Herschel Walker and four late-round picks.

Jay Snider's first pitch to Aubut in January included Rick Tocchet, who had subsequently been moved. But that three-way trade had also netted the Flyers Los Angeles's No. 1 pick, which gave Snider and Russ Farwell the seventh and fifteenth selections in the 1992 draft to include in a revised offer.

The Flyers had become a younger and more promising team through a tumultuous 1991-92 season and had reason to believe they could return to the playoffs in 1993. But Ed and Jay Snider

As far as Nordique president Marcel Aubut was concerned, draft choices would be a critical part of any deal for Lindros.

wanted more than incremental improvement. They desired a contender built around a marquee player.

"We had gotten back to the finals a number of times and didn't win because we didn't have the best player," Jay Snider recalls. "The dynasties had the superstar, and we had not had one in a long time. This looked like a unique opportunity."

In snubbing Quebec, the Lindroses were making their second stand against the hockey establishment. In 1989, the London, Ontario-born and Toronto-bred wunderkind had refused the draft of the OHL Sault Ste. Marie Greyhounds because the family was concerned Lindros's education would suffer while travelling to and from the junior league's most remote franchise.

He played half the 1989-90 season in a Detroit Tier II league before his rights were traded to Oshawa, where in 1990-91, the 6--4, 229-pound center scored 149 points in only 57 games, leading the Generals to the Memorial Cup championship.

Farwell had believed Lindros was playing hard-to-get to extract more money from the Nordiques. But as the 19-year-old played the 1991-92 season with various Canadian national teams, he reinforced both the family's resolve to stay out of Quebec, as well as the virtual certainty of his making an immediate impact in the NHL.

"He did so well playing against the very best guys at the [1991] Canada Cup that I no longer had any doubts about what kind of player he was," recalls Farwell. "As far as what kind of kid he was, it was a big problem trying to sort out the reputation from the guy. Getting to a comfort level about going after him was really difficult.

"Bill Dineen knew [Oshawa coach] Rick Cornacchia a little bit and [Cornacchia] had good things to say. But we talked to everybody we could think of. The pattern was that people who had casual or more distant contact with the kid didn't have very good things to say about him. From the people who knew him well, all you would hear were good things."

Jay Snider also worried about rebuilding around a player who had been labeled as selfish and arrogant. "But the more we asked around about him, the more it seemed the negative stuff was coming from people who were envious," recalls Snider. "What convinced me was how badly Mike Keenan wanted him. Mike was the only guy in the NHL who had actually coached Lindros [for Team Canada in the Canada Cup]."

Keenan, who had coached the Blackhawks to the 1992 Stanley Cup finals, had two superstars, Jeremy

Roenick and Chris Chelios, and any club willing to offer a young, elite veteran of their caliber, a commodity the Flyers did not possess, figured to blow Philadelphia out of the bidding.

"I remember right before the trading deadline, when I had all my various options on my board in my office and Mr. [Ed] Snider was in there and started talking about Lindros," recalls Farwell. "We named the teams that could afford him and then went down the list.

"The Rangers were close to a Cup and wouldn't want to break up their team. Same with Chicago and Detroit. We had no reason to be reluctant. From the beginning Mr. Snider said, 'We have the best chance.'"

The Nordiques had already collected a cadre of talented offensive forwards like Joe Sakic, Mats Sundin, Owen Nolan and Valery Kamensky. To begin winning, Quebec needed goaltending, grit and defense.

"We had been told that Pierre Page really liked Ricci," recalls Farwell. "We had a name goalie in Hextall. We had an offensive defenseman [Steve Duchesne] who was French-Canadian and might be attractive to Quebec. And we had two first-round picks.

"We figured Ricci would have to be in it. But we decided very early on that we weren't going to trade Recchi or Brind'Amour. It was one thing to take a step back and rebuild around a superstar. It was another to bring Lindros into a hopeless situation for years and years. We felt good about the way we were playing at the end of the season. In fact, if Peter Forsberg had been coming to play for us in the fall, we might not have gone after Lindros at all."

Forsberg, Philadelphia's second-guessed sixth-overall pick in 1991, had blossomed into the world's top player outside of the NHL. In April, Farwell and Jay Snider had spoken to the 19-year-old center and his father at the World Championships in Prague.

"We told them we thought he could play in the NHL the next season, but after thinking it over for a week, they decided he wasn't ready to come," recalls Farwell. "If he was, we would have been looking at a center ice of Brind'Amour, Ricci and Forsberg, a pretty good group to build around. Without Forsberg, it became just Ricci and Brind'Amour and we didn't want to go that way for another year."

While the Sniders debated the wisdom of tearing up a nucleus for the second time in two summers, they had reason to feel the organization was again whole. On June 10, 1992, Bobby Clarke came home. The Flyers announced his appointment as senior vice president during a media luncheon at the Society Hill Sheraton.

"I had gotten together in Los Angeles with Mr. Snider when I was out there with the North Stars," recalls Clarke. "And I knew he was sincere in his desire to have me back. So I asked if he still wanted me.

"He was concerned about tampering, but I thought it was okay because I would be leaving the North Stars for a lesser position with the Flyers. I wasn't going to be president or general manager if I came back.

"I made it clear I didn't want to take anybody's job. Russ would be in charge and I would do things for him and the Flyers. [Jay and Ed] both thought there would be lots to do. So did I.

"I explained my feelings to Mr. Green [North Stars' owner Norm]. He said he had seen the way I was greeted [in Philadelphia] during All-Star Weekend and understood.

"I liked managing, but I had gotten frustrated dealing with people who had no interest in the game whatsoever," recalls Clarke. "A guy like Ron Simon [the agent who had instructed North Star goaltender Jon Casey to walk out prior to a game as a renegotiation ploy] leeches off the sport. He just takes money from it.

"But getting the family back home had become the most important thing to me. We met lots of nice people in Minnesota, but I didn't like the climate very much and never really made the commitment to live there. I had gone for the work. I had never sold my [Moorestown, New Jersey] house, although we probably would have if a good offer had come along. It just seemed right to come back."

Clarke, whose GM duties were given to North Star coach Bob Gainey, returned with a small share of ownership in the Flyers and the belief that if his wife and children were content, he would be, too. "You'll never know how happy this makes me and my family," Clarke told reporters after Jay had declared off-limits any questions about their 1990 breakup. The new vice president would begin his duties after conducting Minnesota's draft on June 20 in Montreal.

As D-Day for Lindros approached, Farwell did not publicly deny the Flyers' interest. "I think he's going to have an impact on the game," the GM told reporters during a press get-together at Downey's. "Just like Gretzky and Lemieux made kids want to pivot, Lindros might make kids want to run people over.

"We're following it, but we don't know yet what the price would be."

They endeavored to find out. On June 11, one day after Farwell had attended the Toronto funeral of Mario Ricci, Mike's father, Snider and Farwell flew to Quebec City.

While a chef prepared dinner in a Colisee entertaining room, Aubut cooked up a blockbuster deal on a chalkboard. In addition to an as-yet unspecified amount of cash, Aubut wanted Ricci, Brind'Amour, Ron Hextall, Duchesne, Kerry Huffman, first-round picks in 1992, 1993 and 1994 and either Forsberg or another prospect, Viacheslav Butsayev.

The Nordique boss also wanted options on several other trades: Flyer winger Claude Boivin for winger Herb Raglan, Flyer defenseman Dan Kordic for defenseman Steven Finn, and winger Chris Simon for a choice of ten lesser Nordique prospects.

Snider, Farwell, Aubut and Page discussed other Nordiques, such as defenseman Mikhail Tatarinov, whom Aubut thought might represent value for Huffman, and winger Andrei Kovalenko, the Flyer GM's suggestion of fair exchange for Simon and Boivin.

As each combination came up for discussion, Farwell and Snider drew up hypothetical depth charts. They played with lineups that included not only Lindros, but two free agents, Teemu Selanne and Vincent Damphousse, whom the Flyers were toying with trying to sign.

Realistically, the millions it would take to obtain and pay for Lindros prevented any other massive expenditures. Thus, Farwell and Snider continued to feel Brind'Amour had to be retained. The Flyers also believed the price for Lindros would be so high that any deal would have to be contingent upon his signing a contract. There was also reason to believe the Lindroses were not keen on Philadelphia.

"I had been calling Rick Curran [Lindros's agent] pretty regularly to find out what was going on and to build a relationship," recalls Farwell. "We talked about other things, too, but at one point he had told me that Eric didn't want to come here. Rick didn't say why and we didn't back off, but we felt it was necessary to talk to the kid before we agreed to any deal."

Indeed, the agent had been instructed to do what he could to keep Eric out of Philadelphia. "I was never really told why," recalls Curran, "other than they preferred him playing in a couple of other places.

"I've had my own feelings as to why they felt that way. But except for me to say that it didn't have anything to do with the Flyers, I have to keep my feelings to myself."

In truth, Curran had fallen into disfavor with the Lindros family, which was wary of the agent's recent relocation from Toronto to Philadelphia's Main Line (where Curran's wife had grown up), and feared the agent had too cozy a relationship with the Flyers.

Curran followed instructions and tried to scare the Flyers off. "I had a telephone conversation with Jay in which I told him I had become aware of some recent conversations between him and the Nordiques," recalls Curran. "I begged him not to pursue Eric's rights and said that if the Flyers were to continue, I wasn't sure they had enough money to sign him.

"Jay was perturbed that I was trying to tell him what to do and he didn't give me any assurances. In the meantime, I was trying hard to maintain confidentiality for my client, so I didn't tell Jay why I was trying to discourage him."

Snider does not recall being angry, only concerned. He had no way of accurately gauging the intensity of Lindros's resolve not to land at the Spectrum and was determined to hear his desires first hand. This would create a potential major procedural problem. Under NHL bylaws, a team not holding a player's rights is prohibited from contact with either that player or his representative without prior written permission from the club holding his rights.

During their meeting in Quebec City, Snider and Farwell asked Aubut for permission to speak to Lindros. The Nordique president said he would allow it only after the two teams struck a deal.

Farwell went back to the hotel pessimistic about the Flyers' chances. Aubut was insistent not only on Brind'Amour, but three first-round draft picks. Snider was as uncomfortable as his GM with the concept of giving up any more than two. But Jay still held out hope Quebec would eventually lower its asking price. "He was much more optimistic than anyone else at that stage," recalls Farwell.

Before leaving Quebec City the next afternoon, Snider and Farwell informed Aubut the Flyers would not give up Brind'Amour or more than two first-rounders. The GM put the deal on the back burner in favor of draft preparations.

In a seller's market, Aubut had no need to chase buyers. It was Jay who initiated the next contact five days later, on Tuesday, June 16. Snider called the Nordique boss and set up a meeting for Thursday, when he would be arriving in Montreal for Saturday's draft.

When Snider landed, he went to the headquarters Farwell had established in Suite 2818 of the Radisson Grand and phoned Aubut. The Flyer president was invited to Quebec's suite on the fifth floor.

"There was a security guy right at the elevator and you had to be announced," recalls Jay. "Then, you walked into what looked like the East Wing of the White House.

"There was a big room with secretaries, computers, desks and two lawyers. There were five people working there. On the left, there was a formal conference chamber. On the right was another big meeting room which was just for Marcel and Page.

"Then there was another bedroom with a desk where Marcel was staying. That's where we met with him. He gave me a printed card with all their portable phone numbers on it. There was a diagram, a floor plan, and an administrative overview of how they would conduct the negotiations.

"I thought I would shmooze him, so I told him how impressed I was and that the Flyers would have to look at something like this. And I asked him if we were still in the bidding for Lindros and he said, 'Yes.'"

Ten of the NHL's twenty-four teams had indicated their interest to Quebec, but according to Page, five dropped out before arriving in Montreal. Detroit had turned down a Quebec demand of money, center Sergei Fedorov, defensemen Nicklas Lidstrom and Steve Chiasson, winger Martin Lapointe, goalie Tim Cheveldae and draft picks. The Red Wings had not made a counteroffer.

Calgary had posed a package including cash, draft choices, goalie Mike Vernon, defensemen Al MacInnis or Gary Suter, plus either of forwards Robert Reichel or Joe Nieuwendyk. The Flames dropped out when Quebec asked for still more.

"Montreal was close at one time, but when we asked for one more player, they said, 'Forget it,' and that was it," recalls Page. "New Jersey wanted Lindros, but it really wanted not to give up anything. By Friday, it was pretty well down to four teams — the Rangers, Blackhawks, Leafs and Flyers."

Philadelphia was making intelligent guesses as to who was in the bidding and what was being offered. "Even before we got [to the draft], we thought we had a fair idea," recalls Farwell. "[Flyer scout] Simon Nolet lived in Quebec and he would read us the speculation in the Quebec papers. What one of them reported about our offer was almost exactly right, so we believed that paper was pretty accurate about the other offers."

"We thought all along the Rangers would be the

strongest competition," recalls Snider. "They had a good veteran goalie [John Vanbiesbrouck], plus good prospects and unlimited cash. We knew Keenan wanted Lindros badly and was prepared to offer just about anybody but Roenick. But [Chicago owner] Bill Wirtz had told us that he wasn't going to pay any cash and we believed him. That just isn't Chicago's style."

The negotiations began in earnest. Aubut and Page again asked for Brind'Amour and wanted Forsberg, too. Snider and Farwell pushed Forsberg alone and the Nordiques replied they did not consider the unproven prospect adequate compensation. "We had to sell like hell to convince them that Forsberg carried that kind of value," recalls Farwell. "Pierre later made comments that Philadelphia didn't know how good Forsberg was, but that was the exact opposite of what really happened."

Page says he was well aware of the Swede's potential. "We were trying to downplay his value because we wanted other players," he recalls. "It was all part of the negotiating posture."

As Ed Snider–due in Montreal Saturday night for a Sunday NHL board of governors meeting–stayed in touch by phone from his Montecito, California home, the Flyers and Nordiques traded various proposals. Quebec continued to insist on three No. 1 picks. "We asked that of every team we talked to," recalls Page.

Ricci, Hextall and Duchesne were involved in virtually every offer exchanged. Quebec also asked for winger Boivin and Huffman. The potential loss of Duchesne, Huffman and Mark Howe, a free agent, would wipe out half the Philadelphia defense. If the Nordiques were insisting on three No. 1's, Farwell wanted 25 year-old blueliner Steven Finn and second rounders back.

Quebec wouldn't budge, so the Flyers proposed a scaled-down deal that would have sent Ricci, Hextall, Duchesne, Huffman and Forsberg, their top 1992 pick seventh overall plus their first pick in 1994 for Lindros and Finn. They were turned down again. "We were not going to move Finn," recalls Page. "He was a character guy. And we weren't ahead if we traded what little defense we had."

Snider and Farwell countered by substituting the second of their two first-round picks the next day, fifteenth overall, for Forsberg. That would give Quebec its desired three No. 1's but enable the Flyers to keep the Swedish prospect. But Aubut wanted Forsberg *and* all three picks.

After practically every Quebec demand, Farwell

and Snider would go around the suite asking opinions of the scouts as well as Keith Allen, Bill Dineen, director of pro scouting Bill Barber and chief operating officer Ron Ryan.

"We kept debating the size of this thing," recalls Jay. "Were we getting in too deep? Were we out of our minds? Not only did I wonder whether we could afford it financially, but could we recover from the loss of so many players? We had a lot of second thoughts.

"While this was going on, we were still running around getting opinions on what kind of a kid Lindros was. And Russ and the scouts still had to prepare for a draft the next day. It was frantic. We agonized every step along the way."

The Flyers' competition was wrestling with the same dilemmas. Keenan had dangled two All-Stars–goalie Ed Belfour and winger Steve Larmer–plus defenseman Steve Smith in a five-player, seven-pick offer. In return, Chicago would get not only Lindros, but three Quebec choices, including a 1992 first-rounder, fourth overall, which Keenan planned to use the next day on highly regarded Lithuanian defensive prospect, Darius Kasparaitis.

"Marcel told me he liked our player offer best and would do the deal for $5 million," recalls Keenan. "But Wirtz said no. He didn't want to pay Lindros what he would have wanted, either."

Keenan, hoping his owner would change his mind, kept working through Friday night. So did the Leafs, who made a better offer than Snider believed possible. "Toronto had the cash, but we didn't see how it could have the players," Jay recalls. Still, GM Cliff Fletcher's package included superior goaltending prospect Felix Potvin, winger Wendel Clark, defenseman Dave Ellett, former Flyer tough guy Craig Berube, multiple first-round draft choices and $15 million. Quebec, however, continued to insist on the inclusion of Doug Gilmour, the Leafs' star center.

Meanwhile, Ranger GM Neil Smith remained willing to part with three first-round picks, which is why the Nordiques kept insisting on getting the same amount from every club with which they bartered. Snider and Farwell continued to believe that every offer Quebec received would be weighed against the anticipated ultimate package from New York.

"In [Aubut's] mind, he thought we were never going to be the team because Lindros wouldn't come here," recalls Farwell. "But he wanted to keep us alive because he thought he could use us to get more out of the Rangers in the end."

Despite their suspicions, the Flyers had no hard evidence of any bad-faith bargaining by Aubut, nor any concrete confirmation that they would be rejected by the Lindroses. So they, too, bartered on through Friday evening, haggling over draft picks and players.

The Nordiques were holding firm on Finn, so Philadelphia tried offering draft picks in alternating years. Quebec continued to want them consecutively, but would reduce its demand to two No. 1 choices if the Flyers would include Forsberg and receive Lindros only.

Jay, on the advice of his father, reduced the $15-million offer to $5 million. "We did it to change the psychology of the negotiations," recalls Jay. "They were always asking for more, more, but now we were derailing that process by suddenly offering less."

Aubut called Ed Snider in Montecito. "Eddie, you have to put the money back," the Quebec president pleaded. "You can't afford to let this guy go to the Rangers. You know what that will do to the league salaries?"

Ed Snider said he would discuss the matter with his son.

More than four hours passed without any contact between the Flyers and Nordiques. Jay, assuming final bargaining would take place in the late morning before the noon draft, left the Philadelphia suite just before 1 A.M. and returned to his room. He had just climbed into bed and turned off the lights when the phone rang.

"It's Marcel," said the voice on the line. "Could I come up?"

Five minutes later, Aubut was at the door. He sat down and pulled out a piece of paper. "This is the deal we'll do," he said.

Snider looked at Aubut's note. On it was Ricci, Hextall, Duchesne, Forsberg, Huffman, the Flyers' seventh overall pick the next day, their No. 1 in 1993 and $15 million.

Snider remembers thinking that after almost thirty-six hours of haggling, this deal was awfully close to the one he had come to Montreal prepared to make. The team president's pulse quickened, but he kept his poker face. He told Aubut he still didn't know whether the Flyers could go as high as $15 million, but that he would call his father.

"I was tired and I wanted to sleep on it," recalls Jay. As soon as Aubut left, Jay called Farwell to his room and together, they called Ed. He agreed they should decide in the morning.

Aubut and Page, however, had hardly retired for the night. "Marcel had gone to Jay's room because he got nervous when the Rangers weren't agreeing

to what he wanted," recalls Page. While Snider and Farwell slept, the Nordique GM and his boss had meetings with Keenan, Smith and Fletcher. "At one point Toronto said yes to what we wanted," recalls Page, "but [Fletcher] almost immediately had second thoughts. He said, 'No, we can't do that.'"

So Toronto was out. Keenan, refusing to take Wirtz's no for an answer, continued trying to find a way to make a trade work without cash. "Chicago was offering more [in players and picks] than the Rangers but no money," recalls Page. "The Rangers' offer had four players and the [three] draft choices, but at 4:30 A.M. we told them what we wanted and said to Neil we would meet again with him at 7:30. I thought the Flyers were out of it. I liked the other deals better."

Smith, still unhappy with Quebec's terms, did not show up for his scheduled 7:30 A.M. meeting with Aubut. Farwell, meanwhile, awoke before 8 A.M. and went back to Snider's room. The two men reviewed their positions on the need to speak to the Lindros family, spreading the two draft choices over three years, and once more, whether they should do the deal at all.

When Snider telephoned Aubut at 9:30 A.M. he did not know that Keenan was in the Nordique suite.

Jay tried again to get Quebec to take less than $15 million and to space out the picks, but Aubut wouldn't budge. The list he had presented Jay at 1 A.M. was the deal, take it or leave it. And Jay was thinking he could take it.

"When I hung up, I realized this was it," recalls Snider. "We could actually have Lindros if we wanted him."

He walked into the living room of the suite, where the braintrust–Farwell, Keith Allen, Jerry Melnyk, Bill Barber, Bill Dineen, Inge Hammarstrom, John Blackwell and Simon Nolet–had assembled for a final pre-draft meeting.

"Nobody was exactly jumping forward with their opinion," recalls Snider. So he polled everyone individually.

Allen spoke about how long it had been since the Flyers had a bona fide superstar and what one could mean to the franchise. Dineen, who had coached Ricci and had scouted both Lindros and Forsberg before becoming coach, gave his positive endorsement. "In my mind, Bill was the key guy," recalls Farwell. "He knew the players involved the best."

Hammarstrom, the European scout who had pushed the Flyers to draft Forsberg, was too choked up at the thought of losing him to say yes. But

Hammarstrom didn't plead against the deal, nor did any one else. "They couldn't speak to the money part, but it was all but unanimous that player wise, they would do it," recalls Jay. "When we analyzed it, it really came down to two players, Ricci and Forsberg.

"The three other guys were all assets, NHL players, but they didn't look irreplaceable. We thought we had two young goalies [Dominic Roussel and Tommy Soderstrom]. Huffman was coming off a good year, but we didn't think he was going to get any better.

"There was a lot of agonizing over Ricci. He's a great kid, a great asset, and his father had just died, making the timing unfortunate. But he was a deal point on their side all along. And when we looked at a center ice of Lindros, Brind'Amour and [Viacheslav] Butsayev, who we were really high on, we could give up Ricci and still have three big, young, talented players at the position."

So, at 10:30 A.M., Snider called Aubut and said the Flyers would do the deal as he wanted it. Jay asked if the $15 million could be paid in four installments rather than three. Aubut said he would consider that schedule if the money was "actualized." Snider assumed that meant paying interest and thought that could be arranged.

With ninety minutes remaining before the start of the draft, the two men discussed the loose ends that had to be tied together. The Flyers still had not talked to Lindros, let alone negotiated a contract, making it impossible to announce the deal before the first round's seventh pick came up in less than three hours.

The most expedient way to transfer the choice would be for the Flyers to select the player the Nordiques desired, then transfer him along with the other assets when the deal could finally be announced. Aubut repeated a suggestion he had made earlier: Page could give Farwell prearranged cues so that he would know who the Nordiques wanted. Snider agreed. He then asked Aubut for the Lindroses' telephone number. Aubut said he would get it and call Snider back.

"Does that mean we have a deal?" Snider recalls asking into the phone.

"I was across the coffee table," recalls Farwell, "and I remember Jay's hand pumping: 'Do we have a deal? Do we have a deal?'"

"And the answer was, 'Yeah,'" recalls Snider.

He hung up, walked back into the living room, and informed the assembled aides that Aubut was getting the number. There were nods and smiles, but no reason to celebrate until Lindros said he was willing to become a Flyer.

While he waited, Snider told his GM to call Page and work out the mechanism for making the seventh selection. Farwell dialed and asked for his counterpart. Whoever answered the phone hung up. "I phoned again and they said Pierre would call back," recalls Farwell. "But I had to try a third time before I finally got him.

"He said they had eight players identified and that we picked seventh so they were sure of getting somebody they would want. He said it was no problem and we could work it out on the [draft] floor. I said I didn't think it was quite that simple, but that was how he was prepared to leave it until we got over [to the Forum]."

Meanwhile, as 15 minutes turned to 20, then to 25, Jay was wondering what was taking Aubut so long. "What the hell are those guys doing?" he wondered. "Why are they being so casual?"

Thirty minutes went by. Sylvan Tobin, the Flyers' minority owner, came into the suite. "I wonder what the hell Marcel is doing?" Tobin said. "I just saw him get off the elevator and go to the Chicago suite."

Snider and Farwell looked at each other. "I can't say I was suspicious," recalls Jay, "but I was agitated. The draft was starting in less than an hour."

Aubut, who did not have the phone number, went to Curran's room at the Radisson at 11:20 A.M.

"I need you to call the family," the Quebec president said.

"Who is it?" the agent asked.

"Philadelphia."

Curran was crestfallen. "How the hell could it be Philadelphia?" said Curran.

"Because they had the best offer," said Aubut. "I need you to call the family. I need to know if they will report and that they will do a contract longer than one-plus-one [years]. Please do this right away and call me."

"You can stay," said Curran. "There's nothing to hide."

"I have to go back to my room," said Aubut. "Call me."

The agent, cringing before what he was convinced would be a negative reaction, dialed the Lindros cottage on Georgian Bay, two hours north of Toronto. Eric's father, Carl, answered.

"You're not going to believe this," said Curran. He relayed the news, then Aubut's questions about Eric's willingness to come to Philadelphia on a long-term deal.

The elder Lindros was more dumbfounded than dismayed. "Rick, that doesn't make any sense," he said. He asked Curran to call back in five minutes.

"The three of us, Eric, Bonnie and I, were in a bedroom that is about eight by twelve, all sitting on the bed," recalls Carl. "We were really surprised. There had been no indication the Flyers were in the circle of teams.

"We had directed Rick on Friday morning to tell all the teams we thought were in the hunt that we could not make a long-term commitment. But we did that to put leverage on Marcel to make a deal. Any club would want to talk to us before making a trade and, of course, we wanted to talk to them. From our perceived track record, I'm sure a lot of teams were thinking we were loony enough to do anything.

"I don't want to go into our reservations at that time about Philadelphia. It had nothing to do with the Flyers."

Eric answered when Curran called back five minutes later. "If you don't want it," Curran told his client, "say no. I gotta believe he has a backup."

"What if he doesn't?" asked Eric. He said he would call Curran back. "We've waited a year," the 19-year-old said. "They can wait another five minutes."

The family huddled. Eric, who had been in limbo for virtually a year, wanted to play, and his father had already decided to involve himself in the contract negotiations, lessening their concerns about the supposed relationship between Curran and the Flyers. But they were suspicious, Philadelphia was being used to raise another team's offer. They wanted direct confirmation from the Flyers that they had made a deal.

"We figured we had nothing to lose by talking to them," recalls Eric. When Curran called back the second time, they told the agent to provide the number.

It was 11:33 A.M. when Aubut finally phoned Jay and provided the number. Farwell got on the extension in the suite's bedroom while Snider dialed the cottage.

Carl answered. He exchanged pleasantries with Jay before Snider quickly got to the point: Would Eric play in Philadelphia?

The father said yes, provided the contract was satisfactory. Snider then asked if the Lindroses would be agreeable to a long-term deal.

"My response was that we perceived Eric will play at or above the level of play of [the Rangers'] Mark Messier, and that he should earn a comparable amount of money," Carl recalls saying. "If the Flyers

were willing to pay that, then I said we could sort out a long-term agreement."

Snider's recollection was that Messier made about $1.5 million a year. "That's something we could do," Jay told Carl before the phone was passed down the bed to Eric.

"Who are you trading?" Eric asked Snider and Farwell. "What's left?" Eric asked about his Canadian national junior teammate Ricci, whom Jay conceded was in the trade, and about Brind'Amour, who was not. More than anything, however, Eric wanted reassurance that the ordeal really was over. "Is it definite?" he asked.

Jay hesitated, not wanting to immediately tell Lindros that the Flyers still considered the transaction conditional to his signing a contract. The kid picked up on Snider's waffling and pressed for an answer. "There are just some minor things," Jay said.

He could hear Mom in the background. "Are you a Flyer?" Bonnie asked sweetly. "I hope so," Eric said.

"My bags are packed," he told Snider and Farwell.

Eric passed the phone back down the bed to Carl, who stipulated that he had to be present before any negotiations were to begin with Curran. Snider didn't understand why, but certainly didn't see it as a problem. He was still talking to the Lindroses when Aubut appeared at the door of the suite.

The Nordique president's shirt tail was out, his breath short, his face flushed, and his arms apart in the wordless question, "What's going on?" Snider smiled and flashed the thumbs-up sign. Aubut ran back down the hall.

When Jay hung up, he was ecstatic. "We could do a deal," he recalls thinking. "I felt like a million dollars."

That feeling was almost matched by the Lindroses. "Something had finally happened," recalls Carl. "We were bubbling." Still, Eric remained unconvinced. "I hoped it was done," he recalls, "but I wasn't positive."

Since the Lindroses' cottage, accessible only by water, had no cable television or satellite dish, Bonnie, Eric, his brother Brett and sister Robin were going to a neighbor's house to watch the draft. As they got in the boat and started the motor, Eric's grandmother called. She had heard on television that Eric had been acquired by Chicago. Carl yelled the information down to the boat before it sped away.

Meanwhile, the Philadelphia suite was awash in handshakes, cheers and backslaps. There was no time for a prolonged celebration, however. The draft would start in ten minutes. Farwell, Allen, Blackwell, Barber and the scouts ran to grab cabs for the Forum. Sylvan Tobin took a call in the adjoining room from Ed Snider, who was already on the Spectacor plane headed for Montreal, and relayed the good news.

Jay Snider had too many loose ends to tie up with Aubut to have time to talk with his father. There had been little time to ponder the logistics of the contract negotiations or how long they might delay the trade announcement, but as Snider and Ryan rode the elevator down to the Quebec floor, the Flyer president was feeling so good about his conversation with the Lindroses that he was thinking forty-eight hours would be sufficient to get a deal done.

Jay and Ryan stepped off the elevator into a resounding and eerie silence.

"I expected to see people happy and shaking hands," Jay recalls. "Instead, we were stopped by the guard and escorted to the holding room."

While they waited, what at first seemed strange began to feel troubling. "We smelled a rat now," recalls Ryan.

Finally, an agitated Aubut appeared. He began speaking about his "board" not being willing to go along with the Flyers' condition that they would have to sign Lindros. Since this was the first time he had mentioned anything about needing any board approval, Snider was annoyed. Just at the point where everything was coming together, here came a curveball.

"If Aubut had calmly explained his problem with the condition, then I would have been willing to work with him," Jay recalls. "But at that point I wasn't going to change anything."

Still, he didn't immediately refuse, saying only that he would have to talk to his people. As Snider and Ryan started back for the elevator. Aubut grabbed the arm of Ryan, an old associate from their days together in the WHA. "Ronnie, you have to get them to drop that condition," pleaded the Quebec boss.

Back in the Flyers' suite, Snider's mood was sinking. Something was clearly wrong. "We had gone down there to drink some champagne and iron out the kinks," he recalls. "Instead we got put into a contamination room, saw a raving maniac in the hallway and were ushered back out."

Several minutes later, Aubut was at the door of the Flyer suite. He waved Snider and Ryan out into the hall, where he said his board would not approve the deal with the signing condition. Instead, he had accepted an offer from the Rangers.

Snider exploded. "Bleep you, we had a deal," he said.

Ryan thought Snider was going to choke Aubut, especially after he suggested they ride together to the draft. "I'm going to get in a cab with you?" Snider screamed. He swore at Aubut, who walked off down the hall.

"I was in complete shock," Snider recalls. He called the Flyers' draft table at the Forum and asked to speak to Farwell, who was called back from his as-yet unsuccessful search for Page.

"Marcel is backing out," Snider told his GM.

"Bleep off," Farwell said.

"No, I'm serious," said Snider. "He says he has a deal with the Rangers."

Farwell hung up the phone, called his scouts together, and told them they had to get their heads together quickly. Philadelphia would be exercising the seventh pick in the draft after all.

Within a few minutes, Ed Snider called the suite from the plane. When Jay said what had happened, Ed, too, cursed Aubut, but he quickly rationalized the collapse of the deal. "Maybe it wasn't meant to be," he told Jay. "We were giving up so much. Maybe we're better off."

But then the owner suggested perhaps there might be some recourse through NHL arbitration procedures. "Go talk to John Ziegler and [NHL vice president and legal counsel] Gil Stein and see if anything can be done," Snider said.

Ryan, the Tobins and a seething Jay hopped a cab to the Forum. They walked in just as Moscow Dynamo center Alexei Yashin, the second pick in the draft, was putting on the jersey of the new Ottawa Senators. Snider went right for Ziegler, who was seated at the side of the stage.

"He was ticked," recalls Ziegler. "I had to separate the rhetoric from the problem." And the problem, the league president recognized, was significant.

"The ramifications were enormous," he recalls thinking. "All kinds of rights and liabilities jumped out at you. You had the prospect of different people having different recollections of who said what to whom. It needed a fair hearing."

In seventeen years as NHL president, Ziegler had arbitrated complaints about traded players who were damaged goods and had ruled on various eligibility disputes involving free agency and the entry draft. But he recalled no case where two teams were claiming to have traded for the same player.

Article 6 of the league constitution stipulated that the president had the choice of appointing an arbitrator or hearing the grievance himself. Ziegler would run his final board of governors meeting the next day—he was about to resign due to many owners' unhappiness with his handling of the labor difficulties two months earlier—and had no desire to delay settling the dispute. If the Flyers wanted a hearing, he would appoint an arbitrator.

Ziegler referred Jay to Stein, once Snider's right-hand man, who was found running a meeting in a Forum anteroom. Stein told Snider to declare his intentions to the Nordiques and Rangers before they announced their deal.

Snider approached Neil Smith at the Rangers' table. "You don't have a deal with Quebec," said Snider. "We had one first and we're arbitrating."

Smith, who had not slept, began to curse Aubut. "You can have the kid," the exasperated Ranger GM said. "I don't even care about Lindros."

Jay then walked up behind Aubut on the draft floor and tapped him hard on the shoulder. The Quebec president turned around. "You don't have a deal with the Rangers, you have one with me," Snider said.

"No, no, I have a deal with the Rangers," said Aubut.

"No you don't," said Jay. "Talk to Gil and John, We're going to arbitration."

A tight smile creased the corners of Snider's mouth as he walked away. Aubut, his face in an incredulous half-sneer, stared after Jay for several seconds.

"We were in Montreal," recalls Snider. "He wanted to announce this big, dramatic, Marcel Aubut victory to upstage the Canadiens so he could declare himself emperor or something."

Meanwhile the Nordiques, picking fourth, had taken left wing Todd Warriner, and the Islanders had used the fifth choice on Kasparaitis, scratching two players that had been high on the Flyers' original list, which they were now suddenly forced to refer to. When the seventh selection arrived, the choice, in Farwell's mind, was between left wing Ryan Sittler of the Nicholls School in Buffalo, Russian defenseman Sergei Gonchar or defenseman Jason Bowen of Tri-Cities in the WHL.

Sittler was not an exceptionally strong skater. Then again, neither was his father, the first member of the family to have been first-round material. And Darryl Sittler, who spent three of his twilight seasons in Philadelphia, had earned election to the Hall of Fame.

The Flyers, looking for beef, thought Bowen, a physical defenseman who had played in only 18

games because of torn right shoulder tendons, was a good gamble to let slip to the fifteenth pick. They were right. Eight picks after selecting Sittler, Philadelphia chose Bowen.

Meanwhile, rumors circulating the Forum were delivering Lindros to Philadelphia, New York *and* Chicago, leaving reporters dumbfounded when the first round passed without any announcement of a trade. When the TV cameras of Canada's TSN [The Sports Network] caught the exchange on the floor between Snider and Aubut, with no audio, it only heightened the intrigue. So did Farwell, who had agreed not to say anything publicly about the protest until Ranger governor Stanley Jaffe arrived at the draft later that day.

"It was just left hanging," Farwell told the Philadelphia media on a conference call about a Lindros deal. "[The Nordiques] let it drag right to the end. We didn't know if we were getting a definitive answer."

At midafternoon, Snider, Aubut, Ziegler, Stein and Jaffe met behind the draft stage.

"I told them we are talking about one player here," recalls Ziegler. "'Let's not take this out of the league's control and into the courts. Let's not harm the league,'" he said.

He informed the parties that the constitution allowed each side in the dispute to select an arbitrator, who would then agree on a third to hear the case. But Ziegler urged skipping that step and agreeing directly on a Solomon.

The league had a roster of lawyers and judges to hear disputes, but the president was uncomfortable with the idea of the same person who awarded Lindros's rights being in a position to decide potential compensation or salary dispute involving Lindros at a later date. Ziegler recommended Larry Bertuzzi, a 44-year-old Toronto labor lawyer who had twice represented the NHL in its collective-bargaining negotiations with the officials' union.

"Larry had good people skills," recalls Ziegler, "which was important, because I knew it was going to be contentious."

Bertuzzi—spending the weekend at his Lindsay, Ontario cottage—was driving to pick up a canoe for his son when the NHL president called a little after 1 P.M. The message was waiting when he returned sometime after 5 o'clock.

Over the phone, Ziegler briefed Bertuzzi and asked if he was interested in hearing the case. The lawyer was questioned whether there were any conflicts of interest that would disqualify him.

Bertuzzi lived only a block and a half from the Lindroses in North Toronto and had played college football with Carl at the University of Western Ontario. Nevertheless, while the lawyer had followed the career of Carl's precocious son in the media, the old teammates had not seen each other in many years.

The barrister had no cases until Wednesday, no fear of media headlights and, as a longtime hockey fan, a healthy curiosity about the affair. He asked Ziegler for the rules and was told both the form of the hearing and the arbitrator's fee would be up to Bertuzzi. He said he would take the case if the parties agreed to him, which they did relatively quickly. "The lawyers weren't yet at the scene," said Ziegler. "I think that was to my advantage."

With the hearing scheduled to begin the following day in Montreal, Snider and Ryan left the draft early and returned to the hotel to begin preparing the case. Jay called Phil Weinberg, the Spectacor attorney, and asked him to fly to Montreal that evening. Snider was reminded by the lawyer that Weinberg's wife Terry was expecting.

"When?" Jay asked.

"Tonight," Weinberg said. Still, he could use the Spectacor jet, which at that hour was flying Ed Snider to Montreal, to get back to Philadelphia on short notice. Weinberg agreed to come to Montreal on the early-evening commercial flight.

Obviously, he would need a stand-in if the blessed event occurred, and Snider, figuring Canadian law would be applied at the hearing, felt Weinberg should have local legal help anyway. Snider, through the help of Canadiens president Ron Corey, obtained the name of a Montreal firm and left a phone message asking for its help.

When the league released news of the mess in the early evening, rumors immediately began circulating on the draft floor that the Rangers had put their trade in writing. Nevertheless, because most NHL deals are completed over the phone, pending filing with the league's Central Registry during normal business hours, Jay was not discouraged from pursuing his case. It would be up to Bertuzzi to ascertain whether the Flyers had made a verbal deal conforming to NHL rules or accepted business practices before the Rangers made theirs.

Since Aubut had stipulated there could be no contact with the family until a deal was struck, Ryan and Snider quickly surmised that the granting of permission to make the phone call would be crucial to Philadelphia's case. Jay called back the Lindroses,

who had reunited at their cottage after the first round had concluded. Snider told Carl about the arbitration and asked if he could verify the time of the Flyers' call that morning. Lindros said he could.

To get backup proof, Ryan requested a copy of the phone bill from the hotel. He was dumbfounded when the call to the cottage did not appear on the charge record. When the Flyer CEO pressed house management the following day, he learned that on Saturday afternoon someone had entered the closet where the telephone computer was housed and removed the record of the call. Ryan was subsequently able to get verification through Bell Canada that the phone call had been made.

When the team hosted its annual open house for Philadelphia draft picks and their families on Saturday night, Jay Snider wasn't exactly in a party mood. At stake was not only a hugely valuable asset, but Snider's reputation and credibility.

If the Flyers lost the arbitration, at best they would look like sore losers. At worst, they would be perceived as incompetents, or as the naive dupes of flimflam artists who had used them to get a better trade elsewhere. "The biggest deal in professional sports history," Snider recalls thinking, "and people will think we should have had it in writing. What a bunch of bumbling fools we'll look like."

Weinberg arrived in Montreal in midevening, dropped his bag in his room, checked in with his wife, then went to Jay's room. The attorney set to work taking the stories of Flyer personnel. Around 1 A.M., he went back to Suite 2818 for a nightcap. No sooner was Weinberg in the door, than Farwell handed over the phone. It was Terry. Her water had broken.

Noise abatement regulations at Dorval Airport prohibited takeoffs between midnight and 6 A.M., and the doctor predicted the birth would not occur until morning. Weinberg decided to spend the night and catch the first flight out.

Meanwhile, back at Georgian Bay, the relief of the Lindroses had turned to frustration, to cynicism, to resignation. "After all Marcel Aubut had done to tear our family apart the past year, I thought it was typical," recalls Eric.

"Eric desperately wanted it to be done," recalls Carl. "And it just seemed to go on and on. But at least we would know in a couple of days.

"We started to go over the pros and cons of both teams. New York had been one of the places that most appealed to us, but the Rangers already had a good team, and what if they won a Cup in the first two years he was there? When you are 21 or 22, where do you go from that, what's going to drive you? We thought maybe if it was Philadelphia, it would be an advantage going to an organization that was building.

"But all we could really do was wait."

Weinberg walked into the maternity ward at Pennsylvania Hospital at about 9 A.M., just as the board of governors meeting convened in Montreal. Bertuzzi arrived in Montreal soon afterwards and huddled with the contending parties in the hotel foyer.

The two law firms Jay contacted the previous evening had called back to decline representation, citing conflicts of interest. Ron Corey suggested Yves Fortier, a winner of the Order of Canada, one of the country's highest honors, but he could not be reached, immediately, leaving Snider feeling alone and pressured.

It was Bertuzzi's understanding that he could not begin until all three parties signed a document. "I just needed a simple agreement that they were accepting my rule and we could make up the rules [of the hearing] as we went along," he recalls.

The representatives of the Rangers and Nordiques wanted ground rules. But Snider would agree to nothing without speaking to his lawyer, who was coaching his wife through labor. Weinberg took calls in the delivery room from Bertuzzi and both Sniders. "Jay, this baby is about to come out of here," Weinberg said. "I'll call you back in twenty minutes."

"Great," remarked Terry Weinberg. "You mean I have twenty minutes to finish this?"

Sidney Weinberg came into the world without complication. Her father's client, however, faced many. "We were getting paranoid," recalls Jay. "We still didn't have the phone record at that point and we couldn't get legal help in the province of Quebec."

Ed Snider gratefully accepted Chicago owner Bill Wirtz's offer of the services of Blackhawks' counsel Gene Gozdecki until Weinberg could get back and up to speed. Keenan confirmed to Jay that, as per the Flyers' suspicions, Aubut had solicited another Blackhawk offer not long before the draft. Unfortunately for Snider, Keenan could not pinpoint the time.

The Blackhawks were not the only NHL organization with sympathy for the Flyers' position. Several expressed their disgust at the governors' meeting.

"In the old days you would pull out a gun and shoot a guy who went back on his word," Glen Sather told Jim Matheson of the *Edmonton Journal*. "In this league we do business on the phone over 3,000 miles.

Your word has to be honored. This is a bloody crime. Aubut has been doing these kinds of negotiations for years. I'd like to see the Flyers stick it to him where the sun don't shine."

Unfortunately, the case would not be heard by a jury of the Flyers' peers but by an arbitrator who the Sniders feared would inevitably take the word of two teams over one. Jay made it clear to reporters he did not feel undercut by the Rangers. "They are an innocent party in this," he said. Still, the Rangers obviously would be supporting Quebec's case.

"No, I'm not confident," Ed Snider told reporters on his way out of the governors' meeting. "How do you combat people who deny the truth? Some people are liars. Some people live their lives that way."

But the Sniders were determined to put up a fight. "I know what happened. And I don't see why we should walk away from something we think is ours," Jay said at a media briefing early Sunday evening. "Somehow, we're plowing ahead on adrenaline."

Weinberg was back in Montreal early Sunday evening. The cigars the proud papa passed out did not explode, even as it appeared the arbitration might. The Flyer counsel strongly objected to the terms of reference (the rules for the arbitration) that had been drawn up by Ranger lawyer Kevin Billet and amended by Quebec attorneys Allan Hilton and Gerald Tremblay.

"We couldn't get out of the starting blocks," recalls Bertuzzi. "Everything was becoming a morass. I thought they all might back out."

On Monday morning, just hours before Stein would be named interim president, the arbitrator called Ziegler, explained the difficulties, and asked the outgoing president what would happen if the Flyers, Rangers and Nordiques refused to accept Bertuzzi's rule.

"Then I'll appoint you anyway," said Ziegler.

"Fine, then I can assert myself," said Bertuzzi.

He relayed his conversation to the arbitrating parties that morning, then wrote up the terms of reference. There would be no appeal on his decision. The hearing would be held *in camera* (privately). There would be no discussion of the case with the media before adjournment nor any disclosure of what the losing side's offer for Lindros had been.

Except for minor revisions, the parties agreed to the terms by early Monday afternoon. When the hearing began at 9 P.M., Yves Fortier, one of the lawyers who had been recommended to Snider a day earlier, had joined the Nordiques' legal team.

The Flyers, told by Bertuzzi to present their case

first, opened with the testimony of Sylvan Tobin. The lawyers argued over the manner of cross-examination—U.S. courts allow for a more leading form of questioning—but with lawyers and arbitrator coming from so many jurisdictions, Bertuzzi relied on common sense as much as common law.

"We went with what I was comfortable with," Bertuzzi recalls.

He was the only one in the room who was at ease. "There was an absolute hatred between us and Quebec," recalls Jay. "And while I didn't blame the Rangers for what happened, they were arrogant. Their attitude was like, 'We can't believe what Philadelphia is doing.'"

Ed Snider, who was scheduled to check into New York's Sloan-Kettering Hospital Tuesday for removal of a possibly-cancerous thyroid tumor, testified after Tobin. The owner gleefully recounted being told by Aubut how it would be bad for the NHL if the Rangers obtained and overpaid Lindros.

The length of the witness list and the detailed testimony soon made it obvious that the hearing would last longer than the one to three days the parties originally anticipated. Proceedings resumed daily at 9 A.M. and sometimes lasted until 10 P.M. Snider, Ryan and Farwell would then huddle with Weinberg into the wee hours to plot strategy and prepare testimony for the next day.

The Flyers were convinced their case would be damaged if they could not get Rick Curran and Carl and Eric Lindros to testify. "Our phone call was a very critical piece of evidence," recalls Weinberg, but the Lindroses and their agent feared being witnesses for the Flyers would cause them to appear to prefer that Eric's rights be awarded to Philadelphia. Jay was turned down three times.

"The prevalent suggestion around the hockey world was that Eric was a spoiled brat who wanted everything his way," recalls Carl. "We wanted to let the hockey people fight it out. We did not want to make it appear we were doing anything to influence it one way or the other."

Bertuzzi had no subpoena power, but became convinced of the importance of the Lindroses' testimony. Finally, he asked them to appear. "I told them I was not interested in hearing what their wishes were, we just wanted the facts," recalls Bertuzzi.

They finally agreed and were escorted up the hotel freight elevator, through the kitchen, away from the media and into the hearing room, where Eric testified for ten minutes. Another NHL executive who had been involved in the bidding for

Lindros (the parties are prohibited from identifying him) testified that he, too, had been told by Aubut that the phone number would not be provided until a deal was completed.

As it turned out, the Rangers' rumored written trade document was merely an agreement that gave the team three days following the trade to back out if Lindros was not signed. The draft choices, players and cash to be exchanged had not been recorded. Media reports pegged New York's offer as $12 million, centers Alexei Kovalev and Doug Weight, right wing Tony Amonte, goalie John Vanbiesbrouck (defenseman James Patrick would be substituted if Vanbiesbrouck, a free agent, refused to sign with Quebec), and first-round draft picks in 1993, 1994 and 1996.

The Flyers had no written proof of their own signing condition. They had never committed to a specific time frame. Still, Jay clung to the right to void the trade if no contract settlement could be reached, leaving him open to a perceived contradiction: how could he insist the transaction was completed and still maintain it depended on Lindros's agreement?

The Rangers and Nordiques argued that New York's signing condition was in writing, unquestionably part of their deal, and attempted to poke holes in the Flyers' verbal stipulation. As Fortier challenged Jay on this point, Bertuzzi interceded with a question. "If I was to find that you and Quebec made a deal, is there still a [signing] condition? What is the status of the condition?"

Weinberg immediately objected. "He doesn't have to answer that," said the attorney.

"I *want* to answer that," said Snider. He immediately dropped the signing condition and, along with it, Weinberg's jaw.

"I had been wondering, 'How are we not going to sign this guy now?'" Jay recalls. "Most of the media speculation about who we had traded was pretty much on target. If we didn't win the arbitration or sign Lindros we would have to take those guys back and it would be awkward. If we won after fighting so hard and giving up so much, how would it look not signing him?

"In other words, if I wrote a book called "How to Put Yourself in a Bad Negotiating Position," we could not have come up any worse than where we were. So I decided to go for it. There was a legal importance to dropping the condition, but I think there was a psychological one, too. Maybe it would make the decision cleaner for Bertuzzi."

To make it tidier, the arbitrator recalls, only increased his burden. "Until then, my jurisdiction was to make the final decision as to whether [Lindros] was a Flyer or a Ranger," recalls Bertuzzi, "not if a trade was still dependent on a signing."

Meanwhile, in New York, Ed Snider's thyroid proved cancerous, but he had become so obsessed with the arbitration that there had been no time to fear the diagnosis. After removing the gland and checking the biopsy of surrounding tissue, doctors assured the owner he would yet live a long life. Snider wondered mostly about the quality of that life should he have to endure the sight of Lindros in a Ranger uniform.

"I was so involved with the arbitration that the timing was almost a blessing," Snider recalls. Only hours after surgery, Snider called Jay with a suggestion for the case. Although neither Jay nor Weinberg remember what it was, they remember thinking it was extremely logical for a guy coming out of general anesthesia. "Either that," recalls Jay, "or we were so nuts by that time, anything might have made sense to us."

Snider, Farwell, Ryan and Weinberg ate all but one meal during the week in their hotel suite. When the hearing recessed for bathroom breaks, not a word was exchanged by the Quebec and Philadelphia parties. There was no patience for small talk and escaping the pressure and the eyes of the hockey world was proving impossible. NHL security personnel blocked off the hotel conference level, but witnesses riding up the escalator faced a gauntlet of television lights. One cameraman had even drilled a hole through the kitchen door that opened into the hearing room and shot tape of Lindros testifying before being discovered.

At one point, Snider, Farwell and Ryan took a short break in the park behind the hotel where they animatedly discussed their anger at one of Quebec's contentions. They later saw themselves on the news, agitatedly waving their arms during their supposedly private conversation.

Since Quebec City is only a two-hour drive from Montreal, the French-language media did not see much validity in the Flyer claim. "One column was read to me where I was called a complete jerk," recalls Snider. His wife, Terry, who did not agree, flew to Montreal to help mute distractions, serve meals in the suite and keep her husband sane.

At one point, Jay tried to sound out Jaffe and Aubut about negotiating a settlement. "I'm not sure what I really had in mind," Snider said. "Maybe some kind of a three-way thing where the Rangers would

still get some players or draft choices or money. I mean, we're partners in the league and this obviously wasn't good for hockey. Maybe there was a solution.

"But they just sat there very smugly and said, 'Well, if you want to drop your case.'" The feelers went nowhere.

The Flyers presented as evidence Aubut's own list of the players, draft choices and $15 million that he had given to Snider in the wee hours of Saturday morning. They called nine witnesses: Jay and Ed Snider, Farwell, Allen, Sylvan Tobin, Curran, Carl Lindros, Eric Lindros and the unidentified NHL GM.

Bertuzzi kept handwritten notes of all the testimony. "Using court reporters in an arbitration is an American thing, not Canadian," he recalls. "Besides, it takes too long to retype the transcript and we wanted to expedite things.

"They say if you just listen to something, you will remember 10 percent, but it you write it down, you'll remember 50 percent and if you review that within twenty-four hours, you'll remember 80 percent."

Bertuzzi also slept little during the week, often rising at 4 A.M. to write a small bone of a press release to satisfy the prowling hounds. "I had to tell them something," he remembers. "Usually, it was only how much longer I thought the hearing would take."

He asked for a copy of the NHL bylaws for guidance as to what constituted a trade, but it provided no help. Farwell testified that the Tocchet trade had been completed over a car phone.

Only Jaffe and Smith spoke for New York. The Madison Square Garden boss said he had received a call from Smith at 9:30 A.M. to report the Ranger GM and Aubut had reached agreement on the player and draft-choice components of the deal. Aubut, however, wanted more money and was going to be phoning Jaffe.

When the Nordique president called Jaffe, he said Quebec could get $15 million from another team. But because he liked the Rangers' deal better, Quebec would take less from them–$12.5 million payable over six years.

Aubut asked for that amount at 11:30 A.M., one hour after Snider had called Aubut back to say the Flyers would do the deal as the Nordiques wanted it, and ten minutes after the Lindros number had been obtained from Curran.

Jaffe told Aubut he would call him back. He did at 11:40 A.M., approximately seven minutes after Aubut had relayed the phone number to Snider. Jaffe offered to pay the Nordiques $12 million over six years, an amount accepted after about ten more minutes of negotiations. Jaffe and Aubut then went over all elements of the transaction, including the players and draft choices.

"Do we have a deal?" asked Jaffe.

"We have a deal, trust me," said Aubut.

The Flyers surmised Aubut must have accepted Jaffe's offer, then dashed back to their suite, hoping that the call to Lindros was going badly. Instead, Aubut got the thumbs-up sign, leaving him no out but to deny he had made a deal first with Philadelphia.

"I liked the players and draft choices the Rangers offered better," recalls Page. "And I thought the Flyers were out of it.

"When Russ called me about the draft picks that morning, I didn't know what he was talking about. I guess I should have figured something was cooking, but I was too caught up in the Ranger deal to figure out what Russ was trying to say. You can't be talking with two clubs with ten minutes left.

"But I had no knowledge Marcel had made a deal with the Flyers. People have always phoned each other with trades and the next day backed out. The Flyers just decided to take this one to court."

The Rangers contended before Bertuzzi that when Jay did not immediately drop the signing condition, which Aubut's "board" insisted upon, it proved the deal had not been concluded. The Rangers also argued Snider had not repeated all the components of the trade in supposedly accepting it, had given Aubut only a "thumbs-up" rather than a handshake, and that Farwell had never reached agreement with the Nordiques about how they would choose for Quebec with the draft pick.

Page did not testify for the Nordiques. Aubut, their only witness, said he never thought Lindros would agree to go to Philadelphia and that the terms of the deal he presented Snider at 1 A.M. were an attempt to force the Blackhawks, Rangers, Devils and Leafs to go higher. Aubut insisted he had told all bidders the phone number would be provided when he was close to a deal, not when one was completed.

By the time Aubut completed the testimony at 9:30 P.M. Friday night, Bertuzzi had made 400 pages of notes. "He was incredible," recalls Snider. "He was writing the entire week, yet never lost track of where we were or the salient points.

"Once in a while he would ask a penetrating question that went right to the heart of an issue. He was professional, level, smart, fair. I wouldn't have respected him any less, no matter how it had turned out."

Bertuzzi's manner provided no hints in tone of voice or body language, as to which way he might be leaning. "I didn't try to sort out a decision until I heard all the testimony," he recalls. "It was like a baseball game, not over until the last man was out.

"There were enough surprises along the way that at no point could I say to myself, 'It looks like this, or looks like that.'"

After getting out of the hotel twice in six days, the arbitrator figured home would be the best place to clear his head, read his notes, and consider his decision. So when Bertuzzi said he didn't want to spend half of Saturday, the next day, listening to the closing arguments, he received no resistance from the weary parties. They agreed to present their summaries after only a one-hour break.

Weinberg, one attorney against five for the Nordiques, spent the preparation time alone. Although the decision obviously hinged on Aubut's credibility, the Flyer counsel had decided not to challenge it in his final statement. "I thought that would be a mistake," recalls Weinberg. "I struggled to find a way not to call him a liar so that Bertuzzi would not be faced with deciding whether we or the Nordiques were telling the truth.

"See, there are separate European and North American interpretations of when a deal, which is a meeting of the minds, is struck. In the North American version there is an objective manifestation that there has been an agreement; in this case, the providing of the phone number, which Aubut had said he wouldn't do until a [trade] was struck.

"The European interpretation is more subjective–not what they showed, but what they thought. From that standpoint, Marcel could have believed there was not a verbal contract formed with the Flyers. We could ascertain there was, based on what objectively had been done, but our whole argument took it out of the realm of what the parties believed and into the question, 'Would an outside observer looking at this infer there had been a deal?'

"I tried to find a way that [Bertuzzi] could believe everybody and still award the player to the Flyers."

Weinberg's argument lasted about ninety minutes. Sometime after 1 A.M., Bertuzzi concluded by telling the parties he would take as long as he needed to reach a decision. He flew back to Toronto on Saturday morning, caught a nap, and then attended his uncle's fiftieth wedding anniversary celebration in Hamilton. "I had a great time, too," he recalls.

The next morning, Bertuzzi was in his office by

10 o'clock, going over his notes. By 7 P.M. the answer was staring back at him.

Bertuzzi folded up his books, went home, had dinner, then consulted law books for concepts relevant to the case. He went to bed at 11, figuring he would spend the entire next day writing his decision. But as the arbitrator lay in bed pondering his words, he found himself worrying about losing a particular thought in his sleep, so he went to the kitchen to make a note. He wrote one sentence, then another, then another. By 6 A.M., he had penned the entire decision, except for the introduction.

He showered, went to work, and phoned Stein to give him a progress report. Bertuzzi then called in two secretaries and swore them to secrecy. He had one transcribe what he had already written and dictated the introduction to the other.

In the afternoon, the arbitrator called Stein again to promise delivery of his decision to the league office the following day. The interim NHL president wanted Bertuzzi to read his decision first to the claimants in a private conference call at 9:30 A.M., then to the public a half-hour later.

Bertuzzi edited his eight-page decision until 7 P.M. Satisfied, he slept.

Jay spent the long weekend feeling the Flyers had taken their best shot before a fair judge, but still was afraid to be confident. It was not exactly a carefree group of Flyer executives that crowded into Snider's Spectrum office on Tuesday morning, June 30, 1992. Once the call was placed, Stein reminded all parties of their pledge to accept the decision as final and asked them to behave in a sportsmanlike manner when it was announced.

He then asked the arbitrator to begin.

"Nobody was looking at anybody," recalls Snider. "You could hear a pin drop. Some guys were pacing. I was sitting behind the desk looking at my hands."

Bertuzzi read:

"I have carefully reviewed all of the evidence and I find the facts to be as follows ...

"There was reluctance on the part of bidding clubs to negotiate anything more than a conditional deal for Lindros's rights ... A number of clubs sought Aubut's permission to speak with Lindros before negotiating with Quebec. I heard from Philadelphia and at least one other team that Aubut's position was that such permission to speak with Lindros would not be granted 'until we had a deal.'

"It is important at this point to emphasize that this is not a dispute over whether an oral deal has more or less weight in the NHL than one which pos-

sesses all the trappings of a legal document. It is simply a determination of whether two clubs made a 'deal' in the way clubs in the NHL have been making 'deals' for seventy-five years. I wish to emphasize that no new standards will be created with this decision.

"These dealings were consistent with evidence I heard regarding how deals are made in the NHL ... some of the league's larger trades have been consummated over the phone, in a press box or restaurant."

Jay Snider continued to stare at his hands. Bertuzzi had already acknowledged Quebec's refusal to allow contact with Lindros prior to a deal. This was a good sign.

"It is ... common ground that [the Ranger-Nordique] deal was concluded at approximately 11:50 A.M. on Saturday June 20, during a telephone conversation between Aubut in Montreal and Jaffe in New York. Although the conditional aspects alluded to earlier had been committed to a written agreement three weeks earlier, there was no written agreement between Aubut and Jaffe setting out the essential components of the ultimate agreement at the time when they both agreed they made a binding deal ... Nor, of course, was there a handshake."

Good again, thought Jay. Bertuzzi was acknowledging the Rangers' trade had no more legal trappings than the Flyers'. Still, all this would mean nothing if the arbitrator believed the Flyers never had a deal.

"There is no indication [Jaffe] had any knowledge of Quebec's dealings with Philadelphia, save the fact that Philadelphia was also a 'bidder' and had a draft choice in its offer. The 11:50 A.M. telephone conversation with Aubut was not New York 'one-upping' the Philadelphia terms. There is no evidence to suggest that Jaffe ever knew what the complete Philadelphia terms were.

"Now I turn to the Philadelphia dealings ... Philadelphia asked Aubut early and often for an opportunity to speak to Lindros to determine his attitude about reporting to Philadelphia. Aubut's response was quite clear: 'Not until we have a deal.' ... Secondly, Philadelphia insisted that any deal was subject to a condition that Lindros sign a contract with it. Philadelphia would have a short period of time, a matter of days, to satisfy this condition ... New York went so far as to put this condition in a signed written agreement three weeks earlier, but Philadelphia and Quebec [also] operated on that clear understanding."

Weinberg, pacing up and down the office, turned to Farwell. "We got him," the lawyer said.

"Quebec suggests no deal was made with Phila-

delphia in that there was no meeting of the minds. It suggests that the test is the test of the reasonable man and that the Philadelphia 'deal' was never agreed to by Aubut. Further, it suggests there were two other key items which were still outstanding, namely the time limit of the Lindros contract condition and the mechanism for making the 1992 draft pick.

"Philadelphia on the other hand, says that Jay Snider accepted Aubut's counter position as written (Exhibit P-2—the list of players and draft picks that Aubut had given Snider Friday night as the deal the Nordiques would accept) and that the condition regarding Lindros was understood and agreed. The time frame for satisfying the condition was always described as very short.

"Further, Quebec had suggested the draft pick mechanism was no problem and should be dealt with on the draft floor, thereby, as it turned out, effectively preventing Philadelphia from getting Quebec's input into the pick."

As the recuperating Ed Snider listened from his Bryn Mawr office, he was thinking that every key Flyer argument had been accurately acknowledged by Bertuzzi. "It's going our way," he said to himself.

"New York agreed with Quebec's submissions and suggested that the absence of a time frame on the Lindros contract condition was the key to finding that no Philadelphia-Quebec deal existed. Such a factor was present in the New York-Quebec deal.

"Conclusion:"

Jay's stone-silent office somehow grew even quieter.

"Having considered the matter carefully and having reviewed and assessed the evidence of all witnesses, I find that Philadelphia made an enforceable deal with Quebec ... "

Jay leaped out of his chair and screamed. The office erupted in hugs and high fives. The door opened and Flyer office workers who had been waiting by the door for the reaction poured in.

Bertuzzi continued.

"I do not find the absence of a specific time frame to satisfy this condition to be an impediment to the existence of the deal since I find Snider and Aubut were in agreement that Philadelphia would have a short period of time, a matter of days, to satisfy the condition ... The issue of what period of time would be reasonable does not arise because Philadelphia was given no opportunity to conclude a contract with Lindros.

"If Aubut intended the contact with the Lindros

family to be something other than confirmation of a deal, he did not make that point clear to Philadelphia or Lindros's agent. In fact they were led to believe the contrary.

" ... In some ways, certain post 10:30 A.M. negotiations were understandable since, if Lindros had flatly rejected Philadelphia, Aubut would still have his rights to trade. But in view of the developments involving Philadelphia at 10:30 and 11:30 A.M., Aubut did not have the capacity to conclude the New York Rangers arrangement at 11:50 A.M."

Bertuzzi concluded with his plan to equalize the draft pick the Flyers had used after Quebec had backed out of the deal. The Nordiques did not want Ryan Sittler and had argued that any future Flyer No. 1 picks the Flyers could substitute might not be as high as seventh overall.

"I shall respect [Quebec's] wishes," Bertuzzi said. Believing the two teams could make a better trade than he, the arbitrator directed the Flyers to provide equal value for the 1992 pick—not to include current NHL players or 1992 draftees—within eighteen days. If the two teams could not come to an agreement, Bertuzzi would arbitrate, via a conference call, on July 17.

As he finished reading his decision, Bertuzzi tried to listen for reaction on the speakerphone. He heard no cheers, no curses–nothing but silence. The mute button had been pushed to prevent the parties from hearing each other's reactions. "Is anybody there?" he asked.

Bertuzzi was wrung out from the nine-day ordeal, but had no nagging doubts he had ruled correctly. "It had just stared back at me on Sunday that Jay was right," he recalls. "The signing condition didn't matter.

"There were weak points in everybody's position. But if the Nordiques had a deal with New York, then they had one with Philly first. Whether it was sealed with a handshake, a kiss or in writing didn't matter. The deal the Flyers made was consistent with the way trades were made in the NHL."

As soon as Bertuzzi had read his conclusion, a Ranger source had called Curran with the news. He immediately relayed the information to the Lindroses, who had invited their lawyer, Gordon Kirke, to their home to listen to the decision. "We had no control, so there was no sense in getting caught up in it," recalls Carl. "Either way, Eric was going to be in the NHL within a few months."

Like most of the hockey world, the subject of the arbitration was surprised by the result. "I thought I was going to New York," Eric recalls. Mostly, he was happy it was settled.

Within minutes, Jay Snider called to set up a negotiating session. He and Carl agreed it was best to stay out of the media spotlight. They settled on a rendezvous the following day at a hotel in Syracuse, New York.

The Lindroses had made arrangements to hold a press conference at Eric's high school, St. Michael's. On the way, Eric and Brett stopped to buy a Flyers cap to wear before the cameras. "The clerk at the store was watching the TSN report on the decision," recalls Eric. "And he didn't even recognize me."

Farwell had quickly excused himself from the celebration in Jay Snider's office. He went to his desk and began the dreary task of phoning the players who had finally, officially, been traded. Bertuzzi's ruling did not name the Flyers in the deal but when Hextall's phone rang five minutes after he had heard the decision, he could guess what the call was about. "I was 95 percent sure I was in the trade," recalls the goalie.

Farwell told Hextall what he expected to hear. "Ron, we've traded you to Quebec," the GM said. "I think this is going to be good for your career."

Intellectually, Hextall could agree. "While I was waiting, I was saying to myself, 'If they don't want me, I don't want to be here.'"

Still, as resigned as he had become to leaving, Hextall surprised himself with how disappointed he suddenly felt. "I was a Flyer and I wanted to still be a Flyer and then suddenly that changed," he recalls. "I mean, at one point or another I was going to get traded, and that deal was the right thing to do. But unlike some other guys who had left over the last two years, I wanted to be a part of it when the Flyers came back strong.

"I sensed there were people [in the organization] who didn't want me to succeed anymore. I just didn't have the backing that I'd had before and that was a distraction, too. But I never got to a point where I said I wasn't going to try.

"I was letting in the odd [bad] goal at inopportune times and we couldn't score, so the bad goal was always the winning or tying one. Then, I would feel we had lost the game because of me. Things kept piling up and I got down. There were times I was

real close to where I had been before the injuries, but then it would slip away again. It was frustrating."

Bill Dineen had tipped Ricci during the arbitration hearing that he was part of the trade. When he heard news of the decision, he went back to bed and was sleeping when Farwell phoned. When he awoke, he went fishing, leaving all calls, including the Flyer GM's, unreturned.

"I think if it had happened at any other time in

my life, it would have hit me a lot harder," Ricci recalls. "After my dad's death, hockey wasn't very big for me for a while."

The coach sincerely lamented the loss of Ricci and Hextall and conceded his team virtually would be starting over again. "But I've seen Lindros play forty times and I'll tell you, three years down the road, he's going to be the top player in hockey," said Dineen from his Lake George home to Rich Hofmann of the *Daily News*. "A guy like this only comes along once in a lifetime for any coach. We got a guy who can play against Mark Messier and Mario Lemieux."

Indeed, the sacrifices were swallowed up by euphoria. "We're elated," said a beaming Ed Snider when the Flyers gathered the media at the Spectrum later in the day. "The last time I felt this way was 1969 at our training camp in Quebec. Keith Allen pointed to the ice and said, 'There is our future.' He was pointing at Bobby Clarke. With Lindros on the

A beaming Ed Snider, left, with Lindros: "I feel like we're whole again."

team and Bob back in the organization, I feel like we're whole again."

The Flyer who set the organizational standard of performance felt Lindros could handle the expectations. "There's going to be way more pressure on him than any other player," said Clarke. "Gretzky or Lemieux didn't have the pressure this kid's going to have coming in. But he has been under tremendous pressure his whole career—ever since he was 14, 15, 16 years old. And he's been able to handle it all the way along.

"It's not fair for me to say how many points I think he'll get, but he's the complete package. He's a great skater with skills and more importantly, he has a great feel for the game, for when to do what."

Lindros wore his Flyer hat and a smile when he met the media at St. Michael's. Curran's negative reaction on draft day to Lindros's potential delivery to Philadelphia had been reported by the media, but Eric emphatically denied being disappointed by Bertuzzi's ruling.

"That was my agent's thinking," Lindros said. "There's a little conflict sometimes and Rick did some things ... But I'm happy to go. I told Mr. Snider that my bag was packed and I'm glad I'm in Philadelphia.

"It's not a matter of me going out and scoring 50 goals or scoring 100 points. I'll go out and do the best job I can. If we can improve by fifteen points, I mean, that's a great start."

Lindros said he did not expect to become the NHL's highest-paid player but the Flyers already had reason to be comfortable with paying him at a rate far above the norm for a high first-round draft choice. Within a few hours of Bertuzzi's ruling, the switchboard was already buzzing with ticket requests.

"I've never seen anything like it in my ten years here," said Jack Betson, the Flyers' vice president of sales. "I have five people handling calls. Some people who had canceled their season tickets called to say they want them back." Spectacor spokesman Larry Rubin said inquiries for luxury boxes at the new arena were running 60 percent higher than on an average day.

Thus, there was reason to believe that at $1.5 million a year, Messier's base salary, Lindros would be a bargain. That illusion was shattered, however, when Jay and Farwell arrived in Syracuse the next day to negotiate with Carl Lindros, Curran and Kirke.

The Ranger center's contract called for the yearly rate to be averaged against that of the top three players in the NHL, and adjusted if market values went up. With signing and performance bonuses, Messier's yearly pay was estimated by Curran at $2.5 million a year.

"We weren't really very well prepared," recalls Jay. When an angry Carl Lindros excused himself, Snider assumed it was to cool off. Instead, Lindros got in his car and drove home to Toronto.

"I thought we had an understanding on the phone," recalls Carl. "We were not asking for more or less than what we had talked about."

While he fumed, the Rangers refused to be bitter. "We are naturally disappointed," said Neil Smith. "But I'm not mad, I can't be. There was nothing more that we could have done. We didn't have a deal because someone else had one before we did."

The traded players were invited to a Quebec City press conference the day following the decision, but Huffman and Duchesne, free agents who had only their rights transferred in the deal, declined to attend. So did Hextall, who wanted to get his thoughts together and his contract renegotiated.

Ricci, too, was determined to get an adjustment. Nevertheless, on the advice of his agent, Anton Thun, Ricci agreed to attend the Quebec media gathering. Thun told Quebec reporters his client would require time to adjust to what had happened. Judging from the somber expression on Ricci's face, he would need a long time. "I enjoyed it in Philadelphia," he said. "I just hope I can be happy here."

Aubut said he had wanted the New York deal because his GM thought it superior. "[However] our deal with the Flyers is not a bad one," the Nordiques president said. He added his belief that the decision was an error and that his image would not be damaged by the evidence of his double-dealing.

"There are a lot of people in this league who are envious of me," he said. "We got an awful lot in this trade, and remember that we got it for a player who has still not skated a shift as a pro. We definitely got the better of this trade."

Certainly the Nordiques had obtained a significant part of the Philadelphia defense. Dimitri Yushkevich, a rapidly-developing sixth-round pick from the 1991 draft who had been signed by Clarke while Farwell was tied up in the arbitration, was third on the depth chart behind Garry Galley and Terry Carkner. Suddenly, re-signing Mark Howe was a priority.

"If they had offered me a two-year deal for $600,000 during the season, I'm sure I would have taken it," Howe recalls. Seeing the Flyers' resolve to rebuild, he was surprised not to have been moved to a contender at the March trading deadline.

In May, Farwell and Jay had offered a one-year deal with a $500,000 base salary plus achievable incentives that could boost his pay to between $800,000 and $900,000. Wanting a longer deal, Howe received permission to shop himself prior to July 1, the day he would become an unrestricted free agent.

The defenseman called the Rangers, Blackhawks, Penguins and Red Wings. The Rangers were willing to offer only a one-year contract. Keenan, not in control of the Chicago purse strings, asked for time to free some money. Detroit's response, however, was immediate and heartening. "I called [Red Wing owner] Mike Ilitch and [GM] Bryan Murray called back in five minutes," recalls Howe.

In late June, the Red Wings offered a two-year deal paying $725,000 the first year, $550,000 the second, with reachable bonuses that would bring the defenseman's yield to an average of approximately $800,000 per season. He took a week in the Virgin Islands to think things over and returned as the Lindros decision was made.

"I waited a few days for the hoopla to die down and called to tell the Flyers what I had from Detroit," Howe recalls. "[Philadelphia] offered me a two-year deal at $800,000 a year solid, no incentives. Very comparable to what I had been offered in Detroit. The difference was the Red Wings promised me a job in the organization after I was finished."

Howe did not know what to do. "My mind had been made up," he recalls. "And now the Flyers still wanted me."

The defenseman had happy remembrances of growing up in the Detroit suburbs, but more importantly, he wished to finish up on a contender. It worried Howe a little that the Flyers might have to overuse him. Murray had said not to expect to play 80 games with the Red Wings. At age 37, that was appealing. So was the prospect of Howe's 14-year-old son Travis participating in a superior junior program in Detroit.

Travis, however, did not want to leave his friends. And neither did his father. "Mom had always said to make the list of the pluses and minuses when mak-

Lindros the Flyer: agent Curran wanted to make Eric the NHL's highest-paid player before he had even played his first game.

ing a tough decision," Mark said. "When I did, it was something like five-to-one for Detroit."

Still, he waffled. "Here I was with two great offers, one to a place I had always wanted to go to, the other where I had always loved it, and I was miserable," Howe recalls. "I had a fever, a flu and a migraine that was probably brought on by stress.

"Ilitch called and asked what was going on. I told him I had a comparable offer from Philly and that the thought of leaving was killing me. Ilitch said he

was sending his plane for me the next day, so we could talk.

"Everybody in the Flyer organization called that night. On the way to the airport the next day [July 8], I phoned Ed Snider. We talked for five or six minutes, and then we lost signal, but there really wasn't much left to say. I was at the plane. I knew if I got on, I was signing with Detroit."

Howe got on. At Little Caesar's Pizza headquarters, the owner threw in a free topping: a signing bonus of $350,000 that enabled Detroit to beat the Philadelphia package by $250,000.

"Good enough?" asked Ed Ferrin, Howe's representative.

"More than I expected," said Howe. He flew home to get Ginger for the following day's press conference. The best defenseman the Flyers ever had was gone.

"There was no communication [from Flyer management] the whole season," Howe told Ray Parrillo of the *Inquirer*. "But the most important thing for me right now is to play for a contender. I've enjoyed my time [in Philadelphia], but the Flyers still have holes to fill."

Farwell conceded that showing more interest in Howe earlier might have kept him. "Maybe we entered the race a little too late," he told the media. "We wanted him the whole time, but it wasn't until after the Lindros deal that our situation became clearer."

Still, Howe left with no bitterness. "Duchesne and Huffman made me expendable, then suddenly they needed insurance," he says today. "It's a business, I understand. The ten years I spent in Philadelphia were the most rewarding I had in hockey.

"The only thing missing was a Cup. Otherwise, it couldn't have been more complete. It made you feel good to walk around that town being a Flyer."

Few players in the team's history ever made the club more proud, either. Keith Allen never made a better trade than the one in 1983 that acquired Howe from Hartford.

The team's fortunes had remained tethered to his health until his departure, but the cord was cut. And the player the Flyers had decided to rebuild around had to be signed at almost any cost.

Curran had come to Philadelphia in the week following the Syracuse fiasco and told Farwell and Snider the price would be $3.5 million a year. This would make Lindros the highest-paid player in the NHL before he had even played a game, pending chain-reaction adjustments in the contracts of Mario Lemieux and Wayne Gretzky. The agent reiterated the family was willing to accept a five-year contract.

"They weren't coming in wanting a bunch of money in the short term so they could bargain again," recalls Farwell. "They were offering to give up Eric's freedom under the collective bargaining agreement."

The organization rationalized it would be saving between $1.3 million and $1.5 million in shedding the contracts of Hextall and Howe. It could also recoup some cash if the Lindroses were agreeable to signing over fees from Eric's endorsements of local products.

Curran informed Farwell of Carl's instructions that the agent's fees were not to come out of the contract, but to be paid by the team. When the GM, the Sniders and Bill Dineen went to Toronto on Monday, July 13, the Flyers were prepared to do a deal.

They visited the Lindros home and had lunch at a nearby restaurant. Eric and his coach-to-be excused themselves to play golf while the others got down to business at Kirke's downtown office.

"I won't ask for more than $3.5 million a year and I won't take one cent less," said Curran. He left the Flyer contingent in privacy to think things over. "Let's get it done," said Ed Snider. After Carl agreed to add an option year to the contract and to grant the club's request for Eric's local commercial monies, the deal was essentially completed by 8 P.M. that evening.

Lindros agreed on a contract including a $2.5-million signing bonus (to be paid in increments of $500,000 a year), plus a base salary of $2 million for two seasons and $2.5 million for the next four. An additional $1 million a year was being assigned to the player for promotional activities on behalf of the team (to be be reduced to $500,000 the last four seasons).

Eric could earn incremental bonuses for team regular-season and playoff successes, for surpassing various individual scoring thresholds, for being named to All-Star teams, and for winning or finishing second in the balloting for league trophies such as the Hart and Calder.

The contract stipulated that if the average salary of the three highest-paid players in the league (Wayne Gretzky excepted) became more than Lindros's, he would get a raise to that amount. The player also would receive adjustments in base salary on a sliding scale if he won one or more Hart trophies.

And, oh yes, the agreement stipulated that Lindros could not be traded to the Quebec Nordiques or any team run by Marcel Aubut.

The parties toasted the deal at an English pub near Kirke's office, then the Flyer contingent flew home on the Spectacor jet. Farwell and Dineen were to return to Toronto the next day to fly the family to Philadelphia for Eric's signing and introduction to the media.

After midnight, Eric called his two best friends, Jeff Hardy and Shannon Finn, and invited them along for his first-ever look at his new home.

"Last night was probably the best night we've had

in years," said the denim-clad 19-year-old millionaire when he stepped onto the tarmac at Philadelphia International Airport. "The whole year has been tough not only on me, but on my parents. They tried to act as shields and take the heat."

As he made his way to Farwell's Mercedes, Lindros stopped to sign a trading card for a police officer. He was asked by a reporter if he knew what a cheesesteak was. "I have no idea," Philadelphia's newest sporting hero admitted.

The Lindroses went for dinner at Old Original Bookbinders, strolled the South Street area during the evening, and spent the night at the Four Seasons Hotel. "We were surprised and impressed with Philadelphia," recalls Carl. "We thought the city would be more worn than it was."

The memorandum of agreement was signed the next morning, then Eric faced reporters. He seemed more awed by the lavishness of the hotel bathtub and an encounter with actor Will Smith of the television series *Fresh Prince of Bel Air* than with the size of the media gathering.

"I don't consider myself a celebrity," he said. "I was gawking at Will Smith. Money is just security. You want to be paid what you feel you are worth. I'll earn the money. I'll give the effort."

After Farwell and Jay Snider helped Lindros put on a Flyer jersey emblazoned with his longtime number, No. 88, the kid gave an exaggerated "Whewwwwwwww." Standing at the podium, hands in pockets, he insisted the responsibility of leading the Flyers' resurrection would not be overwhelming. "Pressure is just something you put on yourself," he said. "This is not going to be a one-man team."

Farwell, too, insisted Lindros was not joining a hopelessly stripped-down club. "I know we're taking some risk with young guys in goal," said the GM. "But if people step in and play, we might really surprise teams.

"What we did was take our good, solid guy, our second-best center [Ricci], and replace him with a player who jumps ahead of even our best center [Brind'Amour]. Do I think we're going to step in and compete? I sure do."

Jay gushed about the length of the deal. "By agreeing to a six-year contract, it showed both sides are completely committed to this marriage," he said. "And of course we all feel it is one that will last forever."

Bonnie, wearing a a necklace with a Flyers' pendant, reflected back to having enrolled not-so-little Eric in hockey for no better reason than to allow him

to work off his boundless energy. "He was just a real busy baby," she recalled, "and we wanted to tire him out so he would lay down at night. This [money and attention] wasn't our objective. He just got better and better."

Carl praised the manner in which the Flyers had negotiated. "We think it is really important Eric be surrounded by quality people," the father said. "And we think that's exactly what we have here and we're very happy."

Meanwhile, negotiations between the Flyers and Nordiques to complete the deal had been predictably unfruitful.

"Quebec had made it clear in the arbitration that it didn't want Ryan Sittler," recalls Bertuzzi. "It was a wise position to take because it made it harder for me to rule for Philly.

"I hoped the whole thing would go away, but when I called the teams on Wednesday [before the Friday deadline], they said they wanted to do it live in my office."

The Flyers, arguing that it was not their fault Quebec had backed out of the deal and failed to exercise the agreed-upon No. 1 pick, offered a second-round choice and winger Chris Simon. The Nordiques maintained simply substituting the 1992 first-rounder for a No. 1 in 1994 (Quebec already had Philadelphia's 1993 pick) would not guarantee them choice as high as seventh overall. So they wanted Simon in addition to the 1994 No. 1.

Bertuzzi gave Farwell and Page fifteen minutes to come to an agreement. They took ten before coming out and asking the arbitrator to make the decision. Bertuzzi chose for Quebec.

"He ruled for us the last time," Farwell said. "We weren't going to win this one."

"The [Flyers] let me know they thought I screwed them," recalls Bertuzzi. "But I was trying to do the right thing, not make anything up to Marcel."

As the loose ends of the Lindros acquisition were tied together, the Sniders could only wish the same for their arena project. Thirteen months after city council had approved the deal, not a shovel had touched the ground of the lot where JFK Stadium once stood.

Goldman-Sachs, the investment banking firm hired to obtain financing by July 11, 1992, had run into a nationwide tightening of credit caused by the recession. Sixers owner Harold Katz agreed to extend the deadline until August 23, 1993, at which point he would become free to search for another home.

On Clarke's recommendation, Farwell signed 30-year-old Ric Nattress, the most affordable, experienced and available defenseman in a market thinned by the NHL's second and third additions in three years—the Ottawa Senators and Tampa Bay Lightning. Desperate for depth, the GM recruited two lesser free agents, defenseman Gord Hynes and winger Greg Paslawski. They and other fringe players like Ryan McGill, a former second-round pick obtained from Chicago in a February trade for Tony

Horacek, had become keys to respectability.

Before dealing for Lindros, the Flyers had accepted an offer of a virtually cost-free week of training in O'Leary, Prince Edward Island, Canada. The media attention his debut would draw made a secluded campsite more desirable than ever. Still, it was not exactly in privacy that he would skate with the team for the first time. Every practice at the 1,200-seat O'Leary Recreation Center was sold out.

As the Flyers flew in after physicals at Voorhees,

the most renowned and controversial rookie in NHL history felt every set of eyes on the plane burning holes in him.

"I knew they thought they would have a playoff team (in 1992-93) and now, because I was here, there were gaps," recalls Lindros. "I was really guarded, determined to be as boring as possible. Plus, I didn't know how things were done on this level, what the routine was."

Keith Acton, the squad's oldest member, was Lindros' assigned bunkmate. It had nothing to do with seniority that the new millionaire spent the night on the floor. "I couldn't sleep," he recalls. "When in doubt, go to the floor. Don't ask why."

The big rookie and his little, sage roomie were the first players on the ice in the morning. "Finally, I was going to be doing what I liked, playing hockey, not answering a bunch of questions," remembers Eric. "Besides, the rink was packed and it was already a production. I didn't want to disappoint."

He didn't. During a scrimmage, Lindros released months of pent-up anxiety by scoring his team's only goal and bouncing bodies all around the rink. "He hunts people down out there," said Clarke. "Look at him."

Indeed, the coach couldn't avert his eyes. "[Lindros] is the strongest player I have ever seen," said Bill Dineen after three days of practice. "He skates and shoots and passes the puck like few players ever at that age. I don't think anyone at 19 has ever had everything in order like this."

Because the veterans found the instant star respectful, their skepticism melted quickly. "I had been thinking, 'Holy bleep we're giving up a lot,'" said Kevin Dineen. "But seeing him, all the excitement wears off on on you. I want to get on the boat and go for the ride."

Indeed, when Lindros made his exhibition launch, the only thing missing was a bottle of champagne cracking against the Spectrum. Two thousand game programs, 400 Lindros T-shirts and 50 full dress No. 88 game jerseys were gobbled up by the 17,226 fans, 2,406 more than had attended the exhibition opener the previous season.

Ironically, the opponent was Quebec, and Eric attacked the Nordiques like they were all personal relations of Aubut. Only 1:01 into the game, the rookie was called for kneeing Tim Hunter. On his second shift, he drew a roughing penalty for dumping Valeri Kamensky. Lindros put his first good scoring chance, a late first-period breakaway, off the glass but converted Recchi's goalmouth pass, then set up the right wing for the winning goal in a 4-3 victory. "I think the big guy did everything we thought he could," said Bill Dineen.

The following afternoon at Le Colisee, Ricci scored a goal and four assists and Hextall exchanged angry words with several Flyers as Philadelphia, minus Lindros, was routed 11-4. Farwell had decided to make the embittered fans of Quebec City wait for a regular-season visit two weeks hence.

Meanwhile, Keith Allen, who abided too long proper recognition as the builder of two Cup winners and seven semifinalists in fifteen seasons as Philadelphia GM, was inducted into the Hockey Hall of Fame.

"I've always believed our Stanley Cup teams never got all the credit they deserved," said the 69-year-old Flyer executive vice president before he was presented by Ed Snider in ceremonies at Toronto. "A lot of people didn't like us. It made me wonder if this would ever happen."

Lindros had the opposite problem. Expectations were so high, he found himself practically enshrined before playing a single NHL regular-season game. "I just want to add a couple points toward [the Flyers'] grand total," he told the *Daily News'* Les Bowen. "If I make a difference of seven or eight points in the end, I think that's a pretty good goal."

That seemed a fair ambition to Farwell, who was going into the season with a goaltending tandem of 17-game NHL veteran Dominic Roussel and rookie Tommy Soderstrom. When the latter was found to have an irregular heart rhythm and was sidelined for tests, the GM traded third and fifth-round draft choices to Winnipeg for Stephane Beauregard, who had appeared in 61 contests in three trials with the Jets.

Nattress, who lost camp time with a muscle tear in his abdomen, subsequently hurt his back lifting

himself off the training table. Eklund suffered a broken foot and Galley was playing through a case of chronic fatigue syndrome. Farwell worked the waiver draft to acquire defenseman Shawn Cronin and winger Doug Evans. He also traded a fourth-round choice to Detroit for left wing Brent Fedyk, who had been coached at Adirondack by Bill Dineen. For lack of a better alternative, Fedyk was placed on the first line with Recchi and Lindros.

The opening-night matchup against Mario

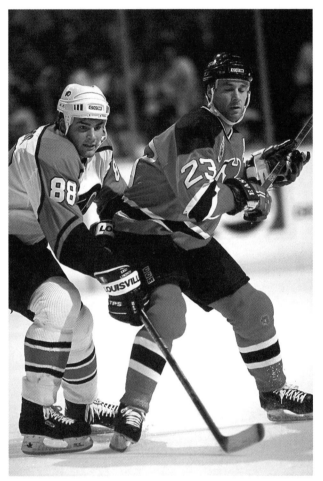

Lemieux and the two-time defending champion Penguins was going to be televised nationally by ESPN, the NHL's new cable rights holder. But as Lindros faced a media pack after the team's morning skate in Pittsburgh, he feigned indifference to the occasion.

"You guys must have a hard time understanding it, but it's just the same game we play as kids," he said. "When you let the atmosphere change you, I think that's when you get into problems."

But when the puck dropped that night, the at-

Lindros brought the Flyers daunting strength, size and the upside potential to be a blue-chip franchise player.

mosphere had changed and the Lindros who had bulldozed his way to 8 goals in 8 exhibition games quickly got into trouble. He lost the opening faceoff to Ron Francis and was caught up ice as Lemieux converted a two-on-one.

"I was just getting my feet wet and I was going against a Hart Trophy winner," Lindros recalls. "When I go into a situation, I like to have a chance. And I had none that night."

After Kevin Stevens made it 2-0, the Civic Arena crowd taunted the high-priced rookie with "Errrrric" chants every time he touched the puck. Rick Tocchet rattled Lindros against the glass. Eric's rush helped set up a goal by Fedyk, but the Flyers were being badly outplayed. Only Roussel's 30 saves held the deficit to 3-1 going into the final period.

But then the struggling Lindros got a break. On the first shift of the third period, Jaromir Jagr fumbled a puck at the goalmouth and Eric tucked his first NHL goal—unassisted—inside the left post. "I think it loosened me up," he said later. It also aroused his teammates. Only 48 seconds later, Evans tied the game.

On Lindros's next shift, he fed Recchi, whose bullet beat goalie Tom Barrasso as Fedyk tumbled into the crease. However, a tape review, the NHL's new procedure on disputed goals, determined Fedyk had used his glove to knock the puck in.

Roussel's hands looked illegal too, when he stopped Lemieux on a breakaway to preserve the 3-3 tie. Afterwards, Eric admitted that he had been a nervous wreck. "Usually, on the day of the game, I sleep like a bear from 1 to 5, but today I didn't sleep too well," he told reporters. "But when our team started to come back in the third period, I thought 'Now *that's* hockey.'"

Despite the game-turning goal, media reviews of Lindros's debut were lukewarm. High expectations would be part of the territory, according to somebody in the Pittsburgh locker room who had suffered a similar experience. "It's pretty tough the first couple of years," Lemieux told Rich Hofmann of the *Daily News.* "You want to do it right away, but you learn that it takes time."

The 17,380 fans who filled the Spectrum three nights later for Lindros' home debut against New Jersey were not demanding instant gratification, only a glimpse of better times ahead. But again Eric disappointed for forty minutes, until Benning's second goal of the game tied the score, 4-4, midway through the third period.

Lindros then stole the puck from Scott Niedermayer, accelerated down the left wing boards and broke in. With Scott Stevens cutting off Eric's angle, goalie Chris Terreri decided on a poke check, but the center pulled the puck back, stepped over the sprawled netminder's stick and scored. The Spectrum exploded. Brind'Amour's goal into the empty net sealed a 6-4 victory and happy days seemed here again.

"I felt like the fans were just sitting there waiting for us to do something good and it wouldn't come," said Lindros. "And finally, it came."

The following night in Landover, Paslawski set up Lomakin, then Dineen, for third-period goals and the Flyers, though outshot 34-15, came from behind to win once more, 4-2. "We're not exactly playing well, but we keep winning." said Lindros.

So were the Nordiques, 2-0 headed into Lindros's visit to Le Colisee. "The fans shouldn't boo him, they should cheer him," said Quebec's Tony Twist. "Look how good he has made us. I don't think he can fill the shoes of the four Flyers we got for him."

Lindros was assigned Dave Brown as a roommate-cum-bodyguard and the center tried to pretend it was just another road game. "I think there's been a lot of overreaction," Eric told a news conference at the hotel after the team's arrival. "It's just a case of one particular player who didn't want to play for one particular owner, that's all. I don't expect roses, just the regular boos. It's just a hockey game."

The *citoyens* didn't see it the same way. To them, Lindros was more than just than an uppity guest who had coldly turned down an invitation. He had become a symbol of anti-Francophone sentiment in Canada. With a referendum for separation scheduled later in the month, a 19-year-old hockey player had become a flashpoint for political controversy.

The Nordiques' radio outlet urged fans to show up with bibs to mock Lindros and handed out 3,000 pacifiers at the door. Some fans dressed in diapers and threw eggs onto the ice as the Flyers came out for the warmup. When Ricci scored only 59 seconds into the game, coins and batteries rained down. A "Bleep You Lindros!" chant began and the organist picked up its rhythm.

The kid played hard, heedless of the ruckus. He knocked down Hextall, who had to be restrained from retaliating, then beat the ex-Flyer on a power-play setup from Recchi, and again on a shorthanded breakaway. Nevertheless, Ricci scored to spark a three- goal Quebec rally in the final four minutes that pulled the Nordiques away to a 6-3 victory. "It wasn't difficult to get ready for this one," Ricci said.

Motivation did not appear to be a problem for the winning goalie, either. "You wouldn't want [fan misbehavior] to happen every night," said Hextall. "But if anybody understands emotion, I can."

Asked if he thought Lindros also did, the former Flyer shrugged. "He scored two goals," said Hextall. "He probably thrives on it."

Farwell, furious at Nordique management's disinterest in crowd control, refused to allow Lindros to come to an interview area. Gil Stein, who had been hit with debris in a seat just above ice level, said the league would take steps to "see that this doesn't happen again."

The only steps Lindros wanted to take were out of town. "I'm going to get the hell out of here," he said. The road, home, and Quebec debuts were behind him. "Good," he said. "Now we can work on other things."

He bought a four-wheel drive truck, rented a condo in the Main Street complex in Voorhees, New Jersey, and quickly seemed to forget just how much toil would be required of him. Lindros skated without passion through consecutive losses, 5-4 at the Spectrum to the Islanders and 2-0 at New Jersey.

A late goal by Evans produced a 5-4 Spectrum victory over Winnipeg, but reality quickly set in for a team with nine new players, most of them marginal. The Flyers rallied from a 3-1 deficit in Uniondale only to go down 4-3 when Paslawski fumbled the puck up the slot on the winning goal.

Roussel began to suffer battle fatigue from the constant shelling. Philadelphia wasted a Paslawski hat trick in a 7-6 home loss to Montreal and collapsed late in an 8-4 defeat at Madison Square Garden. The players closed the locker-room doors to talk things over, and two nights later, Lindros scored twice in his most dominating performance yet, a 5-5 tie in Chicago. The following night, however, he was ejected for hitting from behind early in a 6-4 defeat at St. Louis. When the trip closed with another loss to the Rangers, 3-1, Philadelphia had won only once in 11 games.

Bill Dineen turned to Beauregard and reunited Fedyk with Recchi and Lindros. The big guy came to the aid of Hynes by leveling veteran St. Louis defenseman Lee Norwood with several right hands

and Fedyk ripped in consecutive goals within 1:08 as the Flyers roared from behind to a 4-2 home victory. "I wrestled a bear when I was 20 years old at the Pennsylvania State Fair," said Norwood. "The bear wasn't as strong as that kid."

Recchi scored six points in an 8-5 Spectrum win over the Islanders and the Flyers manufactured a turnaround in the shape of an octagon. Fedyk (wearing No. 18), Lindros (No. 88) and Recchi (No. 8) ran off 12 points in a 7-2 Spectrum blasting of Ottawa.

The Crazy 8's line totaled eight points in a 7-3 pounding of the Rangers that brought Philadelphia's record to .500. "When Eric comes skating at the defense at full speed, they don't know whether to just fall down or get out of the way," said Evans.

A 5-game winning streak ended with a listless 4-3 loss in Boston on November 21. "That's not the way we play," Lindros said. "I'm embarrassed." The following night at the Spectrum, he came out determined to do something about it. Two minutes into

Kevin Dineen's 35 goals ranked fourth on the Flyers in 1992-93.

the game, Eric attempted to make a pancake out of Petr Svoboda just as Recchi was also taking a piece of the Buffalo defenseman.

Lindros tumbled over both players and could rise only as far as one knee. He watched from the Superbox as Len Barrie, called up from Hershey due to an elbow injury to Brind'Amour, scored with 15 seconds remaining to salvage a 4-4 tie.

Dr. Arthur Bartolozzi's initial diagnosis of a stretched medial collateral ligament in Lindros' left knee was confirmed by an MRI the next day. After the Flyers announced their star would be out one to two weeks, he shrugged off suggestions his craving for body contact invited injury. "Everyone gets hurt," he said. "This is the way I've played since I was a kid."

Farwell agreed: "I don't think you can change his style," said the GM. "That's the package." And without Lindros, Philadelphia came in a plain brown wrapper. The return of Eklund did not prevent a 9-3 embarrassment at Uniondale.

When the Nordiques visited, Ricci absent-mindedly started towards the wrong penalty box and Hextall was made aware he no longer was welcome on the Spectrum's home team bench. Standing in front of it jawing with Carkner, Hextall was squirted with a water bottle by McGill. "I got him in the mouth," said the defenseman. "I thought maybe he was thirsty."

Hextall, who skated away, was far more insulted by Claude Boivin's game-winner in overtime. "I'm a little miffed right now," said the goalie. "But [the homecoming] wasn't as difficult as I thought it would be."

This was in contrast to the Flyers, who found winning without Lindros to be almost impossible. The only consolation in a 3-2 loss in Ottawa to the pitiful Senators was the secondary play the defeat received in the newspapers. Police in Oshawa, Ontario, had issued a warrant for Lindros' arrest on a complaint filed by a 24-year-old woman. Lynne Nunney claimed that six days previously, he had spit and poured beer on her at Koo Koo Bananas, a Whitby, Ontario, nightspot.

Lindros, who had been excused to go home for the weekend, was at the bar with several friends, who Nunney said tried to crowd her off the dance floor, causing the confrontation. She complained that instead of apologizing in the parking lot afterwards, Lindros had said, "I make $3.5 million a year. What are you going to do?"

The Flyer flew to Toronto to surrender and was

told to put on handcuffs while being driven to be fingerprinted. Upon returning to Philadelphia, Lindros disputed Nunney's version and said being a celebrity had made him a victim. "If I was a student and beer [was] thrown, I don't think anything would have happened," he said.

His friend Jeff Hardy was subsequently charged, while Lindros filed a countersuit against Nunney. "I just can't let this pass," he said. His teammates, meanwhile, were having trouble completing a pass. Philadelphia was blasted 7-1 at the Spectrum by Boston.

As Farwell traded the little-used Steve Kasper to Tampa Bay for minor-leaguer Dan Vincelette and moved Mark Pederson to San Jose for winger Dave Snuggerud. Bill Dineen turned to Soderstrom, who had undergone three different procedures to correct Wolff-Parkinson-White Syndrome, an abnormality that sends an extra electrical impulse to the heart.

In his NHL debut, the Swede gave up four goals on Pittsburgh's first 13 shots, including two by Rick Tocchet in his Spectrum homecoming. The Flyers fought back to tie, but Jagr's overtime goal sent them down to a club record-tying sixth-consecutive defeat, 5-4.

The next day, Lindros skated without pain. So the following afternoon, he dressed for a home game with Chicago. "He didn't take off his jersey after the warmup, so I just let it be," smiled Bill Dineen after the young star assisted on a goal in the 3-1 victory. But Lindros was dead on his feet the night after in a 4-1 loss at Tampa. And when the Flyers played Santa Claus in a 4-0 December 23 loss to Pittsburgh before a crowd less charitable than the season, rumors of Dineen's demise gained momentum.

"We're certainly not playing hard enough," said Farwell. The players came to their kindly coach's defense. "Guys love Bill, they're not trying to get him fired," said Recchi.

Indeed, Lindros was fond of the man. "I couldn't have asked for a better coach at the time," he recalls. "He set a whole big picture, reminded me this was just the beginning and that things would get better. I loved talking to him. But we had some wrong people in here who were taking advantage of him."

At Landover, Washington goalie Jim Hrivnak did his best to save Dineen's job by surrendering four Philadelphia goals within 5:11 of the second period. Predictably, a 4-1 lead dissolved into a 5-4 deficit before Washington defenseman Al Iafrate pushed the net off its magnets with 18 seconds remaining. Lindros cashed a penalty shot between Don Beaupre's legs to complete a hat trick and salvage a 5-5 tie.

The bus developed a flat tire on the way home, then caught fire as it limped toward an I-95 rest stop on bare wheel bearings. This was exactly the kind of hard driving the Flyers' brass was beginning to believe the team needed. Farwell contacted Mike Keenan, who had been fired the previous month as Chicago GM after failing to agree to a contract extension. Keenan was interested, but when asked if he could go to work immediately, decided not to make a commitment.

Lindros felt his knee give during the morning skate on December 29 in Los Angeles and was told to take another two days off. This time, Brind'Amour picked up the slack, scoring six points in a startling 10-2 rout of the Kings, then adding a goal and two assists in a 6-2 victory at San Jose. Eric returned in Calgary to score a goal, but the Flyers came apart in a 7-3 loss and so did Claude Boivin's knee. The former first-round choice underwent surgery that ended his season, while Lindros continued to tempt the same fate by playing without a brace during a 2-2 comeback tie in Edmonton.

Spurred by a heart-to-heart talk with Coach Dad, Kevin Dineen scored a hat trick in an 8-2 Spectrum rout of the Capitals. Yushkevich was playing like a building block, Galley was getting stronger, Nattress was back in the lineup and Philadelphia was gaining momentum as Lindros played himself into shape. But after helping the franchise to its 1,000th victory, 4-3 over the Rangers on January 9, he reported the next night for a game against Edmonton with a reinjured knee.

A phone tip to WIP reported Lindros had interrupted an altercation between a buddy visiting from Toronto and a bar patron. The young star denied the knee was hurt during the incident and defended his actions. "If one of your friends gets into a little altercation and you tell him, 'C'mon, let's go', are you at fault for that?" he asked. "It's ridiculous."

Dr. Bartolozzi drew fluid from the joint before Eric went home to see Dr. Peter Fowler, a London, Ontario orthopedist and family friend. Fowler ordered Lindros away from the rink for two and a half weeks, while Farwell suggested his 19-year-old franchise player build leg strength by walking away at the first sign of trouble in public places.

When the GM suggested Lindros might be better served living with a Flyer veteran, Eric bristled. "Why do I need a roommate?" he asked. "This is just ridiculous."

Actually, the kid required company, not a babysitter. "There weren't many single guys and everybody would go home to their wives and girlfriends and I would hang at the rink by myself," Lindros recalls. "I had a condo in a ghost town, I cooked meals for myself and had no one to talk to. My phone bills were thousands a month. I would talk my friends into driving down ten to twelve hours. I had nobody else.

"It was horrible. I hated it. It helped that down here the [Koo Koo Bananas incident] wasn't taken very seriously, but back home there was a lot of strain. I felt like the world was caving in on me."

The walls collapsed on the team, too, just as it did during Lindros's first absence. In an attempt to spruce up the league's twentieth-ranked power play, Philadelphia traded Benning to Vancouver for winger Josef Beranek and defenseman Greg Hawgood. And, in an effort to let Farwell know he wasn't expected to rebuild a fallen empire in one day, Philadelphia extended his contract for three more years.

But the Flyers, thinner than the patience of the people running them, remained easily overwhelmed in their own end. The club blew a 3-0 lead to Detroit into a 7-4 loss, then overcame four-goal deficits against Boston and the Islanders and still lost both games. "We're pretty fragile," said Bill Dineen.

Philadelphia's one victory in a 9-game period came at the Spectrum over coach Paul Holmgren's Whalers, 5-4. The warmest cheers during the time were for an ArenaVision message that Tim Kerr, signed by Hartford at the beginning of the season after being released by the Rangers, had announced his retirement. Kerr was given a standing ovation in absentia. "They hold their hockey players special here," said a touched Holmgren.

Soderstrom's heart once again began to manufacture an unwanted beat, so the Flyers turned to Roussel for the first time in six weeks. He failed to part the waters, losing to Buffalo and in Montreal. But after Kevin Dineen's early third-period goal produced a 2-2 tie at Madison Square Garden on February 3, the clouds began to clear, just like Lindros's name in an Oshawa courtroom.

Three independent defense witnesses said they did not see him pour beer on Nunney and, after three days of testimony, the charge of common assault was dismissed. "This could have been resolved before it came to trial," said Ontario Provincial Judge J. Rhys Morgan. He dissuaded Lindros from filing countercharges that Nunney doused him first.

"Being accused of something you didn't commit and getting this much media attention isn't good for anybody," Eric told reporters outside the courtroom. Asked if he was going to be more careful in the future, Lindros remained defiant. "I'm still a kid and I like to do things that kids do," he said. "What was rude and insulting about retaliating?"

Nevertheless, the Flyer brass toasted quietly—beer still in the glass—when Lindros moved in with Kevin Dineen and his wife, Ann. Upon his return, he and his landlord both made themselves at home against Ottawa. Lindros scored two goals and Dineen a hat trick in an 8-1 Spectrum victory.

After a cardiologist cleared Soderstrom's return,

wondered aloud why a captain had never been appointed. "It would be nice if they named somebody," he said. "With 28 games left they could have done this a long time ago."

Bill Dineen had passed for lack of a strong candidate. He questioned whether Recchi could handle the additional responsibility and knew the appointment of his son would be perceived as nepotism. "If I would have made a choice, it would have been Galley," recalls Dineen. "But the assistant coaches (Ken Hitchcock and Craig Hartsburg) felt we didn't have the right guy for it."

As the eventual team captain, Lindros, struggled to recondition himself, the Flyers seemed to take confidence just from his presence. Philadelphia rallied from a 4-2 deficit to tie Calgary in a neutral-site game in Cincinnati, then won a 3-2 thriller in Vancouver when Dineen intercepted a pass by Adrian Plavsic and beat the Canucks and the clock with 1.6 seconds to spare. Four nights later, at Cleveland, the Flyers cut it even closer, pulling out a 5-5 tie against Detroit when Fedyk scored off a scramble with only 0.8 seconds remaining.

Lindros dominated in a 5-2 victory at Hartford, then outslugged Scott Stevens in a 6-2 defeat of New Jersey. Kevin Dineen ran his hot streak to 12 goals in 13 games and Recchi was on his way to becoming the Flyers' first 100-point scorer since 1975-76.

Meanwhile, the guy who set the franchise record that season with 119 was feeling like a relic, and not because seventeen seasons had passed. On the contrary, at age 43, the Flyers' senior vice president was finding himself too young to be a senior anything.

"I was bored," said Clarke. "It wasn't anybody's fault because Russ and Jay both tried to include me. But when I went to the owners' meetings in Florida (in early December), Mr. Snider was there and I realized that I was way down the line in responsibility.

Claude Boivin; Hextall miffed over his game-winner in overtime.

the Flyers took further heart. The 23-year-old Swede combined with Montreal's Andre Racicot for the first scoreless tie at the Spectrum since Bernie Parent dueled St. Louis in 1969. "He's had four heart [procedures] and he never gets rattled," Bill Dineen said. "I can't say enough good things about him."

The coach wasn't as complimentary towards his team as a whole, lecturing it about breaches of discipline before a February 13 game at the Meadowlands. Lindros promptly threw Bernie Nicholls to the ice on the opening face-off, Eklund quickly took another penalty, and the Devils went on to score three power-play goals in a 6-4 victory.

The team obviously lacked leadership and Recchi

Your ego wakes up and you realize you don't like sitting on the side, watching hockey go by."

It was moving quickly, too. Franchises were granted at the owners' session to Miami and Anaheim, creating two more general manager positions. Clarke decided he wanted one of them. Inquiries on his behalf were made by both Stein and Jay Snider. In late January, H. Wayne Huizenga, the Miami owner-to-be, sent a plane for Clarke to come for an interview.

"It went well," he recalls. "And I just figured out the things that bugged me about being a GM, like dealing with agents, you just have to learn to deal with."

In late February, with the new franchises committed to starting the following season, Huizenga asked Clarke to come negotiate a contract. Two days later, on March 1, he was introduced as the general manager of the yet-to-be-named team.

"I've said many times that Bob is like another son to me," Ed Snider said. "I truly love him and I only want what is best for him and at this point in time, taking this job may very well be just that."

Magnanimous as he tried to be, the owner didn't feel any better about Clarke's departure than Lindros did, who had been counselled by Clarke both on and off the ice. Farwell's public lectures about Lindros's living arrangements and the medical handling of his knee problem had provoked some resentment in the young star. But mostly, a 19-year-old not used to losing felt the aloof general manager was not improving the team quickly enough.

"I was bleeped," Lindros recalls. "The team sucked and the only bright light upstairs, the guy I believed in, was leaving. I remember being in the directors' lounge, still out with my knee, when Clarkie told he might be going. Life sucked."

But it went on, with reason to celebrate it, too. Mario Lemieux, diagnosed with Hodgkin's disease in early January, finished his final radiation treatment on the morning of March 2 and rejoined his teammates that night at the Spectrum.

The fans gave the Pittsburgh superstar a standing ovation when he skated onto the ice and another hand when he scored through Roussel's legs early in the second period. The cheers were louder, however,

when Galley broke a 4-4 tie with 3:33 remaining, then blocked a Lemieux shot in the final minute to preserve Philadelphia's first victory over the Penguins in 15 meetings.

Three nights later at Landover, Soderstrom stood on his head, Recchi broke a scoreless tie in the third period, and Lindros and Brind'Amour added goals as the Flyers recorded only their second divisional road victory of the season, 3-0. At 24-30-11, the team still had outside hope at a playoff spot. But when

Lindros came down with the flu at New Jersey, the Flyers turned in a sickly effort that ruined the occasion of Recchi's 100th point. "We didn't do a bleeping thing," said Bill Dineen after the 7-3 loss. "I can't understand it, a game as big as that."

The coach wanted his players to die as hard as the 3,000 fans who ignored what weather experts called the East Coast "storm of the century" to come to the Spectrum on Saturday afternoon, March 13, to watch the Kings. The score was tied 1-1 late in the first period when debris swirling from high winds

Mark Recchi's 53 goals and 70 assists in 1992-93 established new career highs for the right winger.

crashed through a Spectrum windowpane, sending glass flying into the concourse.

Thankful that the only injuries were minor cuts suffered by a concession worker, Spectrum officials decided not to take further risk. They postponed the game to the boos of the all-weather zealots. The NHL also called off Philadelphia's game in Hartford the following evening. After almost three feet of snow was cleared, the Flyers plowed Minnesota under, 4-3, in the final game between the two rivals born simultaneously twenty-six years earlier. The North Stars were moving to Dallas in 1993-94 to become the Stars.

Farwell unloaded Greg Paslawski to Calgary for a late-round pick and Lemieux dumped four goals on the Flyers in a 9-3 loss at Pittsburgh. Lindros and Scott Stevens rammed each other repeatedly—"It looked like rutting season out there," said Devils coach Herb Brooks—but 21 Flyer third-period shots still left Philadelphia short in a 3-2 defeat.

Although Lindros's hat trick brought his total to 35 goals and produced a 5-4 victory over the struggling Rangers at Madison Square Garden, it depressed him to be twelve points out of a playoff spot behind an obviously vulnerable New York club. "This is a team we should beat," Lindros said.

Roussel, no longer the people's choice with the emergence of Soderstrom, and Carkner, never Mr. Popularity in his five Flyer seasons, continued to be booed, which brought Lindros to their defense. Also, to issue a battle cry. "I don't think we've had pride every game," he said. "It's time to make a point about what our team is about." He then went pointless in the next three games.

The signing of Nattress had turned out to be largely pointless, too. The defenseman was lost for the year with knee tendonitis. Frankly, he was missed in Philadelphia about as much as Lindros in Quebec. The Colisee crowd barely noticed Eric as the Nordiques, headed for a 100-point season, blew away Philadelphia, 8-3.

Recchi celebrated his 50th goal in the replay of the snow-canceled game with the Kings, but after the 3-1 loss he criticized the coach for not practicing the power play.

A once-inconceivable fourth consecutive spring without playoffs was virtually assured before the Flyers began to come on. Soderstrom shut out a Toronto team that had lost only three of its last 25 games, 4-0, and Lindros played commandingly in a 4-2 victory at Winnipeg. Following the Flyer Hall of Fame inductions of Ed Van Impe and Joe Scott—

the former minority owner whose moral and financial support of Ed Snider was critical to the fledgling franchise—Lindros was again outstanding in a 4-3 Spectrum victory over Washington.

"The big guy is playing again like he did before he was injured," said Bill Dineen. Indeed, Lindros's enthusiasm was sustained even though the Flyers remained nine points out with five games remaining. "I want to have a good feeling into the off-season," Eric said. "I don't care if it is too little, too late."

For Bill Dineen, it already was. After Soderstrom shutout the Leafs for the second time in nine days, 4-0, at Maple Leaf Gardens, the Flyers returned to the Spectrum for their final home game, where they entertained both Mike Keenan and a strong desire desire to bring him back.

Named Canada's coach for the upcoming World Hockey Championships in Germany, Keenan wanted players from Philadelphia and New York (which was one loss away from elimination) for his tournament team. But he also desired full-time employment in the NHL again.

"[Ed and Jay] knew him better than I did," recalls Farwell. "I was on board with the decision." The day after Recchi's franchise-record 120th point set up Greg Hawgood for the only goal in a 1-0 Philadelphia victory over New York, Keenan went to Ed Snider's Bryn Mawr residence.

"He was the best coach available and I was going to take a shot at him," recalls Ed.

"I had some trepidation," recalls Jay. "I think Russ did, too. But I can't say I was opposed. We had fired him and he was up to a lot of the same shenanigans in Chicago, but we were saying the heck with it, the guy wins."

Keenan's bitterness toward the people who had released him four years earlier had long disappeared. "I'm not a person who holds grudges," he recalls. "I had plenty of time to get over the hurt and a lot of respect for Ed Snider."

Ed Snider put a five-year contract worth $750,000 a season in front of Keenan and wanted him to sign it immediately. Keenan asked for time to think it over.

"Everything was up in the air with my life," recalls Keenan. "My marriage was coming apart, and I had memories of living with (wife) Rita and (daughter) Gayla in Philadelphia. I was too raw from personal things to make a good evaluation."

He flew to Toronto, where Team Canada was gathering, and within twenty-four hours received a call from Bob Gutkowski, the Madison Square Garden president. The following day, Gutkowski and Neil

Smith met Keenan at the Toronto offices of his business advisor, Rob Campbell. Keenan was tendered a five-year deal by the Rangers that began at $750,000 and escalated to $1 million. The contract also called for a $660,875 signing bonus, plus a 5 percent loan to buy a house.

Keenan was told it was a one-time offer, to take it or leave it on the spot. He accepted and called Ed Snider back with his regrets.

The Philadelphia owner was steamed. "I think

delphia braintrust's conviction that the team needed a stronger hand. So Bill Dineen remained a lame duck, even as his son, whose hat trick paced a 7-4 victory in Buffalo, continued to pedal furiously. The following night, Yushkevich's overtime goal in the makeup game in Hartford, enabled the Flyers, 36-37-11, to close the season with an 8-game winning streak,

Recchi won the Bobby Clarke Award and Galley, who had overcome chronic fatigue syndrome to enjoy

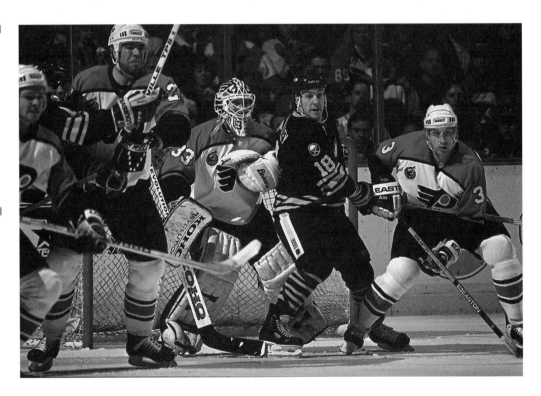

Dominic Roussel in close quarters vs. Buffalo. Roussel appeared in 34 regular-season games in 1992-93.

he used my offer to get what he did from the Rangers," he says today. "I'm not doubting him about what was going on with his personal life, or saying he didn't have valid reasons for not wanting to come back here. I don't think he came here with the intention of using us.

"I just believe that once Mike made the decision that he didn't want to come, he took our offer and used it in New York."

Keenan says that isn't true. "Money had nothing to do with it," he recalls. "The Rangers offered more, but not substantially more. With the Flyers, I wondered between Ed, Jay and Russ where everybody fit in. That would be three people to answer to. But mostly, it was personal. I didn't want to go back to where I'd had a life with my wife and daughter."

Keenan's snub was not going to change the Phila-

an all-star-caliber season, won the Barry Ashbee Trophy. Lindros scored 41 goals and 75 points despite missing 23 games. He finished behind Winnipeg's Teemu Selanne, Boston's Joe Juneau and Toronto's Felix Potvin in rookie of the year balloting, but overall did not disappoint. The Flyers had a .549 winning percentage in games their centerpiece player was in the lineup. "He came through with flying colors," said Jay Snider.

With the benefit of hindsight, Lindros agreed his first season had not been a complete disaster. "I wouldn't say it's too far off what I'd envisioned," he told the *Daily News's* Bowen. "This club missed the playoffs three straight years, then traded five players for me. I'm disappointed in a lot of respects, but not totally."

Dineen, who accompanied Farwell on a scouting

mission to Germany, was reassured his old scouting job would still be there for him, even if the Flyers hired a new coach. "I probably would have liked to keep [coaching]," he recalls. "But I knew my age (60) was a factor and there were a lot of guys out there. I could live with whatever happened."

Farwell, whose drafts had been strongly influenced by his western Canadian background, was naturally drawn to a coach who enjoyed legendary success in the WHL. Terry Simpson made a reputation upgrading a dominant Junior B franchise, the Prince Albert Raiders, into a Junior A powerhouse and had coached Canada to gold and silver medals at the 1985 and 1986 World Junior Championships.

Hired by the Islanders to replace the retiring Al Arbour in 1986, Simpson's first Islander team upset Washington in the first round before extending the division champion Flyers to seven games. A regular-season Patrick Division title followed, but a first-round defeat to the Devils and a 7-18-2 start in 1988-89 brought about his firing.

He had grated on the surviving Islander stars from the Cup teams. But Farwell, who had a one-man list, believed the 49-year-old Simpson, an assistant at Winnipeg for the previous three seasons, would be better as a result of his Long Island experience.

So did the candidate, who was thrilled when Farwell called. "There was really no decision to make," he recalls. "I knew Russ a little bit and had come to respect him from an adversarial point of view. The Flyers were traditionally a good organization and Eric Lindros was just an added bonus. I saw it as a chance to succeed."

Simpson flew to Philadelphia to meet with Farwell and Jay. The GM then negotiated a three-year contract in Toronto with the candidate's agent, Don Meehan. Meanwhile, Dineen still had not been informed of a decision that had been etched in stone since before the Keenan flirtation. "What are you waiting for?" Jay asked his GM.

"Bill knew how we were proceeding," recalls Farwell, "but I underestimated what the public speculation would do to him." It wasn't until Friday, May 21, the day of Simpson's signing, that the GM phoned Dineen at Lake George.

"I thought they could have let me know a little sooner," recalls Dineen. "But Russ had his own problems, probably.

"He was unbelievable to work with and I'm not bitter about it all. And, considering I took over a struggling team, got it straightened out and then

had it torn up by the trade, I have no problem with the job (60-60-20) I did."

Ray Parrillo broke the news of Simpson's hiring in Sunday's *Inquirer.* The next day, at Ovations, he was introduced as the ninth head coach in the team's history.

"I've got a great respect for players," Simpson, 49, told reporters, "but players have to take responsibility for their jobs."

Indeed, Jay Snider, who pronounced the Flyers ready to return to the playoffs by the following spring, made clear his perception that discipline had been lacking.

"Bill is a fabulous guy and he's very bright and a good coach," said the team president. "(But) you try to match a coach with the makeup of your team. We didn't make a change because of Eric. He hasn't been difficult. The issue is the dynamics of the team, dealing with potential jealousies around a superstar."

Garry Galley said what most of the senior players felt: Dineen did not have the commanding presence to handle big, and in some cases immature, egos. "He had to handle a lot of volatile situations this year, especially with Eric and a few other marquee players," said the defenseman. "Some guys took advantage of Billy's good nature."

"You have to demand more of your players," Dave Brown told the *Daily News's* Bill Fleischman. "And they have to play for the team more."

In a cost-cutting mode, the Flyers cut off negotiations with television voice Mike Emrick. They sent Gene Hart back to television to work with Gary Dornhoefer, who in turn had replaced Bill Clement, gone to do full-time work with ESPN.

Jim Jackson, the 30-year-old voice of the AHL Utica Devils, was hired to do the WIP play-by-play. With Bobby Taylor on his way to Tampa Bay, Steve Coates, the pregame and intermission host from 1984 to 1991, became the radio analyst.

Meanwhile Keith Acton, offered only a termination contract by the Flyers, signed with Washington. Farwell lost Andrei Lomakin and Hynes to Clarke's Florida Panthers in the expansion draft, traded Shawn Cronin to San Jose for future considerations and bought out Nattress.

Depth, size and character were of the highest priority and the lowest availability. "About five of the kind of guys we could have used had gone to Florida in the expansion," recalls Farwell. "They just weren't there.

"We were thin in our ability to deal anyway. We talked about (32-year-old) Dave Poulin (who ultimately signed with Washington), Mike Lalor, and almost signed Grant Ledyard. But the dollars weren't worth it for what we would be getting."

The GM settled on working the fringes, picking up defenseman Jeff Finley and center Dave Tippett as free agents and obtaining defenseman Stewart Malgunas from Detroit for future considerations.

The market was poor for arena-building, too. More than two years following city council approval, financing had not been obtained by Goldman Sachs. "They didn't have the right approach," recalls Jay. "The structure they were proposing was not what the money sources were used to seeing for this kind of project."

Ultimately, the investment house offered its own money, but wanted major equity. Ed Snider could not live with such an arrangement. The August 23 deadline that would free Harold Katz to shop elsewhere for a new Sixers home was looming on the spring day that Lindy Snider, Spectrum II's director of sales and marketing, went to pitch Sam Katz to buy a suite for an arena in jeopardy of not being built.

Sam Katz, no relation to Harold, headed Public Financial Management, a firm that had obtained construction loans for several new sporting palaces, including Baltimore's Oriole Park at Camden Yards, Phoenix's America West Arena and Denver's Coors Field. Sam Katz, an unsuccessful 1991 Philadelphia mayoral candidate who had his eye on running for governor, had briefed Spectacor officials that those other projects had been built using deposits on luxury boxes as collateral, but they opted for the more traditional strategy proposed by Goldman Sachs.

"They believed that since Spectacor had been in business for twenty-four years the capital market would trust them," recalls Katz.

The company was wrong and found out the hard way, just as Ed Snider's daughter found out there was no harder way to sell a Spectrum II suite than face-to-face with a person jilted by Spectacor.

"I'm going to make you work like hell," Sam Katz said. He unleashed on Lindy his anger at being ignored for a project in his own backyard and also about a personal run-in he had suffered with an official from Spectacor Management Group.

"I was upset to hear about it," recalls Lindy. "Carl Hirsch (Spectacor's director of development) and I went to him and essentially apologized. We started talking and he pointed out some facts about arena financing that I relayed to Jay."

"Lindy kept bugging me and I finally contacted him," remembers Jay. "We had a meeting and I brought it back to my Dad."

Sam Katz tried to get the project moving again by approaching PNC Bank about become the prime lender. The same institution that had saved the Philadelphia franchise in 1967 by issuing a $500,000 loan two days before the NHL entry fee came due was willing to lead an association of banks offering an eight-year loan, provided luxury box revenue went first toward servicing the debt.

Ed Snider was willing to take a secondary cut, but Harold Katz saw no benefit in subordinating $6.5 million annually in premium seating when at the end of eight years he would have no equity in the building. The day after the August 23 deadline passed, the Sixers owner reopened negotiations with the administration of New Jersey Governor James Florio.

For both Ed and Jay, the proposed South Philadelphia pleasure palace had turned into the Rue Morgue. The senior Snider's personal stake in the arena had become so high, he had been forced to move his primary residence from California back to Bryn Mawr. "There were guarantees that only I could make," he recalls. "It had put Jay in an untenable position."

The junior Snider had been spending 90 percent of his time on a project born out of self-defense, not a family dream. "We loved the Spectrum and had put so much into it to keep it modern," recalls Jay. "And all the additional revenue from the new arena would end up going to the players anyway. The risk was so great that a lot of times, it didn't seem worth it."

Neither did enduring any longer the prison of his father's shadow. "I had never had a career goal to run the Flyers or Spectacor," Jay recalls. "I had a goal to be in my own business, which I did starting Spectaguard. I want to put my own stamp on something. I didn't think I was going to be able to do it [with the Flyers and Spectacor.]

"I wasn't trying to be Ed Snider. His role as a builder of a sports franchise was unparalleled, like his loyalty to the city and fans. The comparisons grew wearisome for me. Now, because of the arena, he had to be here a lot and it kind of forced the issue. I made a decision to do what I wanted. I told him I was moving on."

Ed was surprised. "But I realized he had to do something with his own company," he said, "I came back to focus mostly on the building and then get the hell out of here back for California. But it dragged on and I cast a big shadow. I don't think Jay was getting any personal satisfaction out of [the Flyers] anymore. It's unfortunate."

On September 23, the Flyer president announced he was taking leave of his day-to-day responsibilities to pursue business ventures in the Far East with Steve Flynn, his cofounder and partner in Spectaguard.

Meanwhile, back at the rink, the NHL had regrouped and renamed its divisions and conferences, entering the Flyers with the Rangers, Devils, Islanders, Capitals, Tampa Bay Lightning and new Florida Panthers in the Atlantic. Conferences were designated Eastern and Western and the playoff format changed to seed teams first through eighth within conferences.

Recchi was signed to a six-year, $15-million contract and Soderstrom was given four years and $2.45 million. After ripping up its nucleus in consecutive summers, the only major change Philadelphia was making before the 1993-94 season was an addition. "I thought Mikael Renberg looked good," volunteered Simpson after watching the first scrimmage at Voorhees.

When the Swedish left wing, twenty-five pounds heavier since being selected fortieth in the 1990 draft, reached backwards to deflect a goal in the exhibition opener against the Devils, Recchi quickly recognized this was serious help for a team that needed it. "He's going to be a helluva hockey player," said Philadelphia's leading scorer. "He's big and tough and he's got a lot of skills."

Lindros had spent the summer taking Clarke's advice to reduce from 235 pounds to 229. The sophomore center tried to ignore all the deadweight dressing at the cubicles around him by agreeing with club brass that it was time the Flyers began moving up. "Making the playoffs is something we should expect," said Eric.

Simpson awarded the captaincy to Dineen, but put an *A* on Lindros' shoulder. It seemed lighter to the kid than the yoke he wore in his rookie season. "I was put in a situation where I was expected to act 30 and I'm not," he told reporters. "I'm 20. I was fighting that last year. I'm a little more relaxed now."

Soderstrom came to camp so at ease he fell asleep, losing the No. 1 goaltending job to Roussel. Terry Carkner, who had reluctantly signed a three-year, $1.8-million contract worth $450,000 less than he felt was deserved, moved to Detroit on opening day in exchange for the more mobile Yves Racine and a fourth-round pick.

A third-period goal by Yushkevich gave Philadelphia a 4-3 victory over Pittsburgh in a rousing opener at the Spectrum, then a five-goal explosion

in the first period at Hartford keyed a 5-2 win. The Flyers rallied from a 3-1 third-period deficit to beat Buffalo 5-3 and shut out the Caps in Landover, 3-0, on the way to six victories in the first seven games.

The fast start would have been cause for celebration had anyone noticed it. The Phillies were on their way to the city's first World Series in eleven years, and the front pages were dominated by another turn in the arena saga.

PNC had agreed to lead eleven other banks in financing $134 million of a project that had grown in cost from $170 million to $200 million. Spectacor would foot $50 million of the bill, with the remaining dollars coming from government sources as outlined in the original deal.

Harold Katz, however, was conspicuously absent from the press conference that immediately followed the banks' agreement. "With what we've gone though in the past year, I won't predict anything," Ed Snider said. "But I haven't reason to believe his goals are not the same as ours."

Sam Katz told reporters the basketball owner would be satisfied quickly. At a testy October 12 meeting at the Holiday Inn in Lionville, Harold Katz was presented with suggestions to compensate him for subordinating his suite profits to the bank. Discussed were plans to allow him to keep one-third of his luxury-seating revenue in exchange for personal guarantees from Ed Snider, a rent cap, and the Sixers being allowed to keep all the revenue from 100 premium courtside seats or a share of the luxury-suite catering revenues.

Harold Katz nodded often. Snider left the meeting with the impression the 76er's owner was amenable. "He never really had agreed, though," recalls Sam Katz. "It's like when Japanese businessmen nod. They aren't agreeing. They're just nodding."

Follow-up negotiations broke down and on October 20, the basketball owner said he would go his own way. "I'm extremely disappointed," Harold Katz said. "I tried to make this happen. But the deal I agreed to was changed drastically.

"I'm not going to be made the culprit. I know the guilty party, the Spectrum people, not me. I made a counterproposal. I didn't think I asked for anything the banks couldn't handle."

A fuming Ed Snider told the media that he had already put $17 million of his own money into the arena and would go forward without a basketball tenant. "It's been like a moving target," Snider said. "He gave us a list of things he wanted last Tuesday. We met most of them, and Thursday he had a whole new list. It's obvious now that he was working on something else."

David L. Cohen, mayor Ed Rendell's chief of staff, said it was too early to give up. "This is not the end of the process, but the middle," he told the *Daily News*. Eagles owner Norman Braman volunteered to finance an 80,000 seat football stadium with seat licenses if the city would donate the arena site, but on Wednesday, November 3, at the urging of Sam Katz, Harold Katz and Snider met again at the St.

"But Ed was difficult, too. I remember early in the process driving up to Santa Barbara from Los Angeles and telling him everything he had to do to subordinate to the banks or else he would lose his monopoly. He totally agreed to it, then later saw the details and the fine print and became resistant.

"There had also been so much mistrust between [Snider and Harold Katz] over such a period of time that I was in a difficult position."

Snider angrily called Harold Katz at his Bryn

Rod Brind'Amour averaged 35 goals per season from 1992 to 1994.

Regis Hotel in New York.

Harold Katz was told he could keep all the premium courtside seating revenue and Snider agreed to personally guarantee part of the PNC loan, enabling the 76ers to assume a lesser obligation to the banks. Snider celebrated at a Chinese restaurant with his wife, Martha, and at the Sixers' opener three nights later, Katz told Phil Jasner of the *Daily News* the deal was "real close."

But the terms faxed to Katz disappointed him and another agreement—forged at a meeting between Snider, Phil Weinberg, Harold Katz and his lawyer Larry Shaiman at the Hotel Atop the Bellevue—fell through when Katz again maintained that what had been agreed to verbally was not on paper. He accused Snider of getting cold feet and changing his mind.

"Harold was a moving target," recalls Sam Katz.

Athyn, Pennsylvania home. When told Katz was sleeping, the Flyer owner told the houseboy, "Wake him up!" After an angry conversation and more negotiations between lawyers, on November 14, Harold Katz and Snider agreed to a deal.

In the meantime, the Flyers' old home was being good to them. Roussel, empowered by an intense offseason conditioning program, ran his record to 7-0 in a 4-2 victory over Quebec and Beranek recorded goals in eight straight games. "Joe comes back to the bench laughing like he thinks it's a joke," said Lindros.

Dineen seemed to be enjoying himself, too. He scored four, including one that broke a 6-6 tie as the Flyers won their last-ever visit to Chicago Stadium, 9-6. Brind'Amour, feeding Dineen and Beranek at a prodigious rate, scored once himself in a 4-3 success in Miami over Clarke's Panthers, while Lindros pumped in No. 13 and Renberg No. 6 in a 4-1 Spectrum victory over Quebec.

The Flyers were 11-3 and Snider was miserable. In the ten days following his agreement with Harold Katz, the hockey owner had become convinced the personal guarantee he was making and his subordination to the banks made the deal unworkable for himself. His top advisors agreed.

Snider met with Rendell, Cohen and William Hankowsky, director the city's official development agency, and told them he wanted to start over again developing a new plan. They gave him until May 1, 1994. On November 28, Snider called Harold Katz and told him the deal was off.

"I never felt better in my life," Snider recalls. "[Harold] Katz had a valid point about not wanting to subordinate without equity, so we tried to find ways to make it more palatable. But he kept wanting more and more, until the deal got ridiculous. There was no risk on his part at all."

Publicly, the Flyer owner took the blame. "It's not Harold's fault," said Snider. "It's mine in that we were pushed over the edge. I looked in the mirror and said it didn't make sense for myself or my partners."

Snider said he would develop separate financial formats for one-team and two-team buildings. But Harold Katz said he couldn't wait. And even Sam Katz was sounding pessimistic. "I thought we had found a middle ground," he told the *Inquirer's* Bob Ford. "But it's increasingly apparent to me that there was only a mirage."

Also proving to be a figment of the imagination was the dominating team Flyer fans believed they saw during October. Philadelphia dropped a challenge for first-place overall, 5-3 in Toronto on November 6. Then, five nights later, the team lost Lindros when he was checked by New Jersey's Bill Guerin and fell over Fedyk. This time it was the right knee, the opposite of the one damaged the previous season, that suffered a collateral ligament tear, putting the NHL's fourth-leading scorer (26 points in 17 games) out from three to six weeks.

Butsayev was substituted onto the No. 1 line. "Just put 88 on his sweater and you'd never know the difference," joked Simpson. Buffalo was not fooled during a 7-2 bombing, driving out Roussel in favor of Soderstrom, who had undergone a fifth procedure to cure his arrhythmia.

Simpson almost had the big one during an 11-5 loss at Pittsburgh. "It's like somebody just pricked

a balloon," said Simpson, "The air's gone right out of the guys."

When the NHL officials walked out on strike, the line of Brind'Amour, Dineen and Beranek, which had sparked the fast start, appeared to be conducting a work slowdown in sympathy. When Recchi suggested the team, enduring longer and harder practices under Simpson than Bill Dineen, needed a day off, the coach suggested the opposite. "I would say we should spend more time at the rink," he said.

Recchi dutifully punched his time card—and two goals into the Hartford net—as the Flyers broke a 3-3 third-period tie to beat the Whalers, 6-3. It was hoped the return of Racine, who missed 15 games with a fractured tibia and a torn medial collateral ligament, would steady a clueless defense. But Philadelphia blew 4-1 and 5-4 leads into a 5-5 tie at Boston, then lost to the Islanders and their new goalie, Ron Hextall, when Pierre Turgeon banked the winner off the back of Roussel's leg 24 seconds into overtime.

Recchi tried to rally the troops by leveling Pierre Sevigny early during a 9-2 Spectrum rout of Montreal. And Farwell attempted to steady the backline by picking up veteran Rob Ramage from Montreal while dumping Hawgood to Florida. The referees and linesmen came back, but not before the Flyers were left fuming by an Edmonton replay official's ruling that Soderstrom caught rookie Jason Arnott's game winner over the goal line.

Butsayev aroused himself from his season-long catatonic state to score a startling hat trick in a 6-3 victory at Vancouver. But his interest quickly disappeared, like Simpson's patience. After a 6-0 loss in Calgary, the coach closed the locker room doors for twenty-two minutes. Turnovers at the blue lines were rampant as the Flyers refused to dump the puck.

"The dumb bleeps won't do it," said Simpson. "We're like a strainer, water goes right through us. Just about every [player] told me last summer that when they started playing defensive hockey (under Dineen) they started winning. They haven't got amnesia. If they do, it's selective."

Harold Katz was remembered well in New Jersey, however. The state offered to float bonds to build a $140-million arena just south of the Ben Franklin Bridge. The basketball owner was told the project, to be constructed near the state aquarium and a 25,000-seat open-air music amphitheater being developed by Sony-Pace, would guarantee the 76ers $7 million annually for luxury seating, advertising and concessions.

Katz was pushing for a commitment. Under a contingency agreement mediated by Sam Katz, the 76ers had to give notice by February 24 that they were leaving the Spectrum before the following season or be bound there until 1999. He also had to sweat an upcoming change of administration. Christine Todd-Whitman had just won the New Jersey gubernatorial election on promises of fiscal austerity.

The governor-elect said she would not oppose the arena as long as it could be built without taxpayer money. So, on December 15, Harold Katz and outgoing governor Florio announced jointly in Trenton that the move of the Sixers to the Garden State was imminent. The agreement included a promise to build a temporary 10,000-seat home if Katz was unable to extend his Spectrum lease a year at a time.

Ed Snider had no intention of being flexible. "The only option I was going to give him was to leave," he recalls. Spectacor and Philadelphia officials began a campaign to convince New Jersey voters the idea to move the basketball team across the river would sell them down it, stuck with an arena that could not possibly pay for itself.

"We could be talking about $50 million of taxpayers' money," said Rendell. He teamed with Snider to scoff at the $80-million price tag, saying it did not include road and other infrastructure costs.

Whitman said she would put the project to a referendum before it was given any go-ahead, then sent the proposal to Arthur Andersen Co., an accounting firm, for review. She asked no questions of Harold Katz when she met with him for the first time on December 24, then announced publicly she needed more answers.

Meanwhile, Simpson didn't have to run any inquiries to determine the Flyers' solution. Lindros had returned on December 16 and taken 15 games of pent-up energy out on his old buddies, the Nordiques. The comeback kid picked up a puck Renberg had loosened from defenseman Adam Foote, reversed behind the net, and fed Recchi for the winning goal in a 3-2 victory. "I'll tell you, it's going to be fun around here after Christmas," predicted Recchi.

From experience, he was allowing time for the big guy to get caught up. Lindros dragged through a 2-2 tie with Chicago, then a 4-2 loss at New Jersey. When Soderstrom allowed a softie to Dmitri Khristich during a 4-1 defeat by Washington on December 21, the Spectrum Scrooges offered the worst of what was beginning to look like a fifth consecutive non-playoff season. "We're not showing the determination to come out of this thing," said Simpson.

Lindros, voted by the fans as an All-Star starter, tried to set an example by ignoring a Keith Primeau

stick to the face, roaring down the ice with blood on his jersey and feeding Renberg, but it was only one goal in a 3-1 loss to Detroit. Soderstrom was yanked again in a 4-4 tie at Pittsburgh and Yushkevich and Fedyk were benched.

A three-goal rally to beat Boston 4-3 in a New Year's Eve neutral-site game in Minneapolis did nothing to turn the team around. The Flyers' first-ever league game in Texas turned into an Alamo of an 8-0 defeat to Dallas. While Lindros continued to pack them in on the road—the second-largest crowd in NHL history, 26,023, watched a 4-2 loss to the Lightning in the St. Petersburg SunCoast Dome—Simpson challenged his team not to pack it in, period. "We're going to make the playoffs," he insisted, "but it's going to be a bleep of a battle to do it."

Indeed, the Flyers needed a late goal by call-up Andre Faust to break a 1-1 death struggle with woeful Ottawa and send Philadelphia on to a 4-1 Spectrum victory. Simpson, who had been alternating his goalies, decided to stick with Roussel.

As Lindros, who scored three times in an 8-3 blasting of St. Louis, tried to turn up the heat, Snider continued his flamethrowing across the Delaware. Through Sam Katz, Spectacor hired a public relations firm to issue a twelve-page media memo clarifying "myths" about the proposed New Jersey arena. "If I was the governor ... I would take it with a grain of salt," said Harold Katz. Instead, Snider poured salt into the open wound with two hands, signing long-term contracts with family shows to keep them from playing Camden.

In the midst of all this negative energy, a positive event had restarted the Flyer patriarch's battery. Sam Katz had found a new potential lender for Spectrum II.

Prudential Power Funding Associates had been the company Katz had arranged to finance the Rose Garden Arena in Portland. "I had not tried them originally because I thought there would be more enthusiasm by PNC, a local bank that would make a Philadelphia arena a signature project," recalls Sam Katz. But when Snider pulled out, Sam Katz called Prudential's senior vice president, Marie Fioramonti in Chicago and asked her to fly to Philadelphia.

"She wasn't unfamiliar with what was going on here," recalls Sam Katz. "Goldman Sachs had brought things to her three different times. When Goldman failed, and I called, I think it became a feather in her cap to get it done."

He took Fioramonti to Snider's home. "They had a very social get-together," recalls Sam Katz. "They hit it right off. The relationship between them was the most important thing in solving the problem."

Prudential, which wanted its involvement kept secret until groundbreaking, offered a twenty-year loan. PNC's had been amortized over eight. And in this plan, only the Flyers, not another principal tenant like the Sixers, would have to subordinate luxury-seating proceeds until the debt service was retired.

On January 12, Whitman rejected the New Jersey arena proposal. "Important details are not in place," she said. The governor-elect said she had asked rock star Jon Bon Jovi whether he would be willing to perform in Camden as well as South Philadelphia. He had advised her two concerts in the same market would not work.

"'If [Whitman] felt [there were loose ends], why didn't she discuss it with us?" asked Harold Katz. "At least Ed Snider dealt directly with me. I have no bad blood towards him. If it's right for him and right for me we could possibly get together."

Snider called Ms. Whitman "quite a lady" and invited the 76ers' owner back to negotiations. Instead, Harold Katz went to Camden County officials who were steamed over Whitman's decision and began talks about local government and/or private investment in an arena. "I'll have to call Jon Bon Jovi to see if we can do a deal," Katz said sarcastically.

Two days later, Spectacor wrapped up "Sesame Street Live" for another ten years. Harold Katz's Camden pipe dream was being systematically shoved into the trash can like Oscar the Grouch. If Katz didn't make an arena deal and find an interim home for his basketball team by February 1, he was stuck at the Spectrum for six more years.

"I was going to just wait to hear from Harold on February 1," Snider recalls. Instead, he allowed himself to be pushed by Sam Katz and Spectacor president Jack Williams back to the table.

On January 17, Snider and Harold Katz sat down in the middle room of a suite at the Conshohocken Marriott. Calling upon their advisors from adjoining rooms as needed, they worked out a deal within four hours. The 76ers would get all revenue from premium courtside tickets, but a portion of suite and club seating would be sold on a one-team-only basis, giving the Flyers, who outdrew the woebegone basketball team, an opportunity for additional revenue.

When a verbal agreement had been struck, Shaiman, Harold Katz's lawyer, volunteered he did not see any need to put it into writing immediately. Snider glared at Katz, who, after a conference in another room, told his attorney to get it done.

The press conference was called for the Spectrum on the February 1 deadline. It was delayed six hours in a dispute over who would pay for cost overruns. Finally, at 4 P.M. Snider, wearing a "Spectrum 2 is Happening" pin on his lapel, stepped to the podium. "Somehow, I have the feeling I've been here before," he said.

"I started this deal when I was 19 years old," said Harold Katz. "Now I'm going on 66." Asked what had finally gotten the agreement done, the basketball owner tried a joke. "I took Snider outside, I beat the crap out of him, and then we made a deal," he said.

When Katz finished, Snider leaned across the podium, smiled less than sweetly and said, "Anytime you want to step outside, Harold."

Katz laughed. Snider held his grin. Groundbreaking, scheduled tentatively for early spring, was still contingent on sales of luxury seating passing a 70 percent threshold, but Snider enjoyed a hugely triumphant day.

"It's exhilarating," he said. "It will be an asset to this city that I'm sure will outlast me. That makes me very proud. But if I had known what I was getting involved in and how difficult it was going to be, I might have had second thoughts."

The retail mall connecting the old Spectrum with the new was being put on hold. The parking garage had been scrapped. The arena would still be in its original design, seating 19,500 for Flyer games and 21,000 for 76er contests and most concerts. It would contain 100 mid level suites to be leased for $125,000 to 135,000 per year, twenty-six balcony suites at roof level for $75,000 per year, plus club-level seating (featuring waiter service, but not enclosed) at $12,500 per season.

Prudential, still unidentified to the public, was financing $140 million of the project. The state of Pennsylvania, which had already spent $4.5 million demolishing JFK Stadium and moving the Eagles practice bubble—had come up with an additional $5 million for construction of parking facilities and related arena work, plus a $2-million low-interest loan for sewer and water installation. The city's $6.5-million low interest loan intended for the parking garage was going towards arena construction. Philadelphia had pledged to help Spectacor secure another $10 million in loans to make up for a shortfall.

Asked how he was going to celebrate, Snider offered his only tempered statement of the day. "I'll celebrate when we break ground," he said.

Meanwhile, his hockey team continued to practice for the big day by shoveling itself into a deeper hole. Lindros scored a goal at Madison Square Garden in his premier All-Star Game appearance, but that used up the Flyers' allotment of thrills for a three-week period.

Washington outworked Philadelphia, 4-2, giving new coach Jim Schoenfeld his first victory since replacing Terry Murray behind the bench. In Montreal, a Philadelphia rally from a 3-0 deficit went down the drain when Brind'Amour took the wrong man in overtime, leaving Guy Carbonneau to score the winner.

Simpson, who drilled the team for ninety hard minutes the next morning, was sick of his players losing one-on-one battles. Farwell got tired of looking at Butsayev and traded him to San Jose for 25-year-old defenseman Rob Zettler. When the Flyers blew an early 2-0 lead into a 3-2 overtime loss to San Jose and fell below .500, the losing streak reached five and chants of "Terry Must Go" began.

"I think we have talent on the ice and if I analyze the deals Russ has made, I can't point to any I thought was horrible," said Snider as he worked a booth at the Wives' Carnival. "As far as Terry is concerned, it's too soon to tell. The question is, Why are they blowing their assignments? I think we probably could use a couple more savvy veterans around to help these young guys. We haven't found the right mix of players."

Two days later at Boston, Simpson could find no players, let alone a formula for stirring them. The Flyers bottomed out in an emotionless 4-0 loss.

Kevin Dineen said just because the team's confidence was shot did not mean Simpson should be taken out and shot. "The coaching doesn't have anything to go with it," said the captain. But Jay Snider, who had moved his offices back to Spectaguard and was preparing to announce his resignation, did not agree.

"I knew we had taken a step back trading so many players," he said. "But I saw expansion teams doing well with less talent than we had. I told Russ we should fire Simpson while we still had a chance to make the playoffs and hire Terry Murray.

"He was afraid we had pulled the cord so many times on coaches, we would lose all stability."

After the Flyers snapped a 7-game winless streak the hard way, blowing a 3-1 lead with six minutes left, then beating Florida 4-3 on Lindros's overtime goal Farwell blamed himself, while absolving Simpson. "After five months with a new group that

has so many shortcomings, people think the answer is to to just change the coach," said the GM. "I got the players."

Too many of them were small and weak. And even the promising ones, like Yushkevich, were slipping backwards. Eklund, a noncontributor in what he had already announced would be his final season in North America, underwent hernia surgery and Soderstrom's composure was ruptured, too. He was sent to Hershey and Frederic Chabot brought in from Montreal as backup.

"We were doing it with mirrors," recalls Lindros. And the shortcomings were made even more obvious by the refusal of some veterans to look into the glass.

"Terry put his trust in a group of players that were undermining him in the room," recalls Farwell. "He had been accused in Long Island of not listening enough, so he met regularly with five or six guys that he was counting on to carry the message to the team. They read that as a weakness.

"Eric wasn't part of the group. I don't know if he was 100 percent on board (with Simpson), but Lindros wasn't one of the problems. Recchi was one of the guys. Galley, too. I swept out some of the marginal players who were negative influences, like Paslawski and Nattress, but I tried to patch it up with the important players. That probably was a mistake."

The plane that took the Flyers to the West Coast on February 14 had to fly low to avoid buzzards. But at least Renberg was keeping the faith. When Philadelphia trailed San Jose 4-3 after two periods, he told his teammates during the second period intermission he was going to score two goals. The rookie of the year candidate pumped three in a 6-4 victory. "I said it to get everybody going," he said. "I don't know if I meant it."

Satisfied with their second victory in 11 games, the Flyers lost the next night to the Mighty Ducks of Anaheim, 6-3, in their first visit to The Pond. "Everybody's trying, but we're not understanding that when you do everything well defensively, you're in a better position offensively," said Lindros. "We probably should have done what it would take to get a few old players to stabilize things. (But) it's not Terry, it's us. We lack mental toughness."

He tried to rally the troops by beating up Montreal defenseman Eric Desjardins during an 8-7 Spectrum victory over Montreal. And Farwell attempted to add more input by transferring Bill Barber from scouting to temporary coaching duties.

Simpson followed up a lifeless 4-1 loss at Madison Square Garden by starting the practice the following day at 8 A.M. Beranek, who had not scored in 28 games, did not seem to get the message. "If he doesn't drive to the net, he won't score in 115," said the coach.

The Flyers, 29-31-4 and tied for the last Eastern Conference playoff spot, were not doing much to inspire suite sales for Spectrum II, They moved towards the goal for groundbreaking regardless. A comedy team of Harold Katz and Ed Snider took to the airwaves with a commercial that lampooned

their tortured negotiations.

Meanwhile, Jay Snider decided not to prolong his own agony. On March 1, he officially stepped down as Flyer president after eleven years.

"I should have just announced it in September," he says today. "But I wasn't exactly sure whether I was going to keep some title or move on cleanly. We struggled for a way to handle it. I knew all the stuff that would be written about me being pushed out."

Thus did his father's shadow darken Jay's term

to its very end. Being named to the presidency at age 25 and heading the franchise during its only period of decline were flashpoints of Snider's unpopularity, but the fans also made him a convenient scapegoat for problems he had acknowledged and aggressively attacked.

The Flyers had empty seats and had won a single playoff round in three seasons when Snider took over in April 1983. The same man vilified for firing Clarke as general manager had hired him in 1984, and had done the interviewing that resulted in the hiring of Keenan.

Clarke later acknowledged that Jay's concerns about the administration of Flyer drafts in the mid-to-late eighties were legitimate. The club faced a lengthy rebuilding process and, despite intense impatience by the fans, Snider stayed the course his father had plotted twenty years before: the Flyers would endure steps backward to take big ones towards the Stanley Cup. Unquestionably, Jay was the person most responsible for the determined, tricky and exhausting maneuvering that made Eric Lindros a Flyer.

"The Lindros trade was the gutsiest move in the history of pro sports," says Ed. "Jay had a lot to be proud of. It's painful to me he never got the credit he deserved.

"I guess his big mistake was the handling of the Bob Clarke situation. Bob was the hero and Jay became the boss's incompetent son. That's just not true, but he never recovered."

That decision was Jay's albatross until he left. "I shouldn't have fired him," Jay says. "It wasn't worth it to me personally.

"My dad was on the fence between us, yet still unhappy when I fired Bob. If one of us had to go, maybe it should have been me."

Ultimately, it was. As Jay left, rumors circulated that Clarke was coming back as team president. "I hate even talking about it," Ed told the *Daily News's* Bill Fleischman. "It would be tampering. Everything that has been written about how I felt about Bob is accurate, but I don't know what he's thinking about it. Russ is doing a great job. I'm certainly not looking for a general manager."

This was in contrast to the general manager, who

Galley's two goals helped Roussel rise to the occasion.

was searching everywhere for a goaltender. Farwell's interest in Calgary's Mike Vernon cooled when the Flames wanted Brind'Amour. So Philadelphia began its stretch drive hoping Roussel would rise to the occasion.

Saved by Galley's second goal of the game with 1:07 remaining, the goalie backstopped a 3-3 tie in Landover, then beat the Lightning 3-1 in Tampa. But on the night Tim Kerr was inducted into the Flyers' Hall of Fame, Roussel was beaten in overtime, 4-3, on a goal by Dallas's Neal Broten and went from lukewarm to ice cold.

The goalie surrendered two goals by Brian Bradley in the final three minutes of a 5-5 tie Lindros pulled out with a goal 37 seconds before the buzzer. Six nights later, Roussel gave up two Hartford goals on the first six shots of a 5-3 defeat. Another 5-3 loss, this one to the Panthers in Miami, put Philadelphia four points behind the expansion Panthers for the final playoff spot.

"We're in a dogfight," said Dineen. Bacchus Lindros, Eric's three-and-a-half month-old Great Dane, lifted his head off the locker-room carpet in apparent agreement. Farwell doggedly tried to get help before the trading deadline, but was able to make only marginal moves.

Winger Rob DiMaio was acquired from Tampa for winger Jim Cummins and a fourth-round pick, while center Mark Lamb was picked up from Ottawa for the disappointing Claude Boivin and goalie prospect Kirk Daubenspeck. When Pelle Eklund was sent to Dallas for a draft pick dependent upon the Stars' success in the playoffs, Dave Brown became the only player on the current roster ever to have represented Philadelphia in a playoff game.

"We'll win it in three years, you can bet on it," Ed Snider told Stan Hochman of the *Daily News*. But not with goaltending like this. Simpson tried Soderstrom, back from a mediocre stint in Hershey, and he beat St. Louis and Florida to create an illusion of hope. But the Swede had to be pulled after giving up three quickies in the second period of a 7-2 loss at New Jersey on March 26. Then Roussel allowed a goal from the blue line by Anaheim's Gary Valk, and another one by the same player in overtime in an excruciating 3-2 Spectrum loss.

"Five years!" yelled a fan after the boos finally died.

The Flyers couldn't get a save to save their season. Alexei Kovalev scored with 37 seconds remaining to give Keenan's Rangers, headed for the President's Trophy, a 4-3 Spectrum victory. Soderstrom

gave up a goal on Calgary's first shot, leaving Renberg's 37th goal and (franchise rookie-record) 76th point of the season the only redeeming moment of a 4-1 loss to Calgary.

An Igor Ulanov nailing of Lindros all but put Philadelphia's playoff hopes into the coffin. The Jets' defenseman took a long running start to slam Eric against the boards, spraining his right shoulder. The Flyers, who rallied for a 2-2 tie on Dineen's goal with 1:25 remaining, said they hoped Lindros could play two nights later at the Spectrum against Florida.

The star, who had been told by a second doctor the injury would take three weeks to heal, was furious. "Day-to-day makes it sound like a common cold," he told reporters.

"I didn't want my teammates thinking I could have played and didn't," he recalls. "Maybe [Farwell] didn't understand how it works in a dressing room." The young star was further angered the GM did not send the league office a tape of the hit and seek a suspension of Ulanov.

Instead, Soderstrom provided highlight video material for a season gone south when he was fooled by Gord Murphy's backhander from the top of the circle during a 3-3 tie against the Panthers. Three days later, two more Soderstrom softies in a 4-3 loss to Boston, plus an Islander victory, eliminated Philadelphia.

"Eighty-four games of pure hell is what it was," said Galley. "We never seemed to push ourselves, to give ourselves a chance."

Unnamed players told the *Inquirer's* Gary Miles that Simpson had set double standards for stars and role players, that his attempt to install a neutral-zone trap at midseason were ignored by the team's best players and that constant meetings had diluted the coaching staff's message.

Galley, the Barry Ashbee Trophy winner, was traced as one of the principal sources of the piece and apologized to his teammates. "I was out of line putting the team and Terry under the microscope," he said.

Lindros, who increased his point production by 22 points while playing in 4 more games than he had the previous season, won the Bobby Clarke Award and came to Simpson's defense. When asked if the team needed an overhaul, Eric replied, "It depends on who does it." When Lindros added he was gladdened by the rumors of Clarke's return, the disdain for Farwell was obvious.

"I think he had the right ideas and his heart was in the right spot," recalls Lindros. "But it just wasn't happening. We were a stripped-down '57 Chevy going against Lamborghinis. So much of [building a team] is chemistry, knowing what is needed on and off the ice."

Farwell admitted he had miscalculated. "We're not as close as we thought because we had a lot of guys underperform," he said. Recchi, used as a second-line center over much of the second half, had dropped from 53 goals to 40. Dineen had slipped from 35 to 19 and Beranek had scored only 5 times after December 21. Yushkevich and Soderstrom, centerpieces of the promising 1992-93 finish, had regressed. Stew Malgunas, a journeyman, had been perhaps the team's most consistent defenseman.

Farwell conceded he might have to trade a top-quality forward to get a steady defenseman. Recchi surmised he might be the logical guy to go. "What's the reason to fill one hole and make another one?" he asked.

By the cruel end, Simpson was aware how some of his most trusted players had conspired against him. "I think I may have misread a couple of players that had real strong negative influences," he told reporters. "We have some good guys, but they have to lead under all kinds of circumstances not just when its going well for them personally."

One week after the end of the season, Snider said Farwell would definitely return as general manager and that he had three candidates to become team president. The owner declined to identify them, saying only that Clarke would become one "if he came knocking at our door.'"

In truth, Snider was going to take a battering ram to Florida, if necessary. "I wanted Bob," he recalls. "I thought he was the best guy out there.

"He learned a lot in Minnesota and Florida, did fabulous jobs. He was well connected, highly regarded and I thought he had a feel for every element. Our not making the playoffs didn't have anything to do with it. I wanted to make him president, then let him make decisions about our other personnel."

Twelve days after the end of the season, Snider called Panthers president Bill Torrey and asked if he could approach. According to Clarke, he was given permission by Torrey to come to Philadelphia and talk. "I was going to lunch with Mr. Snider," Clarke recalls. "But he had received notice from one of [Huizenga's] lawyers that we weren't allowed.

"I went back to Bill and told him it was a little bit unfair. He said he understood and would talk to Wayne.

"We had a meeting at Mr. Huizenga's house and he said he wanted to give me a new contract. I said if you want me to honor the old one I will, but Philadelphia is my home and I would like to have the right to talk to Mr. Snider. [Huizenga] gave me permission.

"I told Mr. Snider I had no intention of coming back just as a club president, that I wanted to manage. I thought I could work it out with Russ. I really wanted him to stay."

Clarke went back to Miami to tell Torrey the Flyers had made an offer that included equity in the club. "Bill said he understood that I was going home and told me to go across the street and tell Mr. Huizenga. When I did, he told me to clear out my desk and leave. It was pretty chilly."

"Next thing I knew," recalls Snider, "I got a threatening letter saying we had tampered and weren't allowed to talk to Bob any further.

"I called Huizenga and he told me to go bleep myself. He acted like a goddamn spoiled child. I started to deal with Torrey because I wanted to get it done."

The Panthers demanded $1 million and a No. 1 draft choice. "We had evidence that phone conversations took place between Ed Snider and Bob during the season," recalls team president Bill Torrey. "I had heard rumors as far back as January and confronted Bob and he said he wasn't going anywhere.

"He repeated that after the season. And that was the real problem. Wayne really liked Bob and his feelings were hurt. I wasn't privy to the conversations between Wayne and Bob as far as who said what when, and I want to close the issue. I understood the relationship between Bob Clarke and Ed Snider. Wayne may not have, fully."

"Bill wants to make it seem like I was plotting all winter long and that's not the case," says Clarke. "I was never asked by Mr. Snider until after the season and I told him, 'You have to talk to Mr. Torrey.' He was given permission and then it was taken away."

Snider informed Farwell of Clarke's desire to function as a day-to-day GM. "Mr. Snider thought we could coexist," recalls Farwell, who also received a call from Clarke expressing the same sentiment.

The incumbent general manager understood he had become a temporary caretaker, one who had an unpleasant task left to perform. "Whatever happened with me, there was no chance we were going forward with Terry," recalls Farwell. He called Simpson on Tuesday evening, May 19, in Saskatchewan and told him he would not be retained.

The Flyers informed the media of their third coaching firing in three and a half years—and the quickest in their history—via a conference call the following day. "There's been an awful lot of speculation (about his own future) and that's why the timing of this is so difficult," said Farwell. "But I've been told to go on operating as normal.

"I just wasn't happy with the results. I know [Simpson] knows the game very well and I know he worked very hard. But we weren't responding. With his style and background, I thought it would work," he said. "Why it didn't, I can't answer."

Simpson, who had two years left on his contract, did not return calls from reporters. When finally contacted five days later, he begged off comment. "It doesn't matter what I have to say anymore," he said. "Obviously, I'm disappointed. But let's leave it at that."

Clarke already knew who he wanted as the next coach. After the Caps, citing a need for more emotional leadership, had fired Terry Murray in February after a 20-23-4 start, he had accepted Clarke's offer to complete the season running the bench of the Panthers' Iinternational Hockey League affiliate at Cincinnati.

"His teams were always organized," recalls Clarke. "And he took control for me in Cincinnati."

Clarke called Murray at his home in Maryland and said he would like to talk once the standoff with Florida was resolved.

As Torrey held out for the moon and Snider left on an Alaskan fishing trip, Farwell's frustration began to show. "It's gone on long enough," he told the *Daily News's* Bowen at a GMs' meeting in New York during the Cup finals. "It needs to be clarified."

As NHL commissioner Gary Bettman stood ready to arbitrate if necessary, the object of the tug-of-war urged Snider not to cave. "I had seen other people move freely from organization to organization," Clarke recalls. "I didn't think [Florida] should get something."

But with the draft approaching, the confrontation was becoming self-defeating for both organizations. Finally, they compromised. Philadelphia gave Florida a second-round pick and $500,000, some of which would be provided by the Flyers' playing an exhibition game at the Miami Arena without getting a share of the gate.

On June 15 at Ovations, with Farwell conspicuously absent, Snider welcomed Clarke home for the second time. "I'm hoping once again that he leads us to the promised land," the owner told reporters. "I probably shouldn't say I'm hoping. I should say I'm confident."

Clarke praised the foundation Farwell had put in, reiterated he wanted him to stay. But Farwell told reporters he would be moving on. "My concern is that it would be like having two mothers-in-law in the kitchen," he said. "I like Bob. But I told him that chances might be better for us to be friends at a distance."

Within a few days, Clarke and Farwell had breakfast together at the International House of Pancakes near the Coliseum. Farwell was asked to take the rest of the month to think about taking on new duties within the organization. "I wanted him to handle contracts, scouting stuff, a lot of things. I thought he might consider it."

Farwell did, barely. When Clarke called days later, there had been no change of heart.

"By that time, I wasn't surprised," recalls Snider. "I was trying to make a marriage of two people who didn't want to get married. I was hopeful because Russ was a talent. I think he had the ability to pick a good player in the draft, but not the ability to pick a good coach. There has to be a chemistry to a team and he didn't have that forte."

Farwell recognized the bottom line. "We weren't winning and that's how you are judged," he says today. "I wasn't happy with how it went myself, so I can't sit there and say it was unfair. Everybody wants big players. We didn't have a lot to trade for them. I didn't have any major problems with Lindros. For his age, he handled everything extremely well.

"Jay hired me. Ed was more comfortable with Bob. If I had stayed, Bob would have been put in the position of defending the things I did."

It would not have been difficult. Farwell's bottom line—136-150-42 and no playoff appearances in four seasons—is a reflection of the rundown talent level of the organization he took over in 1990. Left with an aging and brittle nucleus, Farwell still managed to leave a core of Eric Lindros, Mark Recchi, Rod Brind'Amour and Mikael Renberg, fulfilling a mandate to make the Flyers younger and more promising.

Clarke quickly invited Murray for an interview and to play in the Pelle Lindbergh charity alumni golf tournament. They went out to dinner and stayed up late talking philosophy. The following morning, Murray was offered the job.

On June 23, the 43-year-old former Flyer defenseman stood before the cameras at Ovations as their tenth head coach, and fourth in two and a half years. He pronounced the team he was inheriting "ready to take off."

"I think Eric Lindros still has a lot of room to grow," said Murray. "Responsibility is part of this business ... You cannot have success in the NHL—especially under the microscopic eye of the media—without discipline. That doesn't mean a dictatorship, but you have to have the star players take on a team mentality. You need everyone playing for each other. When a team starts believing that, it's a very powerful thing."

Clarke bristled when asked if it would be perceived he was hiring a good friend. "It's important that the manager and coach be comfortable with each other," he said. "How the hell else are you going to be successful?

"I'm not stupid. I know we have to sign some free agents or somehow acquire more size on the wings. Maybe we can get another defenseman or two. And I think our goaltending has to prove itself."

The Flyers–their first pick gone to Quebec, their second to Florida–tried to move up in the draft and select Brett Lindros, Eric's brother. Clarke passed when all counteroffers involved one of his top players. Lindros was selected ninth-overall by the Islanders.

Philadelphia drafted for size and the next day traded for abrasiveness. Racine was dealt to the Canadiens for 23-year-old defenseman Kevin Haller, a former first-round pick of Buffalo who had fallen out of Montreal's regular defensive rotation. Clarke unsuccessfully sought 30-year-old Toronto defenseman Bob Rouse, who signed with Detroit, then tried to reel in 35-year-old center Craig MacTavish with a two-year, $1.6-million deal.

"(Agent) Mike Gillis had asked for more and we had bowed out, but Craig called me, asked what had happened and phoned back later to say he would accept. He could still play. But the real value would be his influence on Eric."

The Flyers also picked up 26-year-old left wing Shjon Podein from Edmonton. "Les Jackson, my chief scout in Minnesota, had always wanted him," recalls Clarke. "I had never seen him play but we needed wingers."

Mike Eaves left to coach at a prep school in Minnesota and Craig Hartsburg became coach of Guelph of the Ontario Hockey League. Bernie Parent, citing business commitments, resigned as goaltending coach, replaced by Rejean Lemelin.

Former Kings coach Tom Webster, who had been in Florida with Clarke, was named one of Murray's assistants. The other position went to Keith Acton,

Lindros' first Flyer roommate. "Every step is in the right direction," Eric said from the family's summer home.

Nevertheless, the people trying to get Spectrum II built were still running in place. Enough suites had been sold to satisfy Prudential Power Funding Associates, but the lender wanted Snider to come up with another $10 million. With interest rates rising, the Flyer owner shopped for a workable rate. The city loaned $5 million and Spectacor came up with the rest.

The company lobbied city council intensely, and on June 23 it ratified the deal. Spectacor was putting up $45.3 million, Prudential was financing $140 million and a total of $32 million was coming in public loans and grants ($8.5 million from the city).

Snider, who had taken a chance by ordering 20 percent of the 7,500 tons of steel to beat a price increase, seemingly had won his final arena battle. The loan paperwork was closed on July 15 and site planning, the final step before groundbreaking, was set to begin.

But when Spectacor requested technical language changes in the approved legislation, city council president John Street seized the opportunity to demand an increase in the proportion of minorities employed in construction from 20 to 25 percent. Street also wanted Spectacor to provide money to promote the twelve events per year for which the city was receiving rent-free use of the arena.

Snider agreed to 25 percent minority participation and Spectacor said it would underwrite city-sponsored events, provided it considered them to be sound ventures. On July 22, 1994, five years after Wilson Goode told Snider the city would be able to approve a new arena in a week, the absolute, final, green light was on.

"I don't know many other owners of professional sports franchises as dedicated to their cities," praised Street. "Ed Snider did not take the money and run."

The only running Snider was doing was to a pay phone outside his daughter Sarena's day camp in Maine so he could participate in the press conference. "I know it got testy," he said, "and it took a lot of sweat."

The occasion was not dampened by anyone asking Snider what had kept him going through all the setbacks. The answer might have been too blunt.

"Stupidity," Snider says today. "I had a sense of duty, but from a personal point of view, I should have threatened to go to Jersey. Every other owner threatens to leave gets a new stadium or arena built for him. We stayed to pay for this one ourselves."

Three days after the deal was done, construction equipment was moved in and work began. The first steel pilings were already in place on September 8, when Spectacor announced it had signed a twenty-nine-year, $40 million agreement with CoreStates Bank for naming rights to both the new arena and the Spectrum. The Flyers would begin their 28th season in the CoreStates Spectrum and in 1996 move into the CoreStates Center.

On September 13, 1994, Snider joined his son Jay,

Harold Katz, Bettman, NBA deputy commissioner Russ Granik, Rendell, and Michael Herschock, the former state budget secretary who had shepherded critical arena legislation in 1990, in the symbolic first turning of the ground.

"All of us at Spectacor share a sense of gratitude to all those who believed in this project," said Snider. On the day one vision became reality, the owner told reporters he had another: "Here I go again, I'm going to get into trouble. But I can see a Stanley Cup final in this building the very first season."

Breaking new ground: Ed Snider and wife Martha turn sod for the new CoreStates Center.

Chapter 12

◆◆◆

Doom and Bloom

As he returned to Philadelphia to prepare for the 1994 training camp, Eric Lindros was adamant the return of Bobby Clarke as president-GM of the Flyers would pull the organization together. "When you talk to him, it's not like you're a player and he's management," said the star center.

But as September began, hockey's athletes and administrators were never so far apart. The players, whose average salary had risen from $232,000 in 1989-90 to a projected $660,000 for 1994-95, were content to keep performing under the terms of their expired collective-bargaining agreement, but the owners were determined to slow runaway talent costs.

After sporadic talks produced no progress by mid-August, NHL commissioner Gary Bettman canceled the players' preseason expenses, as well as medical and disability coverage in an attempt to force bargaining to begin. Camps would start on time but a lockout loomed for opening day of the season if there were no progress. "We'll try to go through camp like nothing is going on," said Lindros. "I don't know how easy it's going to be."

As he buckled his helmet against the gathering storm, the 21-year-old found a *C* on his jersey. "I think he's ready for it," said new coach Terry Murray, and Kevin Dineen, the previous captain, agreed. "It's [Eric's] team and his responsibility to make sure we have some success," said the right wing.

Lindros, who had been careful not to come on strong around older players in his first two seasons, promised he would heed Murray's and Clarke's ad-

vice to be himself, lead mostly by example, and not be overwhelmed by his expanded duties. "I was told not to act like there was a loaded gun in my back," Eric said.

Murray tried to ease his biggest and best player's burden by unholstering his magnum early in the exhibition season, sending Dave Brown after rookie Peter Forsberg following an attempt by Quebec's Chris Simon to goad Lindros into a fight. "You have to support your teammates," lectured the coach, who spoke repeatedly about restoring the pride he had felt as a Flyer two decades earlier.

Privately, Murray was not encouraged by what he saw. "I wanted to scrimmage the first few days to get an idea of what the talent level really was," he recalls. "But the fundamentals were so lacking, I changed everything around to do drills.

"We were real short in a lot of areas, no question about it. Some of the guys who had been here for a year or two were not NHL players."

In Clarke's view, the incumbent goalies had minor talent and more than minor attitude problems. Dominic Roussel refused to blame his wretched 1993-94 finish on himself. "It didn't feel like [management] really wanted me to become No. 1," he said. "I had a couple of bad games and that was it."

Tommy Soderstrom had taken a harder look in the mirror. "Last year was a disaster," he admitted. Still, Clarke was convinced Philadelphia would go nowhere without a change of chemistry in the crease. "They each had something to offer but together they were terrible," he recalls. "They were fighting with each other the whole time about who was going to be No.

1. To me, that's a bunch of crap. Just play for us and don't worry about each other."

Clarke spent the summer checking the market. The top free-agent goalie, Bill Ranford, would command $3 million to $4 million a year. Grant Fuhr, who was in iffy health, was available, as was the player Clarke believed had torched his first run as Flyer GM—Ron Hextall. Nevertheless, the dollars and circumstances were right for the goalie's return.

Hextall, who had been traded by Quebec to the Islanders the previous summer, had been humiliated during the Rangers' first-round sweep of their crosstown rivals. Isles' GM Don Maloney thought the fans would never allow him to go with the veteran another season. "I got talking to Donnie at the draft and he wanted Soderstrom," recalls Clarke.

It was ironic that a goalie whose fall from hero status in Philadelphia began with a bitter contract dispute would five years later represent the best buy on the market. "It wasn't so much that Hexy was affordable," recalls Clarke. "He was making $1 million (including easily achievable bonuses). What made it appealing was that the Islanders wanted to trade him for Soderstrom (earning $600,000).

"I was bleeped off at Hexy (in 1989-90). [His holdout] was one of the reasons I ended up losing my job. Maybe I didn't handle [the renegotiation request] right, either. But once things happen, you get over them and move on.

"The team needed his competitiveness. Despite the last couple of playoffs (Hextall had also played poorly in Quebec's first-round loss in 1993), I thought he was still a good goalie. He was at an age (30) where he should have overcome that stuff about revolutionizing goaltending and come here to be just what he

had always been—a good team player. That's what we needed.

"Worrying about the fan reaction didn't bother me. It would have bothered me a lot more to stay with the two goalies we had."

Hextall was in a hotel room in Jacksonville when Islander goalie coach Bob Froese called and told him not to dress for that evening's exhibition game. Froese didn't say why. But Hextall, already moved twice in two years, had his suspicions. Maloney called an hour

later.

"Ron you've been traded," said the GM. "I think you're going to like the move.

"You're going to Philadelphia."

"It was hard for me to grasp," recalls Hextall. "I heard rumors that the Flyers had been talking to the Islanders at the draft, but I'd pretty much lost hope when training camp began.

"So many things run through your head right away when you're traded. But when I called (wife) Diane, I don't think two people could have been happier."

He was coming back to fans who had booed him, to a general manager who had resented him and to a team that traced its decline to Hextall's own. And still he was thrilled.

"I just figured if Clarkie wanted me back, he couldn't be bitter," recalls Hextall. "And I had a better perspective on fans than when I was younger. The first time they get on you it hurts, but you realize they're just frustrated. You're ten times more frustrated than they are. So you don't take it personally."

Hextall walked into the visiting locker room in Landover the next night wearing a new Vandyke beard but the same old heart on his black-and-orange sleeve. "I guess there's a little bit of me that never did leave," he said, even if the vast majority of his old teammates had. The goalie counted only seven Flyers he had played with before his trade to Quebec two years earlier.

Murray emphasized that Philadelphia had not acquired a savior, only improved a troubled position. "[Hextall's] game probably isn't where it was a few years ago," said the coach. "We're not looking for him to play 75 games or anything like that. We just want him to help us become a playoff team."

Soderstrom, who had appeared to be a key to the club's rebuilding in 1992-93, left saying that the organization had mistaken his cool for indifference. "If I'm screaming on the ice or hitting somebody with my stick, that's not going to help me," he said. "Maybe they think I don't give a bleep, but I do."

While Lindros, who was renting the Voorhees, New Jersey, home Hextall had never sold, went looking for new digs, the sides in the labor dispute shoveled deeper into foxholes. Left wing Patrik Juhlin, a 1989 second-round pick, and Chris Therien, a 6-5, 237-pound defenseman drafted forty-seventh overall in 1990, won jobs with the team. But the desertion of Hextall in the 9-0 exhibition loss to Boston that marked his Spectrum return reflected the attitude of Flyers who knew they were getting ready for nothing.

The owners, insistent on a salary tax for high club payrolls that would provide additional revenue to small-market teams, rejected the players' offer to work a second season without an agreement. On September 30, one day before Philadelphia's home opener against Hartford, Ed Snider and Clarke were among representatives from twenty organizations on a dais with Bettman at the New York Hilton as the commissioner announced a two-week postponement of the start of the season.

The Flyers' owner was just as determined as the small market clubs to gain concessions. He said that despite $30 million in revenue the previous year, his team had lost $3 million.

"(Players' Association director) Bob Goodenow is emphasizing that this is a business," Snider told the *Daily News's* Les Bowen. "He starts talking about the Disney Co. (Anaheim) and Blockbuster (Florida) buying these teams. If that's what the players want, that's what they're going to have. There won't be owners like me left, I'm sure of that.

"They're talking about our rising franchise values. Well, you can't pay salaries with a franchise value. In the lower bowl of our arena now the tickets are all $50. I don't want to raise prices."

At the Coliseum, the players packed up and left. "I fear we could lose half the season," said Rod Brind'Amour.

Clarke was beside himself. "Why is Eric Lindros out of work at three and a half million?" the president-GM asked. "What the hell does he want? What do they want? It's crazy."

When the *Inquirer's* story led with the quotes about Lindros, Clarke called his star player in Toronto to apologize. Eric accepted and enrolled in economics courses at the University of Western Ontario. "I guess I'm kind of learning [the subject] in theory and reality," Lindros said. "And the reality bites."

Eric played with team union representative Mark Recchi in a sparsely attended NHLPA-sponsored tournament in Hamilton, Ontario. Kevin Dineen went off to play for his brother Peter, who ran the IHL Houston Aeros. Clarke spent more and more time in Hershey.

By early November, the league had lopped 14 matches from each team's 84-game schedule and only ten to twelve Flyers were joylessly skating three times a week at Hollydell in Sewell, New Jersey. The concrete foundation walls of the CoreStates Center were almost complete and cranes were adding steel girders, but Snider noted the depressing irony of the building finally rising while the Spectrum next door was dark on hockey nights. "I would be excited, if I wasn't also so discouraged," he said.

While the players remained adamant they would not accept a salary tax, the two sides inched closer on other concerns. Over Thanksgiving weekend, the owners, who had wanted the age at which a veteran could become an unrestricted free agent to be 33, suggested compromises that the age be 31 or 32. After Bettman declared January 16 as the last date a shortened schedule could begin, the union agreed in principle to a rookie salary cap, to eliminate restricted free agency for players under age 24, and to relieve teams from one loss in a salary arbitration case per season.

The concessions made Snider one of seven owners willing to settle when the governors met on Sat-

deal.

In the wee hours, the union offered to allow three arbitration walkaways over a two-year period and an $850,000 salary cap for first-round draft choices. Nearing 5 A.M., the players compromised on the most important issue, offering to set the age of unrestricted free agency at 32 in the first year of the agreement and 31 for the following five seasons.

With the owners preparing for a 2 P.M. conference-call vote, those Flyers who had taken up the

When Hextall returned, only seven of his old teammates remained.

urday, January 7, in New York. Although the doves were still a minority, the hawks insisting on a tax lost their bid to cancel the season immediately. Management made a counteroffer that did not include a tax, but insisted on the rookie salary cap, the right to walk away from two arbitration cases per year and the age of unrestricted free agency being set at 32. They announced a deadline of Tuesday, three days hence, for cancellation of the season.

"None of the differences is major," said Snider. "Any reasonable person can see this. We should find a happy meeting ground and end this ridiculous situation."

The players rejected the owners' compromise. On Monday, one day before the deadline, Bettman and Goodenow, who had virtually ignored each other for thirty-three days, went to New York to try to cut a

team's offer of ice time at the Coliseum gathered for a skate. "This has been the hardest day for me to separate all the ups and downs," said Hextall. "But I can't imagine when two sides are so close, that a year is going to be washed away."

As Bettman began to lay out the compromises to the owners, he was cut off by Washington's Abe Pollin. He wanted to know who had authorized Bettman to make changes in the offer the league had made over the weekend. Pollin moved to tell the players they could take or leave what had been presented to them on Saturday.

"That's the dumbest motion I've ever heard," said Snider.

Although the owners struck down the proposal 14-12, the doves had gained five votes, only two short of what was needed for an agreement. Bettman asked the owners to fax in their suggestions for a counter proposal and at 6 P.M. convened another conference call. The final management offer stipulated the age of free agency would be 32 for the first three years of the agreement and 31 thereafter. The next morning, Goodenow and his executive committee accepted. The players overwhelmingly ratified the deal and the 103-day nightmare was over.

"I think this gives us an opportunity, if we're intelligent, to slow the astronomical growth of salaries," said Snider. He insisted this was a victory for the fans and stable ticket prices. Time would tell whether the customers felt such appreciation, but at least one owner did not have to worry about lingering animosity from his players.

"Mr. Snider did everything he could so we could play," said Lindros.

While the league drew up a 48-game schedule in which teams would play exclusively in their own conference, the Flyers announced they would begin a six-day camp with an open scrimmage at the CoreStates Spectrum. The rescheduled season opener was set for Saturday afternoon, January 21, at home against Quebec.

"It's going to take a month, month and a half before we'll get to the level of hockey we want to be at," said Murray. But he was so delighted to finally have a team to coach that the short-preparation time was a secondary concern. The fans agreed. More than 12,000 attended the scrimmage. "It meant a lot to the players," said Murray.

Although most had skated only lightly during the lockout, the stoppage had provided a few benefits. Dmitri Yushkevich, who had infuriated Clarke and Murray by reporting fifteen pounds overweight in September, had slimmed down playing in Russia. Garry Galley, whose October was in jeopardy following summer shoulder surgery, enjoyed additional recovery time, and Therien had followed up a strong camp with a solid 34 games at Hershey.

The rookie would add size and Kevin Haller could restore grit, allowing Stew Malugunas and Jeff Finley, two bandages on an open wound of a 1993-94 defense, to be sent to the AHL. But Murray said improved personnel was not the only key to tightening up.

"We want to be a team that plays consistently well away from the puck," said the coach. "The numbers last year (314 goals against, fourth-worst in the NHL) were outrageous."

So seemed the compacted 1995 schedule. The Flyers would play 7 games in the first 11 days and

14 in the first 25. "It's not a crapshoot," said Murray. "It's a fire drill."

And the team picked up where it had left off the previous April—sliding down a pole. In the opener, the Nordiques' Andrei Kovalenko beat Hextall after only 1:36.

As the two clubs struggled to complete a pass, Lindros tried to make Forsberg's regular-season debut miserable by knocking the Swede down three times, and Brind'Amour converted a Juhlin rebound to tie the creaking game.

In the end, however, it wasn't only the players who proved rusty. Owen Nolan's winning goal in the third period was clearly kicked in, yet allowed to stand because replay judge Mike Condon was not provided the same view shown on ArenaVision. In the final minute, Bob Bassen clinched Quebec's 3-1 victory by hitting a net that was as empty as Philadelphia's gas tank.

The following afternoon in Boston, Lindros, the erstwhile college student, was taken to school on a hat trick by Cam Neely. "I told Eric two or three weeks before the lockout [ended that] he needed to get himself in shape," said Clarke after a desultory 4-1 loss. "How much work he did, I don't know."

Lindros was struggling almost as much as his mom and dad when the Flyer star faced his younger brother Brett for the first time in an NHL game. "We're in Uniondale, but we're also in Switzerland," said Carl Lindros. "We have to be neutral." Philadelphia, meanwhile, stayed in reverse. Hextall performed strongly before fans who had booed him viciously the previous spring. But despite Eric's two goals, a late rally fell short in a 4-3 loss.

"I hope we start playing better because these are the same questions I've been hearing the last years," the captain told reporters. "You're sick of asking them and I'm sick of talking about them." After he set up Recchi with 2:32 remaining to beat Hartford, Lindros just got sick, period. He struggled with a stomach virus through a 2-1 Spectrum victory over Boston, and couldn't answer the bell the next day in a 2-2 tie at Montreal. "The biggest decision Eric had to make today was which end of his body to put on the toilet," announced Craig MacTavish, who won face-off after face-off as the Flyers ground out the tie.

Lindros felt better two nights later, but the team played decidedly worse in a dismal 5-2 loss in Quebec. "Everything we had been doing well the past few games we did not do tonight," said Murray. "I don't know what the hell is going on. Awful. Awful."

Eric was told by his coach to take shorter shifts

and put more effort into them. But when he looked down the bench, Murray knew he was trying to squeeze blood from the same stone that had failed predecessors Bill Dineen and Terry Simpson. "We would play well for a while and then fall off because the depth wasn't there," Murray recalls.

The Flyers lost at home in overtime to the Islanders when Ray Ferraro's winner deflected off Galley's glove. In Ottawa, the Flyers were victims of the first shutout in Senators history, 3-0.

"[Teams] kept throwing their biggest people out there against Eric. Because we had (6-2, 218-pound Mikael) Renberg, we could spot smaller players with the two of them for a while. But they usually would get handled by the big players on the other team. So we needed a big winger and a defenseman who could work the power play, do a lot of the penalty killing, and take the first and last shift of the period. We were using Galley thirty-five minutes a game and he was tiring out."

Defenseman Eric Desjardins was shocked by the trade that sent him to the Flyers from Montreal.

Murray tried old tactics like juggling lines and threatening benchings, while aware that Clarke was working on a better solution—new players. Knowing Montreal was struggling to score, the president-GM called Canadiens' GM Serge Savard to see if he was interested in Recchi.

"I wasn't down on Mark at all," recalls Clarke. The 27-year-old winger had simply become Philadelphia's most marketable commodity. When Savard asked Clarke what was wanted in return, the Montreal boss was given a shopping list.

"Recchi is a 100-point scorer and we wanted value," recalls Clarke. "We made it clear we were not in a position to accept a one-for-one. We had to get help in a couple of areas."

Clarke asked Savard about 25-year-old defenseman Mathieu Schneider. "We thought he was what we needed for our power play," recalls Clarke. "Serge didn't want to trade Schneider, so he brought up Eric Desjardins. We figured either one. Desjardins wasn't quite at Schneider's level offensively, but he was steadier, more solid."

Desjardins, picked by Mike Keenan to play in the 1991 Canada Cup as a 21-year-old, had fallen short of expectations that he would develop into a dominating defenseman. The Canadiens had depth at the position, plus a big winger who had taken up residence in their doghouse.

John LeClair, 6-2, 215, had scored two overtime winners for Montreal's 1993 Cup champions but had not broken 20 goals or 45 points in his three full NHL seasons. The Canadiens, experimenting with him at center, were disappointed with his poor start.

"We thought we could try him with Lindros," recalls Clarke. "If it didn't work out, then we would make him the checking centerman and use Brind'Amour on the wing with Eric.

"But I was still worried about giving up so much scoring in Recchi, so Serge told me he had been offered a third-round pick for (winger) Gilbert Dionne (who was on the block after criticizing his teammates), so I gave him [a draft choice] to put Dionne into the deal. But we would have done it without him."

Savard and Clarke spoke at midnight on February 8, following the Canadiens' 4-2 victory at Ottawa. They agreed to make the trade—Recchi and a third-round pick for Desjardins, LeClair and Dionne—in the morning so that the three new Flyers could get to Philadelphia for a game that night against Florida.

LeClair, whose sister Nancy went to Penn graduate school and taught at Cherokee High School in Marlton, New Jersey, got the call from Montreal coach Jacques Demers at around 9 A.M.. "We were practicing late and he asked me to come down early," recalls LeClair. "I kind of knew something was up, so I asked why he couldn't just tell me on the phone. Serge got on and told me what the deal was.

"When Bob Clarke called, I asked him if I was going to be playing wing or center. He said they wanted to try me at wing with Eric Lindros and Mikael Renberg and I got really excited."

Desjardins had heard rumors he was going to Winnipeg, but was still stunned. "I knew they had to trade a defenseman" he told reporters, "but it's always too bad when it's you."

Recchi was informed at the Flyers' morning skate. "We all thought something was going to happen," he said. "I didn't think it would be me, though. It's very tough. I think I've brought a lot to this organization."

Savard, who owned part of an airline, arranged a charter to transport the players between the two cities that afternoon. A cab pulled up at the Spectrum just as Lindros arrived for the game with MacTavish. "Must be the new guys," said Eric.

They met with Murray in his office and, with Desjardins paired with Haller, his old Montreal teammate, went out to play their third game in three nights. The three new Flyers received no help from their more-rested teammates. Yushkevich fell down

on Dave Lowry's game-opening goal, Stu Barnes shot between Roussel's legs and Gord Murphy scored off MacTavish. After eleven minutes, Philadelphia was behind by three.

The Flyers had no energy for a comeback. Lindros was benched for all but one shift during the last eight minutes of the 3-0 loss before a booing crowd 1,151 short of capacity. "I don't deserve to play if I'm not real sharp," Lindros said, adding the disruption of the team with a major trade had "made it a long day for everybody."

Clarke did not want to hear about extenuating circumstances from the captain of a 3-7-1 club that had suffered the franchise's first back-to-back shutouts in twenty-two years. "If we want to find excuses, we can," said the GM. "We were [bleeping] outplayed and [bleeping] outworked. They've been blaming the coach and general manager here for five [bleeping] years. At some point it has to be the players' fault."

So, how did Desjardins like it in Philadelphia? "Uh, it's tough to judge from one game," he said. "But it seems to me like the team has to play a little more together."

The coach, however, felt better than after the loss three days earlier in Ottawa. "I don't have a crystal ball, but I have a good feeling about this group of players," said Murray. "I know Desjardins can play in all situations and Lindros and LeClair standing beside each other in the face-off dots looks pretty nice."

LeClair appeared better than he felt. "I was exhausted," he recalls. "It had been a long, weird day. And it looked like it was going to be a long year."

Within twenty-four hours, Clarke and Savard worked a deal of fourth line centers—Mark Lamb to Montreal for Jim Montgomery. The Flyers bused up the New Jersey Turnpike, where U-turns were not only illegal, but unlikely. Philadelphia had not won in 13 visits (0-12-1) to the Meadowlands and had not even scored in the previous two.

But as the new players hung their street clothes in the visiting locker room, Lindros saw three teammates without skeletons in their closets. "When you haven't won someplace in a long time and you've suddenly got some guys who have, there's a different feeling about it," Eric recalls.

When the captain chased down a Desjardins rebound early in the game, his hunch turned into a revelation—LeClair was in front of the goal, unmoved by the big Devil defense. He jammed Lindros's feed past goalie Chris Terreri for a 1-0 lead.

LeClair, Lindros and Renberg dominated their shifts throughout the first period. Stephane Richer tied the game, but Roussel made big stops on four Devil chances before Brent Fedyk put Philadelphia back ahead in the first minute of the third period by redirecting a Haller point drive. Josef Beranek's goal with 2:57 to go wrapped up the 3-1 victory.

Desjardins finishedthe game plus-3 and LeClair had been in the slot all night while Lindros and Renberg muscled and hustled around the New Jersey end. "They looked like the Legion of Doom out there," said Montgomery.

The Flyers left the Meadowlands in a good mood for the first time since 1990. "For the guys who have been around here for a few years, that was a huge win," said Dineen. "I haven't been this excited after a hockey game in a long time."

Two nights later at the Spectrum, Desjardins assisted twice in the team's four-goal first period, while Hextall floored Rob Pearson with a counterpunch in a rousing 5-3 victory over Washington. Philadelphia's postgame charter didn't arrive in St. Petersburg until 2:30 A.M., but the only dragging LeClair did was of Lightning players around the ice.

He cut off a late Tampa Bay rally by charging off the wing, overpowering Cory Cross, stickhandling past Marc Bergevin and scoring on a stuffer, then completed his first NHL hat trick and a nine-point night for his line into the empty net. "This is great," said Lindros after the 5-2 victory. "John is so strong. There aren't a whole lot of people who can stop him."

Murray did not curb his enthusiasm. "I really have visions that line can be together for many years," he said.

Clarke didn't sit back to admire his handiwork. He traded Beranek, who had 10 goals in 62 games since his torrid start of the previous season, to Vancouver for 6-4, 235-pound winger Shawn Antoski, then made his fourth deal in seven days by exchanging minor-league defensemen with Chicago. Acquired was Karl Dykhuis for Bob Wilkie.

"I tried to get [Dykhuis] once for Florida," recalls Clarke. "He was a (1990) first-round pick who could skate and shoot. Chicago had one of the deepest defenses, which might explain why he hadn't won a job.

"GM Bob Pulford called back. He wanted a veteran minor-leaguer and said, 'Give me [Hershey's] Wilkie, and a fourth-round pick if Dykhuis plays 100 games for you.'"

Dykhuis was sent to the farm, while Lindros returned to the doghouse, replaced by Brind'Amour on the top line as Philadelphia's 3-game winning streak ended in a 4-2 loss to Quebec. The fans let Eric know

they were unhappy. "They *should* be booing," said Lindros. "But everybody goes through [a bad streak]. I'll be getting out of it soon."

The coach believed that, too, even as he chastised his star. "We have two big wingers playing at a high level and we need a center doing the same thing," said Murray. "But I think we're real close to having a breakthrough.

"The intensity, the work habits, the focus, the listening skills have improved a great deal. I really sense a camaraderie here now on buses, planes and in hotels. The players can see the direction we're going in. I think they're excited."

A six-day break gave Murray an opportunity to recall, drill and study Dykhuis. "He looks like a pretty complete guy," said the intrigued coach. With Galley's wrist injury putting him out of the lineup for at least two more contests, Dykhuis, who had been tried for only 18 games in two stretches with the Blackhawks, was kept for a two-game swing through Quebec City and Montreal.

His parents used the opportunity to drive down from Sept-Iles, Quebec. The 22-year-old redhead instantly made the trip worthwhile by scoring at Le Colisee the first time he touched the puck. With a hat trick by the awakening Lindros and four power-play goals, the Flyers built a 6-3 lead with 11:36 to go.

But a power-play goal by Owen Nolan reenergized the Nordiques. Adam Deadmarsh scored on a one-timer, then got a step outside Yushkevich and caught Hextall coming off the post. The game ended in a 6-6 tie. "It feels like we lost," said Renberg.

More to the point, Philadelphia had surrendered its poise. "It's amazing what pressure is when you put it on yourself," said Murray. "It's incredible to me we can't play better than that."

As he lamented the frustrating details to Clarke on the phone after the game, the coach did find one positive. "I think Dykhuis can play," he said.

The next day, before the Flyers practiced at the Forum, Desjardins brought closure to his Montreal days by taking a last look around the Canadiens' dressing room. "Next time here, I won't need to do that," he said.

Recchi, who had 10 points in his first 7 games with the Habs, diplomatically told reporters he could see why the Flyers had made the deal. But Murray, still steamed by Yushkevich's misplay on the tying goal in Quebec City, showed no understanding when he found the blueliner shooting pucks instead of concentrating on defensive drills. The impatient coach decided to scratch Yushkevich for the game the following night.

Murray also restored Lindros to the top line, which leaned on the smallish Canadiens through much of a scoreless first period. Early in the second, LeClair, set up by Lindros, beat Patrick Roy over his glove, then converted a Renberg rebound to give Philadelphia a 2-0 lead.

Hextall dumped Recchi in a chase for a loose puck, then stoned the former Flyer on a breakaway.

When Shjon Podein scored 25 seconds into the third period, the floodgates opened. LeClair pumped in his third goal and leaped into the air as *chapeaux*—some thrown in honor, others mocking the poor performance of the Canadiens—littered the ice. "That hat trick will definitely help me remember this," he said after Philadelphia's startling 7-0 rout. "But this win was special anyway."

The shutout was the Flyers' first at the Forum since one by Bernie Parent in 1974. "Hexy was

calmer, more relaxed," said Murray. "I thought he was really on top of the puck and just letting it hit him much better than what he did in Quebec."

The victory did more than boost a veteran goalie's confidence. It turned on a bulb inside the young players' heads. "Whoa," Lindros thought. "We are *gooood*."

Two nights later, on the captain's 22nd birthday, Philadelphia overwhelmed the Caps with 17 third-period shots, broke a 2-2 tie on a goal by Podein and won 4-2, at the CoreStates Spectrum.

Three weeks after the Florida debacle, Murray's team matched the Panthers in patience, rallying for a 2-2 home tie on goals by Renberg and Lindros. Even a 5-3 loss at Madison Square Garden turned into a positive when the big line dominated the Stanley Cup champions in the third period. "When we play our game, we can beat them," said Lindros.

Returning home, the Flyers blasted the Penguins 6-2 with four third-period goals. "[This was] as good an effort for 60 minutes as we've had," beamed Murray.

The Legion of Doom line was becoming a phenomenon. LeClair scored his 10th and 11th goals in his 12th game as a Flyer, a 4-3 victory at St. Petersburg that put the team over the .500 mark. And Lindros had scored 15 points in his last 7 contests.

The defense also came together. The consistent, smart Desjardins was clearly the franchise's best backliner since Mark Howe. The chip on Haller's shoulder added a long-lost dimension, while Therien, the hulking rookie, held his own. Dykhuis proved to be a revelation, and Hextall, who stopped Bryan Smolinski point-blank in the final seconds of a 3-2 victory over Boston, was doing footwork drills that were helping him restore the standup style and confidence of his early NHL seasons.

While Clarke continued to search for scoring depth, picking up veteran forward Anatoli Semenov from Anaheim for Czech defenseman Milos Holan, who had skipped out of Hershey with homesickness, Philadelphia kept finding ways to succeed. When the Devils rallied from a 3-1 deficit to tie the score, Lindros, set up by Haller, blew a winner over Martin Brodeur's glove. After squandering a 3-0 lead at Madison Square Garden, Eric's chip pass from just inside the Flyer line sent LeClair away to fire the winner through Mike Richter with 3:38 to go. "Very big for our morale," said the captain.

With Lindros's huge linemates lightening some of his physical burden, Eric was gleefully racking up points. He ran over two Senators so LeClair could roof the winner with 2:42 remaining in a 3-1 victory in Ottawa, then completed a hat trick to beat Florida 4-3 in overtime. Two nights later, at a delirious Spectrum, the captain recorded three more goals and took over the NHL scoring lead from Pittsburgh's Jaromir Jagr. "It's the most dominating line I've seen in ten years," said Canadiens' coach Jacques Demers after Philadelphia recorded its 8th-straight victory, 8-4 over Montreal.

Finally, the Flyers cooled. A late goal by Hartford's Adam Burt broke the winning streak, 4-3, and a victory got away in Landover when MacTavish lost a face-off to Michal Pivonka and Lindros allowed Peter Bondra to score with only 11 seconds remaining. Philadelphia's last-ever visit to Boston Garden, where great moments in the franchise's history were forged, failed to stir the new generation, which went down 5-1. And a 3-2 defeat in Pittsburgh brought the Flyers' record to 1-4-1 in their last 6 games.

But before old doubts could resurface, Lindros stepped into the Rangers' Brian Leetch, knocking the puck loose and firing in the first of two goals to spark a 4-2 Spectrum victory over New York on April 2.

As rumors circulated that the team was seeking to upgrade its goaltending, Murray designated Hextall as the No. 1 man for the stretch drive. Roussel would have been the more economical choice. After Alexander Semak went around Galley to give Tampa Bay a 2-0 lead over the sleepwalking Flyers, Hextall turned his stick into kindling, repeatedly smashing it over the net. "Now I know why they call him Psycho," Murray said later. Philadelphia scored three goals within the next nine minutes and won 5-3.

The following day, at the trading deadline, Clarke acquired the fifth new defenseman since his return, dealing Galley to Buffalo for 29-year-old Petr Svoboda. "We wanted somebody a little younger, a little quicker," recalls Clarke. "(Sabres GM-coach) John Muckler was looking for more offense. I thought Garry was a good guy, but he had his problems (at the end of the 1993-94 season) criticizing his teammates. Even though he apologized, this would be a fresh start."

Svoboda, ten pounds underweight as he recovered from a broken jaw, debuted by setting up a Brind'Amour goal that started the Flyers to a 3-1 victory at Landover. The team took advantage of a three-day break by going to Hilton Head, South Carolina. "This is Craig MacTavish teaching Lindros how to manipulate the general manager," said a smiling Clarke. But the vacation proved worthwhile after Lindros made a highlight-film quality backhand pass to set up a two-on-one goal by Renberg, then fed LeClair's winner in a 3-2 home victory over Tampa.

Everything was breaking Philadelphia's way. The team was trailing Pittsburgh 3-2 at the CoreStates Spectrum on April 16, when referee Paul Stewart penalized the Penguins twice in the final minute. Desjardins's point drives were deflected by Renberg, in regulation, and Brind'Amour in overtime. The Flyers' latest winning streak was stretched to 7 when Lindros figured in every goal of a workmanlike 3-1 victory at Miami. At 24-13-4, Philadelphia was within two points of guaranteeing itself a playoff spot.

With seven games to go, clinching was only a matter of time, but five seasons had seemed like an eternity to loyalists who were anxious for the blessed event to occur at home.

The Islanders' Kirk Muller jumped on a puck Svoboda couldn't hold at the point and soloed shorthanded, but the Flyer's newest defenseman then made a between-the-legs feed that enabled Desjardins to set up Lindros for a game-tying one-timer.

Midway through the third period, Hextall made a big save on Patrick Flatley and Brind'Amour broke out two-on-one with the deep rebound. He laid the puck onto the backhand of Renberg, who swept the lead goal past Tommy Salo, starting the countdown. Hextall, one of two players (along with Brown) who had been on Philadelphia's last playoff qualifier, raced to the corner to pick up the puck as the buzzer sounded the end of the 2-1 victory and the most painful period in franchise history.

But Clarke had said just after the end of the lockout that a playoff berth wasn't a very high ambition. A team only two points from wrapping up the division title and the conference's second playoff seed had good reason not to be complacent. "Our goal has been refocused," said Lindros. "We can really contend for the Stanley Cup."

Two days later at New Jersey, after the Devils rallied from a 3-1 deficit to force overtime, LeClair came onto the ice during the first line change of sudden death, chased down a Brind'Amour dump, centered to Renberg and hustled to the front of the net to jam the puck under goalie Martin Brodeur. The Flyers, winners of their 9th straight game, raced onto the ice as divisional champions for the first time since 1987.

"We wanted to show we deserve to be where we are right now," said Murray. "To have not made the playoffs for five years, this is a significant step. I just keep wondering at what level this team will plateau, and I don't know."

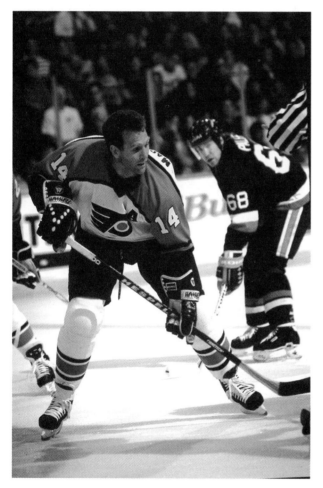

With all regular-season goals accomplished, a letdown was inevitable. A 4-2 loss in Buffalo ended Philadelphia's streak. Following a pregame ceremony at the Spectrum awarding Lindros the Bobby Clarke Award and Desjardins the Barry Ashbee Trophy, the team slept through a 5-2 loss to inept Ottawa. Thus, when the struggling Rangers arrived for the next-to-last game still needing two points to wrap up a postseason spot, the Flyers were determined to put on their playoff face.

Instead, Lindros was hit in the face. Only 4:25 into the game, his shot boomeranged off the hip of New York's Jeff Beukeboom and back into the captain's cheekbone, striking dangerously close to the left eye. As Eric exited with a towel to his face, the Flyers' ambition went with him. Two goals by Leetch and Glenn Healy's goaltending gave the visitors a 2-0 victory.

At Wills Eye Hospital, specialists drained a small amount of blood from the eye and sent Lindros home to bed with a patch, drops and no promise that he would be able to start the playoffs in seven days. "They were worried, more than they let on to the public, about the pressure buildup," he recalls.

Without its captain, Philadelphia finished the season with a 2-0 victory at Nassau Coliseum, the team's first win on Long Island in 12 visits (0-11-1). Lindros' opportunity to record the Flyers' first-ever league scoring title, disappeared when Jagr got 3 points in his final 2 games and forced a dead heat at 70. The Pittsburgh star was awarded the Art Ross Trophy because he had scored 32 goals to Eric's 29. "There are more important things now," said Eric.

His sore eye tired easily after he was allowed to take off the patch. "With all the precautions they'd normally take, we're talking two and a half weeks," Lindros told reporters when he visited practice. "We don't have time for that. When we finally get into the playoffs, I'm not going to be sitting on my butt watching them on TV."

As the week went by, the doctors told Lindros otherwise, ruling him out for at least the first two games of the series against the Sabres. But before the Flyers could feel sorry for themselves, the real world brought a dose of perspective. Nathan MacTavish, Craig's 3-year-old son, miraculously escaped with only a fractured hip bone and bruises when he pushed through a screen and fell from a second-floor window of the family home in Voorhees, New Jersey.

The players practiced with "Get Well Nathan" patches on their uniforms, figuring Eric would recover in due time without their making a fuss over him. After closing the strike-shortened season with a 25-

Craig MacTavish played 55 games before being traded to St. Louis for Dale Hawerchuk on March 15, 1996.

9-3 rush, Philadelphia was confident it could get the jump on Buffalo without Lindros. "He's won us a lot of games this year," Murray said. "Now it's time for us to step up and do something for him."

Indeed, there could be no passengers, even if the Sabres came into the series carrying most of the baggage. Buffalo had gotten past the first round only once in eleven years. Leading scorer Pat LaFontaine, struggling back from a knee reconstruction, was nowhere near top form and Dale Hawerchuk, who anchored the second line, would not be ready for the early matches after missing 25 games with an arthritic hip.

Still, no matter who was absent with regrets from the Spectrum's first playoff game since 1989, there were 17,380 fans who wouldn't have missed it for the world. The place was wired and so were the Flyers, perhaps to their initial detriment.

After Alexander Mogilny deked Desjardins to the ice, the Sabres' Jason Dawe converted a two-on-one in the first two minutes. Rob DiMaio, on a setup from Podein, tied the game, but Haller and Desjardins were spread too wide, leaving LaFontaine time to fake Hextall and put Buffalo back ahead, 2-1.

Philadelphia, holding clear size and strength advantages over a small Sabre defense, settled down and pressed the attack. Dineen was taking Richard Smehlik into goalie Dominik Hasek when Fedyk's pass bounced off the defenseman to tie the score. Only 1:28 later, Haller one-timed a deep rebound of a Desjardins point blast past Hasek to give the Flyers a 3-2 lead.

But it did not hold up. LaFontaine intercepted a Desjardins pass and flipped it to Dawe who converted and Philadelphia had to scramble to survive until overtime. The Flyers came out strong in sudden death, however. Buffalo had not managed a shot in the first ten minutes when Hasek wrapped the puck up the boards and Brind'Amour pinched. He dropped a pass to Dykhuis, who fired as Dineen was taking defenseman Alexei Zhitnik into Hasek. The Sabre goalie was on all fours as the puck deflected off LaFontaine and in to win the game, 4-3.

Even after five years, the fans had no trouble remembering how to celebrate a playoff victory. But Buffalo's GM-coach could not recall seeing a goalie so physically abused in a playoff game. "There were people sitting on him for three goals," Muckler complained.

While Hasek was having a load taken off his feet, the Flyers, getting a jump in the series without Lindros, were removing a monkey from their backs.

After Brind'Amour controlled a DiMaio feed from the point and beat Hasek with a wrist shot to give Philadelphia a 1-0 lead in Game 2, Hextall robbed LaFontaine and Dawe. Brind'Amour then leaped over a fallen Galley at the Buffalo blue line and fed a two-on-one pass to DiMaio, who scorched a one-timer under the crossbar.

Brian Holzinger cut the 2-0 advantage in half from the edge of the crease on a power play, but Semenov redirected a LeClair crossi-ice pass to make the score 3-1. That was one more goal than a superb Hextall needed, as he calmly reached up and robbed Dawe on a third-period rebound attempt to preserve the victory.

The following day, Lindros practiced with a full face shield, but the doctors still held him out of Game 3 in Buffalo. Before six minutes had been played, Renberg assisted Dykhuis to end an 0-for-13 power-play drought, but four more Philadelphia manpower advantages fizzled before the Sabres' Donald Audette tapped in a cross-ice pass from teammate Garry Galley to tie the game.

Less than two minutes later, Yushkevich let up when the linesman missed an obvious offside call and Wayne Presley beat Hextall from the circle. Buffalo, determined to step up its physical game, threw 19 second-period shots at Hextall, who kept the Flyers within a goal until Mogilny hit the empty net to sew up the Sabres' 3-1 triumph.

Philadelphia barely bemoaned the linesman's mistake that led to the winning goal. "Those things happen," said Murray, secure in the knowledge that he was on the verge of a real happening—the return of Lindros. The Sabres, able to step out of character for one game, but not two, visibly shrunk in the presence of the big man in Game 4.

Eric dominated from the first shift and Brind'Amour set up on a backhand pass by Dineen and scored on the second. Fedyk, from Haller, made it 2-0 early in the middle period, then Desjardins beat Hasek on the power play from the high slot. Lindros took the puck from a clearly frightened Zhitnik and fed LeClair to build the lead to four.

Mogilny scored on a scramble and 37 seconds later, LaFontaine converted a gift that Hextall had cleared off Dykhuis's skate to pull Buffalo within two. But when Lindros immediately carried the puck into the Sabre end, they quickly backed up and gave up. Statistically, Eric counted only two assists, but he was a commanding presence in Philadelphia's 4-2 victory and 3-1 series lead.

Buffalo was "Doomed." Eleven seconds into Game

5 at the Spectrum, Lindros slammed Smehlik into the boards. LeClair then flattened LaFontaine and Renberg rattled Doug Bodger. Brind'Amour put the Flyers on the board, then Haller gloved down a Lindros feed from the Philadelphia side of center ice and stuck the puck past Hasek's stick side to make the score 2-0. Hasek stopped Lindros on a breakaway, but the captain retrieved and scored off Galley's stick. Juhlin completed a four-goal first period.

LeClair converted a clear by the frazzled Hasek to build the lead to five before the Flyers let up. A giveaway by Hextall just before the second-period buzzer helped Buffalo creep back to within two goals, but before things could get tense, Dineen put the series away. Philadelphia, winning 6-4, had overpowered the Sabres in five games. "When we saw the kind of desire [Lindros] had to end it, we basically latched onto his coattails," said Murray.

As the eighth-seeded Rangers reached back to their 1994 performance level to finish off conference champion Quebec in six games, the Madison Square Garden fans chanted, "We Want Hextall."

"They can have him," said Lindros. "He's been incredible for us."

The goalie, who had given up 16 goals in his three starts during the Rangers' sweep of the Islanders the previous spring, wasn't interested in redemption. "You guys keep bringing it up," he told reporters. "But whether I had a successful playoff or a bad one last year, it still would be behind me."

It was also up to the Flyers to prove that the Stanley Cup champions' best days were behind them. New York's depth had diminished in eleven months' time and Philadelphia had a significant edge in size. But the Rangers had peerless leadership from Mark Messier, the reigning Conn Smythe Trophy winner in Leetch, and a successful track record when competing under pressure.

"I thought as long as a few of their guys didn't catch fire, we would win," recalls Lindros. He tried to hose down Leetch's enthusiasm early in Game 1 at the CoreStates Spectrum, but drew a cross-checking penalty which the Ranger star converted past Hextall's glove. With Dineen in the box for elbowing Kevin Lowe, Petr Nedved got away from Lindros and scored on a pass from Sergei Zubov to make the score 2-0 New York.

LeClair converted a cross-crease pass from Renberg after a Richter turnover to cut the lead in half. But Dykhuis was caught holding, Brind'Amour coughed up the puck to Messier, and Pat Verbeek scored the Rangers third power-play goal of the game to rebuild the lead to 3-1.

The Flyers kept coming, though. LeClair jammed his own rebound between Richter's legs, then took a behind-the-back feed by Lindros to tie the game and complete a hat trick. Eric had Leetch in his sights again when Richter decided to save the defenseman from death by clearing a dump-in up the boards. But Renberg pinched in and Desjardins steamed up the slot to put Philadelphia ahead, 4-3, with 4:49 remaining.

New York had not managed a shot in twelve minutes when it pulled Richter and forced the puck into the slot. Verbeek roofed a backhander with only 19.1 seconds remaining and, for the second consecutive series opener, the Flyers had been caught from behind,

But just as against Buffalo, Philadelphia had too much energy and confidence to be shaken. Seven minutes into overtime, MacTavish beat Nedved on a face-off, dropped the puck back to Desjardins at the point, and went to the net. Desjardins came down the right boards, fired through the screen, and scored just under the crossbar on the near side to give the Flyers the 5-4 win.

MacTavish, who had carried the Cup with the Rangers, knew they would be better the following night in Game 2. "Winning creates excitement," he said. "But losing creates desperation."

Indeed, it looked like Leetch would not let New York go down. He controlled the first period and scored twice on power plays. Six minutes into the second period, Philadelphia had managed only 6 shots. Nevertheless, Murray kept matching Lindros against Messier, and playing six defensemen to the Rangers' four. As Hextall held down the damage, the younger team powered its way off the ropes.

Lindros knocked Lowe off the puck behind the goal, then came around to put in Renberg's rebound. Ten minutes later, Brind'Amour dug out the puck along the endboards and Yushkevich tied the game.

Renberg put Philadelphia ahead 25 seconds into the third period, but Leetch refused to die. He cut diagonally during a four-on-four and came back across his body to tie the score off Dykhuis's stick. For the second straight game, there would be overtime.

New York won the face-off, but LeClair stopped a rush at the blue line trapping Beukeboom, and Renberg broke out to feed Haller on a two-on-one. The defenseman lifted the puck over the sliding Leetch and underneath the crossbar after only 35 seconds, creating a 4-3 victory and a 2-0 Flyer edge going into Madison Square Garden.

Philadelphia had outscored New York 8-1 at even strength, a sign of physical dominance. Still, at 5-for-10, the champions had their power play clicking and were going home to the amenities of last change and a roaring house.

But Dineen quieted the crowd almost immediately. Before three minutes had been played, the Flyer picked off an up-the-middle clear by Beukeboom and beat Richter with yet another Philadelphia shot just under the crossbar. The Rangers shook it off and carried the play the rest of the period until the final minute, when the overeager Beukeboom stepped up just inside the Flyer line to nail Lindros.

Eric withstood enough of the hit to get the puck ahead to LeClair. The winger broke out two-on-one against Leetch and laid an exquisite pass to Renberg at the right post for a tap-in 16 seconds before the end of the period.

New York, down 2-0, deflated with startling speed. Brind'Amour, playing most of his shifts against Messier as New York coach Colin Campbell endeavored to keep his captain from Lindros, stole the puck from the fatigued Ranger leader. Dineen converted from fifty feet out through the legs of Lowe and the rattled Richter. Brind'Amour then tipped home Yushkevich's point drive to make the score 4-0.

Campbell replaced Richter with Healy and Messier chipped a goal over Hextall's shoulder. But Brind'Amour and MacTavish forced a giveaway, and Haller finished off a shorthanded goal. The Flyers rolled to an astonishingly easy 5-2 victory and a 3-0 command of the series.

"I didn't even dream about this," said Murray. Lindros had been a presence, but his line had hardly dominated. Still, Philadelphia was on the verge of a sweep.

The Flyers spent the off-day in New York insisting the series wasn't over. "Can't let your foot off the rattlesnake," Lindros thought. The fans refused to be venomous, giving their team a standing ovation as it took the ice for what looked like the last time as champion.

The Rangers put up a fight. Verbeek sent Svoboda to the medical room in need of twelve stitches in his chin. Fedyk went to the hospital for a precautionary spinal checkup after his head snapped backwards on a check by Jay Wells. New York took 10 of the game's first 14 shots, but Hextall, playing his strongest match of the series, was unbeatable.

Inevitably, the Rangers began to gasp. Verbeek

gave the puck away, Zubov was caught up ice, and Dykhuis finished off a three-on-one pass from DiMaio. Four minutes later, New York was caught with too many men on the ice. On the power play, Dykhuis gloved down a Leetch clearing attempt, moved into the slot, and fired his second goal, the Flyers' 12th of the playoffs by a defenseman, off Healy's glove.

It was over. Renberg chopped Haller's shot out of the air past the screened Healy, then Semenov–set up by Desjardins after Philadelphia's third line pinned the Messier unit–scored from the slot to build the lead to four. Mark Osborne broke the shutout, but Hextall easily cleaned up the Rangers' feeble chances in the third period, then shook his glove in the air triumphantly as the buzzer went. With a 4-1 victory, the Flyers had pulverized the defending champs in four straight.

"It's incredible what has happened with this group of guys," said Murray. "They have grown by incredible bounds."

Kids like Dykhuis, rescued from minor-league obscurity, had come far to be part of the exhilarating sweep. Yet no Philadelphia player had traveled as difficult a path as Hextall in returning from injuries, lean seasons, and rejection by three teams in three years.

"Hexy was the MVP of this series in my mind," said Murray. "You're playing against a team with a tremendous amount of speed and skill. And he played with poise and made the big stops time after time."

Hextall patiently shook his head to the waves of Big Apple media who asked if he felt personal vindication for his humiliation the previous April. "I don't think about that," he said. "But this does mean more to me than beating Buffalo. We proved something as a team. People were concerned about me, concerned about us having only one line, but we beat a great team with a lot of playoff experience."

The Flyers had hit the Rangers with so many body checks that their brains had shut off. "They wore us down," said winger Adam Graves. "When they come in that hard on the forecheck, there's not a whole lot you can do."

Still, as overpowering as Philadelphia had been, mistakes up ice by freewheeling New York had led to most of the goals. In the Eastern Conference final, the Flyers would have to contend with a different animal—big, strong, deep and disciplined New Jersey.

The Devils, who twelve months earlier had lost Game 7 of the conference final to the Rangers in double overtime, were hitting their stride after struggling through the short season. With the irascible Claude Lemieux blanketing and infuriating Neely and Jagr, New Jersey had beaten both Boston and Pittsburgh in five games.

Philadelphia, playing into June for the first time in its history, had eight days to enjoy the status of reaching the Final Four. "This is something you're going to remember for the rest of your life, you know?" said Lindros, whose team then went out and played a Game 1 to forget.

From the opening face-off, Eric hit any visitor he could find, but turned up no scoring chances for his efforts. When Semenov lost the puck to Sergei Brylin in the corner and Antoski missed Bill Guerin coming up the slot, the Devils jumped ahead. Svoboda then turned over the puck in New Jersey's neutral-zone trap and Scott Niedermayer finished off a two-on-one.

Center ice was a swamp for the Flyers, who made bad decisions on the slushy Spectrum surface and were counterattacked all night. Hextall sprawled to stop Randy McKay and wound up knocking the puck into the net with the butt end of his goalie stick, then flopped to allow Guerin to go upstairs and make the score 4-0.

When Lindros went on strafing runs in the final minutes of the Devils' 4-1 victory, Scott Stevens, who was matched every shift against the Flyer captain, sneered at his frustration.

Lindros, who admitted he would have to pick his spots better in Game 2, delivered the opening goal off a circle-to-circle pass from Dineen. But MacTavish was given a spearing penalty following a joust with Bobby Holik and McKay cashed in on the power play to even the score.

Renberg jammed in a Lindros rebound and Philadelphia carried the play until, with Juhlin off for slashing, Niedermayer knocked down a Lindros clear and fed John MacLean's game-tying goal only 12 seconds before the first period buzzer.

The Flyers, their hard-earned lead gone, sagged. Bruce Driver broke up a poorly advised Lindros pass on a shorthanded two-on-one, catching Philadelphia in transition and allowing Shawn Chambers to feed Neal Broten for a gimme. One minute later, Holik made it 4-2, and a goal by Ken Daneyko sealed New Jersey's 5-2 domination.

"I've played worse," said Hextall after Murray fingered the veteran for a bad night. But clearly the goaltending would have to improve if the Flyers were to make a series of it. So would Lindros who, after a good start, had again allowed Stevens to be-

come a preoccupation.

"We have to make sure we do what we're told to do," said Desjardins. Perhaps that would be easier at the Meadowlands, where Philadelphia could escape pressure from its home fans to force the play. Murray reminded his team that it had to pass, not carry, the puck through center ice. He also challenged his players to handle adversity. "One of the problems we've had is that in the first two series, everything was going our way," he said.

In Game 3, Philadelphia was tested almost immediately with another bad break. After Brodeur stopped Yushkevich on a golden opportunity, the rebound kicked deep, trapping LeClair and allowing Lemieux to blow a shot through Hextall's pads.

But the Flyers bounced back. Dykhuis and Svoboda carefully tiptoed through the minefield between the blue lines and Dineen shoved home a rebound. McKay walked out from the side boards to put New Jersey ahead 2-1 early in the second period, but Hextall settled down and Philadelphia played the Devils' waiting game. Still, as the clock ticked deep into the third period, the Flyers' patience appeared to be putting them closer only to a third straight loss.

Instead, their perseverance paid off. Brind'Amour took a drop pass at the Devils' blue line and, for lack of a better option, tossed the puck at the net. It bounced through Semenov and Broten, then over Martin Brodeur's glove to tie the game with 6:03 remaining.

Philadelphia had sudden life going into sudden death. Four minutes of overtime had been played when Lindros disentangled himself from Lemieux, raced up ice to take a trailing pass from Renberg, and perfectly placed a shot just inside the post on Brodeur's stick side. The Flyers' fourth consecutive victory in overtime cut New Jersey's series lead to 2-1.

"It's amazing how things work out," said Lindros, who had been invisible most of the night. "It might have been boring for people to watch and it might seem like I'm not doing much, but that's the way the coach wanted us to work and it worked out fine."

A struggling Therien was in the box when Brian Rolston scored on the power play to put the Devils up 1-0 in Game 4, but Hextall remained sharp, stopping 15 first-period shots. After Podein deflected Dykhuis's drive to tie the score, Philadelphia began to win the center-ice chess match.

Brodeur twice had to make good saves against Renberg on outnumbered breaks before the winger one-timed a Lindros setup to put the Flyers ahead late in the second period. New Jersey, behind late in a game for the first time in the series, was making the same mistakes Philadelphia had at the Spectrum. Montgomery forced a bad pass by Chambers, springing Brind'Amour on a breakaway. He pulled the puck in from Brodeur's attempted poke check and scored to build the lead to 3-1.

Desjardins' goal cemented a series-tying 4-2 victory. The rejuvenated Flyers and suddenly worried Devils went back to Philadelphia the following afternoon for a Game 5 that was as steamy as the ninety-degree weather. MacLean, picked up by neither Juhlin or Yushkevich, scored on New Jersey's first shot of the game, but Yushkevich's power-play point drive bounced in off Dineen's shin to even the score.

Antoski, annoyed by Ken Daneyko's interference, stupidly tore the defenseman's helmet off and drew a Flyer penalty and Bobby Carpenter beat a charging Hextall to put the Devils up 2-1 before the end of the first period.

Murray tried to awaken his team's offense by exchanging Brind'Amour for the slumping LeClair on the Doom line, but Philadelphia was doing more retaliating against New Jersey's bodychecking than counterattacking with the puck. Through forty minutes, Philadelphia had only 8 shots.

Nevertheless, early in the third, Dineen saved a clearing attempt by Brodeur and fired a blast through a screen just under the crossbar to tie the game. The next goal would probably turn the series.

Dineen, with Brodeur at his mercy, shot wide on a LeClair rebound. Richer hit the crossbar on a breakaway with 3:54 remaining. Overtime looked inevitable when Lemieux picked up the puck in the Devil end, shouldered Lindros, and raced up the right wing. Svoboda gave up the blue line, and the winger was barely across it when he fired, catching Hextall before he could completely cut down the angle.

The perfect shot came across the goalie's body, hitting just inside the post, inches off the ice, with 44.2 seconds remaining. "I should have had it," said Hextall after the Devils sealed off Brodeur and left the silent Spectrum with a 3-2 series lead.

After the game, Murray defended the increasingly criticized Lindros. "We would like him to shoot the puck more," the coach said, "but [the Devils] are following him all over." The next day, however, Murray joined the chorus and challenged his star. "He's got to get himself going at a higher level."

Going into Game 6 at the Meadowlands, the home team still had not won a contest, but the young Fly-

ers were facing elimination for the first time. The Devils, meanwhile, were back where they had been a year earlier, when New Jersey had lost Game 6 and ultimately Game 7 to the Rangers. "Everybody has that on his mind," said Lemieux, "and the lesson we should learn from it is you just keep pounding away until it's over."

So the Devils did not panic when Montgomery's shot from the point bounced off Tommy Albelin's stick to give Philadelphia the early 1-0 lead. Richer converted a tap-in from Broten while Podein was in the penalty box for tripping to tie the game, and New Jersey went ahead when Rolston chipped a rebound off the sprawled Hextall's glove.

Murray juggled lines to try to find some offense, but LeClair fanned on two good chances and No. 88 never had the puck. The Flyers went almost nineteen minutes without a shot. "We were a fragile group," recalls Lindros. "They really took it to us."

Halfway through the second period, Chambers blocked a MacTavish shot and the puck caromed past three trapped Philadelphia players to Holik, who fed McKay at the right post for an easy tap-in. Lemieux then scored on a breakaway before Renberg's late power-play goal set a 4-2 final that ended the Flyers' season.

"The Devils right now are a better club than we are," said Murray. The numbers showed just how blanketing New Jersey had been—in 16 of the 18 full periods, the Flyers were held to fewer than 10 shots; in two of the games, the Legion of Doom did not have a point.

"It does wear on you mentally," said Lindros about the Devils' style. "You go out there and you don't touch the puck. You feel you haven't done anything. It's not for lack of effort."

New Jersey's superior concentration had been practiced. "This is the Devils' time," said Daneyko. "Eric may be a superstar, but he wasn't going to beat us the way Mark Messier did last year. We were too determined. I'm sure in the future Eric is going to do it to somebody. But not us. Not tonight."

The Flyers shed some tears. "It's tough when you're two games away from the finals and now you're 100 games away from the finals," said Dineen. But outside the locker room, Clarke was more proud than disappointed.

"We did lots of good things, made lots of strides," said the president-GM. "The closer you get to the top of the pyramid, the better team you play against. They show you the cracks that you have.

"Eric had to go through this himself. The coaches

told him what to do, but in the end it's you out there learning the hard way. We have all these kids who had never seen the playoffs before making it to the conference finals. I think they did a really good job."

The Professional Hockey Writers Association agreed, elevating the Flyer captain into the most elite company of the franchise's history. Lindros joined Bobby Clarke as the second Flyer to be named the NHL's most valuable player.

"Thank you to the fans of Philadelphia who sup-

"When you look at some of the names on it, there's a lot going on there," said Eric, who also joined LeClair on the first All-Star team.

Clarke, who had enjoyed a pretty good season himself, spent a busy summer signing big players to sizable contracts. He made sure 6-2, 225-pound Joel Otto, the best anti-Lindros device on the free-agent market, didn't fall into the wrong hands, signing the ten-season veteran away from Calgary for three years and $4.9 million. "I would rather play with Eric than

The Legion of Doom poses with Ed Snider to promote World Cup of Hockey games set for the CoreStates Center. LeClair (USA) and Lindros (Canada) joined their World Cup teams. Injuries forced Mikael Renberg to withdraw from Team Sweden.

ported us when we weren't so good," said Eric, pausing as his eyes welled up at the end of his acceptance speech at a black-tie gala at the Metropolitan Toronto Convention Center. "We're getting better. And we're going to do it."

Since the honor activated a clause in Lindros's contract that raised his yearly salary by $600,000, it was suggested to Snider that perhaps he should cry along with his star. Not a chance. "When we've got the best player in the league, he's worth it," said the beaming owner, "don't you think?"

Lindros, who collected 63 voting points to 27 for Jagr and 23 for Hasek, became the second-youngest Hart Trophy winner in history to Wayne Gretzky.

against him," said the 33-year-old Otto.

A two-year, $2.3 million offer outbid Mike Keenan's Blues and brought back 37-year-old Kjell Samuelsson, who had been released in a Penguin economy move. "[Philadelphia] made a better offer and I liked it here, too," Samuelsson recalls. "I knew I wouldn't have to play as many minutes, and that it would be good for me at this stage of my career."

Samuelsson's acquisition allowed Clarke to recycle the stubborn and disappointing Yushkevich and a 1996 second-round pick to Toronto for the Leafs' first- and fourth-round choices in 1996 and a 1997 No. 2. The president-GM then responded to Roussel's request for a substantial raise by acquiring 25-year-old goalie Garth Snow from the Colorado Avalanche—the relocated Quebec Nordiques—for 1996 third- and sixth-round choices. Roussel took the hint and agreed to a one-year, $600,000 deal.

Dave Brown was let go to sign as a free agent with San Jose. And at age 64, a Flyer original, Gene Hart, was replaced as the team's television play-by-play announcer by Jim Jackson, who was moving over from radio. "You can't be unhappy with twenty-eight years," said Hart, who would continue to do community and public relations work for the team. Steve Carroll, formerly the voice of the East Coast Hockey League Nashville Knights, was hired to do the WIP call.

Glen Seabrooke, Philadelphia's first-round pick in 1985, won a $5-million lawsuit against Dr. John Gregg, the team's former orthopedist. The player claimed that Gregg's advice to do "aggressive therapy" on his injured shoulder had left him crippled. "I would never hurt anybody," Gregg wept during his testimony.

Clarke opened the cash register for the team's nucleus. LeClair ($7 million, five years), Desjardins ($6 million, four years), and Haller ($4 million, five years) signed new contracts. So did Renberg ($6.4 million, four years), soon after undergoing surgery to repair a hernia during training camp. "I think this group of guys wants to stay together," said Clarke. "And we want to keep them together."

The club received excellent value for its dollar as it raced from the 1995-96 gate. Patrick Roy and the Canadiens were routed 7-1 in the season opener at the Forum. Then, behind Hextall's 25 saves, 8-for-9 penalty killing and a shorthanded goal by Brind'Amour, the Flyers began their twenty-ninth and final year at the Spectrum with a 2-1 victory over Washington.

Roussel, who had outplayed Snow during the exhibition season for the backup job, shut out the Islanders, 3-0, in Uniondale. A 7-1 rout of Edmonton, pushed Philadelphia to its first 4-0 start since 1988-89.

When Hextall strained a hamstring in a 4-2 victory at Anaheim, Murray looked to Roussel. He turned a 3-1 third-period lead in the Flyers' first-ever game at Chicago's new United Center into the initial loss of the season, 5-4. Roussel had problems

again in a 5-5 tie at Nassau Coliseum, so the coach tried Snow. In his Philadelphia debut, the rookie beat Ottawa, 5-2.

The Legion of Doom accumulated 26 goals as the team went 7-1-3 in its first 11 games. Nevertheless, when the attentions of LeClair and Renberg meandered during a 2-1 home loss to Florida on November 2, the wingers were benched for long stretches of the second and third periods. "We're going to treat people the same here," said Murray. "Ice time is

earned."

The coach had no grievance with Lindros, the NHL's player of the month for October, but with referees who did not take action when opponents tried to goad the captain into fights. In the Florida loss, the big guy became a victim of a low-bridge by Jason Woolley, whose hit tore a medial collateral ligament in a left knee that was already bruised by a collision with a Nassau Coliseum goalpost.

Lindros, expected to be out two weeks, would be absent for the third time in four years with a knee problem. Just as in the two previous instances, his team struggled without him. Murray yanked Roussel after he gave up four goals in a 7-4 defeat in Pittsburgh, and Snow couldn't overcome a cluster of third-period turnovers in Miami that converted a 2-1 lead into a 4-2 loss.

Hextall returned, as did Otto after a week's absence with a strained knee. Murray moved the checking center to the Doom Line for a game against his former Calgary teammates and Otto scored in the 3-1 Spectrum victory. But the Flyers then flunked both ends of a home-to-home series against the Stanley Cup champion Devils.

Although LeClair's goal with 17 seconds remaining pulled out a 2-2 tie in Landover, Philadelphia's 2-4-1 record without its captain didn't earn the team any perseverance medals. All was well in Metropolis again, however, when Superman flew in on November 16, scored after only 1:33, and netted a third-period winner during the 5-3 victory over Ottawa at the CoreStates Spectrum. "The Big E is back," said Therien. "Now, we'll get going again."

"No one wears a cape around here," insisted Lindros.

Meanwhile, Murray had used everybody but Lois Lane and Jimmy Olsen in an attempt to get production from a second line. Juhlin, who the organization hoped would develop into a scoring threat, was floundering and Brind'Amour had not scored in 11 games. So Clarke traded one of his two No. 1 picks in what was expected to be an unexciting 1996 draft to San Jose for 23-year-old Pat Falloon, the struggling second-overall choice in 1991.

"He had good hands," recalls Clarke. "And he had been a high pick. We thought it was worth a shot."

The new Flyer showed up ten pounds above ideal playing weight but contributed a goal in his second game, which Therien won 3-2 in overtime against visiting Vancouver. When Hextall strained a buttocks muscle and was again unable to play, Snow stepped in capably and Philadelphia went on another roll. Two goals by Lindros sparked a 4-1 home victory over Detroit, the league's first-place team, and the Flyers moved to within one point of Atlantic Division-leading Florida when Haller scored with 30 seconds remaining in overtime for a 2-1 victory at Miami.

An unbeaten streak reached 9 (8-0-1) when the Legionnaires scored four goals in a 6-1 Spectrum pasting of Boston. "I haven't been on a real good team in a while," said Hextall, who returned to lower his NHL-best goals-against average to 1.62. "It's a

great feeling knowing I don't have to go out there every night and stand on my head."

Brent Fedyk scored his 4th and 5th goals in 4 games as Detroit ended Philadelphia's streak, 5-3, at Joe Louis Arena. Nevertheless, Clarke moved the left wing to Dallas for the bigger (6-1, 205), more durable and grittier Trent Klatt, a right wing who had played for the Flyer GM when he was at Minnesota.

While Clarke continued to change players, the organization decided upon a means to turn over new customers. Realizing that ticket costs had eliminated the NHL as a family night out, and wanting to fill 40 dates a year at the Spectrum, the team announced on December 19 that it would operate an AHL franchise in Philadelphia beginning in the 1996-97 season. "We'll be developing fans and players at the same time," said Snider.

As Hershey shopped for a new NHL affiliation after twelve years of working with Philadelphia, the Flyers were forced to renew their working agreements with each other. They were clobbered, 6-2, at home by the woeful Islanders. "We'll suck it up and move on," said Lindros, after spending thirteen minutes in the penalty box.

In Montreal, before the vans backed up to take the Canadiens to the new Molson Centre, Brind'Amour scored twice to make Philadelphia's final visit to the storied Forum a 4-2 success.

The Flyers blew 2-0 and 4-3 leads into a 5-4 overtime loss at New Jersey, then were strangled at home, 2-1, by the perfect checking effort of the Rangers. Philadelphia dropped its fourth game in a row, 3-2 in Edmonton, and the next day lost a former captain.

Kevin Dineen, who had become a part-time fourth-liner, waived a no-trade clause so Clarke could give the 32-year-old veteran a chance to rejuvenate his career in Hartford, his pre-Flyers' home. "He's a quality person, always smiling, always thinking of others first," said Lindros as he bid goodbye to his friend and former landlord.

Otto tortured his ex-teammates for the second time in two meetings, scoring to break a third-period tie and the losing streak, 3-2, at the Canadian Airlines Saddledome. Just when it appeared Philadelphia was about to ring in the New Year with a resolution to buckle down, it blew a three-goal lead in the final 10 minutes at Vancouver, settling for a 5-5 tie when Mogilny scored with 5 seconds remaining. Three nights later, the Flyers tried to squander another game with a sloppy effort against the woebegone Sharks, but Hextall saved a 3-2 victory.

"I don't think anybody in this locker room is under the illusion that what we're doing right now is anywhere near good enough to win a Stanley Cup," said MacTavish. The big line had tailed off, the second line still lacked consistency and the defense—missing Haller for 9 games with a severely strained chest tendon—was not playing as it had in 1995. Svoboda had been in and out of the lineup with various injuries, and the play of sophomores Dykhuis and Therien had dipped from their rookie seasons.

Samuelsson scored in the third period to save a 2-2 tie as Philadelphia closed the trip against the Colorado Avalanche, but a goal by St. Louis' Stephane Matteau with 25 seconds remaining forced a fifth tie in eight games and pushed the frustration level still higher. "We're not putting teams away," complained LeClair. The team's record against New York, Pittsburgh and Florida—the top competition in the Atlantic Division—fell to 2-8 with a desultory 4-0 home loss to the Rangers.

Brind'Amour forced yet another deadlock, 1-1, when he scored late against the Panthers, then Renberg suffered a lower-abdominal strain that was expected to leave him out two weeks. Clarke shuffled his cards again, sending Roussel and Juhlin to Hershey to play for Bill Barber, who had replaced Jay Leach as the Bears' coach. Center Dan Quinn was then reacquired from Ottawa for future considerations.

The Flyers rallied on another late goal by Brind'Amour to gain a 4-4 saw-off in a playoff-level game at Madison Square Garden, yet the effort proved exhausting. A hat trick by Mario Lemieux, leading the NHL in scoring after sitting out an entire season to recover from back problems and cancer treatment, chased Snow in a 7-4 defeat at Pittsburgh. Samuelsson and Therien were on for three goals against, including Steve Konowalchuk's overtime winner, during a 3-2 loss in Landover.

"I think we've got to keep it all in proper perspective," said Murray, as his team's confidence fell with the 1-3-5 slump, "We've still got a lot of games ahead of us."

The players were in need of a rallying point. Montreal's Marc Bureau provided one by taking a long run to knock Svoboda unconscious with an elbow midway through the second period of a February 1 game at the CoreStates Spectrum.

As the defenseman lay on the ice, blood oozing from a two-inch cut in the back of his head, MacTavish went after Bureau, precipitating a brawl. Desjardins' goal won the game with 30 seconds remaining in overtime, but Lindros vowed the book was not closed.

"Dave Brown told me my rookie year that you never forget something like that," said Lindros. "There will be a time and there will be a place."

Svoboda was not aware of either when he woke up. "It's an ugly feeling when you're coming back to normal and you see people looking at you and you don't even remember why you're there," he said after being released from the hospital the following day.

Angry as he was at the Canadiens, Lindros had no quarrel with the Blues. He turned down several fistic challenges, scored a hat trick and made Philadelphia's first-ever visit to the Kiel Center a 7-3 success. "My job isn't to be sitting in the box," said Eric.

Armchair vigilantes lectured on talk radio that the team was going soft, but Murray continued to preach discipline while Clarke looked for more size, not just goons. Minor league left wing Chris Herperger and a 1997 seventh-round pick were sent to Anaheim for 6-2 center Bob Corkum, who scored on his first shift as a Flyer. Nevertheless, he provided the only Philadelphia offense in a 2-1 home loss to Buffalo and goalie Andrei Trefilov.

An annoyed Clarke suggested the Flyers stop the drop passes and begin blasting away. Sufficiently chastened, they whipped Boston, 6-2, in their maiden visit to the FleetCenter. The following night, Svoboda was hit into the boards and suffered nausea. So did Murray after Claude Lemieux scored with 1:53 remaining in a disheartening 5-3 home loss to Colorado. Philadelphia was only 3-9-3 against clubs with a record superior to its 27-16-11.

A 4-2 victory over the slumping Panthers was the Flyers' first over an Atlantic Division foe in two months, but a 5-2 defeat at Tampa Bay kept the team on the seesaw.

When Renberg's stomach muscle problem did not respond to rest, Murray moved Lindros to wing on a line with Quinn and LeClair and the team promptly played its best game in two months, beating the slumping Devils, 4-1. After Joe Watson was inducted into the Flyers' Hall of Fame, the reawakening LeClair pushed a goal-scoring streak to 4 games in a 5-3 victory over Washington.

Snow was buried in a 7-2 Buffalo blizzard, but Clarke decided to move Roussel to Winnipeg for Tim Cheveldae. The president-GM, in assigning the 29-year-old goalie to Hershey, insisted he was only acquiring insurance, not making a big deal. Certainly it was nothing compared to what Snider was working on behind the scenes.

Pat Croce, the former Flyer and 76er strength and conditioning coach who had expanded his physical fitness and therapy center in Broomall, Pennsylvania, into a 40-franchise chain before selling it in 1993, had lunched with Sixers' owner Harold Katz on November 8. The beleaguered Katz spoke wearily of the franchise's problems. Croce began thinking. Soon, Katz was approached by Croce, who suggested that the owner sell him a share of the club and name him president.

Katz replied that the Sixers weren't up for bid, adding that if he ever decided to divest, he would liquidate completely, not take on a partner. Croce continued to make his interest known in repeated meetings, and began trying to line up capital.

He approached Ron Rubin, the center city real estate magnate whom he had met 15 years earlier when his wife had sought rehabilitation from a skiing accident. Rubin, who had developed the Bellevue Hotel complex and Suburban Station building among other ventures, had looked with Croce into buying the Philadelphia Eagles before their 1994 purchase by Jeffrey Lurie.

Rubin had studied the prospectus from the 1994 sale of Madison Square Garden, the Rangers, Knicks and MSG Network to ITT Corporation and Cablevision. He began thinking of the value a similar deal in Philadelphia would have to a media company. Rubin joined Croce at Katz's Huntington Valley, Pennsylvania, home in yet another attempt to talk the basketball owner into getting out. "He was still adamant the team was not for sale," recalls Rubin. "But Pat kept working on him."

Finally, the basketball owner relented. On February 5, Katz signed an agreement that gave Croce and Rubin thirty days to consummate a sale.

Rubin then told Snider, a longtime friend, that he planned to approach Comcast, the cable conglomerate, about financing Croce's bid to buy the 76ers. Would the hockey owner be willing to include the Flyers and CoreStates Center in a megadeal?

Snider had been thinking perhaps the time was right to give up majority interest. "Jay had gone his own way, and my other children had gotten involved in other things," he recalls. "I wanted to spend more time in California. For estate planning, for overall planning, I had already explored a few avenues."

Rubin next approached Ralph Roberts, the chairman of Comcast. Within the last two years, the company—third-largest in the cable industry and the dominant one in the Philadelphia market—had paid $1.4 billion for a 57 percent share of the QVC home shopping network and had agreed to pay $1.59 billion to acquire cable rival E.W. Scripps. Inc. With other media companies, such as Turner Broadcasting and Cablevision already owning sports teams, Roberts, 75, and his son Brian, the 38-year-old company president, became interested.

Snider met with Ralph and Brian Roberts, Comcast vice chairman Julian Brodsky, and Rubin on Saturday, February 24, at the Comcast offices in Center Square. "Ed went there with the idea of exploring the options," recalls Rubin. "He was going through some lifestyle dilemmas, but wasn't sure how much control he wanted to give up.

"They talked. Then [Brian and Ralph Roberts and Brodsky] excused themselves, leaving Ed and me sitting there by ourselves. When they came back and asked if Ed would be interested in continuing to run the operation, it struck a chord. Deep down, Ed wanted to stay active."

Negotiations began.

Meanwhile, the time behind the bench at Hershey had intrigued Barber, who committed to coaching

Philadelphia's new AHL team, the Phantoms. Jerry Melnyk, weary after twenty-eight years of watching juniors, gave up his position as head scout to take over Barber's old job of evaluating the pros.

Samuelsson returned on February 25 after sitting out two games with a strained neck, and probably caused whiplash from doubletakes when he beat Chicago, 3-2, with a slap shot 21 seconds before the buzzer. "If he'd been lefthanded, I'd have thought he was Bobby Orr," said Hextall.

Lindros celebrated his 23rd birthday with two goals in a hard-earned comeback 4-4 tie at Dallas, but the Flyers lost their wits when Lindros went skull-first into the boards as a result of a check by Boston's Sandy Moger. While Philadelphia chased the Bruin around the FleetCenter seeking vengeance, Boston scored two goals to pull out a 3-2 victory. "The lack of poise lost the game, nothing else," said Murray.

The following night, Guerin's overtime goal, the Devils' third on the power play, gave New Jersey a 3-2 victory at the CoreStates Spectrum, leaving the Flyers only 16-14-8 since their 21-7-4 start. "The hockey gods aren't smiling too brightly on us right now," said Murray.

One phone call fixed that. Keenan rang Clarke, asking if he still wanted Dale Hawerchuk, whom the Flyers had pursued as a free agent the previous summer before he had agreed to go to St. Louis. "Mike said he needed to free up some money to sign Wayne Gretzky (a free-agent-to-be who had just been traded to St. Louis)," Clarke recalls. "I would have been interested even if Renberg wasn't hurt. [Hawerchuk's] an intelligent player who could fit into the power play and he could play the wing."

Keenan asked for MacTavish. Clarke wanted the Blues to provide some financial relief from the 33-year-old Hawerchuk's three-year, $7.8 million contract. Blues' president Jack Quinn agreed to pick up part of the forward's salary. In a straight swap for MacTavish, the Flyers had obtained the NHL's ninth all-time leading scorer.

Hawerchuk was in his hotel room in San Jose early in the afternoon of a night game with the Sharks when Keenan called with the news. "I had no clue anything was up," Hawerchuk recalls, "but I wasn't playing that much and I thought if anybody was interested it would probably be Philadelphia.

"I was really close to signing there over the summer, but the Blues jumped in with a deal that was $1.5 million more over three years. You always have mixed feelings about a trade, but I felt pretty comfortable with Philadelphia."

Hawerchuk missed a 3 P.M. plane out of San Jose, took a fifty-five-minute cab ride to the San Francisco airport, where he waited another three hours for a red-eye that got him into Philadelphia at 6 A.M. "On the plane, I really had time to get excited about it," he recalls. "And when I walked into the locker room for the morning skate (at Voorhees), it was a much happier, looser atmosphere than in St. Louis. I just had a good feeling about being there."

Renberg's abdominal muscle could not withstand game stress when he tried it out during Hawerchuk's debut that evening, a 3-0 Hextall shutout of Winnipeg, but the team's newest member stepped onto the top line and reenergized its offense. Hawerchuk assisted on one of LeClair's three goals in an 8-2 rout of San Jose the following night, then the power play clicked three times in a 4-1 CoreStates Spectrum victory over the Islanders on March 19.

The largest power play in Philadelphia sports history was finalized and announced earlier that day at Ovations. After twenty-nine years, Ed Snider was giving up majority ownership in the Flyers. Sixty-six per cent of the hockey team, the 76ers, the CoreStates Center and the CoreStates Spectrum had been acquired by Comcast for $250 million.

Snider was remaining in charge under a five-year contract as managing partner. His share of the entire package, including the Sixers, would be 34 percent, including Croce's 2 percent interest and the continuing minority shares in the Flyers of Fran and Sylvan Tobin and Clarke. Croce was being named president of the basketball club..

"I didn't need a partner in what I'm doing now," Snider said at the news conference. "There are no financial problems. But I felt what Comcast brings into the fold will be very important to our future.

"We have a legal, contractual agreement that we are totally in charge of managing this thing without interference. We don't have to talk to anybody about anything. I probably will, because I've always done that with any partners I've had. No matter what your legal rights are, they're not worth the paper they are written on if you're not getting along. I believe these people when they say that if we do our job, they're going to be be really happy.

"No, I'm not excited about basketball. I'm excited about the opportunity the deal affords. I believe that we can do a lot of marketing things together that we were not able to do as two separate organizations.

"We now have a better building than [Madison Square Garden]. We now have the teams. We're going to have a great network. In fact, we're going to do some things that some people are going to be pretty amazed at. We have to find every avenue of income to compete in today's world of professional sports."

Snider bristled at an anonymous published quote by a Spectacor official who said the owner's willingness to reduce equity reflected his waning passion for the Flyers. "Contrary to what I have read, I do not have one foot in the grave," Snider told reporters. "Anybody who says I don't care about losing, I'll throw them right through the wall."

He was also angry at media speculation that getting out of debt was his motivation for selling. "To read that I did this because of that rankles me," he said. "It's unadulterated bullbleep. We could handle the arena [obligation] and the Flyers didn't owe a penny, despite what was reported. I kept one-third instead of one-half ownership for tax reasons.

"The whole deal just made sense for me and my family in overall planning. It was also a very attractive price. In eighteen months, either [Comcast or I] can opt out of the deal. It's just a good way for me to go, all the way around."

Brian Roberts confirmed it was still Snider's "whole show." The Comcast president spoke of the desirability of the cable company owning sports programming, plus the immediate cross-marketing opportunities presented by Comcast's ownership of QVC.

Five weeks later, the new Comcast-Spectacor venture announced it would begin a regional sports channel in October 1997 featuring Flyers and Phillies games. The 76ers games would be added when the basketball team's PRISM contract ran out in 2000 or earlier if a deal could be worked out.

At the trading deadline, Clarke continued to tinker with his support players, moving Semenov and prospect Mike Crowley for right wing Brian Wesenberg, who had been Anaheim's second-round pick in 1995. Philadelphia also reacquired Kerry Huffman from Ottawa to be its seventh defenseman. Additionally, the Flyers picked up 30-year-old right wing John Druce, a former Capital under Murray, from Los Angeles for a No. 4 choice in 1996. "He's an honest player," said Clarke.

As opponents continued to do dishonest things to Lindros, Murray attempted to take steps. When Eric was goaded into a fight by Keith Tkachuk during Roussel's 4-1 revenge over Philadelphia on March 22 at Winnipeg, the coach sent out Antoski. When the policeman failed to confront a Jet, he

earned a seat back on the bench and expressed conflict over his role. "They stress poise and discipline here every day," he said. "Do I take an instigator penalty? I'm lost. I really am."

But his teammates were beginning to find themselves. Despite an early-morning arrival in Toronto from Winnipeg, they held the Leafs to only two first-period shots in a 4-0 shutout. Two nights later at the CoreStates Spectrum, Lindros reached 100 points for the first time in Hextall's 3-0 blanking of Hartford— the first set of back-to-back shutouts recorded by a Flyer goalie since Bernie Parent in 1973.

Foot soldiers became heroes in Buffalo, where Klatt's goal forced an overtime won by Corkum, 6-5, and LeClair pumped his goal total to 47 with his second hat trick in four games, delivering a 4-1 home victory over Pittsburgh.

Otto, in and out of the lineup with an almost season-long knee problem, and Podein scored consecutive shorthanded goals in a 6-2 pasting of the Islanders at Uniondale. When Marty McSorley, one of several beefy players acquired by the Rangers before the trading deadline, drew Lindros into a fight and Otto and Messier tangled, the Flyers answered the challenge with a 4-1 win.

New York won the rematch, 3-1, at Madison Square Garden the following night to end Philadelphia's 7-game winning streak. Two days later, Lindros had to sit out with a bruised right calf and Boston left the CoreStates Spectrum with a 4-2 triumph. But LeClair didn't need his regular center to score Nos. 49 and 50 in a 5-1 swamping of the gasping Devils at the Meadowlands on April 10. "It's something I never anticipated accomplishing in my career," said LeClair.

Eleven victories in 14 contests had brought the Flyers to the brink of the Atlantic Division and Eastern Conference titles when they played their last regular-season NHL game ever at the Spectrum. After Lindros—back from a two-game absence—won his third Bobby Clarke Award and Desjardins was honored with his second consecutive Barry Ashbee Trophy, Renberg returned in a now-or-never test to see if he could be of any help in the playoffs.

Podein and Druce then provided Philadelphia a 2-0 lead over Montreal. Appropriate for the finale in one of the homiest venues (696-294-141 during regular seasons) in professional sports history, the Flyers never trailed as they won 3-2 and clinched the Atlantic Division title.

After the buzzer, the crowd watched a highlight video of thrills from twenty-nine years, and goose bumps rose for one last occasion when the late Kate

Smith appeared on ArenaVision singing "God Bless America." Then, each of the 1995-96 Flyers paired off with a player from the past, and Clarke and Lindros led a lap around the ice.

Gary Dornhoefer said he was honored to take his skate with Podein, the winner of the Pelle Lindbergh Most Improved Player award and the latest overachiever of a franchise trademarked by them. "When you become a Flyer, it's like you're part of a family," said Lindros after the ceremony.

Two days later, the team learned Hershey left wing Yanick Dupre, who had played 12 games with Philadelphia during injury callups, was diagnosed with leukemia and would need a bone marrow transplant. "He is a member of our organization and he is not alone," said Clarke.

A 3-1 Flyer victory at Tampa Bay in the final regular-season game, coupled with Pittsburgh's 6-5 loss in Boston, gave Philadelphia (45-24-13) the Eastern Conference championship. The first-round match-up would be against the Lightning, which had gone 16-8-4 down the stretch to beat out New Jersey for the final playoff spot.

Despite the midseason travails, the Flyers were going into the playoffs healthy, hungry, and slightly favored to be the conference representative in the finals. "It's weird," said Brind'Amour, "because it all came together so fast at the end."

Renberg became a late scratch from Game 1 when his girlfriend, Stina Sundstrom, went into labor. Hawerchuk, still in the right wing's place on the top line, put in LeClair's rebound after a pregnant pause of only 55 seconds. Lindros, Corkum and Podein threw big body checks, Otto deflected a Desjardins power-play drive and Klatt put a shot through Tampa Bay defenseman Roman Hamrlik's legs to make the score 3-0 after 6:27.

LeClair's second-period score chased Lightning netminder Daren Puppa in favor of Jeff Reese, who was unable to slow the barrage. Lindros and Falloon added goals and Philadelphia built its lead to 6-0 until Jason Wiemer's power-play tip-in finally settled down the overwhelmed visitors. The Lightning crept back to 6-3 before Brind'Amour put away a

Druce rebound.

Seven different Flyers delivered goals and Renberg's girlfriend chipped in a daughter, Emmy, as Philadelphia won the rousing opener, 7-3. "The guys were fired up," said Lindros in the understatement of the night. "But it's only one win."

Accumulating three more looked like it would be snap when Hawerchuk picked off a bad clear by Rob Zamuner and scored after only 1:48 of Game 2. This time, however, Puppa buckled down and Flyers be-

gan going down, too. Otto skated off in the middle of a power play with a knee strain, then Lindros, flipped on a hip check by defenseman Igor Ulanov, limped to the locker room. Ulanov, whose March 1994 slam of Lindros into the boards from a full running start ended his season with a sprained shoulder, next nailed Druce, putting a third Philadelphia player out of the game with a knee injury.

Lindros returned early in the second period and almost immediately high-sticked Ulanov, but LeClair went down with an ankle sprain when he was tripped from behind by Michel Petit into Puppa and the goal post. The depleted Flyers suddenly had become an even match for Tampa Bay, which tied the game 1-1 when Alexander Selivanov deposited a John Cullen rebound early in the third period.

Philadelphia failed to cash a two-man advantage and several two-on-one breaks. In sudden death, Lindros, on a power play, put what looked like a winner off Puppa's mask and over the glass. Nine minutes had been played when Chris Gratton picked off a Haller outlet pass and fed Brian Bellows. The veteran winger forced Hextall to move laterally, then scored between the goalie's legs from the right circle to give the Lightning a series-evening 2-1 victory.

Under questioning by the media, Lindros said he believed Ulanov had gone for his knees, while LeClair thought bad ice at the CoreStates Spectrum had contributed to the other injuries. Whatever the causes, a team that had been in the process of mashing Tampa Bay suddenly could fill a M*A*S*H unit to capacity. "When you look down the bench and you don't have to ask guys to shove over, there's a problem," said Lindros.

A scheduled two-day break and the hyperbaric chamber revived Otto for Game 3 at St. Petersburg's Thunderdome. Seven minutes after a power-play goal by Petr Klima had given Tampa Bay a quick lead, the big Flyer center squeezed a wrist shot through the pads of Reese, a starter because of Puppa's back problems.

Klatt retrieved his own deflection of an Otto drive and stuffed in the rebound to put Philadelphia ahead, 2-1. Falloon converted a power-play two-on-one pass from Renberg 39 seconds into the second period, building the lead to two, and the Flyers had another man-advantage opportunity to build their lead. But Zamuner stole the puck from Hawerchuk, faked Hextall down, and struck shorthanded to put the Lightning back to within a goal.

Reese then stopped Falloon and Brind'Amour on point-blank chances before Renberg and Lindros knocked each other off a puck in the Philadelphia slot and Zamuner scored again, off Hextall's glove, to tie the score.

Lindros tipped home a Hawerchuk drive early in the third period and the Flyers nursed their one-goal lead into the final two minutes. But Brind'Amour kicked and missed at a puck Brian Bradley had forced in front, and Hextall swiped it into the slot, where Bellows put in a backhander. To the joy of an NHL playoff-record crowd of 25,945

in the cavernous indoor baseball facility, the first post-season home game in Tampa Bay's history was going into overtime.

The Lightning had outshot the Flyers 4-0 in sudden death when Desjardins failed to get the puck past Bill Houlder, who floated a shot through a screen. The blast hit the blinded Hextall and fell at the feet of Selivanov, who tapped the puck home at 2:04, giving the Lightning a 5-4 victory and a 2-1 series lead.

"Every goal that they scored was a puck we had possession of," said a frustrated Murray. Lindros had been on the ice for the final four goals-against and in the penalty box for the other. Renberg, forced back onto the first line because of LeClair's injury, was rusty and tender, while the team's best defensive pair of Desjardins and Haller was struggling. Even more disturbingly, Philadelphia had shown signs of not bearing down.

"A playoff game should be so intense you should be unable to move after it's over," said Otto.

Fortunately, LeClair proved ambulatory before the start of Game 4. The ace left wing climbed out of the hyperbaric chamber in Voorhees and jetted southward, a sight for eyes even more sore than his ankle. After Gratton was penalized for giving Samuelsson a shot after the whistle, LeClair took a Lindros pass and wristed the puck behind Reese before eight minutes had been played.

Otto made the score 2-0 after Podein fought his way off the end boards, but very quickly Philadelphia was in the middle of another crisis. With Therien in the penalty box, Brind'Amour inadvertently poked the puck up the slot to Klima, who cut the lead in half.

As soon as the Flyers killed a Haller penalty, Samuelsson took another, so Murray used Philadelphia's time-out to calm his team. "Anytime you've got 28,000 or 155 billion of whatever fits in this place going nuts, it can really change the momentum of a hockey team," said Lindros. But he and his teammates refocused.

The Lightning was held without a good chance on the power play, Hawerchuk restored the two-goal lead by tipping in a Renberg drive and, in the third period, LeClair scored his second goal. "I think with or without me they would have played a strong game," he said after the Flyers, exhibiting the maturity they had failed to show in Game 3, squared the series 2-2 with a 4-1 victory. His teammates, however, were in awe of how LeClair had come to their rescue. "John's hurting pretty bad and he wanted to play," said Otto. "This is one I'll remember when I retire."

Ulanov and his partner Petit had spent Games 3

and 4 running at Lindros, who had absorbed considerable abuse to allow LeClair and Hawerchuk skating room. But as Game 5 began at a fomenting CoreStates Spectrum, the Philadelphia captain had a chance at Ulanov and nailed it perfectly, knocking off the Tampa Bay villain's helmet and drawing a standing ovation. Just 28 seconds later, Lindros lined up antagonist No. 2, Petit, bouncing the defenseman with a shoulder check while crashing a stick into his nose.

Petit left bleeding, so Bellows retaliated by roughing Dykhuis, drawing a penalty. Lightning tough guy Rudy Poeschek then high-sticked Quinn in the face. Fifteen seconds into the five-on-three, Renberg shot between Puppa's legs for the game's first goal.

Podein made it 2-0 early in the second when he soloed off a steal from Ulanov. Hextall came up with a big stop on Cullen during a Tampa Bay five-on-three before Wiemer punched Svoboda. On the power play that spilled into the third period, Falloon stickhandled around Puppa and scored to build the lead to three.

Whatever control the two teams had remaining vanished. With the Lightning already shorthanded, Poeschek slashed Lindros. After LeClair skated around John Tucker to make the score 4-0, Antoski went after Petit and kicked at Ulanov, drawing a match penalty that presented Tampa Bay with an eight-minute power play. David Shaw shortened it by drawing a minor with a slam of Hextall to the ice.

Referee Bill McCreary whistled 139 penalty minutes, yet called fewer than half of the infractions during a 4-1 Philadelphia victory that was out of a twenty-year time warp. Flyer fans, longing for the good ol' days and pleased to have their team up 3-2, had no complaints about what they witnessed. But Clarke wasn't singing "Auld Lang Syne" with Lightning coach Terry Crisp, his former Broad Street Bully teammate.

"[Tampa Bay] didn't try to win," said Clarke. "They tried to bleep people up. When a bleeping player like Poeschek swings with two hands at a bare hand of Lindros, then he's trying to break his hand."

Crisp admitted his team lost its composure. "I preach discipline," he said, "but they're the guys getting hit. We definitely took dumb penalties that killed us. One thing you have to give us, though, is that we stick together and look out for each other."

The underdogs stayed loyal and hostile to their bitter end. Soon after Game 6 began, minus a broken-thumbed Haller, Hamrlik flattened Renberg. Cory Cross then knocked down Antoski, and Zamuner

ran at Hextall, drawing a penalty. Five seconds into the power play, Dykhuis, performing his best hockey of the season, gave Philadelphia a 1-0 lead. Antoski jammed home a Klatt rebound less than one minute later.

After Cullen got one goal back, Klatt made the score 3-1 before the end of the first period. When the Flyers flawlessly killed off a major to Podein for breaking Shawn Burr's nose with a high stick and Puppa muffed an unthreatening Corkum drive into the net, only the final score—and personal scores—remained to be settled. Lindros converted a pass from Dykhuis and then with 2:04 to go went after Ulanov.

Both players received majors that sent them to their locker rooms early, sparing any phony civility in the handshake line. Philadelphia routed Tampa Bay 6-1 to end the series in six games.

"Our backs were to the wall there for a while and we battled back," said Therien. Thirteen different Flyers had scored in the first round, a tribute to the team's depth. Philadelphia's own breaches of discipline had been overcome by 32-for-35 penalty killing.

Despite the hot collars the first round had generated, the Flyers knew they had only survived a warmup. "You almost want to forget about this one," said Brind'Amour, "because the next one will take more and more [energy]."

Indeed, the fourth-seeded Florida Panthers, who finished off Boston in five games, had spent most of the season ahead of Philadelphia in the standings. Ten players Clarke, the former Panther GM, had helped choose in the most successful expansion draft in history were playing key roles on a disciplined 3-year-old team anchored by goaltender John Vanbiesbrouck.

If a 2-2-1 split of the season series between the two teams had not made all Flyers fully aware of what they were up against, their eyes were opened in Game 1, even as the conservative Panthers put the CoreStates Spectrum to sleep. After a scoreless first period, Ed Jovanovski, the hulking first-overall choice in the 1994 draft, picked up a misdirected Otto-to-Podein pass as Dykhuis and Svoboda were leaving the ice on a badly timed change. Stu Barnes, two-on-one with Dave Lowry against Huffman, swung wide and slid a backhander past Hextall.

Center Brian Skrudland and Jovanovski had bumped Lindros constantly, sealed off his passing options and limited Philadelphia to virtually no scoring chances until Lowry put the 2-0 victory away with four minutes remaining.

"This was as complete a game as any team in the NHL can play in such a tough building," said Vanbiesbrouck.

"They play zone defense," said Hawerchuk. "You have to bust through the holes and we didn't bust through tonight."

When Jovanovski knocked Lindros down along the boards early in Game 2, the captain came right back and leveled the rookie with a thundering body check. Eric and linemates LeClair and Hawerchuk

fought through Florida's interference to create more chances in the first ten minutes than Philadelphia had in all of Game 1.

Still, Vanbiesbrouck sparkled to stop Renberg on the Flyers' best chance and kept the game scoreless until Ray Sheppard finished off a two-on-one pass from Barnes with only 23 seconds left in the period.

Philadelphia refused to deflate. LeClair, on his knees after being tripped by Radek Dvorak, got the puck to Lindros, who went around two Panthers and fed Dykhuis at the right post to tie the game 4:47 into the second period. Ten minutes later, Lindros forced the puck to the front of the goal, where a falling Terry Carkner could only clear partway up the slot. LeClair turned and cranked with all his might to beat the partially screened Vanbiesbrouck over his glove.

After two periods, the Flyers had taken 31 shots—12 by the big line. Still, they led by only one goal. When Lindros went to the penalty box for high-sticking and Samuelsson didn't get enough of the puck on an attempted clear, Sheppard knocked the puck down, went behind the net and fed Lowry to tie the game 4:36 into the third.

John LeClair: 57 goals in the regular season and playoffs.

"My fault," said Lindros as he came back to the bench. On his next shift, the captain drove Jovanovski to the ice with a slash between the thigh and knee pads. Svoboda then intercepted a Panther clear and fed LeClair going for the net. He dropped the puck for Lindros, who overpowered the stick check of Jody Hull and wristed his second goal and third point of the night off the leg of defenseman Rhett Warrener.

"You can tell when something special is going to happen," said Murray after Lindros won eight of nine face-offs down the stretch of Philadelphia's 3-2 series-evening victory. "There was fire in his eyes before the game," said the coach. "It was incredible—the intensity, the work, the strength. I don't know if there has ever been a better playoff game [by an individual]."

Or a dirtier one, either, according to Florida. Jovanovski showed off a Lindros-created welt above his left knee, and coach Doug MacLean seethed. "I know we had three guys cut and two guys with deep bruises because of slashes," he said. "When three guys get cut, I think that speaks for itself."

After ex-Flyer Scott Mellanby had killed a rodent in the Miami Arena locker room on the season's opening night, then scored what Vanbiesbrouck had termed a three-goal "rat trick," Panther fans developed a custom of throwing plastic replicas of the creatures onto the ice to celebrate goals. As the playoff series switched to South Florida, the Mighty Mouse who wore No. 88 in the orange road jersey was deemed worthy of extermination.

"Broad Street Butcher" signs hung in the arena. Vulgar chants aimed at Lindros drowned out the national anthem while spectators littered the ice with debris. Yet when the game started, it was the Flyers who were doing all the pelting—of Vanbiesbrouck.

Fourteen minutes into the period, Skrudland, trying to lift Brind'Amour's stick, inadvertently hit the Philadelphia center in the face, drawing a double minor. On the power play, Desjardins made a strong move to keep the puck in at the point and fired. Otto poked the rebound to an unchecked Quinn, who jammed in the lead goal. During the second of the Brind'Amour penalties, Vanbiesbrouck poked a rebound away from LeClair to Lindros, who shot the puck through the goalie's legs from a sharp angle to put the Flyers ahead, 2-0.

The Panthers, outshot 17-2 in the first period, cut the lead in half when Paul Laus intercepted a blind clearing pass by Corkum and scored off Therien's leg. Florida was coming on until Brind'Amour got the puck to Quinn, who fed Klatt as he fought off Dvorak in front. Klatt beat Vanbiesbrouck between the pads to restore the two-goal lead that Philadelphia protected the rest of the way with minimal anxiety.

Lindros cross-checked Jovanovski with 5 seconds left, precipitating a six-player brawl, and triggering another explosion of fan venom. Klatt was hit by a glancing blow from a liquor bottle. "Did you see the sparklers?" asked Ed Snider. "Two things that were on fire were flying through the air. The [Florida management] doesn't know if those people are throwing a rat or a damn bomb. They ought to be ashamed of themselves. And they don't care."

Lindros caught a cup thrown at him as he left the ice and crushed it as defiantly as the Flyers, 3-1 winners, had done to the home team. Two consecutive dominating performances seemed to have established which was the better team.

"We won't be in the driver's seat until we win Game 4," warned Klatt. And indeed the Panthers played desperately to keep Philadelphia from seizing control. Rob Niedermayer blocked a pass by Desjardins, went around the defenseman, and beat Hextall with the first shot of the night. After LeClair—who had taken food intravenously before the match in an attempt to play through a stomach ailment—bowed out early, Jovanovski leveled Lindros, Svoboda and Dykhuis took penalties, and Niedermayer scored again on a five-on-three to put Florida up 2-0.

The Flyers found their legs in the second period, bombarding the ultra-cool Vanbiesbrouck. But what few rebounds the goalie left were just out of Philadelphia's reach until Renberg took a pass from Lindros, drove down the right side and got his team on the board at 16:18 of the second. Only 1:18 later, with Mellanby off for hooking, Brind'Amour worked a give-and-go with Quinn and beat Vanbiesbrouck into the top of the net to tie the game.

Lindros dislodged Jovanovski's helmet and Florida's heads appeared ready to come off. But in the final seconds before the second intermission, Huffman, taking shifts in place of the injured Haller, unnecessarily tried to force the puck up the right sideboards. Mellanby got position on Brind'Amour and fed Laus, whose point shot was bunted by Barnes past Hextall with 5.5 seconds remaining. Despite Philadelphia's hard work and 24 shots in the period, one horribly-timed giveaway had again put the Flyers behind.

They were a discouraged, unfocused team in the third period, taking four penalties and playing most of the twenty minutes in their own end. But as the clock wound down to the one-minute mark, Renberg, back on the big line in LeClair's absence, fought to the net and whacked in his own rebound to create a 3-3 tie.

Vanbiesbrouck beat Hawerchuk twice on chances early in overtime before Jovanovski's shot was redirected by Lowry past Hextall. As the shot went across the line, the back of the net was up as a result of Mellanby pushing Huffman. But referee Rob Shick asked the replay official only if the puck had been kicked in, not about the dislodged cage. Florida had won 4-3 to tie the series 2-2.

"We got ourselves in a jam with the turnovers," said Murray. "It's disappointing we did that after all the intensity we showed."

"Obviously, we deserved better," Lindros said. "[We've] got to shake this off."

But the Flyers didn't. Only 2:27 into Game 5, Laus

was given a major for elbowing Falloon, giving Philadelphia five minutes to seize early control. An unchallenged Desjardins fumbled away the puck at the point, however, and the suddenly jittery home team managed only 2 shots on the advantage. The determination to fight through the always well-positioned Panthers was suddenly and curiously gone.

Hextall, the best Flyer on the ice, dove to rob Niedermayer as the puck bounced off the end boards and kept the game scoreless. In the second period, after referee Don Koharski quickly followed a tripping penalty on Lowry with a kneeing call on Mike Hough, Lindros put a wrist shot through LeClair, Gord Murphy and Vanbiesbrouck to give Philadelphia a 1-0 lead.

But the Flyers were not playing well enough to build on it. After Svoboda, the team's most consistent defenseman in the series, left with a groin strain early in the third period, the struggling Desjardins lost the puck at the point. The Doom line did not get back quickly and Barnes scored off Hawerchuk's knee to tie the game.

Florida, matching Carkner against Lindros after using Jovanovski in that role for the first four games, was getting stronger as the contest went into overtime. Philadelphia's puck movement ground to a halt and the one-on-one game was being controlled by the Panthers' speed, not by the Flyers' size. "We were scared to make a mistake instead of going at them in overtime," Hawerchuk would say later.

Therien gave his team a reprieve by sweeping a broken-down drive by Lindsay away from the goal line, but during the first sudden-death period, Philadelphia was outshot 12-4. As the second extra session began, the home team was on its heels waiting for the inevitable. It came in the eighth minute, after Skrudland got his stick on Samuelsson's attempted hard wrap up the boards.

Hull intercepted and put a drive on net. Hextall stopped the puck with his right skate and left a fat rebound to Hough. The Florida winger had an eternity to turn to his forehand and lift the winner over the flopping goalie at 28:05 of overtime.

A fan threw a chair onto the ice, but it went unused by a home team that had already sat back too long. It was Philadelphia's fourth straight playoff loss in overtime after going 4-0 the previous spring.

"We were a little disoriented," a somber, haunted Lindros told reporters before he was asked to predict the outcome of Game 6. "We're coming back home," he said. "We're going to win."

Hextall made the same guarantee and the fol-

lowing day Murray challenged the Flyers' best players to "step up." Meanwhile, Clarke expressed bafflement at the wild fluctuations in his team's performance. "Keeping our emotional level up has been a constant battle right from the beginning [of the playoffs]," said the president-GM. "How can you be so high one game and so low the next?"

Philadelphia had Haller and Svoboda back for Game 6 at the Miami Arena. The team played steadily, but without the gumption of Games 2 and 3. The Panthers were skating evenly with the Flyers late in the first period when, with Skrudland off for tripping, Svoboda attempted to play the puck at center and missed. Bill Lindsay broke down the right wing shorthanded and beat the challenging Hextall to the far side.

Dykhuis slammed Lindsay into the boards after he scored, but Philadelphia killed the penalty and stayed within a goal. Desjardins had the best chance, but put his blast up where Vanbiesbrouck could handle it. As Florida sealed its slot even tighter, the Flyers dodged a bullet when Tom Fitzgerald fanned on a late second-period breakaway.

Early in the third, with Samuelsson off for tripping, Brind'Amour lost a draw to Niedermayer, then looked down for the puck instead of screening the Panther center away from the goal. Niedermayer stepped ahead, was not picked up by either Desjardins or Svoboda, and was incredibly alone when he received Martin Straka's tip. Niedermayer hit the net from the edge of the crease without being touched to make the score 2-0.

Philadelphia was forced to gamble and Lowry scored on an odd-man break. LeClair, on a rare Flyer appearance at the goalmouth, put in his own rebound with 4:17 remaining and skated back to the bench holding up a finger, trying to ignite a miracle. "That's one," he said. But it was all Philadelphia would get. Johan Garpenlov scored into the empty net and a season of promise had come to a crushing, second-round halt in a 4-1, Game 6 loss.

"I've been around too damn long and I'm getting sick of this," said Hextall in a stricken locker room. "I want to win the last game, not lose."

"It was so bad that I don't have any answers," said Svoboda. Held to 11 goals in 6 games, the Flyers credited Florida's success to its discipline, perseverance and goaltending, but could not understand what had happened to themselves from the series' midpoint on.

"We felt we had enough balance, enough experience, enough strength to go further than we did," said Lindros.

Two days after the loss, Philadelphia's captain blamed himself for scoring only three goals in the series and suggested that the team had not developed the inner strength required of champions. "What we needed at different times of the series we couldn't find," he said.

LeClair thought Hextall and Lindros had been the only Flyers able to reach down for something extra. And Murray, while stressing there was no need to tear the club apart, agreed that his team, which had used anger to work its way out of the corner against Tampa Bay, could not sustain the controlled determination needed to grind past a patient opponent.

"The emotion that we took from Game 2 should have [provided] enough energy and enthusiasm to play that kind of game the rest of the series," said the coach. "And we didn't do it."

Still, the Flyers chalked up the defeat as a learning experience and moved on. The rebuilt team hit a snag like the many that had delayed the groundbreaking of the CoreStates Center by two years. Despite those problems, the massive, gleaming arena, opening to the public on August 31 with a World Cup of Hockey game between the U.S. and Canada has risen as a monument to the organization's persistence and resourcefulness.

Only time will tell whether the Flyers can benefit from the playoff loss that brought the Flyers' twenty-nine years at the Spectrum to a disappointing end. But considering the team's talented young nucleus and the franchise's track record for resiliency, the 1995-96 season closed only an era, not an opportunity.

Set for a new era: Bob Clarke and Ed Snider, backed up by the newly-completed CoreStates Center.

ACKNOWLEDGMENTS

Ed Snider's endless enthusiasm for this project saved it. Jay Snider hatched the idea, trusted me with it, kept his promise that this be an objective history, and never said die as the team's 28th and 29th years passed without completion of the 25th anniversary book.

Without Bobby Clarke's deeds and words, this would be a pamphlet. Were it not for Keith Allen, there would never have been 25 truly great Flyers nor enough goosebumps for 25 legitimately glorious victories. I had to make some tough cuts on both lists, a reflection on the volume of accomplishments by the organization.

Ed, Jay, Bob and Keith all willingly provided me with hour after hour of memories, both good and bad, so I could retell how they were not only successful, but human. I appreciate their understanding of the scope of this work and congratulate them on their candor.

I can never adequately thank my wife, Mona, who edited chapters 1 through 9, chapter 12, and the profiles of the 25 greatest Flyers, but I have every day to try.

Mott Linn relentlessly, painstakingly and unselfishly checked most of the facts in this tome, which he cared about almost as if it were his own.

My gratitude is also extended to Dan Diamond for impressively framing a cumbersome amount of words and for not panicking down the stretch; Stu Hackel, for helping to edit chapters 7 to 11; Ron Ryan, for sticking it out; John Brogan, for encouragement, insights and clear memories of the early days; Scott Lauber, for fact-checking, outlining, editing and being a lifesaver in the final hours; Mark Piazza and Joe Klueg for always returning my calls and coming up with the needed facts and phone number; Linda Held, for assisting with the pictures; and Scott Morrison at The Toronto *Sun* and Dick Klayman at The New York *Post* for juggling my work schedules when I needed a day for my side project.

Elizabeth and Stephanie have deserved more from a father over the last six years than this thank you for being incredibly understanding about all the time we will never get back. Midas, our golden retriever, earns a lifetime of belly rubs for enjoying my company through one of the most stressful periods of my life and for never wanting to change a word that I wrote. My appreciation also goes out to friends and colleagues who did not flash that grin I grew to hate whenever I had to say "No, I'm not finished."

I covered the Flyers on a daily basis from 1975 to 1989. For other years, the text relies on the accounts of the Philadelphia *Evening* and *Sunday Bulletin*, Philadelphia *Daily News*, Philadelphia *Inquirer* and the words of Stan Hochman, John Brogan, Jack Chevalier, Ed Conrad, Frank Dolson, Bill Fleischman, Chuck Newman, Ray Didinger, Al Morganti, Ray Parrillo, Les Bowen, Rich Hofmann, Gary Miles and Tim Dwyer. Credit was given for exclusives when they were obtained.

In the course of conducting 168 interviews, I was turned down only twice, a winning percentage even better than the Flyers' during the year they went 35 games without losing. The co-operation was fantastic, especially from the following persons who forechecked long and hard into their memories and in some cases, filing cabinets and attics: Bill Barber, Larry Bertuzzi, Jim Cooper, Rick Curran, Russ Farwell, Carl Hirsh, Paul Holmgren, Mike Keenan, Bill Levine, Eric Lindros, Brad Marsh, E.J. McGuire, Jerry Melnyk, Bob McCammon, Gunnar Nordstrom, Pierre Page, Bernie Parent, Ed Parvin Jr., Dave Poulin, Jack Prettyman, Bill Putnam, Pat Quinn, Lou Scheinfeld, Joe Scott, Kerstin Somnell, Gil Stein, Joe Watson, Phil Weinberg and Larry Zeidel.

To everyone else who fed goalmouth setups or chipped in a second assist, my everlasting appreciation. And to all 326 players who have worn the black and orange, thank you for making this a story worth telling.

Jay Greenberg
July 1996

PHOTO CREDITS

Photos courtesy: Bruce Bennett Studios, Dan Diamond and Associates collection, Philadelphia Flyers archives, Bill Putnam collection, Len Redkoles.

Author's jacket photo: Nathan Kushner, The Portrait Shoppe of New Jersey.

FLYERS ALL-TIME REGULAR-SEASON SCORING
1967-1996

PLAYER	GP	G	A	PTS	PIM
B. Clarke	1144	358	852	1210	1453
B. Barber	903	420	463	883	623
B. Propp	790	369	480	849	669
R. MacLeish	741	328	369	697	384
T. Kerr	601	363	287	650	577
G. Dornhoefer	725	202	316	518	1256
R. Leach	606	306	208	514	276
M. Howe	594	138	342	480	323
R. Tocchet	531	215	247	462	1683
P. Eklund	589	118	334	452	107
M. Craven	523	152	272	424	315
I. Sinisalo	526	199	210	409	180
D. Poulin	467	161	233	394	303
* R. Brind'Amour	375	143	243	386	417
Ron Sutter	555	137	223	360	854
* E. Lindros	245	161	196	357	473
M. Bridgman	462	118	205	323	971
R. Lonsberry	497	144	170	314	403
P. Holmgren	500	138	171	309	1600
B. Kelly	741	128	168	296	1285
M. Recchi	200	105	157	262	171
P. Zezel	310	91	170	261	230
O. Kindrachuk	360	79	181	260	465
K. Linseman	269	73	184	257	585
D. Saleski	476	118	117	235	602
T. Bladon	463	67	163	230	281
B. Wilson	339	59	155	214	873
S. Nolet	358	93	108	201	129
Joe Watson	746	36	162	198	397
S. Mellanby	355	83	114	197	694
B. Dailey	304	56	138	194	397
D. Crossman	392	35	158	193	255
B. McCrimmon	367	35	152	187	355
Jim Watson	613	38	148	186	490
* M. Renberg	181	87	95	182	101
D. Sittler	191	84	94	178	148
A. Dupont	539	42	135	177	1505
K. Dineen	284	88	88	176	533
G. Galley	236	28	144	172	260
A. Lacroix	245	72	98	170	36
J. Johnson	266	66	102	168	67
D. Smith	494	80	87	167	338
J. Gendron	278	69	86	155	203
* J. LeClair	119	76	70	146	84
R. Flockhart	167	65	80	145	108
B. Flett	167	71	68	139	130
L. Carson	346	61	76	137	495
T. Carkner	376	29	103	132	867
* K. Samuelsson	462	31	100	131	740
R. Allison	168	47	81	128	210
G. Murphy	261	31	97	128	254
E. Van Impe	617	19	107	126	892
B. Fedyk	200	59	65	124	160
K. Acton	303	45	71	116	424
D. Schultz	297	51	64	115	1386
M. Bullard	124	50	63	113	127
B. Marsh	514	14	96	110	636
T. Gorence	291	57	52	109	89
B. Clement	229	53	52	105	166
T. Eriksson	208	22	76	98	107
M. Ricci	146	41	56	97	157
A. Hill	221	40	55	95	227
M. Dvorak	193	11	74	85	51
J. Beranek	134	46	38	84	137
K. Huffman	207	23	61	84	158
Rich Sutter	204	36	47	83	381
B. Ashbee	270	15	67	82	277
T. Crisp	194	25	54	79	78
D. Brown	552	39	39	78	1382
L. Rochefort	139	35	42	77	26
G. Cochrane	257	16	61	77	1110
D. Yushkevich	197	15	61	76	204
S. Bernier	123	35	40	75	130
B. Sutherland	123	42	29	71	40
L. Goodenough	129	15	56	71	104
* E. Desjardins	114	12	58	70	57
D. Quinn	102	18	40	58	48
S. Duchesne	78	18	38	56	86
G. Peters	229	27	28	55	209
D. Sarrazin	100	20	35	55	22
L. Hachborn	78	16	38	54	27
B. Selby	119	25	28	53	47
Y. Racine	67	9	43	52	48
A. Lomakin	108	22	28	50	60
M. Pederson	84	20	30	50	33
R. LaPointe	146	8	42	50	183
B. Lesuk	123	24	25	49	118
B. Dunlop	69	20	29	49	16
L. Angotti	70	12	37	49	35
* P. Falloon	62	22	26	48	6
J. Latal	92	12	36	48	24
D. Ververgaert	95	23	24	47	30
L. Hillman	149	8	39	47	112
L. Hughes	122	5	41	46	88
D. Blackburn	115	16	29	45	59
F. Kennedy	132	18	25	43	325
G. Hawgood	59	9	34	43	58
C. Berube	235	16	26	42	948
B. Dean	86	11	31	42	54
L. Hale	196	5	37	42	90
L. Morrison	202	19	22	41	70
* J. Otto	67	12	29	41	115
B. Benning	59	11	29	40	128
B. Hoffmeyer	94	9	31	40	182
J. Wells	126	5	35	40	313
P. Evans	103	14	25	39	34
V. Butsayev	99	14	23	37	119
D. Quinn	67	11	26	37	26
E. Hoekstra	70	15	21	36	6
R. Foley	58	11	25	36	168
* C. Therien	130	9	27	36	127
J. Miszuk	140	6	30	36	149
* S. Podein	123	18	17	35	122
G. Paslawski	60	14	19	33	12
* R. DiMaio	109	12	21	33	117
N. Lacombe	92	11	22	33	34
M. Taylor	64	8	25	33	24
W. Hillman	258	8	25	33	170
* P. Svoboda	84	1	31	32	115
T. Murray	115	1	30	31	69
C. Boivin	114	11	18	29	320
* K. Dykhuis	115	7	21	28	138
N. Barnes	82	4	24	28	77
P. Hannigan	72	11	16	27	58
R. Fleming	65	9	18	27	134
J. Potvin	64	6	21	27	16
F. Bathe	198	3	24	27	502
* R. Hextall	365	1	26	27	421
J. Daigneault	105	8	18	26	68
M. Busniuk	143	3	23	26	297
C. LaForge	65	9	16	25	36
C. MacTavish	100	8	17	25	85
T. Ball	62	7	18	25	20
E. Heiskala	127	13	11	24	294
D. Kushner	82	10	13	23	213
A. Conroy	114	9	14	23	156
T. Horacek	116	9	14	23	217
* K. Haller	105	7	16	23	140
D. Cherry	139	12	10	22	41
G. Adams	39	7	15	22	113
H. Bennett	53	13	8	21	67
D. Evans	65	8	13	21	70
J. Chychrun	199	3	17	20	608
D. Hoyda	108	4	16	20	257
K. McCarthy	90	3	17	20	57
M. Baron	83	10	10	20	86
C. Schmautz	30	8	12	20	23
* D. Hawerchuk	16	4	16	20	4
D. Sulliman	80	9	10	19	8
A. Semenov	70	4	15	19	20
A. Faust	47	10	7	17	14
R. Nattress	44	7	10	17	29
B. Jones	48	7	10	17	44
A. Stanley	64	4	13	17	28
R. McGill	134	4	13	17	363
T. Bergen	14	11	5	16	4
G. Morrison	43	1	15	16	70
E. Hospodar	112	8	7	15	321
M. Freer	59	6	9	15	18
D. Tippett	73	4	11	15	38
B. Dobbin	56	6	8	14	39
M. Botell	32	4	10	14	31
M. Hostak	55	3	11	14	24
M. Parizeau	38	2	12	14	10
J. Paddock	47	5	8	13	49
W. Huber	10	4	9	13	16
J. Gauthier	65	5	7	12	74
B. Parent	486	0	11	11	95
L. Zeidel	66	1	10	11	68
B. Wesley	52	3	8	11	109
* T. Klatt	49	3	8	11	21
M. Mantha	35	3	8	11	35
Y. Preston	28	7	3	10	4
J. McIlhargey	128	3	7	10	497
D. Stanley	89	2	8	10	216
D. Nachbaur	65	2	8	10	194
J. Finley	55	1	8	9	24
R. Paiement	43	4	5	9	74
S. Kasper	37	4	5	9	12
W. Hicks	32	2	7	9	6

FLYERS ALL-TIME REGULAR-SEASON SCORING

CONTINUED

PLAYER		GP	G	A	PTS	PIM
M.	Lamb	27	1	8	9	18
P.	Guay	16	2	7	9	14
F.	Arthur	74	1	7	8	47
M.	Roupe	40	3	5	8	42
T.	Young	20	2	6	8	12
D.	Michayluk	14	2	6	8	8
* J.	Druce	13	4	4	8	13
T.	Harris	70	1	6	7	48
* J.	Bowen	69	2	5	7	91
G.	Smyth	49	1	6	7	192
G.	Hynes	37	3	4	7	16
* B.	Corkum	28	4	3	7	8
E.	Joyal	26	3	4	7	8
C.	Foster	25	3	4	7	20
R.	Fitzpatrick	20	5	2	7	0
G.	Seabrooke	19	1	6	7	4
G.	Dionne	22	0	7	7	2
* P.	Juhlin	14	3	3	6	17
B.	Froese	144	0	6	6	22
D.	Fenyves	58	1	5	6	32
J.	Montgomery	13	2	3	5	15
* D.	Kordic	59	2	3	5	162
P.	Lindbergh	157	0	5	5	10
R.	Zettler	65	0	5	5	103
W.	Brossart	47	0	5	5	12
R.	MacSweyn	45	0	5	5	10
M.	Stankiewicz	19	0	5	5	25
P.	Lawless	8	0	5	5	0
D.	Favell	215	0	4	4	86
P.	Peeters	179	0	4	4	77
D.	Roussel	139	0	4	4	23
K.	Wregget	107	0	4	4	18
S.	Antoski	89	1	3	4	265
S.	Malgunas	71	1	3	4	90
M.	LaForest	38	0	4	4	12
R.	Bailey	27	1	3	4	78
P.	Plante	26	1	3	4	15
P.	Murray	25	3	1	4	15
D.	Callander	18	3	1	4	5
A.	Stratton	12	0	4	4	4
B.	Wilkie	10	1	3	4	8
L.	Barrie	9	2	2	4	9
* R.	Romaniuk	17	3	0	3	17
L.	Wright	38	1	2	3	6
S.	Cronin	35	2	1	3	37
K.	Daniels	27	1	2	3	4
B.	Root	24	1	2	3	16
C.	Jensen	21	2	1	3	2
L.	Mickey	14	1	2	3	8
D.	Schock	14	1	2	3	0
G.	Roberts	11	1	2	3	15
S.	Sandelin	15	0	3	3	0
G.	Meehan	12	0	3	3	4
* Y.	Dupre	35	2	0	2	16
R.	St. Croix	82	0	2	2	2
T.	Soderstrom	78	0	2	2	4
D.	Richter	50	0	2	2	138
D.	Snuggerud	14	0	2	2	0
P.	Crowe	16	1	1	2	28
L.	Keenan	14	1	1	2	2

PLAYER		GP	G	A	PTS	PIM
D.	Biggs	11	2	0	2	8
B.	Collins	9	1	1	2	4
* J.	Stevens	9	0	2	2	14
M.	Holan	8	1	1	2	4
* A.	Brimanis	18	0	2	2	12
B.	Berglund	7	0	2	2	4
M.	Byers	5	0	2	2	0
C.	Winnes	4	0	2	2	0
A.	Brickley	3	1	1	2	0
D.	Gardner	2	1	1	2	0
W.	Stephenson	165	0	1	1	17
B.	Taylor	44	0	1	1	16
D.	Jensen	30	0	1	1	2
M.	Belhumeur	23	0	1	1	2
A.	Secord	20	1	0	1	38
S.	Beauregard	16	0	1	1	0
R.	Ramage	15	0	1	1	14
S.	Smith	14	0	1	1	15
M.	Stothers	12	0	1	1	23
* D.	Rumble	8	1	0	1	4
G.	Inness	8	0	1	1	0
D.	Lucas	6	1	0	1	0
K.	Maguire	5	1	0	1	6
R.	Moore	5	0	1	1	0
B.	Sirois	4	1	0	1	4
M.	Suzor	4	0	1	1	4
D.	Patterson	3	0	1	1	0
T.	Hlushko	2	1	0	1	0
W.	Walz	2	1	0	1	0
D.	Gillen	1	1	0	1	0
B.H.	Armstrong	1	0	1	1	0
P.	Myre	57	0	0	0	37
B.	Gamble	35	0	0	0	2
R.	Holt	26	0	0	0	74
* G.	Snow	26	0	0	0	18
N.	Fotiu	23	0	0	0	40
G.	Resch	22	0	0	0	0
J.	Hanna	15	0	0	0	0
J.	Harding	15	0	0	0	47
L.	Brown	12	0	0	0	0
J.	Paterson	11	0	0	0	43
B.	Hoffort	9	0	0	0	2
W.	Young	6	0	0	0	0
S.	Lajeunesse	6	0	0	0	2
A.	MacAdam	5	0	0	0	0
F.	Chabot	4	0	0	0	0
C.	Fisher	4	0	0	0	6
J.	Mair	4	0	0	0	0
D.	McLeod	4	0	0	0	0
M.	Lamoureux	3	0	0	0	0
M.	Boland	2	0	0	0	0
R.	Dallman	2	0	0	0	5
D.	Ederstrand	2	0	0	0	0
M.	Larocque	2	0	0	0	0
S.	Sabol	2	0	0	0	0
G.	Swarbrick	2	0	0	0	0
T.	Tookey	2	0	0	0	0
C.	Vilgrain	2	0	0	0	0
G.	Williams	2	0	0	0	0
S.	Anderson	1	0	0	0	0

PLAYER		GP	G	A	PTS	PIM
D.	Carruthers	1	0	0	0	0
J.	Cunningham	1	0	0	0	2
M.	D'Amour	1	0	0	0	0
R.	Drolet	1	0	0	0	0
J.	Gillis	1	0	0	0	0
C.	Mokosak	1	0	0	0	5
J.	Mrazek	1	0	0	0	0
G.	Mulvenna	1	0	0	0	2
M.	Murray	1	0	0	0	0
R.	Osburn	1	0	0	0	0
R.	Pelletier	1	0	0	0	0
B.	Ritchie	1	0	0	0	0
R.	Simpson	1	0	0	0	0
D.	Wilson	1	0	0	0	0
K.	Wright	1	0	0	0	0

* Still active on Flyers roster

FLYERS ALL-TIME PLAYOFF SCORING
1967-1996

PLAYER	GP	G	A	PTS
B. Clarke	136	42	77	119
B. Propp	116	52	60	112
B. Barber	129	53	55	108
R. MacLeish	108	53	52	105
T. Kerr	73	39	31	70
R. Leach	91	47	22	69
K. Linseman	41	11	42	53
M. Howe	82	8	45	53
P. Holmgren	67	19	31	50
R. Tocchet	71	22	26	48
M. Bridgman	74	13	30	43
P. Eklund	57	10	33	43
R. Lonsberry	83	19	22	41
O. Kindrachuk	76	20	20	40
B. Dailey	56	10	30	40
D. Poulin	63	17	22	39
Jim Watson	101	5	34	39
T. Bladon	86	8	29	37
G. Dornhoefer	80	17	19	36
Ron Sutter	62	6	27	33
B. Wilson	43	8	24	32
I. Sinisalo	66	21	10	31
P. Zezel	56	10	21	31
D. Crossman	60	9	22	31
D. Saleski	82	13	17	30
A. Dupont	108	13	15	28
* E. Lindros	24	10	17	27
D. Smith	75	13	11	24
M. Craven	44	9	15	24
* J. LeClair	26	11	12	23
B. Kelly	102	9	14	23
* M. Renberg	26	9	13	22
* R. Brind'Amour	27	8	14	22
S. Mellanby	50	9	11	20
A. Hill	50	8	10	18
T. Crisp	47	5	13	18
L. Goodenough	21	3	15	18
B. Marsh	60	5	12	17
D. Schultz	61	7	9	16
* K. Samuelsson	64	4	12	16
T. Gorence	37	9	6	15
Joe Watson	84	3	12	15
* E. Desjardins	27	4	10	14
B. McCrimmon	46	7	6	13
T. Bergen	17	4	9	13
B. Flett	33	3	10	13
* K. Dykhuis	27	6	6	12
M. Bullard	19	3	9	12
E. Van Impe	57	1	11	12
L. Carson	44	3	8	11
K. Dineen	15	6	4	10
* P. Svoboda	26	0	10	10
S. Nolet	31	6	3	9
* K. Haller	21	4	5	9
* D. Hawerchuk	12	3	6	9
G. Murphy	19	2	7	9
* S. Podein	27	2	5	7
M. Busniuk	25	2	5	7
J. Patterson	17	3	4	7
* J. Otto	12	3	4	7

PLAYER	GP	G	A	PTS
D. Sittler	10	4	3	7
T. Carkner	19	1	5	6
* R. DiMaio	18	2	4	6
A. Semenov	15	2	4	6
D. Yushkevich	15	1	5	6
* R. Hextall	75	1	4	5
Rich Sutter	19	5	0	5
K. Acton	16	2	3	5
C. MacTavish	15	1	4	5
R. Allison	12	2	3	5
* T. Klatt	12	4	1	5
* P. Falloon	13	3	2	5
D. Quinn	12	1	4	5
F. Kennedy	7	1	4	5
D. Brown	54	2	2	4
F. Bathe	27	1	3	4
T. Murray	18	2	2	4
B. Ashbee	17	0	4	4
T. Harris	16	0	4	4
A. Secord	14	0	4	4
T. Tookey	10	1	3	4
B. Fedyk	9	2	2	4
J. Gauthier	7	1	3	4
J. McIlhargey	26	0	3	3
R. LaPointe	22	0	3	3
S. Antoski	20	1	2	3
T. Eriksson	19	0	3	3
* B. Corkum	12	1	2	3
D. Blackburn	11	3	0	3
J. Miszuk	11	0	3	3
P. Hannigan	7	1	2	3
L. Hachborn	7	0	3	3
C. LaForge	5	1	2	3
R. Paiement	3	3	0	3
J. Mair	3	1	2	3
E. Hospodar	23	1	1	2
J. Chychrun	19	0	2	2
B. Clement	18	2	0	2
J. Wells	18	0	2	2
M. Dvorak	18	0	2	2
R. Bailey	14	0	2	2
G. Cochrane	11	1	1	2
L. Rochefort	10	2	0	2
D. Nachbaur	9	1	1	2
B. Dunlop	8	1	1	2
A. Lacroix	8	0	2	2
R. Flockhart	7	1	1	2
B. Selby	7	1	1	2
J. Johnson	7	0	2	2
D. Ververgaert	5	0	2	2
G. Peters	4	1	1	2
S. Bernier	4	1	1	2
G. Sutherland	4	1	1	2
L. Hillman	4	0	2	2
J. Paddock	3	2	0	2
* J. Druce	2	0	2	2
P. Lindbergh	23	0	1	1
W. Stephenson	23	0	1	1
P. Juhlin	13	1	0	1
B. Froese	12	0	1	1

PLAYER	GP	G	A	PTS
K. McCarthy	10	0	1	1
J. Daigneault	9	1	0	1
J. Gendron	8	0	1	1
E. Hoekstra	7	0	1	1
J. Montgomery	8	1	0	1
L. Zeidel	7	0	1	1
G. Morrison	5	0	1	1
R. Moore	5	0	1	1
B. Lesuk	4	1	0	1
D. Cherry	4	1	0	1
M. Beyers	4	0	1	1
A. Stanley	3	0	1	1
B. Hoffmeyer	2	0	1	1
B. Parent	63	0	0	0
* C Therien	27	0	0	0
C. Berube	21	0	0	0
P. Peeters	20	0	0	0
D. Stanley	17	0	0	0
D. Favell	16	0	0	0
N. Barnes	12	0	0	0
R. St. Croix	10	0	0	0
D. Hoyda	9	0	0	0
R. MacSweyn	8	0	0	0
K. Huffman	8	0	0	0
B. Cowick	8	0	0	0
W. Hillman	8	0	0	0
L. Hale	8	0	0	0
L. Angotti	7	0	0	0
P. Myre	6	0	0	0
G. Smyth	6	0	0	0
K. Wregget	5	0	0	0
M. Stothers	5	0	0	0
W. Huber	5	0	0	0
D. Richter	5	0	0	0
A. Stratton	5	0	0	0
D. Sulliman	4	0	0	0
F. Arthur	4	0	0	0
H. Bennett	4	0	0	0
B. Hughes	4	0	0	0
G. Meehan	4	0	0	0
L. Morrison	4	0	0	0
D. Sarrazin	4	0	0	0
G. Dionne	3	0	0	0
P. Guay	3	0	0	0
G. Resch	3	0	0	0
D. Dobbin	2	0	0	0
B. Gamble	2	0	0	0
M. Laforest	2	0	0	0
B. Root	2	0	0	0
M. Mantha	1	0	0	0
M. Belhumeur	1	0	0	0
A. MacAdam	1	0	0	0
* R. Romaniuk	1	0	0	0
* G. Snow	1	0	0	0
M. Stankewicz	1	0	0	0
* D. Roussel	1	0	0	0
R. Zettler	1	0	0	0

* Still active on Flyers roster

FLYERS ALL-TIME ROSTER
1967-1996

JERSEY #	PLAYER	SEASON(S)
25	ACTON, Keith	1988-93
36, 25	ADAMS, Greg	1980-82
19, 36	ALLISON, Ray	1981-85, 86-87
37	ANDERSON, Shawn	1994-95
7	ANGOTTI, Lou	1967-68
8	ANTOSKI, Shawn	1994-**
58	ARMSTRONG, Bill H.	1990-92
6	ARTHUR, Fred	1981-82
4	ASHBEE, Barry	1970-74
34,35,36,9	BAILEY, Reid	1980-82
24	BALL, Terry	1969-70
7	BARBER, Bill	1972-85
23, 25	BARNES, Norm	1976-77, 79-81
8	BARON, Murray	1989-91
20, 34	BARRIE, Len	1990-93
21, 31, 5	BATHE, Frank	1977-84
35	BEAUREGARD, Stephane	1992-93
30, 35	BELHUMEUR, Michel	1972-73
22	BENNETT, Harvey	1976-78
19	BENNING, Brian	1991-93
42	BERANEK, Josef	1992-95
19, 42	BERGEN, Todd	1984-85
37, 19	BERGLUND, Bo	1985-86
19, 21	BERNIER, Serge	1968-72
34, 17	BERUBE, Craig	1986-91
46	BIGGS, Don	1989-90
8	BLACKBURN, Don	1967-69
4, 23, 3	BLADON, Tom	1972-78
33	BLOSKI, Mike (DNP)	1985-86
40, 10	BOIVIN, Claude	1991-94
17, 5	BOLAND, Mike A.	1974-75
28	BOTELL, Mark	1981-82
28,53	BOWEN, Jason	1992-**
34	BRICKLEY, Andy	1982-83
10	BRIDGMAN, Mel	1975-82
40	BRIMANIS, Aris	1993-94, 95-**
17	BRIND'AMOUR, Rod	1991-**
25, 3, 10	BROSSART, Willie	1970-73
32, 21	BROWN, Dave	1982-89, 91-**
3	BROWN, Larry	1971-72
10	BULLARD, Mike	1988-90
21, 28	BUSNIUK, Mike	1979-81
22, 26	BUTSAYEV, Viacheslav	1992-94
22	BYERS, Mike	1968-69
28	CALLANDER, Drew	1976-79
29	CARKNER, Terry	1988-93
21	CARRUTHERS, Dwight	1967-68
18	CARSON, Lindsay	1981-88
35	CHABOT, Frederic	1993-94
5	CHERRY, Dick	1968-70
40, 6	CHYCHRUN, Jeff	1986-91
36, 16	CLARKE, Bobby	1969-84
15, 10	CLEMENT, Bill	1971-75
44,9,35,29	COCHRANE, Glen	1978-79, 81-84
23	COLLINS, Bill	1976-77
46, 15	CONROY, Al	1991-94
22	CORKUM, Bob	1995-**
27	COWICK, Bruce	1973-74

JERSEY #	PLAYER	SEASON(S)
32	CRAVEN, Murray	1984-91
29, 15	CRISP, Terry	1972-77
44	CRONIN, Shawn	1992-93
3	CROSSMAN, Doug	1983-88
26	CROWE, Phil	1995-96
12	CUMMINS, Jim	1993-94
21	CUNNINGHAM, Jimmy	1977-78
15	DAIGNEAULT, J-J	1986-88
2	DAILEY, Bob	1976-82
24	DALLMAN, Rod	1991-92
49	D'AMOUR, Marc	1988-89
46, 14	DANIELS, Kimbi	1990-92
29	DEAN, Barry	1977-79
37	DESJARDINS, Eric	1994-**
20, 9	DiMAIO, Rob	1993-**
20, 11	DINEEN, Kevin	1991-96
45	DIONNE, Gilbert	1994-96
7, 18	DOBBIN, Brian	1986-92
24, 12	DORNHOEFER, Gary	1967-78
23	DROLET, Rene	1971-72
26	DRUCE, John	1995-**
19, 28	DUCHESNE, Steve	1991-92
32	DUNLOP, Blake	1977-79
28, 6	DUPONT, Andre	1972-80
66, 15, 18	DUPRE, Yanick	1991-92, 94-**
9	DVORAK, Miroslav	1982-85
24	DYKHUIS, Karl	1994-**
21	EDESTRAND, Darryl	1969-70
9	EKLUND, Pelle	1985-94
6, 8, 27	ERIKSSON, Thomas	1980-82, 83-86
15	EVANS, Doug	1992-93
23, 25	EVANS, John	1978-79, 80-81, 82-83
15	FALLOON, Pat	1995-**
36	FAUST, Andre	1992-94
1	FAVELL, Doug	1967-73
18	FEDYK, Brent	1992-96
39	FENYVES, Dave	1987-92
25	FINLEY, Jeff	1993-94
7, 15	FISHER, Craig	1989-91
32,22,34,39	FITZPATRICK, Ross	1982-86
9	FLEMING, Reggie	1969-70
21	FLETT, Bill	1971-74
43, 11	FLOCKHART, Ron	1980-83
22	FOLEY, Rick	1971-72
44	FOSTER, Corey	1991-92
35	FOSTER, Norm (DNP)	1993-94
29	FOTIU, Nick	1987-88
45, 37	FREER, Mark	1986-92
35	FROESE, Bob	1982-87
3	GALLEY, Garry	1991-95
30	GAMBLE, Bruce	1970-72
23	GARDNER, Dave	1979-80
5	GAUTHIER, Jean	1967-68
20, 11	GENDRON, Jean-Guy	1968-72
21	GILLEN, Don	1979-80
34	GILLIS, Jere	1986-87

JERSEY #	PLAYER	SEASON(S)
30	GILLOW, Russ (DNP)	1971-72
49	GILMOUR, Darryl (DNP)	1987-88
4,23,5,29	GOODENOUGH, Larry	1974-77
22, 36	GORENCE, Tom	1978-83
35	GREENLAY, Mike (DNP)	1994-95
25, 34	GUAY, Paul	1983-85
11, 36	HACHBORN, Len	1983-85
17, 23, 19	HALE, Larry	1968-72
5	HALLER, Kevin	1994-**
6	HANNA, John	1967-68
14	HANNIGAN, Pat	1967-69
34	HARDING, Jeff	1988-90
25	HARRIS, Ted	1974-75
18	HAWERCHUK, Dale	1995-**
20	HAWGOOD, Greg	1992-94
19	HEISKALA, Earl	1968-71
27	HEXTALL, Ron	1986-92, 94-**
17	HICKS, Wayne	1967-68
37,15,28,36	HILL, Al	1976-82, 86-88
3	HILLMAN, Larry	1969-71
6	HILLMAN, Wayne	1969-73
10	HLUSHKO, Todd	1993-94
18	HOEKSTRA, Ed	1967-68
24, 34, 35	HOFFMEYER, Bob	1981-83
68, 30	HOFFORT, Bruce	1989-92
41	HOLAN, Milos	1993-94
17	HOLMGREN, Paul	1975-84
24	HOLT, Randy	1983-84
43, 21	HORACEK, Tony	1989-92
17	HOSPODAR, Ed	1984-85, 86-87
26	HOSTAK, Martin	1990-92
2	HOWE, Mark	1982-92
8	HOYDA, Dave	1977-79
47, 44	HUBER, Willie	1987-88
5, 2	HUFFMAN, Kerry	1986-92, 95-96
5	HUGHES, Brent	1971-73
26	HYNES, Gord	1992-93
30	INNESS, Gary	1975-77
45, 14	JENSEN, Chris	1989-92
33, 30	JENSEN, Darren	1984-86
21, 20	JOHNSON, Jimmy	1968-72
47	JONES, Brad	1991-92
20	JOYAL, Eddie	1971-72
12	JUHLIN, Patrik	1994-**
15	KASPER, Steve	1991-93
23	KEENAN, Larry	1971-72
9	KELLY, Bob	1970-80
22	KENNEDY, Forbes	1967-70
12	KERR, Tim	1980-91
26	KINDRACHUK, Orest	1972-78
20	KLATT, Trent	1995-**
6, 21	KORDIC, Dan	1991-92, 93-94, 95-**
35	KUNTAR, Les (DNP)	1994-95
36,10,8,15	KUSHNER, Dale	1990-92
68, 36, 20	LACOMBE, Norman	1990-91

FLYERS ALL-TIME ROSTER

CONTINUED

JERSEY #	PLAYER	SEASON(S)
15, 7	LACROIX, Andre	1967-71
33	LaFOREST, Mark	1987-89
16	LAFORGE, Claude	1967-68
5	LAJEUNESSE, Serge	1973-75
22	LAMB, Mark	1993-95
37	LAMOUREUX, Mitch	1987-89
5	LAPOINTE, Rick	1976-79
33	LAROCQUE, Michel	1982-84
62, 11	LATAL, Jiri	1989-92
18	LAWLESS, Paul	1987-88
5, 27	LEACH, Reggie	1974-82
10	LeCLAIR, John	1994-**
28	LEMELIN, Rejean (DNP)	1977-78
18	LESUK, Bill	1970-72
31	LINDBERGH, Pelle	1981-86
88	LINDROS, Eric	1992-**
26, 14, 18	LINSEMAN, Ken	1978-82, 89-90
23	LOMAKIN, Andrei	1991-93
18	LONSBERRY, Ross	1971-78
15	LUCAS, Danny	1978-79
25	MacADAM, Al	1973-74
19, 21	MacLEISH, Rick	1970-81, 83-84
19,4,21,24	MacSWEYN, Ralph	1968-72
14	MacTAVISH, Craig	1994-96
20	MAGUIRE, Kevin	1989-90
3, 25	MAIR, Jimmy	1970-72
43, 23	MALGUNAS, Stewart	1993-**
8, 42	MANTHA, Moe	1988-89, 91-92
8	MARSH, Brad	1981-88
25, 36, 5	McCARTHY, Kevin	1977-79, 85-87
10	McCRIMMON, Brad	1982-87
27, 29	McGILL, Ryan	1992-95
29	McILHARGEY, Jack	1974-77, 79-81
30, 24	McLEOD, Don	1971-72
23	MEEHAN, Gerry	1968-69
19	MELLANBY, Scott	1985-91
35, 13	MICHAYLUK, Dave	1981-83
15	MICKEY, Larry	1971-72
4	MISZUK, John	1968-70
36	MOKOSAK, Carl	1985-86
22	MONTGOMERY, Jim	1994-96
39	MOORE, Robbie	1978-80
21	MORRISON, Gary	1979-82
8	MORRISON, Lew	1969-72
33	MRAZEK, Jerome	1975-76
41	MULVENNA, Glenn	1992-93
3	MURPHY, Gord	1988-92
39	MURRAY, Mike	1987-88
23, 24	MURRAY, Pat	1990-92
25, 24	MURRAY, Terry	1975-77, 78-79, 80-81
31	MYRE, Phil	1979-81
42	NACHBAUR, Don	1985-90
5	NATTRESS, Ric	1992-93
22,21,14,17	NOLET, Simon	1969-74
17	OSBURN, Randy	1974-75
29	OTTO, Joel	1995-**

JERSEY #	PLAYER	SEASON(S)
21, 12, 32	PADDOCK, John	1976-77, 79-80, 82-83
20, 18, 19	PAIEMENT, Rosaire	1967-70
30, 1	PARENT, Bernie	1967-71, 73-79
7	PARIZEAU, Michel	1971-72
12	PASLAWSKI, Greg	1992-93
6, 28	PATERSON, Joe	1984-85
34	PATTERSON, Dennis	1979-80
41, 14	PEDERSON, Mark	1990-93
33	PEETERS, Pete	1978-82, 89-91
19	PELLETIER, Roger	1967-68
15	PETERS, Garry	1967-71
25, 20	PLANTE, Pierre	1971-73
25	PODEIN, Shjon	1994-**
25	POTVIN, Jean	1971-73
34, 20	POULIN, Dave	1982-90
18	PRESTON, Yves	1978-79, 80-81
14, 26	PROPP, Brian	1979-90
14, 10, 11	QUINN, Dan	1991-92, 95-96
29	RACINE, Yves	1993-94
5	RAMAGE, Rob	1993-94
8	RECCHI, Mark	1991-95
19	RENBERG, Mikael	1993-**
33	RESCH, Glenn	1985-87
18	RICCI, Mike	1990-92
34, 5	RICHTER, Dave	1985-86
31	RITCHIE, Bob	1976-77
36	ROBERTS, Gordie	1987-88
9	ROCHEFORT, Leon	1967-69
42	ROMANIUK, Russ	1995-**
48, 34	ROOT, Bill	1987-88
10	ROUPE, Magnus	1987-88
33	ROUSSEL, Dominic	1991-**
36, 3	RUMBLE, Darren	1990-92, 95-**
47	SABOL, Shaun	1989-90
25, 11	SALESKI, Don	1971-79
28	SAMUELSSON, Kjell	1986-92, 95-**
50	SANDELIN, Scott	1990-91
21, 24	SARRAZIN, Dick	1968-70, 71-72
10	SCHMAUTZ, Cliff	1970-71
22	SCHOCK, Danny	1970-71
25, 8	SCHULTZ, Dave	1971-76
11	SEABROOKE, Glen	1986-89
21	SECORD, Al	1988-89
10	SELBY, Brit	1967-69
34, 44	SEMENOV, Anatoli	1994-96
30	SETTLEMYRE, Dave (DNP)	1989-90
48	SIMPSON, Reid	1989-92
23	SINISALO, Ilkka	1981-90
21	SIROIS, Bob	1974-75
9, 27	SITTLER, Darryl	1982-84
24	SMITH, Derrick	1984-91
24, 5	SMITH, Steve	1981-82, 84-87
40, 6	SMYTH, Greg	1986-88
30	SNOW, Garth	1995-**
14	SNUGGERUD, Dave	1992-93
30	SODERSTROM, Tommy	1992-94
23	STANKIEWICZ, Myron	1968-69

JERSEY #	PLAYER	SEASON(S)
6	STANLEY, Allan	1968-69
28, 34, 29	STANLEY, Daryl	1983-84, 85-87
30	ST. CROIX, Rick	1977-83
35	STEPHENSON, Wayne	1974-79
41	STEVENS, John	1986-88
44	STOTHERS, Mike	1984-88
19	STRATTON, Art	1967-69
15	SULLIMAN, Doug	1988-90
11, 10	SUTHERLAND, Bill	1967-71
15	SUTTER, Rich	1983-86
14	SUTTER, Ron	1982-91
4	SUZOR, Mark	1976-77
3, 23	SVOBODA, Petr	1994-**
22	SWARBRICK, George	1970-71
30	TAYLOR, Bobby	1971-76
35, 15	TAYLOR, Mark	1981-83
6	THERIEN, Chris	1994-**
14	TIPPETT, Dave	1993-94
22	TOCCHET, Rick	1984-92
37	TOOKEY, Tim	1986-87
2	VAN IMPE, Ed	1967-76
43, 28, 11	VERVERGAERT, Dennis	1978-80
43	VILGRAIN, Claude	1993-94
36	WALZ, Wes	1991-93
20	WATSON, Jimmy	1972-82
3, 14	WATSON, Joe	1967-78
7	WELLS, Jay	1988-90
8, 6	WESLEY, Blake	1979-81
24	WILKIE, Bob	1993-94
35, 34	WILLIAMS, Gordie	1981-83
3	WILSON, Behn	1978-83
1	WILSON, Dunc	1969-70
32	WINNES, Chris	1993-94
35	WREGGET, Ken	1988-92
20	WRIGHT, Keith	1967-68
10,15,21,20	WRIGHT, Larry	1971-73, 75-76
6	YOUNG, Tim	1984-85
30	YOUNG, Wendell	1987-88
2	YUSHKEVICH, Dimitri	1992-95
24	ZEIDEL, Larry	1967-69
26, 20	ZETTLER, Rob	1993-95
25	ZEZEL, Peter	1984-88

	Denotes Flyers retired number
**	Still active on Flyers roster
(DNP)	Dressed, but did not play

FLYERS ALL-TIME GOALTENDING STATISTICS
COACHES, CAPTAINS, GENERAL MANAGERS

REGULAR-SEASON GOALTENDING, 1967-96

PLAYER	GP	MINS	GA	SO	AVG	W	L	T
Marc D'Amour	1	19	0	0	0.00	0	0	0
Robbie Moore	5	237	7	2	1.77	3	0	1
Gary Inness	8	330	12	0	2.18	3	0	2
Bernie Parent	486	28,276	1141	50	2.42	232	141	103
Bob Froese	144	8,108	370	12	2.74	92	29	12
Wayne Stephenson	165	9,192	424	10	2.77	93	35	26
Doug Favell	215	12,053	559	16	2.78	76	87	37
* Garth Snow	26	1,437	69	0	2.88	12	8	4
Glenn Resch	22	1,054	52	0	2.96	7	7	2
Dunc Wilson	1	60	3	0	3.00	0	1	0
* Ron Hextall	365	21,164	1086	9	3.08	178	132	42
Bruce Gamble	35	1,846	95	2	3.09	10	14	4
* Dominic Roussel	139	7,507	398	5	3.18	62	49	14
Pete Peeters	179	9,987	531	5	3.19	85	57	20
Michel Belhumeur	23	1,117	60	0	3.22	9	7	3
Rick St. Croix	82	4,808	259	2	3.23	38	26	16
Pelle Lindbergh	157	9,151	503	7	3.30	87	49	15
Ken Wregget	107	5,834	345	0	3.55	42	47	9
Tommy Soderstrom	78	4,248	259	7	3.66	26	35	10
Phil Myre	57	3,267	202	0	3.71	24	12	19
Bruce Hoffort	9	368	23	0	3.75	4	0	3
Wendell Young	6	320	20	0	3.75	3	2	0
Darren Jensen	30	1,496	95	2	3.81	15	10	1
Mark LaForest	38	1,905	124	1	3.91	10	16	4
Michel Larocque	2	120	8	0	4.00	0	1	1
Bobby Taylor	44	2,190	148	0	4.05	15	16	7
Frederic Chabot	4	70	5	0	4.29	0	1	1
Stephane Beauregard	16	802	59	0	4.41	3	9	0
Don McLeod	4	181	14	0	4.64	0	3	1
Jerome Mrazek	1	6	1	0	10.00	0	0	0

PLAYOFF GOALTENDING, 1967-96

PLAYER	GP	MINS	GA	SO	AVG	W	L
* D. Roussel	1	23	0	0	0.00	0	0
* G. Snow	1	1	0	0	0.00	0	0
M. Laforest	2	48	1	0	1.25	1	0
K. Wregget	5	268	10	0	2.24	2	2
B. Parent	63	3824	152	6	2.38	35	28
P. Myre	6	384	16	0	2.50	5	1
G. Resch	3	43	2	0	2.79	0	0
W. Stephenson	23	1362	65	2	2.86	10	10
* R. Hextall	75	4462	219	2	2.94	41	33
R. St. Croix	10	561	28	1	2.99	4	6
D. Favell	16	969	50	1	3.10	6	10
P. Lindbergh	23	1214	63	3	3.11	12	10
P. Peeters	20	1199	66	1	3.30	11	8
B. Froese	12	593	37	0	3.74	2	6
R. Moore	5	268	18	0	4.03	3	2
B. Gamble	2	120	12	0	6.00	0	2
M. Belhumeur	1	10	1	0	6.00	0	0

* Still active on Flyers roster

COACHES

Keith Allen	1967-68	through	1968-69
Vic Stasiuk	1969-70	through	1970-71
Fred Shero	1971-72	through	1977-78
Bob McCammon	1978-79		
Pat Quinn	1978-79	to	1981-82
Bob McCammon	1981-82	through	1983-84
Mike Keenan	1984-85	through	1987-88
Paul Holmgren	1988-89	to	1991-92
Bill Dineen	1991-92	through	1992-93
Terry Simpson	1993-94		
Terry Murray	1994-95	to	present

CAPTAINS

Lou Angotti	1967-68		
Ed Van Impe	1968-69	through	1972-73
Bobby Clarke	1972-73	through	1978-79
Mel Bridgman	1979-80	through	1980-81
Bill Barber	1981-82	to	1982-83
Bobby Clarke	1982-83	through	1983-84
Dave Poulin	1984-85	to	1989-90
Ron Sutter	1989-90	through	1990-91
Rick Tocchet	1991-92		
Kevin Dineen	1993-94		
Eric Lindros	1994-95	to	present

GENERAL MANAGERS

Bud Poile	1967-68	to	1969-70
Keith Allen	1969-70	through	1982-83
Bob McCammon	1983-84		
Bob Clarke	1984-85	through	1989-90
Russ Farwell	1990-91	to	1993-94
Bob Clarke	1994-95	to	present

FLYERS ALL-TIME TOP 25 GAMES
INDEX

1. **May 19, 1974:** Rick MacLeish's first-period goal and the goaltending of Bernie Parent defeat Boston 1-0 in Game 6 at the Spectrum, bringing the Stanley Cup to Philadelphia for the first time. *page 83.*

2. **May 27, 1975:** Bob Kelly scores 11 seconds into the third period to break a scoreless tie and Parent records his second Cup-clinching shutout in two years as the Flyers win Game 6 at Buffalo, 2-0, to repeat as champions. *page 95.*

3. **May 9, 1974:** Bobby Clarke's goal at 12:01 of overtime in Boston caps a rally from a 2-0 deficit, evens the 1974 finals at a game apiece and gives underdog Philadelphia the home-ice advantage it uses to go on to claim Cup No. 1. *page 83.*

4. **January 11, 1976:** The Stanley Cup-titlist Flyers dismantle perennial Soviet champions Central Red Army, 4-1, saving the NHL's honor at a Cold War-charged Spectrum. *page 99.*

5. **December 22, 1979:** Philadelphia establishes the longest unbeaten streak in NHL history, 29 games on the way to 35, with a smothering 5-2 victory at Boston Garden. *page 144.*

6. **May 5, 1974:** The Flyers become the first expansion team to eliminate a pre-1967 club from the playoffs, holding off the Rangers 4-3 in Game 7 at the Spectrum to advance to the finals for the first time. *page 81.*

7. **May 13, 1975:** Gary Dornhoefer scores after only 19 seconds and the Flyers, dominating an Islander team that had come back from a 3-0 deficit, win 4-1 at the Spectrum to reach the finals a second-straight year. *page 92.*

8. **May 16, 1985:** Dave Poulin electrifies the Spectrum by scoring with his team two men short and Philadelphia goes on to a 3-0 Game 6 victory over Quebec that lifts the team to its first finals berth in five years. *page 195.*

9. **May 14, 1987:** The superlative goaltending of rookie Ron Hextall produces a 4-3 victory in Game 6 at Montreal, dethroning the champions and giving the Flyers a second crack at the Cup in three seasons. *page 221.*

10. **May 6, 1976:** Reggie Leach ties an NHL record with five goals as Philadelphia eliminates Boston, 6-3, in Game 5 at the Spectrum and advances to the finals for the third consecutive spring. *page 106.*

11. **April 10, 1973:** Gary Dornhoefer's overtime goal at the Spectrum defeats Minnesota 3-2, inspires the Score statue outside the building, and puts the 6-year-old Flyers one victory away from their first series victory. *page 69.*

12. **May 14, 1974:** Bill Barber's wrist shot from along the boards explodes over Boston goalie Gilles Gilbert's shoulder with 5:35 remaining, breaking a tie and sending the Flyers on a 4-2 victory that leaves them one game from the Cup. *page 83.*

13. **April 13, 1985:** Tim Kerr scores an NHL-record four goals in the second period at Madison Square Garden as the Flyers break a string of three consecutive first-round defeats with a 6-5 victory and a sweep of the Rangers. *page 191.*

14. **May 28, 1987:** Philadelphia rallies from a two-goal deficit for the third time in the finals, forcing Game 7 against Edmonton with a 3-2 victory at the Spectrum. *page 224.*

15. **May 26, 1995:** Back in the playoffs after a five-year absence, the rebuilt Flyers complete a sweep of the defending champion Rangers, 4-1, at Madison Square Garden. *page 354.*

16. **April 17, 1977:** The Flyers, behind 5-2 at Maple Leaf Gardens with 7:16 remaining, pull off their second miracle rally in as many games, winning 6-5 in overtime, before going on to a 6-game quarterfinal triumph. *page 116.*

17. **April 29, 1989:** Ken Wregget steps into Game 7 for the injured Ron Hextall and Philadelphia advances to the Wales Conference final with a 4-1 victory at Pittsburgh. *page 253.*

18. **May 2, 1987:** Dave Poulin puts on a flak jacket to protect broken ribs that sidelined him for six games and, with the help of three assists by Brian Propp, sparks a 5-1 victory that puts away the Islanders in Game 7. *page 218.*

19. **April 28, 1985:** Pelle Lindbergh shuts out the four-time champion Islanders 1-0 in Game 5 to advance the Flyers to the Wales Conference finals. *page 193.*

20. **December 8, 1987:** Ron Hextall becomes the first NHL netminder ever to shoot and score a goal as Philadelphia defeats Boston 5-3 at the Spectrum. *page 229.*

21. **April 16, 1968:** The first-year Flyers, down to their last 15 seconds in Game 6 at St. Louis, tie the score on a goal by Andre Lacroix, then win 2-1 when Don Blackburn scores in double overtime. *page 36.*

22. **November 14, 1985:** Five days after the death of Pelle Lindbergh, Flyers memorialize the Vezina Trophy-winning goalie at the Spectrum, then defeat the Stanley Cup-champion Oilers. *page 204.*

23. **April 12, 1973:** Behind the goaltending of Doug Favell, Philadelphia wraps up its first-ever playoff series victory with a 4-1 victory at Minnesota. *page 70.*

24. **May 4, 1980:** Bill Barber scores four goals in Game 3 of the semifinals at Minnesota, sparking a 5-3 victory and pivoting the series Philadelphia's way. *page 149.*

25. **December 11, 1977:** Tom Bladon scores eight points in a 10-1 victory over Cleveland, breaking the NHL record for most points in a game by a defenseman. *page 122.*